Nonverbal Communication

Judee K. Burgoon
University of Arizona

Laura K. Guerrero
Arizona State University

Kory Floyd
Arizona State University

Routledge
Taylor & Francis Group

LONDON AND NEW YORK

First published 2010 by Pearson Education, Inc.

Published 2016 by Routledge
2 Park Square, Milton Park, Abingdon, Oxon OX14 4RN
711 Third Avenue, New York, NY 10017, USA

Routledge is an imprint of the Taylor & Francis Group, an informa business

ISBN: 9780205525003 (pbk)

Cover Designer: Bruce Kenselaar

Library of Congress Cataloging-in-Publication Data

Burgoon, Judee K.
    Nonverbal communication / Judee K. Burgoon, Laura K. Guerrero, Kory Floyd.
        p.   cm.
    Includes bibliographical references and index.
    ISBN 978-0-205-52500-3 (pbk.)
    1. Body language. 2. Nonverbal communication. I. Guerrero, Laura K. II.Floyd, Kory.
III. Title.
    BF637.N66B86 2010
    153.6'9—dc22   2009028235

CONTENTS

PART THREE   Nonverbal Communication Functions

13   Relational Messages: Power, Dominance, and Influence   343

14 Managing Conversations   373

PREFACE

Communication plays a central role in our lives. In fact, being a skilled communicator enhances one's prospects for sustaining a happy, healthy, and productive life. This isn't just our opinion. A local conciliation court recently reported that, for the 14th year in a row, the most reported problem among troubled marriages is the lack of good communication. Successful relationships are built on a solid foundation of communication skills. Communication is also instrumental to our success or failure in the workplace. Surveys among business leaders, major employers, and employment counselors emphasize the importance of communication skills in acquiring jobs and performing effectively on the job. A study by the Administrative Management Society, for example, found that 80% of managers rated communication skills as among the most important qualifications of prospective employees; 65% also cited interpersonal and leadership skills. Another study involved asking female managers about the strategies or techniques that they credited with helping them reach their current positions. Rated as very or extremely important were communication skills (89%), personal power (78%), and charisma, charm, and social skills (53%). In a study by a college placement service, several hundred alumni reported that communication abilities were more important to their job success than the major subject they studied.

These testimonials probably pale in comparison to the vividness of your own firsthand experiences. What could be more persuasive evidence of the importance of communication than the recollection of butterflies in your stomach when you fretted about what to say on your first date, the flush of pleasure after making a well-received presentation in class, the exhilaration of receiving a job offer after a grueling interview, the satisfaction of winning an argument with your parents, or the sadness of losing a friendship over a silly disagreement? Clearly, communication plays a pivotal role in the significant—as well as insignificant—moments in your life, and the nonverbal dimension is a major contributor to the success or failure of communication.

The fascination with nonverbal communication has spawned thousands of legitimate books and articles on the subject. Knowledge about nonverbal communication now springs from such fountainheads as psychology, psychiatry, sociology, anthropology, linguistics, semiotics, and biology, in addition to the field of communication itself. In fact, the unceasing interest in nonverbal communication has created a state of information overload. Trying to make sense of this diverse body of information is no small task, especially given that scholars from different fields approach nonverbal behavior with differing perspectives, assumptions, and methodologies. At the same time, the popularity of "body language" has spawned a slew of charlatans and self-proclaimed nonverbal "experts" who purport to read politicians' every move like a book. It is our hope that by the time you finish reading this textbook, you will be able to tell fact from fiction and distinguish valid scientific conclusions and complexities from simplified assertions and suppositions that often trivialize the topic.

Our mission in writing this textbook, then, has been to sift through the mountains of literature on the subject and, while attempting to be comprehensive and current, to distill the most valid and valuable information into understandable and usable principles. Because we believe that different disciplines offer unique perspectives and insights, our "take" on nonverbal communication is integrative and eclectic. In the process, we hope to have escaped the plight of the three blind men trying to describe an elephant, each with only a limited experience of one part of the elephant's anatomy.

This does not mean, however, that there is no underlying perspective that unifies our orientation to nonverbal behavior. We believe that nonverbal *communication* can best be understood according to the functions—the goals and purposes—it serves. This approach, which other scholars have increasingly embraced, was initially introduced in the first version of this textbook, Burgoon and Saine's *The Unspoken Dialogue* (1978). We are indebted to Tom Saine for his role in developing this original approach to nonverbal communication, just as we are indebted to co-authors David Buller and Gill Woodall for amplifying and updating this approach in a second edition, *Nonverbal Communication* (1996).

In this latest edition, we have made significant changes to the previous volumes. In Chapter 1, we define nonverbal communication and lay the foundations for studying it. In Chapters 2 and 3, we introduce sociocultural and bio-evolutionary influences as the twin pillars on which so much of nonverbal communication rests. These two chapters examine the respective nurture and nature influences on nonverbal displays and interpretations. Chapters 4 through 7 then present the foundations of the codes that we regard as most central to nonverbal communication. Covered in these chapters are the body codes of physical appearance and adornment (Chapter 4), the visual and auditory codes of kinesics and vocalics (Chapter 5), the contact codes of proxemics and haptics (Chapter 6), and the time and place codes of chronemics, the environment, and artifacts (Chapter 7). These four chapters examine the structural and normative features of each code before considering how they interrelate with the verbal code in the remaining chapters.

The remaining eight chapters each tackle a different function of nonverbal communication. They answer the question, "What can nonverbal communication do for me or to me?" We suspect you are far more interested in knowing how to use nonverbal communication to make a good impression on an employer, influence a group, keep a conversation going, interpret a friend's emotional expressions, or woo a mate than to know how many different ways people use eye contact or how frequently they touch. Consequently, the second half of this textbook is organized around the communication functions in which nonverbal behavior plays a central role. It covers the various purposes of nonverbal communication that loom largest in people's communication lives. Chapter 8, on message processing and production, looks at all the ways in which the verbal and nonverbal codes work together to help people create, perceive, and interpret messages. Chapter 9 considers the kinds of impressions we form from nonverbal cues and the principles of social cognition that govern the impression formation process. Chapter 10 delves into how we use nonverbal cues to express our "real" and desired identities, from presenting such aspects of our personal identity as our gender, age, and personality to presenting ourselves as we want others to see us. Chapter 11 covers the ways in which we express and interpret emotions from nonverbal visual, auditory, and tactile cues. Chapters 12 and 13 address two major facets of what is called *relational communication*. Relational communication refers to the ways in which we define our interpersonal relationships through communication. Chapter 12 explains how we express the degree of intimacy and affection in our relationships. Chapter 13 describes how we express power, dominance, and influence nonverbally. Chapter 14 examines the ways in which nonverbal behavior regulates interpersonal interaction, including how we initiate and terminate interaction and how we manage turn-taking nonverbally. Finally, Chapter 15 provides an ideal culmination for this introduction to nonverbal communication, because it covers deception, which is an amalgam of impression management, interaction management, and influence functions.

Beyond our dedication to a functional approach, another feature unifying our perspective on nonverbal communication is our emphasis on scientific knowledge rather than anecdotal experience. This book is dedicated to giving you the most current and comprehensive coverage of theories and research findings related to nonverbal communication and behavior. Many popular books and self-proclaimed experts promise to divulge how you can "win friends and influence people." But the truth is, humans cannot be "read" like a book, and there are as many questions about nonverbal communication as there are answers. The cookbook approach to communication may make its promoters a bundle of money, but it is unlikely to give you surefire guidance on how to craft your own nonverbal messages or interpret those of others. Much of what we know about nonverbal communication is tentative, because new research is daily challenging or disconfirming old beliefs while creating new ones. The best we can offer you, then, is the latest thinking and scientific evidence that is supplemented rather than replaced by anecdote and personal experience. Although the absence of abundant clear-cut prescriptions about how to behave nonverbally may be unsatisfying to some readers, we are comforted by Voltaire's statement that "doubt is not a very agreeable status but certainty is a ridiculous one."

Although this book is intended to be reasonably comprehensive, we have organized it in a way that should permit instructors the option of using all or only parts of it and to order the chapters in a sequence best suited to their sense of the unfolding story of nonverbal communication. The current organization, which is modified from the previous one, is based on the assumption that it is best to introduce basic principles and individual codes before considering how the various codes work together to accomplish various communication functions. But this ordering can be adjusted according to an instructor's preferences.

ACKNOWLEDGMENTS

The process of producing this book has involved the labors and contributions of many people who we wish to acknowledge most gratefully. We are grateful to Mark Bobrov, Erin Burgoon, Josh Carlson, Lauren Hamel, and Beth Waldrop, who assisted us with everything from library research to editing to candid appraisals of our revisions. Special thanks goes to Marilyn Stringer, whose wonderful photographic eye captured many of the candid photographs seen throughout this text, and to Cindy Hill, Daniel Hill, and Angelica Saavedra, who allowed us to use multiple photographs of them in this book. Gabrielle and Kristiana Guerrero are also thanked for their help in identifying children's faces that best show various emotions for Chapter 11. We are also indebted to our many graduate and undergraduate students who, through their curiosity and classroom discussions, helped us sharpen our own thinking and organization.

We also wish to thank the following individuals for their thoughtful and helpful reviews of the book: Nick Backus, Western Oregon University; Dwayne Cornelison, Clemson University; Marcia D. Dixson, Indiana University—Purdue University, Fort Wayne; Norah Ellen Dunbar, University of Oklahoma; Valerie Manno Giroux, Ph.D., University of Miami; Shelly Lutzweiler, Guilford Technical Community College; Kristen Norwood, University of Iowa; Narissra Maria Punyanunt-Carter, Texas Tech University; Daniel Schabot, William Carey University; David C. Schrader, Oklahoma State University; Robert J. Sidelinger, West Virginia University; Jason Teven, California State University, Fullerton; Amy Veuleman, McNeese State University.

Finally, we are most grateful to our editors at Allyn and Bacon for their patience, encouragement, and guidance. Karon Bowers, Jeanne Zalesky, and Megan Lentz have remained supportive and upbeat through all the various obstacles and distractions that have slowed our progress. We can only hope that the final product was worth the wait.

ABOUT THE AUTHORS

Judee K. Burgoon is site director for the Center for Identification Technology Research, Eller College of Management, University of Arizona. She holds appointments as professor of Communication, Family Studies, and Human Development, and as distinguished visiting professor at the University of Oklahoma. Dr. Burgoon has written eight books and more than 250 articles, chapters, and reviews on nonverbal and relational communication, deception, and computer-mediated communication. Her current research, funded by the National Science Foundation, the Department of Defense, and the Department of Homeland Security, examines ways to automate analysis of nonverbal and verbal communication to detect deception. Honors include the International Communication Association's Fisher Mentorship, Chaffee Career Achievement, and ICA Fellow Awards, and the National Communication Association's Distinguished Scholar Award, Golden Anniversary Monographs Award, Woolbert Award for Research with Lasting Impact, and Knapp Award in Interpersonal Communication.

Laura K. Guerrero is professor of Human Communication at Arizona State University. Her research focuses on relational, nonverbal, and emotional communication, including both the "dark" (jealousy, hurtful events, conflict, intimate partner violence) and "bright" (nonverbal intimacy, maintenance, forgiveness) sides of personal relationships. She has written five books and more than 80 articles and chapters on these topics. Dr. Guerrero has received several research awards, including the 2001 Gerald R. Miller Award for Early Career Achievement from the International Association for Relationship Research, the Dickens Article Award from the Western States Communication Association, and the Outstanding Doctoral Dissertation Award in Interpersonal Communication from the International Communication Association. She received her PhD from the University of Arizona in 1994.

Kory Floyd is professor of Human Communication and director of the Communication Sciences Laboratory at Arizona State University. His research focuses on the communication of affection in personal relationships and on the interplay between interpersonal behavior and health. He has written nine books and nearly 75 journal articles and book chapters on the topics of interpersonal communication, nonverbal communication, family communication, and health. He is immediate past editor of the *Journal of Family Communication* and was the 2006 recipient of the Gerald R. Miller Award for Early Career Achievement from the International Association for Relationship Research. He received his PhD from the University of Arizona in 1998.

DEDICATION

To all of our students. They have taught us well.

—*Judee, Laura, and Kory*

1 Introduction to Nonverbal Communication

Silent Meaning

> The word not spoken
> goes not quite unheard.
> It lingers in the eye,
> in the semi-arch of brow.
> A gesture of the hand
> speaks pages more than words,
> The echo rests in the heart
> as driftwood does in sand,
> To be rubbed by time
> until it rots or shines.
> The word not spoken
> touches us as music
> does the mind.

—Sen. William S. Cohen (R., Maine)
The New York Times

Humans are social creatures. We spend most of our waking hours in contact with other people—learning, working, playing, dating, parenting, negotiating, buying, selling, persuading, or just plain talking. We not only communicate with people face to face, we watch them on television and videos, listen to them on talk radio, and interact with them through cell phones and webcams. With so much of our daily lives consumed by communication, it should be intuitively evident that our ability to navigate the waters of daily living—indeed, our prospects for happy, healthy lives—depends on how well we communicate. And a major part of that communication process is the "unspoken dialogue," the nonverbal aspects of communication to which Senator Cohen's poem alludes.

This textbook is about the unspoken dialogue, all those messages that people exchange beyond the words themselves. Whether it involves mundane requests at the grocery store or delicate international negotiations, the nonverbal side of communication is crucial and often overshadows the verbal communication that is going on. Successful human relations hinge on the ability to express oneself nonverbally and to understand the nonverbal communication of others.

Some consider the study of nonverbal communication trivial or suspect, a view fueled by charlatans who claim that your every move "talks" and promise to teach you how to "read others like a book." Take, for example, this sardonic observation by Aldous Huxley (1954):

> When it comes to any form of non-verbal education more fundamental (and more likely of some practical use) than Swedish drill, no really respectable person in any really respectable university or church will do anything about it. . . . Besides, this matter of education in the nonverbal humanities will not fit into any of the established pigeon-holes. It is not religion, not neurology, not gymnastics, not morality or civics, not even experimental psychology. This being so, the subject is for academic and ecclesiastical purposes, non-existent and may be safely ignored altogether or left, with a patronizing smile, to those whom the Pharisees of verbal orthodoxy call cranks, quacks, charlatans and unqualified amateurs. (pp. 76–77)

Much to our relief, such cynicism has been countered by the publication of literally thousands of articles, books, documentaries, and investigative reports on the subject. In contrast to Huxley's gloomy assessment, there is a strong scientific body of knowledge about nonverbal communication that springs from such disciplinary fountainheads as communication, psychology, psychiatry, sociology, anthropology, linguistics, semiotics, and biology. The body of information is so vast and diverse, in fact, that making sense of it is no small task, especially given that scholars from different fields approach nonverbal behavior with differing perspectives, assumptions, and methodologies. Consequently, nonverbal communication is best understood by taking a multidisciplinary approach.

That is the approach adopted in this text. We explore multiple facets of nonverbal communication—the various codes (systems of cues) that comprise it, the many kinds of messages it can send, the purposes or functions it can serve, and the processes whereby people generate, exchange, and interpret such messages. Throughout, however, our emphasis is on the communicative aspects of nonverbal behavior.

The Importance of Nonverbal Communication

We need not rely on intuition to know that nonverbal communication is a major force in our lives. One popularized estimate often quoted in magazines and on television is that 93% of all meaning is nonverbal. This estimate would mean that only 7% of meaning comes from verbal content, that is, the words themselves. Common sense tells us that this is unlikely and that there are many circumstances in which the words themselves carry far more weight. It turns out that this often-cited estimate is a faulty one, based on an erroneous extrapolation of results from two very early studies by Mehrabian (Mehrabian & Ferris, 1967; Mehrabian & Wiener, 1967). Other estimates put the number closer to 66%, with two-thirds of the meaning in human interactions being derived from nonverbal cues (Birdwhistell, 1955b;

Philpott, 1983), which still places substantial weight on the nonverbal side of the meaning equation.

Regardless of the actual percentage, plenty of evidence documents that people rely heavily on nonverbal cues to express themselves and to interpret others' communication. Research shows that when verbal messages contradict nonverbal ones, adults usually believe the nonverbal messages over the verbal ones and rely on nonverbal behavior to judge another's attitudes and feelings. For example, the student who professes to be tolerant of all races, ethnicities, and sexual orientations but always chooses to sit at a distance from African American, Latino, and gay classmates may be judged to be bigoted and homophobic. As Photo 1.1 shows, politicians are often suspected of speaking with "crossed fingers," which would be a clear nonverbal signal of their insincerity if visible. Unfortunately, we seldom have such clear nonverbal signs to help us interpret mixed and contradictory messages. Nevertheless, we place a great deal of stock in what is being expressed nonverbally.

Communication experts regard the power of nonverbal messages as indisputable. There are several possible reasons why they are so influential.

1. *Nonverbal communication is omnipresent.* Nonverbal facets pervade virtually every communicative act. In face-to-face interactions, all the nonverbal channels come into play. Body, face, voice, appearance, touch, distancing, timing, and physical surroundings all play a part in creating the total communication. A friend's gestures, facial expressions, posture, and eye contact may signal interest. A supervisor's vocal pitch, loudness, and tempo may signal dominance. A job candidate's physical attractiveness, dress, and grooming may connote credibility. A lover's close proximity and touch may establish intimacy. A group leader's

PHOTO 1.1 *Crossed fingers are a nonverbal way of saying "you can't believe what I am saying." This slick politician's nonverbal expressions of conviction and sincerity are likely to be believed because the audience can't see that he is speaking with "crossed fingers."*

temporal behaviors, such as pacing and giving undivided attention, may create conversational coordination. A church's architecture, furnishings, and artifacts may dictate what degree of decorum and formality is to be observed.

When a communication channel becomes mediated, as with television broadcasts, webcam conversations, or telephone calls, some nonverbal features are lost, but several important ones remain. For example, the decision to talk to someone by phone rather than in person can be a nonverbal message of detachment or nonurgency. Chronemic (temporal) and vocalic features are still present, and the choice of medium itself can send a message precisely because the person chooses to communicate in a way that either includes or excludes certain types of nonverbal cues.

Even written communication can have nonverbal features. The decision to write a nasty letter rather than confront someone in person can be a delaying tactic. E-mails and text chats can have features embedded in them to capture some nonverbal nuances. Using different font colors, stationery, emoticons, and capitalization to "yell" at someone can all add nonverbal cues into a completely verbal medium.

Some have argued that one "cannot not communicate" (Watzlawick, Beavin, & Jackson, 1967). According to this view, all behavior is communicative. Choosing not to interact with someone, for instance, carries a message in itself, and the absence of a greeting is as meaningful as the presence of one. Although the authors of this book do not subscribe to this liberal view, it does underscore the ever-present possibilities of nonverbal communication, for it indicates that any behavior can be interpreted by someone as a nonverbal message. Even when people are not talking to each other, it is possible to read nonverbal meaning into their actions. In short, every encounter between two or more people is a potential nonverbal exchange, regardless of whether any verbal exchange takes place.

2. *Nonverbal behaviors are multifunctional.* Nonverbal cues are part of almost every communication purpose one can imagine. They can be enlisted to create a favorable first impression during a job interview, persuade a pedestrian to sign a petition, prevent an overbearing member from monopolizing a group meeting, show one's excitement about winning an award, flirt with a new acquaintance, or signal one's confusion over what someone has just said. In fact, nonverbal cues may do several of these things at once. Because many different nonverbal channels can be used to send simultaneous messages, they are often pressed into service to do just that—handle multiple responsibilities in conjunction with, or as a substitute for, verbal communication.

3. *Nonverbal behaviors may form a universal language system.* Many scholars believe nonverbal signals are part of a universally recognized and understood code. This view is evident in an oft-quoted statement by Edward Sapir (1949):

> We respond to gestures with an extreme alertness and, one might almost say, in accordance with an elaborate and secret code that is written nowhere, known to none and understood by all. (p. 556)

Behaviors such as smiling, crying, pointing, caressing, and staring in a threatening manner are examples of nonverbal signals that appear to be used and understood the world over. They allow people to communicate with one another at the most basic level regardless of their familiarity with the prevailing verbal language system. Such nonverbal actions thus transcend cultural differences, forming a kind of universal language. This capacity of nonverbal communication to cross geographic boundaries is evident to anyone who has traveled abroad. As one former student wrote in a postcard penned from Italy, "When sitting at the dinner table with 25 relatives, it struck me how much I relied on the nonverbals."

Clearly, not all meaning can be gleaned from nonverbal cues alone, and there are differences between and within cultures. But the fact that exclusive reliance on nonverbal cues can produce a sense of commonality and understanding in a foreign situation is a testament to their universal character. When words fail us, we can always fall back on our nonverbal communication system to achieve some degree of mutual understanding.

4. *Nonverbal communication can lead to misunderstanding as well as understanding.* Although nonverbal signals can aid us greatly in making sense out of the world, they are equally important because of the misunderstandings they can cause. These can sometimes be tragic, as the following true anecdote illustrates.

A young photographer, accustomed to working alone, was flown into a remote part of Alaska for the summer. He so prized his solitude that on a previous survival retreat, he had chastised his father for sending a search party after him. On this trip, he failed to make clear arrangements for being flown back out of the wilderness. When the weather began turning cool, his father reluctantly sent a plane looking for him. The pilot soon located the camp. As he neared it, the young man waved a red jacket liner, which to pilots is a signal to wave someone away. The young man then gave a thumbs-up gesture and walked casually to his campsite. The pilot concluded that everything was okay and flew away.

A diary the young man kept revealed a very different interpretation of the encounter. He was thrilled to see the plane, and to ensure being seen, waved his jacket in the air. He gave the thumbs-up gesture as a sign of his elation and his victory over his growing fears. He then jaunted to his campsite, expecting the plane to land, and was totally disbelieving when it flew on. Weeks later, when the weather turned bitter cold and he ran out of firewood, the young photographer used his last bullet to take his own life. The diary was found with his frozen body.

Not all nonverbal misunderstandings have fatal or even serious consequences. But the potential for nonverbal cues to mislead and be misread is there, and such misreadings can often have a more profound impact than the accurately exchanged cues. This is especially true when people believe they can "read another like a book" and draw lots of inferences from a person's unintentional behavior. Many mistakenly believe that nonverbal behaviors all have obvious meanings and that everyone interprets nonverbal cues the same way. Recognition of the potential for misunderstanding is a prerequisite to successful communication.

5. *Nonverbal communication has phylogenetic primacy.* Nonverbal communication predated language in the evolution of human communication. That is, before humans developed the capacity to speak and use language, they were able to communicate nonverbally. Although numerous theories have addressed the issue of whether vocalizations preceded gestural communication or vice versa, there is no question that nonverbal forms of expression preceded verbal ones (Dew & Jensen, 1977; McBride, 1975; McNeill, 1970). According to ethologists, many forms of nonverbal expression have, through an evolutionary history spanning perhaps 150 million years, became specialized as ritualized communication signals. Ploog (1995) explains:

> . . . in the beginning, the most basic modes of social behavior were nothing but approach and avoidance among members of the species. The outcome of such encounters was always unpredictable and depended upon each partner's actions and reactions. . . . Because communication between partners was advantageous, social signals evolved—as the theory goes—to permit more flexibility in encounters and a greater degree of information about the outcome. (p. 27)

Because nonverbal communication came first to the species, it can be argued that we are inherently programmed to attend first and foremost to nonverbal signals. This primacy of nonverbal cues should cause us to give them more weight in interpreting communicative events, especially in times of stress, when we are likely to revert to more primitive (phylogenetically older) response patterns. If we as humans rely more heavily on nonverbal than verbal messages, it may be because we are innately predisposed to do so.

6. *Nonverbal communication has ontogenetic primacy.* Just as the species first turned to nonverbal forms to communicate with one another, so too do infants rely first on nonverbal means to interact with their caretakers and environment. Nonverbal communication is literally our first communication system. Before birth, the fetus develops awareness of its mother in utero through the senses of touch and hearing. At birth, the infant's primary interactions with caregivers continue to center around sounds and touches. Nursing, grasping, rocking, holding, crying, cooing, singing—all these experiences contribute to the infant's awakening recognition that humans communicate with one another.

As the infant's vision improves, visual cues are added to the nonverbal mix; sequences of separations and contacts and other routines add rudimentary understanding of spatial and temporal messages. Long before a child has begun to grasp the concept of verbal language, she or he has already acquired a rich communication system that is strictly nonverbal in nature. The importance of nonverbal modes of expression at this critical and vulnerable stage of life doubtless contributes to our continued dependence on them even when we acquire more sophisticated means of expression. For we do not abandon the nonverbal system; rather, as we mature, we broaden our communicative repertoire to include more complex verbal and nonverbal forms.

7. *Nonverbal communication has interaction primacy.* Besides being the first form of communication in the history of the species and in the lifespan of the individual, nonverbal behavior usually precedes verbal behavior in the opening minutes of human encounters. Before people even open their mouths, their nonverbal behaviors are supplying a wealth of information to onlookers. Everything from posture to gait to hair style to voice quality paints a picture for the observer and provides a frame of reference for interpreting the words that are spoken.

BOX 1.1

Flouting the System Nonverbally

Ray Birdwhistell, one of the pioneers of the field of nonverbal communication, was fond of telling anecdotes about how people can express themselves nonverbally in ways they can't get away with verbally. One example he used was the courtroom, where attorneys try to introduce illicit messages to influence the jury:

> The present system of restricting admissible evidence to exhibits and words still leaves the way open for the introduction of non-admissible ideas and attitudes. The trial lawyer often is a master of the raised eyebrow, the disapproving headshake, and the knowing nod. In many cases, these gestures, if translated into words, would be inadmissible as evidence. Yet, as presented, they have a definite effect on the judge and jury. (Birdwhistell, 1955, p. 56)

Lawyers aren't the only masters of flouting the formal requirements of the system. Soldiers, too, know how to get their message across while still appearing to conform to the rules:

> The salute, a conventionalized movement of the right hand to the vicinity of the anterior portion of the cap or hat, can—without occasioning a court martial—be performed in a manner that can satisfy, please, or enrage the demanding officer. By shifts in stance, facial expression, the velocity or duration of the movement of salutation, and even in the selection of inappropriate contexts for the act, the soldier can dignify, ridicule, demean, seduce, insult, or promote the recipient of the salute (Birdwhistell, 1970, p. 79–80)

Especially important in early interaction are the visual nonverbal cues such as physical appearance and gestures that are available at a distance. These begin working before a communicator is within speaking range. Environmental nonverbal cues may also set the stage. For instance, when the President holds a news conference, the American flag, the red carpet, and all the other symbols of the White House create an image of power; they evoke respect from the gathered press prior to the President starting his remarks. This ability of nonverbal cues to "get in the first word," so to speak, gives them a temporal primacy that may also cause their meanings to take precedence over verbal ones.

8. *Nonverbal communication can express what verbal communication can't or shouldn't.* There are many occasions when verbalizing our thoughts and feelings would be risky, rude, or inappropriate, so we use nonverbal channels instead. In the case of a budding romance, people are hesitant to commit themselves too quickly for fear of being rejected. If a friendly smile is unreturned, one can retreat to a less intimate level without embarrassment. Similarly, nonverbal cues can be used to satirize, criticize, or leak information without the communicator being held accountable for his or her acts (see Box 1.1). A good example is the use of the eye roll to signal disbelief or scorn for what someone is saying. In another example, two athletes used a "black power" gesture during a medal ceremony at the 1968 Olympics to express nonverbally something that they were otherwise prohibited from communicating (see Photo 1.2).

We entrust the expression of our most deep-seated emotions to nonverbal channels. Witness Steven Spielberg's powerful portrayal of the horrors of

PHOTO 1.2   *Tommie Smith and John Carlos, gold and bronze medalists in the 200-meter run at the 1968 Olympic Games, engaged in a victory stand protest against unfair treatment of blacks in the United States. With heads lowered and black-gloved fists raised in the black power salute, they refused to recognize the American flag and the national anthem.*

Auschwitz in his classic film, *Schindler's List*. No verbal description could compare to the palpable terror evident in the faces, postures, and touches of 300 women and children clinging desperately to one another in the showers, waiting for the deadly gas to overtake them. Political protests and demonstrations also are a prime illustration of this use of nonverbal communication. Note the range of expression shown in Photos 1.3a, 1.3b and 1.3c.

9. *Nonverbal communication is trusted.* The naive belief exists that nonverbal behaviors are spontaneous and uncontrolled; that they are the "windows to the soul." As we shall see later, this is a fallacious belief. Many nonverbal behaviors are intentionally manipulated, some for deceptive purposes, and people who are image-conscious work scrupulously to suppress behaviors that make a bad impression. Nevertheless, there is a prevailing faith in the authenticity, truthfulness, and candor of nonverbal behaviors. Consequently, people believe them over verbal behaviors. In fact, the bulk of research shows that when verbal messages contradict nonverbal ones, adults usually believe the nonverbal messages (Burgoon, 1985). Throughout history, skillful nonverbal communication has been a hallmark of some of the most influential world leaders. Ronald Reagan, for example, was dubbed "The Great Communicator" less for what he said than for how he said it.

a. Iraqi men shouting and brandishing AK-47 assault weapons to protest the US-led war in Iraq.

b. Members of the UNAM Workers Union link arms and march in protest in Mexico City.

c. Basque nationalists carrying flags and showing their displeasure at the outlawing of a pro-independence youth group in Spain, 2001.

PHOTO 1.3   *Nonverbal expressions speak louder than words in conveying people's emotions and attitudes during political demonstrations, as these examples show.*

These nine reasons for the significant impact of nonverbal communication, although not exhaustive, highlight the need to understand how nonverbal communication works together with verbal communication and independently of it. Given that few people receive formal training in this subject in their primary or secondary school education (with most attention being devoted instead to the verbal side of communication), this text may serve to remediate "nonverbal illiteracy." Although this text is about nonverbal communication, the authors are committed to a more integrated approach to verbal and nonverbal communication, and so you will find a variety of general communication principles and some specific findings about verbal communication interspersed throughout the book.

Definitional Issues

So far, we have been referring to nonverbal communication as if there were some commonly accepted definition for it. In reality, there may be as many definitions of it as there are nonverbal textbooks. Before we proceed, it is

BOX 1.2

Do Definitions Matter?

For those involved in legal matters, the answer to that question is a resounding "yes." Consider the matter of James B. Daniels, an attorney before the Union County Superior Court, whose nonverbal actions earned him a contempt citation. It seems that during early proceedings, he responded to a judge's repeated denial of his motions by shaking his head and smiling. The judge declared his behavior disrespectful and warned him that further displays of disapproval would land him in jail. The attorney apologized, excusing his behavior as "a very human response" and not intended as disrespect. But the next day, when he was overruled again, his reaction prompted the judge to hold him in contempt of court. The ruling was not based on anything the attorney said, but on what he did— "laughing, rolling his head, and throwing himself back in his chair"—all of which was recorded in the court records. The attorney appealed the ruling, but it was upheld by the New Jersey Supreme Court.

This ruling is consistent with recent court decisions that many nonverbal behaviors qualify as "symbolic expressive conduct," in other words, as behavior that is communicative. Often considered in the context of what behaviors are protected as free speech, the courts have ruled that such widely varying forms of "expressive conduct" as burning the American flag, engaging in sit-ins, wearing black armbands, and shaving one's head in protest qualify as "free speech," that is, they

are equivalent to verbal acts and therefore covered by the First Amendment. Tiersma (1993) suggests that such acts qualify as communication if they (1) are conducted within view of an *audience* (with whom eye contact is usually established), (2) are done in a *ritualistic* or exaggerated way, (3) are *repetitive* (occur more than once), (4) are of longer than normal *duration*, (5) have no other evident *function* than a communicative one, and (6) occur within a *communicative context*.

The extent to which nonverbal behaviors can be regarded as equivalent to verbal acts is evident in the criminal case of United States v. Arshad Pervez, in which the defendant was unobtrusively videotaped nodding in response to questioning by undercover agents. The government contended that his nods were an affirmative answer confessing his guilt. The defense argued instead that the nodding should not be construed as a "yes" but rather as merely a gesture of attentiveness typical of what listeners do during conversation. The defense further claimed that the agents' own behavior, by reinforcing the suspect's listener response pattern, had entrapped him.

The defense filed a motion to preclude the agents from giving their interpretation of the nods. Should the judge side with the defense or the prosecution? Given the other rulings on nonverbal conduct, what do you think the outcome was? This illustrates that the way in which nonverbal communication is defined can have very real consequences.

---

important that we come to a common understanding of the terminology being used. Although discussing definitional issues may seem as useful as debating how many angels can dance on the head of a pin, definitions can make quite a difference in how actions are interpreted (see Box 1.2). Consider the following scenario:

> **GIRLFRIEND:**   Our relationship is falling apart. You have become totally distant and cold.

BOYFRIEND: How can you say that? Give me just one example.

GIRLFRIEND: I'll give you several. You sit silently when we go out to eat together. You spend more time with your buddies than you do with me. You don't look at me when we do talk and you never hold my hand anymore.

BOYFRIEND: You're just imagining things. I've had a lot on my mind between school and my job, but I haven't changed how I behave toward you.

She interprets his actions as nonverbal messages of distance and lack of affection. He claims his behaviors are unchanged or merely indicative of being preoccupied with other things; any "messages" are her imagination. If his actions are defined as nonverbal communication, even though he may be unaware of them, he might be faulted for communicating detachment. Under a different definition, however, she might be seen as reading too much into unintentional and noncommunicative activity. In this very practical way, then, definitions can make a difference.

Definitions of Nonverbal Communication

Exactly what is this thing called nonverbal communication? Experts at a National Communication Association convention, queried about their definition of nonverbal communication, offered this potpourri of responses:

- Jerold L. Hale of the University of Georgia described nonverbal communication as "the study of behaviors other than words that create shared meaning between people who are interacting with one another" (Hale, 2003).
- Brant Burleson of Purdue University defined it as "any kind of expression, gesture or symbolic behavior that is either intended to convey meaning or happens to convey meaning" (Burleson, 2003).
- Daniel Canary of Arizona State University defined it as "intentional behavior that's used to symbolically convey an idea" (Canary, 2003).
- John Greene of Purdue University said "it is everything we do except the words that we use in our face to face interactions, so it includes facial expressions, gestures, eye contact . . . even our artifacts, the clothes that we wear, the rings and jewelry that we carry around with us" (Greene, 2003).

A starting point for arriving at a sound definition is the concept of communication itself. This term is a slippery one, because people use it to refer to everything from communing with nature, to "dialoguing" with oneself, to linking computers, to transmitting via satellite. We limit the domain to *human* communication, that is, exchanges between two or more people. This eliminates a lot, including "intrapersonal" communication, human-computer interaction, and animal or animal-human communication. Apart from philosophical justifications for such exclusions, this restriction is pragmatic. It makes it far more likely that we will uncover general principles if the types of communication phenomena to be explained have some commonality. It is difficult to find principles that explain bee signals and computer interfaces in the same way as nonverbal exchanges between humans. Nevertheless, we may learn some things about human communication processes by studying nonhuman interactions, and we will draw on these observations when they serve as useful illustrations or analogues.

Within the domain of human communication, most scholars agree that communication refers to the *process of creating meanings between senders and receivers through the exchange of signs and symbols*. Messages originate as sender cognitions that are *encoded* (transformed into signals) *through commonly understood codes* and *decoded* by receivers (the signals must be recognized, interpreted, and evaluated). Formal languages, American Sign Language, and Morse code all meet these requirements. Nonverbal codes, then, must include the same properties.

At this stage, it might seem that defining nonverbal communication is easy. But consider the following possibilities and determine for each whether you think it is a nonverbal message or not:

- wearing one red and one blue tennis shoe
- sneezing
- squinting in bright sunlight
- slumped posture
- crying
- breaking out in a rash
- standing close to others because of a hearing impairment

To some people, these may seem obvious instances of communication; to others, none may qualify. Additional criteria are necessary to resolve the issue.

Information, Behavior, and Communication

One way to clarify the matter is to distinguish among the concepts of information, behavior, and communication. Information can be conceived of as *all stimuli in the environment that reduce uncertainty for the organism*. That is, information is anything individuals use to gain predictability about the environment and to guide their behavior. The position of the sun in the sky is information about the time of day, but one would normally not call it a "message," because the sun did not establish its position for the purpose of signaling to observers what hour of the day it is on Earth. It is simply there as an environmental stimulus from which observers can draw inferences and adjust their own behavior.

Unfortunately, when the source of the information becomes a human, people are inclined to label the inference-making process as communication. For example, a red rash on a child becomes a "nonverbal message" to the doctor that the child has measles, even though the information being gleaned is no different than that obtained by a botanist diagnosing leaf blight on a tree. The child does not "will" the measles into being nor can he or she choose to suppress the appearance of the disease. Similarly, a sneeze may be symptomatic of an allergy, and a close conversational distance may be indicative of a hearing problem, but in the absence of other knowledge about the situation, these are behaviors that should be regarded only as informative and not as communicative. In short, the passive or involuntary display of cues that an observer might want to interpret should be treated only as information or behavior and not specifically as communication. It is "given off" rather than "given." To be communication, the behavior must be *volitional* and *other-directed* (targeted to a receiver or receivers). This distinguishes it from what others have labeled informative, expressive, indicative, or incidental behavior (see Andersen, 1991; Bavelas, 1990; Ekman & Friesen, 1969b; Knapp, 1983, 1984b; Motley, 1990).

This is not to say that communication is not informative, because it is. In fact, all communication is potential information. But all information is not communication. Having green eyes, for example, may be informative about one's ancestry, but it is not a message. Communication is a subset of information rather than something synonymous with it.

In the same vein, many forms of behavior are informative, but only some of them qualify as communication. Here the confusion is even more likely, partly because of the perspective that regards any and all nonverbal activity as messages. If one subscribes to this view, there is no need for a separate concept of communication, because it is totally redundant with behavior. It seems more useful to distinguish between the broad category of behavior, which encompasses *any actions or reactions performed by an organism*, and the more specific category of communication. The difference is that behavior can take place without others witnessing it, responding to it, or understanding it. Typically, routine activities such as sleeping and eating would be classified as behavior rather than as communication unless they were done in a manner or context designed to turn them into "statements." It is doubtful that a person taking a nap in the privacy of her own home intends to communicate something to an accidental observer; however, if she chooses to do it in the middle of a political science lecture, the "publicness" and inappropriateness of the act may suggest it is a message. Similarly, holding one's dinner fork in an idiosyncratic manner is unlikely to be a message, but using it to stab food off a dinner guest's plate *is* a message, whether it is one of playfulness or boorishness. Other actions like sneezing or blinking are likewise regarded as behavior, not communication, because they are involuntary acts that neither convey a consistent meaning nor can be used deliberately to send a particular meaning.

The important point is that not every behavior should be regarded as communication; as with information, *communication is a subset of behavior, which is itself a subset of information*. The relationship is shown graphically in Figure 1.1. This perspective reduces the number of things that qualify as nonverbal communication to a manageable level.

Source, Receiver, and Message Orientations

Another helpful distinction in defining nonverbal communication is the general orientation one holds on defining communication. This distinction revolves around issues of *intent, consciousness,* and *awareness.* Those who hold a *source orientation* believe that communication includes only those messages that the source intends to send. At minimum, a sender must direct a message toward someone, and a receiver

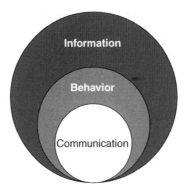

FIGURE 1.1   The relationship among information, behavior, and communication

must attend to that message (Motley, 1991). Unintended or unconscious messages don't count.

The issue of whether communication must be intentional or not is hotly contested (see Andersen, 1998a; Kellermann, 1992; Motley, 1991; Stamp & Knapp, 1990). A major difficulty with imposing intentionality as a criterion is deciding what is or is not intentional behavior and who decides which is which. With verbal communication, one can at least assume an intent to communicate if a person vocalizes or writes something, even if the purpose or meaning of the message itself is unclear. With nonverbal communication, determining intent is much more difficult. As Knapp, Wiemann, and Daly (1978) noted:

> Some messages, for instance, are planned and sent with a high degree of conscious awareness; others seem more casually prepared; some messages are designed to look casual or unintentional; still others are more reflexive, habitual, or expressive responses; and some are "given off" rather than "given." (p. 273)

Is the boss who frowns whenever his employees express a concern communicating or not? He would probably say no; the employee would probably say yes. And who decides—the frowning employer, the disgruntled employee, or an impartial observer? This example shows how easy it is to disavow intent for much of what goes on nonverbally. It also shows how difficult it is to determine what the "right" interpretation is, if there is one. There is no clear arbiter to say the sender's interpretation is any more "correct" than the receiver's or observer's interpretation.

The challenge of discerning intent is compounded by the fact that most nonverbal expressions and patterns are well-learned habits that require little forethought or conscious awareness. Just as we apply a car's brake automatically when approaching a red light, so, too, do we perform numerous nonverbal behaviors without thinking. We do not have to remind ourselves to smile and make eye contact when greeting a friend, for example. This low level of awareness raises the question of whether such routine activity is intentional communication or not. Intent can readily be claimed when the behavior is first learned, as when a child learns not to bump into people. But whether an adult's avoidance of contact with strangers can then be regarded as a deliberate message or just an ingrained, unconscious habit is less clear. It may be that our larger goals and plans are intentional (strategic) but that the particular behaviors used to achieve them may be enacted automatically (Bargh, 1989; Kellermann, 1992). For instance, we may have as a conscious goal making someone else like us, but we may not pay attention to the particular nonverbal behaviors we use to achieve this goal.

There are additional problems with trying to identify intent (Knapp et al., 1978). One is timing. During an encounter, we may not be fully aware of our actions but in retrospect may admit that we purposely committed a particular behavior, such as snubbing someone. If questioned at the time of the act, we might deny intent but at a later time concede it. This suggests that a person's self-report of intent is of questionable value and can vary greatly, depending on when the person is asked. Another problem is that circumstances may alter whether the same behavior is seen as intentional or not. For example, you are probably more likely to see a "hard sell" in the effusive handshake of an insurance salesperson than in the same warm handshake from your friend. But if you meet the salesperson at a social event, you are less likely to attribute ulterior motives to her handshake than if you meet her in the office. Some situations and some people cause us to be more sensitive to intent than others, and we may recognize intent when the communicator does not.

These issues demonstrate that if all behaviors for which a source disclaims responsibility or professes lack of awareness are ruled out as communication, the nonverbal domain may become overly narrow, especially considering how poorly many people monitor their own nonverbal behavior. For this reason, many nonverbal communication scholars find the source orientation unsatisfying.

At the opposite extreme of the source orientation is the *receiver orientation*, which holds that anything a receiver interprets as a message is communication, regardless of source intent or awareness (Andersen, 1991). This perspective originated with a highly popularized postulate of interpersonal communication that "one cannot not communicate" (Watzlawick, Beavin, & Jackson, 1967), which quickly became translated into "all nonverbal behavior is communicative." According to this perspective, accidental and unintended behaviors are included as long as a receiver chooses to read something into them. For example, if a hypersensitive classmate mistakes a squint for a frown and interprets it as a personal rejection, the receiver orientation would say communication has taken place.

The "one cannot not communicate" postulate has generated considerable debate (see Andersen, 1991; Bavelas, 1990; Clevenger, 1991; Motley, 1990). Although in face-to-face contexts it may be true that our behavior at minimum signals whether or not we are willing to interact with another, many find the receiver orientation too broad. From a practical standpoint, we again face the problem of trying to derive some general principles about communication if everything from involuntary and idiosyncratic behaviors—such as allergic sneezing and frequent blinking—to physical traits over which a person has little control—such as buck teeth, short stature or a bow-legged walk—counts, as long as someone draws an inference from them. Imagine, too, our personal discomfort if we truly believed that all of our actions could be "read" by someone. In addition to constantly monitoring our own behaviors, we would have to be on constant alert for signs that a receiver attached meaning to something we did. Common sense tells us that not everything we do is a "message," and such a sweeping perspective would lead us to studying a lot of trivial actions. Perhaps for this reason, many nonverbal experts insist that behaviors have to be intentional to count as communication. Nonverbal communication expert Maureen Keeley of Texas State University put it this way, "I'm not interested in people scratching their head because they have an itch" (Keeley, 2003).

In another respect, the receiver orientation is too narrow. Just as the source orientation downplays the role of the receiver in comparison to the sender, the receiver orientation privileges the receiver over the sender. Given that communication entails both sender and receiver, a definition ought to take both parties into account.

The third perspective, which we follow in this text, is a *message orientation* (Burgoon & Hoobler, 2002). Three decades ago, psychologists Wiener, Devoe, Rubinow, and Geller (1972) distinguished between nonverbal communication and nonverbal behavior. The message orientation draws upon those distinctions. Communication is viewed as only including those behaviors that form a socially shared coding system. This includes behaviors that (1) *are typically sent with intent*, (2) *are used with regularity among members of a given social community, society, or culture*, (3) *are typically interpreted as intentional*, and (4) *have consensually recognized meanings*. The operative terms are "typically," "regularity," and "consensually recognized." Behaviors need not be intentional or regarded as intentional every time they are used. But they must be ones that senders routinely select when they want to encode an intentional message and ones that receivers routinely recognize as constituents of intentionally crafted messages. They should also have a definable set of common interpretations associated with them (such as might be found in a dictionary) and be used frequently enough for those meanings to achieve normative status. In short, they should form the "lexicon" of nonverbal communication.

The properties of a message orientation form the foundation for the *social meaning model of nonverbal behavior* (Burgoon & Newton, 1991), which holds that many nonverbal cues and constellations of cues have meanings that transcend context. This does not deny that meanings are also negotiated between sender and receiver within a particular interaction context (see Stamp & Knapp, 1990) but it does place constraints on the meanings that are possible and probable.

From a message orientation, an unconscious frown would not qualify as communication if it occurred while a person was working alone, or was merely overseen by an onlooker, or could be attributed to a person being "lost in thought." But it would count if viewed by a recipient as an expression of irritation, even if the sender were unaware of betraying his feelings, because a frown is part of the "vocabulary" of nonverbal communication. A teenage busboy wearing unmatched tennis shoes would be too idiosyncratic to produce consistent meaning among observers and by itself might lead merely to the inference that the wearer is disorganized or socially inept. However, if coupled with such other nonconformist actions as wearing spiked blue hair and a dog collar, it could become a "statement" of rebellion, especially if worn around authority figures. Context, then, guides whether and how to interpret specific acts. Nonverbal expert Cindy White of the University of Colorado sums it up this way:

> If you roll your eyes during an interview, that could either be a joke or it could be taken to mean that you are disgusted with something. Some of that depends on the context but we have shared meanings of those that we come to understand, and we also don't typically think of people as rolling their eyes accidentally because it requires a certain amount of action and because it's used in strategic ways. (White, 2003)

We find the message orientation most practical for studying nonverbal communication because it sidesteps the trap of trying to discern communicator intent for every action and includes both habitual and mindful actions. It also avoids the problem of the relative skill, self-monitoring, and perceptiveness of communicators determining whether their behavior qualifies as nonverbal communication or not. At a more theoretical level, this perspective also reflects our belief that although different communicators will bring various connotations and experience-shaped interpretations to a given behavior, without some common "nonverbal vocabulary and grammar," communication between people would be impossible.

Symbols and Signs

A final issue is the distinction that is made between signs and symbols. *Signs* are things that stand for something else and produce at least some of the responses that the referent produces. Used in this general sense, signs include language (linguistic signs). However, for our purposes, it is more useful to limit signs to referents that are *natural and intrinsic representations of what they signify,* such as smoke being a sign of fire. Signs may be an attribute of a larger entity and index its presence or index the relationship between meaning and form. For example, nonverbal emotional expressions such as crying and smiling are often outward manifestations of internally experienced feelings or actional tendencies (Buck, 1994). Signs also may have an *iconic* relationship with the referent, in which case there is a physical resemblance between the sign and the referent. For example, a sculpture is a highly iconic sign of the person represented; a photograph is a somewhat less iconic version (because it is only two dimensional). What some refer to as expressive behavior and others call behaviors with intrinsic meaning generally qualify as signs.

By contrast, *symbols* are *arbitrarily assigned representations that stand for something else.* The word "fire" is an arbitrarily selected label or symbol for the substance of fire (unlike the iconic visual representation on campground billboards). Nonverbal symbols include such things as the hitchhiker's thumbing gesture, the cleric's white collar that signifies a religious occupation, and the "give me five" hand slap used as a congratulatory gesture. Recall that the New Jersey Supreme Court upheld a contempt citation against an attorney because it considered his laughing, rolling his head, and throwing himself back in his chair during the judge's rulings as clear messages of disrespect.

Buck (1991) makes an important distinction between our *biologically shared signal system* and our *socially shared signal system*. Biologically based displays such as territorial defense, anger displays, and play behavior are involuntary, spontaneous, and indicative of emotional or motivational states. Usually the right hemisphere of the brain is dominant for processing such signals. The socially shared signal system consists of symbols that (1) are voluntary and intentional, (2) have an arbitrary relationship between the reference (symbol) and the referent (the thing itself), (3) are part of a socially shared coding system, (4) have propositional content, which means they are capable of logical analysis and can be declared true or false, and (5) are processed primarily by the left hemisphere of the brain. Nonverbal author Ross Buck (2003) of the University of Connecticut elaborates:

> I think of communication as proceeding in two simultaneous streams, one of which is symbolic in which there is an encoding process; information is encoded into symbols and is decoded by the receiver. Then the other way is a spontaneous process where emotion is displayed and is picked up by pre-attunements in the receiver. This is very different because the emotional, the spontaneous process is based upon evolved sending and receiving mechanisms. The sender is not consciously aware of sending an intentional message. The receiver is often not intentionally aware of receiving a message. They often get the message in terms of vibes and feelings.

Some nonverbal behaviors fall into a gray area that Liska (1990) would call *rituals*—"sign behaviors that are neither totally arbitrary nor totally symbolic" (p. 174) and that Buck and VanLear (2002) have labeled as "pseudo-spontaneous." Rituals include spontaneous emotional expressions and species-wide displays such as threat stares that are naturally occurring behaviors the individual need not learn to produce or interpret but that are intentionally shown. Pseudo-spontaneous expressions are ones that appear to be impromptu but are actually deliberately expressed. Posed or controlled emotional expressions such as the feigned sadness at the death of a despised coworker are deliberate and voluntary, have socially shared meaning, and are propositional in that they can be judged as true (honest) or false (deceptive) but are not arbitrarily manufactured expressions. Similarly, the smile may have originated as a natural expression of pleasure or affection, but the smiling face also expresses such nonspontaneous sentiments as approval, congratulations, and well wishes on bumper stickers saying, "Have a Nice Day." Moreover, one can take an essentially spontaneous expression and intentionally overintensify it (e.g., the person who gushes over a gift) or deintensify it (e.g., masking one's pleasure at besting an opponent). In short, nonverbal behaviors originating as biological signals can become social ones when used in conventional or strategic ways.

Because the authors believe that biological and social factors are equally important in shaping nonverbal communication, we devote two separate chapters to these influences. Chapter 2 covers sociocultural influences; Chapter 3 covers bio-evolutionary influences. Everything else we cover needs to be understood within the context of these influences on our behavior.

Nonverbal Codes

The foregoing definitions become much more concrete if we consider the specific codes that are used to produce and interpret them. A code is a set of signals that is usually transmitted via one particular medium or channel. Nonverbal communication codes are often defined by the human sense or senses they stimulate (e.g., the visual sense) and/or the carrier of the signal (e.g., the human body or artifacts). The various codes in combination form the structure of nonverbal communication.

A number of different systems have been advanced for classifying nonverbal codes and channels. One of the earliest approaches, proposed by Ruesch and Kees (1956), grouped nonverbal cues into the three categories of *sign language*, which included any type of gesture that replaces specific words, numbers, or punctuation marks; *action language,* which included all other body movements (e.g., eating, running) not used as signs; and *object language*, which included the intentional or unintentional display of objects (e.g., clothing, architecture, implements, footprints) that could act as statements about their user. Subsequent theorizing has greatly expanded this classic work to refine the categories, ungroup dissimilar types of cues, add important facets of nonverbal communication such as vocal behavior and use of time, and exclude unintentional and noncommunicative behavior. Harrison (1974), for example, identified four categories of *performance codes, spatiotemporal codes, artifactual codes,* and *mediatory codes* (special effects of media when interposed between sender and receiver).

Today, most textbooks differentiate nonverbal codes according to the medium being used to transmit the signal. *Kinesics,*[1] or what is known in the popular vernacular as body language, refers to body movements that are used to convey messages. Included here are facial expressions, head movements, eye behavior, gestures, posture, and gait. (Some people use a separate category of *oculesics* for eye behavior.) Vocal activity forms another category of performance codes known variously as paralanguage, prosody, or *vocalics.* This code includes such features of the voice as dialect, pitch, tempo, resonance, pauses, dysfluencies, and intonation patterns.

The body itself is also a vehicle for conveying messages through *physical appearance, adornments,* and *olfactics.* Included in this code are natural features of the body as well as grooming, hair styling, clothing, adornments such as tattoos, personal artifacts such as jewelry, and use of body odors and fragrances.

Two closely related codes that form the opposites of an approach-avoidance continuum are haptics and proxemics. *Haptics* refers to the use of touch as a communication system, whereas *proxemics* refers to the use of space and distance to communicate. Together these form the contact codes.

Two final codes are *chronemics,* which is the use of time to communicate, and *artifacts* (sometimes called objectics), or the use and arrangement of the physical environment and objects to communicate. Together these form the time and place codes.

In this text, we will first examine the nonverbal codes separately, defining each in more detail, discussing various taxonomies of their constituent parts, and considering norms related to their use. We have grouped together the visual and

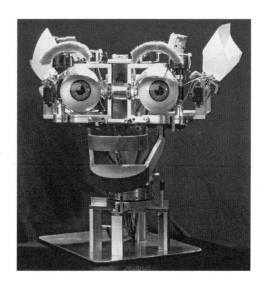

PHOTO 1.4   *Kismet is an expressive robotic creature with humanlike nonverbal inputs and outputs. The robot is equipped with visual, auditory, and proprioceptive sensory inputs to recognize human movements such as hand waving. The motor outputs include vocalizations, facial expressions, and motor capabilities to adjust the gaze direction of the eyes and the orientation of the head and to display moods and emotions such as surprise (shown here with open mouth and raised eyebrows).*

auditory performance codes (kinesics and vocalics), body codes (appearance, adornments, and olfactics), contact codes (proxemics and haptics), and time and place codes (chronemics and artifacts). Although it is necessary temporarily to decompose nonverbal communication into its component codes, we want to emphasize that ultimately, it is critical to look at the interrelationships among codes if any understanding of nonverbal communication is to be achieved. As Cherry (1957), a pioneering communication theorist, rightly observed,

> The human organism is one integrated whole, stimulated into responses by physical signals; it is not to be thought of as a box, carrying independent pairs of terminals labeled "ears," "eyes," "nose," et cetera. (pp. 131–131)

The various nonverbal channels simultaneously send forth a stream of information, and it is the totality of all the channels, of their juxtaposition to one another and their degree of congruence or incongruence, that produces the meaningful pattern. People working in the fields of artificial intelligence and robotics are keenly aware of how much the various nonverbal modalities must be integrated to be able to express and respond in a comprehensible way. Kismet, a robot developed at MIT (shown in Photo 1.4), is one example of emerging devices that can show and recognize human expressions. Thus, the second half of this textbook will take an integrated view by looking at how the codes work together to achieve specific communication functions.

Functions and Processes

Functions are the purposes, motives, or goals of communication. An analysis of functions answers the question, what does nonverbal communication *do*? Processes are the patterns of behavior between interactants and across time.

A functional perspective makes several assumptions. First, *the nature of the specific communication function determines the nonverbal behaviors to be observed.* Some nonverbal codes may be irrelevant or inconsequential for some functions. For example, hair style would be a "bit player" in expressing emotions. Second, *every function has situational characteristics.* Certain contexts tend to be associated with certain functions and have associated verbal and nonverbal behaviors. An interview, for instance, typically occurs face to face and has a fairly structured turn-taking pattern. Third, *functions are dynamic and transcend single time frames.* Although it is convenient to study episodes that cover a finite period of time, a given function rarely begins or ends in a single occasion. It may be influenced by previous functions, may evolve as the transaction unfolds, and may influence subsequent episodes. That said, the immediate situational features and the behaviors of other participants that might elicit one's own nonverbal behavior are considered more revealing about communication than are "initial" causes, such as a traumatic childhood. Fourth, *a single nonverbal cue may serve multiple functions.* Direct gaze, for example, may express relational involvement while facilitating learning and behavioral change. Fifth, *a single function may be accomplished through multiple nonverbal cues.* Fear may be expressed vocally, facially, posturally, proxemically, haptically, or through any combination of these channels. Sixth, and perhaps most importantly, *a single function typically requires the coordination of verbal and nonverbal behaviors.* Communication is usually a cooperative venture among several nonverbal channels and the verbal channel. To understand how communication goals are enacted, it is necessary to study how the various codes work together to attain their aim.

Early analyses of functions focused on the subsidiary role of nonverbal behavior to verbal communication. Ekman and Friesen (1969b) proposed five functions that became the popular view of the primary functions of nonverbal behavior. They include *redundancy* (duplicating the verbal message), *substitution* (replacing the verbal message), *complementation* (amplifying or elaborating on the verbal message), *emphasis* (highlighting the verbal message), and *contradiction* (sending opposite signals of the literal meaning of the verbal message). This set of functions highlights the close linkage between verbal and nonverbal communication and the ways in which nonverbal cues clarify and amplify verbal meanings.

However, nonverbal behaviors need not be relegated to auxiliary status. Not only do they hold equal partnership with verbal behavior in accomplishing numerous communication functions, they often operate independently in achieving communication goals. Scholars have proposed a variety of functions that nonverbal behaviors fulfill (see Argyle, 1967, 1972a; Burgoon & Saine, 1978; Eisenberg & Smith, 1971; Harrison, 1974; Higginbotham & Yoder, 1982; Patterson, 1983, 1990; Scheflen, 1967; Scheflen & Scheflen, 1972; Sebeok, 1964 for earlier typologies). The ones we will cover in this textbook represent a synthesis of the primary ones that have been identified and studied.

Message production and processing builds on the Ekman-Friesen typology by considering in greater depth the integral role that nonverbal behaviors play in creating and interpreting a total message. The physiology of the brain's processing of nonverbal cues, how nonverbal cues "prime the pump" to make an utterance possible, and how they aid in initial comprehension and subsequent recall of information are among the topics considered under this function.

Social cognition and impression formation addresses the ways in which people form initial impressions of others. It considers which judgments are accurate and which are stereotypic. It also covers which nonverbal cues are responsible for impressions of others.

Expressing real and desired identities combines the way we signal to others who we think we are and who we would like them to think we are. This function covers how people identify their personality, gender orientation, age, and socioeconomic status through their nonverbal behavior. Part of this process arises from conforming to social norms for one's sex, age, ethnicity, and culture. Stereotypic identities—for example, as a conservative Christian, a young Arab male, or a feminist—set expectations that influence greatly how people communicate with one another. This function also includes how people present themselves to foster attraction and credibility, especially as it might pertain to interviews and other professional contexts.

Expressing emotions concerns the ways in which nonverbal cues transmit our emotions and mood states to others. Kinesics, vocalics, and haptics certainly play a starring role in expressing people's various emotions, so much so that laypeople often associate nonverbal communication exclusively with showing how people feel. The cues that are responsible for these expressions and the accuracy with which emotional messages are sent and received are part of the emotion function. Also included are the ways in which people manage or fail to manage those expressions and the role of nonverbal cues in the "dark side" of communication—conflict, aggression, jealousy, and the like.

Communicating relational messages is one of the primary functions of nonverbal behavior. Relational communication concerns how people define their interpersonal relationships, signaling how they regard one another, their relationship, and themselves within the context of the relationship. Because this topic is so large, we subdivided it into two chapters. The first focuses on the liking and intimacy aspects of relational communication, including attraction, courtship, and affection. The second examines how people exert dominance, power, and influence, and includes the range of nonverbal behaviors that are used to foster credibility, persuade, and dominate others.

Making connections and managing conversations covers conversations from the first hello to the last good-bye and all the ways in which nonverbal cues regulate interaction in between. Greeting rituals, turn-taking patterns, leave-taking, and patterns of matched or mismatched interaction are part of this function. Also included here are the ways in which the environment can be structured to produce different kinds of interactions. Before communication even begins, nonverbal cues define the setting and serve as implicit guidelines for how to behave. They can tell participants what roles are expected, how formal the setting is, what behaviors are proscribed, and so forth.

A final function of *deceiving others* is a culmination of emotional expression, relational communication, impression management, influence, and interaction management principles. Although we typically expect people's communication to be "the truth, the whole truth, and nothing but the truth," much communication falls short of that standard. In the last chapter, we consider how actual deception and suspicion of deception are expressed nonverbally, how receivers utilize nonverbal cues to make truth and credibility judgments, how accurate those judgments are, and how deceptive interactions are likely to be played out.

Although we have selected the previous functions for inclusion in this book, we want to emphasize that these do not represent an exhaustive or even mutually exclusive list. For example, other authors (e.g., Patterson, 1990) propose such other unique functions as *providing information* and *facilitating task and service goals*. The former refers to nonverbal indicative behavior (as opposed to communication). Because such behaviors sometimes become communicative, we address them under the other functional categories. The latter function refers to behaviors that might be used in the process of completing some task or service activity—such as the use of touch during physical examinations or golf instruction. Because these are not truly communication, we leave these to other authors to discuss.

Equally important to taking a functional approach to nonverbal communication is taking a processual one. That is, we need to understand nonverbal communication as an ongoing, dynamic process rather than just a static snapshot of cues or final outcomes at one moment in time. Unfortunately, even though most scholars pay lip service to looking at interaction sequences and longitudinal patterns of nonverbal behavior, little research has actually done so. Exceptions include developmental research, which looks at the acquisition of nonverbal behaviors in childhood and changes in communication ability over the lifespan; dyadic interaction research that examines interaction sequences, especially turn-taking and adaptation patterns; and relationship development research that investigates how nonverbal behavior changes during the course of relationships.

Individual Differences, Emotional Intelligence, and Nonverbal Skills

Individual Variability

We have all had experiences interacting with individuals who are rude, impolite, or socially inept. We have also been around people who are charming and charismatic, drawing others to them like moths to light. Individuals clearly have their own communication styles and differ in their nonverbal prowess. Does this mean that there is so much variability in nonverbal performance that it is too complex to make sense of? And does it mean that we are stuck with whatever talents (or lack thereof) that nature has given us?

The answer to both questions is no. It is true that no two individuals are exactly alike in their nonverbal styles and that the same individual may change from one moment to the next. Moreover, when two or more people come together, their joint interaction pattern takes on additional uniqueness. Yet a moment's reflection reassures us that there must be some consistency in human behavior within and between individuals or we could never carry on a conversation; each encounter would be a new and foreign event.

Many of the differences between people are what Berger (1977) referred to as *irrelevant variety*. That is, there are many interesting differences that actually don't make a difference as far as communication goes. It doesn't matter, for example, that some people at a dinner gathering hold their fork in the European manner and others do not. LaFrance and Mayo (1978b) proposed that there are essentially three layers of human behavior that range from complete commonality between people to great dissimilarity, depending on whether they bear "content" or relate more to "form." The innermost core represents nonverbal behaviors considered to be universal and innate; facial expressions of some emotional states belong to this core. These are behaviors that all humans exhibit and recognize. Next come nonverbal behaviors that show both uniformity and diversity; members of all cultures display emotions, express intimacy, and signal status, but the particular signs for doing so are variable. Finally, there are nonverbal behaviors that are highly dissimilar across people and cultures—language-related acts, certain gestures, and personality-related actions show this diversity most clearly.

As we move from the universal to the particular, our ability to predict and explain a given person's nonverbal behaviors becomes more complicated and imprecise. Nevertheless, we are able to form expectations that people will commit certain behaviors and omit others. These expectations are grounded in the normative or typical behavior patterns for a given class of people. Although it may be difficult to say exactly how Person A will respond to Person B in Situation X, it is possible to develop some predictions about how people *like* Person A typically respond to people *like* Person B in Situation X. These predictions are based on the average response pattern of similar people under a given circumstance. If Person A is an extrovert and extroverts usually reciprocate direct eye contact, we can anticipate that Person A will do the same when Person B gazes at A. Our predictions will obviously not be error-free, but imperfect knowledge is better than none in navigating the waters of our social world. In addition, the more familiar we are with people, the better we can adjust our predictions about their actions to take into account their own idiosyncrasies.

Emotional Intelligence and Nonverbal Skills

In the past, it has been common to rely on personality traits to explain and predict individual differences. We will consider some of these individual personality differences when we discuss identities in Chapter 10. But there has been a noticeable shift in the nonverbal and interpersonal communication literature away from personality-based predictions and toward the concepts of communicator competence (knowledge of what behaviors are expected, appropriate and effective in a given context) and skills (how someone puts that knowledge into practice). Social skills, communicator style, expressiveness, empathy, sensitivity, interpersonal orientation, self-monitoring, rapport, and charisma are all labels for this general constellation of individual abilities that is now being identified in some quarters as another aspect of human intelligence called *emotional intelligence* (Goleman, 1995; Mayer, Salovey, & Caruso, 1999; see also Chapter 11, where we consider emotional intelligence in more detail).

Unlike variables that look only at the sending side of the equation, however, nonverbal skills and emotional intelligence encompass both sending and receiving abilities that influence the course of a social interaction so that the interactants' goals are more likely to be achieved (Feldman, Philipott & Custrin, 1991). Nonverbal sending abilities—also called *nonverbal expressivity*—entail the capacity to encode and express oneself in ways that can be received and decoded correctly by others, whereas nonverbal receiving abilities—also called *nonverbal sensitivity*—entail the capacity to accurately decode the expressions of others (Rosenthal, Hall, DiMatteo, Rogers, & Archer, 1979). The former may be rooted in a biologically based system of temperament that is further shaped by social learning processes, whereas the latter may be especially subject to social learning and cultural practices (Buck, 1983, 1984).

Numerous standardized performance and self-report measures have been developed to tap into these abilities (see Burgoon & Bacue, 2003). Curiously, subjective judgments of ability do not show a high correspondence with objective measures of ability (Marangoni, Garcia, Ickes, & Teng, 1995). People who report being empathic, for example, may not actually score higher on empathic accuracy than others. Conversely, people who are very accurate in judging the emotions and intentions of others may not rate themselves as particularly sensitive or empathic. Still, both types of measures predict communicative performance with some reliability and correlate with a wide range of measures that conceptually should relate to social skills (Riggio, 1986). People who perceive themselves as nonverbally sensitive are better at role-playing and creating impressions of warmth, dependability, and supportiveness. They are also better able to judge other people's social competence and to accurately interpret other people's behavior (Hall, 1998).

Just how important are these social skills? The brief synopsis in Box 1.3 gives some indication: They affect everything from people's ability to make themselves understood and the quality of their social life to their ability to get along with and influence others. Given this crucial importance in successful nonverbal communication, we will return to the role of nonverbal skills throughout several of the later chapters. Given their relevance to emotions, we will return to them in more detail in Chapter 11, where we present Riggio's (1992) dimensions of nonverbal skill, which include expressivity, control and sensitivity, and approaches to emotional intelligence developed by Mayer, Salovey & Caruso (2004) and Goleman (1995) that center on self-awareness, self-regulation and motivation. For the moment, however, we can draw a few generalizations about the role of general skills from over one hundred studies that have been summarized in several volumes (Burgoon & Bacue, 2003; Hall, 1998; Rosenthal, 1979):

1. *Individuals vary substantially in their encoding and decoding ability.* Some people are very expressive and easy to read; others are "opaque." Some people have excellent ability to interpret the expressions of others accurately; others are very poor interpreters.

2. *Better encoders tend to be better decoders and vice versa.* Encoding and decoding skills are correlated. However, the relationship is a modest one. The best encoders

BOX 1.3

Are You a Skilled Communicator?

How can you tell if you have the makings of a skilled communicator? Research shows that, in addition to gender, encoding and decoding ability are related to personality, self-esteem, social predispositions, occupation, age, training, verbal elements of academic intelligence, familiarity, and nonverbal style (e.g., DePaulo & Rosenthal, 1979a; Gallaher, 1992; Riggio, Watring, & Throckmorton, 1993; Stinson & Ickes, 1992; Sullins, 1989).

Good encoders tend to be well-adjusted, extroverted, outgoing, nonreticent, and physically attractive. They have higher self-esteem, hold a more complex view of human nature, and are less dogmatic. They are social participators, have a large social network, and are less lonely. Their communication is generally more expressive, animated, and coordinated. Their nonverbal behaviors are more novel, intense, complex, changeable, and noticeable. They personalize emotional experiences more, engage in more self-monitoring, and are more persuasive. They also may be more socially anxious and more likely to seek help.

Good decoders are more gregarious and sociable, less Machiavellian and dogmatic. They are good at role-playing and creating favorable impressions as well as sizing up other people's social competence, experience, age, and training. Interestingly, those who see themselves as persuasive may be good at sending nonverbal messages but often are not particularly skilled at receiving them, suggesting that more careful listening and observation of others may be warranted.

If you see yourself among the categories of less skilled communicators, take heart. Maturation, experience, training, and instruction do improve ability. The contents of this book offer much practical information on how you can send the messages you mean to send and how you can more accurately interpret the nonverbal messages of others. If you see yourself among the categories of more skilled communicators, we congratulate you, but we hope you, too, realize that you can improve your success with more education and experience.

---

are not necessarily the same people who are the best decoders. Although it is often reported that encoding and decoding skill go hand in hand, research findings have actually been all across the board, with the most likely conclusion being a positive but modest correlation. In other words, if you are a good encoder, you are somewhat more likely to be a good decoder (and vice versa).

3. *Encoding ability in a given channel is positively related to decoding ability in the same channel.* People who are good at expressing themselves vocally, for example, tend to be good at also "reading" others' vocal expressions. People who are good at decoding messages of liking and disliking tend to be more accurate in judging ambivalent messages and deception.

4. *Encoding and decoding abilities are positively related to a variety of personality traits.* Those who are more extroverted, nonreticent, expressive, high in self-esteem, high in self-monitoring and public self-consciousness, nondogmatic, and physically attractive tend to be more skillful in nonverbal encoding. Those who are sociable, nonanxious, publicly self-conscious, empathic, independent, psychologically flexible, and intellectually efficient tend to be better decoders.

5. *Women are more skilled at nonverbal communication than are men.* Women are typically more expressive nonverbally than men when in public or social settings, and their expressions are read more accurately by others. Put differently, women have an advantage over men in sending ability, an advantage that is especially true of facial cues. This difference between males and females is not very pronounced in early childhood but becomes more so past preschool. Women are also better decoders of nonverbal cues than men, regardless of the age and sex of sender. This decoding superiority is greatest for facial expressions, followed by body movements, vocal cues, and brief visual cues. Women may have less of an advantage in identifying discrepant or deceptive messages.

Various theories have been advanced for why women are generally more skilled at nonverbal communication. One is that women may be more "accommodating" than men, causing them to attend most closely to the intentional nonverbal messages of others and not to eavesdrop on unintentionally leaked cues. Another plausible explanation is that women's expressiveness is a function of their adherence to learned gender roles. Their social positions give them greater practice than men observing nonverbal communication because they are more often in passive or submissive roles and they learn to adopt friendly expressions that appease those in positions of power. Other explanations are that they have an innate advantage; that they have different cognitive styles, possibly including greater ability to match affects with verbal labels; and that brain lateralization may differ for males and females.

6. *Other individual differences show weak relationships to encoding and decoding.* Encoding skill is somewhat related to occupation in that more skilled individuals gravitate to people-oriented jobs. It is unrelated to race, education, or intelligence. Decoding skill shows a modest positive relationship to mental abilities, as measured by standardized IQ tests or amount learned from a teacher, and is characterized by a stronger relationship to cognitive complexity. Decoding ability is curvilinearly related to age. It is poorer among the very young and the elderly. Decoding ability also improves with maturation, practice, and training.

These relationships bolster the conclusions that a significant component of individual social skill is attributable to abilities to encode and decode nonverbal behaviors and that certain individuals and subgroups (such as women) have a significant advantage.

Of course, identification of skills isn't the whole picture. People also differ in their preferences, goals, and level of motivation, which will introduce considerable variability from one interaction to the next. As the study of nonverbal communication advances, we should gain greater understanding of how some of these other factors explain individual differences in behavior.

Summary

This chapter lays the groundwork for studying the codes, processes, and functions of nonverbal communication. Nonverbal behaviors are a central and essential part of the communication process. They contribute significantly to the meaning that is extracted from communicative episodes and they influence communication outcomes. Possible reasons for this powerful impact include nonverbal cues being omnipresent, forming a sort of universal language system, adding to misunderstanding as well as understanding, expressing what verbal communication can't or shouldn't, having phylogenetic, ontogenetic, and interaction primacy, and being a trusted system of communication.

Before beginning a detailed study of nonverbal communication, it is first necessary to clarify what constitutes it. A wide range of definitions is possible, some of which use the concepts of information, behavior, and communication interchangeably. In this text, we distinguish among these three. It is also possible to generate different definitions depending on whether one takes a source, receiver, or message orientation. In this text, emphasis is on the latter approach, which regards as communication those behaviors that are used with regularity by a social community, are typically encoded with intent, and are typically decoded as intentional. In analyzing these perspectives, we have addressed a number of issues related to intentionality, awareness, propositionality, and meaning, including whether nonverbal behaviors are signs or symbols. The position advanced here is that the total nonverbal communication system includes a mix of signs and symbols with varying degrees of awareness, volition, and propositionality. Some emanate from our biological heritage. Others are the result of social forces. Together, they create a complex set of influences on how we communicate nonverbally.

The mix of signals derives from the various nonverbal codes that work together to produce a wide range of communication functions. To gain the fullest understanding of how these codes coordinate with one another and with the verbal code to achieve desired outcomes, nonverbal communication should be studied as a dynamic system that is highly integrated with verbal communication and should take into account cultural, contextual, and individual differences. This is the approach that will be followed throughout this text.

SUGGESTED READINGS

Buck, R., & VanLear, C. A. (2002). Verbal and nonverbal communication: Distinguishing symbolic, spontaneous, and pseudo-spontaneous communication. *Journal of Communication, 52,* 522–541.

Ekman, P., & Friesen, W. V. (1969b). The repertoire of nonverbal behavior: Categories, origins, usage, and coding. *Semiotica, 1,* 49–98.

Knapp, M. L., & Hall, J. (2010). *Nonverbal communication in human interaction.* (7th ed.) Orlando, FL: Harcourt Brace Jovanovich.

Morris, D. (1985). *Bodywatching.* New York: Crown.

Patterson, M. L. (1991). A functional approach to nonverbal exchange. In R. S. Feldman & B. Rimé (Eds.), *Fundamentals of nonverbal behavior* (pp. 458–495). New York: Cambridge University Press.

Wiener, M., Devoe, S., Rubinow, S., & Geller, J. (1972). Nonverbal behavior and nonverbal communication. *Psychological Review, 79,* 185–214.

2 Sociocultural Influences on Nonverbal Communication

A culture may be conceived as a network of beliefs and purposes in which any string in the net pulls and is pulled by the others, thus perpetually changing the configuration of the whole.

—Jacques Barzun, educator and author

People from different nations and various cultural backgrounds have distinct ways of using nonverbal communication. These differences in nonverbal behavior help groups of people create unique identities that often reflect shared values and cultural history. For example, in some Asian cultures, bowing symbolizes much more than a simple greeting or departing behavior; bowing is based on a long-standing tradition of showing respect to high-status individuals. The lower and longer the bow is, the greater the show of respect.

To be able to appreciate nonverbal behaviors such as the bow, one must first understand their meaning within a given culture or community. It is difficult, however, for people from outside a particular culture to understand fully all the nuances—let alone the basic meanings—behind various forms of nonverbal communication. In this chapter, we hope to give you a basic understanding of the complex role that culture plays in shaping nonverbal communication. We begin by discussing the importance of nonverbal communication in cross-cultural interaction. Then we define the terms *culture* and *co-culture*, describe five cultural dimensions that influence nonverbal communication, and outline some important points to keep in mind when interpreting cultural differences in communication. The chapter ends with a summary of cultural differences in each nonverbal code, ranging from gestures to chronemics. Our review of these differences is by no means complete, and we do not pretend to understand all of the nuances of communication across different cultures, especially since we are viewing these differences through our own cultural lenses. We do, however, hope that this chapter will help you appreciate and be sensitive to the diversity of nonverbal communication across different cultures.

The Importance of Nonverbal Communication in Cross-Cultural Interaction

In the 21st century, advances in technology, telecommunications, and transportation have increased the frequency of cross-cultural communication. Many cultures that only a few decades ago led isolated existences now find themselves thrust onto the world stage and into the global economy. Individuals who might have had little contact with other cultures only a generation or two ago are now confronted with media images of people worldwide who have different values and engage in different behaviors than they do. And world leaders are meeting for face-to-face summits and engaging in video conferencing more than ever. When cultural values clash, as seems often to be the case, a better understanding of cultural differences in nonverbal communication is foundational to successful international relationships and communication.

Indeed, there are many famous accounts of nonverbal communication being misinterpreted in international settings. These misunderstandings can lead to embarrassment and sometimes even have political consequences. One well-known example involves President Richard Nixon disembarking from Air Force One in South America and displaying the "OK" hand gesture that is commonly used in the United States. This gesture is considered obscene in South America, where it symbolizes the female genitalia. In another famous case, the Soviet Premier, Leonid Brezhnev, visited the United States to meet with President Nixon. When he exited his plane, he clenched his hands together over his head in a gesture that people from the United States regard as a sign of superiority and victory. However, Brezhnev had not meant to offend his audience; he was simply using a gesture that in Russia signals gratitude for a warm welcome.

These types of misunderstandings also have political ramifications for current events, such as the ongoing tensions in the Middle East. To illustrate cultural differences in greetings, Axtell (1998) gave an example of a 1994 meeting between Yasser Arafat, the leader of the Palestinian Authority, and Yitzhak Rabin, the Israeli prime minister. The media reported that there had been considerable discussion regarding if and when the two leaders should shake hands. In line with cultural customs, Arafat was reportedly comfortable with a high-contact greeting (such as a hearty handshake accompanied by cheek kissing), but Rabin was more comfortable with a reserved handshake. Rabin reportedly agreed to the handshake only after being assured that there would be no cheek kissing. Still, when the time came to shake hands in front of the world media, Arafat stepped forward with his hand outstretched and Rabin hesitated before accepting it (see Photo 2.1). Rabin's hesitation could easily be viewed as insulting rather than as a cultural difference in nonverbal communication. Similarly, Arafat's expressiveness could be viewed as aggression rather than enthusiasm.

The business world is another place where cultural differences in nonverbal communication can create misunderstanding. Businesspeople are increasingly meeting on the global stage, where they must cope with differences in the ways they conduct business. For example, the owner of a Japanese computer company might come to the United States to negotiate a deal with the president of a software

PHOTO 2.1   *Israeli Prime Minister Yitzhak Rabin and Palestine Leader Yasser Arafat shake hands while President Clinton and the world watch.*

company in San Francisco. How should they greet one another? Are there different cultural rules for exchanging business cards or displaying emotions while negotiating and closing the deal? By knowing the answers to these types of questions about nonverbal behavior, these two business executives would be better equipped to engage in a smooth and mutually satisfying negotiation. The Japanese executive might extend his hand in greeting, and the software company president might bow slightly as she shakes hands with him. When he offers her his business card, she might examine it for a few moments before carefully placing it in her wallet. This type of interaction would show that both parties respect one another's norms and customs, which would pave the way for a successful business transaction.

Defining Culture and Related Terms

Of course, culture influences our behavior across a wide variety of situations, ranging from business interactions to personal relationships. Culture is a pervasive force that affects all humans, usually at a subconscious level. Scholars in fields such as anthropology and communication often define *culture* in terms of a learned and enduring pattern of beliefs, values, and behaviors that influences a large group of people (Andersen, 1988; Geertz, 1973; Lustig & Koester, 2003). Hofstede (1984, 1991, 2001) explained that this shared set of beliefs, values, and behaviors is rooted in the way a group of people interacts with the social environment. Thus, culture is learned through interaction with one's family and friends, as well as with social and religious institutions such as schools and churches. As such, culture can be thought of as a socially constructed phenomenon that is passed on from generation to generation (Philipsen, 1992).

Within any culture, there are a number of co-cultures. A *co-culture* refers to a group of people within a given culture who share particular ways of thinking and behaving. These sociological groupings can be tied to religion, ethnicity, age, social class, geographic location, sexual orientation, or gender, just to name a few types of co-culture. People are influenced by both the broad culture in which they live and the co-cultures to which they belong. For example, if Winona is a young Native American mother living on a reservation in Arizona, she is likely to have different values and cultural experiences than Terrell, who is an African American activist living in an affluent suburb of Chicago. Yet both Winona and Terrell are likely to be affected by broader cultural values that characterize the United States. In this chapter, we focus primarily on culture at a broad, national level, although we acknowledge that co-cultures play a critical role in determining one's cultural identity.

Winona and Terrell would also belong to different social groups. The term *ingroup* refers to the groups to which an individual belongs, and the term *outgroup* refers to the groups to which an individual does not belong. Often, people within the same ingroup communicate in ways that reflect their identification with the group. For example, when Winona is with a group of young mothers, she might talk about certain issues related to parenthood that outgroup members, such as Terrell, would not understand or appreciate. Similarly, Terrell might show identification with other African Americans by using certain gestures, accents, and slang that Winona would not understand.

Characteristics of Culture

At the broad level, cultures are distinguished from one another by a number of different characteristics, including educational level, tolerance for uncertainty, and respect for tradition (e.g., Andersen, 1988; Hofstede, 1980, 2001). Some cultures are more homogeneous than others. For instance, the United States is highly diverse, given that its population comes from a variety of ethnic and cultural backgrounds. This can lead to more variation in nonverbal communication. Some cultures have more traditions than others. Places such as Japan and the Middle East draw on ancient history and philosophies to guide their values and behaviors, whereas the United States has a relatively short history. Thus, some of the gestures used by people from countries such as Japan, India, China, Iran, Lebanon, or Saudi Arabia originated in customs or social practices that are centuries old.

Although many cultural dimensions have been identified, research has shown that five dimensions in particular are connected to nonverbal communication: (1) individualism versus collectivism; (2) immediacy versus nonimmediacy; (3) low versus high power distance; (4) low versus high context; and (5) femininity versus masculinity (Andersen, Hecht, Hoobler, & Smallwood, 2002; Andersen & Wang, 2006). Each of these dimensions is reviewed in the following sections.

Individualist Versus Collectivist Cultures

This distinction reflects the degree to which a culture is oriented toward individual versus group needs. People in individualistic cultures value personal space, autonomy, privacy, freedom (including personal choice), and the right to express themselves verbally and emotionally. In Hofstede's (1980) study of 40 non-communist nations, the United States rated the highest in terms of individualism, followed by Australia, England, Canada, the Netherlands, New Zealand, Italy, Belgium, Denmark, and France. Not surprisingly, all of the countries on this list have been classified as "Western" in terms of thinking. Because people in individualistic countries value privacy, they regulate personal space. Because they value freedom of expression, they tend to express both positive and negative emotions more spontaneously than do those in collectivistic cultures, especially when with friends and loved ones (Matsumoto, 2006). Some research also suggests that people in individualistic cultures have more interactions with different people during the course of a typical day (Wheeler, Reis, & Bond, 1989).

Eastern countries, in contrast, tend to be characterized by collectivism, as do some countries in South America. According to Hofstede's (1980, 2001) work, Venezuela, Colombia, Pakistan, Peru, Taiwan, Thailand, and Singapore are all good examples of collectivistic cultures. Other scholars have described both Japan and China as collectivistic cultures (e.g., Andersen & Wang, 2006; Lustig & Koester, 2003; Matsumoto, 1991). People in collectivistic cultures value harmony among people and between people and nature. They value togetherness, loyalty, and tradition, so the needs of the collective group are perceived as more important than the needs of any one person. Extended families play a key role in people's lives within collectivistic cultures, and expressions of negative emotions that could upset the balance of harmony within one's family or broader social group are inhibited (Matsumoto, 2006). In fact, individuals from collectivistic cultures have a harder time recognizing and identifying other people's facial expressions of negative emotion than do people from individualistic cultures (Beaupre & Hess, 2005).

Immediate Versus Nonimmediate Cultures

Early work by Hall (1966, 1990) identified different nations as *contact* or *noncontact* cultures based on how much people from various countries touched, as well as how close people stood to each other during conversation. Later, Andersen and his colleagues expanded this idea by noting that cultures differ to the extent that they are *nonverbally immediate* (Andersen et al, 2002; Andersen & Wang, 2006). People in nonverbally immediate cultures touch more and stand closer together, and they also use more eye contact, face one another more directly, and talk in louder voices than do people in less nonverbally immediate cultures. Overall, people in immediate cultures are more comfortable with higher levels of sensory stimulation through nonverbal cues. Think about how distance is connected to sensory stimulation: People who stand closer together can also touch one another easily, smell one another, hear the nuances in one another's voices, and get a close-up view of one another's facial expressions. In contrast, people who stand farther apart see more of the other person's body. Hall suggested that people in high contact (or highly immediate) cultures rely most on tactile and olfactory modes of communication, whereas people in noncontact (or nonimmediate) cultures rely most on visual communication. Thus, the distinction of a culture as contact versus noncontact, or immediate versus nonimmediate, is based on touch and proxemic distancing, as well as other behaviors that show engagement within an interaction, such as gaze and expressiveness.

Research suggests that the Middle East, the Mediterranean area of Europe (Greece, southern Italy, southern France, southern Spain, and Portugal), eastern

Europe (including Russia), North Africa, Mexico, Central America, and South America are generally characterized as contact cultures. In contrast, northern Europe (Finland, Sweden, Norway), Germany, Great Britain, and most Asian counties (China, Japan, South Korea, the Philippines, Thailand, Vietnam, and Taiwan) have been classified as primarily noncontact cultures (Andersen, 2008; Andersen, Andersen, & Lustig, 1987; Barnlund, 1978; Hall, 1990; Hecht, Andersen, & Ribeau, 1989; Heslin & Alper, 1983; Patterson, 1983; Remland, Jones, & Brinkman, 1995). Although the United States was classified as a noncontact culture in early work (e.g., Hall, 1990), more recent studies suggest that the United States is a moderately immediate culture (Andersen, 2008; Andersen & Wang, 2006; McDaniel & Andersen, 1998).

You may be surprised that Asian countries are characterized as relatively nonimmediate. More than half of the world's population lives in Asia, and cities such as Tokyo and Beijing are crowded with people. One way that Asians may compensate for their crowded conditions is by reducing immediacy cues, such as smiling and eye contact. A recent study compared how people from the United States and Japan reacted to pedestrians who walked by them (Patterson et al., 2007). The confederates who were helping the experimenters were trained to look and smile at the oncoming pedestrian, look without smiling, or avoid looking by keeping their eyes focused on something straight ahead. People from the United States looked back more than people from Japan. In fact, only 1% to 2% of the Japanese people smiled, nodded, or spoke to the confederate, compared to 9% to 25% of the people from the United States. In addition, the Japanese tended to respond with low levels of immediacy regardless of what the confederate did. People from the United States had strong responses to increasing levels of immediacy. They were more likely to smile, nod, or greet the confederates who glanced at them rather than looked straight ahead, and they were even more likely to engage in these types of immediacy behaviors when the confederates had looked at them and smiled.

Low- Versus High-Power Distance Cultures

Power distance refers to the degree of social inequality that exists within a given culture. The degree of power distance is also related to how much people value social status and authority, and how evenly (or unevenly) resources are distributed within a particular society. Hofstede (1980) coined the term *power distance index* to refer to the degree to which a co-culture or individual member of a culture is separated from another co-culture or individual in terms of power.

Cultures characterized by high levels of power distance are typically authoritarian, with power and resources held by only a few high-status members of society. There are usually sharp distinctions between the lower, middle, and upper classes within high-power distance cultures. Hofstede (1980, 2001) identified the following countries as high in power distance: the Philippines, Mexico, Venezuela, India, the former Yugoslavia, Singapore, Brazil, France, Hong Kong (prior to it being a district of China), and Colombia. In high-power distance cultures such as these, communication functions to reinforce status differences. For example, people of lower status are likely to engage in submissive nonverbal behavior and to hide negative emotions, especially when in the presence of high-status others

(Basabe et al., 2000). Compared to people in low-power distance cultures, people in high-power distance cultures are more likely to use both nonverbal and verbal behaviors to try to save face when they think they are being perceived negatively (Merkin, 2006).

In contrast, cultures characterized by low levels of power distance are more egalitarian, with power and resources spread out among different individuals and various groups of people, and less distinctions between classes. Hofstede (1980) identified the following countries as lowest in power distance: Austria, Israel, Denmark, New Zealand, Ireland, Sweden, Norway, Finland, Switzerland, and England. In these cultures, nonverbal communication sometimes functions to minimize status differences. For example, people in northern European countries might show more symmetry in their nonverbal behavior as a way to stress similarities rather than status differences.

Some countries possess characteristics that are related to both high- and low-power distance. In Japan, for instance, people with high status are revered, making distinctions between those of low and high status important. Yet wealth is distributed fairly evenly. Indeed, the gap between the salaries of entry-level employees and executives is much smaller in Japan than it is in countries such as Mexico, India, and the United States. In Japan, subordinate employees are also perceived as making important contributions to their companies despite their relatively low status. The United States is also moderate in terms of its power distance score. On the one hand, in the United States people believe that everyone deserves an equal opportunity to prosper, but on the other hand, there are definitely distinct differences in the wealth and resources connected to different social classes.

High- Versus Low-Context Cultures

Cultures also differ in terms of how much information is explicitly communicated within the environment (Hall, 1981). In high-context cultures, information is found in the physical environment or within people rather than in messages themselves. Thus, there is a heavy reliance on nonverbal forms of expression in high-context cultures (Hall, 1981). To interpret a message, individuals must be familiar with the meanings that are embedded within a given context. Meanings must also be allowed to evolve over time. Hall often used Japanese culture as a prime example of a high-context culture. For example, the Japanese glean a lot of important information about people by looking at their formal rock gardens. The Japanese also send subtle messages of respect and liking through nonverbal behaviors such as bowing, conversational distancing, and subtle facial expression. Artifacts used in Japanese ceremonies, such as teacups, tablecloths, and traditional dress, are replete with meaning.

In contrast, people in low-context cultures do not rely as much on context to interpret messages. Rather, the majority of information needed to interpret a message is found within the message itself. People emphasize the spoken word, and direct forms of communication, such as language and emblems, are relied on more in low-context than high-context cultures. This distinction does not mean that nonverbal communication is unimportant in low-context cultures, but subtle, indirect forms of communication do go unnoticed more often in low-context versus high-context cultures. As you might guess, Hall referred to the United States as a good example of a low-context culture. In the United States, many people value "getting to the point," "saying what you mean," and "being specific." Artifacts are more likely to reflect personal taste and individualism rather than culture or tradition.

Collectivistic cultures tend to be more high-context than individualistic cultures (Hofstede, 1980, 2001). In addition to Japan, other Asian countries such as China, South Korea, and Taiwan have been classified as high-context cultures. The United States is joined by Canada and many northern European regions (including Scandinavia, Germany, and Switzerland) as low-context cultures (Gudykunst & Kim, 1992; Hall, 1981; Levine & Wolff, 1985). Countries in the Mediterranean region, such as France and Italy, appear to use both contextually and noncontextually based message systems about equally. As is the case for many cultural differences in nonverbal communication, it would be a mistake to assume that all people within a given region subscribe to the norm of the mainstream national culture. Indeed, in the United States, African Americans, Mexican Americans, and Native Americans are high-context co-cultures (Lustig & Koester, 2003).

The low- versus high-context distinction is evident in cross-cultural and interpersonal communication (Andersen, 2008) as well as political advertisements (Tak, Kaid, & Khang, 2007). In the study by Tak and colleagues, television spots for political candidates in the United States and Korea were compared. The Korean advertisements were more subdued and contained more subtle messages than the U.S. advertisements, which reflects the high- and low-context orientations of these countries. In another study, when people from Japan were trying to determine how someone was feeling, they paid particular attention to the subtle cues sent by the eyes (Yuki, Maddux, & Masuda, 2007). People from the United States, on the other hand, paid more attention to the mouth, which sends more direct and obvious clues about how someone is feeling through expressions such as smiles, grimaces, and frowns.

Feminine Versus Masculine Cultures

Within every culture, people learn what roles men and women are expected to play in society. They also learn stereotypes about how men and women are supposed to behave. There are two basic cultural orientations toward gender: feminine and masculine (Andersen, 2008; Andersen & Wang, 2006; Hofstede, 1980, 2001). Cultures with a *feminine* orientation are more androgynous, have more flexible gender roles, and value stereotypically female traits such as compassion, care-giving, and cooperation. In contrast, cultures with a *masculine* orientation have more rigid gender roles and value stereotypically male traits such as ambition, strength, and competitiveness.

According to Andersen and his colleagues, cultural orientations regarding gender are related to a number of trends within a culture, including how educated men and women are, the types of occupations men and women have, and attitudes about the distribution of household labor (Andersen, 2008; Andersen et al., 2002; Hecht et al., 1989). A culture's gender orientation is also related to patterns of nonverbal communication. For example, in highly masculine cultures, women are expected to display more submissive behaviors than men and to avoid immediate interaction with men whom they do not know well. Men are expected to inhibit stereotypically feminine expressions, such as overt shows of affection or crying during a sad movie. There are also likely to be fewer sex differences in nonverbal communication in cultures or co-cultures characterized by feminine gender orientations. Importantly, in feminine cultures, both men and women have more freedom of nonverbal expression (Andersen, 2008; Andersen & Wang, 2006). Women can exhibit nonverbal cues reflecting power without penalty, whereas men can display nonverbal cues reflecting affection and care-giving without being seen as unmanly.

As you might be able to guess from this description, the United States is generally regarded as a moderately masculine culture. However, many countries are more masculine than the United States, including Japan, Austria, Venezuela, Italy, Switzerland, Mexico, Ireland, England, and Germany (Hofstede, 1980). Muslim countries in the Middle East also tend to have masculine orientations (Andersen, 2008). The countries with the most feminine gender orientations are located in northern Europe and include Sweden, Norway, the Netherlands, Denmark, and Finland. Countries that fall along the coastal regions of the Pacific Ocean in South America, such as Chile and Peru, also tend to have feminine gender orientations. (For a summary of where various regions fall on the five cultural dimensions, see Table 2.1.)

TABLE 2.1   Cultural Characteristics of Selected Regions

Region	Individualistic/ Collectivist	Immediacy	Power Distance	Context	Gender
Mediterranean Area of Southern Europe	individualistic	high		moderate	
Mexico		high	high	high	masculine
Middle East (excluding Israel)	moderately collectivist	high*		high	masculine
Northern Africa	moderately individualistic	high		high	
Northern Europe (Finland, Sweden, Norway)	moderately individualistic	low	low	low	feminine
Pacific Coast of South America	collectivistic	high		high	feminine
United States**	highly individualistic	moderate	moderate	low	somewhat masculine

*Although many countries in the Middle East are highly immediate, members of the opposite sex exhibit relatively low levels of immediacy in public.

**Canada, Great Britain, and Australia have similar cultural orientations to the U.S., although the U.S. is the most individualistic.

Note: The blank cells indicate that there is not enough information to classify a certain region on a dimension.

Interpreting Research on Culture and Nonverbal Communication

As shown in Table 2.1, different regions of the world are characterized by unique combinations of cultural dimensions. However, it is important to keep in mind that these generalizations are simplistic. Many cultures are rich in diversity and complex in terms of the mix of characteristics that shapes them. Therefore, although the distinctions we make among various cultures should be helpful, you should recognize that differences in nonverbal communication cannot be traced to a single factor such as how individualistic or immediate a particular culture is. Similarly, when you read about differences in nonverbal communication across cultures, it is critical to keep in mind that there are some inherent risks involved in making such comparisons. These risks include emphasizing differences over similarities, overgeneralizing, viewing cultural norms as static, and viewing cultural norms through an ethnocentric lens.

Emphasizing Differences over Similarities

Whenever cross-cultural comparisons are made, there is a tendency for people to think about "us" versus "them" or "Group X" versus "Group Y," although there are likely to be just as many similarities between these groups as differences. For instance, smiling is a universal sign of happiness and friendliness even though the situations under which people suppress or exaggerate smiles vary by culture. Similarly, in most cultures, people tend to stand closer to relational partners than acquaintances, even though people exhibit closer overall distancing in some cultures than others. In other words, two Canadian friends might stand talking to one another with about 18 inches between them, whereas two Brazilian friends might have only 10 inches between them. But both the Canadians and the Brazilians would likely stand closer to a good friend than to an acquaintance.

Overgeneralization

When people learn about cultural differences, they also have a tendency to overgeneralize or stereotype; that is, they may view everyone within a given group similarly. These stereotypes are all around us. You may have heard that Germans are meticulous and punctual, Greeks are vivacious and outgoing, and Polynesians are happy and easygoing. Although stereotypes such as these are sometimes based in cultural values, they ignore differences between individuals and co-cultures. So the German student you meet might really be unorganized, your friend's Greek roommate might be quiet and withdrawn, and when you visit Tahiti you might run into some locals who seem anxious and uptight.

As these examples illustrate, is it important to remember that there is enormous variability within a given culture based on factors such as personality, co-culture, geographic location, and sex. Similarly, when reading our review of cultural differences in nonverbal communication, it is critical to keep in mind that our overview paints a picture of the "average" person within each culture. Yet this average person is a myth. It is unlikely that any one person always communicates in ways that are normative for her or his culture.

Viewing Cultural Norms as Static

Another danger lies in interpreting results from past research as representative of a culture today. Cultures develop and change over time, and this change is often reflected in nonverbal communication. Sometimes this change occurs within a culture or co-culture. For instance, in the mid- to late-1960s in the United States, a new youth co-culture emerged. College students began embracing less traditional values, rebelling against authority, and engaging in more open forms of communication. Other times, a culture is affected by other cultures. Due to technology such as television, the Internet, and air travel, as well as an increasingly global economy that allows people from different cultures to trade goods, people around the world have the opportunity to learn about, and perhaps adopt, each other's customs and communication patterns. For example, although styles of dress still vary quite a bit across the world, people living in North America and Europe have become more similar in terms of the clothing they wear.

In some cases the media promotes understanding of nonverbal behaviors. One of our European students once told us that although people in her country do not "give someone the finger" the way people in the United States do, she had seen the gesture enough times in Hollywood movies to know what it meant. Moreover, she and her friends sometimes used the gesture with one another, but as more of a joke than an insult. Thus, it is important to recognize that cultures themselves, as well as people's understanding of other cultures, are constantly evolving.

Viewing Cultures Through an Ethnocentric Lens

When people are first exposed to cross-cultural differences, they sometimes fall into the trap of evaluating these differences in reference to their own culture. This ethnocentric bias leads people to perceive "foreign" behavioral patterns as odd or inferior. This bias, of course, cuts both ways. You might think that the "over-friendly" way an acquaintance from another culture greets you is presumptuous and inappropriate, but your acquaintance may think that you are "unfriendly" and have a problem showing affection.

One of the authors of this textbook witnessed this type of ethnocentric bias firsthand while traveling in Europe. While in a train, some tourists from the United States commented that Mediterranean people are "backward" because they do not cover up their body odor as well as people in the United States do. Later that evening, a large group of French students was dining in a restaurant where tourists frequent. As they were exiting the restaurant, a few of these students were heard commenting in French that Americans are "savages" who have "disgusting" table manners. In each of these cases, people were making judgments based on the norms within their own culture rather than considering that a behavior can be perfectly acceptable in one cultural setting but inappropriate in another.

BOX 2.1

Arab Hijab: A Sign of Oppression or Pride?

To Westerners, the use of *hijab*—the headscarf traditionally used by Muslim women in Middle Eastern countries—signifies the oppression of women who are not even allowed to show their faces in public in those cultures. Do American women who veil themselves feel the same way, however? To find out, communication professor Rachel Droogsma interviewed 13 American Muslim women who voluntarily veil their heads when in public. She asked each woman to explain why she wore the headscarf and what meanings it signified for her. Contrary to what many Westerners might expect, the women in Droogsma's study said they didn't perceive the veil to be a sign of female oppression. Rather, they reported that wearing the veil helped them express their Muslim identity and their commitment to Muslim principles. It also freed them from worrying about their physical appearance, protected them from being sexually objectified, and allowed them to save their beauty for their husbands. Far from signifying oppression, therefore, hijab functioned as an empowering symbol of the women's Muslim identity.

Source: Droogsma (2007).

Another illustration of viewing nonverbal behavior ethnocentrically is the perception by Westerners that wearing the veil or hijab by women in the Middle East is a sign of oppression. Although in many cases it may be imposed by law or cultural stricture, that is not always the case, as Box 2.1 reveals. Learning more about some of these cultural differences may encourage you to keep an open mind and refrain from making ethnocentric evaluations.

Patterns of Nonverbal Communication Across Cultures

In the next section of this chapter, we discuss some of the key cross-cultural differences in nonverbal communication that have been identified in the literature. As we discuss these differences, you will notice that we often discuss groups of countries that are similar to one another in terms of nonverbal behavior. For example, several countries have been identified as "contact cultures" in which touch and close proxemic distancing are encouraged, and other countries have been identified as "noncontact cultures" in which touch and close proxemic distancing occur less frequently. Keeping both cross-cultural differences and similarities in mind will help you develop clearer expectations about the nonverbal behavior you might see in different parts of the world. Similarities and differences work together to create a unique set of nonverbal cues that act as cultural identifiers. These nonverbal cues are often the primary means by which people signal their identification with cultural or co-cultural groups.

Gestures

Gestures provide one of the most obvious cases of cross-cultural differences in nonverbal communication. Emblems, in particular, tend to differ by culture. As discussed in Chapter 4, *emblems* are gestures that substitute for language. Examples of emblems include waving to say "hello" or "good-bye," nodding to say "yes," putting your hand out so that someone stops, and crossing your fingers to wish a friend "good luck." If you are from the United States, all of these emblems should make sense to you. However, if you are from a different country, some of these examples might not fit the way gestures are used in your country. Because emblems have literal translations, they are tied to language. Therefore, it should not be surprising that emblematic gestures are used differently across cultures, just as different words make up different languages. For example, Jandt (1995) reported that the "come here" gesture used in the United States (which involves moving one's fingers and palm back and forth toward one's body) means "good-bye" in countries such as Italy, China, and Colombia. In Algeria, the wave that signals "hello" and "good-bye" in the United States means "come here" (Martin & Nakayama, 1997). In Box 2.2 we provide a sampling of other emblems that are used in the United States and have different meanings in other cultures.

People also use different emblematic gestures within co-cultures. For example, surfers were initially the primary group who used the Hawaiian "hang loose" gesture. Eventually, this gesture (which involves holding the thumb and little finger up with the three middle fingers down) became popular with a broader segment of the population, but it is still more recognizable in some parts of the United States than others. In fact, one of the authors of this textbook showed this gesture to her classes at universities in Arizona, California, and Pennsylvania. Nearly all of the students in California and most of the students in Arizona recognized this gesture, but only about half the students in Pennsylvania did. Other emblematic gestures are only understood within certain ethnic groups, clubs, families, or circles of friends.

Cross-cultural differences have not been identified as frequently for illustrator gestures as for emblems. However, some research suggests that people from certain countries use expressive gestures more frequently. Arabs use expansive gestures frequently as a way to show involvement and express themselves (Almaney & Alwan, 1982). For Arab women who are wearing veils, gesturing substitutes for facial expression as a way of conveying emotional information. Italians and inhabitants of other countries in southern Europe, and particularly people from cities on the Mediterranean Sea, have been identified as frequently using expressive gestures (Efron, 1972; Morris, Collett, Marsh, & O'Shaughnessy, 1979). This finding fits with research showing that people from warm climates may generally be more expressive than people in cold climates. In fact, Pennebaker, Rimé, and Blankenship (1996) found that within many different countries, including Croatia, Italy, Japan, Serbia, Switzerland, and the United States, people living in southern regions were more expressive than people living in northern regions. Research also suggests that kinesic expressiveness is a learned

B O X **2.2**

Global Interpretations of Selected U.S. Gestures

Using a gesture that has a common meaning in the United States can lead to misunderstanding if used in another culture, as the following examples suggest.

U.S. Gesture	Meanings in Other Cultures
The A-OK Gesture	"Money" or "coin" (Japan) "Worthless" or "zero" (France and parts of Switzerland) An obscene gesture in various places around the world
The Thumbs-up Gesture	"Speak up" or "turn up the volume" in parts of South America Used when counting in parts of Central Europe (where it means "one") and in parts of Asia (where it means "five") An insult in many places (Iran, parts of South America and Europe), especially when the thumb is pumped up and down
The "V" Sign	"Victory" or "peace" in many Western countries If made with the open palm toward one's face, it is an insult in Australia, Great Britain, and South Africa (where it means that you are acting like an animal with horns)
The "Good Luck" Gesture	Is a religious symbol (because it resembles a partial cross) in some parts of the world Is a sexual symbol or a sign of lesbianism in some cultures Represents being "close" or "best friends" in some cultures
The "Hang Loose" Gesture	Is associated with alcohol in some parts of Mexico and the Caribbean Means "six" in some parts of Asia (five for the thumb, plus one)

FIGURE 2.1   Cut-off gestures common in Japan and other Asian countries

behavior. For instance, although first-generation immigrants from areas such as Italy and Lithuania use highly expressive gestures similar to those used in their homeland, second-generation immigrants do not, presumably because they have been enculturated into U.S. society (Efron, 1972; Shuter, 1979).

Another gesture that shows some cultural specificity is the facial cut-off gesture (see Figure 2.1). This gesture, which involves covering all or parts of the face with one's hand or hands, communicates shy femininity, caution, coyness, and self-consciousness (Morsbach, 1973; Ramsey, 1981). In Japan, women use a wide variety of cut-off gestures. The more traditionally oriented a Japanese woman is, the more likely she is to use this type of gesture frequently, especially when interacting with men. In other places, including the United States, Europe, Africa, South America, and Indonesia, a limited number of cut-off gestures function as flirting behaviors (Eibl-Eibesfeldt, 1972; Moore, 1983). People from North America and Europe also sometimes use cut-off gestures when they are aroused and want to reduce environmental stimuli (Morris, 1977). For example, in one study people tended to use blocking gestures (such as covering their faces with their hands) when an opposite-sex friend became overly flirtatious (Andersen, Guerrero, Buller, & Jorgensen, 1998). Whether cut-off gestures are used to communicate submissiveness or self-consciousness, to flirt, or to block out arousing stimuli, women appear to use them more than men regardless of culture.

Eye Behavior

Relatively few studies have examined cultural differences in eye contact. However, some tentative conclusions can be drawn based on the work that has been conducted.

Research suggests that Arabs generally engage in more frequent and extended eye contact than do North Americans (Almaney & Alwan, 1982; Hall, 1959). People in North America are taught to look at people who are speaking, whereas people in many Asian and African countries are taught to avoid looking a speaker directly in the eye when speaking and to avoid eye contact altogether when listening, especially when the person speaking is of high status (Byers & Byers, 1972). This difference in eye contact norms caused problems for at least one Peace Corps teacher in an African village. The teacher required her students to look her in the eye when she reprimanded them. This was such a violation of social norms that the elders of the tribe insisted that the teacher be sent elsewhere. Thus, in some cultures giving direct eye contact to a speaker is perceived as a sign of attentiveness or respect, whereas in other cultures it is perceived as a sign of disrespect.

Within various cultures, different co-cultures have also been found to interpret eye behavior differently. For example, in the United States people generally view eye contact as a sign of respect. However, some Native American tribes perceive direct eye contact as disrespectful (Martin & Nakayama, 1997). Research also suggests that African Americans engage in less eye contact than European Americans, and like Native Americans, regard too much eye contact as impolite, arrogant, and/or disrespectful (Byers & Byers, 1972; Ickes, 1984; Vrij & Winkel, 1991; Winkel & Vrij, 1990).

Facial Expression

In contrast to eye behavior, facial expression has received considerable attention in terms of both cross-cultural similarities and differences. In a landmark book, Darwin (1872) argued that facial expressions of emotion are innate, inherited, and therefore universal. Most researchers agree that facial expressions of happiness, and to a lesser extent sadness, anger, fear, surprise, and disgust, are universally understood (Boucher & Carlson, 1980; Ekman, 1993; Ekman & Friesen, 1986; Ekman, Friesen, & Ellsworth, 1972; Izard, 1971, 1992; Scherer & Wallbott, 1994), although some research suggests that the accuracy of decoding these emotions is highest for Western cultures (Russell, 1994). The universality of emotional expression may also be limited to these primary emotions. LaFrance and Mayo (1978a), among others, found that blended facial expressions, such as a smug or sarcastic smile, may only be accurately interpreted in certain cultures or co-cultures. Izard (1971) concluded that although many primary emotions like happiness, anger, and sadness are expressed and decoded similarly across cultures, there are important cultural differences. For example, the Japanese have difficulty decoding expressions related to shame, presumably because Japanese people are taught to hide these feelings. In Izard's study, people from Africa had difficultly decoding facial expressions of disgust/contempt, probably because Africans are discouraged from showing this emotion.

A more recent study suggests that people have *nonverbal accents* that help others identify their country of origin (Marsh, Elfenbein, & Ambady, 2003). In this study, people from the United States looked at photos of individuals from the United States and Australia. In some of the photos, people were smiling. In the other photos, people had neutral expressions on their faces. The participants in this study could only differentiate between American and Australian faces when people were smiling, suggesting that the smile is somehow accented. The presence of nonverbal accents helps explain why some studies have shown an *ingroup advantage* when it comes to identifying emotional expressions. Specifically, several studies have shown that people are better at recognizing and interpreting the facial expressions of people who are from the same culture or co-culture as they are (Dovidio, Hebl, Richeson, & Shelton, 2006; Elfenbein & Ambady, 2002a, 2003).

Despite the existence of nonverbal accents and an ingroup advantage, the weight of evidence suggests that there is still considerable similarity in the way people from different cultures express and decode the six primary emotions listed previously (Beaupre & Hess, 2005; Elfenbein & Ambady, 2002; Matsumoto, 2006), as well as pride, which has been identified at above-chance levels in the United States, Italy, and a remote part of West Africa (Tracy & Robins, 2008). Some scholars have argued that the facial expression of emotion is innate (e.g., Ekman, 1993; Scherer & Wallbott, 1994), as Darwin (1872) originally suggested. Evidence from blind children supports this claim (Charlesworth & Kreutzer, 1973). For example, Eibl-Eibesfeldt (1974) found that blind children tend to display facial expressions that are similar to those displayed by sighted children, especially in terms of the primary emotions. Similarly, Galati, Scherer, and Ricci-Bitti (1997) compared the posed expressions of sighted adults and adults who had been blind since birth. They found virtually no differences between these two groups in the expressions used to communicate happiness, sadness, anger, fear, surprise, or disgust. Thus, although there may be nonverbal accents in people's facial expressions of emotions, there are still some common universal features (see Photo 2.2).

PHOTO 2.2 *Although there may be "nonverbal accents" when it comes to smiling, the general attributes of happy faces are similar across cultures.*

Keep in mind, however, that the vast majority of studies examining the cross-cultural identification of emotion have relied on posed facial expressions in photographs. This shows that there is universal knowledge regarding how to make one's face look happy, sad, angry, afraid, surprised, or disgusted, and that people around the world have enough of this knowledge to decode the facial expressions of primary emotions fairly accurately—or at least at levels better than chance. However, facial expressions do not always reveal the emotions that people are feeling (Parkinson, 2005). Sometimes people hide or fail to express the emotions they are experiencing. For instance, one study showed that people who had just won an Olympic gold medal tended not to smile despite being happy (Fernández-Dols & Ruiz-Belda, 1995).

Some researchers have argued that facial expressions are more closely related to social motives than to the emotions people are experiencing (Fridlund & Russell, 2006). According to this perspective, a smile is related to one's readiness to affiliate with someone more than it is related to feelings of happiness. Similarly, an aggressive expression is related to one's readiness to attack more than it is related to feelings of anger. This perspective, which has been called the *behavioral ecology view*, is discussed in more detail in Chapter 11. According to this perspective, people use facial expressions to show their intentions to others. Certain intentions (such as showing group harmony or asserting one's rights) may be more valued in some cultural groups than others, leading to differences in facial expressions. For instance, aggression may be tolerated or expected more in one culture than another. This might explain why people from collectivistic cultures are more likely to inhibit facial expressions of negative emotion than are people from individualistic cultures (Matsumoto, 2006).

People also communicate emotions differently depending on the rules and norms of their culture (Ekman & Friesen, 1975; Ekman, Sorensen, & Friesen 1969; Saarni, 1993). The same emotion might therefore be encouraged in one culture but discouraged in another. Expressions of grief are a prime example, as can be seen in Photo 2.3, where grief is expressed in varying ways. One of our students shared an excellent example of how cultural norms shape emotional communication. The student had a roommate (we'll call her Mary) who had tragically lost two close friends in a car accident when she was in high school. One of the friends was a foreign exchange student, and the other was a student from the United States. Mary attended funeral services for both students. At both services, Mary felt extremely upset and sad. At the service for the U.S. student, people were expected to be sad and subdued during the service because they were grieving a loss, so Mary felt free to show her feelings of sadness. She cried and held on to other friends for support. However, at the service for the foreign student, Mary learned that people in this student's culture are expected to be in a festive and joyful mood during a funeral because they are celebrating the life of someone who is now in a better place. So Mary hid her feelings of sadness and tried to smile and think of good memories.

The extent to which a culture is collectivist or individualist also has been theorized to influence the way people display emotion (Matsumoto, 1991, 2006).

PHOTO 2.3   *Grief expressions*

As discussed previously, people in collectivistic cultures value group cohesion, cooperation, and harmony more than individual needs. Maintaining good relationships with ingroup members is particularly important to those in collectivistic cultures. In contrast, people in individualistic cultures place a higher value on personal freedom and the fulfillment of individual goals and needs. Making good impressions on outgroup members (such as strangers and acquaintances) is more important to people in individualistic than collectivist cultures. Thus, people in collectivist cultures are likely to inhibit or mask negative emotion when with ingroup members such as close friends or family members (Matsumoto, 2006).

The reverse holds true for people in individualistic cultures, who are more likely to inhibit negative emotion with strangers than with friends. If you live in an individualistic culture such as the United States, you may be able to relate to this difference. Think about whom you are more likely to communicate anger to—a romantic partner or a casual acquaintance. According to cultural norms, people in individualistic cultures would be more likely to communicate anger to a romantic partner. They would likely believe that communicating both positive and negative emotions is an appropriate form of expression in close relationships because partners in an intimate relationship are expected to be at liberty to be open with one another and share rather than withhold their feelings. For someone in a collectivistic culture, however, such an expression of anger would likely be perceived as a threat to the harmony of the ingroup, so expressing anger to an outgroup member (although also not desirable) would be preferable.

Research has shown that collectivism and individualism are related to emotional expression, with a number of studies suggesting that people from the United States (an individualistic culture) express emotion more directly or freely than those from collectivistic cultures such as South Korea, Japan, and Russia (Matsumoto, Takeuchi, Andayani, Kouznetsova, & Krupp, 1998; Matsumoto, Yoo, Hirayama, & Petrova, 2005). Friesen (1972) had groups from Japan and the United States view highly stressful films alone and with another person. When alone, people from Japan and the United States expressed emotions such as fear, disgust, anger, and sadness similarly. However, when they were in the presence of another person, people from the United States tended to express negative emotions, whereas people from Japan tended to inhibit the expression of negative emotion or to smile.

Individuals within cultures also vary in terms of how individualistic versus collectivistic they are, so Matsumoto and Kupperbusch (2001) tested to see whether white women from the United States would vary in their reactions to films depending upon their level of individualism or collectivism. Similar to the earlier study by Friesen, they found that women with individualistic and collectivistic orientations exhibited similar facial expressions when alone, but collectivistic-oriented women tended to smile or display a neutral facial expression when watching the film with someone else.

Matsumoto (1991) also believed that cultural differences in emotional expression were partially based on differences in power distance. Recall that cultures with high-power distances emphasize status differences, whereas cultures with low-power distances emphasize equality. Matsumoto theorized that individuals in cultures characterized by high-power distance would tend to display positive emotions to higher status others as a way of showing respect. Individuals in these cultures would feel freer to express negative emotion and criticism to lower status others. The opposite pattern was theorized to characterize low-power distance cultures. To minimize status differences, positive emotions should be shown to low-status individuals, whereas negative emotions should be shown to high-status individuals.

To put this in context, think about a situation in which a manager is upset because one of her company's entry-level employees made a clerical error that a fellow manager failed to catch, and the error embarrassed the entire department. Assuming that both of them were to blame, would it be more appropriate for her to express her anger to the entry-level employee or her equal-status colleague? People in a low-power distance culture would be more likely to express anger to the equal-status employee because they ultimately see the error as this individual's responsibility and because they would feel bad derogating an employee who is below them. However, people in a high-power distance culture would be more likely to express anger (if they expressed anger at all) to the lower-status employee because it is this person's job to handle these details and it would be a sign of disrespect to show anger to someone who is of equal status.

Differences in cultural orientations toward immediacy may also help explain why some cultures encourage emotional expression more than others. People in cultures that value high levels of immediacy also tend to value open emotional expression. Therefore, it is not surprising that people from nonimmediate Asian cultures, particularly the Japanese, tend to inhibit their expression of negative emotion (Barnlund, 1975, 1978, 1989; Morsbach, 1973). The Japanese avoid conflict and often smile to mask negative emotions such as shame, anger, and disgust.

Even expressions of happiness are more restrained in Japan than in Western or Middle Eastern countries. For example, Japanese women often use cut-off gestures to hide their faces and/or muffle laughter when they are smiling. The relative inexpressiveness of Japanese people is consistent with cultural values related to politeness, respect, and harmony. On the other side of the expressiveness continuum, people from Arab countries tend to express emotions in an uninhibited manner with facial expressions, expansive gestures, touch, and loud, animated voices. Arabs also tend to approach rather than avoid conflict. Such uninhibited emotional expression is consistent with Arabic cultural values, which include living life to the utmost and showing pride in oneself and one's culture (Almaney & Alwan, 1982; Feghali, 1997). Interestingly, being hospitable appears to mean two different things to Japanese and Arab people. For the Japanese, being hospitable entails showing polite respect; for Arabs, being hospitable entails being outwardly expressive and providing sensory stimulation through nonverbal communication.

People in so-called Western countries, such as those in Europe and North America, and in Australia, fall somewhere between Asian and Arab cultures when it comes to emotional expression. To Westerners, people from Asia may be stereotyped as too reserved and withdrawn, as well as difficult to read. By contrast, Westerners are likely to stereotype Arabs as too loud and domineering. Of course, people from Western cultures are likely to be seen as too "pushy" or too "reserved" in the eyes of people from Asian and Arab cultures, respectively. Finally, people from Asian cultures may not be as inexpressive as those from immediate cultures think. Because Asian countries tend to be high-context cultures, they likely express emotions in more subtle, nuanced ways than people from low-context cultures do. Thus, in some cases it may be more correct to say that people from Asian cultures express emotions more subtly, whereas people from immediate cultures express emotions in more direct, obvious ways.

Proxemics and Haptics

People from different cultures also stereotype one another based on patterns of touch and preferences for personal space. For example, people from Arab countries have different rules regarding appropriate conversational distancing than do people from the United States, with Arabs preferring closer distances (Almaney & Alwan, 1982; Feghali, 1997). Watson (1970) found that this cultural preference led Arab students to regard students from the United States as condescending and aloof, whereas U.S. students regarded Arab students as arrogant and overbearing.

BOX 2.3

Why Arab Men Hold Hands

Hassan M. Fattah,
New York Times, May 1, 2005
Permission to reprint this article was granted
by the author.

When President Bush and Crown Prince Abdullah of Saudi Arabia met in Crawford, Tex., last week, they did something very un-Texan: they walked hand in hand.

Americans may raise an eyebrow at men holding hands, but in the Arab world, affection among men is common, and without sexual connotation.

"Holding hands is the warmest expression of affection between men," said Samir Khalaf, a sociology professor at American University of Beirut in Lebanon. "It's a sign of solidarity and kinship."

In fact, if a man chooses not to touch another in a greeting, it can be interpreted as a sign of distance or disdain. Kissing cheeks, long handshakes and clutching hands are meant to reflect amity, devotion, and most important, equality in status, noted Fuad Ishak Khuri, a social anthropologist, in his book, "The Body in Islamic Culture" (2001).

Strangers, on the other hand, do not kiss or hold hands, and the strong do not kiss the weak, wrote Mr. Khuri, who died in 2003.

And because the sexes are segregated, men rarely have the chance to touch or show affection toward a woman.

"Arab culture has historically been segregated, so emotions and feelings are channeled to the same sex," said Musa Shteiwi, a sociology professor at the University of Jordan. "Men spend a lot of time together and these customs grew out of that."

But as the Arab world changes, so do the customs. With growing urbanization and increased contact between the sexes, Professor Shteiwi noted, such gestures are slowly becoming dated. It's rare to see men holding hands in a city like Beirut, where the sexes mingle openly, though it is still commonplace in Saudi Arabia and other countries where sex segregation remains strong.

Some expatriates have learned to blend in. As militants targeted Westerners in Saudi Arabia last year, one Saudi businessman gave a friend advice: "Stroll like you have nowhere important to go, and if you see a friend's hand next to you, grab it."

Of course, within each culture, other factors such as sex and relationship play important roles in regulating the appropriate use of space. In many Middle Eastern cultures, for instance, same-sex touch is culturally appropriate, but opposite-sex touch among unmarried individuals is strictly prohibited. In contrast, female friends in the United States are more likely to touch each other than are male friends. This explains why many people in the United States were surprised, or even shocked, to see President George W. Bush walking hand in hand with Crown Prince Abdullah of Saudi Arabia on his Texas ranch in 2005 (see Box 2.3 and Photo 2.4).

Haptic and proxemic norms also change over time. The United States is a good example of this. Early studies suggested that North Americans (excluding Mexicans), like their northern European counterparts, used little tactile communication (Hall, 1959; Jourard, 1966a). Jourard observed people interacting at cafes in various places around the world. According to these observations, people in San

PHOTO 2.4 *President George W. Bush holding hands with Saudi Crown Prince Abdullah at his Texas ranch.*

Juan, Puerto Rico averaged 180 touches per hour, and people in Paris, France averaged 110 touches per hour, but people in the United States rarely touched. More recent work by Field (1999) found similar results when observing adolescents at McDonald's restaurants in Miami, Florida, and Paris, France. The teenagers in Paris touched one another significantly more often than did the teenagers in Miami.

However, over the past few decades, the United States has been moving toward becoming a more contact-oriented society (Willis & Rawdon, 1994), making Hall and Jourard's early observations, which were originally found in the 1960s, outdated. Indeed, although the Miami teenagers in Field's study touched less than the Paris teenagers, chances are that they touched more than Miami teenagers did back in the 1960s or 1970s, which is when Hall and Jourard conducted their studies. Andersen (2008) contended that the part of the Americas that is north of Mexico is now closer to the contact end of the continuum, even though contact patterns in the United States vary based on generation (e.g., people in their 20s versus their 60s). In fact, younger people in both North America and northern Europe may be more contact-oriented than older people (Andersen, Lustig, & Andersen, 1990; Lustig & Koester, 2003).

Geographical features, such as being in sunny Hawaii versus snowy Colorado, also play a role in shaping haptic and proxemic behaviors. In fact, some research suggests that people living in warm climates are more contact-oriented than people living in colder climates. People living in warmer areas of the United States touch more and have more positive attitudes toward touch than do those living in colder areas of the United States (Andersen, Lustig, & Andersen, 1990; Lustig & Koester, 2003). Similarly, studies of patterns of touch in the United States have shown that 85% of Westerners and 80% of Southerners classify themselves as having used moderate to high levels of touch in their families when growing up. In contrast, 90% of Northerners and 80% of Midwesterners describe themselves as coming from families using low to moderate amounts of touch (Leathers, 1997).

Regional and co-cultural differences are likely to exist in most, if not all, countries, making the distinction between contact and noncontact cultures somewhat simplistic. For example, in a study by Boyer, Thompson, Klopf, and Ishii (1990), people from Japan reported using less immediacy (touch, direct body orientation, close distancing) than did people from the United States, but within both cultures women reported being more immediate than men. Sex has also been shown to be an important factor in Italy, Germany, and the United States. Specifically, Shuter (1977) found that Italian men were more contact-oriented than Italian women. However, the reverse held true in the United States and Germany, where women were more contact-oriented than men. The more masculine orientations of the United States and Germany may help explain why women are more immediate than men in these countries.

Other studies suggest that there is more diversity in touching patterns within regions than suggested by the classifications of broad geographical areas into contact versus noncontact cultures. As a case in point, people from South America, Central America, and Mexico are often lumped together as "Latin Americans" in the research on cultural differences in touch and distancing. Yet Shuter (1976) found that, when compared to Panamanians and Colombians, Costa Ricans interact at closer distances and engage in more touch. Similarly, there is considerable ethnic diversity in the United States, and it would be a mistake to think that people with different cultural backgrounds would behave similarly. For example, African Americans are generally more nonverbally immediate than are European Americans (Lustig & Koester, 2003), although European Americans who come from places along the Mediterranean, such as southern Italy or Greece, are even more immediate than people of African descent.

Some research also contradicts Hall's classifications of European countries in comparison to one another and to the United States. Shuter (1977) found no differences in the contact patterns of women from the United States versus Italy or men from Germany versus Italy, even though Hall classified Italy as a contact culture and the United States and Germany as noncontact cultures. Remland, Jones, and Brinkman (1991) looked at dyads seated in public places. They found that Dutch people sat farther apart than French and English people, but that contrary to expectations, French people sat farther apart on average than did English people. Consistent with these findings, some nonverbal scholars have argued that contact patterns in North America and Europe are more similar than different (Andersen, 2008). However, southern Europeans, especially those in Mediterranean areas, may touch and stand closer to one another than northern Europeans or North Americans. For example, Remland, Jones, and Brinkman (1995) found Greek and Italian people to touch more than do Dutch, English, or French people.

Some research also suggests that the real distinction is between Asian countries and the rest of the world. McDaniel and Andersen (1998) examined touch patterns during departures at a large international airport. In their research, Asians stood out as the group who engaged in the least contact. Similarly, Barnlund (1975) found college students in the United States to engage in about twice as much touch as college students in Japan, and Regan, Jerry, Narvaez, and Johnson (1999) found

Latino couples to engage in more public touch than Asian couples. McDaniel and Andersen suggested that British, Northern European, and North American (except for Mexico), countries may actually be more moderate in terms of contact than previously thought. Although people from these countries generally exhibit less touch and greater conversational distance than do people in areas such as the Middle East, South America, and the Mediterranean region, they typically exhibit more touch and smaller conversational distance than do people from Asian countries.

Although Asian countries are generally considered to be noncontact, there appears to be at least one notable exception—Japanese mothers engage in high levels of contact with their infant sons and daughters, including holding them continuously and letting them sleep on their laps or with them in bed (Caudill & Weinstein, 1972), which is in contrast to mothers in the United States who commonly place their children in separate rooms to sleep. In fact, tactile contact between Japanese mothers and their children is common through childhood. As an example, the daughter of one of the authors of this textbook has a friend (we will call her Lu) who recently moved to the United States from Japan. Lu's "bedroom" has a desk, a little playhouse, and a lot of toys, but no place to sleep. When asked why she did not have a bed in her room, Lu replied that she is only seven years old, so naturally she still sleeps with her mom. When Lu's friends from the United States heard this, many of them thought this was a great idea and wanted to sleep with their moms, too.

In the United States, mothers are generally more mobile than mothers in other countries, making products such as baby carriers that transfer from the car into a stroller popular items for U.S. mothers. The use of such carriers allows sleeping babies to remain undisturbed while moms run errands. Interestingly, in certain countries, such as Australia, groups have advocated against the overuse of these baby carriers, cautioning that they reduce the amount of physical contact between infants and their mothers. As discussed in Chapters 3 and 6, positive tactile stimulation plays a critical role in the healthy psychological and physical development of children.

Greeting behaviors also reflect a culture's norms regarding the level of contact that is appropriate. For example, people from Mediterranean countries often greet one another by kissing cheeks, often kissing one side of the face and then the other. Similarly, people in South American countries often engage in a hug called the *abrazo* when greeting one another. This type of hug involves putting one's arms fully around another person and then patting their back heartily two or three times. In contrast, people in the United States often greet one another with handshakes or brief hugs (depending on the intimacy level associated with the relationship), and people in some Asian countries greet one another by bowing, with the lowest and longest bows reserved for people who are the most highly respected.

Vocalics

Although there are obvious cultural differences in vocalics based on accent and the characteristics of one's native language, little research has explored cross-cultural differences in vocalics (Scherer, 1984). A few interesting differences, however, were identified by studies done in the 1960s. Arab cultures are characterized by louder speech than most cultures, presumably because loudness connotes strength and sincerity to Arabs, whereas softness communicates weakness and deviousness (Almaney & Alwan, 1982; Hall & Whyte, 1966). Britons and other Europeans use softer voices than North Americans (Hall, 1990). If these findings still hold true today, it is likely that people from the United States would sound brash to many Europeans, and that Arabs would sound overly aggressive to non-Arab people.

Communication Accommodation Theory has been used to explain how people adjust to cultural and co-cultural differences in a variety of nonverbal behaviors, including vocalic cues. The theory was first developed by Howard Giles and his colleagues, who sought to determine why people's accents change when they are exposed to people from different cultural groups (Giles, 1973; Giles, Mulac, Bradac, & Johnson, 1987; Shepard, Giles, & Le Poire, 2001). According to the theory, people often accommodate their own communication style to the communication style of others in an effort either to converge or diverge.

Convergence occurs when an individual adapts her or his style so that it becomes more similar to another person's or group's style. People can converge using a variety of nonverbal behaviors, including facial expression, smiling, eye behavior, dress, touch, posture, gait, speech rate, pitch, and accent (Giles & Wadleigh, 1999). For example, if you visit Japan you might adapt to some of the Japanese's customs, such as bowing, inhibiting emotional expression, and speaking in a soft, polite voice. Generally, individuals exhibit more convergence when they are with ingroup members and people they like.

Divergence, in contrast, occurs when an individual adapts his or her style so that it becomes less similar to another person's or group's style. People typically practice divergence when they dislike a particular person or group, when they want to distance themselves from others, or when they want to emphasize their identification with a particular ingroup. For instance, Brittany might disapprove of the way Marcia says "like" all the time and twirls strands of hair around her finger. As a result, Brittany might avoid using these behaviors herself. Or Tyler might try to disassociate himself from a group of troublemaking friends by using nonverbal behaviors that are different from theirs and similar to those of his new friends.

Patterns of vocalic accommodation are also related to power. Specifically, the person with less status and/or power usually converges to the style of the more powerful person (Giles, Bourhis, & Taylor, 1977). For example, researchers studied tapes of *The Larry King Show* on CNN to determine patterns of vocalic accommodation between King and his guests. Consistent with principles from Communication Accommodation Theory, King was found to converge more to the pitch of higher status guests such as President Clinton, but lower status guests were more likely to converge toward King's speaking style (Gregory & Webster, 1996). Thus, patterns of convergence may be particularly strong in cultures characterized by high-power distances.

People also perceive others differently depending on which speaking styles are valued more within their culture and co-culture. For example, in a given culture, certain accents are often perceived as the most powerful and prestigious. Within most of Europe, it is considered more prestigious to speak "the Queen's English" than "American English." In fact, one of the authors of this textbook has a friend (we'll call her Sarah) who is a U.S. citizen living in Germany with her British husband and their two children. Sarah was appalled when a teacher told her daughter that she should only practice speaking English with her father, since her mother did not speak proper English! Within Great Britain itself, certain accents are perceived as more prestigious than others. The same is true for the United States and many other countries, where people have different perceptions of others based on accents (such as a New England accent versus a Brooklyn accent).

Although there is a preferred speaking style in most cultures, some co-cultural groups have distinct styles that separate them from the mainstream and help them identify with other ingroup members. These styles are generally rated lower in terms of prestige and status, but high in terms of group solidarity (Giles, 1973; Thakerar & Giles, 1981). So if you encounter someone who speaks in a style similar to your own, you will likely view that person as friendlier, more attractive, and more similar to yourself than someone who speaks differently than you do.

Chronemics

People from various cultures perceive and use time differently. Hall (1984) argued that cultures differ in terms of whether they perceive time as monochronic (M-time) or polychronic (P-time). In monochronic cultures, people tend to focus on one task at a time and to adhere to schedules. As Hall and Hall (1990) put it, people in cultures ruled by M-time tend to see time as a road that extends from the past to the future and can be divided into segments. People adhering to M-time rules usually see time as a tangible commodity that can be compartmentalized, spent, or saved. For example, students in the United States are expected to attend classes on time, many carry organizers with them, and most work on one class project at a time until it is completed, before beginning their next project. Cultures adhering to M-time include those in northern and central Europe (Finland, Norway, Sweden, Great Britain, and Germany) as well as the United States and Canada.

By contrast, people in polychronic cultures tend to focus on multiple tasks simultaneously and to avoid strict scheduling. Rather than seeing time as linear, cultures adopting a P-time orientation see time as flexible and diffused, giving more focus to human interaction than to schedules. Thus, students in P-time cultures feel free to arrive late for classes and often go back and forth between different class projects before completing one. Levine, a psychology professor from the United States, witnessed this cultural difference firsthand when teaching in Brazil. The Brazilian students would arrive as late as 11:00 for a class held from 10:00 to noon, and many would stay past noon asking questions and settling in for more discussion (Levine & Wolff, 1985). Cultures adhering to P-time include France, Brazil, Mexico, and Saudi Arabia. In general, most countries in the Mediterranean and Middle East regions, as well as those below the U.S. border in the Western Hemisphere, tend to use P-time.

Cultures may also differ in the extent to which they are focused on the present, past, or future. Gonzalez and Zimbardo (1985) argued that people from the

United States are oriented toward the future. In their large-scale survey, only 9% of people from the United States reported being primarily oriented toward the present, and only 1% reported being oriented toward the past. Instead, most people from the United States reported having either a balanced orientation that focuses on both the present and future, or an orientation that focuses primarily on the future. Gonzalez and Zimbardo found that being oriented toward the future was associated with higher income and a greater sense of being in charge of one's destiny, whereas being oriented toward the present was associated with less income and less control of one's destiny. They argued that in "industrial, technologically based societies such as" the United States, "a present-oriented time sense dooms most people to life at the bottom of the heap. There is no place for fatalism, impulsivity, or spontaneity when the marketplace is run on objectives, deadlines, budgets, and quotas" (p. 24). In other cultures, however, present and past orientations toward time are the norm. People in some South American and Mediterranean cultures value the present and perceive people from the United States as overly obsessed with work, efficiency, and future gratification (Gonzalez & Zimbardo, 1985). People in some Asian cultures, such as China, place much more emphasis on tradition and learning lessons from history.

Of course, within any given culture there are differences in time orientation based on co-culture. Take the United States as an example. Many Native American tribes are characterized by time systems that are flexible and focused on the present. For example, the Sioux have no words for *late* or *waiting* in their language. Pueblo Indians start many of their ceremonies "when the time is right" rather than at a scheduled time. For the traditional Navajo, time and space are very much the same concept; only the here and now is real, and the future is a foreign concept (Hall, 1959). Native Hawaiians operate under two time systems: *Haole time* is similar to the linear and fixed orientation of mainstream U.S. culture, but *Hawaiian time* is more diffused and relaxed. In Hawaii, it is important to know which time system is operative. For example, if an islander says "see you at three," you can expect to meet at that time. But if the islander says, "see you at three, Hawaiian time," you can expect to see each other whenever you both happen to arrive.

Summary

Cultures vary on a wide variety of characteristics, including collectivism versus individualism, immediacy, power distance, low- versus high-context, and gender orientation. These characteristics provide a partial explanation for some of the differences and similarities found when comparing nonverbal behavior across cultures. Some global patterns of cultural differences emerge in the literature. For example, Asian countries can be distinguished from other countries by their subtlety in expression and their relatively low levels of immediacy, especially when interacting in public contexts. The Mediterranean regions of Europe and Africa, the Middle East, Mexico, Central America, and South America stand out in terms of being highly expressive and immediate, whereas the United States stands out as the most individualistic. Of course, it is important to remember that these broad cultural comparisons ignore the diversity that occurs within cultures. Nonetheless, we hope this chapter has helped you appreciate and be sensitive to cultural variation in nonverbal behavior so that you can step away from your own cultural stereotypes when communicating with people from other cultural and co-cultural groups.

SUGGESTED READINGS

Almaney, A. J., & Alwan, A. J. (1982). *Communicating with the Arabs: A handbook for the business executive*. Prospect Heights, IL: Waveland Press.

Andersen, P. A., Hecht, M. L., Hoobler, G. D., & Smallwood, M. (2002). Nonverbal communication across culture. In N. B. Gudykunst & B. Mody (Eds.), *Handbook of international and intercultural communication* (pp. 89–106). Thousand Oaks, CA: Sage.

Andersen, P. A., & Wang, H. (2006). Unraveling cultural cues: Dimensions of nonverbal communication across cultures. In L. A. Samovar, R. E. Porter, & E. R. McDaniel (Eds.), *Intercultural communication: A reader* (pp. 250–266). Belmont, CA: Wadsworth.

Axtell, R. E. (1998). *Gestures: Do's and taboos of body language around the world*. New York: John Wiley & Sons.

Elfenbein, H. A., & Ambady, N. (2002). On the universality and cultural specificity of emotional recognition: A meta-analysis. *Psychological Bulletin, 128,* 205–235.

Elfenbein, H. A., & Ambady, N. (2003). When familiarity breeds accuracy: Cultural exposure and facial expression recognition. *Journal of Personality and Social Psychology, 85,* 276–290.

Hofstede, G. (2001). *Cultures consequences: Comparing values, behaviors, institutions, and organizations across nations*. Thousand Oaks, CA: Sage.

Marsh, A. A., Elfenbein, H. A., & Ambady, N. (2003). Nonverbal "accents": Cultural difference in facial expressions of emotion. *Psychological Science, 14,* 373–376.

Matsumoto, D. (2006). Culture and nonverbal behavior. In V. Manusov & M. L. Patterson (Eds.), *The Sage handbook of nonverbal communication* (pp. 219–235). Thousand Oaks, CA: Sage.

Scherer, K. R., & Wallbott, H. G. (1994). Evidence for universality and cultural variation of differential emotion response patterning. *Journal of Personality and Social Psychology, 66,* 310–328.

3 Bio-Evolutionary Influences on Nonverbal Communication

Evolutionary theory provides a powerful and fertile framework for understanding common patterns of nonverbal exchange between individuals.
—Miles Patterson (2003)

As the previous chapter detailed, nonverbal communication is strongly influenced by the social and cultural contexts in which it is enacted. Learning, socialization, and enculturation all have robust effects on many nonverbal behaviors—however, they don't tell the whole story. Although some nonverbal behaviors vary from culture to culture, others do not. For instance, many nonverbal emotion displays are encoded and decoded similarly across societies (Fridlund, 1994). Certain facial features are considered attractive in all cultures (Etcoff, 1999). And, as seen in Photo 3.1, parents around the world use a similar vocal and gestural pattern, known as *babytalk*, when communicating with their infants (Grieser & Kuhl, 1988). Much of the variation in these and other behaviors can be attributed not to cultural and social influences but to biological and evolutionary causes. In this chapter, we will explore bio-evolutionary explanations for nonverbal communication and see how they complement social and cultural theories.

We begin our discussion by addressing the characteristics of a bio-evolutionary perspective. The dual influences of evolution and biology/physiology are explained, and the assumptions of each approach are made clear. Next, we summarize research demonstrating bio-evolutionary effects on a number of specific nonverbal behaviors. We conclude the chapter with a discussion of how bio-evolutionary and social/cultural explanations can work together to increase our understanding of nonverbal communication.

PHOTO 3.1   *Although many non-verbal behaviors vary by culture, some—such as the tendency to speak in "babytalk" to infants—do not. Behaviors such as these may have their roots in biology and evolution more so than in enculturation.*

Biology and Evolution in the Study of Nonverbal Communication

All theories of nonverbal communication are concerned with explaining why people enact the particular behaviors they do. Why do we scowl when we feel disgusted? Why do we hug people we love? Why do our jaws fall open when we're surprised or shocked? As Chapter 2 described, theories in the sociocultural paradigm answer these types of questions with reference to how people in a given culture are socialized into that culture's traditions, values, and expectations. By contrast, theories in the bio-evolutionary paradigm answer these and other questions about communication by explaining how and why patterns of human behavior have evolved over the millennia and how these patterns are reflected in physiological processes. The bio-evolutionary approach is therefore broad and specific at the same time. On one hand, it looks at how the development of certain behavioral and emotional tendencies have provided advantages for survival and procreation over very long spans of time. On the other hand, it focuses on how behaviors and emotions are related to specific genes, hormones, neurological structures, and immune system activities.

We have adopted the term *bio-evolutionary* to describe the theories and research in this paradigm, because this term takes into account the broad influences of evolution and the more specific influences of biology simultaneously. Although the forces of evolution and biology work together to explain several aspects of nonverbal behavior, the principles and assumptions of each are somewhat different. We begin this section with a detailed overview of evolution and evolutionary psychology. Following that is an overview of the biological/physiological approach to understanding behavior and a discussion of how these forms of explanation converge into what we call the bio-evolutionary paradigm.

The Evolutionary Approach

Although you've probably heard of the "Theory of Evolution" before, there actually is no such theory. Rather, several different theories explain how various aspects of the evolutionary process work. The term *evolution* refers to changes observed over time in the physical characteristics of organisms. For instance, changes over time in the average length of the giraffe's neck, the average coloring pattern of the moth's wings, or the average height of the adult human would all be examples of evolution. Contrary to popular belief, evolution wasn't discovered by Charles Darwin—in fact, scientists had been studying evolution for many decades prior to Darwin's work. What Darwin offered with his *theory of natural selection* (Darwin, 1859) was an explanation for *how* the process of evolution works to change the characteristics of various species. We begin this section by describing the principles of natural selection. We then focus on how they can be used to explain human behavior, including nonverbal communication, through evolutionary psychology.

Natural Selection

Darwin's theory suggests that certain members of a species have traits that provide them advantages, relative to others in their species, with respect to survival and reproduction. Which traits are advantageous depends on the specific survival challenges of that species. Size and strength are advantages for some; the ability to camouflage oneself is an advantage for others. For humans, strength, intelligence, and physical attractiveness might all give one person advantages over others in terms of survival and reproductive opportunity, as depicted in Photo 3.2. Many of the traits that provide advantages are (at least partially) *heritable*, which means they are passed from parents to their offspring genetically, instead of through socialization. The gist of Darwin's theory is that, because organisms with advantageous traits will be more likely than others to survive and reproduce, then those advantageous traits will be passed on to future generations while less advantageous traits will eventually die out.

Let's look at a brief example to illustrate this process. One of the major survival challenges for a giraffe is access to food, which often consists of leaves growing at the tops of very tall trees. The longer a giraffe's neck is, therefore, the

PHOTO 3.2   *For humans, heritable traits such as strength, intelligence, and physical attractiveness are often advantageous for survival and reproductive success.*

better chance that giraffe has of getting the food necessary to survive. Those who survive are the most likely to procreate, so all other things being equal, those with the longest necks should produce the most offspring over the course of their lives. Since neck length is passed from parent to offspring genetically, the average neck length should increase from generation to generation. This is the process of *natural selection*, wherein a certain trait that has proven advantageous (such as a long neck) gets "selected for."

Several theories developed since Darwin's time have clarified the process of natural selection. One of the most important of these is *inclusive fitness theory* (Hamilton, 1964), which points out that the goal of procreation is to replicate *one's genes*, not necessarily to replicate *oneself*. As a result, people can contribute to their reproductive success not only by producing offspring of their own but also by providing aid to those who carry their genes, such as their siblings or cousins. In reproductive terms, having one daughter is equal to having two nieces, because in either case, the same proportion of one's genes (50% in this example) is passed on to a succeeding generation. Therefore, one can have reproductive success even without producing any children. As long as one's genetic relatives are producing offspring, one's own genes are still being passed along. Inclusive fitness theory helped to explain why many organisms (including humans) have evolved the tendency to give more love, attention, and resources to their family members than to nonrelatives (Buss, 1999; Simpson & Gangestad, 2001).

Applications to Human Behavior

What does natural selection have to do with human behavior? Researchers in the field of evolutionary psychology have applied Darwin's theory to the task of explaining several aspects of human emotions, cognitions, and interpersonal behaviors (for reviews, see Buss, 1999; Floyd & Haynes, 2005). Evolutionary psychologists argue that the human mind has been shaped by natural selection just as much as the human body has. Physical characteristics such as strength, speed, and good eyesight might give someone advantages when it comes to survival and procreation, but evolutionary psychologists believe that cognitive and emotional characteristics like intelligence, sensitivity, and even humor could also be advantageous. To the extent that these traits are passed from parent to child genetically—even partially— they should be subject to the pressures of natural selection, according to evolutionary psychologists. See Box 3.1 for a brief description of natural selection.

As we will see in more detail in the following sections, natural selection can explain many aspects of human emotions, cognitive patterns, preferences, and social behaviors. Something as simple as the preference for sweets, for instance, may have an evolutionary basis. Sugar doesn't taste sweet because it *is* sweet— rather, sweetness is a sensation created by our brains when our taste buds come into contact with sugar. Sugar is an essential fuel for the body, so the fact that it is pleasant to the taste would have encouraged our hunter-gatherer ancestors to consume the sugar necessary to survive. Those for whom the taste of sugar wasn't as pleasant would not have been as motivated to eat it and would not, therefore, have been as successful in surviving (all other things being equal). Those with a

BOX 3.1

Natural Selection at a Glance

The process of evolution and natural selection might seem complex, but it's actually a function of only four principles. If you understand these, then you understand the gist of the natural selection process.

1. In any generation, more of a given species (including humans) are born than can survive to reproductive maturity, which creates a struggle for existence.
2. Individual organisms vary, one from another, in several cognitive, emotional, and physical ways.
3. Some of the variation in these cognitive, emotional, and physical characteristics is passed genetically from parents to offspring.
4. Genetically inherited characteristics that provide advantages for survival and/or procreation will therefore be passed on to future generations with greater frequency than disadvantageous characteristics.

As one example of natural selection at work, let's consider the characteristic of physical attractiveness. Physical attractiveness is one of the ways individuals vary from one to another, and it is largely genetic: Highly attractive parents tend to produce highly attractive children, and less attractive parents produce less attractive children. Volumes of research have shown that being physically attractive gives people advantages when it comes to securing jobs, attracting mates, and currying favor with others in their social networks. Other things being equal, therefore, physically attractive people are advantaged when it comes to survival (because of the resources they attract) and procreation (because of mating opportunities), relative to less attractive people.

When an advantageous characteristic begins to appear with greater and greater frequency in each new generation, we say that it has been "selected for," because it is increasing due to the survival or reproductive advantages it provides. When a disadvantageous characteristic begins to die out over time in a population, we say that it has been "selected against."

---

preference for sugar would have been more likely to survive and, therefore, to procreate, passing along their preference to their offspring. As an aside, although this preference for sugar was advantageous for our hunting and gathering ancestors, it is less advantageous for people living in industrial countries today where there is an abundance of food. In fact, this preference may contribute to health problems such as obesity. Thus, it is important to recognize that evolution takes place over many millennia and changes are slow.

With respect to social behavior, evolutionary psychologists suggest that natural selection has shaped human tendencies related to things like affiliation, attachment, altruism, dominance, and sexuality. For example, teamwork was important to our ancestors, who worked in groups to accomplish basic tasks related to hunting food, gathering supplies, providing shelter, and protecting each other from danger. Those whose personalities helped them bond and cooperate with each other were probably more likely to survive and reproduce than those whose dispositions were more antisocial. Individuals whose intelligence or attractiveness made them highly valued by the group may have been most likely to be protected and to be given their share of resources. Thus, as we will see, nonverbal behaviors related to liking and cooperation, including smiling and touch, may have evolved as key ways of connecting with group members.

The evolutionary approach provides "big picture" explanations for why certain cognitive, emotional, and behavioral traits or tendencies might have evolved in humans and other species. The two key elements are (1) that the trait or tendency be at least partially genetic and (2) that it helped to solve a problem related to survival and/or procreation. Exactly *how* these traits or tendencies confer their advantages is often less clear, however. How does sugar feel pleasant to the taste? How might a smile contribute to feelings of affiliation? To address these types of questions, we turn to the other part of the bio-evolutionary paradigm: that related to biology and physiology.

The Biological/Physiological Approach

When you think about it, it's easy to see how biology and communication influence each other. Consider the last time you got into a heated argument with someone, for instance. You probably felt your pulse and breathing rate increase and your skin temperature go up (giving you that "hot under the collar" feeling). You might also have experienced some of the physical effects of stress, such as nervousness or agitation. Those physical effects, in turn, likely influenced how you behaved during the argument. Many communicative situations are accompanied by a distinctive set of physical experiences—for example, you can probably describe what it feels like to share affection with a loved one, hear a juicy piece of gossip, or deliver disappointing news to someone else. These examples illustrate the idea that our bodies and our behaviors are intimately connected. As we described earlier, principles of natural selection can often explain *why* that is the case, but to understand exactly *how* communication behavior and the body influence each other, we must turn to the study of psychophysiology. We begin this section by describing the principles of psychophysiology and their relationship to evolutionary psychology. Next, we briefly describe some of the primary methods used by researchers to identify how biology and behavior intersect.

Psychophysiology

The field of psychophysiology assumes that cognitive, emotional, behavioral, and social events are all reflected in the body's physiological processes (see Floyd, 2004). As an example, consider the emotion of fear. Experiencing fear is associated with several hormonal reactions, nervous system activities, and muscular responses that distinguish it from other emotional experiences, such as sadness or surprise. By the same token, falling in love causes neural and hormonal activities that differ from those associated with falling out of love. Researchers in the field of psychophysiology focus their attention on these and many other ways that psychological and social events interface with the body's physiological systems (Hugdahl, 1995). Box 3.2 describes some of the methods.

BOX 3.2

Ways of Studying Psychophysiology

Researchers use a variety of methods to discover how social, psychological, or behavioral events are related to physiological activities. These methods vary greatly, depending on which physiological system is being studied. Learning how emotions or behaviors are associated with different hormones, for instance, requires a researcher to collect and analyze body fluids. Many hormones and immune system chemicals can be measured in saliva, whereas others require samples of blood, urine, or other fluids (sweat, semen, spinal fluid, tears, etc.).

Examinations of other bodily systems require much different approaches. To measure activity in the brain, for example, researchers can use several different methods, including electroencephalography (EEG), positron emission tomography (PET), computed tomography (CT), magnetoencephalography (MEG), and functional magnetic resonance imaging (fMRI). Each method works on a different principle and

produces a different type of outcome. When researchers want to study muscular movement (such as movement of the facial muscles associated with a certain emotion), they often use an electromyograph (EMG), which uses electrodes positioned on the surface of the skin to detect electrical signals produced by muscle contractions.

Several studies also focus on nervous system activities, such as heart rate, blood pressure, and perspiration. An electrocardiogram (EKG) is often used to measure how fast a heart is beating. Blood pressure can be measured manually or electronically, using a device called a sphygmomanometer. Changes in perspiration are usually measured using a skin conductance response (SCR) monitor. Many studies in psychophysiology make use of several of these methods at once, so that researchers can see how a certain behavior or emotion affects multiple physiological systems simultaneously.

Being affiliative, for instance, helps people form social bonds that provide important resources (such as support, shelter, and protection) that are critical for survival. Similarly, enhancing one's physical attractiveness helps people to attract potential mates, which is important for procreation. The field of psychophysiology focuses on the physiological processes that go along with these behaviors and emotions and are often responsible for their survival or procreation benefits.

Let's return to the example of fear. From the perspective of evolutionary psychology, the ability to experience fear is advantageous for survival because it increases a person's surveillance of threatening situations. Physiologically, the experience of fear activates several processes that improve one's ability to examine and respond to a threat. When you're afraid, for instance, your pupils dilate, increasing your visual acuity so you can better assess the threat. Increases in your heart rate and respiration provide extra fuel to your muscles in case you have to fight or flee. You perspire more, so that your body doesn't overheat. And, your adrenal gland increases production of the hormone *cortisol*, which suppresses nonessential bodily systems so that your energy can be used more efficiently. According to evolutionary psychology, these physiological reactions would increase your ability to assess and respond to a threat, giving you an advantage over those who don't experience the same reactions.

In this section, we have explored what it means to take a bio-evolutionary approach to explaining behavior. We have learned that, unlike the sociocultural approach described in the previous chapter, bio-evolutionary explanations focus on why tendencies for certain emotions and behaviors (including nonverbal behaviors) are beneficial for survival and procreation. The bio-evolutionary approach also examines the physiological processes that bring those advantages about. We have examined the ideas behind evolutionary psychology and psychophysiology and have looked at several examples showing how these approaches help explain emotions and behaviors. In the next section, we will explore several specific categories of nonverbal communication and illustrate how bio-evolutionary explanations can be used to illuminate them.

How Nonverbal Behaviors Are Affected by Evolution and Biology

In Chapter 2, you saw examples of several nonverbal behaviors that show variation across cultures, suggesting they are affected by socialization and enculturation. In this section, we will look at a number of nonverbal communication behaviors that can be explained using the principles of biology and evolution. Some behaviors examined in the previous chapter are also covered here, and you might find yourself wondering how a certain behavior can be explained by both approaches. It might seem as though a given behavior is *either* a product of one's culture *or* a product of one's biology—but as we will illustrate, behaviors can often be influenced by both. Bear in mind, therefore, that sociocultural and bio-evolutionary theories are not necessarily competing explanations. Rather, they often explain different aspects of a nonverbal behavior. In this section, we will look at several categories of nonverbal behavior, including facial displays of emotion, touch, vocalics, eye behaviors, olfactics, and physical appearance.

Facial Displays

The human face is remarkably expressive and is used to communicate a variety of messages. One of the most important nonverbal functions of the face is the expression of emotion. As we noted in Chapter 2, researchers have found high levels of consistency from culture to culture in how specific emotions are communicated through facial displays, and scientists have long thought that displays of basic (or primary) emotions (such as joy, fear, anger, surprise, or disgust) may have evolved for specific reasons. One of the most famous scientists to investigate the expression of emotions was Charles Darwin (1872). He acknowledged that people perform certain behaviors to meet certain needs, such as plugging your nose in the presence of a foul odor to keep yourself from smelling it. This behavior is adaptive because it prevents the foul odor (which might be toxic or otherwise harmful) from entering your nasal passages. Darwin speculated that, when people experience a similar state of mind, they will perform a similar behavior. When someone has a spectacularly bad idea, for instance, you might plug your nose to express contempt, if your state of mind in the presence of the bad idea is similar to your state of mind in the presence of the foul odor. In this way, Darwin proposed, people became conditioned to perform specific facial displays when they experience specific emotions.

Darwin also believed that some facial displays of emotion are the direct result of nervous system arousal. As we mentioned, for instance, being frightened can arouse the nervous system and lead to some of the typical components of the fear expression: dilated pupils, an open mouth, increased muscular tension, and increased perspiration. We can appreciate these reactions in Photo 3.3. Why should these reactions be associated with fear? Pupil dilation allows for the increased intake of visual information that can help the person to gauge the threat. Increased muscular tension readies the body either to fight the threat or to flee from it, and an open mouth allows for increased oxygen intake to fuel those efforts. Increased perspiration ensures that the body doesn't overheat while engaging in fight or flight. From the vantage of evolutionary psychology, these specific functions are adaptive, because they would each increase the chances that you would survive whatever threat had caused you to be afraid in the first place.

Darwin proposed that some facial displays of emotion are conditioned through states of mind, whereas others are the product of nervous system arousal. In either case, though, he argued that emotion displays of emotion are rooted in biological and evolutionary causes. This doesn't mean that other influences, such as culture, aren't operative—in fact, Darwin believed that even some innately based expressions required practice and were adaptive to the social environment. Importantly, however, Darwin proposed that there are underlying bio-evolutionary reasons why we express emotions the way we do.

At least three forms of evidence support Darwin's proposal. First, if displays of emotion are primarily rooted in bio-evolution, they should be fairly consistent across cultures. Many investigations have reported that, across cultures, people

PHOTO 3.3 *Facial displays of many emotions, including fear, are related to arousal of the human nervous system.*

express basic emotions (joy, sadness, anger, fear, surprise, disgust) with remarkable consistency and are also highly consistent in how they interpret these displays (e.g., Ekman, Friesen, & Ellsworth, 1972; Scherer & Wallbott, 1994). Some research suggests that the accuracy of decoding these emotions is highest for Western cultures, although investigations in non-Western and even pre-literate cultures have also identified consistency (Russell, 1994; see also Chapter 2).

Second, if displays of emotion are rooted in biology and evolution, then infants should use the same displays as adults, even though they haven't yet learned them. Several studies have shown that children's displays of emotions begin resembling adults' displays early in life. For example, research has found that infants begin smiling in response to external sights, sounds, and other stimuli around the end of their first month (Sroufe, 1984), and that by the end of their third month, they begin smiling in response to familiar persons and newly mastered skills (Lewis, Sullivan, & Brooks-Gunn, 1985). Similar results have been found for displays of surprise (Camras, 1988), interest (Sullivan & Lewis, 1989), disgust (Rosenstein & Oster, 1988), anger (Stenberg, Campos, & Emde, 1983), and fear (Schwartz, Izard, & Ansul, 1982).

Also informative is research on children born blind, who lack the ability to imitate visually observed expressions in others. If facial displays of emotion were primarily learned, then those born blind should have an impaired ability to learn those displays. Research has found just the opposite, however. Eibl-Eibesfeldt (1973) reported that blind children tend to display facial expressions that are similar to those displayed by sighted children, especially in terms of the primary emotions, and Freedman (1965) found this consistency to appear at 6 months of age. Similarly, Galati, Scherer, and Ricci-Bitti (1997) compared the posed expressions of sighted adults and adults who had been blind since birth. They found virtually no differences between these two groups in the expressions used to communicate happiness, sadness, anger, fear, surprise, or disgust.

Third, if facial displays of emotion are grounded in bio-evolution, then certain facial expressions should be associated with specific physiological effects. Looking happy should therefore make you feel happy, for instance. This is the idea behind the *facial feedback hypothesis*, which suggests that merely engaging in a facial display of emotion will spark physiological changes that are consistent with that emotion. In one experiment, Ekman, Levenson, and Friesen (1983) told participants to enact facial expressions of six different emotions while their nervous system arousal was measured. They had participants hold the expression of each emotion for 10 seconds. The researchers found that facial displays of fear, sadness, anger, surprise, and happiness were accompanied by increases in heart rate, whereas displays of disgust produced decreased heart rate. Displays of anger, sadness, and happiness also caused increases in skin temperature, whereas displays of surprise, fear, and disgust caused skin temperatures to go down. Importantly, these physiological responses to *displaying* each emotion closely resemble those involved in *experiencing* the emotion (Levenson, 1992). Several subsequent studies have replicated these results (e.g., Hess, Kappas, McHugo, Lanzetta, & Kleck, 1992).

BOX 3.3
Why We Cry

Many animals whine or howl when they're in distress, and a few produce tears when their eyes get irritated. But human beings are the only creatures who tear up in times of sorrow—that is, we're the only ones who genuinely cry. Why do we cry, though? From the bio-evolutionary perspective, it's because crying contributes to our survival by calming us down in times of distress.

When we cry sorrowfully, it's often because we have suffered some type of loss, such as the loss of a job, the death of a favorite pet, or the termination of a significant relationship. These situations don't feel good, and it might seem as though we cry because the loss has upset us. Many researchers now believe, however, that we cry not because we're upset but because we're trying to *recover from being upset*. Perhaps you've noticed that, even if you're in distress, you often feel a little better after having a good cry.

One reason crying has this calming effect relates to your tears. You might not realize that

you actually produce three different kinds of tears. *Basal tears* are what keep your eyes moist every time you blink, and *reflex tears* are the ones you produce when you smell an onion or get a speck of dust in your eyes. These two types are very similar chemically, but *emotional tears* are quite different. They contain up to 25% more types of protein and 400% more potassium than basal or reflex tears, and they also have as much as 30 times more manganese than you have in your blood stream.

Why does this matter? Researchers speculate that crying emotional tears might be nature's way of flushing out high concentrations of chemicals that accumulate in our bodies when we're upset. This is one reason why we often feel better after crying—that is, the act of crying itself has helped us to get over whatever was bothering us in the first place. This is significant from the evolutionary point of view because it keeps us from being immobilized by our distress, so that we can attend to our health, our safety needs, and our relationships.

Touch

Touch is the first of the five senses to develop and it is the most important sense for survival. Many people survive—and even thrive—without the ability to see, hear, taste, or smell. Without the ability to feel touch, however, one would constantly be susceptible to injury, temperature extremes, and other environmental threats that could easily prove fatal. As we learned in the previous chapter, touch in interpersonal relationships is strongly influenced by cultural and gender norms. Social groups vary widely in how, and how much, people touch each other. What is consistent across genders, cultures, and even historical periods, however, is the importance of interpersonal touch for human survival and well-being.

Why do we use touch to communicate? From the bio-evolutionary perspective, it's because touch comforts and stimulates us in ways that are essential to our health and development. If touch conveys these benefits, then those who receive adequate touch will be more likely than those who don't to survive, thrive, and reproduce (see Prescott, 1971). Is touch really that important to our health? A bizarre experiment from the 13th century suggests that it is. Emperor Fredrick II of

Germany wanted to know what language humans would speak naturally, if they weren't taught any particular language. To find out, he put 50 newborn babies in the care of nurses who were told only to feed and bathe them but not to hold, comfort, or speak to them. The emperor never learned the answer to his question, though, because all the infants died (Perry, 2002). Research conducted since that time has convincingly shown that touch is critical for infants' survival and healthy development (see Field, 2001). After analyzing evidence from orphanages around the world, in fact, Spitz (1945) found that infants who were not touched tended to die before their first birthdays or to develop psychological problems. By contrast, those who were cuddled frequently tended to thrive (also see Chapter 6).

Indeed, touch is important for health and well-being not only in infancy but well into adulthood. At the Touch Research Institute at the University of Miami School of Medicine, a scientific team led by Dr. Tiffany Field studies the health benefits of touch therapy. In most of their studies, participants receive some form of massage, either from a massage therapist or from someone they know, such as a parent or a romantic partner. The massage is usually given once every day or every few days for a period of weeks, and the researchers measure what kinds of physical benefits the recipients experience. Their work has identified benefits of touch therapy on a huge range of physical conditions, including anorexia (Hart et al., 2001), asthma (Field et al., 1998), dermatitis (Schachner, Field, Hernandez-Reif, Duarte, Krasnegor, 1998), and sleep disorders (Field & Hernandez-Reif, 2001). Whether the touch came from a professional massage therapist or from someone the participants knew well, it led to measurable improvements in each of these conditions.

Field and her colleagues have mostly studied the health benefits of touch therapy, such as massage. But research shows that even more mundane forms of touch, such as hand-holding, can be beneficial. In two studies with young adults, for instance, Drescher, Gantt, and Whitehead (1980) found that participants had a relaxation response (in the form of decreased heart rate) when touched on the wrist for 30 seconds by an experimenter. The participants didn't get the same benefit when they touched themselves on the wrist, though, suggesting that it was the contact with another person that produced the result.

Hand-holding can also reduce the physical and psychological effects of stress by creating or reinforcing a sense of emotional security. In one study, Coan, Schaefer, and Davidson (2006) subjected happily married women to threats of electric shock while they were in an fMRI machine that measured their brain activity. At different times during the experiment, the women held their husband's hand, held a male stranger's hand, or did not hold anyone's hand. The researchers found that when the women were holding hands with someone, they experienced significantly less neurological arousal in response to the threat than when they weren't holding someone's hand. In other words, holding hands lessened the extent to which they felt physically threatened. This was especially true when the women were holding their husband's hand as opposed to a stranger's hand.

However, even holding a stranger's hand was significantly better than holding no hand at all, and this seems to demonstrate (as Field and her colleagues have shown with touch therapy) that some of the benefit of touch resides in the touch itself, independent of the relationship in which it is occurring. This is an important point, because a sociocultural explanation for the benefits of touch would focus on what the touch means to you within the context of your relational or cultural history. That matters, of course—most of us would probably rather hold hands with someone we know than with someone we don't, and the women in the study conducted by Coan et al. received a greater benefit when they held their husbands' hand. However, as many of these studies have demonstrated, even touch from a stranger can be beneficial, and this suggests that *some* of the benefit of touch resides at the physiological level. This is particularly important in therapeutic settings, such as hospitals or clinics, where research has shown that hand-holding and other forms of touch from health care providers can reduce patient anxiety and facilitate recovery even if the providers don't have a personal relationship with the patients (Groër et al., 1994).

In interpersonal communication, we often use forms of touch for the purpose of expressing affection to loved ones. From the perspective of evolutionary psychology, it is adaptive for people to initiate and maintain significant long-term relationships, since they contribute not only to our survival but also to our reproduction success. One of the most important communicative behaviors for the formation and maintenance of personal relationships is the expression of affection. This includes those behaviors that convey feelings of love, fondness, and appreciation, and although there is social and cultural variation in how people express affection, it is an ubiquitous human behavior.

Why do we communicate affection in the first place? Researchers working in the bio-evolutionary paradigm have speculated that affection behaviors (especially nonverbal ones) evolved largely from maternal protective behaviors (for review, see Floyd, 2006). As mothers have protected, cuddled, and attended to their infants for centuries, these behaviors gradually evolved into hugging, kissing, caressing, and other nonverbal behaviors that carry messages of affection. And the more these behaviors contribute to the formation and maintenance of significant relationships with friends, relatives, and romantic partners, the more important they are for our ability to survive and procreate.

If personal relationships are important to our well-being, then one would expect that behaviors aimed at forming and maintaining such relationships—like affectionate behaviors—should be physiologically rewarding. Several studies have shown that nonverbal affection has specific physiological benefits. You've probably noticed, for instance, that hugging, kissing, and holding hands with someone you love feels good—not just emotionally, but physically, too. One of the reasons why appears to be that these nonverbal behaviors elevate levels of the hormone *oxytocin*. Oxytocin is released by the pituitary gland and it has stress-alleviating effects on the body. Specifically, it lowers blood pressure and heart rate, increases metabolism, suppresses pain, and promotes a feeling of calmness and pleasantness (Altemus, Deuster, Carter, & Gold, 1995). Oxytocin is best known for the role it plays in childbirth (McCarthy & Becker, 2002); however, it is also produced when people engage in relationally significant behavior. For instance, it is released into the bloodstream of both women and men at sexual orgasm (Carmichael et al., 1987), and it appears to contribute to the physical and emotional pleasure of sexual interaction. Several researchers have also suggested that that oxytocin may be stimulated by warm, affectionate behavior and may be one of the major reasons why love and intimacy feel so good (e.g., Uvnäs-Moberg, 1998).

In one study, Grewen, Girdler, Amico, and Light (2005) had heterosexual romantic partners take part in a 10-minute affectionate interaction. The participants were asked to hold hands, sit close to each other, talk about significant times in their relationship, watch a romantic video together, and hug each other. Before and after the interactions, the researchers took blood samples to measure oxytocin levels, and participants also reported on how much emotional support they received from each other. The researchers found that levels of oxytocin were directly related to perceived emotional support for both women and men. This suggests that people who have more supportive, satisfying relationships have higher average levels of oxytocin than those with less supportive bonds. They also discovered that oxytocin levels increased significantly as a result of the affectionate interaction, but for women only. In addition, both sexes experienced a decrease in the stress hormone cortisol as a result of the affectionate interaction. Although a part of the affectionate interactions was verbal (i.e., talking about significant times in the relationship), most of the interaction focused on nonverbal behaviors such as hugging, hand-holding, and sitting in close proximity. This research suggests that this type of cuddling behavior can increase oxytocin—at least for women—which may be one reason why nonverbal affection behaviors often feel so good.

Kissing is another nonverbal behavior that is often used to convey affection. Kissing is seen (in various forms) in a range of relationships, including those with romantic partners, friends, family members, and even strangers (as in cultures where kissing on the cheek is part of a ritual greeting). How, why, and where kissing occurs is largely dependent on social and cultural expectations, and people in some cultures kiss significantly more often than do those in other cultures. Research shows that kissing not only has stress-alleviating effects, but it can actually strengthen your immune system. In one study, Kimata (2006) found that kissing a spouse or romantic partner for 30 minutes reduced the production of allergic agents in the immune system. Cuddling and embracing without kissing did not produce the same effects. Other research has suggested that the exchange of bacteria involved in an open-mouth kiss can strengthen your immunity by stimulating your immune system to develop antibodies to bacteria introduced by your kissing partner (see Davis, 2007).

Some research suggests that affectionate communication is particularly beneficial when you're stressed. Taylor et al. (2000) proposed that engaging in "befriending" behaviors, such as snuggling and hugging, helps reduce the physical effects of stress. To test this idea, Floyd, Mikkelson, Tafoya et al. (2007) put a group of college students through a series of stressful activities and found that the students had reduced hormonal reactions to the stress if they reported high degrees of affectionate communication in their closest relationships.

Vocalics

The voice is a powerful instrument for communication. Some vocalic characteristics are culturally determined—for instance, the accent you adopt depends on the accent your family and friends had when you were learning to speak. Some of the acoustic properties of the voice, however, are biologically determined. For instance, the *pitch* of your voice relates to how high or low your voice sounds, which is determined by the length of your vocal folds. The longer your vocal folds, the lower your voice. This is why men's voices are usually lower than women's and why adults' voices are usually lower than children's (see Charpied, 2007). Each of us also has a unique "voice print," or combination of acoustic properties that distinguishes our voice from every other voice. This has enabled law enforcement officials to design software that recognizes and identifies samples of the voice, even if the speaker is trying to disguise it (Evans, 1996).

Aside from the words we use, the sound of our voices sends certain messages. What does an excited voice sound like? How about an aggressive, dominant voice, or a loving, affectionate voice? Chances are, you can hear in your mind how each type of voice sounds. The excited voice probably sounds loud and high pitched; the dominant voice probably sounds loud and low pitched; and the loving voice probably sounds soft and high pitched. Why? According to the bio-evolutionary perspective, it is because these vocal properties are most efficient at conveying these states of mind.

To understand how, think about animals for a moment, instead of people. When a group of animals gets excited, it's usually because something has happened that demands their immediate attention. This could be something good, like the discovery of food, or something bad, like the presence of a predator. In either case, the animals are physiologically aroused and are motivated to communicate that arousal with others in the group (either to join in eating the food or to flee from the predator). Communicating with a group is done most efficiently with a louder voice than a quieter one, and physiological arousal pushes the pitch of a voice up—thus, an excited voice sounds loud and high pitched (Charpied, 2007).

Think about a predator now. The extent to which a predator is threatening is, in some measure, a function of the predator's size relative to its prey. A canary wouldn't pose much of a threat to a mountain lion, nor would a mouse to a polar bear. The larger an individual animal is, the longer its vocal folds are and the lower its pitch is. This is why physically small organisms, such as house-cats, small birds, and human infants, have high-pitched voices, whereas large dogs, bears, and lions have lower-pitched voices. Larger organisms are also more capable of producing loud sounds than smaller organisms are. According to evolutionary logic, these are the reasons why we think of aggressive, dominant voices as being loud and low pitched—because the organisms that can produce these sounds are the ones who are capable of being a threat. And, if aggression is conveyed by loud, low-pitched voices, then it stands to reason that an opposite state of being, such as affection, would be communicated by softer, higher-pitched voices.

Several studies have suggested that the same vocal patterns apply to humans. Loud, low-pitched voices are associated with perceptions of aggression and dominance (Tusing & Dillard, 2000). High-pitched voices are perceived as conveying warmth and affection when quiet and as conveying excitement when loud (Fernald & Simon, 1984), although Floyd and Ray (2003) found that pitch was directly related to perceived affection only for women.

Eye Behaviors

Many eye behaviors convey meaning in interpersonal settings. Engaging in eye contact with someone, for instance, might communicate interest, attraction, or anger, whereas failing to make eye contact may denote submissiveness, respect, or shame. As the previous chapter suggested, eye behaviors are strongly subject to social and cultural influences, but one eye behavior that appears to transcend those influences is *pupil dilation*.

The pupil is the dark circle in the middle of the visible eye. It changes size nearly constantly to regulate the amount of light allowed to enter the eyeball. You've probably noticed, for example, that your pupils dilate, or open wider, when you're in a dark environment. This automatic response helps you to see as well as you possibly can in the dark. You've probably also noticed that your pupils contract, or become smaller, in bright environments; this response helps prevent too much light from entering your eyes (Marieb, 2003).

What you might not know is that, besides being affected by light, pupil dilation is also affected by attraction. When you look at someone you find attractive, your pupils open up wider than normal (Hess, 1972). This happens because your nervous system becomes aroused when you look at someone attractive (that's why you can sometimes feel your heart rate go up in the presence of a good looking person; Guyton, 1977). Why should our pupils dilate when we look at someone attractive? From the bio-evolutionary perspective, it's because attraction is often the first step toward developing a relationship with someone, and pupil dilation allows us to take in more visual information about that person to help us decide whether he or she is a potential relational partner. All of this happens outside of your conscious control—you can't feel your pupils dilate or contract, and most of the time you're completely unaware of how your pupil size is changing when you look at someone. From the vantage of bio-evolution, however, your awareness doesn't matter—your body is responding to the visual stimulus of an attractive person in an automatic and adaptive way.

There's a second part to this effect, which is that having dilated pupils makes you more physically attractive to others (Hess, 1975). All other things being equal, we find people with wide, dilated pupils to be more physically appealing than people with narrow, contracted pupils. In fact, women in earlier centuries sometimes used a toxic herb called *belladonna* to dilate their pupils for cosmetic effect. The evolutionary explanation for this part of the effect is that when you see someone with dilated eyes, that means he or she might find you attractive and might therefore be a prospective relational partner, so we have evolved to be attracted to large, dilated pupils.

Olfactics

You might not think about your sense of smell as a communication tool, the way your senses of sight, hearing, or touch are. Humans have one of the dullest senses of smell in the animal kingdom, so you might be surprised that we use our olfactic ability in social interaction at all. The truth is that our sense of smell plays an important role—and a largely subconscious one—in physical and romantic attraction.

We develop romantic relationships for many reasons, but from an evolutionary perspective, the most important reason is to procreate. It's not enough just to produce offspring, though; we want to produce *healthy* offspring who will grow up and have children of their own. One way to ensure that our future children will be healthy is to choose a healthy romantic partner; therefore, the process of natural selection has made us attentive to signs of health in the opposite sex. Many of these signs are visual (which we will discuss in the following section), but some are olfactic—and even though we may not pick up on these consciously, research indicates that they influence who we find sexually attractive.

Each of us has a set of genes known as the *major histocompatibility complex* (MHC), which plays an important role in the health of our immune systems (Klein, 1986). Biologically, it is most adaptive for you to be sexually attracted to a partner with an MHC that is dissimilar to your own. The reason is that any children you might produce together would inherit the strengths of both of your immune systems (see Wedekind, Seebeck, Bettens, & Paepke, 1995). In contrast, when parents are too genetically similar to each other, their children are at higher risk for a range of health problems and are less likely to survive to sexual maturity. Therefore, it's in our best evolutionary interests to find mates who are genetically dissimilar to us.

People can subconsciously detect differences in MHC through body odor, and these differences affect the judgments they make about other people's attractiveness. In one study, Wedekind and Furi (1997) had several men each wear the same t-shirts for a week without washing them. Afterward, a different group of men and women smelled each shirt and rated its odor for pleasantness. Both women and men rated the odor of each t-shirt as more pleasant if the man had MHC genes dissimilar to their own than if he had similar MHC genes. In a replication of this study, Thornhill and Gangestad (1999) had both women and men wear t-shirts for several days after they had taken facial photographs of the participants. Afterward, male and female raters smelled each shirt and rated the pleasantness of the body odor. The researchers found that the pleasantness of the body odor was directly related to facial attractiveness for both men and women. They also found that women's preference for the scents of facially attractive men was strongest when the women were ovulating. This is significant from the evolutionary point of view, since it would be the time when a woman's choice of mate would be the most consequential.

These results show clear links between smell and sexual attraction. In many Western cultures, however, it is common for people to mask or eliminate their natural body odors (Hirsch, 1998). What effect might this have on perceived attractiveness? To find out, Aune and Aune (2008) had female research assistants approach students on a college campus and ask if they could be interviewed. The assistants said they were enrolled in an interviewing class and that they would be asking the students to evaluate them at the end of the interview. The evaluations included assessments of the women's physical attractiveness. The assistants conducted the interviews wearing either a low amount of perfume (one spray in the neck/chest area), a moderate amount (two to three sprays), a high amount (five to six sprays), or no perfume (control condition). Aune found that female students rated the assistants as most physically attractive in the no-perfume condition, less attractive in the low-perfume condition, even less in the moderate-perfume condition, and least attractive in the high-perfume condition. Men's evaluations showed a similar pattern, except that their ratings of attractiveness were highest in the low-perfume condition rather than in the no-perfume control group (see also Baron, 1981). What is especially noteworthy about these results is that how the women *smelled* affected people's judgments of how attractive they *looked*, even though nothing about their visual appearance changed from interview to interview. This is an example of how the effects of smell on interpersonal attraction are often subconscious. We will take a more detailed look at the visual aspects of attractiveness in the following section.

Physical Appearance

Attraction is the force that draws us to other people, encouraging us to form personal relationships. As we mentioned previously, the development of friendships, and particularly romantic relationships, is highly adaptive—so what determines who we'll find attractive? Many believe that "beauty is in the eye of the beholder," or that what one person finds physically attractive will not necessarily appeal to another. This commonly held notion suggests that our ideas of attractiveness are purely subjective, meaning we would expect to find very little agreement from person to person, and from culture to culture, in what is physically attractive and unattractive.

In fact, just the opposite is true: people show strong agreement in what they find physically attractive, and many of our judgments about beauty are highly consistent across cultures and even across time periods (see Buss, 1989). What are the major predictors of attractiveness, and why? Research suggests that, in general, we are most attracted to physical features that signal health and fertility—in other words, signs that someone would be a good potential mate. As we mentioned earlier, the primary reason for forming romantic relationships (from the evolutionary perspective) is procreation, so we have evolved to be attracted to those physical characteristics that suggest that someone would produce healthy offspring.

We have already discussed the link between sexual attraction and smell, but two visual features, in particular, also tend to be strongly associated with

B O X **3.4**

Measuring Symmetry

Body symmetry is an important measure of genetic health, but how easy is it to see? Some asymmetries are obvious, such as having one amputated arm or a large scar on one side of the face. Much of the time, however, we can't really appreciate asymmetries with the naked eye—so how would researchers determine how symmetrical you are?

The most common method is to use a set of calipers to measure the length and width of several features on your left and right sides. Calipers take very precise measurements of length; some electronic calipers are accurate to within 1/10,000th of an inch. Using this instrument, a researcher would take measures of things like the width of your ear, the thickness of your wrist, the length of your fingers, the breadth of your foot, or the size of your ankle on the left side of your body and compare them to the same measures taken from the right side. The smaller the difference, the more symmetrical you are. Researchers usually measure several features like this, because asymmetries can appear almost anywhere on your body. Perhaps one ear is one 500th of an inch wider than the other, or your left ring finger is one 2,000th of an inch shorter than your right. These differences are too small for most people to pick up on consciously without the use of an instrument—but research suggests that we notice them subconsciously and that they play a role in our perceptions of attractiveness.

attractiveness. The first is *symmetry*, or the extent to which two sides of the body mirror each other (See Box 3.4). On a genetically perfect body, the left and right sides would match each other exactly in their outward appearance (with the exception in men that one testicle normally hangs lower than the other). No such perfect body exists in real life, however; genetic abnormalities and environmental stressors encountered during development cause the two sides of the body to deviate from perfect symmetry. Only the most genetically fit people can maintain symmetric development in the face of genetic and environmental challenges, making symmetry an important marker of genetic quality (Møller, 1997).

We are therefore attracted to symmetry, even if only subconsciously, because symmetrical bodies are more likely than asymmetrical ones to be free of infections and genetic defects. In fact, symmetry in the face and body are directly associated with genetic, physical, and mental health, as well as with IQ and cognitive ability (Shackelford & Larsen, 1997). We find symmetry to be attractive, therefore, partly because children produced with symmetrical partners will be more likely to survive to sexual maturity than will children produced with asymmetrical ones (for more on facial symmetry and attraction, see Chapter 4).

A second visual feature that is strongly associated with attractiveness—at least for women—is waist-to-hip ratio (WHR), or the ratio of waist width to hip width. Across cultures, and even across time periods, the preferred WHR for adult women has been about .70. This means that women are seen as maximally attractive when their waists are approximately 70% as wide as their hips (Singh, 1993). This is true no matter what the absolute measurements of the waist and hip are. Audrey Hepburn (at 31.5-22-31) and Marilyn Monroe (at 36–24–34) both had a .70 WHR—so do Sophia Loren, Elle Macpherson, and Kate Moss. In a study of WHR, Singh (1993) analyzed the body measurements of Miss America winners from 1923 to 1987 and found that every single one had a WHR between .69 and .72. He also examined measurements of *Playboy* centerfolds from 1955 to 1965 and 1976 to 1990 and found that every one had a WHR between .68 and .71. Later research by Singh and Luis (1995) demonstrated cross-cultural applicability for the .70 WHR, suggesting that it is seen nearly universally as a sign of female attractiveness.

Why do we find symmetry and a .70 WHR to be attractive? From the evolutionary perspective, it is because mating with people who have these characteristics gives us an advantage when it comes to producing healthy offspring. If that's true, then we should find that symmetry and a .70 WHR aren't simply attractive, but are actually related to reproductive success. Research indicates that this is the case. Several studies have demonstrated that body symmetry exerts several direct influences on reproduction and reproductive opportunity. In one investigation, Thornhill and Gangestad (1994) found that people with more symmetrical bodies have more sexual partners than those with less symmetrical bodies. This was true for both women and men, and after controlling for the effects of participants' ages (see also Gangestad & Thornhill, 1997). In a later study, Thornhill, Gangestad, and Comer (1995) found that men's body symmetry was the strongest predictor of whether their female partners would achieve orgasm during intercourse. The effect of symmetry was stronger than that of all other variables measured in the study, including the man's attractiveness, his height, earnings, and sexual experience, and the couple's ratings of their mutual love. This is important for reproduction because a female's orgasm retains her partner's sperm in her reproductive tract, boosting the likelihood that she will become pregnant (Baxter & Bellis, 1993).

Research has also found that a WHR close to .70 corresponds to maximum reproductive success for women. In one study, Zaadstra et al. (1993) found that women whose WHR was under .80 were more than twice as likely to get pregnant following 12 rounds of artificial insemination as were women with WHR over .80. Married women with WHR higher than .70 also report difficulties becoming pregnant and tend to be older when they deliver their first child (Kaye, Folsom, Prineas, Potter, & Gapstur, 1990). Lower WHR also corresponds to higher levels of estrogen (Krotkiewski & Björntorp, 1978) and lower levels of testosterone (Kirschner & Samojilik, 1991), both of which are important for women's reproductive success.

These data suggest that people are attracted to symmetry and a .70 WHR not simply for cultural or social reasons, but because these characteristics are associated with the likelihood of producing healthy offspring. Photo 3.4 depicts an example of a symmetrical—and therefore healthy—face.

PHOTO 3.4   *People across cultures find symmetrical faces to be more attractive than asymmetrical ones, because facial symmetry is a signal of genetic health and strength.*

Summary

The bio-evolutionary perspective explains the tendency to enact a given behavior, first by examining why that behavior might contribute to survival and/or procreation, and second by investigating the physiological correlates of the behavior through which those contributions are made. We have seen, for instance, that crying might ultimately contribute to our survival by preventing us from being immobilized by distress, and that the chemical composition of emotional tears may be responsible for the calming effect that crying often has on us. We've seen how being affectionate with a loved one can help bond us to that person emotionally, increasing our security and our reproductive opportunity, and how the hormone oxytocin plays a part in creating the feelings of bonding and attachment that go along with affection. And we have seen that our evaluation of someone's body odor predicts our physical attraction to that person, which discourages us from mating with people whose genetic information is too similar to our own.

The fact that these and other behaviors are affected by bio-evolutionary forces doesn't mean they aren't also subject to the influences of culture, however. Engaging in affectionate behavior is good for you and your relationships, but cultures still vary in *how* they show affection. As you consider the influences of culture and biology on nonverbal behavior, we want to encourage you not to adopt an *either/or* perspective, as though the cause of a given behavior were either culture or biology. Humans aren't that simplistic. As you learn more about nonverbal communication in this text, keep in mind that most behaviors are subject to multiple causes. The goal of research, therefore, is not to pin down which cause is the true cause, but rather to identify how influential each cause is. How much of the variation in a given behavior can we attribute to culture, for instance? How much to biology? How much to their interaction? These are all intriguing—and ongoing—questions for researchers in the field of nonverbal communication.

All explanations have their strengths and weaknesses, and the bio-evolutionary perspective is no exception. One of its most important strengths is its ability to account for behaviors that are consistent across cultures and time periods. If a behavior doesn't differ from culture to culture, it cannot be said to be culturally determined, which means that there is a good chance it is based on something broader than culture, such as a biological drive. Indeed, some of the behaviors we have discussed in this chapter—such as the preference for symmetry, for instance—are observed across cultures, across centuries, and even across species (nearly all species, in fact, are attracted to symmetry). A sociocultural explanation may be able to account for why people in a given culture prefer symmetry, but it cannot adequately explain the universality of this preference, whereas the bio-evolutionary perspective can.

One of the limitations of the bio-evolutionary approach is that it deals with causes that are sometimes difficult to see and appreciate. For example, consider the fact that aggressive parents tend to raise aggressive children. If you saw that occur, it would be easy to point to the aggressive environment in the household as the cause of the children's aggression. The parents always fought, they were abusive toward each other, they watched a lot of violent television—no wonder the children grew up to be aggressive. They obviously learned it

from their parents. In this case, socialization is an obvious cause of the children's aggression, but is it the biggest cause? Perhaps the parents' genes predisposed them to be aggressive, and the children are aggressive because they inherited those genes. This isn't quite as apparent a cause as socialization or environment, but it may actually be a more influential one, and scientists would have ways of determining if it is. One of the keys to using a bio-evolutionary perspective, therefore, is to remember that cause-and-effect relationships aren't always obvious—sometimes we have to dig deeper than the environment, the culture, the media, or the politics to really understand human behavior.

SUGGESTED READINGS

Andreassi, J. L. (2000). *Psychophysiology: Human behavior and physiological response* (4th ed.). Mahwah, NJ: Lawrence Erlbaum Associates.

Beatty, M. J., McCroskey, J. C., & Valencic, K. M. (2001). *The biology of communication: A communibiological perspective*. Cresskill, NJ: Hampton Press.

Floyd, K., Mikkelson, A. C., & Hesse, C. (2007). *The biology of human communication* (2nd ed.). Florence, KY: Thomson Learning.

Miller, A. S., & Kanazawa, S. (2007). *Why beautiful people have more daughters*. New York: Penguin.

Pinker, S. (2002). *The blank slate: The modern denial of human nature*. New York: Penguin.

4 The Body as a Code: Appearance and Adornment

Appearances can be deceiving.

—Aesop

Personal beauty is a greater recommendation than any letter of reference.
—Aristotle

There are various forms of personal beauty. Inner beauty refers to qualities such as being honest, fair, friendly, and empathetic. Outer beauty, on the other hand, refers to how people look based on physical characteristics such as facial structure, height, weight, and coloring. Although people often perceive that individuals who are outwardly beautiful are also inwardly beautiful, sometimes, as the saying goes, appearances can be deceiving. Yet right or wrong, people often place considerable weight on first impressions, which are largely a function of how people look.

It is not surprising, then, that considerable research has examined outer beauty, or physical attractiveness, as a form of nonverbal communication. Physical attractiveness is part of a larger code of nonverbal communication that focuses on how appearance and adornment are encoded and decoded. Appearance cues include physical features, such as facial structure, height, weight, and coloring. Adornment cues, such as clothing, jewelry, and perfume, are worn on the body.

In this chapter, we begin our examination of nonverbal codes by looking at one of the codes that relates to our visual senses: physical appearance and adornment. (Chapter 5 discusses the other visual code, kinesics.) Our bodies and how we dress, groom, and decorate them are among the most primal signals of who we are, how attractive we are to others, and what our place is in the social hierarchy, among other messages. These bodily features are also the basis for some powerful perceptions of others, perceptions that we sometimes regard as messages and sometimes draw on as context for interpreting messages. That makes appearance and adornment a good place to start our exploration of the coding systems available for the exchange of nonverbal messages.

Whereas some of the other codes we cover will have elaborate and precise systems that have been developed for describing how messages are encoded and decoded, no such formalized system exists for physical appearance and adornments. Therefore, we offer what we regard as features that are part of the coding system. In some cases, these are fixed, natural features—such as body type or skin color—that do not truly meet our criteria for communication because they are not intentionally selected or manipulated cues nor are they directed to a specific target, as would normally be true of other encoded messages. Nevertheless, humans often act as if even naturally arising features are chosen or can be modified. So, people assume that the obese individual could diet and therefore chooses to be overweight, or the pasty-white complexioned person chooses not to acquire that "healthy glow" of a tan. These are not necessarily conscious judgments but instead may insidiously permeate implicit thoughts and judgments and may even creep into assessments of features that cannot be selected or manipulated, such as being tall or having dark skin. We discuss these kinds of judgments more when we address stereotypes in Chapter 9. Other body-based features such as clothing, jewelry, and tattoos more closely conform to our definition of communication because they are message vehicles, intentionally selected and modified by their senders and interpreted as intentional by receivers.

We start by discussing the importance of these cues, followed by a summary of research on how physical attractiveness is perceived. The rest of the chapter focuses on specific aspects of physical appearance—the body, coloring, adornment, and olfactics (odors and fragrances). These are the elements that comprise the physical appearance and adornment code. Because they have interaction primacy—they are noticeable at a distance before any other nonverbal or verbal messages have been exchanged—they have great power to set the stage for any human interaction.

The Importance of Physical Appearance and Adornment

The need to project a positive appearance often follows closely behind needs for food and shelter in importance. This may seem like an overstatement, but the survival of the human race and of our genetic line relies on the ability to attract others, and physical appearance is a key component in attracting mates (Buss, 1994; see also Chapter 3). People in the United States are highly conscious of their physical appearance. A study by Cash (1988) showed that 82% of men and 93% of women are actively oriented toward developing and maintaining an attractive appearance. In the United States, multibillion-dollar industries are built around the need to look and smell good. Think of all the money spent on clothing, jewelry, shoes, makeup, perfume, deodorant, and dieting products. Many people are employed by businesses designed to help people look their best, including the fashion industry, beauty salons and spas, barbershops, orthodontic offices, exercise clubs, and plastic surgery clinics. These businesses often continue to thrive when economic times are hard, because even when money is tight, people still want to look and feel their best.

People develop a sense of the importance of physical appearance early in life. Even in preschool, children are able to point out who the better-looking kids are, and these children are often the most popular in their classes (Berscheid & Walster, 1974). Children are born with a sense of what is physically attractive. Infants react positively to beautiful faces and look away from ugly faces. Children also learn appearance norms from parents, from other adults, and eventually from peers. From the time they are babies, they are taught to wear clothing appropriately rather than to run around naked. They learn gender stereotypes related to appearance. In the United States, boys learn not to wear skirts, dresses, or makeup, whereas girls learn how to fix their hair and wear jewelry. Elsewhere, as girls and boys move through childhood and adolescence, they are learning their culture's and peer group's norms for fashion, grooming, and accepted appearance.

As we shall see, physical appearance also plays a critical role in the formation of initial impressions, with people often actively manipulating their physical appearance to create a particular image. Despite the critical role that appearance and adornment cues play in fostering impressions, however, these cues are more static than other forms of encoded nonverbal communication. Thus, the communicative potential of appearance and adornment cues is somewhat limited. Unlike kinesic and vocalic cues, for example, appearance and adornment cues often stay fairly consistent throughout the course of interaction. For example, if you feel overdressed when you meet with a potential employer for an interview, there is little you can do to alter your appearance during the interview. In contrast, if you noticed that your body was tense and your voice a bit high pitched, you could make adjustments so that you appeared more relaxed. Because appearance and adornment cues are often static, they constitute a somewhat inflexible communication channel after an interaction has begun. Some appearance cues are also limited because the communicator has little control over them. For example, although people can wear high heels or elevator shoes to try to look taller, they cannot change their actual height. Similarly, it is difficult to change facial features such as the shape of one's eyes or the size of one's nose. Adornment cues, such as clothing, perfume, and cosmetics, are somewhat more flexible, however. People can intentionally manipulate these cues to try to create a positive impression.

Perceptions Associated with Physical Attractiveness

Fairly or not, people tend to associate all sorts of positive internal characteristics, such as friendliness, ambition, likeability, and intelligence, with an outwardly attractive appearance (Dion, 1986; Dion, Berscheid, & Walster, 1972; Hatfield & Sprecher, 1986; Wilson & Nias, 1976). This beauty bias, which has been termed the *halo effect* or the *"what is beautiful is good" hypothesis*, is present from childhood through older adulthood (Larose & Standing, 1998), although it may be less pronounced in adulthood than in childhood and adolescence (Zuckerman & Hodgins, 1993). Eagly, Ashmore, Makhijani, and Longo (1991) demonstrated that the "what is beautiful is good" stereotype is stronger for perceptions of social competence (such as extraversion and self-confidence) than perceptions of one's cognitive abilities (such as intelligence and adjustment). Moreover, when it comes to judgments about integrity and concern for others, being good looking does not seem to matter.

Of course, it is important to keep in mind that the halo effect is a perceptual bias; beautiful people may be *perceived* as more friendly and competent than average-looking people, but this does not mean that they *actually* possess these positive traits. In fact, although physically attractive people are generally more self-confident and socially skilled than average looking or unattractive people, there is no evidence showing that physically attractive people are actually nicer or more trustworthy than other people (Feingold, 1992). And although there is evidence that physically attractive people tend to be intelligent (Kanazawa & Kovar, 2004), this does not mean that good-looking individuals are always smarter than average-looking individuals. Think of the smartest people you know. Chances are that some of them are good looking, but others are not.

Research also suggests that people behave differently when they feel attractive. In particular, people are more self-confident when they believe they look good. People also expect good-looking people to act confident and sociable. A pair of researchers tested these ideas by examining communication between avatars in a virtual environment (Yee & Bailenson, 2007). Avatars are digital representations of a person. In this study, people who were assigned attractive avatars engaged in more self-disclosure and used closer distances with other avatars than did people who were assigned less attractive avatars. Yee and Bailenson called this *the proteus effect*—people's actions reflected how they thought a person with their avatar's characteristics should act.

Of course, people also believe that attractive people have negative characteristics. Really good-looking people are perceived to be vain, self-centered, materialistic, and snobbish (Dermer & Thiel, 1975). Cash and Janda (1984) called this the *"what is beautiful is self-centered" hypothesis*. Thus, being physically attractive comes with advantages and disadvantages, as is illustrated by research on physical attractiveness in relationships and professional contexts.

Physical Attractiveness in Relationships

Research suggests that good-looking people have certain advantages when it comes to initiating and developing romantic relationships. Considerable research suggests that physical appearance is one of the best predictors of romantic attraction (Dion, 1986; Sprecher, 1989). Sprecher and Regan (2002) examined characteristics that people look for in romantic relationships and friendships. Across various types of relationships, people preferred partners who were warm and kind, expressive and open, and had a good sense of humor. Physical attractiveness was most important in romantic relationships and cross-sex friendships. Sprecher and Regan's results also suggest that women who consider themselves to be highly desirable are most likely to be choosy about physical appearance in potential mates. Men are likely to be choosiest when they perceive that there are a lot of attractive women available for them to date.

Physical appearance often acts as a screening device for determining who qualifies as a potential romantic partner. In a study of videodating (Woll, 1986), physical appearance and age were the two biggest predictors of whether a person would click on someone's link to view their videotape. Studies of speed dating have produced similar results, showing that appearance is a better predictor of attraction than personality-related factors (see Box 4.1). People are so cognizant of the role that physical attractiveness plays in the initial stages of romantic relationships that they sometimes exaggerate or lie about their appearance. Rowatt and his colleagues found that over 1/3 of women and nearly 46% of men admit deceiving someone in order to initiate a date, with deception often revolving around physical appearance or status (Rowatt, Cunningham, & Druen, 1999). Men are more likely to exaggerate (or lie about) how successful and sincere they are; women are more likely to enhance their appearance by using tactics such as covering blemishes with makeup or wearing clothes that make them look thinner (Tooke & Camire, 1991). Perhaps even more interestingly, people are most likely to engage in deception and impression management when the potential dating partner is high in physical attractiveness (Rowatt et al., 1999). Apparently, people feel a stronger need to project a positive image to people who are physically attractive.

When interacting with physically attractive individuals, people also work harder to manage their appearance, because they perceive good-looking people to be harder to get. Thus, although people tend to be attracted to people who are especially good looking, they also realize that good-looking individuals may be more difficult to attract. The results from Sprecher and Regan's (2002) study (discussed previously) support this logic; women who considered themselves to be highly desirable were choosier, as were men who believed that they could chose from many highly attractive potential partners. People who are less physically attractive and have fewer alternatives are likely to settle for someone who is less attractive than the ideal. This is one of the ideas behind the *matching hypothesis* (Berscheid, Dion, Walster, & Walster, 1971; Berscheid & Walster, 1974), which is the tendency to search for partners who are within a similar range of our own level of attractiveness. The matching hypothesis does *not* specify that we look for partners who look like us; instead it suggests that we look for partners who have about the same level of physical attractiveness as we do. So if you are tall, blond, and moderately attractive, you will not necessarily look for a partner who is tall or blond, but you will look for a partner who is moderately attractive.

Research has shown that the matching hypothesis applies to various types of relationships, including both friendships and marriages (Cash & Derlega, 1978; Feingold, 1988). In the first test of the matching hypothesis, Murstein (1972) had the participants in his study rate the physical attractiveness of people in photographs. He then compared the attractiveness scores of partners who were actually dating to create a difference score. For example, if the woman was rated a 7 and the man was rated a 6, their difference score would be 1. Murstein also created random pairs of people who were not dating each other. He found that the difference scores were smaller for the real couples than the randomly paired couples. In another classic study (Berscheid & Walster, 1974), college students were matched

BOX **4.1**

Dating Really Is Like a Meat Market

Faye Flam, *Seattle Times*, August 22, 2005, p. E8
Permission to reprint this article was granted by
the author.

Is dating really a search for that special match, or is it more like a commercial venture—meat market with the hottest-looking holding all the capital? Science has found an answer using "speed dating," a singles event in which [members of the opposite sex] are matched up for a series of encounters of three to four minutes.

Psychologist Robert Kurzban of the University of Pennsylvania says his goal was to distinguish between two possible models of mating behavior. One, called the "matching hypothesis," suggests people seek partners like themselves. If you're an ugly green ogre, for example, you'd choose an ugly green ogress over a beautiful princess. "It's kind of the Disney model," says Kurzban.

The other possibility is the "market model." Everyone agrees on who's most attractive, but in the end we're forced to settle for the best we can get. Cyrano wants pretty Roxanne, not a woman with a huge proboscis. Failure to settle ends tragically.

To determine which scenario most closely resembles the real world, Kurzban turned to HurryDate, a speed-dating provider. He and colleague Jason Weeden got 2,650 participants to fill out surveys revealing weight, height, age, number of children, previous marriages, and attitudes toward premarital sex. It also asked participants to rate their own faces, bodies, and personalities on scales from 1 to 7.

The mechanics of speed dating gave the psychologists a chance to see which participants were chosen most often and by whom. In HurryDate, you rotate through a series of three- or four-minute conversations with each of about 25 possible suitors. After each encounter, you mark a card "no" or "yes." On average, men got a "yes" from 34 percent of the women, while women got the approval of 49 percent of the men. If two yeses match up, the pair can exchange e-mail addresses or phone numbers.

The most important factor determining how many "yeses" one got was weight in proportion to height. It made the biggest difference for women, but looks and fitness mattered for men, too. What didn't seem to matter much were personality, religion, education, income, drinking, smoking, or number of children.

In the end, the market model won. The same people were consistently deemed desirable. When it comes to first impressions, at least, beauty is not in the eye of the beholder but in the body of the beholdee.

Florida Atlantic University psychologist Todd Shackelford puts it bluntly: People who are 1s and 2s (on a scale from 1 to 10) don't want other 1s and 2s. If you're a 6, say, your partner would rather have a 10, but has to settle for you.

What a cold, calculating world it is . . . Still, [Kurzban] says, the extreme emphasis on looks characterizes only the first phase of mate selection, a "first-pass filter." At this stage we're driven by animal instincts to find fertile and healthy mates . . . .

But what about love? Is it really just a beauty contest? Here it might help to turn from science to the poets. As Antoine de Saint-Exupéry wrote: "Life has taught us that love does not consist in gazing at each other but in looking outward in the same direction." Love, once established, is about sharing life. But you have to brave the mating market to get there.

Note: See Kurzban and Weeden (2005) for information regarding the HurryDate study.

up for a date at a dance using a computer program. The students completed predance questionnaires about what they wanted in a partner. They also completed post-dance questionnaires asking about the date. Unbeknownst to the students in this study, they were matched based on their level of physical attractiveness. The study showed that especially good-looking people desired and had a better time with dates who were highly physically attractive, whereas average-looking people desired and had a better time with dates who were moderately physically attractive. Finally, some research suggests that couples who are similar in physical attractiveness have happier relationships (Patzer, 1985; Zajonc, Adelman, Murphy, & Niedenthal, 1987).

Research on the matching hypothesis suggests that the most physically attractive people might not always get the most dates, even if they do get the most attention. Even so, if you do not consider yourself to be especially good looking, many of the other research findings discussed in this section may be disheartening. You may wonder if your partner is settling for you. You might also lament the unfairness of the situation. Before despairing too much, however, consider two additional findings: (1) good-looking people sometimes have a hard time living up to the high expectations of their partners; and (2) having a good relationship and a positive style of communication may actually make you seem more physically attractive to your partner.

According to research on the "what is good is beautiful" hypothesis, people expect good-looking people to possess an array of desirable characteristics. Over time, however, people may come to realize that the attractive person has strengths and weaknesses, just as everyone else does. When this happens, the attractive person may fall off his or her pedestal and suddenly appear less desirable. This *pedestal effect* has been supported by research showing that people tend to expect and demand more from especially good-looking people (Solnick & Schweitzer, 1999). As Guerrero, Andersen, and Afifi (2007) put it:

> People notice those who are physically attractive, and are more likely to initiate communication with attractive people, but that does not guarantee that highly attractive people will continue to be valued after the initial attraction fades. In fact, they can be at a disadvantage in trying to live up to the high expectations imposed by the halo effect. For example, Hatfield (1984) wrote about a beautiful woman who was insecure because she worried that men would be disappointed if they saw her for what she really was, rather than what they dreamed a beautiful woman should be. Physical appearance only goes so far. (p. 54)

Physically attractive individuals are not the only people who have an edge in developing and maintaining relationships; good communicators also have an edge. Albana, Knapp, and Thenue (2002) advanced the idea that positive interaction can actually enhance people's perceptions of their partner's physical appearance. To test their ideas, they advanced *interaction appearance theory*. The theory rests on four principles. First, most people believe that an ideal partner is physically attractive and a good communicator. Second, people feel free to communicate with a range of people, some of whom fall outside the range of what one considers optimally physically attractive. Third, if someone starts to develop a satisfying relationship with a good communicator who is not highly physically attractive, the original belief structure about what constitutes an ideal partner is challenged. Fourth, to resolve this discrepancy, the initial perception of the partner's level of physical appearance is altered to be more favorable. In other words, if you are in a satisfying relationship and have positive interactions with someone, you are likely to see that person as more attractive. For example, you might focus on that person's best physical features so that you start to see him or her as more attractive. Some of these features may even be accentuated during positive social interactions. You might think someone looks sexy when he or she gives you a certain look, or you might think your partner looks especially cute when laughing or smiling.

Albana and her colleagues conducted three studies to test interaction appearance theory. In addition to finding general support for their theory, they showed that negative interaction had an even stronger effect on ratings of physical appearance than did positive interaction. For example, if a person was initially rated around an 8 (on a scale of 1 to 10) for physical appearance, the rating would drop down to around a 6 after an uncomfortable or negative social interaction. Because expectations may be higher for physically attractive individuals to be competent communicators, good-looking people may be especially likely to be seen as less attractive when they violate those expectations.

Other research supports that idea that people in satisfying relationships perceive their partners to be especially attractive. For instance, people in happy relationships often view their partners as more attractive than other people do (Simpson, Lerma, & Gangestad, 1990). So if you are in love with your partner, you are likely to rate her or him as better looking than your friends or an objective observer would. People in happy relationships also derogate the physical attractiveness of other potential partners (Simpson et al., 1990). If a good-looking man or woman approaches you, and you are already in a happy relationship, you are less likely to rate him or her as a 9 or 10 than you would be if you were not already in a happy relationship. Simpson and his colleagues argued that this type of derogation helps people stay loyal and maintain healthy relationships. These studies also suggest that beauty is sometimes in "the eye of the beholder" as the old adage suggests.

Physical Attractiveness in Professional Contexts

Physical appearance is also important in professional contexts such as the classroom and the workplace. Some of the earliest research on the benefits of physical appearance examined people's perceptions of attractive and average-looking children (Berscheid & Walster, 1974; Dion, 1972). These studies showed that people generally have more favorable impressions and more positive expectations for attractive versus average-looking or less-attractive students. Teachers were more likely to call on and encourage the better-looking students. Dion's work suggests that people may also be more lenient when good-looking students misbehave. In her study, people read a description of a 7-year-old's bad behavior. Some descriptions included a picture of an attractive child and others included a picture of a less-attractive child. Although the misbehavior was exactly the same, people believed that less-attractive students were more chronically aggressive, dishonest, and unpleasant, whereas attractive students were viewed as less likely to engage in aggressive behavior again in the future. In short, people attributed bad behavior to personality characteristics when judging unattractive children; when judging attractive children, they blamed their misbehavior on external factors (e.g., they were having a bad day or were provoked by others).

Some research also suggests that beauty is an asset for teachers. For example, Hamermesh and Parker (2005) had a group of undergraduate students look at pictures of the instructors for 463 courses and then rate those instructors on physical attractiveness. They found that beauty had a substantial effect on undergraduate ratings of the overall quality of college courses, with classes taught by better-looking instructors regarded as better than classes taught by less-attractive instructors. This effect was stronger for male than female instructors.

However, other research has shown that other factors may outweigh physical attractiveness in student evaluations of teachers. Ambady and Rosenthal (1993) examined how people evaluate teachers based on "thin slices" of nonverbal behavior and physical appearance. Specifically, people rated teachers after viewing silent video clips that lasted from 6 to 30 seconds. Rather than being influenced by physical attractiveness, judges tended to evaluate teachers more positively when they used warm and expressive nonverbal behaviors. Ambady and Rosenthal suggested that studies that involve showing people still pictures of teachers may produce different findings than studies that involve video clips. They argued that "when people actually interact with [teachers], the effects of physical attractiveness become diluted by the other information available" (p. 439).

Physical attractiveness can be an asset during employment interviews. When two people are equally qualified, the better-looking applicant is more likely to get the job, especially if the position requires interpersonal skill and/or contact with the public (Bardack & McAndrew, 1985; Cash & Kilcullen, 1985). Interestingly, this beauty bias may be stronger for female interviewers than male interviewers (Heilman & Saruwatari, 1979). A *glass ceiling effect* may also modify the beauty bias for women applicants, such that good looks are an asset when interviewing for entry-level positions but a disadvantage when interviewing for top managerial positions (Frieze, Olson, & Russell, 1991; Kaiser, 1997). If a woman is too attractive, she may be falsely judged as too feminine to take on a traditionally masculine role, or too involved in her social life to put much effort into work. Some research also reinforces the idea that attractive blondes are stereotyped as unintelligent (Weir & Fine-Davis, 1989), and at least one study suggests that brunettes are judged as more competent than blondes or redheads (Kyle & Mahler, 1996).

The effects of appearance extend beyond the initial interview. Several studies conducted in different countries (Canada, England, and the United States) have demonstrated that attractive people earn, on average, more money than average-looking people, and that average-looking people earn more than unattractive people (Frieze et al., 1991; Hamermesh & Biddle, 1994; Harper, 2000). In one of these studies, men earned $2,600 more and women earned nearly $2,200 more per unit of attractiveness, with each unit representing a number on a 5-point scale (Frieze et al., 1991). So if Paul and Steve are both customer service representatives, but Paul is a "5" on the attractiveness scale and Steve is a "3," we would expect Paul to earn about $5,200 more than Steve on the basis of the study by Frieze and colleagues. In the study done by Hamermesh and Biddle (1994), women and men who were classified as below average in physical appearance made 5% and 9% less money, respectively, than their average-looking counterparts. In addition, beautiful women earned about 4% more than average-looking women, whereas handsome men earned about 5% more than average-looking men. Notice that in both of these studies, men paid a higher penalty for being unattractive than women. Men also received a larger premium for being good looking.

Height and weight are also linked to wages (Averett & Korenman, 1996; Harper, 2000; Hamermesh & Biddle, 1994). Tall people, especially tall men, generally make more money than shorter people. Overweight and obese people, especially women, make even less money. Having a healthy weight in proportion to height, in contrast, is associated with higher salaries and better positions. Another study showed that women who make high salaries and are highly educated tend to be taller and thinner than average (Fulwood, Abrahams, & Johnson, 1986). For men, height and a slightly heavier frame were associated with both higher salary and more education. The findings for height can be interpreted as reflecting a stereotype that tall people are dominant and competent. The results for weight may reflect that educated, professional women have more resources to exercise and eat healthy food, whereas educated, professional men have the resources to join health clubs, build up more muscle and eat more food.

Several explanations have been offered for the beauty premium in the workplace. Some scholars have suggested that *lookism* is an unconscious form of discrimination in the workplace (e.g., Hamermesh & Biddle, 1994). As the "what is beautiful is good" stereotype suggests, employers may associate all kinds of positive characteristics with good looks. They may also associate negative characteristics with below-average looks. The glass ceiling effect may help explain why the premiums and penalties associated with looks are stronger for men than women—when women compete for upper-level positions, beauty is no longer an advantage and can even be a disadvantage.

The pedestal effect, which was discussed previously, is another disadvantage for attractive people in the workplace. According to the pedestal effect, people have high expectations for how good-looking people will perform; when these expectations are not met, people are especially disappointed. A study by Shanani and Plumitallo (1993) supports this logic. In their study, bank supervisors read memos describing a problem with an employee who was described as attractive, average-looking, or unattractive. The supervisors were more likely to believe that attractive people failed because they did not try hard enough, whereas unattractive people failed because they had bad luck. Thus, supervisors may expect that attractive people will be able to perform well if they put the appropriate level of effort into a task. Shanani and Plumitallo also suggested that people might perceive attractive individuals to have more control of the situation than unattractive individuals.

Despite findings showing that beauty comes with certain drawbacks, the overwhelming consensus is that attractiveness is more of an advantage than a disadvantage in the workplace (Shahani-Denning, 2003). A study by Mobias and Rosenblat (2006) probed further into the reasons why beauty is an advantage in the workplace. In their study, people assigned as "employers" observed "potential employees" as they worked through a maze-solving task. Although a person's success at this task was completely unrelated to her or his physical attractiveness, better-looking people were still assigned higher wages. The attractive individuals appeared more confident during the task; they also were more skilled at communication and were judged as more able to complete the task (even if there was no objective evidence to support this judgment).

Attractiveness Features

So far we have been discussing physical attractiveness as if everyone knows what it is. This may not be a bad assumption; counter to the popular saying that "beauty is in the eye of the beholder," scholars have determined that some features of physical attractiveness are universal. In other words, people from various countries around the globe agree that these features are attractive. Thus, people seem to make two assessments related to beauty: (1) a subjective assessment based on interpersonal and cultural factors, such as how much they like someone and what their society tells them is attractive; and (2) an objective assessment related to features that are universally regarded as good looking. Let us examine five features that are universally associated with attractiveness: koinophilia, facial neoteny combined with sexual maturity, face and body symmetry, the Golden Ratio, and waist-to-hip ratios. These are all static features that cannot be readily encoded as a message but nonetheless influence judgments of attractiveness.

Koinophilia

Researchers have found that faces with "average" female or male characteristics within a given population are considered attractive (Langlois & Roggman, 1990; Langlois, Roggman, & Musselman, 1994; Rhodes, Harwood, Yoshikawa, Nishitani, & McLean, 2002; Rubenstein, Langlois, & Roggman, 2002). The tendency to perceive faces with average features as attractive is known as *koinophilia* (Koeslag & Koeslag, 1994). This may seem odd to you; most people probably assume that beautiful and handsome faces are anything but average. However, the idea that average is beautiful makes sense when you consider what makes a face unattractive. Features that are too large, too small, too close together, and so forth, detract from the aesthetic beauty of a face.

In the first major study of the beauty of average faces, researchers used a computer program to configure different faces so that features represented mathematical averages (Langlois & Roggman, 1990). Specifically, they took photographs of 96 college-age men and 96 college-age women. They then created new pictures using a computer program that reconfigured the features on faces to represent the mathematical average of 4, 6, 8, 16, or 32 different faces. For instance, in the composite pictures of women, the size of the eyes, nose, and mouth, as well as the height of the forehead and structure of the cheekbones, represented the average across groups of 4, 6, 8, 16, or 32 individual women. These new composite faces were generally rated as more attractive than individual faces, with the composite faces generated by averaging across 16 or 32 individuals rated as the most attractive overall. In this and other studies, female faces that represented average configurations of all the female facial characteristics in the population were rated as most attractive. Average configurations were also evaluated most favorably for men.

Facial Neoteny and Sexual Maturity

Research also suggests that facial attractiveness is influenced by the degree to which a face displays both baby-like features (facial neoteny) and sexual maturity. In one study, researchers used a computer program that allowed the participants in their study to create an ideally beautiful face for a woman (Johnston & Franklin, 1993). The participants looked at numerous faces of real women and then chose the features they liked best and least. A composite of the best features was then used to create an ideal woman's face. Compared to actual faces, the ideal faces had more baby-like features, such as fuller lips, wider eyes, small chins, shorter distances between the eyes and nose, and larger distances between the eyes and hairline. Other studies suggest that facial neoteny is viewed as attractive across diverse cultures, including Austria, Brazil, Germany, Great Britain, Japan, Russia, and native peoples in Paraguay and Venezuela (Fauss, 1988; D. Jones, 1995; Jones & Hill, 1993; Perrett, May, & Yoshikawa, 1994; Riedl, 1990). Some facial neoteny is also attractive in men's faces. For example, Cunningham, Barbee, and Pike (1990) found that women prefer men with large eyes.

Although facial neoteny is attractive, a face that is too babyish is often seen as immature. Therefore, to be viewed as optimally attractive, faces need to have a combination of baby-like and sexually mature features. In the study by Cunningham and his colleagues, the most attractive women had the baby-like features we discussed previously (such as full lips and large wide eyes) combined with high cheekbones, which is a sexually mature feature. Take a look at Photo 4.1 to see how a young girl's babyish facial features are different from a young woman's combination of sexually mature and babyish features. For men, attractiveness is related to having sexually mature features such as prominent cheekbones, a strong jaw line, and large chin, combined with the less mature features of large eyes and a wide smile. According to these studies, the ideal woman's face consists of baby-like features and high cheekbones, whereas the ideal man's face consists of sexually mature features and large eyes. Thus, baby-like features are more prized in women than men. Importantly, faces that are too feminine and babyish, or too masculine and harsh, are perceived negatively (Cunningham, Barbee, & Pike, 1990; Langlois et al., 1994). The key appears to be to have mostly average features along with the right combination of babyish and sexually mature features.

PHOTO 4.1   *How are the features in this little girl's face and this young woman's face similar and different? What makes them each attractive?*

Symmetry

Researchers are currently examining the extent to which symmetry is related to attractiveness in both faces and bodies. Facial symmetry refers to how similar the two sides of a person's face are. If you divide a face into two halves and one side of the face is a perfect mirror image of the other, then the face is perfectly symmetrical. Most people, however, do not have perfectly symmetrical faces. For example, one eye might be slightly farther away from the midpoint of the face than the other eye, or one cheek might be slightly fuller than the other cheek. The larger these differences are, the more asymmetrical a face is, and the more likely it is that the face will be judged as unattractive (Grammer & Thornhill, 1994; Perret et al., 1999; Rhodes, Proffitt, Grady, & Sumich, 1998). For instance, some researchers have used photograph retouching or morphing techniques (which involve putting electronic graphic images of each side of the face onto the other side) to create more symmetrical versions of real faces. The symmetrical faces they created were judged as more attractive than the real faces (Hume & Montgomerie, 2001; Perrett et al., 1999; Rhodes et al., 1998).

However, there is also evidence that a face can be too symmetrical. Zaidel and her colleagues have conducted several studies of symmetry using photos of professional models and college students to represent beautiful versus ordinary faces (Zaidel & Choi, 2007; Zaidel & Cohen, 2005). Using a computer program, the photos were altered to create two additional faces for each person: a right-right version that represented the right side of the face plus its mirror image, and a left-left version that represented the left side of the face plus its mirror image. People who viewed these photographs actually rated the natural faces as more attractive than either the left-left or right-right faces, regardless of whether they were viewing beautiful or ordinary faces (Zaidel & Choi, 2007). Similarly, Zaidel and Cohen (2005) found that people perceived minor asymmetries in faces they rated as especially good looking. In addition, when people compared the left-left and right-right faces of beautiful people, they tended to see one of those faces as more beautiful than the other, even though there was no consistent pattern. In other words, some people preferred the left-left version, whereas others preferred the right-right version. When judging ordinary women's faces, however, there may be a preference for the right-right version (Zaidel, Chen, & German, 2005).

Overall, these findings suggest that although high levels of facial asymmetry are related to judgments of unattractiveness, faces do not have to be perfectly symmetrical to be rated as good looking. In fact, slight asymmetries may be preferable to perfect symmetry. This may be because perfect symmetry is rarely, if ever, found in real human faces. Symmetrical faces that are generated by computer may look unnatural to the human eye. This would explain why people are rated as more attractive when their photos are touched up or morphed (with the two sides averaged together) to look more symmetrical, but less attractive when a computer program is used to create a perfect mirror image of either side of the face. In the former case, the natural quality of the face is still preserved; the image is more symmetrical but not an exact mirror image. Take a look at the three faces shown in Photo 4.2. Which images do you perceive as most and least attractive?

Less research has focused on symmetrical bodies, but so far it appears that more symmetrical bodies are rated as better looking. For example, hands that are mirror images of one another are more attractive than hands that are asymmetrical, and legs and arms that are the same length and proportion are perceived as more attractive than those that are dissimilar. There appears to be a biological basis for preferring symmetrical bodies (see Chapter 3). People with symmetrical bodies not only are perceived to be more physically attractive, but they also tend to be more coordinated, more fertile, and even more intelligent than people with less symmetrical bodies (Furlow, Armigo-Presitt, Gangestad, & Thornhill, 1997; Shackelford & Larsen, 1997; Thornhill & Gangestad, 1994; Thornhill & Møller, 1997). In fact, star athletes tend to have more symmetrical bodies than the average population, which accounts for some of their talent in running faster, jumping higher, and so forth.

| left symmetrical | natural | right symmetrical |

PHOTO 4.2 Which version of this person's face do you find the most attractive?

Proportion and the Golden Ratio

Another universal feature of beauty is the *Golden Ratio*, or *Phi*, which is a ratio of 1 to 1.618. The Greek philosopher and mathematician Pythagoras is credited with discovering the association between Phi and beauty (Livio, 2002). According to Pythagoras, Phi is related to beauty in nature as well as in faces and bodies. Research supports Pythagoras's early observations (see Guerrero & Floyd, 2006, for a summary). Attractive bodies are marked repeatedly by the Golden Ratio. If you have an ideal body, the distance from your belly button to the bottom of your feet would be 1.618 times the distance from the top of your head to your belly button. Similarly, the distance from the top of your head to your elbow would be 1.618 times the distance from your elbow to the end of your middle finger. Beautiful faces are also marked by Phi. For instance, in especially beautiful faces, the mouth is 1.618 times as wide as the nose. In the most attractive faces, the Phi ratio creates a series of triangles that defines the shape of the mouth, the nose, the space between the eyes, and the cheekbones, among other facial features. The more balanced these triangular regions are across the face, the more attractive a face is regarded. Elizabeth Hurley and Tom Cruise, among other celebrities, have faces that conform closely to this pattern.

Waist-to-Hip Ratio

Although there are cultural differences in preferences for weight and height, men from various countries around the world prefer women with waist-to-hip ratios of about .70 (Buss, 1989, 1994; Singh, 1993; Singh & Young, 1995). This means that the waist is 70% as wide as the hips. This ratio is preferred in countries where thinness is prized as well as in countries where heavier weight is preferred. As we discussed in Chapter 3, the key is not what the actual measurements are, but rather what the ratio is. Importantly, a waist-to-hip ratio of .70 is associated with health and fertility (see Guerrero & Floyd, 2006, for a review, as well as Chapter 3). Although less research has examined the ideal waist-to-hip ratio for men, scholars who have looked at this issue suggest that men are perceived as most attractive when their waist-to-hip ratio is in the .90 to 1.0 range (Asthana, 2000; Buss, 1989, 1994). In other words, women tend to prefer men whose hips are slightly wider or the same width as their waists (Lavrakas, 1975). The preference for V-shaped men (broad shoulders with small waist and hips) appears to be as universal as the preference for hourglass-shaped women.

Body Features

In addition to the waist-to-hip ratio, height and weight influence how attractive a person is judged to be. Height appears to be a universally attractive feature in men (e.g., Pawlowski, Dunbar, & Lipowicz, 2000; Shepperd & Strathman, 1989). Preferences for weight are more culturally variable. In some places, thinness is stigmatized and heaviness is valued; in other places, the opposite is true. For example, obesity may be a sign of affluence and status. Within many cultures, including the United States, people evaluate their bodies by comparing them to an ideal body image that is a socially constructed representation of health, status, and beauty.

Body Types

Early research on body types focused on how people are stereotyped based on their height and weight. The original work of Sheldon and his colleagues (Sheldon, 1940; Sheldon, Stevens, & Tucker, 1942) identified three prototypical body types: endomorph, mesomorph, and ectomorph. *Endomorphs* are overweight compared to their height, *mesomorphs* are balanced in terms of weight and height, and *ectomorphs* are underweight compared to their height. Two classic studies (Cortes & Gatti, 1965; Wells & Siegel, 1961) examined stereotypes associated with these three body types. These studies showed that endomorphs tend to be judged as lazy, old-fashioned, friendly, warm, agreeable, trusting, and forgiving. Think about how some of the characters in animated movies, such as Mrs. Potts in *Beauty and the Beast,* fit this stereotype. The U.S. stereotypes associated with the mesomorphic body type include being strong, adventurous, assertive, self-reliant, confident, competitive, hot-tempered, and argumentative. Many famous athletes, such as Tiger Woods and Venus Williams, fit this stereotype. Finally, *ectomorphs* are thin and frail. Many supermodels fit this description, as do cartoon characters such as Olive Oyl from *Popeye* or Ling from *Mulan.* In the United States, ectomorphs are stereotyped as sensitive, cautious, nervous, precise, shy, serious, quiet, and introspective.

As these stereotypes suggest, a mesomorphic body type is generally preferred by people in the United States and other Western countries. However, there are sex differences in the preferred body type. For men, the muscular body type of the mesomorph is preferred, as is tallness (Asthana, 2000; Jackson & Ervin, 1992; Shepperd & Strathman, 1989). In fact, women are more likely to respond to personal ads if men advertise that they are tall (Lynn & Shurgot, 1984). Therefore, a tall mesomorphic man is often preferred to a mesomorphic man of average height. For women, a body type somewhere between an ectomorph and a mesomorph is preferred. In two studies conducted 30 years apart in Great Britain (Iliffe, 1960) and Australia (Huon, Morris, & Brown, 1990), men preferred women who were around 5 feet 5 inches tall and weighed around 120 pounds, with bust, waist, and hip measurements of 35, 23, and 35 inches, respectively. A study of senior citizens (55 years old and older) also revealed a preference for the mesomorphic and ectomorphic body types (Enid, 1993). In this study, people were shown silhouettes of the three body types. They then rated them on physical attractiveness (how good they looked), social attractiveness (how much they would enjoy getting to know them), task attractiveness (how good they would be at helping them get things done), and communicative attractiveness (how much they would like to talk with them). The endomorphic body type was rated lowest on all four types of attractiveness, but was rated especially low on physical attractiveness.

Despite preferences for average and somewhat thin bodies, many people in the United States have the endomorphic body type. In 2007, the Harvard School of Public Health reported that there is an epidemic of obesity in the United States. In most states, between 20% and 25% of the population are overweight. Even more troubling is the trend for adolescents, with 17% of children between the ages of 2 and 19 years old being overweight or obese. The discrepancy between one's actual weight and one's ideal weight can be distressing, leading to health problems, depression, or lack of self-confidence. In the United States, obese people, and obese women in particular, are perceived as lazy, insecure, sloppy, and lacking in self-discipline (Jasper & Klassen, 1990), even though many of these individuals have weight problems that are genetically or physiologically determined.

However, in some places, such as the Ivory Coast, plumpness is prized rather than stigmatized. In the United States, many women diet to get thin enough to fit into their wedding dresses. In Nigeria, women diet for the opposite reason—they go on a high-fat diet so that they are plump enough for the wedding ceremony (Rosenblatt, 1974). Scholars have suggested that people prize the body type that is associated with status and wealth in their culture (see Guerrero & Floyd, 2006, for a summary). In places such as North America and Western Europe, food is abundant, so having the resources to eat right, the time to exercise, and the money to join a fitness club are all associated with high status. The next time you are at the grocery store, compare the prices of sugary drinks versus real fruit drinks, or extra lean sirloin versus regular hamburger meat. Nutritious food costs more than unhealthy food. Because high status is associated with mesomorphic and ectomorphic body types in industrialized countries, these body types are prized. In contrast, in cultures where food and nutrition are scarce, such as parts of Africa, a more endomorphic body is preferred. As Cahnman (1968) put it long ago, "Where affluence is attainable only by a privileged few, obesity, especially in women, is likely to be regarded as prestigious and therefore attractive" (p. 287). In cultures where affluence is available to many, obesity is stigmatized.

Body Image

Cultural standards for beautiful bodies influence people's body images. *Body image* is a broad term that represents how people "think, feel, and behave with regard to their physical attributes" (Muth & Cash, 1997, p. 1438). Within this broad term, there are two specific components of body image: *body image evaluation*, which refers to the judgments people make about their physical appearance, and *body image investment*, which refers to behaviors people engage in to enhance their appearance (Cash & Szymanski, 1995).

Body Image Evaluation.   Paradoxically, even in the United States, where a sizable portion of the population is overweight, individuals who are thin or at a healthy weight sometimes evaluate themselves as too fat. Studies have shown that the weights women perceive as ideal for their body type often fall below the range of healthy weight for their size (e.g., Huon et al., 1990). For example, a woman with a medium frame who is 5 foot 5 inches tall might perceive her ideal weight to be 115 pounds, when actually a weight of 125 to 140 would be considered healthy, depending on her frame and age (Harvard School of Public Health, 2007). In another study, women who were within a healthy weight range perceived themselves as 11.8% over their preferred weight (Galgan, Mable, Ouellette, & Balance, 1989). Women who are preoccupied with their weight and perceive themselves to be heavier than they actually are may be especially likely to develop eating disorders such as anorexia nervosa or bulimia nervosa (Galgan et al., 1989).

Scholars have advanced two primary explanations for women's dissatisfaction with their bodies: sociocultural theory and social comparison theory (Morrison, Kalin, & Morrison, 2004). According to *sociocultural theory*, Western societies promote the idea that thinness is good. The "thin is good" assumption perpetuates the belief that people are rewarded for being thin and punished for being overweight. Many scholars consider the mass media to be one of primary sources of the "thin is good" assumption. Morrison et al. summarized research showing that around 70% of actresses are thinner than the average woman. Moreover, although women in the United States have become heavier since the 1980s, "media images of women have become progressively thinner" (Morrison et al., 2004, p. 572). Although most thin women with small waists tend to have small breasts, women on television and in magazines often have thin waists and hips combined with larger-than-average cup sizes. To complicate matters even more, actors in television programs and advertisements are often shown eating unhealthy foods (Kaufman, 1980). Together, these studies suggest that the media, and society in general, promote unrealistic ideas about what constitutes an ideal body.

Social comparison theory further explains how media images lead to dissatisfaction with one's body. According to social comparison theory, people have an innate need to compare themselves with others (Festinger, 1954). Although the original theory focused on how people compare their abilities and opinions to individuals within their own peer group, more recent applications of the theory have focused on comparisons to dissimilar others in a variety of domains, including physical appearance (Martin & Kennedy, 1993; Morrison et al., 2004; Wheeler & Miyake, 1992). Thus, people compare their looks to the appearance of their peer group, but they also compare themselves to the ideal images they see in the media.

In fact, research suggests that people tend to make more upward than downward comparisons (Wheeler & Miyake, 1992). In other words, people are more likely to compare themselves to individuals who look better than they do (an upward comparison) than to individuals who look worse than they do (a downward comparison). People who make upward comparisons tend to be less satisfied with their bodies than people who make downward comparisons. In addition, people feel more pressure to conform to the standards that are presented in sources such as the mass media; these standards are perceived to be more universal than the standards that exist within one's family or peer group (Irving, 1990). People are likely to be more dissatisfied with their bodies if they spend a lot of time watching television and/or looking at magazines (Martin & Kennedy, 1993; Myers & Biocca, 1992; Thornton & Moore, 1993). This effect appears to be especially strong for adolescent girls. In some of these studies, adolescent girls rate their bodies as less attractive after viewing pictures of thin models in magazines.

Research also suggests that both women and men overestimate the extent to which potential romantic partners are looking for someone with perfect body dimensions. In one study, heterosexual college students were asked to rate physical characteristics in terms of what they were looking for in an ideal mate and what they thought potential mates were looking for in them (Jacobi & Cash, 1994). Women overestimated the extent to which men prefer thin, muscular, and large-breasted women, whereas men overestimated the extent to which women prefer tall and muscular men. So although some body types are generally preferred for men and women based on waist-to-hip ratio, height, and weight, within these general types there is variability in what people find attractive. For example, one woman might prefer a tall, slightly thin man, but another might prefer a large, muscular man, as long as each man falls within a healthy weight range for his height. Indeed, aside from the waist-to-hip ratio, the most important aspect of body type may not be any one specific feature, such as having large breasts or broad shoulders, but rather whether one's weight is in proportion to one's height (Kurzban & Weeden, 2005).

Body Image Investment.   People use various methods to try to achieve and maintain a physically attractive body. Many businesses in the United States revolve around exercising and dieting as ways of enhancing one's body. Studies of the general population as well as studies that isolate teenagers have found that approximately one-third of females report currently dieting as a means of improving their body's appearance (Cash & Henry, 1995; Schwartz, Thompson, & Johnson, 1982). This is not surprising given that a national survey of more than 800 women in the United States found that almost half of these women were unhappy with their bodies and preoccupied with being or becoming overweight (Cash & Henry, 1995).

Some individuals, particularly women, go to greater lengths to alter their appearance by undergoing cosmetic procedures. The American Society of Plastic Surgeons (2002) reported that more than a quarter of a million liposuction procedures were conducted in the United States in 2001, and nearly 220,000 women had breast augmentations in the same year. People also undergo cosmetic procedures to improve their facial appearance. In fact, according to the American Society of Plastic Surgeons, the number of people who had elective cosmetic facial procedures steadily increased from 1992 to 2001, partially because of improved techniques and increased availability. In 2001, over 1.1 million chemical peels were performed on women in the United States. This procedure involves removing the skin's outer layers to improve texture. A similar procedure, called microdermabrasion, which involves smoothing out and refinishing the skin by scraping the skin's outer layers, was performed over 900,000 times on women in the United States in 2001 (American Society of Plastic Surgeons, 2002). Other top nonsurgical procedures for women in 2001 included Botox and collagen injections, which are used to plump up skin and lips and to reduce the appearance of wrinkles. Although men also undergo these procedures, they do so to a much lesser extent.

Chemical peels, microdermabrasion, and injections are nonsurgical procedures that are typically performed in a doctor's office. Other procedures to improve one's facial appearance involve surgery and hospitalization. The most popular form of cosmetic surgery in 2001 was nose reshaping, with over 230,000 women and 136,000 men having this surgery (American Society of Plastic Surgeons, 2002). Eyelid surgery was also among the most popular types of cosmetic surgery for both women and men, as were facelifts for women and hair transplantations for men.

The fact that so many people are willing to undergo surgery or uncomfortable cosmetic procedures in an attempt to enhance the appearance of their bodies and faces is a testament to the public's awareness of the importance of physical attractiveness. As you might suspect, people who have a strong need to present a positive image of themselves to others are particularly likely to have cosmetic surgery (Culos-Reed, Brawley, Martin, & Leary, 2002). Cosmetic surgery can boost people's confidence in their ability to attract and interact with others, but it cannot counterbalance or hide all of one's insecurities (Thomson, Knorr, & Edgerton, 1978).

Coloring

Like preferences for weight and body type, preferences for coloring vary by culture and individual taste. In fact, the same principle of scarcity that explains cultural differences in preferences for weight helps explain why people from different cultures vary in what skin, eye, and hair coloring is perceived as most attractive. Specifically, people often like coloring that conveys status or is scarce within their ethnic or co-cultural group. Such preferences can change over time. For instance, prior to the 20th century, people in many Western cultures (including the United States) prized pale white skin because skin tanned by the sun indicated poverty or outdoor labor. If you've read the *Little House on the Prairie* books by Laura Ingalls Wilder, you may remember Caroline Ingalls telling daughters Laura, Mary, and Carrie to put their bonnets on when they went outside so their faces would not get tanned. Queen Elizabeth I, who reigned in England from 1558 to 1603, is another example. She wore white powder makeup to accentuate her fair complexion. Interestingly, research suggests that primitive European peoples had dark skin. Lighter skin colors emerged around 6,000 to 12,000 years ago ("European skin," 2007). Thus, in European cultures, lighter skin would historically be perceived as rarer than darker skin.

Beginning in the middle of the 20th century, however, tanning became popular in Western cultures partially because it is associated with having leisure time. Studies from the 1990s suggested that people with tanned skin are judged as more attractive, healthy, popular, sexy, and socially active (Broadstock, Borland, & Gason, 1992; Miller, Ashton, McHoskey, & Gimbel, 1984). Tanning continues to be popular today, even though skin cancer is on the rise. However, consistent with the scarcity principle, tanning only appears to be valued by cultures and ethnic groups characterized by fair skin. In India, where darker skin is the norm, people prize light skin and women carry parasols to prevent tanning. Marriage advertisements in India often highlight preferences for a light-skinned bride. Within the United States, people from Hispanic and Latin American cultures, as well as African Americans, tend to prize lighter skins (Porter, 1991).

The *scarcity principle* is also applicable to preferences for certain hair and eye colors. In 2006, only around 1 in every 6 people living in the United States had blue eyes, only around 2% of the world's adult population was redheaded, and only about 6% of the world's population was naturally blond (e.g., Belkin, 2006; "Extinction of blondes," 2002). In fact, throughout the 20th and early 21st century, there have been newspaper and media reports that blondes, redheads, blue-eyed, or green-eyed people would become extinct within the next 60 or so years. Such reports are hoaxes ("Extinction of blondes," 2002).

B O X **4.2**

Blue-Eyed Men Have Clear View of Their Ideal Partner

New Scientist, January 20, 2007, p. 16
Copyright New Scientist, RBI Ltd.

JEALOUS man seeks partner for meaningful relationship. Tall, handsome, blue eyes, looking for blue-eyed women only.

Why? Because men with blue eyes are drawn toward blue-eyed women, and prefer to choose them as their partner because this can provide reassurance that the woman's babies are theirs too.

When surveyed, blue-eyed men find pictures of women with the same eye color significantly more attractive than those with brown eyes, whereas neither brown-eyed men nor brown-eyed women show any preference for eye color, Bruno Laeng of the University of Tromsö, Norway, and his team, have discovered.

The effect is seen in real relationships, too. Blue-eyed men are more likely to be romantically involved with a woman of the same eye color than they are with brown-eyed women, or brown-eyed men are with a partner of any eye color (*Behavioral Ecology and Sociobiology, vol. 61*, p. 371).

Blue eyes are a recessive trait, Laeng explains, so two blue-eyed parents should produce a blue-eyed child, while a child with any other eye color must have been fathered by another man. Blue-eyed men seeking a partner unconsciously know this, Laeng claims, and select women of similar eye color to ensure they can more easily spot if they have been cuckolded.

Note: For more information about this study, see Laeng, Mathisen, and Johnsen (2007). It should also be noted that, although uncommon, it is possible for two blue-eyed parents to produce a brown-eyed child.

Recessive genes produce lighter eye and hair colors, which are rarer than the darker colors carried in dominant genes. However, recessive genes do not disappear. They are still carried by one's offspring even if they are not reflected in their coloring.

Although there is no danger that people with blue or green eyes, or blonde or red hair, will become extinct, people still recognize that these types of coloring are rare within certain societies. In cultures such as the United States, where there is a diverse array of coloring, people sometimes alter their appearance toward rarer coloring. For example, many women lighten their hair and some people even wear colored contact lenses. In the United States, as well as in countries where dark coloring is the norm, the scarcity principle suggests that people perceive light hair and eyes as especially attractive. This principle has generally been supported for blondes, but not redheads. Of course, in countries such as Sweden and Norway, where blond hair, blue eyes, and fair skin are common, people (and especially men) with darker hair and eyes are often viewed as sexy and exotic. There are also sex differences in preferences for coloring. In the United States, a study showed that men are more likely to favor women with light hair, skin, and eyes; whereas women are more likely to prefer dark hair and skin (Feinman & Gill, 1978). A more recent study showed that blue-eyed men are likely to look for blue-eyed mates (see Box 4.2).

Of course, people also have individual preferences for hair and eye color. One of your friends might prefer dark eyes, whereas another might prefer light eyes. Thus, preferences for coloring show considerable variability across individuals and cultures. The scarcity principle only explains a small portion of these preferences.

Finally, it is important to note that coloring is an inherited and largely static cue. Thus, it has limited value as a communication cue, although it can be manipulated slightly by engaging in activities such as tanning, applying makeup, and wearing colored contact lenses. When people do try to alter coloring, their actions often reveal the individual and cultural preferences that they and those around them have. Despite the limited communicative value of natural features such as coloring, people use these features to make judgments about others, including their ethnic background, health, and status. For example, one of the authors of this book knows someone who is part Polynesian, part Spanish, and part German. Growing up, this person noticed that people often made judgments about him based on his coloring. Some people called him a "coconut" (brown on the outside and white on the inside) and other people assumed that he was from Mexico when actually his ancestors immigrated from Spain to the Polynesian Islands, and then to the United States. As this example illustrates, making assumptions about people based solely on physical appearance cues is often error prone.

Adornment and Olfactics

Earlier in this chapter we discussed how people alter their bodies and faces by dieting and undergoing cosmetic procedures to try to achieve a more attractive appearance. People also adorn themselves in ways that promote preferred images. For example, people engage in primping behaviors such as straightening ties, reapplying lip gloss, and brushing their hair out of their eyes when preparing to approach someone in whom they are romantically interested (Givens, 1983). When they start interacting with the person to whom they are attracted, they might engage in behaviors such flipping hair back and patting or smoothing clothing. At work, people often dress to project an image of competence and professionalism.

People also adorn themselves with makeup and fragrances. As the information in Box 4.3 suggests, the practice of using makeup to enhance appearance dates back as far as 6000 B.C. As we discussed in Chapter 3, olfactic cues, such as body odors and cologne, also can influence people's impressions of one another by affecting the sense of smell.

Compared to physical attributes such as facial features, natural skin color, and height, adornment cues are more dynamic and easily changeable. People are born with certain facial features and body types, but they can intentionally manipulate adornment cues to enhance and sometimes even alter their natural features. Tanning salons, colored contact lens manufacturers, jewelry and clothing stores, and the cosmetics industry offer people a multitude of choices about how to change people's perceptions of their faces and bodies through the use of

---

BOX 4.3

Glamor and Beauty Through the Ages

Throughout the ages, people have emphasized their facial features with makeup. Archaeologists have found evidence of Egyptian perfumeries and beauty parlors dating to 4000 B.C. and makeup paraphernalia that dates to 6000 B.C. The ancient Egyptians preferred green eye shadow, which was topped with a glitter made from crushing the iridescent carapaces of certain beetles, kohl eyeliner and mascara, blue-black lipstick, red rogue, and fingers and feet stained red with henna. They shaved their eyebrows and drew false ones.

Roman men adored cosmetics; field commanders had their hair coiffed and perfumed and their nails lacquered before they went into battle. A second-century Roman physician invented cold cream, whose formula has changed little since then.

We may remember from the Old Testament that it was Queen Jezebel who "painted her face" before embarking on her wicked ways, a fashion she learned from the hightoned Phoenicians around 850 B.C. In the 18th century, women were willing to eat Arsenic Complexion Wafers to make their skin whiter, which worked by poisoning the hemoglobin in the blood so they developed a fragile, lunar whiteness. Rouges often contained such dangerous metals as lead and mercury.

Source: Ackerman, 1990.

---

adornment. Next, we discuss how three forms of adornment—makeup, clothing, and perfume—function in relationships and in the workplace, followed by a discussion of other olfactic cues.

Cosmetics

Within the United States, men usually accept their facial shortcomings and do not try to change their facial appearance much, except through shaving and grooming facial hair. Women, on the other hand, often apply makeup to enhance their femininity and correct perceived flaws. Lipstick can make lips look fuller, mascara and eye shadow can add dimension to eyes while making them look closer together or farther apart, and blush accentuates cheekbones. Smooth, evenly textured and youthful-looking skin is related to facial attractiveness (Fink, Grammer, & Thornhill, 2001), so it is not surprising that women often use makeup to conceal dark circles under their eyes and even out skin texture, and that they use special facial cleansers and moisturizers to try to keep their skin fresh and young looking. Even though today's women generally use less makeup than did the generation of women before them, cosmetics still generate millions of dollars in sales each year within the United States. In fact, in 1996 alone women spent over a billion dollars in drug stores on nearly 26 million cosmetic items (Dortch, 1997), and this statistic does not include dollars spent in beauty salons or department stores. The use of these products represents one way that women try to alter their appearance to make positive impressions on others.

Using makeup can make women feel more attractive and self-confident during social interaction (Miller & Cox, 1982). Makeup may also enhance how attractive others perceive a woman to be. In one study, researchers compared the influence of natural facial characteristics with the use of cosmetics on facial beauty (Osborn, 1996). This study showed that for women with average-looking faces, wearing makeup had a positive effect on the degree to which others rated them as attractive. In fact, for women within the average range of facial attractiveness, wearing makeup had as powerful an impact on attractiveness ratings as did structural features. Other studies have shown that women wearing makeup are judged to be more generally attractive, feminine, friendly, healthy, and sexy than women not wearing makeup (Cash, Dawson, Davis, Bowen, & Galumbeck, 1989; Cox & Glick, 1986; Dellinger & Williams, 1997). The use of makeup, however, needs to be appropriate. Research suggests that too much makeup looks phony and detracts from facial beauty; a natural look that accentuates feminine features is best (Cox & Glick, 1986).

Wearing too much makeup can backfire in the workplace. Kyle and Mahler (1996) examined how cosmetic use and hair color influence people's perceptions of female job applicants. They had people look at identical resumes with one of six photographs of the same 40-year-old woman attached. The woman, who had blond hair, was photographed twice—once without makeup and once with a moderate amount of makeup (light foundation, blush, lipstick, mascara, and eyeliner). These photographs were then altered to create four more pictures—two with the woman's hair color changed to brown and two with her hair color changed to red. The people who viewed the resumes and pictures thought all three hair colors looked equally natural, and they rated the various versions of the woman in the photos as equally attractive, friendly, happy, healthy, or stressed. However, participants rated the woman as less capable and assigned her a lower starting salary when she was wearing makeup, regardless of whether she was depicted as a blonde, brunette, or redhead. Kyle and Mahler suggested that cosmetic use is associated with femininity, which in turn is associated with perceptions of less competence in the workplace. For women, wearing a minimal amount of makeup may be the best prescription for presenting a capable professional image.

Another study examined whether beauty expenditures, which were defined as the percentage of household income spent on cosmetics and clothing, are associated with earnings (Hamermesh, Meng, & Zhang, 2002). In this study, Chinese women who spent more of their income on cosmetics and clothing were generally rated as somewhat more physically attractive than those who spent less money. However, the amount of "payback" these women received for beauty expenditures was minimal. As Hamermesh and colleagues put it, "spending on beauty items generates only a small payoff in the form of higher wages. Primping clearly does pay; but the payoff is only a small fraction of what is spent" (p. 366). Women who made average investments into their appearance earned back the most, followed by those who made low investments. Interestingly, women who spent the most on cosmetics and clothing received the smallest payback.

Body Modifications

People also make investments into their appearance by having the surfaces of their bodies modified by tattoos or piercings. Throughout history, people from various cultures have used body modifications such as piercings, tattoos, and branding as part of cultural and social rituals. Within Western cultures such as the United States and Europe, these types of body modifications were relatively rare until tattooing and piercings become popular among the mainstream culture in the 1980s (Wohlrab, Stahl, Rammsayer, & Kappeler, 2007). By the 1990s, around 10% of high school students, 20% of college students, and 37% of military personnel had at least one tattoo (Armstrong & Pace-Murphy, 1997; Armstrong, Pace-Murphy, Salle, & Watson, 2000; Johnson, 2007). In fact, Marin (1995) estimated that around 5% of the general population in the United States had tattoos by the mid-1990s; and Wohlrab et al. noted that approximately 10% of the population in modern Western societies had tattoos and/or body piercings by the mid-2000s. In the United States, one study showed that around 30% of college students had at least one tattoo or piercing in 2001 (Forbes). Most people who have tattoos or piercings have only one or two, but some people become "collectors" who make extensive body modifications. As suggested in Photo 4.3, people are more likely to have tattoos or piercings if their friends and/or family members have them as well (Koch, Roberts, Armstrong, & Owen, 2005).

As tattoos and piercings have become increasingly commonplace, their meaning has changed. People with body modifications were once viewed as deviant and rebellious. Now, however, the types of individuals who modify their bodies have become so diverse that most people see tattoos and body piercings as a form of self-expression that communicates one's identity to others (Fredrick & Bradley, 2000). As Johnson (2007) put it:

> Tattoos are a form of self-expression, a way to touch the depths of one's feelings and bring those feelings out for one's own observation or for the observation of others. Tattoos are a way of expressing thoughts, beliefs, triumphs, and trials, and a way of memorializing a loved one. (p. 59)

PHOTO 4.3   *What stereotypes might you have about these people based on their tattoos?*
Photo courtesy of J. K. Burgoon.

In addition to being a means of self-expression, tattoos are commonly used to communicate group affiliation or love for someone (Bell, 1999; Johnson, 2007). For example, members of sports teams, gangs, fraternities, and sororities sometimes get similar tattoos to show group identification, and people sometimes memorialize a loved one with a tattoo of his or her name. People report getting piercings for a wide variety of reasons, including self-expression, group affiliation, rebellion, sexual enhancement, desire to have a spiritual experience, and desire to prove that one can endure pain (Myers, 1992).

Early research suggested that people with body modifications are more likely to suffer from psychological problems or substance abuse, and to be perceived as deviant (Johnson, 2007; Wohlrab et al., 2007). However, recent research has shown that body modifications are associated with a number of positive and negative characteristics. Compared to un-tattooed people, individuals with tattoos are more likely to be perceived (by themselves and others) as adventurous, artistic, creative, impulsive, independent, open, politically liberal, sexually liberal, and unique, and they are less likely to be perceived as agreeable or conscientious (Drews, Allison, & Probst, 2000; Manuel & Sheehan, 2007; Tate & Shelton, 2008; Wohlrab et al., 2007). They also report being more angry (Carroll & Anderson, 2002), less depressed (Fredrick & Bradley, 2000), and more sexually active (Koch, Roberts, Armstrong, & Owen, 2005), although some of these findings may be limited to adolescents and young adults. Compared to non-pierced people, individuals with piercings rate themselves as more open and flashy, higher in sensation seeking, and as less conscientious (Manuel & Sheehan, 2007; Tate & Shelton, 2008; Wohlrab et al., 2007). Women with piercings also perceive themselves as having a higher need for social recognition than do women without piercings (Tate & Shelton, 2008).

There are also sex differences in the types of tattoos women and men get. Women are more likely to get softer, smaller, and more personal images in discreet places on their bodies, such as their belly button area or lower back. In contrast, men are more likely to get larger, more macho images on highly visible parts of their body such as their upper or lower arms (Bell, 1999; Wohlrab et al., 2007).

Clothing

As with body modifications, clothing can send a variety of messages and serve a number of functions. At a basic level, clothing provides us with protection from the sun or cold weather. Clothing can be a form of self-expression or group identification. Take a look at Photo 4.4, which shows a group of Peruvian Indians. The musicians in this picture are wearing traditional costumes that reflect cultural traditions and values. These costumes help them achieve a variety of goals, including showing that they are a group, establishing credibility and authenticity with the audience, and creating a mood that is conducive for enjoying their music.

Clothing can also be used to enhance physical attraction. During courtship, people often dress provocatively and manipulate dress as part of the flirtation game. For instance, some observational research has shown that women sometimes loosen buttons on their blouses or adjust their skirts to show more leg when

PHOTO 4.4   *What messages do the costumes worn by these Peruvian Indian musicians communicate?*
Photo courtesy of J. K. Burgoon.

flirting with someone (Moore, 1985; Scheflen, 1965; see Chapter 12). Other research suggests that although provocative dress enhances one's attractiveness as a sexual partner, it may be counterproductive when trying to attract a long-term relational partner. In one study, researchers manipulated the extent to which people dressed to display their physique versus their socioeconomic status (Hill, Nocks, & Gardner, 1987). Physique display was manipulated by altering the extent to which people wore tight, skin-revealing clothing; status display was manipulated by the extent to which people wore neat, fairly expensive clothing rather than sloppy, inexpensive clothing. College students then rated opposite-sex models in terms of physical, dating, sexual, and marital attractiveness. Across all four types of attractiveness, both men and women found the models wearing high-status clothing to be the most appealing. In contrast, physique display only enhanced sexual attractiveness. For marital attractiveness, a combination of high-status clothing and low to moderate physique display produced the most attraction. Of course, there may be differences in how people rate public versus private dress. People may want their romantic partners to dress provocatively when they are alone in private settings, but not when they are in public interacting with others.

Style of dress is also related to job satisfaction and career advancement, especially for women. Early research in this area determined that women's clothing predispositions fit the categories of clothing consciousness, exhibitionism, practicality (Rosenfeld & Plax, 1977), conservatism, and dressing for fun (Molley, 1977). *Clothing consciousness* involves making careful choices about what to wear. Women who endorse this style like to dress up, spend a considerable amount of money on clothes (relative to their income), think it is important to be "in style," and believe that other people notice what they wear. *Exhibitionism* involves using clothes to attract attention by wearing unique, tight-fitting, or revealing outfits. *Practicality* refers to dressing more for comfort than to impress other people or be "in style." Women identifying with *conservatism* report that they wear professional clothes to work in an effort to be taken seriously. These women are more likely to report wearing dark or neutral colors, blazers and skirts, and simple pumps. *Dressing for fun* involved wearing sexy clothing and/or clothes that would be appropriate for a party.

Contemporary research on clothing in the workplace reveals that conservative dress is related to impressions of effectiveness and dominance. For women, a skirted suit makes a professional impression, and women wearing such suits were rated as more forceful, self-reliant, assertive, and decisive (Kaiser, 1997). However, when a woman dresses too conservatively, she may be seen as unapproachable and uncreative. Clothing that reflects both professionalism and feminism may project the most positive images for women on the job (Rucker, Taber, & Harrison, 1981).

Men have less latitude in business clothing than women do. In most organizations, men typically wear a suit or a professional-looking shirt and pants. Colors are also more limited for men than women, with most men dressing in neutral, dark, or blue tones (Kaiser, 1997). This lack of flexibility may partially explain why men are not judged based on clothing to the extent that women are. Since most men tend to dress within a similar range of clothing selections, there may be little variability in the impressions they make using their clothing.

Just as women tend to be more conscious of clothing in the workplace, some research suggests that certain groups of people may face special challenges when it comes to professional attire. For example, ethnic minorities may feel a stronger need to "dress to impress" than white employees. In a study by Rucker, Anderson, and Kangas (1999), ethnic minorities reported that dressing to fit the corporate image was a way of showing that they fit in and were ready to move up the corporate ladder. These researchers also reported that older women found it increasingly difficult to dress professionally and be comfortable at the same time.

Perfume

Perfume can also be used as a means of attracting others. However, research suggests that too much perfume, like too much makeup, is actually a turn-off. In one study (Aune & Aune, 2008), people were interviewed by women who either used no perfume, light perfume (1 spray), moderate perfume (2–3 sprays), or excessive perfume (5–6 sprays). Men rated the women interviewers as most physically attractive when they were wearing light perfume, while women rated the interviewers as most physically attractive when they were wearing no perfume. For both men and women, the interviewers were perceived the least positively in the excessive perfume condition. Since most perfume users apply moderate levels of fragrance (Aune & Aune, 2008), this study suggests that people may generally use too much perfume.

A study by Baron (1981) also suggests that there can be "too much of a good thing" when using adornment to attract others. In this study, clothing and perfume use were manipulated so that some women wore pleasant-smelling perfume and others wore no perfume; some women dressed formally in professional-looking skirts and blouses while others dressed casually in jeans and sweatshirts. Men interacted with one of the women and then rated them on a number of personality traits. The casually dressed women were rated as more attractive when they wore perfume. However, for the formally dressed women, perfume use seemed to decrease their attractiveness. Thus, using formal dress and perfume together was not as effective as manipulating either of these adornment cues separately, perhaps because the simultaneous use of these cues could suggest that the woman is trying too hard to manage impressions. Another explanation for these findings is that the men preferred women who were similar to them in terms of formality. Well dressed women wearing perfume may have been perceived to be overly well groomed compared to the men's less formal grooming.

Other Olfactic Cues

Although perfume and cologne are used to intentionally alter the way people smell, other olfactic cues related to body odor are naturally occurring. Researchers have found that every person has a unique smell, similar to a fingerprint or "voice print." These smell prints are called *olfactory* or *chemical signatures* (Niolaides, 1974) and they are influenced by body odors, secretions (such as sweat and tears), and genetic factors. Like fingerprints and voice prints, olfactory signatures may be useful in identifying people. The U.S. Government's Defense Advanced Research Projects Agency (DARPA) is even examining the potential usefulness of olfactory signatures (see Box 4.4). Olfactory signatures are also an important part of communication within families (Filsinger & Fabes, 1985). Studies by Porter and his colleagues have demonstrated that mothers and their children are able to identify t-shirts worn by each other versus strangers (Porter & Moore, 1981), and that mothers can identify which t-shirts were worn by their infants (Porter, Cernock, & McLauglin, 1983) simply by smelling them. Other studies have shown that very young infants can identify the smell of their mother. Specifically, week-old infants turn their heads toward their mother's breast pads rather than the breast pads of a stranger (MacFarlane, 1975; Russell, 1976). Some researchers have claimed that olfactory communication, like tactile communication, is developed well before visual and auditory communication (Filsinger & Fabes, 1985).

Olfactory communication also appears to play a subtle yet important role in the process of human attraction. The term *pheromone* was created by Karlson and Luscher (1959) by combining the Greek words "pherein" and "hormone," which mean "to carry" and "to excite," respectively. Pheromones are "chemical messengers that are emitted into the environment from the body where they can then activate specific physiological or behavioral responses in other individuals of the same species" (Grammer, Fink, & Neave, 2005, p. 136). Pheromones are secreted by the apocrine glands that are located in the armpits and genital areas (Filsinger & Fabes, 1985; Grammer et al., 2005). According to Bohannon (2005), the "best candidates" for human pheromones are androstenes, which are related to testosterone, and a molecule called EST, which is related to estrogen (p. 4).

One function of pheromones is to regulate our own bodies and the bodily responses of those around us. For example, studies suggest that women who live together often converge toward one another's menstrual cycles over time. McClintock (1971) was the first to explain this phenomenon as a side effect of

---

BOX **4.4**

The Olfactory Signature as a Tool Against Terrorism and Disease

According to an article in *Seed Magazine,* the U.S. government is exploring how to utilize the olfactory signature to combat both terrorists and disease.

Specifically, the Defense Advanced Research Projects Agency (DARPA) is involved in a "Unique Signature Detection Project." The project seeks to take advantage of the unique smell emitted through a person's bodily fluids, such as sweat, tears, and urine. Researchers believe that olfactory signatures may provide a superior method for identifying terrorists and other criminals. Detecting scent is less invasive than fingerprinting and retinal scans. In addition, Gary Beauchamp, a researcher on the project, noted that a person's scent can linger for a considerable time after a person has left the scene of a crime.

Because our olfactory signatures are linked to the major histocompatibility complex (MHC), the DARPA researchers believe that their project could also lead to major advances in health care. The MHC is a complex group of genes found on T-cell surfaces. T-cells are an integral part of the immune system—they attack diseases and foreign substances. Each person's MHC is as unique as his or her DNA. Therefore, anything that identifies MHC, including scent, is a critical determinant of identity. The uniqueness of the MHC also complicates matters when it comes to organ transplants. If the donated organ contains a pattern of MHC that is too different from the recipient's own MHC, it will be rejected. Beauchamp argues that matching people based on olfactory signatures may help doctors identify matches between potential donors and recipients. He also noted that changes in a person's olfactory signature could signal the onset of diseases and perhaps even aid physicians in pinpointing which part of the immune system is under stress.

Note: For more information, see Cohn (2006).

---

olfactic communication. Later, Russell, Switz, and Thompson (1980) formally tested McClintock's hypothesis. They had one group of women repeatedly smell the pheromones of a woman who had a consistent and strong menstrual cycle. A second group of women smelled a completely different substance unrelated to pheromones. Russell and his colleagues found that women in the first group tended to move toward the menstrual cycle of the woman whose pheromones they had smelled; those in the second group showed no such reaction.

Pheromones also act to attract or repel others. Early research in this area used a surgical mask technique that involved some participants wearing masks that were odorless and other participants wearing masks sprayed with androstenol. In one study, men were asked to wear one of these masks while rating descriptions of female job candidates (Cowley, Johnson, & Brooksbank, 1977). Men rated women more favorably when they were wearing an odorless mask. However, in another study, women were judged as sexier and more attractive when being rated by someone wearing a mask sprayed with androstenol compared to an odorless mask, and both men and women were judged as warmer when wearing the pheromone-sprayed mask (Kirk-Smith, Booth, Carroll, & Davies, 1978).

More recent research has focused on explaining the inconsistency found in early work on pheromones and attraction. One line of research has focused on sex differences. Men and women react differently to various types of pheromones. For instance, research by neuroscientists in Sweden examined how molecules related to androstenes (AND) and an estrogen-related steroid (EST) are processed by the brain. In this study, gay men, straight men, and straight women were exposed to AND and EST while their brains were scanned. The results were striking. As Bohannon (2005) summarized:

> When it comes to deep-seated sexual attraction, the nose knows. A whiff of AND increased blood flow to the primitive mating center of homosexual men and heterosexual women, but did nothing for heterosexual men . . . In contrast, EST activated the same part of the brain in heterosexual men, but left the brains of homosexual men cold. (p. 5)

In other words, AND, which is related to testosterone, was a turn-on for straight women and gay men, who are attracted to men. EST, which is related to estrogen, was a turn-on only for straight men. This suggests that the same pheromone that is attractive to one person may be unattractive to another. Based on these findings, it is not surprising that men in the Cowley et al. study rated women more favorably when wearing odorless versus androstenol-sprayed masks.

The major histocompatibility complex (MHC) is another important component of pheromones. As we discussed in Chapter 3, the MHC is a set of genes that plays an important role in immune system functioning (Klein, 1986). People can detect differences in MHC through body odor, and these differences are related to sexual attraction. Specifically, people are most sexually attracted to individuals whose MHC is different from their own (Wedekind, Seebeck, Bettens, & Paepke, 1995). From an evolutionary perspective, being attracted to people with dissimilar MHC is adaptive; when genes are too similar, certain genetic diseases and malformations are more likely to occur in offspring. For a child, having parents with dissimilar MHCs also strengthens immunity by giving her or him resistance to more diseases.

To test the hypotheses that people are most attracted to those with a different MHC than themselves, and that this difference is transmitted through pheromones and other body odors, scholars have conducted "smelly t-shirt" studies. Wedekind and his team conducted experiments in which men were asked to wear the same cotton t-shirt to bed for consecutive nights. The men were instructed not to smoke, drink, have sex, wear deodorant, use cologne, eat spicy foods, or wash the shirts until their part of the experiment was over. The men were also asked to sleep alone. Later, their t-shirts were placed in bags, and another group of men and women smelled each shirt and then rated the odor. Both women and men rated the odors of men with dissimilar MHC genes as being more pleasant than the odors of men with similar MCH genes, and women rated the odors of men with dissimilar MHC genes as sexier and as similar to the scents of past dating partners (Wedekind & Furi, 1997; Wedekind et al., 1995). These studies have also shown that the effects of body odor are most pronounced when women are not using hormonal birth control and are ovulating.

Summary

In most interactions, appearance and adornment are the first nonverbal cues people notice. Because of this, appearance and adornment play a pivotal role in the formation of first impressions. People frequently make judgments of others based on appearance cues. Physically attractive people are often evaluated in accordance with the "what is beautiful is good" hypothesis, which specifies that outer beauty is associated with a host of positive internal qualities, ranging from likeability to intelligence. However, physically attractive people are also judged to be vain and materialistic, as the "what is beautiful is self-centered" hypothesis suggests. Thus, beauty comes with both advantages and disadvantages. Beauty is also both universal and in the eye of the beholder. Features judged as universally attractive include koinophilia, facial neoteny combined with sexual maturity, face and body symmetry, the Golden Ratio, and waist-to-hip ratios of .70 for women and .90 to 1.0 for men. Preferences for body type and coloring are more culturally and individually variable, and people tend to evaluate people they like and people who are good communicators as more physically attractive. People are aware of the importance of physical appearance, leading them to make body image investments such as dieting and cosmetic procedures. Adornment cues, such as makeup, clothing, and perfume, are also used to intentionally project particular images. Finally, other olfactic cues, such as pheromones, can influence processes related to attraction even though they are emitted unintentionally.

SUGGESTED READINGS

Albana, K. F., Knapp, M. L., & Thenue, K. E. (2002). Interaction appearance theory: Changing perceptions of physical attractiveness through social interaction. *Communication Theory, 12,* 8–40.

Ambady, N., & Rosenthal, R. (1993). Half a minute: Predicting teacher evaluations from thin slices of nonverbal behavior and physical attractiveness. *Journal of Personality and Social Psychology, 64,* 431–441.

Cash, T. F., & Henry, P. E. (1995). Women's body images: The results of a national survey in the U.S.A. *Sex Roles, 33,* 19–28.

Cunningham, M. R., Barbee, A. R., & Pike, C. L. (1990). What do women want? Facialmetric assessment of multiple motives in the perception of male facial physical attractiveness. *Journal of Personality and Social Psychology, 59,* 61–72.

Eagly, A. H., Ashmore, R. D., Makhijani, M. G., & Longo, L. C. (1991). What is beautiful is good, but . . .: A meta-analytic review of research on the physical attractiveness stereotype. *Psychological Bulletin, 110,* 109–128.

Grammer, K., & Thornhill, R. (1994). Human (homo sapiens) facial attractiveness and sexual selection: The role of symmetry and averageness. *Journal of Comparative Psychology, 108,* 233–242.

Hamermesh, D. S., & Biddle, J. E. (1994). Beauty and the labor market. *American Economic Review, 84,* 1174–1194.

Kaiser, S. B. (1997). *The social psychology of clothing: Symbolic appearances in context* (3rd ed.). New York: Fairfield Publications.

Kurzban, R., & Weeden, J. (2005). HurryDate: Mate preferences in action. *Evolution and Human Behavior, 26,* 227–244.

Livio, M. (2002). *The Golden Ratio: The story of Phi, the world's most astonishing number.* New York: Broadway.

Mobias, M. M., & Rosenblat, T. (2006). Why beauty matters. *American Economic Review, 96,* 222–235.

5 Visual and Auditory Codes: Kinesics and Vocalics

The dominant organ of sensory and social orientation in pre-alphabet societies was the ear—"Hearing was believing." The phonetic alphabet forced the magic world of the eye. Man was given an eye for an ear . . . . The rational man in our Western culture is a visual man.

—Marshall McLuhan and Quentin Fiore

Imagine for a moment that you have been hired as a consultant at a medical facility. A new emphasis in medicine to be more service oriented includes teaching doctors to be better communicators. Your charge is to improve the "bedside manner" of new residents by improving their nonverbal communication. Where would you begin? Research suggests you should begin with two of the most powerful nonverbal codes: kinesics and vocalics. This chapter provides some beginning answers to what features you would want to take into account.

Kinesics

The eyes of men converse as much as their tongues, with the advantage that the ocular dialect needs no dictionary, but is understood the world over.

—Ralph Waldo Emerson

The term *kinesics* derives from the Greek word for "movement" and refers to all forms of body movement, excluding physical contact with another's body. The popular term *body language* is almost exclusively concerned with this code. Kinesics includes facial, eye, head, trunk, limb, hand, and foot movements, as well as postures and gait.

Scope and Importance of Kinesics

Kinesics is perhaps the most commanding and influential of the nonverbal codes. The face and eyes are commanding because they are always visible and always "on"—even in repose or in solitude the body still presents useful information and can reveal internal mood states or emotions (Cohn & Ekman, 2006). Kinesics is also influential because of the wealth of features available for bearing messages. The richness of this code is underscored by the following estimates and observations:

- An estimated 700,000 different physical signs can be produced by humans (Pei, 1965).
- Physiologists have estimated that the 30 or so muscles in the face are capable of displaying 20,000 different expressions (Birdwhistell, 1970). Birdwhistell claims that up to 250,000 expressions are possible.
- Krout (1954a, 1954b) observed 7,777 distinct gestures in classroom behavior and 5,000 hand gestures in clinical situations.
- Hewes (1957) reported that 1,000 steady human postures are possible.

These estimates highlight the nearly limitless kinesic means for sending nonverbal signals, especially if one considers that a person displays more than a single behavior at any instance. For example, how many ways can you show a friend you approve of something he or she has just done? You might engage in a very brief, almost imperceptible head nod or nod your head vigorously. You might smile or combine head nodding and smiling. You might choose to be more enthusiastic by giving two thumbs up or shaking both arms overhead with hands clenched in fists. All of these actions can signal approval to the other person, although each transmits a slight variation on that theme.

The human capacity to recognize kinesic signals is also large. Vision accounts for around 80% of our sensory perception; the remaining 20% comes from our senses of hearing, touching, tasting, and smelling combined. Observers can distinguish movements as short as 1/50th of a second. Air Force pilots purportedly can identify a plane flashed as briefly as 1/200th of a second (How many frames, 2009) and even fleeting facial expressions and body movements of 125 microseconds that seem to escape conscious observation may still be registered by the brain (McLeod & Rosenthal, 1983).

As well, humans have a strong bias to attend to kinesic cues, as a result of the innate tendency to orient to others visually, the overtly noticeable and attention-getting characteristics of kinesics, and the many functions kinesic cues serve. Consequently, people rely more on kinesic cues than any other code to derive meaning from nonverbal messages (Burgoon & Hoobler, 2002).

This multiplicity of cues and meanings makes for a very rich code but one that is also fraught with ambiguities and misunderstandings. See Box 5.1 for an amusing example of such a misunderstanding.

Origins and Acquisition of Kinesics

One reason kinesics is such a powerful coding system derives from its central place in the development of communication, whether at the level of the species or the individual. Charles Darwin was one of the first scholars to become interested in the evolutionary origin of kinesic behavior. In his book *The Expression of the Emotions in Man and Animals*, Darwin (1872) noted similarities between emotional expression of humans and those of primates and lower animal forms. It was his

BOX 5.1

A Zen Parable

In a temple in the northern part of Japan, two brother monks were dwelling together. The elder one was learned, but the younger one was stupid and had only one eye.

A wandering monk came and asked for lodging, properly challenging them to a debate about the sublime teaching. The elder brother, tired that day from much studying, told the younger one to take his place. "Go and request the dialogue in silence," he cautioned.

So the young monk and the stranger went to the shrine and sat down.

Shortly afterward, the traveler arose and went in to the elder brother and said: "Your young brother is a wonderful fellow. He defeated me."

"Relate the dialogue to me," said the elder one.

"Well," explained the traveler, "first I held up one finger, representing Buddha, the enlightened one. So he held up two fingers, signifying Buddha and his teachings. I held up three fingers, representing Buddha, his teachings, and his followers, living the harmonious life together. Then he shook his clenched fist in my face, indicating that all three come from one realization. Thus he won. . . ." With this, the traveler left.

"Where is that fellow?" asked the younger one, running in to his elder brother.

"I understand you won the debate."

"Won nothing. I'm going to beat him up."

"Tell me the subject of the debate," asked the elder one.

"Why, the minute he saw me, he held up one finger, insulting me by insinuating that I have only one eye. Since he was a stranger, I thought I would be polite to him, so I held up two fingers, congratulating him that he has two eyes. Then the impolite wretch held up three fingers, suggesting that between us we only have three eyes. So I got mad and started to punch him, but he ran out and that ended it."

---

belief that in the course of human development, facial expressions were programmed into the brain due to their importance to survival. For example, closing the eyes, flaring the nostrils, expelling breath, and extending the tongue in the disgust expression were useful in protecting early humans from such harms as rotten food. Tongue showing is another case of a kinesic behavior with innate origins. When people are intensely involved in activities requiring concentration, are under stress, feel a loss of control, or are being reprimanded, they often display their tongue. Michael Jordan was known for sticking out his tongue while playing basketball. As illustrated in Photos 5.1a through 5.1e, the gesture is a common one that both infant and adult humans and other primates display under similar conditions (Smith, Chase, & Liebach, 1974).

Studies of infants provide further evidence for inborn elements of kinesic behavior. In the first few months of life, newborns display many kinesic reflexes. One is the imitation of face and head movements (Bjorklund, 1987; Meltzoff & Moore, 1989). Only 72 hours after birth, infants imitate adults' tongue protrusions and head movements, and they imitate facial gestures as early as 2 months. This imitation is innate and requires little cognitive function. Imitation of facial

PHOTO 5.1   *Tongue showing by (from left to right) (a) Michael Jordan, (b) human infant, (c) Maori warrior, (d) mother and child, and (e) adult gorilla.*

gestures helps newborns to maintain social interaction with adults in the period before their abilities to control gaze, head, and mouth movements develop. When infants achieve the ability to make these other kinesic movements, the imitation reflex is no longer useful and declines. This reflex also may help newborns learn to integrate information from different senses; this is referred to as *intermodal matching*. That is, newborns practice matching the visual information gained from seeing adult gestures with the internal feelings received from the movement of face and head muscles as the newborns imitate these perceived gestures.

Newborns also display many facial expressions that are similar to adult expressions and are linked directly to emotional states (Barrett, 1993; Camras, Sullivan, & Michel, 1993). The infant quickly learns to emit positive feelings and distress or anger in response to other people and to use these expressions to control others' behaviors (Cappella, 1981; Denham & Grout, 1993). Positive expressions are displayed more frequently than negative expressions.

Gestures originate at a very early age (Hannan, 1992; Wood, 1981). In the first week of life, infants reflexively open and close their eyes, grasp reflexively, and smile spontaneously. Within the first 3 months, they smile, stare at faces, visually follow people around a room, make eye contact, and display such emotional states as distress, delight, and excitement. During the next 3 months, other emotions such as fear, disgust, and anger emerge; the infant begins to discriminate faces from one another and from other stimuli; and the infant begins to imitate facial expressions. Imitation continues through the next 6 months and expands to include gestures of adults and other children.

One of the most important early gestures, the pointing gesture, usually emerges in the first year. It provides the child with a bridge between nonverbal and verbal expression as the child acquires more language skills. Pointing is also a sign of cognitive development, something that differentiates humans from other lower primates. Children use pointing to name or express interest in an object. Before pointing, children often look at a caregiver, as if first checking to see that the caregiver is paying attention. Thus, gestures become enmeshed in the interaction process even before language develops.

Gestures continue to develop in the first five years of life. Age four appears to be an important developmental period. Prior to this time, children use more body-part gestures, such as describing tooth-brushing by extending the forefinger and rubbing it back and forth along the front teeth. After age four, children switch to imagery-object gestures, such as clenching the hand to the side of the mouth and moving it back and forth as if it is holding a toothbrush (Boyatzis & Watson, 1993).

Eye contact, too, has innate properties. Within a few days of birth, infants appear to fixate on the caregiver's eyes, and simply seeing the eyes of a caregiver is sufficient to produce a smiling reaction (Argyle & Cook, 1976). Interestingly, the distance at which newborns focus best is the distance they are from the infant to the mother's eyes when breast-feeding. At this very young age, it is likely that the child's gaze is more a signal of attention than any more complex social message. Further, eye gaze from others innately arouses infants. Eye contact is invaluable for the maturation of infants. The lack of mutual gaze impairs infant interaction and perceptual and social development (Andersen et al., 1985; Robson, 1967).

Not all kinesic behaviors displayed by adults and children are inborn. Many are learned through environmental and social experiences. Ekman and Friesen (1969b, 1972) have suggested that some behaviors, though not innate, arise from experiences that all humans acquire through interacting with any environment. Two examples: all humans eat with their hands and all humans have witnessed death. Thus almost all people possess kinesic expressions representing eating and dying.

However, as noted in Chapter 2, many behaviors vary greatly from culture to culture because life experiences and conditions differ from place to place. A case in point is the enormous variety across cultures in common sitting and standing postures that have arisen from the conditions and tools present in a culture. The chair-sitting posture in the United States differs from the deep squat common in parts of Asia and Africa, indicating the lesser importance of chairs in the latter regions (see Figure 5.1). Other behaviors that are culture-specific include greeting and parting rituals, occasions for when facial displays are permitted, and kinesic turn-taking behaviors, to name only a few. Many behaviors are specifically taught to children by older members of the culture. Others are learned through imitation. Either way, by school age, children appear to possess a rich repertoire of kinesic behaviors.

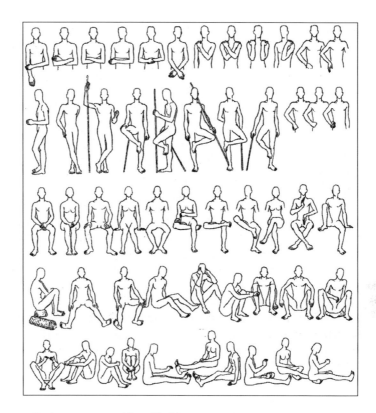

FIGURE 5.1 Various postures identified by Hewes (1957).

In sum, kinesic expressions are acquired in three ways:

- From innate neurological processes passed on genetically and developed through evolution
- From experiences common to all humans as they interact with the environment
- Through culture-specific tasks and social interactions that vary across cultures, co-cultures, and individuals

So far we have been focusing on the sending side of the kinesic equation. Equally important is the receiving side—how we come to recognize and interpret kinesic behavior. Humans come well equipped to decode visual nonverbal cues. Orienting gaze toward others appears very early in a newborn's life, and between the ages of 6 weeks and 3 months, infants begin smiling in response to other faces (Stern, 1980), suggesting an ability to decode face and head cues during this earliest stage of life. By 3 months, infants recognize familiar faces. Recognition of affect displays also comes quickly (Andersen et al., 1985). The ability to decode kinesic cues also continues to develop with age, peaking during the teens (Hoots,

McAndrew, & Francois, 1989). By adulthood, then, the human capacity to encode and decode kinesics is quite extensive.

Features of the Kinesics Code

Place yourself back in the same medical facility as in the opening scenario. This time, your task is to develop computer agents (avatars) to greet, educate, and interact with patients as they wait in their clinic to see their doctor. You want these "embodied conversational agents" to be as lifelike as possible so that patients arc willing to "talk" with them. It might seem an impossible task to distill all the potential kinesic behaviors into a subset you can manage. Fortunately, a lot of that groundwork has been done over the course of centuries.

Delsarte's System of Oratory.   One of the first efforts to provide a detailed cata-log of gestures, postures, and facial expressions grew out of the elocutionary movement of the 1700s and 1800s. Intended to be a scientific approach to public oratory, the Delsarte (1882) system of oratory was intended to teach lecturers, preachers, lawyers, and actors how to properly use their voice, body, and lan-guage during their public recitations. Delsarte produced an elaborate classification scheme and associated "laws" for elocution so that gestures, movements, and voice would appear quite natural, even though carefully calculated: "The orator should not even think of what he is doing. The thing should have been so much studied, that all would seem to flow of itself from the fountain." Examples from Delsarte's catalog include the "eccentric attitude" (head elevated), which was said to be indicative of vehemence if the head is bent backward, but indicative of aban-don and confidence if inclined toward the interlocutor. The elbow turned out-ward was said to signify strength, audacity, and abruptness, whereas an elbow drawn inward signified impotence, fear, and subordination. Gestures and postures had to be positioned in specific directions and regions of space to convey precise meanings (see Figure 5.2).

This stylized approach to public elocution, which reached its zenith late in the 19th century (see, e.g., Hyde & Hyde, 1886), lives on today in farcical melo-dramas. Although many of the configurations intuitively fit what we are accus-tomed to seeing today and match ethologists' observations of many kinesic displays among nonhuman vertebrates, many others were highly contrived. The overly stylized nature of the expressions, coupled with the nonscientific designa-tion of different body regions as related to life, soul, and mind, ultimately led to its disfavor. Still, Delsarte's writings significantly influenced the thinking and approaches of those who subsequently attempted to reduce the voluminous range of kinesic movements into a more manageable set of categories.

Two basic approaches emerged. The structural approach attempts to classify the constituent components of the kinesic code. The functional approach exam-ines kinesics according to what various expressions, gestures, and postures *mean* or *do*. The classification systems we will introduce provide a critical foundation and vocabulary for understanding everything that is discussed in the second half of the textbook.

FIGURE 5.2   The elocutionary movement specified precise curves for each gesture. The sphere shows the various gesture trajectories. For example, *F* represents the front curve of gesture, *O* represents the oblique curve, *L* represents the lateral curve, *O.B.* is the oblique backward curve of gesture, *A.H.* is the upper or ascending horizontal, and *D.H.* is the downward or descending horizontal curve.

Source: http://www.inkleaf.net/images/blog/gesture_sphere.gif

Structural Approaches.   The system developed by Birdwhistell (1955a, 1955b, 1970) over half a century ago is by far the most detailed and famous example of a structural approach. Birdwhistell sought to identify discrete, universal kinesic behaviors that are combined to produce nonverbal communication. He followed a linguistic-kinesic analogy in that he modeled his approach after the linguistic classification system that distinguishes discrete units of language behavior like phonemes and morphemes. (Phonemes are units of sound in human speech and morphemes are combinations of phonemes, such as words and sentences, that carry meaning.) Birdwhistell reasoned that since kinesics units appear to be tied to speech, they should exhibit structures similar to language.

In Birdwhistell's system, the smallest meaningful unit of behavior is the *kineme*. Birdwhistell identified 50 to 60 kinemes that he considered culturally universal. That is, cultural differences in kinesic behavior come from variations within kinemes, not from the use of different kinemes. Birdwhistell divided the body into eight regions, each with its own set of kinemes: (1) total head; (2) face; (3) neck; (4) trunk; (5) shoulders, arms, and wrists; (6) hands and fingers; (7) hips, legs, and ankles; and (8) feet (including walking). Figure 5.3 shows his notation system for expressions in the face region alone.

Kinemes are equivalent to morphemes—the smallest meaningful units within language. Kinemes in turn can be broken down further into *kines*. Kines are equivalent to phonemes, which are the smallest sound units—the voiced

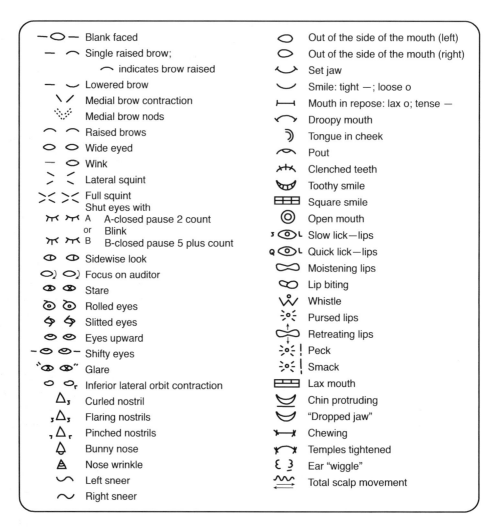

FIGURE 5.3   Birdwhistell's notation scheme for kinemes

alphabet—that are recognizable in a culture's language but do not possess unique meaning. Variations in the intensity, duration, or extent of these behaviors are called *allokines* or *kine variants*. For example, although trained observers have noted as many as 23 different eyelid positions (Birdwhistell himself claimed to have observed 15), only four positions appear to change the meaning. Thus, muscular adjustments of the eyelid around these four kineme positions are considered allokinic. Other groups of allokines are based on the sides of the body used to display the kines. Winks by the left and right eye can be considered allokines, as can movements by left and right forefingers. The test is whether it makes a difference which side of the body displays the kine. If it does not, the kines are allokines.

One of the most important kinemes to have received special attention in terms of its allokinetic features is the smile. Can you tell a fake smile from a genuine one? You probably answered yes, but you might be hard-pressed to say what makes the difference. Researchers think they can now tell you, based on analysis of the muscles in the face. Groundbreaking work by the French anatomist Duchenne de Boulogne (Duchenne, 1991/1862) identified two muscle groups involved in smiling—the zygomaticus major (lip corners) and orbicularis oculi (eye corners). These two muscle groups distinguish felt from fake smiles, with genuine or spontaneous smiles referred to as *Duchenne smiles* (Ekman & Friesen, 1982). Experiments, perceptual observations, EMGs, and automated facial image analyses have shown that the Duchenne smile differs from deliberately posed (or fake) ones in terms of the onset, offset, duration, and possibly asymmetry of the muscle groups that are engaged (Cohn & Schmidt, 2004; Schmidt, Ambadar, Cohn, & Reed, 2006; Hager & Ekman, 1997). Posed smiles, when compared to spontaneous smiles, are "turned on and off" more quickly but are longer in duration, are "bigger," tend to be more lopsided, and are less likely to engage the corners of the eyes (see Photos 5.2a, 5.2b, and 5.2c). Duchenne and non-Duchenne smiles factor significantly into our judgments of everything from a loved one's true affection for us to the genuineness of a teacher's praise to the sincerity and credibility of a politician running for office. It is also a relevant indicator of deception. Knowing the difference is therefore a valuable skill to cultivate.

When used, kinemes are combined into kinemorphs, which are similar to words in the linguistic system. Kinemorphs are grouped by classes and often occur in concert with other kinemorphs to produce complex kinemorphic constructions similar to sentences. It is at the level of kinemorphic constructions that the meaning

PHOTO 5.2 *Examples of (a) posed (fake) smiles; (b) and (c) Duchenne (genuine) smiles.*

of kinesic behavior becomes fully understandable. For instance, if you want to comfort a distraught friend, you might bow your head, lower your eyelids slightly, and lean your body in her direction. These behaviors singly and separately may not communicate sympathy, but displayed together, they convey compassion and understanding.

Another class of behaviors identified by Birdwhistell, called *parakinesics,* is similar to syntax in language. These are movements that aid our understanding of spoken language. Included in this set are kinesic *markers, stress,* and *juncture.* Markers can occur with or take the place of a variety of syntactic features. They can mark pronouns, indicate pluralizations, mark verbs, designate area, and indicate the manner of events. Subtle head movements are common parakinesic markers. For example, try describing what you did for your last school break and then what you plan to do for the next one. You may notice yourself gesturing backward slightly with your head when talking in past tense and then nodding forward when using future tense to describe your future plans. Kinesic stress includes movements that occur regularly, marking special linguistic combinations such as clauses, phrases, and adjectives with nouns. Four levels of stress are *primary stress* (strong movements), *secondary stress* (weak movements), *unstressed* (normal flow with speech), and *destress* (reduction of kinesic behavior below normal). These head movements may serve to create stressed and unstressed syllables, just as the voice does. Kinesic junctures serve to connect or separate kinesic phenomena, such as a slight lengthening of a gesture at the end of a complex kinemorphic stream.

Various other systems have been developed to describe facial expressions, postures, and gestures. Davis (1982) has applied Laban's (1975/1956) system for analyzing dance (Labanotation, Kinetography Laban) to the analysis of nonverbal movements. This system uses abstract symbols to specify on a staff like a musical score, each with detailed subcomponents: (1) the body part doing the movement; (2) the direction of movement; (3) the duration of movement; and (4) the effort involved (e.g., its sustained or sudden timing, the lightness or strength of weight).

Other structural approaches to classifying kinesics have focused on more specific body regions, such as gestures, facial behaviors, and the eyes. One recent effort to catalog gestures is a Gestionary, a dictionary of symbolic gestures developed by Poggi and Magno Caldognetto (1997; Poggi, 2002c). In it, each of the pictured gestures is analyzed according to these parameters: verbal translation, hand shape, orientation of hands in relation to interlocutor, location, and movement. Figure 5.4 illustrates two such gestures.

Eye behavior is one of the most important facets of kinesic behavior. The eyes are used to perform many of the same functions as other kinesic behaviors, including expressing interpersonal attitudes or emotions, regulating interactions, signaling attention, and producing anxiety or arousal in another person (Argyle & Cook, 1976). However, gaze also performs unique surveillance and information-gathering functions (Rutter, Pennington, Dewey, & Swain, 1984).

Although eye behavior has been the subject of a good deal of research, very few systems identifying the units of eye behavior exist. Von Cranach and Ellgring

Gesture	Verbal formulation	Handshape	Orientation	Location	Movement	Non-manual components
 1	They have an understanding with each other.	extended index fingers (both hands)	palms down, metacarp to Hearer	neutral space	parallel index fingers get close to each other	
 2	I am very sorry.	right index finger extended	palm to Speaker, fingertip up	on zygoma	down from zygoma to cheek	inner parts of eyebrows raised, lip corners down

FIGURE 5.4 In Poggi's Gestionary, each emblematic gesture can be described according to its specific meaning and how it is formed.

Source: Poggi, 2001–2002, *Toward an alphabet and the lexicon of gestures, gaze, and touch.* From http://www. semioticon.com/virtuals/index.html

(1973) proposed a structural system based on the length, direction, duration, and reciprocation of gaze:

- *One-sided look*—a gaze in the direction of the interlocutor's face that is not reciprocated by the partner.
- *Mutual look*—gaze by both partners directed at each other's faces.
- *Eye contact*—gaze by both partners directed at each other's eyes that both partners are aware of.
- *Gaze avoidance*—one person intentionally avoids the other interlocutor's eyes.
- *Gaze omission*—a person fails to look at an interlocutor but without intent to avoid eye contact.

In another system that was developed specifically for coding visual behaviors related to emotions, Noller (2004; Noller & Gallois, 1986) distinguished between the *gaze* and the *stare*, and also added three behaviors related to the brows: *eyebrow raise, eyebrow flash*, and *eyebrow furrow*.

The advent of computer vision techniques for identifying specific features of faces, gestures, and postures has brought a need for more refined structural analysis of kinesic features. Automated methods, such as the automated facial image analysis used for analyzing smiles, are revolutionizing the precision with which nonverbal behaviors can be examined. One common method, called blob analysis, is described in Box 5.2.

BOX **5.2**

What's in a Blob?

A "blob" may seem to be a peculiar and humorous name for what computer vision experts use to identify human hands and faces automatically from video, but that is what they call the ellipses that their techniques are able to superimpose on human body parts.

Here's how it works. Computers scan the pixels in a video sequence, and using either color look-up tables that match skin colors or other filters and algorithms, the software identifies candidate regions of a frame that could be skin tones or body parts. An ellipse is formed around the head, and the x and y coordinates of the ellipse are calculated in terms of pixels. Other algorithms then can calculate the width of the head and use its position, along with knowledge of the body's geometry, to infer where the hands, forearms, shoulders, trunk, and legs are likely to be located within the frame.

Sometimes it is useful to calculate whether an ellipse is in the trunk region, head region, or to the left or right of the body. A single frame from such an analysis in which calculations are made for each of four quadrants might look like the accompanying screen capture of a blob analysis. For example, it might be useful to know that a speaker's right hand is doing most of its gesturing in Quadrant 2, rather than engaging in a lot of hand-to-face adaptors, which would result in

the right hand ellipse merging with the head ellipse in Quadrant 1.

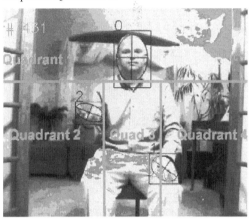

Changes from one frame to the next enable calculations of such parameters as changes in location, direction of movement, velocity of movement, and smoothness or abruptness of movement. These various parameters can be used to describe how frequently people gesture, nod, or shift postures, as well as what those movements look like. Such techniques can be used to analyze surveillance videos, public speeches, media broadcasts, or even "babycams" in daycare centers. These techniques have brought nonverbal analysis front and center into a "Brave New World."

Functional Approaches.   An alternative approach favored by many nonverbal researchers focuses instead on the functions of kinesic behaviors. This approach considers the meanings or purposes of the behaviors. Most scholarly attention has focused on the meanings of hand gestures, perhaps because they are such a rich vehicle for conveying symbolic and syntactic information as well as creating an interdependent exchange between speaker and listener. However, gestures need not be confined to the hands. They can be displayed by the face, eyes, or posture. To illustrate: a "blank face" can signify irony or sarcasm when accompanying a sarcastic voice that contradicts the words being spoken (Attardo, Eisterhold, & Hay, 2003). A smile can signify pleasure or friendliness (Poggi & Chirico, 1998).

And all children recognize "the look," often accompanied by hands on hips, from a disapproving parent.

Drawing on centuries-old essays on oratory, long-standing strictures on gesturing from the elocutionary movement, ethnographic observations by Efron (1941) and Kendon (1981), and other works, Ekman and Friesen (1969b) proposed five distinct types of kinesic behavior—emblems, illustrators, regulators, affect displays, and adaptors—each of which performs different functions or displays different meanings. These categories are not mutually exclusive. A single gesture, for example, may do more than one thing at the same time.

Emblems are gestures that have a clear symbolic meaning and can stand alone as a speech act (i.e., they need not be accompanied by words). Emblems meet the following criteria:

- They have a direct verbal translation and can be substituted for the words they represent without affecting the meaning.
- Their precise meaning is known by most or all members of a social group.
- They are most often used intentionally to transmit a message.
- They are recognized by receivers as meaningful and intentionally sent.
- The sender takes responsibility for them.
- They have clear meaning even when displayed out of context.

Emblems express greetings (a wave hello), requests (a "come here" beckoning gesture), insults (the cuckold horns), threats (the pistol shot gesture with forefinger and thumb), physical states (stomach rubbing to signal hunger or satiation), death (slashing the throat), promises ("cross my heart" or crossed fingers to nullify a promise), thought processes (palms turned up and lifted shoulders meaning "I don't know"), and emotional states (the eye widening to express "beware"). Emblems serve the same functions in all cultures, but as noted in Box 5.3, the number, forms, and meanings of particular emblems differ from culture to culture (see also Chapter 2). For example, there are 200 Persian emblems in use in present-day Iran. Culture and ethnicity also influence the ability to distinguish genuine from fake gestures (Molinsky, Krabbenhoft, & Ambady, 2005).

Regulators are kinesic behaviors designed to maintain or regulate turn taking between two or more interactants. They are the "traffic cops" of conversation. Rather than comment on the verbal stream, they coordinate and pace the flow of conversation. These behaviors are learned at a very early age, are displayed at a low level of awareness, and are produced almost automatically.

A useful expansion and clarification of the concept of regulators comes from Bavelas and Chovil, who introduced a typology of *conversational gestures and facial displays* (e.g., Bavelas & Chovil, 2000, 2006; Chovil, 2004). These typologies place gestures and facial displays within an interactive context and take into account their interdependent and adaptive nature.

Conversational gestures can be divided into *topic gestures*—ones that relate to the content itself—and *interactive or social gestures*—ones that function to distinguish true dyadic interaction from monologues and that are nonredundant with the information conveyed by words. Speakers use interactive gestures within

---

BOX **5.3**

Emblems and the Savvy Traveler

When visiting another culture, you may be struck by the fact that some emblems help you bridge communication difficulties while others add confusion. Paul Ekman and colleagues (Ekman, 1976; Ekman & Friesen, 1969b; Friesen, Ekman, & Wallbott, 1979) reported that emblems are common in every culture. Some cultures, such as middle-class U.S. culture, have fewer than one hundred emblems, whereas others, such as Israeli student culture, have over 250 emblems. Luckily for you, some emblems carry cross-cultural meaning. Ekman reported that emblems perform six functions in all cultures: (1) insulting others; (2) giving interpersonal directions ("come here" or "be quiet"); (3) greeting others; (4) signaling departure; (5) replying positively or negatively to requests; and (6) commenting on physical or emotional states. Further, all cultures seem to use emblems in similar places in conversations—at the beginning or end of a turn, in filled pauses, and preceding or accompanying the words they repeat. Emblems such as those deriving from facial affect displays carry common meaning across cultures. Other emblems, such as eating and drinking emblems, bear some cross-cultural similarity because they arise from common experiences with the environment. However, most have unique meanings in each culture.

If you want to avoid embarrassment when traveling abroad, you should learn in advance what that culture's emblems mean and what emblems might be misread as insults. Take a look at the Gestionary (Poggi, 2001–2002) or *Gestures* (Morris et al., 1979) to learn the country-specific meanings of various gestures.

---

their speaking turn to refer to receivers, so they feel included in the dialogue, without speakers giving up their turn. Interactive gestures may invite receivers to fill in an unstated part of the message, figuratively hand over the speaking turn to them, indicate that a receiver's question is being answered, refer to a previous topic, signal a word search, request agreement from the receiver, or mark a rhetorical question. Interactive gestures occur more frequently in face-to-face interaction than when the receiver is not visually available or when people are alone, evidence that they are more oriented to the receiver than to the content of the message.

Chovil's (1991a, 2004) taxonomy of facial expressions is based on observing 1,184 expressions from videotaped interactions. It includes *syntactic displays*, which display grammatical information; *speaker semantic displays*, which display content and can be *redundant* or *nonredundant* with the verbal information; *listener semantic displays* (which are by definition nonredundant with the speaker's words); and *adaptors* (which have no meaning). Syntactic displays include emphasizers, underliners, question markers, story announcers, and so on. Semantic displays include indications of personal reactions, portrayals of the action being described (such as scrutinizing a photograph), facial shrugs, agreement, and so forth. Listener displays signify understanding or personal reactions. For example, a quizzical look by the listener says, "I don't understand you."

Ekman (1997), too, now recognizes this separate category of conversational signals that are part of the structure and flow of conversation and are governed by the same rules that govern verbal communication. In Chapter 14, we present a different division of regulatory cues according to their turn-taking role: turn-yielding, turn-denying, turn-requesting, and backchannel cues.

Illustrators (also called gesticulations) are kinesic acts accompanying speech that are used to aid in the description of what is being said, trace the direction of speech, set the rhythm of speech, and gain and hold a listener's attention. They may accent, complement, repeat, or contradict what is being said. They are a resource on which speakers draw to clarify and eliminate ambiguous meanings for their listeners (Holler & Beattie, 2003).

Ekman and Friesen (1969b) proposed several types of illustrators: *pictographs* sketch a picture of the referent; *kinetographs* display a bodily action; *ideographs* draw the direction or path of thought; *spatial movements* show a spatial relationship among objects; *emblematic movements* repeat or substitute for words in illustrating the spoken words; *deictic movements* point to an object; *batons* emphasize a phrase or word; and *rhythmic movements* show timing or rhythm of an event. Taking more of a discourse-oriented perspective, McNeill (1992) offered a modified taxonomy that combines a speech versus motor distinction with several of the Ekman-Friesen illustrator categories and adds a unique category related to tying together parts of extended discourse. In Table 5.1, we have combined the various taxonomies, added our own take on them, and noted their relationship to the Ekman-Friesen or Birdwhistell categories. Chovil's (1991a) category of adaptors is omitted, as it is unrelated to content and duplicative of the Ekman-Friesen category.

Affect displays reveal emotions. As we will see in Chapter 11, many facial expressions have been declared to be universal. A major controversy regarding affect displays is whether they signal emotional states or are instead social signals intended to convey affectively toned messages to actual or imagined recipients (Fridlund & Russell, 2006). For example, is an authentic smile a "read-out" of an individual's felt happiness, a message of affiliation to another person ("It's great to see you," "Let's get together"), or a sign of embarrassment ("I can't believe I messed up that badly")? A variety of systems have been developed for classifying and coding affect, among them, the previously mentioned system by Noller (2004) and other systems discussed in Chapter 11 that examine how emotions are expressed.

Adaptors are behaviors that satisfy physical or psychological needs. They have their origins early in life. Adaptors satisfy personal needs (e.g., need for comfort), respond to internal states (e.g., anxiety, relaxation, perceptions of crowding, feelings of submissiveness or defensiveness), perform bodily functions, structure the body's external aspect, shield the individual from interfering stimuli, manage emotions (e.g., discomfort, guilt), maintain interpersonal contact and personal image, and complete instrumental activities (McBrayer, Johnson, & Purvis, 1992). Because they are designed to help the individual adapt to stresses and needs, adaptors are habits that usually are not intended to communicate. However, they

TABLE 5.1   An Intergrated Taxonomy of Gestures and Facial Expressions

Display Category	Definition	Relationship to Ekman-Friesen Categories	Example
Iconics	Pictorial gestures that bear a close resemblance to a concrete object that is being depicted.	Includes pictographs and kinetographs.	Showing the size of the "fish that got away."
Metaphorics	Pictorial gestures that present an abstract concept or thought process.	Incorporates ideographs, spatial movements, rhythmic movements, and emblematic movements.	Using hands to form a container metaphor when describing wanting to break out of a confining relationship.
Deictics	Pointing gestures.	Same as deictics.	Pointing with one's head or index finger toward the defendant in a courtroom.
Beats	Hand movements that follow the rhythmic pulsation of speech. Form is the same regardless of speech content.	Same as batons and possibly rhythmic gestures.	Using rhythmic, emphatic gestures like a baton while giving a public speech.
Cohesives	Repetitions of gestures, movements, and locations in gestural space to tie together related but separated discourse themes. All of the above forms can be included here as long as they create continuities across extended discourse.	Not in Ekman-Friesen taxonomy.	During a narrative about trolley cars, repeating the same pictograph of the crossed wires when later referring to them as "these."
Syntactic displays	Facial expressions or gestures that accompany and perform a parakinesic function (punctuation, emphasis, pausality). Includes subcategories such as emphasis, underlining, question markers.	Not in Ekman-Friesen taxonomy; same as Birdwhistell's parakinesics.	Raising eyebrows and opening eyes to emphasize a word.
Speaker semantic displays	Nonrepresentational facial expressions or gestures that add in personal sentiments to neutral statements and/or allude to thoughts or memories, and interactive displays that recruit interlocutor's attention.	Includes but goes beyond regulators in Ekman-Friesen system.	Frowning when recalling and retelling an unpleasant event.
Listener semantic displays	Backchannel displays, personal reactions to what speaker is saying, shows of understanding, motor mimicry.	Includes but goes beyond regulators in Ekman-Friesen system.	Head nod plus smile to signify agreement with speaker.

Note: These categories are based on integrating work by Bavelas and Chovil (2000, 2006) and McNeill (1992).

can be quite informative about the sender's internal state, and they are occasionally used with intent as an insult or message of disrespect.

There are three types of adaptors—*self-adaptors, alter-directed adaptors*, and *object adaptors*—distinguished by the target of the behavior. Scratching your arm, playing with your hair, working your jaw, biting your lip, or picking your nose are self-adaptors. Alter-directed adaptors are movements directed toward another person during interpersonal interactions, often to make interactants more comfortable or to release energy. Examples include tucking in a tag that is sticking up out of a friend's shirt, wiping dirt off a child's nose, or releasing anger by swiping at someone. Finally, object adaptors involve the manipulation of objects, such as smoking a cigarette or tapping a pencil while concentrating. Although not truly communicative, these behaviors can be very revealing about a person's level of comfort and cognitive difficulty. They will show up repeatedly in later chapters as unconscious and unintended acts that are nevertheless often regarded as "messages." They can also be pressed into service as intentional acts—such as burping to be funny or loudly "passing wind" as a sign of disrespect.

Meaning-Based Approaches. A final way that gestures and facial expressions have been examined, but one that does not lend itself to a specific taxonomy, is a semantic approach. In contrast to describing what kinesic behaviors look like (structural approach) or what they do (functional approach), they can be described according to the meanings they convey. In other words, the categories are the meanings themselves, rather than the nonverbal features or the functions they fulfill.

Because meaning is inherently context specific, generic meanings usually cannot be specified. Fridlund (1991), for example, challenges the notion that many kinesic behaviors convey standard meanings. He argues that smiles, facial expressions, gestures, and body movements are strictly social signals that are selected for what they can communicate in a given circumstance rather than being read-outs of internal states. Burgoon and Newton's (1991) social meaning model is also of this type in that it recognizes that behaviors can have a wide range of meanings and that the specific meaning being communicated in a given interaction is dependent on a number of contextual factors such as the purpose of the interaction and the relationship between actors.

Nevertheless, some meaning-based approaches have been created. One is Gottman's Specific Affect (SPAFF) coding system, developed to measure affect in close relationships (Gottman, Woodin, & Coan, 1998; Jones, Carrère, & Gottman, 2004). This system specifies the facial, postural, gestural, and vocal behaviors associated with different negative interpersonal affects such as whining, contempt, stonewalling, belligerence, or domineeringness and positive affects such as validation, joy, and humor. SPAFF differs from other systems that focus on the individual by narrowing (or broadening) its attention to what happens within couples.

Another meaning-based approach has been proposed by Poggi and Chirico (1998). They contend, for example, that all smiles boil down to one of two general types and meanings: those that are pure expressions of a basic emotional state that can be paraphrased as "I feel pleasure," and those that are communicative signals and express essentially the message of "I'm your friend." These two alternative meanings coincide with our distinction between emotional expressions and relational messages, which we address in Chapters 11 and 12, respectively.

Kinesic Norms and Expectations.   Although individual variability exists, kinesic behaviors are highly normative at the cultural and co-cultural level. In general, cultures can be classified as to whether they are high-frequency or low-frequency cultures in terms of the amount and complexity of gesturing (Kendon, 1981; Pika, Nicoladis & Marentette, 2006). Italy, France, and Israel are high-frequency cultures; England and the United States are low-frequency ones.

Beyond culture, several personal factors shape norms and become the backdrop against which to assess a given behavior. Personality, sex, age, culture, race, and ethnicity have received the majority of attention (see, e.g., Burgoon & Hoobler, 2002; Manusov & Patterson, 2006; Poggi, 2002a; and Chapter 10).

Other factors that exert significant influence on kinesic norms and usage are characteristics of the interpersonal relationship and the communication context. For example, how well two people like each other and the degree to which they have equal or unequal status will affect what kinesic patterns are normative and preferred. Chapters 12 and 13 examine relationship factors that affect behavior selection. Whether the interaction is task-oriented or social-oriented and formal or informal also calls up different sets of kinesic behaviors. Features of the setting further constrain and shape what kinesic patterns emerge. A more extended discussion of the impact of environmental features is presented in Chapter 14. Finally, the modalities available for expression and receipt of signals will also influence their selection and frequency. For example, use of a videophone may shift more expression of content and parakinesics to the face and away from gestures, voice, and words.

The interrelationships among these factors produce a complex system in which no behavior exists in isolation. With this qualification in mind, let us take quick stock of some of the norms and standards that have been observed for the various kinesic categories.

Emblems.   We noted earlier that emblems serve the same functions in all cultures. However, many emblems have meaning only for members of a particular culture. Generally, this simply means that the person to whom you are communicating may not understand your meaning when you use an emblem from your native culture. Among the more complete catalogues of emblems used in a wide variety of cultures are Morris, Collett, Marsh, and O'Shaugnessy's *Gestures* (1979), Morris's *Bodytalk* (1995), and Poggi's (2002c) Gestionary.

Illustrators.   Norms of illustrator usage have not been well documented, although it is evident that some cultures and co-cultures are more "illustrative" than others. Although exaggerated and stylized gestures are less common now among actors and public speakers, the close handling that presidential candidates are subjected to during their public addresses suggests that there may be less leeway than one would expect.

Outside the public arena, friends of the same sex reportedly use more illustrators and overall animation in conversation than do friends of the opposite sex or romantic partners, and romantic partners appear to nod the least (Guerrero, 1994).

Regulators. Regulators are the most rule-governed of all kinesic behaviors and are usually displayed automatically in interaction. Early research (e.g., Ellsworth & Ludwig, 1972; Kendon, 1978; Rutter & Stephenson, 1979) identified the following norms:

- The normal amount of gaze in an interaction ranges from 28% to 70% of the time.
- Under stress conditions, the range broadens to 8% to 73% of the time.
- Eye contact increases when listening (30% to 80% of the time) and decreases when speaking (25% to 65% of the time).
- Gaze increases when information is needed from another person, when monitoring another, and when needing to be seen by another.
- Individuals are consistent in their looking patterns.
- Interactants coordinate their looking patterns.
- Gaze aversion is more frequent when discussing difficult topics, when uncertain, or when ashamed.
- Sex, race, personality, and interpersonal relationship affect the amount of eye contact.

Affect Displays. At a basic level, all cultures share a limited set of facial affect displays (Ekman, Sorenson, & Friesen, 1969). However, cultures develop rules governing when affect displays are appropriate, when they are inappropriate, and what forms they should take (Buck, 1984; Ekman & Friesen, 1969b). For example, as part of their "emotional education," boys in the United States are encouraged to mask negative emotions such as sadness or grief and not to display an overabundance of tenderness, affection, or emotionality. Conversely, girls are encouraged to show more emotions than boys but are trained to maintain a pleasant front and to minimize aggressive displays such as anger. Chapter 11 provides a more extended discussion of gender and other differences in affect displays.

Adaptors. The primary norm governing adaptor displays is to avoid using them in public. This is especially true of self-adaptors, which normally are permitted only in the privacy of one's own home and in the presence of intimately familiar others. The comedian Bill Cosby once noted that at home, only fathers are allowed to have "gas." Alter-oriented and object adaptors are more permissible in public, although mores are constantly changing, as witnessed by new legal restrictions on smoking in public places in the United States. Gum chewing varies in its acceptability in many social situations, but it is considered déclassé behavior in many countries, such as Germany, and until recently was actually illegal in Singapore. Burping, considered rude in the United States, is an expected expression of appreciation for a good meal in parts of Africa and the Middle East. Often object adaptors are used to signal membership in a particular group. Beyond the public versus nonpublic and group-specific rules, few other norms for adaptor behavior exist.

PHOTO 5.3 *Can you recognize these common expressions? Which are emblems and which are affect displays?*

Source: Top l., r.; Marilyn Stringer, photographer

Vocalics

most people are perfectly afraid of silence.

—e. e. cummings

There is no index so sure as the voice.

—Tancred

I have never fallen in love with my own voice, but I've always had an attraction for it.

—Tom Snyder

The voice is a powerful instrument of communication, with or without the accompaniment of language. Not only can it be used to complement, accent, emphasize, and contradict what is said, it can also send messages independently. Pitch, loudness, pauses, laughs, and sighs are a few examples of cues in the code. Vocal cues communicate emotional reactions, comment on relationships, indicate social attitudes, and regulate the back-and-forth exchange in conversations.

The analysis of the voice as an instrument of communication occurs under many different guises. Some call it paralanguage ("along-with language"); some, prosody; some, noncontent speech; and some, vocalics. We find the term "paralanguage" problematic, because in some usages it encompasses kinesic behaviors, which makes the term unnecessarily broad, and in other respects it is too narrow because it ties the voice strictly to language. Prosody, too, is usually linked to the words that are spoken. It refers to the melody and rhythm of an utterance and is often described in terms of the timing, amplitude, and frequency spectrum of an utterance (Cutler, 2002; Cutler, Dahan, & van Donselaar, 1997). Although prosodic features can also describe vocalizing that lacks verbal content—such as the screech of joy at unexpectedly seeing a long-lost friend or the purring of contentment in the arms of a loved one—it is usually associated with language rather than with expressions that are devoid of words. Noncontent speech implies that the vocal aspects of speech do not in themselves have any content, which is also inaccurate. For these reasons, we prefer the label *vocalics*, as it encompasses any vocal-auditory behavior except the spoken word.

Vocalics rivals kinesics in number and variety of signals, the human ability to encode and decode the signals, and the inborn tendency to rely on them. The human ear is capable of perceiving frequencies ranging from 16 Hz to 20,000 Hz (Hz is the abbreviation for *hertz*; 1 Hz = 1 cycle per second; 20,000 Hz = 20,000 cycles per second). Humans can also recognize incredibly minute variations in sound, to the point that law enforcement and speech scientists have worked to perfect a voice print that would rival the fingerprint in producing reliable identification of people. You can test this capacity informally for yourself. Think about the last 20 phone calls you received. How many of the callers did you recognize immediately from the sound of their voice (and not from caller ID)?

The highly popularized (though faulty) estimate that 93% of all meaning resides in nonverbal cues was based in part on a study that found that 55% of the meaning of an utterance was conveyed visually and 38% was conveyed vocally (Mehrabian & Ferris, 1967). Although the extrapolation process led to some faulty conclusions, the fact remains that the voice is probably second only to kinesics in the ranking of nonverbal codes on their communicative power. The voice is thought to have preceded formal language as a means of communication and has been retained throughout evolution for its communicative function. Besides this phylogenetically based advantage, the voice has primacy in human development. An infant begins to communicate with vocal cues long before words appear, and reliance on vocalics as a communication channel continues throughout life. Interactionally, the voice can also be heard at a distance and so holds primacy in many cases. Vocalic behaviors are also ever-present during conversation and are essential to the comprehension of oral (as opposed to written) language use. These factors, plus the frequency of manipulation, number of cues, and range of information and functions that vocalic behaviors can perform, are the reasons for the potency of this code.

Origins and Acquisition of Vocalics

Communication through vocalizations is by no means exclusive to the human species. Many living beings depend on vocalics for communication with other members of their species. Vocal-auditory communication has been observed in crickets, grasshoppers, finches, thrushes, doves, mynahs, whales, and porpoises (Thorpe, 1972). Vocal behavior in primates is strikingly similar to that in humans. van Hooff (1972) documented numerous examples of laugh-like behavior in primates, consisting of a relaxed open-mouthed facial expression accompanied by screeches and squeals. In fact, during play involving children and chimpanzees, children engage in laughter, whereas chimps engage in the relaxed open-mouthed facial expression with squealing. Moreover, pitch levels and contours appear to be used for the same purposes by humans and other vertebrates. Vocalic threats and dominance displays invariably entail deep-pitched, harsh vocal patterns, whereas nonthreatening, nurturing contexts—such as mothers cooing to infants—entail high-pitched, softer patterns.

Developmentally, newborns have an amazing ability to communicate vocally with parents. Infants also can change their vocalizations (principally crying) to reflect physiological needs during the *prebabbling* period. Parents (especially mothers) are able to distinguish between different types of cries and respond to crying in some characteristic ways. The attempt to comfort a crying baby may be an innate response. When a mother hears her baby crying, the milk in her breasts also becomes warmer.

Beyond communicating basic needs, crying helps the baby develop the use of pitch, pausing, loudness, and tempo. Children begin picking up the rudiments of prosody in infancy. Research using intonagrams, which measure the fundamental frequency, duration, and intensity of vocalic cues, has found that by 2 months of age infants produce intonation patterns similar to those of adults. Babies begin as universal listeners, able to pick up all the sounds of different languages, but then lose this ability as they age. Fundamental frequency (pitch) changes from birth to puberty, with the greatest changes taking place between infancy and 2 years and again at puberty. By the time a child enters kindergarten, pausing, hesitations, tempo, and loudness are almost adult-like and typically match the patterns of conversational partners (Wood, 1981).

Ability to decode vocalizations is also a fundamental facet of child development. Infants appear to attend to vocalic cues innately from birth (Harris & Rubenstein, 1975), and the ability to discriminate between intonation patterns improves markedly during the babbling period (Menyuk, 1972). Critically important to language acquisition is auditory feedback (Oller & Eilers, 1988). Children listen to their own voices as they pronounce words. This feedback helps them adjust vocal sounds to conform to adult standards. Whereas hearing infants have developed proper pronunciation of syllables by 10 months of age, deaf children have not. Thus the lack of auditory feedback results in delayed speech development of deaf infants.

In the first year, then, there is a rich communication exchange between the infant and its caregivers. This exchange enables the infant to signal its needs and desires. The exchange also helps the parents care effectively for the infant. Finally, in this exchange, the infant learns important basic communication skills from the parents that it will continue to use once it develops language.

Features of the Vocalics Code

Next to kinesics, the vocalic code possesses the largest number of nonverbal cues and, like kinesics, has attracted its fair share of analysis. Writings during the elocutionary movement, for example, had much to say about the relevant features of the voice, and the linguistic approach taken to analyzing kinesics in the late 1950s was also applied to the voice. Here we examine a few of the basic classification systems again, because they are responsible for the vocabulary we use in describing vocalics and because they are foundational to the material we cover in all the chapters on nonverbal communication functions.

Structural Approaches. Depending on one's purposes and disciplinary perspective, the voice can be described according to its perceptual, linguistic, or acoustic properties. Perceptually, the voice can be described according to the qualities that the average person would mention when describing a speaker's voice. Think of some famous people with distinctive voices—such as President Barack Obama, sportscaster John Madden, actress Fran Drescher (from *The Nanny*), radio show host Delilah (from *Delilah After Dark*), or actor James Earl Jones, who was the voice of Darth Vader in *Star Wars*, the voice of Mufasa in *The Lion King,* and says, "This is CNN." Or, what about the celebrities shown in Photos 5.4a through 5.4d? Chances are, you can hear these voices in your mind, and you can describe each of them by such qualities as loud, accented, lilting, lisping, halting, twangy, nasal, raspy, or smooth. These are the kinds of perceptual qualities we are accustomed to using when we talk about someone's "tone of voice."

In the course of centuries of expounding on those voice qualities that were thought to be part of effective speaker delivery, proponents of the elocutionary movement identified several vocal features (Hyde & Hyde, 1886) that a good speaker was expected to master (see also Box 5.4 for a critique of how these qualities were misused by teachers of the day). These included *pitch* (the tone

PHOTO 5.4 *Can you recognize these people with distinctive voices? How do their voices sound? (a = Barbara Walters, b = Arnold Schwarzenegger, c = Whoopi Goldberg, d = Rush Limbaugh)*

BOX 5.4

Speaking Naturally, or Do Neither As I Say Nor As I Do

Throughout recorded history, philosophers and rhetoricians have held strong opinions about what makes for effective speaking voices. In their *Natural System for Elocution and Oratory* (1886), Hyde and Hyde offer up this scathing critique of the vapid and listless way in which public teachers speak and how they wrongfully encourage their pupils to follow suit (p. 416):

> Observe public teachers while speaking, and you will not fail to discover many inflections and peculiar changes of voice, which, although they resemble some phases of natural conversation yet are extremely unnatural. There appears to be a sort of calculated emphasis, a stated recurrence of the upward and downward slides of the voice, and an affected precision in the enunciation of vowels and consonants. The same way of beginning and closing a sentence which leads to monotony, even amid variety. It is very easy to discover a school teacher by her mode of delivery. This false style of delivery arises from the desire to imitate the changes of voice occurring in

ordinary conversation; those which appear on the surface are the ones most readily imitated. Inflection and force-emphasis, because habitually used by most people are thought to contribute grace of natural delivery, hence they form the prevailing elements in the imitative natural delivery. The expressions of the passions are never conveyed by this style of enunciation, because by its very nature it does not recognize the manifold changes of voice necessary to express passion. It often happens, that those who have formed this false conception of what constitutes natural delivery, undertake to criticize pupils who have a gift for speaking, and almost ruin the style of such pupils by insisting on the adoption of their imitative mode.

Does the style described in this passage fit teachers of today? Notice, ironically, that these advocates of an elocutionary approach were castigating teachers for imitating a natural delivery style rather than following their dictums for a more deliberate "natural" style that would properly express the passions.

---

level from high to low) and pitch variation, *inflection* (the tonal patterns of the voice), *loudness* (the amplitude of the voice), *emphasis* (specific points of stress), *tempo* (speed of speaking), *pauses* (silences between words and clauses and at the ends of sentences), and *voice coloring* (qualities of the voice that convey passion and emotional overtones, accomplished partly through modulation and inflection), among others. To these, twentieth-century researchers added *accent* (a distinctive pattern of pronunciation that is usually associated with a regional dialect, culture, co-culture, or socioeconomic group), and *fluency* (the presence or absence of filled pauses such as "um" or "uh" and other dysfluencies like repetitions and garbled sounds).

Linguists and psycholinguists take a somewhat different approach to the voice, describing it in terms of its role in segmenting language into its constituents. *Segmentals* are the essential sounds of a language—phonemes—and the features that describe those sounds (e.g., tongue height, lip rounding). For example, English has around 40 phonemes that include the consonants in the alphabet plus variations in how various vowels are pronounced. *Nonsegmentals* (which is what many people refer to as prosody or paralanguage) are the nonlinguistic features— what most people think of as "voice quality," by which they might mean such things as pitch, loudness, tempo, or resonance. They include *suprasegmentals*— features such as combinations of stress, silences, pitch height, pitch range, tempo, and intonation patterns that produce the melody of speech—and *registers*—voice qualities such as a falsetto, breathy, or denasal voice.

At the same time Birdwhistell was developing his linguistic-kinesic approach, Trager (1958, 1961) proposed a complementary linguistic-based classification system that encompassed both speech and body movement. Trager believed that vocalic behavior was only one facet of speech and was intimately related to language, kinesics, and background characteristics of the speaker. In his system, analysis begins with *voice set,* which consists of the mental, physiological, and physical characteristics of a speaker, against which all vocalic and speech behaviors are judged. In other words, speech must be judged within the context of the speaker's traits and states such as sex, age, state of health, body build, and geographic location. For instance, older people have more jitter in their voice than those who are junior to them. Although other taxonomies don't include voice set because it is not a feature of the voice per se, the concept underscores that voices must be described and analyzed in relative terms.

The next level of analysis is *speech*. Trager saw speech as a combination of language and paralanguage. *Paralanguage* includes what he labeled as voice qualities and vocalizations. *Voice qualities* describe a given utterance along a continuum (e.g., narrow to spread pitch range, slurred to precise articulation control, resonant to thin resonance, slow to fast tempo). *Vocalizations*, by contrast, describe nonlinguistic sounds or noises associated with brief utterances, such as how loud or long an utterance is or whether it is voiced in a whiny, whispering, or laughing manner. Utterances also can include sounds such as pauses, clicks, snorts, and vocalic emblems such as "uh-uh" for no, "uh-huh" for yes, and "sh" for quiet that Trager called *vocal segregates.*

Poyatos (1991, 1993), an anthropologist, followed Trager's lead in advancing his triple structure of language. The triple structure refers to words, voice, and kinesics. His elaborate taxonomy for suprasegmentals distinguishes between *primary qualities* and *voice qualifiers*. Primary qualities are characteristics of speech style that are always present in the human voice and include timbre, resonance, loudness, tempo, pitch (level, range, registers, intervals), intonation range, syllabic duration, and rhythm. *Voice qualifiers* refer to how the voice produces specific sounds (e.g., laryngeal, velopharyngeal, labial) that are heard as breathy, strident, hoarse, shrill, husky, and so on. These prosodic features are determined by biological, physiological, and sociocultural factors. Other features are equivalent to Trager's categories.

These various taxonomies have produced a large number of terms, many of which refer to the same phenomenon. Table 5.2 presents our compilation of the basic units or attributes that are used to describe vocalics and how they relate to one another.

TABLE 5.2   Structural Features of Vocalics

Linguistic Category	Definition	Acoustic/Linguistic Attributes	Perceptual Attributes
I. Segmentals	Building blocks of language		
A. Phonemes, phones, & allophones	Fundamental units of sound in a language	Vowels, consonants	
B. Morphemes	Fundamental units of meaning in a language:	Syllables, words, affixes (prefixes, suffixes, infixes)	
C. Paralinguistic alternants	Word-like sounds like "brrr" for cold or "aaagh" for pain		
D. Vocalizations	Discrete sounds like sighs or belches		
II. Nonsegmentals	Features that transcend a specific utterance or are interjected as word-like constructions		
A. Suprasegmentals	Prosodic and paralinguistic features		
1. Frequency spectrum	Energy concentrations and patterns in the speech wave	Fundamental frequency (F_0) Formants $(F_1, F_2, \ldots)$	Pitch, pitch height Resonance, voice qualities
		Intensity/energy	Loudness, stress
2. Time spectrum	Temporal features of a segment of speech or voice	Length of sound portions Silence portions Sound and silence sequences Duration plus peak energy	Extent, utterance length Pauses, terminal junctures Tempo, fluency Intonation, rhythm, accent
B. Registers			Falsetto, whispery, creaky, harsh, hoarse, whiny, shrill, strident, tense
C. Vocal segregates	Voiced fillers such as "ah," "um," or other interruptive sounds such as clicks or snorts		Nonfluencies

Finally, the voice can be described acoustically, according to frequencies of the sound waves that are produced and their timing. Sound waves consist of various *frequencies* and include multiple *formants*, which are concentrations of acoustic energy around a particular frequency in the speech wave. Formants occur at roughly 1000-Hz intervals and correspond to a resonance in the vocal tract. The lowest frequency is the fundamental frequency, labeled as F_0, and is what we naturally hear as pitch. (It is also referred to as the first harmonic.) Higher formants or harmonics produce different voice qualities. See Figure 5.5, which shows a spectrogram of an utterance and its multiple formants. *Intensity* or loudness refers to the concentration of energy during voicing. *Tempo* refers to the rapidity of on-off sound-silence sequences and changes in frequencies.

One of the pioneers of research on vocalics, Scherer (1986), enumerated acoustic parameters related to the expression of arousal and emotions. More recently, research in computational linguistics and communication has advanced to the point that many features of the voice can be analyzed automatically. For example, in one of the most comprehensive experiments to be conducted, Shriberg et al. (1998; see also Shriberg et al., 2005) measured a wide range of features to detect discourse acts with automated tools. Combining these two systems, the following features can be identified:

- *Duration features*—duration of utterance, durations of voiced speech, number of frames at fundamental frequency, number of voiceless frames, number of accented frames
- *Pause features*—frequency of noticeable pauses (100 milliseconds length or greater); sum, mean duration; number of frames in continuous speech regions

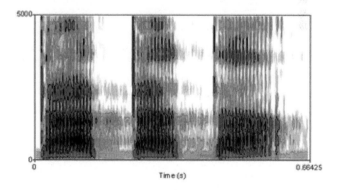

FIGURE 5.5   Spectrogram of a male voice saying "TaTaTa"

Note: The horizontal axis represents *time*, the vertical axis is *frequency*, and the *intensity* of each point in the image represents amplitude of a particular frequency at a particular time. Here the diagram is reduced to two dimensions by indicating the intensity with more intense lines and gray values. Each set of dark bands, moving up the vertical axis, represents another formant.

Source: http://en.wikipedia.org/wiki/Spectrogram

- F_0 *features (pitch)*—mean, standard deviation, minimum, maximum, range, perturbations, contour over time (intonation) ratio of F_0 to other values, various boundary measures, various accent measures
- *Formants*—F_1 mean, F_2 mean, bandwidth (width of spectral band), precision
- *Intensity (energy or loudness)*—mean, standard deviation, minimum, maximum, range, proportion of energy in upper frequency, differences in energy in different regions, ratio of energy in different ranges, spectral noise
- *Tempo features*—mean, standard deviation, minimum, maximum

Other voice qualities such as dialects, nonfluencies, and vocal tension are the result of how the voice mechanism produces combinations of these sound waves. Emotional states can be described in terms of acoustic-prosodic combinations as well. For example, anger is displayed through higher intensity, higher mean F_0, greater F_0 range and variability, downward contours, higher frequency energy, and clearer articulation (Scherer, 2003).

As new technologies become available for capturing and analyzing the voice automatically, research has been moving toward this more objective method of describing human vocal activity, which will doubtless become a standard part of researching vocal communication.

Functional Approaches.   Perhaps because the voice is so often treated as part of language rather than nonverbal communication, it has been analyzed less often from a functional standpoint. However, we can apply some of the same categories that we use for gestures to classify the functions of the voice.

Emblems.   A variety of vocalizations can stand alone and have well understood symbolic meaning within a culture. Four examples are the rapid trilling of the lips ("blowing raspberries") that can be an expression of delight from a child but disappointment or disgust from an adult; "brr" to signify cold; "shh" to hush someone; and "tsk-tsk" to chide someone. Vocalizations such as belches might also be considered emblematic as an insult, taunt, or show of appreciation. Silences are particularly powerful symbolic messages. They can be used to express negation without having to say "no" or to establish a sense of being "simpatico" and in complete harmony. They can also be used to slight someone. One of the authors had the experience of an otherwise very proper department head entering the mail room, looking right past her, saying nothing, and hitching up his underwear—a strong signal that he had become so accustomed to giving her the "silent treatment" that she had become a nonperson whose presence he failed to recognize.

To our knowledge, no one has catalogued vocal emblems in the way that gestures have been catalogued, so it is yet unknown whether these vocalizations are universal or culture specific.

Regulators.   The role of the voice in the turn-taking process will be discussed in more detail in Chapter 14, but suffice it to say that vocal features are central to the way people engage in conversation. Intonation and silence patterns regulate the flow of conversation and the fluidity of turn-exchanges. Even a feature as slight as audible inhalation can serve a turn-taking role.

Illustrators. All of the features described as vocal characterizers or registers can function to illustrate verbal content. A tense voice adds intensity to what is being expressed and may supply emphasis. A soft, lilting voice may add a feeling of whimsy. In fact, many of the adjectives used in literature to describe direct quotes—he said harshly, she said winsomely, they whispered—conjure up clear "voice pictures" of how something is to be heard.

Affect Displays. As you will learn in much greater detail in Chapter 11, the voice is also a superb mechanism for expressing emotional tone and emotional states. Many descriptors of the voice—laughing, giggling, yelling, moaning, wailing—implicitly or explicitly convey the emotional state of the speaker. Poggi (2002b) also introduced the concept of "mind markers" that might fit into this category. *Mind markers* are indications through voice, gesture, and other non-verbal signals of a speaker's thoughts, goals, plans, and emotions. One can imagine a variety of vocalizations that tap into a speaker's current state of mind: a "hrmpp" that reveals disgruntlement at a proffered solution during a heated negotiation, or a cooed "oooh" that reveals pleasure in response to exciting news, for instance.

Cognitive State Indicators. Poggi's category of mind markers also includes indicators of thoughts, goals, and plans that are not necessarily affective in nature. It seems reasonable to add a category to reflect this distinction. An elongated "hmmm" while someone is trying to recover a fact from memory might signify the extent of the cognitive difficulty in retrieving it. A long response latency (delay before answering a question) when stating one's plans, on the other hand, might be indicative of uncertainty regarding those plans. Silences during interactions often signify that a communicator needs time to think or has nothing to say. Other vocal features could be analyzed for their cognitive signification.

Adaptors. Adaptors are behaviors that satisfy personal psychological or physiological needs. Burping, weeping, and sniffling are a few examples of vocalizations that fit this function. (You might see how many terms like this that you can generate in a few minutes.) Given that what is appropriate in one culture can be considered rude or crude in another, it is important to understand the norms and rules that govern vocal adaptors, just as it is critical to know which kinesic behaviors are appropriate or inappropriate within certain contexts or cultures. Although adaptors are not intended to be communicative, the fact that they can be read as intentional, if only because the person emitting them has failed to exercise self-control, warrants analyzing which ones might be taken as messages.

Vocalic Norms and Expectations. Every culture has what are considered standard and nonstandard forms of speech. These are tied to the languages that are considered standard or prestigious. British English, European English, Castilian Spanish, and classical Arabic are preferred languages in Britain, Quebec, Spain, and Egypt, respectively (Thakerar & Giles, 1981). The preferred dialect (which combines accent and prosody with grammar and vocabulary) is usually also considered the most prestigious, even among speakers of nonpreferred dialects. What features are considered the most attractive and prestigious? In an empirical study by Zuckerman and Miyake (1993), voices that were perceived as the most attractive had higher articulation and resonance, low to moderate shrillness, moderate pitch, small to medium pitch range, and low nasality.

An interesting example of the preference for a particular vocal style comes from Britain. In the 20th century, accent training became an unofficial requisite of the British educational system. To promote the elitism of the educated class, students from London to Liverpool were subtly encouraged to adopt the accent of their Oxford masters. This "official" accent connoted intelligence and distinction. Many newscasters for the British Broadcasting Corporation adopted this vocal style; hence it acquired the nickname "BBC English." Newscasters in the United States are likewise trained to remove any sign of an accent from their voice and to speak general American dialect (which is speech devoid of any noticeable regional accent). By contrast, talk-radio and television talk show hosts tend to retain their accented speech as a distinctive part of their on-air personas. Reporting the news calls for competence, education, and standard speech; hosting a talk program calls for different qualities like amiability or assertiveness.

Of course, not every member of a culture follows the language and vocalic norms of the preferred pronunciation. Co-cultural variations persist in every culture. For instance, Southern, Appalachian, New England, Brooklyn, Texan, Mexican American, Hoosier, and Ebonic variations exist in U.S. culture. If you encounter someone who speaks with an accent similar to your own, you are likely to view that person as friendlier, more similar to you, a member of your co-culture, and more attractive (Thakerar & Giles, 1981). The maintenance of group identity promote the continuance of these nonpreferred patterns in a culture.

Beyond cultural patterns, vocalic norms depend on the nature of the interpersonal relationship. Guerrero (1994) showed that conversations between opposite-sex and same-sex friends were characterized by more fluency, shorter response latencies, fewer silences, and more vocal interest than conversations between romantic partners.

Communication Potential of Kinesics and Vocalics

Kinesics and vocalics are two of the most powerful nonverbal coding systems. Both codes share a high attention-getting and arousal value that increases their communication potential. On the encoding side, the enormous number of behaviors at a sender's disposal presents a communicator with a rich array of signals from which to fashion highly precise and subtle messages. These codes easily exceed the others in the sheer number of possible features that can be utilized in forming messages. In addition, a single sender can perform many kinesic or vocalic cues at the same time. This produces a multichanneled message capable of many shades of meaning.

A sender can also perform multiple functions simultaneously. At a given point in a conversation, kinesic and vocalic cues each can signal an emotion, coordinate the switch between speaker and listener, comment on the relationship between speaker and listener, maintain a desired front, or persuade an audience. Finally, the innate basis of many kinesic and vocalic cues makes them an automatic, often unconscious choice to transmit many messages. Although some cues are unintentional, children learn very early in life to manipulate kinesic and vocalic cues to affect the people around them.

There is, however, a downside to the communication potential of these two performance codes. First, many cues and their various combinations are often ambiguous or confusing, leading to inaccurate decoding, misunderstandings, and conflict. Second, intentionality is not always certain, but vocalics seems to be used intentionally more often than many other codes, probably because of the intimate connection to language, which is almost always encoded deliberately, and the continuous attention to the voice that processing of speech requires. As people listen to words, they cannot help but process vocalic meaning, giving vocalic cues a perceptual advantage over other nonverbal channels. However, the awareness of vocalic cues is probably less than the awareness of the words they accompany, and nonlinguistic expressions, such as emotional cues, may be far less intentional or conscious.

Third, the intrinsic relationship between many of the cues and communicators' feelings and emotions often leads to unintentional displays. Since receivers are likely to consider kinesic cues as intentional and truthful, communicators are sometimes faced with unexpected or undesirable reactions due to unwitting displays. Fourth, people learn to mask, minimize, exaggerate, or substitute in new kinesic and vocal cues, which makes accurate decoding more difficult. This is especially true for facial expressions and thus does not bode well for accurate interpretation by those communicators who are biased toward attending to facial cues. Finally, humans are capable of making very fine discriminations among vocal cues.

Summary

Kinesics and vocalics relate to the visual and auditory senses for encoding and decoding messages. Each draws on strong nature and nurture tributaries and each is critically important to the development of children's ability to communicate. Centuries of treatises on the methods and features of public oratory, combined with modern-day scientific approaches to analyzing nonverbal behavior, have resulted in numerous ways to categorize or group the nearly limitless possibilities for expression into more manageable units of analysis. The main approaches identify either (1) specific structures—movements or vocal features—that are part of the human's expressive "equipment," (2) specific communicative functions that kinesic and vocal expressions accomplish, or (3) specific meanings that constellations of behaviors convey. These basic coding systems introduce essential vocabulary for the study of nonverbal communication and the building blocks from which nonverbal expressions are crafted or comprehended. The large number of structural, functional, and meaning-based approaches is testament to the importance of these two coding systems. Each approach has its virtues in showing how many features are available for use in our kinesic and vocalic repertoires and how they can be put to use to communicate.

Despite a strong, innate foundation, the codes are governed powerfully by cultural, co-cultural, contextual, and personality norms that are learned at an early age. The visual and auditory codes play a major role in accomplishing all the communication functions we discuss in Part Three.

SUGGESTED READINGS

Bavelas, J. B., & Chovil, N. (2006). Hand gestures and facial displays as part of language use in face-to-face dialogue. In V. Manusov & M. L. Patterson (Eds.), *The Sage handbook of nonverbal communication* (pp. 97–115). Thousand Oaks, CA: Sage.

Birdwhistell, R. L. (1970). *Kinesics and context.* Philadelphia: University of Pennsylvania Press.

Ekman, P. (Ed). (1973). *Darwin and facial expression: A century of research in review.* New York: Academic Press.

Giles, H., & Coupland, N. (1992). *Language: Contexts and consequences.* Pacific Grove, CA: Brooks/Cole.

Goffman, E. (1971). *Relations in public.* New York: Basic Books.

Guerrero, L. K. (2008). Gestures and kinesics. In W. Donsbach (Ed.), *The international encyclopedia of communication* (pp. 1967–1971). Malden, MA: Blackwell.

Kendon, A. (2004). *Gesture: Visible action as utterance.* New York: Cambridge University Press.

Morris, D. (1995). *Bodytalk.* New York: Abrams.

Poyatos, F. (1993). *Paralanguage: A linguistic and interdisciplinary approach to interactive speech and sounds.* Amsterdam: Benjamins.

Meservy, T., & Burgoon, J. K. (2008). Paralanguage. In W. Donsbach (Ed.), *The international encyclopedia of communication, Vol 8* (pp. 3496–3501). Malden, MA: Blackwell.

6 The Contact Codes: Haptics and Proxemics

Touch is our most intimate and involving form of communication and helps us to keep good relationships with others. That is why we use expressions like "Let's stay in touch," "I'll contact you when I get back," and "I was touched" by what another person said or did.

—Stanley E. Jones, 1999, p. 192.

That all are aware of personal space to some degree is readily apparent from some of the verbal usages in our language. We talk about someone "keeping his or her distance," or complain when we perceive others "invading our territory"...When someone is pressing another on an issue, the other may (impolitely) respond, "Keep out of my face," or (certainly more politely), "Give me breathing room."

—Larry Smeltzer, John Waltman, & Donald Leonard, 1999, p. 184.

As these quotes suggest, touch and space are such important forms of communication that people use words such as "close" and "distant" to describe their relationships and feelings. One reason that touch and distance are referred to so often in our language is that both of these communication codes engage our senses in a particularly strong way. When we are close enough to touch someone, our senses are stimulated and we are usually highly involved in the interaction. Of course, sometimes people do not want to be involved in an interaction. Instead they prefer to be distant. Too much physical closeness can make people feel uncomfortable and vulnerable. Our senses can become so highly engaged that we need to decrease sensory stimulation by looking away, backing up, or even pushing someone out of our way.

In this chapter we discuss two nonverbal codes that are related to sensory stimulation and people's needs for closeness and distance: haptics and proxemics. *Haptics* refers to the perception and use of touch as communication. *Proxemics* refers to the perception, use, and structuring of space as communication. In addition to having the ability to increase sensory stimulation, these two nonverbal codes are similar in that they help make interaction engaging and immediate, and they can lead to either positive or negative evaluations. For example, when someone stands close to you, it can be a "turn-on" or a "turn-off," depending on the situation, the attractiveness of the person, and the type of relationship you share. Similarly, sometimes you welcome people into your private territory (such as your home or apartment), but other times you would be upset if someone invaded your space. To help you better understand how these two nonverbal codes function, we discuss why each is important in our every day life. We also describe the types of messages that are commonly communicated through each of these codes.

Haptics

Touch is the first sense to develop and probably the last sense to leave us when we die; it is also the most intimate and sophisticated of our senses (Hansen, 2007; Reite, 1990; Sachs, 1988). As Sachs (1988) put it, touch is "the foundation for communication with the world around us, and probably the single sense that is as old as life itself" (p. 28). Children can cope without sight or hearing, but, as discussed next, they are likely to suffer grave psychological and physical consequences if they are deprived of touch.

The Importance of Touch

Desmond Morris once noted that we are a touch-starved society. Indeed, research suggests that many people do not receive enough touch. Yet touch is important for emotional and psychological well-being, starting from the time we spend in the womb and extending into old age (Reite, 1990). Not only does touch provide the first means of communication between infants and their mothers, but it also helps children understand and explore their environment, including their social relationships with others (Hertenstein, 2002; Hertenstein, Verkamp, Kerestes, & Holmes, 2006; Moszkowski & Stack, 2007). Children first learn how to classify objects, people, and experiences as soft, warm, harsh, rough, and so forth based on their early tactile experiences. Learning to be comfortable with touch is also a key ingredient in the recipe for developing healthy personal relationships. In fact, numerous studies have shown that touch stimulates infants to reach their full social and intellectual potential and helps children grow up to be emotionally secure (e.g., Caulfield, 2000; Fisher, Rytting, & Heslin, 1976; Frank, 1971, 1972; Montagu, 1978; Morris, 1967, 1971; Perry, 2002).

A series of famous studies by Harlow and his colleagues helps illustrate the importance of touch to mammals (Harlow, 1958; Harlow, Harlow, & Hansen, 1963; Harlow & Zimmerman, 1958). In these studies, infant monkeys were raised in isolation from their mothers. The experimenters then set up two types of "surrogate mothers": a hard wire mesh "mother" that supplied food through a bottle, and a soft terrycloth-covered "mother" equipped with a light bulb for warmth. The infant monkeys spent up to 18 hours a day clinging to the warm terrycloth-covered mothers. In contrast, they visited the wire mothers only long enough to get nourishment. Harlow and his colleagues concluded that contact comfort was a primary need in higher-order mammals. The infant monkeys in these studies were clearly more attached to the mothers who provided them with warmth and touch than to those who provided them with food. Therefore, although food is essential for survival, touch is more important when it comes to providing emotional security.

Research on humans leads to similar conclusions. Early evidence for the importance of touch in human development comes from Montagu's (1978) book on the human significance of the skin. Montagu summarized evidence from orphanages and children's hospitals in the 19th and early 20th centuries. During this time, the mortality rate among infants in these institutions was a staggering 90 to 100%. Many of these children died from a disease called marasmus, which means "wasting away." Although these children received adequate food, they were seldom held. There were simply not enough caregivers to tend to the tactile needs of the large number of infants in these institutions. As a result, many of them died from problems that were spurred by a lack of loving touch. These children often became depressed and nonresponsive, and some of them would sit rocking back and forth in a daze for hours, whereas others bit themselves or banged their heads against their cribs. These types of actions, along with depression and a lack of motivation to live, probably made these infants more susceptible to catching disease and less likely to recover when they did. In a set of classic reports, Spitz (1945, 1946) summarized statistical evidence from various orphanages throughout the world and came to similar conclusions. When children were not touched, they tended to die before their first birthdays. Even if they survived, they tended to develop psychological problems. However, Spitz found that babies thrived in an environment where women from the community came to the orphanage to cuddle them on a consistent basis.

More recent research has demonstrated that tactile stimulation during the first year and a half of life is essential for healthy brain development; children who fail to receive adequate stimulation have underdeveloped pathways in the parts of the brain that process social and emotional information (Gerhart, 2004; Perry, 2002). Some research even shows that people who suffered from tactile deprivation during early childhood have brains that are about 20% smaller than children who have received normal or high levels of stimulation (Honig, 2005).

The consequences for children who are raised in isolation are even more severe. One famous case involves a girl named Genie who was locked up in a dark room in her Los Angeles area home for more than 10 years (Rymer, 1994). Genie had virtually no social interaction with others. She was given just enough food and water to survive, and she spent much of her time strapped onto a toilet seat. When Genie was finally rescued, psychologists and language specialists worked with her extensively. Although there was every indication that Genie was born without any physical or mental problems, she struggled to learn language and to interact socially. She was able to learn words, but she was never able to string them together to make sentences. Similarly, she displayed some social behaviors, such as smiling, and was able to show affection, but she also engaged in abnormal behavior, such as excessive rocking and banging her body against walls. Scientists concluded that Genie's emotional and cognitive development was irrecoverably harmed by her lack of early social interaction.

Whether or not children grow up in orphanages or suffer from some degree of social isolation, touch appears to be essential to their well-being and future happiness (Caulfield, 2000). When babies have mothers who consistently come and comfort them when they cry, they are more likely to be cooperative and independent as toddlers. By contrast, when babies have mothers who do not comfort them very much, they tend to be uncooperative as toddlers, and when babies have mothers who are inconsistent (sometimes they comfort them; other times they don't), they are likely to be anxious and clingy as toddlers (Ainsworth, Blehar, Waters, & Wall, 1978). Studies of low birth-weight infants show that children develop better coordination and stronger motor skills if their mothers hold them longer and stimulate them more during feedings (Weiss, Wilson, & Morrison, 2004). Low-weight infants are also less likely to be aggressive at 2 years old if they received frequent affectionate touch, rather than harsh touch, when they were 3 months old (Weiss, Wilson, St. John-Seed, & Paul, 2001). Similarly, premature babies gain weight more quickly and go home earlier when nurses massage them frequently (Honig, 2005). When children are raised by warm and affectionate parents who cuddle them when they are young, they are also more likely to develop the ability to maintain happy relationships with spouses, children, and friends when they are adults (Goleman, 1991). People who have positive recollections about being touched by caregivers when they were children are more likely to report being self-confident as adults (Jones & Brown, 1996). Thus, the type of touch shown in Photo 6.1 is essential for healthy social and emotional development in childhood and beyond.

Research also suggests that touch is important to one's health throughout the lifespan. Studies have shown that when people pet an animal or breast-feed a baby, their blood pressure goes down and they feel content (Collins & McNicholas, 1998; Guerrero, 2000). Holding hands with a relational partner or caregiver can lessen the threat response that is stimulated in the brain in reaction to stress, fear, or medical procedures (Coan, Schaefer, & Davidson, 2006; Moon & Cho, 2001). Heart patients may experience a reduction in anxiety when they receive comforting and task-related touch from nurses (Weiss, 1990). Female patients reported

PHOTO 6.1   *Loving touch is essential for healthy social and physical development.*

feeling less fearful about having surgery if a nurse touched them in a comforting manner when explaining the procedure (Whitcher & Fisher, 1979). Many other studies have examined the effects that touch by nurses has on patients (for review, see Routasalo, 1999). These studies suggest that a nurse's touch has little effect on biological states, such as heart rate and blood pressure. However, patients report being comforted and feeling calmer after being touched by nurses. Patients also report having more positive attitudes and engaging in friendlier behavior toward nurses who touch them (Routasalo, 1999).

People who express affection to others also experience health benefits, as a series of studies by Floyd and his colleagues has shown. For example, people who express affection show quicker physiological recovery from stress and have better metabolic and cardiovascular health (Floyd, Hesse, & Haynes, 2007). Expressing affection is also related to being happier, having less fear of intimacy, and feeling less depressed (Floyd et al., 2005).

Dimensions of Touch

Although touch can undoubtedly promote physical and psychological well-being, not all touches are the same. Touch can be affectionate and loving, condescending, or violent. Just as warm, loving touch can lead to positive outcomes, violent touch can lead to negative outcomes such as lowered self-esteem, stress, and illness.

Touches come in many different forms. We use everyday language to help us describe various forms of touch, including "hitting," "tugging," "caressing," "tapping," "pinching," "tackling," "guiding," "biting," "kissing," "rocking," and "pushing," just to name a few (Argyle, 1975; Morris, 1977). Although these terms are helpful in describing different types of touch, they do not tell the whole story. The same type of touch can send different messages. For example, a pat on the shoulder can be comforting when given by a good friend who is providing you with social support, or it can be condescending when administered by a rival who says "better luck next time" after being promoted instead of you. Similarly, you might welcome a kiss from someone you love, but back away immediately when someone you dislike tries to kiss you. As these examples show, the relationship between two people and the context in which the touch occurs are both important when people interpret touch.

People also interpret tactile behavior based on various dimensions of touch (Hertenstein, 2002; Weiss, 1979). These dimensions include intensity, duration, location, frequency, and the instrument of touch. *Intensity* refers to how soft or hard a touch is. For example, a "punch" can be playful if it is delivered softly or violent if it is delivered with force. *Duration* refers to how brief or prolonged the touch is. A couple might hold hands for a moment or for an hour. In this case, the duration might help define how much intimacy the relational partners communicate to each other. *Location* refers to the place where a person is touched. Touches to various body parts are interpreted differently. For example, a study showed that elderly residents in a nursing home evaluated touch above the wrist by nurses more positively than touch below the wrist (Hollinger & Buschmann, 1993). Another study showed that students evaluated male professors especially negatively when they were depicted as touching a student's thigh, yet men had positive reactions when female professors were depicted as touching a student's arm (Lannutti, Laliker, & Hale, 2001). *Frequency* describes the number of touches that occur. Does a father kiss his daughter once when he picks her up from daycare, or does he kiss her multiple times? Finally, the *instrument of touch* makes a difference. Although people usually touch with their hands, they can also touch with other body parts, such as feet, lips, and shoulders, or with objects, such as the tip of a pencil. For example, a mother might laugh and say "I'm going to get you" while tickling her son with a teddy bear.

Functions of Touch

Knowing the type of touch (such as a pat, caress, or shove) and the dimensions of touch (such as frequency, duration, and location) helps researchers understand the meanings behind various forms of tactile behavior; however, these two pieces of information do not always reveal the *purpose* of the touch. Researchers who are primarily interested in determining the purposes behind touch have taken a functional approach. A functional approach may also help explain sex differences in touch, as covered in Box 6.1.

At least three systems have been developed for classifying touch according to function. In the first of these systems, Heslin and Alper (1983) categorized touch based on the level of intimacy it displayed. Sexual touches were seen as the most intimate, followed by touches conveying love, and then friendship. Touches used to show social politeness were classified as fairly low in intimacy, whereas professional touches were seen as the least intimate of all. A more extensive classification system was developed by Jones and Yarbrough (1985), who based their categories on diary entries that included nearly 1,500 descriptions of actual contacts over a period of several days. Jones and Yarbrough identified seven main types of touch: positive affect, playful, control, task-related, ritualistic, accidental, and hybrid. A third study by Guerrero and Ebesu (1993) extended Jones and Yarbrough's study by observing young children interacting in public parks. They found that children used many of the same types of touch as adults, although as would be expected, they used less ritualistic forms of touch such as handshakes. The children also engaged in negative affect touches, which were not found in either the Heslin or Jones and Yarbrough studies. The following categories represent an integration of the findings from these three studies.

Instrumental Touch.   This type of touch, which was termed "professional-functional" by Heslin and Alper (1983) and "task-related" by Jones and Yarbrough (1985), is typically one-sided, task-oriented, and has little if any personal meaning. Simply put, this type of touch is instrumental because it helps people complete necessary tasks. When a doctor examines a patient, an usher guides people to their assigned seats, a teacher helps a student hold a pen properly, or a parent puts a child in a high chair, the touch is primarily task related. Jones and Yarbrough noted that some task-related touches are helpful but not necessary in accomplishing a task (hand-to-hand contact when a cashier returns money to a

---

BOX 6.1
Sex Differences in Touch

When men and women interact with one another, who is more likely to initiate touch—the man or the woman? The answer to this question is not as straightforward as you might expect. In public settings, men may initiate touch more often than women (Henley, 1973; Hertenstein, Verkamp, et al., 2006; Major, Schmidlin, & Williams, 1990). However, in private settings, women appear to initiate touch just as much or more than men (Major et al., 1990; Stier & Hall, 1984). Indeed, in their summary of the literature, Burgoon and Bacue (2003) concluded that, in general, women touch and are touched more than men.

The stage of the relationship also makes a difference. Three different observational studies examining couples in places such as movie theaters, shopping malls, and zoos, have demonstrated that men are more likely to initiate touch in the beginning stages of romantic relationships, whereas women are more likely to initiate touch in marriages (Guerrero & Andersen, 1994; Willis & Briggs, 1992; Willis & Dodds, 1998). One explanation for this difference is that men use touch as a means of social control in the early stages of relationships, whereas women use touch as a way to communicate affection and maintain relationships after relationships are established. In line with the second part of this explanation, a study by Hanzal et al. (2008) showed that married women rated touch as

more affectionate (loving, warm, and pleasant) than unmarried women.

In another study, Hall and Veccia (1990) found that although men and women touched one another equally overall, there were dramatic differences when age and body part were considered. For touches involving the hand, males tended to touch females more. Non-hand touches seemed to be initiated by females, although these differences were small (57% and 56%, respectively). It is also important to realize that people in the under 30 group were less likely to be married or in long-term relationships, so the findings could be related to the stage of the relationship. Willis and Dodds (1998), who examined both age and relationship type, found that men under 20 who were in the courtship stage of their relationship tended to initiate the most touch, especially to intimate body parts such as the lips, face, and knees. Among the women, those in their 40s were more likely to initiate touch than those in their 30s, 20s, or under 20. Finally, there are also differences in touch when the sex composition of a dyad and the setting are considered. Many studies have found that, in the United States, female friends touch each other considerably more than male friends do (Floyd, 2000). The exception is during sports, when men pat, hug, and bang against one another. The masculine context of a sporting event appears to make man-to-man touch socially appropriate.

---

customer), but other task-related touches are necessary to accomplish the task (helping a person put on a coat).

Edwards (1981) described several specific forms of instrumental touch. *Information pickup* touches involve tasks such as taking a pulse or feeling someone's forehead to see if he or she has a fever. Here touch is used to gain information. *Movement-facilitation* touches involve giving someone a boost or carrying someone to safety, such as a firefighter carrying a child out of a burning building. *Prompting* touches involve providing manual guidance in learning. A golf pro might use manual touch to help clients with their swings. Similarly, a preschool teacher might guide children's hands as they learn to place blocks in a shape sorter. Finally, Edwards discussed *ludic* touches, which occur as part of games, such as playing patty-cake or tackling someone during a football game. Guerrero and Ebesu (1993) found that these kinds of touches were an integral part of children's play, with children touching one another during games such as tag and ring-around-the-rosy, as well as touching while engaging in tasks such as building a sand castle or stacking blocks.

Socially Polite Touch.   These touches are relatively formal and governed by social norms and rules of politeness. In fact, Jones and Yarbrough (1985) labeled this type of touch "ritualistic." Many forms of socially polite touch occur during greetings and departures. Handshakes are a common type of ritualistic touch used in business situations or when meeting people at social functions for the first time. Across two studies, between 61% and 78% of patients reported that they prefer having a doctor who shakes their hand when greeting them (Davis, Wiggins, Mercado, & O'Sullivan, 2007; Makoul, Zick, & Green, 2007). Increasingly, people are using virtual handshakes in situations involving teleconferencing or other technologies (Paterson, 2006), which shows how important touch is in business situations. (For more on new technologies and handshaking, see Box 6.2).

Research has shown that individuals develop a fairly consistent handshake, so that the way you shake hands with one person is similar to the way you shake hands with another person (Bailenson & Yee, 2007; Chaplin, Phillips, Brown, Clanton, & Stein, 2000). During initial interactions, there is a fairly strong relationship between style of handshaking and first impressions. Specifically, people who shake hands with a firm, complete (but not hard) grip while giving eye contact are rated more positively than people who offer a weaker handshake (Chaplin et al., 2000). Individuals who are extroverted and open to new experiences are more likely to have firm handshakes, and men tend to give firmer handshakes than women (Chaplin et al., 2000).

Pats to the shoulder, arm, or lower back are also sometimes used as part of greeting and departure rituals. Although these types of touch are common within U.S. culture, some research suggests that overweight individuals receive less casual touch, such as handshakes and pats on the arm, than do other individuals (Holmes, 2005). This discrepancy in tactile behavior directed toward overweight and non-overweight individuals is a subtle form of discrimination that most people probably do not notice.

Researchers have also examined the timing of haptic behavior in relation to verbal statements during greetings and departures. Jones and Yarbrough (1985) found that people tend to verbally greet ("Hi, it's nice to meet you") or depart ("I'll miss you") from others before or during the touch, rather than after. Thus, if you observed people's behavior at a business meeting, you would likely see people introduce themselves right before or during a handshake. Similarly, if you observed behavior at airports, you would likely see people touching right before the passenger moved toward the departure gate.

BOX **6.2**

New Technologies and Virtual Interpersonal Touch

New technologies are being developed to incorporate touch into virtual environments, including gaming and chat rooms. Joysticks can function as one such haptic device. In a study by Bailenson and Yee (2007), a joystick was used to simulate a handshake. In some cases, the joystick was programmed so that people received their own virtual handshake back. Interestingly, men liked the handshakes that mimicked their own handshake more than women did. Other new technologies include sending vibrations from one computer keyboard or object to another; creating avatars (which are digital representations of oneself, such as a cartoon-type character) that other people can touch and feel; using hand-held objects to play touch-based games; and employing forced-feedback techniques so that it feels like two (or more) people are sharing an object over distance.

Imagine the possibilities these new technologies hold. Partners in a long-distance relationship may be able to "touch" each other across the miles. Businesspeople from around the globe could share a virtual handshake. Indeed, Bailenson and Yee noted that virtual interpersonal touch has many unique features. In the future, people may be able to produce "handshakes" that mirror their partners, "hold" a potential dating partner's hand without worrying about sweaty palms, or shake hands with 10 people at once. Haptic devices can also help people in cyberspace communicate their emotions more clearly (Bailenson, Yee, Brave, Merget, & Koslow, 2007).

Virtual interpersonal touch may also revolutionize computer-mediated communication by creating a greater sense of immediacy, togetherness, and trust than currently exists in such environments. For example, studies have shown that people who engage in collaborative tasks or play games in virtual environments perform better and feel closer to one another if haptic devices are utilized (Basdogan, Ho, Slater, & Shrivinvasan, 1998; Sallnas, Rassmus-Grohn, & Sjostrom, 2000). In another study, people worked on a screen-based maze with a collaborative partner or against an opponent. Interpersonal virtual touch increased trust in the competitive situation, but decreased trust between partners in the cooperative situation. As other findings on interpersonal virtual touch emerge, researchers will get a clearer picture of the role that haptic devices may play in the virtual interaction of the future.

Other types of socially polite touches include guiding an elderly person or child across the street, touching someone's arm in a crowded room to avoid bumping into them, and lining up and touching the hands of the players of an opposing team after a ball game. All of these types of touch coincide with rules of social appropriateness. Therefore, they typically send a message of politeness rather than of intimacy. Interestingly, Guerrero and Ebesu (1993) found that young children do not use socially polite touches very often, presumably because they have not yet learned all the rules of social appropriateness.

Touch can also be used in conjunction with verbal messages to help people present socially polite messages. A study by Trees and Manusov (1998) examined how nonverbal behaviors, including touch, help soften messages that could threaten a person's self-image. In their study, people evaluated how polite a criticism about a friend was. When the criticism was delivered using supportive nonverbal behaviors, including touch, a pleasant facial expression, and a soft voice, the study's participants perceived it to be more polite.

Affectionate Touch.   This type of touch reflects general friendship, warmth, and intimacy without necessarily conveying sexual attraction. Moreover, this type of touch is primarily used to show affection, rather than to give comfort, show appreciation, or congratulate someone. Common forms of affectionate touch include hugs, hand-holding, and some forms of kissing (Derlega, Lewis, Harrison, & Costanza, 1989; Floyd & Morman, 1998; Morris, 1977). Putting an arm around another person's shoulder or waist or softly touching someone's face can also reflect intimacy (Lee & Guerrero, 2001). Indeed, face touch, hand-holding, arm around the shoulder, and arm around the waist are perceived as highly to moderately intimate forms of touch (Burgoon, 1991; Burgoon & Walther, 1990). This is probably because these forms of touch are fairly invasive. The face is a vulnerable part of one's body, so letting someone touch your face involves trust. Letting someone invade your space by reaching around your waist or shoulders requires a similar level of trust. Thus, it is no wonder that people back away when those they dislike or do not know try to engage in these forms of touch.

Stroking, rubbing, interlocking fingers while holding hands, and hugging are also special ways of showing love and affection (Derlega et al., 1989; Floyd & Morman, 1998). In a creative series of studies by Hertenstein, Keltner, App, Bulleit, and Jaskolka (2006), people from the United States and Spain tried to identify the emotions of a person who touched them from behind a curtain. Love was associated with strokes, rubs, and interlocked fingers. In fact, of the eight emotions people had to choose from, love was the only emotion that was associated with interlocked fingers. Think about how you hold hands with different people. Holding hands without interlocking your fingers is generally considered to be less intimate than having your fingers entwined.

Some types of hugs are also more intimate than others. Floyd (1999) conducted a study that compared people's perceptions of three different types of hugs: neck-waist, criss-cross, and engulfing. Imagine that two sisters, Rachel and Andrea, meet and hug. Rachel puts her arms around Andrea's neck, while Andrea puts her arms around Rachel's waist. Floyd labeled this the neck-waist hug (see Photo 6.2, left). Now imagine that each woman puts one arm over her sister's shoulder, and the other arm under her sister's shoulder. Floyd called this the criss-cross hug (see Photo 6.2, middle). Finally, imagine that Rachel has her arms on her own chest while Andrea hugs her. This is called an engulfing hug (see Photo 6.2, right). Which of these hugs do you think reflects the most intimacy and closeness? Floyd found the criss-cross hug to be perceived as the most affectionate, followed by the neck-waist touch. The engulfing hug was rated as conveying the least affection, perhaps because it was perceived as more one-sided than the other two types of hugs.

Friends, family members, and romantic couples are all likely to use hugs to show affection, but romantic partners may have the widest latitude in terms of

PHOTO 6.2 *Variations of the hug; from left to right: the neck-waist hug; the criss-cross hug; and the engulfing hug.*

the types of touch they can use to display affection. Guerrero and Andersen (1991) found that hand-holding was the most frequent type of public touch used by romantic couples. The couples in their study also commonly put their arms around one another's waists or shoulders and touched one another's backs or buttocks. In Guerrero and Andersen's study, seriously dating couples used these types of touch more than casually dating or married couples. A recent study by Hanzal, Segrin, and Dorros (2008) also suggests the type of relationship two people have influences perceptions of touch. In their study, people were surveyed to see how they would react to touch in different body regions by their significant others. Married women perceived touch to reflect more warmth and love than did unmarried women. The reverse was true for men; unmarried men perceived touch to reflect more warmth and love than did married men.

Comforting Touch. These types of touch are intended to provide social support and comfort to a distressed other. Jones and Yarbrough (1985) found that most touches reflecting social support involved using the hand or an arm and were directed to one or two body parts. For example, patting someone on the shoulder, reaching out and squeezing someone's arm, and giving someone a hug can all express comfort. In the study by Hertenstein, Keltner, et al. (2006), in which people identified the emotions of someone who touched them from behind a curtain, the following forms of touch were related to expressing sympathy or comfort: patting, stroking, and rubbing.

In a study of nonverbal comforting behaviors, Dolin and Booth-Butterfield (1993) had college students describe how they would react if they were trying to comfort a roommate who was distressed over a recent romantic breakup. The students frequently mentioned that they would use touch to comfort their distressed roommates. In fact, the most common behavior mentioned was hugs, with 42%

of the students saying that they would hug their roommates by either engaging in a full-body hug or hugging them around the shoulders. Recall that hugs can also be a type of affectionate touch. This shows that the same form of touch can have different functions depending on the context. Hugs are likely to be interpreted as comforting only in contexts in which the recipient is in need of comforting.

The same is true for other types of potentially comforting touch, such as pats and handholding. In Dolin and Booth-Butterfield's study, *pats*, which were defined as using short, repetitive movements such as patting the distressed roommate's arm or shoulder, were mentioned by 27% of the students. Nearly 35% of the students mentioned other forms of touch, such as holding the person's hand, stroking the roommate's hair, or letting the roommate cry on their shoulder. This study clearly suggests that people perceive touch to be an important vehicle by which to express comfort and social support.

Appreciative and Congratulatory Touch.   Although people use comforting touches in response to a person's distressed state, they also use touch in response to something positive a person does. Jones and Yarbrough (1985) gave several examples of appreciative touches, such as when a boss touches a worker on the shoulder and says, "you did a really great job handling things today" or when a woman kisses a close male friend on the cheek to thank him for cooking her dinner. In Hertenstein, Keltner, et al.'s (2006) study, people communicated messages of gratitude from behind a curtain by using touches with patting, stroking, and rubbing movement.

Congratulatory touches are also fairly common. We often hug our close friends, family members, and romantic partners when they do something that makes us feel proud. Or we might squeeze someone's hand in congratulations when we find out that he or she won an award or is about to be promoted. In Guerrero and Ebesu's (1993) study, elementary school-age children sometimes gave one another "high fives" as a way of saying "congratulations" during play.

Sexual Touch.   Heslin and Alper (1983) refer to sexual-arousal touches as the most intense and intimate form of physical contact. Sexual touch can be distinguished from friendly or affectionate touch in two primary ways. First, sexual touch is usually concentrated in more vulnerable areas of the body, such as the mouth, thigh, or genitals. Thus, the behaviors most associated with this form of touch include French kissing; "petting," which involves touching private body parts; and sexual intercourse. Second, sexual touch usually involves multiple kinds of touches that occur together and in sequences. For instance, Jones and Yarbrough (1985) gave the example of lovers embracing and then caressing as a prototypical expression of sexual intimacy. Sexual touch is a unique form of touch that is especially important in close, romantic relationships, but is also used during one-night stands, hookups, and friends-with-benefits relationships. In fact, sexual touch helps define all of these types of relationships as including a sexual (but not necessarily romantic) element. As Prager (1995) argued, sexual touch is particularly intimate because it allows lovers to share private aspects of themselves with one another in a way that is not shared with close friends and nonspousal family members. In general, both married and unmarried men tend to see touch as more sexual than women do (Hanzal et al., 2008).

Playful Touch.   This type of touch is designed to lighten an interaction and possibly give double meaning to a verbal message (Jones & Yarbrough, 1985). For example, you might tell a friend, "I hate always losing to you" while punching her or him playfully on the arm. Jones and Yarbrough classified playful touch as affectionate or aggressive. Both forms of touch help lighten an interaction. *Playful affection* includes behaviors such as saying, "how about a kiss?" in a joking way to an opposite-sex friend, followed by a quick kiss on the forehead. *Playful aggression* includes behaviors such as "getting someone back" by tickling them, engaging in mock aggression such as wrestling in a playful way, or curbing aggressive verbal comments with touch. For example, one of Yarbrough and Jones's participants reported following an aggressive comment to a waitress ("No, we don't want the check—tear it up") with a smile and light touch to her arm. Some studies suggest that certain types of touch, such as sitting on one's lap, tickling someone, or play wrestling are often interpreted differently by women and men. Women are more likely to perceive these types of touch as playful, whereas men are more likely to perceive them as sexual (Pisano, Wall, & Foster, 1986).

Control Touch.   These touches direct the behavior, attitude, or feeling state of another. Some control touches focus on persuading or gaining compliance from others. Yarbrough and Jones gave the example of a boss touching an employee on the shoulder and saying, "Could you get this done by 5 o'clock?" In this case, the touch to the shoulder communicates that the boss really wants the job done. Such touch may also be persuasive (Segrin, 1993). Other times control touches focus on gaining the attention of others and either shifting their perceptual focus or emphasizing a particular feeling state. For example, you might pat your companion on the shoulder and say, "Look at that!" (Jones & Yarbrough, 1985). This form of control touch appears to be fairly common among children. In Guerrero and Ebesu's (1993) study, young children were especially likely to pat someone on the back or arm with a hand or finger to try to gain attention.

Negative Affect Touch.   Neither Jones and Yarbrough (1985) nor Heslin and Alper (1983) included aggressive or negative affect touch in their classification systems. Perhaps this is because many adults have learned to inhibit these types of touch because they are hurtful and socially inappropriate. Adults who do engage in negative forms of touch may not report them in diary studies, because they know they are socially inappropriate. However, studies on relational violence suggest that physically aggressive touches do indeed occur. In fact, a national survey suggests that 16% of married couples experience physical violence within a given year, and surveys of high school students suggest that somewhere between 12% and 36% of these students have enacted or experienced physical violence in a dating relationship (Christopher & Lloyd, 2001). Relatively common types of violent touch include pushing, pulling, and pinching. Slapping, punching, and kicking are less common, whereas behaviors such as stabbing or beating up someone are less common still (Marshall, 1994).

Research on violence in romantic relationships indicates that men and women differ in the types of violent touch they are most likely to use. Although grabbing the partner suddenly or forcefully and pushing or shoving the partner are common forms of violent touch for both men and women, women are more likely to scratch or slap with the palm of their hand. Men, in contrast, are more likely to hold or pin down the partner, shake the partner, or otherwise handle the partner roughly (Marshall, 1994). It is also important to note that people can use touch as an aggressive or controlling action, or they can use touch to defend themselves against violent attacks.

Interestingly, children may use aggressive touch more often than adults, especially when in public situations. Guerrero and Ebesu (1993) found that aggressive touches, such as pushing someone or touching another child while trying to pull a toy away, are fairly common among preschool-age children. Young children also displayed negative affect by engaging in affection withdrawal. For example, one boy in the study pushed a girl away and said "no" when she tried to hug him. A study of a daycare center produced similar results, showing that children use spatial withdrawal and negative forms of touch to communicate dislike or preference for another person (Meyer & Driskill, 1997). For instance, during a conflict situation, a child moved to a different place in the circle so that she would be away from another child. In another instance, a child moved when another child tried to sit next to her. Some hitting and kicking were also observed in Meyer and Driskill's study. Negative forms of touch such as these appear to be used less frequently as children get older and learn norms of social appropriateness (Guerrero & Ebesu, 1993).

Hybrid Touch.   Hybrid touch combines various types of touch. According to Jones and Yarbrough's (1985) study, the most common type of hybrid touch combines affectionate and socially polite touch. In these cases, people use touch to say hello or good-bye while communicating intimacy and affection. Husbands and wives might kiss each other in the morning and evening when leaving for and returning from work. Friends might hug each other when reunited after a separation. Jones and Yarbrough noted that these types of hybrid touches tend to be more intense and affectionate the longer people have been separated from one another.

Although Jones and Yarbrough did not identify any other specific types of hybrid touches, other combinations could occur. Studies have shown that instrumental touch often fulfills multiple functions in interactions between adults and young children. A caregiver might hug a child after catching him or her during a game of tag (Meyer & Driskill, 1997) or tickle a child's feet while swinging the youngster (Guerrero & Ebesu, 1993), both of which are instrumental touches that also show affection. Studies of children undergoing cancer have also identified a hybrid type of touch that functions in both an instrumental and controlling way. For example, a caregiver may need to hold a child down during a treatment (Peterson et al., 2007). Parents were more likely to engage in these types of instrumental/controlling touches before and during procedures that were painful and distressing to the child, and they were more likely to engage in supportive touches after a painful procedure as a way to provide comfort (Peterson et al., 2007).

Other examples of hybrid touch abound. Teammates use high fives and pats on the butt to say "good job" (fulfilling a congratulatory/appreciative function) and to try to "psyche one another up" to win the game (fulfilling an instrumental function). A mother might slap her son's hand to keep him from touching the stove, which could signal both control and negative affect. You might put suntan lotion on your romantic partner's back, which accomplishes a task but also shows affection. Thus, in everyday life, it is often difficult to categorize a particular type of touch as falling under a single category. It can also be difficult to interpret some types of touch. For instance, how do you know when someone is using real versus mock aggression? If your romantic partner is wrestling with you, when does it cross the line and become threatening rather than playful? The answers to questions such as this would help us understand the communication dynamics behind haptic behavior even better than we do today.

Proxemics

Haptics, or touch, occurs when there is no space between people. When there is space between people, the amount of space and the degree to which space is connected to one's territory have implications for the interaction at hand. Just as people need touch to feel close and connected, so too do people need space to maintain privacy and personal space.

The Importance of Space and Territory

Several studies suggest it is important for animals (including humans) to have adequate space. The need to regulate and protect territory and personal space may be especially prevalent in crowded urban areas. As Rosenbloom (2006) put it, "with the population in the United States climbing above 300 million, urban corridors becoming denser and people with wealth searching for new ways to separate themselves from the masses, interest in the issue of personal space—that invisible force field around your body—is intensifying" (p. G1).

Defining Territory. Before considering the extent to which people need space, we should distinguish between the concepts of territory and personal space. A territory is a fixed geographic area that is occupied, controlled, and defended by a person or group as their exclusive domain (Altman, 1975; Altman & Haythorn, 1967; Goffman, 1963a; Hall, 1959; Hediger, 1961; Lyman & Scott, 1967; Sommer, 1966, 1969; Stea, 1965). Territories often house valuable resources or possessions, such as food and water, diaries, computers, jewelry, or money. Other times territories are simply spaces that allow people some level of privacy. Whether the resource is shelter, food, possessions, or privacy, the owner(s) of the territory guard and protect these resources from invaders.

A complex set of social rules guides how people should use various territories. Take, for example, a home that is occupied by a family of three: a single mother and her son and daughter. The three of them are likely to guard the home as their mutual territory. However, within the home, each person will likely have mapped out his or her own special territorie The mother may view her bedroom, bathroom, and den as private territories that the children should not enter without permission. Similarly, the children may view their bedrooms as private territories that the mother should only enter under certain circumstances (such as after knocking or to put laundry on their beds without going into their private dresser drawers). These types of territorial norms and rules are negotiated within groups or social units.

Defining Personal Space.   In contrast to territory, *personal space* is an invisible, adjustable bubble of space that people carry around with them. Individuals actively maintain this personal space bubble as a way to protect themselves from physical harm and emotional discomfort (Burgoon & Jones, 1976; Ciolek, 1983; Dosey & Meisels, 1969; Hall, 1990; Hayduk, 1978; Horowitz, Duff, & Stratton, 1964; Sommer, 1959). Recently, social scientists have extended the definition of personal space to include "not only the invisible bubble around the body, but all the senses," with personal space being violated by loud noises, unpleasant smells, people's cell phones ringing, or someone staring at you in an elevator (Rosenbloom, 2006). Imagine you are walking down a fairly crowded street at sunset. Even though the street is a bit crowded, you are likely to feel threatened if a stranger walks too closely behind you or if a car suddenly backfires. In very crowded places, such as subways during rush hour, it can be difficult for people to maintain comfortable levels of personal space. To compensate, people often sit still and avoid eye contact with others. As these examples illustrate, personal space can be thought of as an individual's *perceived self-boundary* or *body-buffer zone* (Horowitz et al., 1964; Katz, 1937) in that it provides a buffer against physical and emotional threats. Similarly, Scott (1988) conceptualized personal space boundaries as invisible boundaries that separate a person's internal self (body, mind, and spirit) from the external environment.

Of course, personal space boundaries vary depending on an individual's culture, personality, and the situation at hand (Petronio, 1991). Some people need more space than others, and thus have larger personal space bubbles. For instance, shy people generally have stronger needs for personal space than do outgoing people, and women generally require less space than men (Andersen, 2008). The situation also makes a difference. Generally, you will require less space in informal settings with close relational partners than in formal settings with strangers or acquaintances. This can easily be seen at a movie theater. When you enter with your friends, you are likely to look for a place in the theater where you can sit together but where there will still be a seat or two between your group and other people. In contrast, think how uncomfortable you would feel if a stranger sat right next to you in an uncrowded movie theater! As we shall see next, a number of studies suggest that this type of discomfort is a common response to crowding and invasions of personal space. (For more on how personal space impacts our daily lives, see Box 6.3.)

Territorial Crowding and Personal Space Invasion.   Two famous classic studies provide particularly vivid illustrations of the adverse effects that crowding, territorial invasion, and the lack of personal space can have on animals: Christian, Flyer, and Davis's (1961) study of Sika deer, and Calhoun's (1962, 1966) study of rats.

BOX **6.3**

Proxemics in the Modern World

In a *New York Times* article, Stephanie Rosenbloom describes some of the ways that proxemics and personal space operate in the modern world by discussing the following findings:

- A survey conducted in 2006 on the website TripAdvisor found that airline travelers would rather pay for larger seats and increased leg room than for better food or luxuries such as massages.
- A recent study by Stanford University researchers showed that people playing a virtual reality game called Second Life moved their avatars (the digital representations of themselves in the game) when other avatars or objects got too close to them, which mirrors what people do in real life when their space is invaded.
- Researchers can predict a variety of behavioral choices based on their knowledge of proxemics, including what areas of an elevator fill up first, where people will sit at library tables (a corner seat first followed by the chair that is diagonally opposite to it), and why people find some restaurants more comfortable than others.

- Researchers have also used proxemics to explain the popularity of devices such as iPods, which allow people to create their own private space in the midst of a crowd. The concept of personal space also helps explain why dimming the lights makes an environment more conductive for getting acquainted with someone—it reduces the overall level of sensory stimulation. Proxemics and the idea of freeway crowding has even been used to explain road rage.
- Research also provides examples of times when crowding is pleasant, including seeing a funny movie in a crowded rather than empty theater, running alongside dozens of other athletes in a marathon, and dancing at a busy nightclub. As Dr. Robert Krauss told Rosenbloom, personal space violations make enjoyable situations more enjoyable and aversive situations less tolerable.

Source: Information summarized from Rosenbloom (2006).

In the 1950s, Sika deer were thriving on James Island in the Chesapeake Bay. They lived in an ideal habitat that was free of natural predators, and they had ample supplies of food and water. These conditions caused the deer population to swell until living space became very crowded and the deer started to die off. In fact, the population suddenly decreased from 300 to 80 deer, with large numbers of deer dying around the same time. You might suspect that the deer died from some type of contagious disease, but that was not the case. Autopsies revealed that the deer had greatly enlarged adrenal glands. Most likely, these glands became enlarged because of the increased adrenaline produced during stressful situations such as overcrowding. Since high levels of adrenaline can become fatal over time, Christian and his colleagues concluded that overpopulation and the resultant lack of living space created the stress that eventually led to the demise of so many deer. In a way, nature was correcting the problem of overcrowding.

Calhoun's study of the effects of overcrowding on rats found similar results. He created a seemingly ideal environment for a group of rats by building a pen that had plenty of water, food, air, nesting materials, and opportunity for social contact. As with the Sika deer, the rat population initially thrived under these circumstances. However, these conditions eventually led to high levels of reproduction and overcrowding, which then led to a host of destructive behaviors among the rats, such as sexual dysfunction, cannibalism, hyperactivity, and vicious attacks. There was also an increase in illness among the rats, as well as an increase in premature births and miscarriages.

Although research suggests that humans are better able to adapt to overcrowding and the lack of personal space than are other animals (Altman, 1975; Edney, 1976; Vine, 1975), humans also show signs of discomfort and stress when their privacy is invaded. Early research showed that the combination of crowding and heat reduces social interaction and makes it more likely that people will dislike one another and act aggressively (Griffit & Veitch, 1971). A study by Stokols, Ohlig, and Resnick (1978) suggested that students living in crowded dormitories were ill more often and earned lower grades than students living in more spacious accommodations. Of course, these effects are probably not only due to the discomfort experienced because of crowding, but also due to the greater likelihood of having more germs around and being more distracted in the crowded environment.

Yet even subtle differences in crowding appear to affect discomfort. For instance, Aiello, Epstein, and Karlin (1975) examined the effects of crowding on dormitory residents by comparing the experiences of those who had one dorm mate with the experiences of those who had two dorm mates. The rooms were set up identically except for the number of occupants. These researchers found that students in the three-person rooms experienced more stress, although they did not fare worse academically. Follow-up studies by Aiello and his colleagues also demonstrated that crowded dormitories promote social tension, stress, relationship dissatisfaction among roommates, helplessness, and competitiveness, especially when dormitory residents had little control over their environments (Aiello, Baum, & Gormley, 1981; Baum, Aiello, & Calesnick, 1978; Reddy, Baum, Fleming, & Aiello, 1981). These studies also suggest that crowding produces the most aversive effects when people do not see themselves as part of a smaller group or coalition within the crowded environment. A more recent study by Tripathi and Tripathi (2005) examined crowding in various types of social situations. As in the earlier dormitory studies, crowding was related to higher levels of stress.

Some studies have also shown that juvenile delinquency and crime increase as crowding increases (Sadalla, 1978). Other researchers have argued that housing projects in urban areas foster crime because large numbers of people live in high-rise buildings with no sense of uniqueness or territorial ownership (Newman, 1972). In contrast to these studies, Franklin, Franklin, and Pratt (2006) found that when the results of different studies on prison overcrowding were analyzed together, there was little evidence for a connection between crowding and increased violence. Nonetheless, the swelling population at many prisons is an important political and social issue, as is the need to revitalize urban areas across the United States.

The swell of people who left urban areas for suburbia in the 1960s and 1970s provides some evidence of people's desire to live in less crowded territories.

Crowding also has implications for consumer satisfaction while shopping. In general, people are less satisfied with their shopping experience when a store is crowded (Eroglu & Machleit, 1990). However, the relationship between crowding and having an unpleasant shopping experience is not always straightforward, as three later studies by Machleit, Eroglu, and Mantel (2000) showed. People are more likely to experience dissatisfaction due to spatial crowding as opposed to social crowding. *Spatial crowding* is related to the number of nonhuman elements in the environment, such as clothing racks, narrowness of lanes, and the number of products being displayed. *Social crowding*, on the other hand, refers to the number of people and interactions in the retail environment. People are also more likely to experience dissatisfaction when the crowding leads to stress and negative emotions like anger and frustration. Some people have a higher tolerance for crowding than others; those individuals are less likely to experience negative arousal than are those with a lower tolerance experience. Finally, the type of retail store makes a difference, with the link between crowding and dissatisfaction with a shopping experience stronger in non-discount stores than discount stores. In discount stores, crowded conditions may symbolize more merchandise at better prices, with consumers eager to buy the store's products (Machleit et al., 2000).

Positive Effects of Crowding and Close Proximity. Despite the evidence linking crowding to discomfort and other negative emotions, it is important to keep in mind that people do not always experience discomfort in crowded situations. Altman (1975) made an important distinction between density and psychological crowding. *Density* refers to the number of people who occupy a certain territory and can be measured in terms of the number of people per square foot or square mile. The more people per square foot or mile, the more crowded the territory is on a physical level. However, on a psychological level, *crowding* is only partially related to density. In some situations, such as trying to find a wave to surf or trying to concentrate while taking a test, you might feel crowded if only one or two people are near you. In other cases, such as in a nightclub or at a sporting event, you might not feel crowded even though hundreds of people are around you. In fact, Hocking (1982) found that many people feel excitement rather than discomfort when they are part of a large crowd. Think of a college football game or a political rally. Would you have more fun at these functions if they were sparsely attended or if they were packed with other people who cared about the game or the political issue at hand? Research suggests that the latter environment would be more stimulating and exciting.

In interpersonal encounters, close proximity can be a sign of great attraction and liking. A considerable body of literature suggests that people show liking and attraction through *nonverbal immediacy behaviors* (Mehrabian, 1981), such as smiling, touch, eye contact, and close proximity. These behaviors signal approachability, convey interpersonal warmth, are arousing, and create both psychological and physical closeness (Andersen, 1985). A number of proxemic behaviors have been classified as immediate and involving, including close interpersonal distancing, forward lean, and direct body orientation (Coker & Burgoon, 1987; Patterson, 1983). In fact, some studies have shown that proxemic behaviors are the most important immediacy behaviors when it comes to showing attraction and liking (Burgoon, Buller, Hale, & deTurck, 1984). Similarly, behaviors such as voluntarily sharing space with someone, letting someone enter your private territory, and moving in with someone send messages of closeness and trust (Andersen, 1985).

Types of Territory

In addition to examining the effects proximity has on people and relationships, researchers have focused on categorizing different types of territory and conversational distancing. We will begin by looking at types of territory. The two most popular systems for categorizing territory were developed by Altman (1975), who distinguished among primary, secondary, and public territory; and Lyman and Scott (1967), who discussed body, home, interactional, and public territories.

Body Territory.   As the name implies, body territory encompasses a person's physical body as well as the personal space bubble that surrounds it. Of all types of territories, Lyman and Scott (1967) argued that body territory is the most private and is defended the most vigorously when invaded. People want to be able to control who touches them, where they are touched, and how close others get to them. In most societies, laws protect people's body territories by punishing people who assault and/or rape others, and many companies in the United States have formal policies regarding touch and sexual harassment. People also believe that they have a right to adorn their body territories in ways they see fit. Branding oneself with a tattoo and piercing one's ears, navel, or tongue are seen by many as extremely personal ways of expressing oneself using body territory.

Research has also examined different types of body territory that relate to people's personal space bubbles. Goffman (1971), in particular, defined several body territories (which he labeled "territories of self") that regulate how large or small our personal space bubbles are. The body territories Goffman defined generally revolve around environmental structures, social norms, tasks, and adornments. Sometimes, environmental structures (or "stalls" as Goffman called them) delineate the amount of personal space that should be considered private. For example, when people are in confessionals, showers, or partitioned workspaces, they expect these environments to be for their private use. Perhaps this expectation adds to people's irritation when someone takes up two parking spaces at the local mall or grocery store. Other times, personal space bubbles are regulated by social norms. We expect people to wait their turn in line rather than cutting in, and to maintain an appropriate amount of space between themselves and the person in front of them while waiting. Similarly, when we withdraw money at an ATM, we expect the person behind us to give us adequate space to conduct our transaction in privacy. Sometimes personal space is regulated more by the task at hand than social norms. Some examples of this include giving someone enough space to perform a double axel at the skating rink or staying out of the kitchen while your partner is cooking a complicated meal. Finally, Goffman described several kinds of adornment that help regulate body territories, including clothing, jewelry, briefcases, and purses. People know that these objects should not be touched without the owner's implicit or explicit permission.

Primary Territory. Primary or "home" territories are central to people's daily lives. These territories include places such as houses, offices, and cars, where people spend a great deal of time. These territories clearly "belong" to a particular person or group of people, and others know that they are not supposed to enter without permission. As with body territories, most societies have laws that protect people's primary territory. For example, breaking and entering, grand theft auto, and to a lesser extent, vandalism, are serious crimes.

People also use primary territory as a place to retreat, both physically and psychologically. In our homes, for example, we can let down our guard and not worry so much about the impressions we are making on others. Think about the way people behave in their cars. They might sing loudly to music, scratch themselves in private places, or blow their noses loudly—all behaviors they would be less likely to engage in when in public places. This is because cars are treated as primary territories that afford a relatively high degree of privacy. Of course, if someone pulls up beside your car and hears you singing off-key or sees you wipe your nose against your sleeve, you will probably experience embarrassment as well as some sense of privacy invasion.

Secondary Territory. In contrast to primary territories, secondary or "interactional" territories are more peripheral to people's daily lives. Typically, these types of territories are semipublic and have somewhat loose rules regarding who can occupy them. Nonetheless, certain people are more likely to be in the territory than others. For example, on a typical day, most of the people you see on your college campus are students and professors. If you see a group of preschool children walking around campus, you will likely notice them because they do not fit the typical profile of who normally occupies the territory. Similarly, when your nonverbal communication class meets, you only expect to see fellow students in your classroom. If someone new enters the room, you would probably wonder why that person was there. Perhaps this is one reason why children get a lot of attention (either positive or negative) when they are the "new kid" in school.

Sometimes secondary territories are marked by group membership and/or repeated interaction. For example, members of sororities and fraternities have access to territories that nonmembers do not, as do people who have country club memberships. Similarly, if you take your child to gymnastics class, you probably expect that only students enrolled in the class will be there to occupy the instructor's time and attention. Places such as restaurants or bars sometimes serve as secondary territories for a group of "regulars" who often frequent these establishments. For example, in the 1980s television series *Cheers*, there were several customers (e.g., Norm, Cliff, and Frasier) who were in the bar on a regular basis after work each day. For them, the Cheers bar was at least a secondary territory. This illustrates an important point: The same territory can be used differently by various people. The regular patrons in a neighborhood bar probably treat the bar as a secondary territory, the employees at the bar might treat it as a home territory, and the occasional customers may treat it as a public territory, as defined in the following section.

Public Territory.   Public territories are open for use by anyone. Examples include public parks, beaches, sidewalks, and shopping malls. The use of such spaces is typically transitory. In other words, most individuals only occupy the space for relatively short periods of time, and different groups of people are likely to inhabit the territory on any given day. Of course, public territories are home or secondary territories for certain people, such as lifeguards working at the beach or gang members who believe that a particular street is off limits to a rival gang. Sometimes conflict arises when one group of people believes that a territory is public but another believes it is private. For instance, a group of surfers might believe that a certain swell is their "home turf," whereas a group of tourists might insist that they have a right to be there as well.

Nonetheless, public territories tend to be regulated mostly by society's laws and customs rather than by rules imposed by certain groups of people. Public parks and beaches often have signs indicating how the territory should be used (e.g., "no glass containers" or "no dogs allowed"), and people who break the law are sometimes removed by security guards or police officers. In more subtle ways, social norms guide the ways that people use public territories. Within shopping malls, people typically follow rules of politeness such as waiting in line. And at beaches, people typically space themselves out so that one group is not sitting right next to another. Thus, even in public territories, people respect other people's needs for personal space (see Photo 6.3).

PHOTO 6.3   *In public territories, such as this beach, groups of people position themselves in ways that maximize personal space.*

Conversational Distances

In addition to describing how different types of territory relate to privacy and social norms, scholars have described how different conversational distances affect communication. Most notably, Hall (1959, 1990) proposed that there are four perceptual categories of conversational distance: intimate, personal-casual, social-consultative, and public. These categories refer to the amount of space that a communicator places between her or himself and others. As you will see, conversational distance affects the overall tone of an interaction by influencing how the senses are engaged, what channels of communication are most noticeable, and how intimate and formal the interaction is.

Intimate Distance. The intimate range stretches from 0 to 1½ feet, meaning that people are literally at or within arm's reach when communicating at this distance. In the intimate zone, sensory stimulation is particularly high. You can smell your partner and might even be able to feel her or his breath or sense body heat. Your partner's face is in close range, making facial expressions (even small or fleeting ones) more noticeable if not blurred. Depending on the situation, you might be focused primarily on the partner's face so that you miss nonverbal signals from other channels, such as the legs or arms. Because you are in such close proximity, your vocal tone is likely to be soft and you can easily touch your partner. Clearly, intimate distance is typically reserved for private, informal interaction with people we like and trust. Of course, there are some exceptions. For example, when dentists, barbers, or chiropractors use instrumental touch, they will necessarily move into the intimate zone. Sometimes, then, intimate distance does not imply intimacy. However, when strangers or acquaintances move into this intimate zone without seeming to have a good reason, we often feel uncomfortable. Perhaps this is why people feel anxious in crowded situations with strangers; they may be forced to occupy the intimate zone even though the relationship is not intimate. Moving out of the intimate distance zone can also send powerful messages.

Personal-Casual Distance. This zone ranges from 1½ to 4 feet, and is divided into two categories: a "personal" distance that reaches from 1½ to 2½ feet, and a "casual" distance that reaches from 2½ to 4 feet. Personal conversation is likely to take place in both of these distances; however, the content of conversation is likely to be somewhat less intimate at the casual distance than the personal distance. Friends, family, and romantic partners are likely to communicate in the close distance on a regular basis, whereas the far distance is more common for casual acquaintances and coworkers. As one moves toward the 4-foot edge of casual distance, it becomes increasingly difficult to touch or smell the partner, and soft voices become less functional. Still, partners are probably focused primarily on one another's faces. At this distance, it is somewhat more comfortable to look into the partner's eyes than it is at closer ranges, and it would be socially impolite to frequently look away from the partner.

Social-Consultative Distance.   The range for this zone is 4 to 10 feet. Again, Hall divided this zone into a close and far distance, with the "social" distance ranging from 4 to 7 feet. It is at this distance that most impersonal social conversations take place. The social zone provides people with sufficient space to maintain some level of privacy in that others are not close enough to touch or smell them. Yet the social zone also allows people to engage in casual conversation and perhaps get to know one another. In the consultative zone, which ranges from 7 to 10 feet, more formal interaction such as business transactions takes place. In both the social and consultative zones, communicators have easier access to multiple communication channels (e.g., they are less restricted to looking at the face), and they can more easily avert their attention from the conversation at hand. They do not, however, have access to minute facial expressions.

Public Distance.   Hall's last category encompasses 10 feet and beyond. Public distance typically occurs in formal settings, such as between speakers and their audiences, celebrities who are blocked off from their fans, or powerful CEOs meeting with groups of lower-level employees. In these situations, communication often involves many people focusing on a single communicator. The audience has an overall view of the person, rather than being able to focus on the communicator's facial expressions or eye behavior. Unless the person is famous, there is unlikely to be much sensory stimulation, and audience members may be easily distracted. This forces the communicator to speak louder, and perhaps more dynamically, to try to keep the audience's attention.

Finally, it is important to note that these conversational distance zones were created based on observations in North America and may not be generalizable to other cultures. People in other areas of the world have different comfort zones when it comes to touch and distancing, so in some cultures the intimate zone may only extend to a foot, whereas in others it might extend to 2 feet. (For more on cultural differences in haptics and proxemics, see Chapter 2.)

Summary

Touch and distance are important forms of nonverbal communication. Haptic behavior is extremely powerful. Throughout the lifespan, positive forms of touch associate with health and social development. Touch can show love and affection or hate and violence. We use touch to comfort and congratulate others, to greet and depart from others, and to help us engage in instrumental tasks. Proxemic cues are also powerful. In fact, these cues are omnipresent in that there is always some measure of space (or no space) between communicators. Even when talking on the phone, communicators are aware that the partner is separated from them by space, and this alters the way communication occurs. People defend their private territories and personal space, and when they welcome people into these spaces, this welcoming behavior often signals some level of friendship, trust, and/or intimacy. Indeed, the nonverbal cues of haptics and proxemics are instrumental in helping people manage their dual needs for privacy and closeness. There are times when we want to put as much distance between ourselves and another person as possible, and there are other times when it may seem impossible to get close enough. These two nonverbal codes help us achieve both of these goals.

SUGGESTED READINGS

Burgoon, J. K. (1991). Relational message interpretations of touch, conversational distance, and posture. *Journal of Nonverbal Behavior, 15,* 233–259.

Chaplin, W. F., Phillips, J. B., Brown, J. D., Clanton, N. R., & Stein, J. L. (2000). Handshaking, gender, personality, and first impressions. *Journal of Personality and Social Psychology, 70,* 110–117.

Dolin D., & Booth-Butterfield, M. (1993). Reach out and touch someone: Analysis of nonverbal comforting responses. *Communication Quarterly, 41,* 383–393.

Floyd, K. (1999). All touches are not created equal: Effects of form and duration on observers' perceptions of an embrace. *Journal of Nonverbal Behavior, 23,* 283–299.

Guerrero, L. K., & Andersen, P. A. (1991). The waxing and waning of relational intimacy: Touch as a function of relational stage, gender and touch avoidance. *Journal of Social and Personal Relationships, 8,* 147–166.

Guerrero, L. K., & Andersen, P. A. (1994). Patterns of matching and initiation: Touch behavior and touch avoidance across relational stages. *Journal of Nonverbal Behavior, 18,* 137–154.

Hall, J. A., & Veccia, E. M. (1990). More "touching" observations: New insights on men, women, and interpersonal touch. *Journal of Personality and Social Psychology, 59,* 1155–1162.

Hanzal, A., Segrin, C., & Dorros, S. (2008). The role of marital status and age on men's and women's reactions to touch from a relational partner. *Journal of Nonverbal Behavior, 32,* 21–32.

Hertenstein, M. J. (2002). Touch: Its communicative functions in intimacy. *Human Development, 45,* 70–94.

Machleit, K. A., Eroglu, S. A., & Mantel, S. P. (2000). Perceived retail crowding and shopping satisfaction: What modifies this relationship? *Journal of Consumer Psychology, 9,* 29–42.

Sachs, F. (1988). The intimate sense. *Sciences, 28*(1), 28–34.

Willis, E. N., & Briggs, L. E. (1992). Relationship and touch in public settings. *Journal of Nonverbal Behavior, 16,* 55–62.

CHAPTER

7 Place and Time Codes: Environment, Artifacts, and Chronemics

We shape our buildings and they shape us.

—Winston Churchill

Time is at once the most valuable and the most perishable of all our possessions.

—John Randolph

All communicative behavior has an underlying temporality, as time in its many forms is central to human beings and their lives.

—Tom Bruneau (2007)

Imagine that you have just reported for your first day on a new job. You arrive promptly at the appointed time. After waiting 20 minutes for the Human Resource Manager to meet with you, you are ushered into her plush corner office with one hand while she holds a phone in the other. You are directed to sit on the Italian leather sofa while she concludes her phone conversation. You glance out the windows of this 14th-floor office, then idly take in the cherrywood desk, the crystal clock, and the matching desk accessories. Ten minutes later, she concludes her phone call, hands you your badge and a packet of paperwork to complete, and then directs you to your basement office where you punch in and find your windowless cubicle in the middle of a large bullpen of desks occupied by a corral of other young employees. In the span of less than an hour, how many nonverbal messages have been exchanged?

This chapter explores how we use our physical environment, other artifacts, and time as messages. You may not be accustomed to thinking of these as aspects of communication. It is relatively easy to see how facial expressions, gestures, vocal behaviors, and touch can convey meaning, but we often overlook the communicative value of things such as architecture, decorations, color, time cycles, or punctuality. In truth, however, the ways we manipulate our physical world and time can send profound messages about who we are, what we value, and how we want others to treat us.

We will begin our discussion by looking at how people communicate through use of physical artifacts. We will identify norms and expectations for the environment and artifacts code and discuss how they convey messages in their own right, as well as influence the meaning and significance of other nonverbal and verbal messages. Next, we will explore the meaning and uses of time in human interaction. We will address the importance of naturally occurring time cycles, describe cultural variation in conceptions of time, and give examples of intentional and unintentional messages conveyed through the use of time.

Environment and Artifacts

It is typically human to affect and change our environment (Photo 7.1). We decorate our homes and offices, landscape our yards, build roads and buildings, harvest trees for wood, and plant new trees in their place. The environment, in turn, affects us. We value space, privacy, and security in our homes, we enjoy certain climates and landscapes more than others, and we are emotionally and physiologically affected by temperature, noise, and color. As a nonverbal code, environment and artifacts includes a very diverse set of elements. We can define the environment and artifacts code as *the physical objects and environmental attributes that communicate directly, define the communication context, and/or guide social behavior in some way.*

Environments include both natural and built, or human-made, features. The natural environment is not in itself a code. It only becomes a potential element in our nonverbal coding system when we as humans act on it, as when we create formal or informal gardens, arrange rocks in a symbolic form such as at Stonehenge, or festoon the landscape with colorful flags to create performance art. Likewise, our built environment and human-made artifacts become potential coding elements when they are used by their designers, owners, or occupants to convey messages about self or the kinds of communication that are expected within their surrounds. All features of the environment and human artifacts,

PHOTO 7.1 *Physical objects and environmental attributes in the home or other contexts can communicate messages, define the communicative context, and guide social behavior.*

then, do not qualify as messages. Our interest here is in those that do. A broad range of disciplines, including architecture, urban planning, environmental psychology, cultural anthropology, and communication, offer insights into how these physical features can act as communication.

Origins and Acquisition of the Environmental Code

Unlike other nonverbal communication codes, we don't really "acquire" the environmental code in any direct sense. Rather, we acquire *reactions* to the environment, by learning (a) that we can interpret meaning from the environment; (b) that certain contexts prompt different kinds of interaction; and, (c) that certain environment cues imply sets of rules and guides for behavior. Our reactions to the environment are learned through socialization and involve a mix of classical, operant, and modeling learning strategies. The meanings we ascribe to the environment are also heavily influenced by our cultural background. For example, westerners may not draw much meaning from a formal Japanese rock garden, whereas the Japanese draw quite important meanings from it. Similarly, most westerners find the formal Japanese teahouse ceremony simply a quaint way to enjoy tea in a serene setting. For the Japanese, however, the teahouse and ceremony constitute a rich context, full of cues and prompts for appropriate behavior.

Anthropologist Edward Hall spent much of his career investigating the cultural dimensions of the environmental code (see Hall, 1959, 1981). One distinction Hall made is between *high-context* and *low-context* cultures:

> A high-context communication (HC) or message is one in which most of the information is either in the physical context or internalized in the person, with very little in the coded, explicit, transmitted part of the message. A low-context (LC) communication is just the opposite; that is, the mass of the information is vested in the explicit code (1981, p. 91).

High-context cultures—which include the Japanese, Arab, and French cultures—use messages with implicit meanings that the communicators are presumed to know or meanings that are obvious in the context of the interaction. Instead of using words or gestures with explicit meanings, people can hint, imply, or suggest meanings and expect to be understood. In such cultures, context and environment assume a very important role in helping people interpret a communicator's behaviors accurately. By contrast, low-context cultures—including the German, Swiss, and U.S. cultures—use explicit verbal messages that depend very little on the environment or context for their meaning. The expectation in these cultures is that people should be clear and explicit about what they mean (whether that is done through language or nonverbal behaviors), and that ambiguity in communicative behavior is undesirable. This doesn't mean that environments and artifacts are meaningless for people in low-context cultures; it simply means that they are less important than for people in high-context cultures. The distinction between high- and low-context cultures indicates that one's culture guides how much attention is paid to the environmental context and how much communicative meaning is invested in it as compared to verbalized messages. Children often begin learning the culturally appropriate rules and expectations about the environment at an early age. For instance, parents teach children how to behave in different environments (such as when to use "inside" voices versus "outside" voices).

Although the specifics of the environmental code are learned, its fundamental basis is more innate. Humans have always altered the environment for their purposes, imbued it with meaning, and relied on environmental cues for guides to behavior. These are all adaptations to the environment that have survival value. For example, the way a culture works out the issues of shelter, crowding, privacy, and allocation of space allows the culture to mediate conflict about those issues, helping people to survive and coexist (Kusmer, 2003). Different cultures have evolved different forms of adapting to the environment, but all cultures have had to adapt. In sum, most of what we consider to be pertinent to the environmental code is learned and culture-bound; however, the basic factor of making some kind of adaptation to the environment has had survival value and may be innately based.

Moreover, Mehrabian (1976), one of the pioneers of nonverbal communication research, proposed that there are three basic dimensions along which we respond emotionally to environments, and these kinds of reactions may be inborn. The three dimensions are *pleasure-displeasure, dominance-submissiveness,* and *arousal-nonarousal*. Environments can all be judged according to how much they make us feel happy, satisfied, and contented, or annoyed, melancholic, and distressed (the pleasure dimension); the extent to which they make us feel dominant, important, and in control, or restricted, weak, and impotent (the dominance dimension); and the degree to which they make us feel active, stimulated, alert, and responsive to external stimuli, or unaroused, relaxed, sluggish, or inattentive (the arousal dimension). We may manipulate environments and the artifacts within them to accentuate or diminish these kinds of reactions. Health spas, for example, give attention to every detail, from the landscaping of grounds, gardens, pools, and other water treatments to the soothing colors of interiors, use of smooth or soft rather than hard surfaces, and simple rather than nerve-jangling décor. All these features are meant to communicate that this is a place for relaxation and rejuvenation.

Elements of the Environment and Artifacts Code

Many features of artifacts and the environment can play a role in communication. Research in architecture, urban design, environmental psychology, and other areas gives us clues about the relevant features to consider, and we will discuss several in this section. When we talk about the *environment*, we will generally mean the characteristics and conditions of one's physical surroundings, such as a home, an office, an outdoor space, or other surroundings in which a person lives, works, or interacts with others. *Artifacts* include those physical (and usually human-made) objects that one places in an environment for either functional or aesthetic purposes, such as chairs and lamps in a home, desks and rugs in an office, or sculptures in a public park. They can also include personal artifacts such as one's car, notebook computer, or hiking gear.

The uses and importance of environment and artifacts may vary from culture to culture, and even across co-cultures. Hall (1959) offered that environmental and artifactual features can be classified into three distinct categories: *fixed-feature elements, semifixed-feature elements,* and *nonfixed-feature elements.* The last category, which Hall called "informal elements," largely coincides with proxemics and so is covered in Chapter 6.

Fixed-Feature Elements.   The category of fixed-feature elements consists of everything that is relatively permanent or slow to change. Standard architectural elements, such as floors, ceilings, and walls, fall into this category. As Rapoport (1990) indicated, the *spatial organization* of such basic elements may communicate something about the people who inhabit an environment or those who designed it. The ways in which urban and suburban areas are spatially organized vary greatly, even within one culture. The spatial organization of a New England town differs quite dramatically from that of a Hopi pueblo or a large city such as Los Angeles. These spacial organizations have a very basic effect on the communication networks people develop. Cross-culturally, even greater differences exist in the degree to which space is highly segmented functionally and partitioned physically (Kent, 1991).

Another fixed-feature element is *size* or *volume of space.* We have all been in rooms and other spaces that we considered too big or too small for the activity taking place in them. Having too many students in a small classroom can be distracting, for instance. A public event, such as a political rally, can be erroneously perceived as a failure if the space makes a substantial turnout appear small. How smoothly and successfully an event unfolds can often depend on how appropriate the amount of space is. The kind of communication that is expected and transpires also depends on the spatial scale. Small spaces with low ceilings invite intimate and informal communication. Moderately sized spaces are appropriate for a wide range of social and task-oriented interactions. Large-scale spaces are appropriate for public events such as rallies, public addresses or large banquets. The space signals to occupants just what kind of communication is expected (see Figure 7.1).

The volume of space and size of architectural features in an environment can have other effects as well. Large, high-ceilinged rooms, a huge pipe organ, or

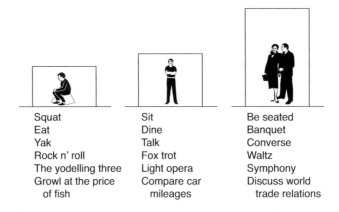

Squat	Sit	Be seated
Eat	Dine	Banquet
Yak	Talk	Converse
Rock n' roll	Fox trot	Waltz
The yodelling three	Light opera	Symphony
Growl at the price of fish	Compare car mileages	Discuss world trade relations

FIGURE 7.1   The volume of space and expected communication

a long staircase may create feelings of expansiveness and grandeur, leaving a person feeling insignificant. Perhaps you have had the experience of visiting a magnificent cathedral or palace and feeling awe or humility inspired by its sheer scale.

Linear perspective is another fixed-feature element. The linear perspective of an environment has to do with the lines created by walls and objects and the relationship of these lines to each other. Various kinds of lines in an environment can create different impressions, mood states, and types of interaction. In U.S. society, there is a heavy and almost exclusive use of right angles and straight lines. Notice the layout of your own home or school; most likely, nearly every room consists of four walls, a ceiling, and a floor, all of which are at 90° angles to each other. This design preference may reflect a culture in a modern and technologically oriented stage of development. Rooms such as the Oval Office in the White House (Photo 7.2) or the rotunda of the U.S. Capitol are notable partly because of their departure from this pattern.

By contrast, many traditional cultures prefer curved lines in their designs and architecture, which may reflect closer ties to the natural environment. Europeans also favor street layouts that create picturesque views at every turn. Thus, linear perspective may reflect a culture's positions on issues such as tradition versus technology, or efficiency versus leisure. Another possibility is that contemporary straight-line architecture reflects the standardization of building materials that we have at our disposal to construct environments, even though the work of Buckminster Fuller showed that straight-line architecture is not always the most desirable or efficient. Interestingly, drawings and conceptions of futuristic American architecture, such as those featured in movies, television shows, or comic books, largely portray buildings that favor curved lines and spheres more similar to those seen in traditional cultures (Corn & Horrigan, 1996). Contemporary efforts to "go green" architecturally may also be moving toward greater use of round floor plans because they maximize space utilization, leave the smallest footprint, and are energy efficient. Thus circular buildings and spaces may soon lose their novelty, whereas straight-angle designs may come to connote datedness, wastefulness, selfishness, or affluence.

PHOTO 7.2 *The Oval Office in the White House is notable not only for being the ceremonial office of the U.S. president, but also for departing from the right angles and straight lines that characterize most North American architecture.*

Linear perspective may also vary in aspect and in balance—whether horizontal or vertical lines predominate and whether the overall design is symmetrical or asymmetrical. Asymmetrical designs may be more complex and exciting, whereas symmetrical designs may be simpler and more soothing.

As for the influence of linear perspective on communication within a space, little has been investigated empirically. However, curved lines in a space create more lines of convergence and perhaps more opportunity for eye contact and communication between individuals.

Materials used in the environment—permanent materials used in the walls and floors and changeable items such as wall hangings and carpet—have both fixed and semifixed aspects. Nonverbal communication pioneers Ruesch and Kees (1970) described the effects of this element in the following way:

> Wood, metal, brick, and textiles produce a variety of anticipation of touch sensations. Wood against wood, metal against brick, a stiffened fabric against a soft and pliable one—all set up "chords" of tactile images that often produce sharp and immediate physical and emotional reactions. Metal may be highly polished or finished with a dull patina; containers may be opaque, translucent, or transparent. Surfaces—whether raised, carved, rough, or smooth—when exposed to light reflections, are likely not only to express the moods of those who shaped them, but also to suggest such subtle and abstract manners as interpenetration or merely the simple adjoining of boundaries. (p. 146)

As Ruesch and Kees suggested, materials have much to do with setting up how the context "feels." Soft, plush, and textured materials may create a relaxed atmosphere that is more inviting for conversation, whereas hard surfaces and bright, angular objects may create feelings of energy or anxiousness. Materials may also have symbolic values, reflecting everything from one's social class to one's interpersonal style and need for creative expression (Sadalla & Sheets, 1993).

All of the previous elements combine to form a final feature, *architectural style*. Greco-Roman architecture differs from contemporary styles, for example, not only in its aesthetic and functional properties but also in the kinds of interaction it promotes or inhibits. Even contemporary styles vary dramatically. For example, traditional modern homes create more pleasant, familiar, informal, and nonarousing perceptions than do postmodern and deconstructivist homes (Buslig, 1991). Homes, like other forms of architecture, also carry significant symbolic meaning (Sadalla, Vershure, & Burroughs, 1987). Indeed, one might think of the home as an extension of the self, and personal artifacts such as motorcycles, trucks, or sailboats perform the same function.

Semifixed-Feature Elements. The category of semifixed-feature elements comprises relatively mobile and changeable features of an environment. One such element is the *arrangement of objects and artifacts*. The placement of furniture, paintings, rugs, and so forth can affect the kind of interaction that takes place and can determine if any particular object in the environment will be perceived as significant. Several studies have shown that the placement of partitions, chairs, desks, or sofas in a room can encourage or discourage interaction. *Sociofugal* *arrangements* direct people away from each other (just like a centrifuge spins particles away from one another); *sociopetal arrangements* bring people together. For example, teachers at Phillips Exeter Academy (a private preparatory school in New Hampshire) practice the Harkness Method of teaching, which involves arranging up to 12 students and a teacher around an oval table. This arrangement is meant to de-emphasize the separation between students and teachers and to encourage students to interact with each other in an open, engaging way. In contrast, people who want to discourage conversation at their worksites may arrange their desks so that their backs are to others. Figure 7.2 shows sociofugal and sociopetal spatial arrangements.

The arrangement of objects may also provide a focal point for people in a particular environment. For example, judges in courtrooms often sit behind a high desk, called a bench, that is placed on a large dais at the front of the room, elevated above everyone else. This environment clearly indicates who is most important in the room. The focal point in an environment may also be occupied by an object intended to signal one's values or status. Michael Jackson placed the Best Picture Oscar for the film *Gone with the Wind* (which he bought at an auction) on a pedestal in his foyer.

Objects also can be rearranged to encourage different types of interaction within the same space. At a wedding, for instance, it is common to have rows of chairs facing forward so that guests can see the wedding party during the ceremony, but then to rearrange the same space with round tables, chairs, and a dance floor for the reception. Each arrangement of objects within the environment encourages a different type of social interaction between the guests.

A second semifixed-feature element is *selection of objects and artifacts* used in the environment. Beyond their arrangement, the objects and artifacts themselves can provide strong and distinct messages about an environment and the people who inhabit it. Objects and personal possessions may be used to "personalize" an environment. For example, some people create an "ego wall" in their home or office, on which they display diplomas, awards, photographs of them with famous people, and other artifacts that signal their status or achievements. Others might cover a wall with pictures of their families and friends. Each of these arrangements might send a different signal about the person and what he or she values. Even something as simple as one's choice of holiday decorations can send signals about values, beliefs, and sociability (Werner, Peterson-Lewis, & Brown, 1989).

Impressions can be created not only by what objects and artifacts are displayed in an environment but also by how tidy and organized they are (see Photo 7.3). In a study of students' perceptions of teachers' credibility and communication style, Teven and Comadena (1996) had participants visit an instructor's office and then rate the instructor after watching a videotaped lecture. Some participants visited a "high aesthetic office," which was attractive, clean, and neatly arranged. Others visited a "low aesthetic office," which was disorganized, untidy, and generally unattractive. Participants then observed a videotaped lecture by the ostensible occupant of the office they had visited. Those who had visited the high aesthetic office rated the instructor as significantly more trustworthy, authoritative, and friendly than those

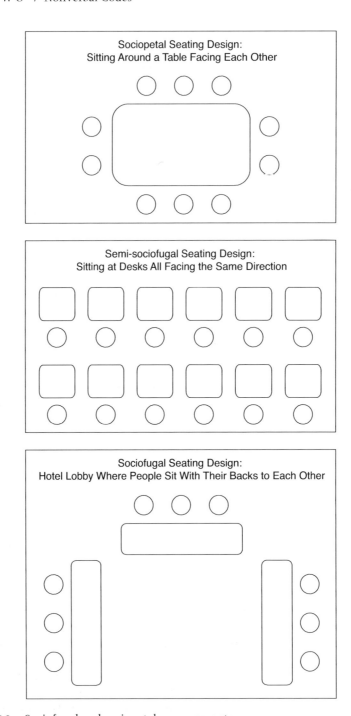

FIGURE 7.2   Sociofugal and sociopetal arrangements

PHOTO 7.3 *Research indicates we form impressions of people based on how tidy and organized their work spaces are. What impressions would you form of this person after seeing the condition of his office?*

who had visited the low aesthetic office. It is possible that participants who visited the organized, attractive office "projected" those qualities onto the instructor, leading them to evaluate the instructor more favorably.

Light and shade in an environment comprise a third semifixed feature. Several studies have investigated the effects of amount of light on work performance, but relatively few have explored the effects of lighting level on communication. Lighting may influence whether a setting is seen as social or task-oriented. All other factors being equal, lower levels of light are conducive to social conversation, whereas higher levels of light set a task tone. This is why you often find lower levels of lighting in a restaurant or bar than in an office or classroom. Similarly, low levels of light in the restrooms of a restaurant or club may make customers feel more confident about their personal appearance when they look in the mirror, encouraging them to be more outgoing and perhaps to purchase more food or drink (see Ryu & Jang, 2007). Sometimes lighting is set inappropriately, such as in a bar where the lights are too bright for social and intimate conversation. Similarly, many of us have found ourselves in a classroom with inadequate lighting. Academic performance can suffer under such situations (Kobayashi & Sato, 1992). Inadequate lighting in the workplace also has a negative influence on employees' moods, an effect that has been demonstrated cross-culturally (Kuller, Ballal, Laike, Mikellides, & Tonello, 2006).

Researchers have known for many years that *color*, a fourth semifixed feature, can significantly affect human behavior (Birren, 1950). The available evidence suggests that color is associated with people's mood states (Mehrabian & Russell, 1974), level of arousal (Acking & Kuller, 1972), and even their cognitive processing ability (Soldat, Sinclair, & Mark, 1997). Specifically, "cool" colors such as blues and greens have calming effects on people, whereas "warm" colors such as red, orange, and yellow are arousing (Davidoff, 1991). Some researchers have suggested that these associations may have been formed early in human history, when humans associated blues and greens with nature and nighttime (and therefore, with passivity), and bright colors with sunshine and daytime (and therefore, with

BOX **7.1**

Pink Jails and Inmate Violence

One controversial example of the use of color to affect behavior occurred in corrections institutions in the United States. Several jails and other penal institutions around the country painted some of their inmate cells pink (actually, *hot pink*; Johnston, 1981). On the advice of Alex Schauss, a corrections consultant, jails in New Orleans, LA; Mecklenberg County, NC; San Bernardino, CA; San Jose, CA; and elsewhere instituted pink holding cells for inmates. According to Schauss, the specific shade of pink he advocated dramatically reduced inmates' violent behavior by weakening their muscles, therefore calming them. This reasoning is based on the possibility that visual processing of light may affect neurologi-

cal and hormonal functions and that shades of pink and orange can result in loss of muscle strength. Anecdotal reports by some jail directors supported Schauss's claims. One empirical study of the pink jail (Pellegrini, Schauss, & Miller, 1978) failed to show any long-term effects due to the color, however, and a number of environmental design researchers expressed skepticism. Although the "pink clink" controversy has yet to be resolved, it appears that changing environmental colors from the usual industrial green to another color (even hot pink) can have some effect on inmates, even if it is only to make them think that corrections officials are more responsive to their environmental needs.

arousal) (Luscher & Scott, 1969). Knowledge of the physiological effects of colors has enabled institutions to use color to create certain states of being. For instance, dentists might use blue walls to calm their patients, and prison officials might use pink walls to reduce aggression among inmates (Costigan, 1984; see Box 7.1).

The human eye can distinguish a very large range of colors (Pointer & Attridge, 1998), and most humans form preferences for certain colors over others. Although you might guess that color preferences vary widely from person to person, or from group to group, research shows that people's preferences are quite similar. Eysenck (1981) summarized findings from investigations involving a total of 21,060 participants and found a consistent rank order of color preferences among adults. Regardless of sex or ethnicity, the preferred color was blue, followed (in order) by red, green, purple, orange, and yellow. It isn't just humans who prefer the color blue; researchers have also demonstrated a preference for blue among other species, including moths (Kelber, 1997), bumblebees (Keasar, Bilu, Motro, & Shmida, 1997), and robins (Murray, Winnett-Murray, Cromie, Minor, & Meyers, 1993). Some researchers have suggested that we prefer blue not because of the color itself, but because of the calmness we associate with it (Crozier, 1999).

In addition to affecting physiology and arousal, color also affects behavior. One example is purchasing behavior; market researchers have known for years that the color of a product or a product's package influences people's tendencies to buy it (Trent, 1993). This is true for a range of products, from clothing (Mundell, 1993) to food (Scanlon, 1985) to cars (Triplett, 1995) to school supplies (Roland, 1993). Color also affects our perceptions of other dimensions of the environment, such as temperature. Indeed, people consistently judge a blue room to be three to four degrees cooler than a red room, and vice versa (Porter & Mikellides, 1976).

The actual *temperature in the environment* is a fifth semifixed feature. People report feeling most comfortable at 79°F and feeling only "slightly cool" to "slightly warm" across a range of temperatures from a low of 68°F to a high of 80°F (Rohles, 1971). Other factors, such as humidity level, physical activity level, air movement, and amount of clothing worn, also affect how comfortable a temperature feels (McCormick, 1976).

Temperature probably affects communication in much the same way that color does—by affecting people's moods and prompting certain modes of interaction. Although no systematic research has directly addressed the effect of temperature on communication, extended exposure to uncomfortable temperatures may cause people to feel fatigued, bored, and irritable (Holahan, 1982). We would expect communication to become more difficult and less effective under those circumstances. We might also expect temperatures to be related to people's perceptions of the social context, with warm temperatures being associated with social interaction and cooler temperatures with task interaction. Restaurants that want patrons to linger may set the thermostat at 72 degrees; those that want rapid turnover may turn the thermostat down. Similarly, employers who want to inhibit idle socializing and encourage more work output by employees may opt for cooler temperatures. Cold and hot temperatures outside the comfort range have been shown to have detrimental effects on task performance, although the evidence suggests these relationships are complex (see Holahan, 1982, pp. 137–138, for a review).

As one illustration, heat appears to have a direct relationship to aggressive behavior (for a review, see Anderson, 1989): As the temperature rises beyond a comfortable zone, so does one's temper. Reifman, Larrick, and Fein (1991) examined archival data from major league baseball games during the 1986 through 1988 seasons. They found a strong and positive linear relationship between temperature and the number of batters hit by a pitch during these games. As temperatures rose, major league pitchers apparently became more aggressive, hitting batters more often. Phrases such as "hot under the collar" and "steamed" may be more than just idle descriptions. In fact, anger is one of several emotions that researchers refer to as a "hot emotion" because experiencing anger typically increases one's skin temperature (Ben Ze'ev, 2000).

A sixth semifixed element is *noise*. This factor has been heavily investigated in recent years, probably because of government regulations on noise levels. But what precisely is noise? Holahan (1982) suggested that noise is any sound that a listener doesn't want to hear. Noise, therefore, isn't just sound; instead, it is sound that one finds psychologically aversive. Rap music is art to some and noise to others; likewise, some people enjoy opera and others think of it as noise.

Noise typically has stress-inducing effects. When people are subjected to noise, especially if it is repeated and uncontrollable, they commonly experience physical symptoms of stress, including increased heart rate and blood pressure and elevated adrenaline production (Stansfeld, Haines, & Brown, 2000). Some researchers have argued that "noise pollution" is actually a public health threat (Carter et al., 2002).

In fact, constant noise bombardment has been used as a form of torture in military prisons, since it subjects the body to continual stress (Conroy, 2001). Perhaps unsurprisingly, we expect noise to have negative and detrimental effects on many communicative processes. We have all tried to carry on a conversation in a noisy room, felt too distracted to do so, and given up. Most research on noise has examined its effects on performance of simple mental and psychomotor tasks or more complex experimental tasks that require attention and vigilance rather than communication (for review, see Cohen & Weinstein, 1981). However, designers or managers may send tacit messages about the kind of communication expected in an interior depending on whether the noise level is more suitable for simple or complex tasks. Beyond task complexity, other studies have shown that the effect of noise on performance is moderated by such factors as the type and quality of the noise (Lysaght, Warm, Dember, & Loeb, 1983), as well as its loudness and predictability (Kohfeld & Goedecke, 1974). Baker and Holding (1993) found, in fact, that "white noise" (such as the sound of static on a television) actually enhanced performance on tasks with simple short-term memory demands, such as solving anagrams.

A seventh semifixed element is *overall level of sensory stimulation* in the environment. It is a composite of fixed and semifixed elements, such as lighting, windows, color, materials, odors, and noise, all of which contribute to the level of stimulation present. A certain amount of stimulation in an environment is necessary for people to feel comfortable and be productive. Too much or too little is undesirable. In fact, studies indicate that total lack of sensory stimulation over a period of time can be uncomfortable and frightening, which is why torture techniques that involve sensory deprivation (such as hooding or solitary confinement) are so harmful (Grassian, 1983).

Moderate rather than extreme stimulation appears to be the ideal. Sensory stimulation affects the inhabitants' level of arousal, which in turn affects performance. The Yerkes-Dodson Law (Yerkes & Dodson, 1908), developed in early experimental psychology, posits an inverted U-shaped function between level of arousal and performance: moderate levels of arousal are optimum for good performance, whereas low or high levels of arousal are detrimental. Thus, environments that provide a moderate level of stimulation, and hence a moderate level of arousal, should be optimal for communication. Voluntary short-term sensory deprivation can be beneficial, however, and is used in alternative medicine and for meditation, relaxation, and prayer. In one technique, practitioners use an isolation chamber, a lightless, soundproof tank in which a person floats in tepid saltwater, typically for one hour. This practice has been shown to significantly reduce stress (van Dierendonck & Te Nijenhuis, 2001) and decrease muscle tension pain (Kjellgren, Sundequist, Norlander, & Archer, 2001).

Norms, Expectations, and Standards for the Environmental Code

Norms and expectations for the environmental code in any given culture are reflected in how environmental elements are used for communicative purposes.

These become part of the culture's scheme for environmental perceptions and affective reactions (Purcell, 1986), and we can examine these with reference to both fixed feature and semifixed feature norms.

Fixed Features and Norms.   A useful way to understand fixed feature norms is to analyze specific environments and the effect these norms have on the communication processes that occur in these environments. Two such environments are homes and schools.

Homes.   Residences are among the most important environments for members of a culture. As noted in Chapter 6, they are primary territories that provide the most environmentally direct expressions of crowding and privacy functions in a culture, and in U.S. culture, they allow the highest degree of personalization and communication of identity (Wright, 1981). Such elements as the styles of furniture, colors, level of lighting, objects in the environment, and materials and textures do not always communicate (unless used symbolically), but they clearly provide a great deal of personal information about the inhabitants of a residential space. Research shows that people are happiest when their home environments allow flexibility of use and opportunities for personalization, as well as privacy, security, and contact with neighbors (see Box 7.2).

Another fixed feature of homes that communicates information about their inhabitants is their size. The average home in the U.S. grew from 983 square feet in 1950 to 2,349 square feet in 2004, a 140% increase in size. This increase cannot be accounted for by necessity, because the size of the average American family decreased during the same period. People may use the size and grandeur of their homes to send signals about their prosperity, particularly when their homes are more spacious and grand than those in the surrounding neighborhood. In the last quarter century, this has given rise to the American architectural trend of building "McMansions." This term has been used to describe new homes that are substantially larger than (a) what is appropriate for the size of the lot, (b) the size of the surrounding homes, and (c) what is necessary for the number of occupants.

Schools.   Another significant environment in which many of us spend a great deal of time is the classroom. The standard classroom features the teacher at the front and students arranged in a rectangle of columns and rows. In older classrooms, little use of color (other than industrial green and tan) is evident, and often there is little variation in the other semifixed features. The overall effect is to produce a somber, almost boring environment that hampers communication among students and limits the possibilities for communication between students and teacher. One alternative classroom design, the *open-space* classroom, has been employed in some schools. This design is literally a school without walls, in which large open spaces are partitioned into smaller usable spaces for as many as five classes. The aims of this classroom design are to create more flexibility in use of space for educational processes and to encourage more interaction among teachers and between teachers and students. Although open-space designs result in a greater level of visual and auditory distraction (Burns, 1972), Barnett and

---

B O X   7.2

Making a House a Home

The home environment is one of the most important—if not *the* most important—environment for humans. People live in all sorts of dwellings, from mansions to house-boats, studio apartments to mud huts. What is it that makes some people happy with their home environments and others dissatisfied? Environmental psychologists such as Aragonés, Francescato, and Gärling (2001) point to five factors in particular that influence whether we see our dwelling place as a "good home." These include the following:

- Features such as yards and courtyards that facilitate positive contact with one's neighbors—but also features that reduce the amount of noise one neighbor hears from another.
- The ability to create privacy when you want it. This includes privacy from

passersby (facilitated by shrubbery or window dressings) and also privacy within the home (facilitated by interior walls and doors separating one space from another).
- Flexibility in how the living space is used. For example, one might turn a spare bed-room into an office or art studio.
- The option to personalize your space. This includes being able to choose decorations and furnishings that reflect your personality and help you feel that your living space is "yours," whether you actually own it or not.
- Features that promote security, such as locks, fences, and alarm systems. This also includes the ability to see or be notified when others approach your home.

Source: Aragonés, Francescato, & Gärling (2001).

Nichols (1982) found that children from open-space classrooms scored better on a selective attention task than did children from a traditional classroom. Also, when open-space classroom design was modified with sound-absorbing partitions to correct for some of the noise, distraction, and privacy problems, students asked more work-related questions, and the rate of verbal and nonverbal interruptions in the classroom dropped off sharply (Evans & Lovell, 1979).

Semifixed Features and Norms.   According to Rapoport (1982), in U.S. culture semifixed elements are likely to be used for communication:

> Thus in our own culture, both in domestic and non-domestic situations, semi-fixed feature elements tend to be used much—and are much more under the control of *users*; hence they tend to be used to communicate meanings. Yet they have been ignored by both designers and analysts who have stressed fixed-feature elements. (p. 92)

As a result of the different viewpoints of creators and users, environments often do not fulfill the functions and purposes for which they were designed. Sommer (1974) labeled architecture that does not respond to the needs of the user as "hard architecture," whereas "soft architecture" is a design that takes user needs into account.

In some cases, users are denied the ability to modify semifixed elements to meet their needs. When CBS designed its headquarters in New York City, an aesthetician was placed in charge of choosing art, colors, plants, furniture, and all other environmental elements so that the semifixed elements would be consistent with the overall building design (Rapoport, 1982). The designers prohibited the use of any personal objects (calendars, pictures, plants, etc.) by the workers in order to preserve the aesthetic ideal of the building. As you might guess, the users of the building disagreed with the designers and attempted to bring in personal effects anyway. Some of the workers even filed lawsuits against the company. To the users of the environment, the prohibition against modifying the semifixed elements of their workspace went too far. Similarly, many tenants of apartments or dormitories, and even many homeowners who belong to homeowner associations, are prevented from making certain changes to their residences. These prohibitions can violate inhabitants' needs to personalize the environment and to give it meaning, and may have negative effects on motivation and productivity (de Botton, 2006). Incidentally, CBS eventually relented and allowed the workers to personalize their office, but not before a very open and public quarrel.

We might wonder whether this state of affairs is found in other cultures. The answer seems to be: *not always*. As Rapoport (1990) indicated, in cultures that are less technologically standardized and specialized, decisions about both fixed and semifixed features of the environment are still often left to the user. The culture may prescribe a range of choices, but it is the user who makes those choices. One broad overall norm, then, has to do with the environmental and artifactual elements that are considered relevant to environmental meaning in a culture. Developed and specialized cultures appear to place the most emphasis on semifixed elements, whereas more traditional cultures emphasize both fixed and semifixed elements. For example, in Navajo culture, both the dwelling's structure (the hogan) and the settlement pattern (very dispersed) are laden with meaning and reflect historical values of the culture.

Communication Potential
of the Environmental Code

Encoding Potential.   Now let us consider the degree to which the structural elements we have discussed actually meet the criteria for a nonverbal code in the strict sense of the term. The elements we have considered often play a contextual and situational role and are not part of the communicative act itself. Sometimes they clearly do play a communicative role, however, as when they communicate symbolically or prompt the use of certain rules for interaction.

As we have said, one criterion for deciding if something is communication is whether it has consensually recognized meaning. It is clear that we all have perceptions of the environment and its elements, some of which are very detailed and elaborate (for a review of work on environmental perception and cognition, see Holahan, 1982). Those that have symbolic value, such as architectural forms for churches, colors, and certain artifacts, will be interpreted consensually. The environment and its artifacts may also communicate on a sign level. A very common example is international signs. These signs often employ icons (visual images), such as the shape of males and females on restroom doors, to communicate content.

Additionally, environment and artifacts have great communication potential by virtue of the behavioral routines that they cue. Rapoport (1982) described the "mnemonic function" of the environment: the environmental cues elicit appropriate emotions, behaviors, interpretations, and transactions. These environmental cues remind people of what is expected of them. Goffman (1963a) referred to "occasioned places" as environments that contain regulative indications of how to behave. Such environmentally based prescriptions to behave confirm that we all share perceptions of indicators in the environment.

Decoding Potential.   The communication potential of environment and artifacts can be demonstrated on other grounds as well. First, there are structural elements to be considered. As we have already discovered, the potential combinations of those elements to produce different communication messages and effects are numerous. Second, humans have the visual and tactile capacity to decode subtle variations in artifactual patterns. Third, most of the senses—sight, sound, touch, and smell—can be stimulated by the structural elements we have been discussing. Since most of the senses are stimulated by the structural elements, the decoding potential is bolstered. Fourth, our reactions to environment and artifacts cues are not only cognitive and perceptual but also emotional and attitudinal, which indicates a strong coding potential. Reactions to the environment are often not simply a matter of taste but a function of the attitudes we have about environmental elements. For instance, when we see a home decorated with lime green carpet, art deco clocks and lamps, and floral print furniture, we know immediately whether we like it or not, an opinion that reflects our attitudes about living spaces. Finally, environmental and artifactual elements, because of their static nature, serve as a constant statement in any communicative setting and may serve as a framework for interpreting the interactions that take place.

However, many environmental and artifactual elements may be mistaken for communication when they are merely information. Moreover, their static nature means that they can make only one statement at a time and are incapable of adapting to the ongoing interaction. Finally, although environmental and artifactual elements are relevant to several social functions, there are some for which they are irrelevant (e.g., expressive communication, relational communication). Compared with codes such as kinesics and vocalics, then, they may be somewhat more limited in their communication potential.

Chronemics

Philosophers, biologists, physicists, and even songwriters have been intrigued by the concept of time. Our interest is in its biological, psychological, and cultural implications for communication. Fisher's (1978) comment that "Time is, without a doubt, one of the most crucial, yet most neglected, variables of communication" is still true 30 years later (pp. 79–80). The very concept of communication as process implies that it is a time-bound activity. The way time is structured may in itself also send messages to others. As Tom Bruneau (in press), one of the key scholars studying chronemics, notes, "Human processes are deeply embedded as temporalities. All genetic, biological, perceptual, psychological, social, or cultural processes show, indeed, that we are *homo temporalis.*" Chronemics, then, is *how humans perceive, structure, and use time as communication.* It concerns its "semiotic" or meaningful aspects.

Consider a few examples of how time affects our daily communication. Our work and school activities revolve around schedules and deadlines. Waiting too long for an appointment may make us impatient or angry. We regard the amount of time a friend spends with us when we are in need as a statement about the importance of our relationship. Experts urge parents to spend "quality time" with their children. In so many ways, time acts as a fundamental organizing principle for social interaction, but how and why does it do so, and what relational messages do we send and receive through our use of time? We will explore these questions in this section.

Origins and Acquisition of the Chronemic Code

For most of us, our lives are so intertwined with time that we rarely stop and think about what time is, exactly. Rather, we take it for granted as one of those natural forces—like the weather or the earth's rotation—that structures and influences our existence. The truth, however, is that *time is a human invention.* This may seem counterintuitive because we so often associate time with its natural correlates, such as the development of a child or the changing of the seasons. These and many other naturally occurring events do provide a basis for the concept and measurement of time, as we will see in the next section—however, they are *markers* of time, not time itself. The very idea that a naturally occurring process ought to be recorded and punctuated in a way that helps us understand cycles and structure our behavior is entirely human. Likewise, the measurement of time—seconds, days, months, years, millennia—is also a human invention that has varied dramatically from civilization to civilization. Before we look at how people acquire the chronemic code, it is important to understand how its origins are, themselves, a product of social interaction.

A Brief History of Time.   Human civilizations began conceiving of and measuring time, well, a long time ago. It appears that the concept of time was first linked to the movement of celestial bodies, such as the sun, the moon, other planets, and the stars. Ice Age hunters in Europe gouged holes and scratched lines in bones and sticks over 20,000 years ago, possibly to count the light-dark cycles (days) between phases of the moon. Around 1500 B.C., Romans and Egyptians began using sundials (Photo 7.4) to mark passages of time (minutes, hours) according to the movement of the sun across the sky. Eventually, other physical and biological patterns and processes became part of the experience and measurement of time, as we will see in the following two sections.

PHOTO 7.4   *Early attempts to measure time relied heavily on the movements of the sun, the moon, the planets, and the stars. Today, technology gives us the ability to measure time with unprecedented precision.*

Physical Cycles.   Think for a moment about some processes that occur in the physical world. Infants are born, mature into adults, and then die. The earth rotates on its axis, producing alternating periods of light and dark. Weather patterns change as one season ends and another begins. The moon goes through phases of light and shadow as it revolves around the earth. The earth revolves around the sun. What is significant about each of these processes is that it is cyclical—that is, it happens over and over again in a fairly consistent way that can be recorded, segmented, and used as a standard against which to measure other processes. What we call a day, for instance, corresponds to one complete rotation of the earth on its axis. What we know as a month corresponds to the phases of the moon, and what we call a year corresponds to the revolution of the earth around the sun. In modern times, a physical cycle also underlies what we call a second. Since 1967, the International System of Units has defined a second as the duration of 9,192,631,770 periods of the radiation corresponding to the transition between two energy levels of the ground state of the caesium-133 atom (Bureau International des Poids et Mesures, 2006). This cycle forms the basis of the atomic clock, currently the most consistent means of measuring units of time.

Even though these physical cycles are naturally occurring and somewhat consistent, humans have used them to denote time in some rather arbitrary ways. Why, for instance, do we have 60 seconds in a minute and 60 minutes in an hour? It is because the Babylonians used a counting system with a base of 60. Had the British invented time with the base-10 system we are more familiar with today, we would likely have hours composed of 100 minutes and minutes composed of 100 seconds. Calendars have likewise varied based on arbitrary divisions of the natural cycles. Around 3000 B.C., for instance, the Sumerian calendar was based on days that were divided into 12 periods (each like two of our hours) and further subdivided into 30 parts (each like four of our minutes). The Babylonians established a calendar composed of a 354-day year, whereas the Mayans used both 365-day and 260-day calendars that were based on the movements of the sun, the moon, and the planet Venus. Even today, the practice of observing Daylight Saving Time arbitrarily changes the time of day in reference to the rising and setting of the sun.

BOX **7.3**

Morning Person or Night Owl?

One way in which biology influences our behavior is by varying how alert we are throughout the day. You might have noticed, for instance, that you feel happier and more invigorated in the afternoon than in the morning, or that you are energized in the morning but fall into a slump in the early evening. These variations are a function of changes in your body temperature, and your level of the stress hormone cortisol, among other things. For most of us, body temperature is lowest first thing in the morning, and it gradually increases throughout the day, reaching its highest point in the late afternoon, when it starts to taper back off. Cortisol, in contrast, is highest in the morning, declines sharply during the midday, then tapers off, reaching its lowest point around midnight. Variations in these and other physiological

factors, however, can produce two distinctly different tendencies: high alertness and energy in the morning (i.e., being a *morning person*) or high alertness and energy in the evening (i.e., being a *night owl*).

These patterns are rarer than you might think: 70 to 85% of people fall into neither category (Brown, in press). For those who do, however, social behavior can vary dramatically over the course of the day. Morning people are often the most outgoing and social in the early morning and may curtail or avoid social interaction later in the evening, when their bodies are ready for sleep. For night owls, it's just the opposite; they can be social and outgoing late into the night, but they may be less pleasant to be around come morning.

Source: Brown (in press).

Biological Cycles.   The perception of time is also affected by biological cycles. Chief among these is the *circadian rhythm* (*circadian* meaning "about a day"), also known as the *diurnal rhythm*. This is a biological cycle that governs changes in sleeping and waking patterns, eating behaviors, hormone and catecholamine levels, urine excretion, blood pressure, cell division and growth, body temperature, blood sugar levels, and cognitive and mental alertness. Many circadian processes are ordered by cues in the physical environment—most notably, by the alternation of light and dark corresponding to night and day, but also by human-made signals, such as clocks and schedules. Since these *zeitgebers*, or time givers, correspond to the 24-hour day, humans typically maintain circadian rhythms that follow a cycle approximately 24 hours long (Dunlap, Loros, & DeCoursey, 2004). When these zeitgebers are removed, however (as in a controlled laboratory setting), and people no longer have any external signals as to the time of day, their circadian processes actually approximate a 25-hour cycle (e.g., Bernstein, Zimmerman, Czeisler, & Weitzman, 1981).

The circadian rhythm governs many biological processes, but humans experience other types of biological rhythms as well. *Ultradian rhythms* govern processes that begin and end multiple times every day, such as your breathing pattern, the beating of your heart, or your alternation between REM and non-REM stages of sleep. *Circalunar rhythms* influence biological processes that transpire approximately monthly, such as menstruation.

Developing Awareness of Time.   By using physical and biological cycles as referents, humans have been able to construct the concept and measurement of time by linking it to processes that are not human-made. (Human orientation toward time also includes psychological and cultural elements, which we review in the section on norms and expectations later in this chapter.) How is it that we become aware of time and its influence on behavior, however? Infants have no sense of time other than their awareness of their own biological cycles. Young children likewise have limited understanding of the passage of time and future events. They may be disturbed, for example, when a parent goes away on a brief business trip because they fail to understand that the parent will return shortly. By around age 6, however, children have learned such formal time categories as the days of the week, and by age 12, they have typically mastered the key elements of their culture's time system.

Piaget (1981) suggested that children's sense of time depends on their operational stage of development. Cognitive maturation is partly a biological process: a child cannot develop a mature sense of time until the higher stages of cognitive development are reached, at around age 12. Nevertheless, ideas, expectations, and rules about the chronemic code are likely to be learned through socialization. Thus the great cultural diversity that exists in chronemic behavior is best explained through social and cultural learning.

Elements of the Chronemic Code

Chronemics operates at many levels: the physical, biological, personal, social, and cultural. At the physical and biological level are the aforementioned rhythms and cycles of the earth and the human body that govern not only the tempo and timing of our daily activities but also our responsiveness to temporal messages. At the personal level are the unique temporalities of each individual, including individual differences in time orientations and usage. Because these are idiosyncratic to the individual, by definition they are not part of a socially shared coding system. Nevertheless, they also shape the ways people communicate through time and respond to the chronemic messages of others. For example, people may fall into one of two basic categories: those who follow a *displaced point* pattern and those who follow a *diffused point* pattern. The former see appointed times as a fixed end point. If they were due for a meeting at 1:00 p.m., they might show up anytime between 12:45 and 1:00 p.m. but anything past that would be considered late. By contrast, those who follow a diffused pattern view appointed times as rough approximations. They might show up for the 1:00 p.m. appointment anytime between 12:45 and 1:15. You can judge for yourself which patterns you and your own classmates follow by observing who shows up for class early or on time and who is chronically late.

At the sociocultural level, time can be organized according to technical time, formal time, or informal time (Hall, 1959). *Technical time* is what we think of as clock time—it is the scientific and precise measurement of time. For example, all computers and cell phones can now be synchronized to an atomic clock set at Greenwich Mean Time. In industrial societies, a high premium is placed on this level of precision, as is evident in our heavy reliance on calendaring, time zones, clocks, and scheduling. This highly objective view of time is diffusing worldwide, replacing more traditional and natural ways of measuring time based on seasons, phases of the moon, and other natural cycles. Although technical time is not part of a communication code per se, adherence to or deviation from technical time can be a message in itself.

Formal time refers to the traditional ways that time is viewed and organized within a given culture. It is the conscious, formally taught system for measuring time. In western cultures, time is often organized in a highly segmented, linear, ordered, and hierarchical fashion (seconds form minutes, minutes form hours, hours form days, days follow in specific order to form weeks, weeks follow specific order to form months, and so on). In more agrarian societies, time might be organized around the spring and fall equinoxes or what is currently being sold at the market. The Anasazi, an ancient Indian civilization in the U.S. Southwest, arranged their pueblo buildings so that the angle of the sun would strike portals in a kiva wall to signal that the time had arrived for an important ceremony. Members of a given cultural or co-cultural group learn how their culture values time and how it views concepts like duration. Take waiting, for example. In the United States, people are impatient if they have to wait and learn to apologize if they are over five minutes late for an appointment. In Asian and Middle Eastern cultures such as Japan, Indonesia, and Saudi Arabia, however, waiting is seen as neither unproductive nor bothersome. The duration of an event is for us a matter of clock time, but it may be "as long as it takes" for people of other cultures.

Cultures also imbue their members with understandings of how concrete and tangible time is regarded (can you save it, waste it, spend it?) and how much "depth" it has. Arabs, for example, view time as an endless process and the individual as an insignificant speck along a huge expanse (Hall, 1959).

Because the formal time system is deeply rooted in traditions, it has the power to evoke strong emotions, and alterations in familiar ways of viewing time can be quite disturbing. When Daylight Saving Time was first instituted, for example, a Kansas farmer wrote to the state legislature to protest that the extra hour of sunlight would burn up his tomatoes.

Informal time is the loosely defined system of time that is implicit, learned through experience with a culture, and usually outside conscious awareness. These are the "rules" and meanings that children pick up or are taught by caregivers rather than being formally taught in school. For example, there are no culture-wide rules about what is an acceptable wait time or how punctual you need to be for various appointments and activities. Instead, people learn how their community deals with wait time and may teach their young about what it means to be "on time" or what counts as an excessive amount of waiting. These mores are also changeable. It used to be that people often waited up to an hour to see their doctor. Now if the wait is that long, an apology is often forthcoming. Because we prize time as a valuable commodity, we expect others to apologize for squandering our time and to show up promptly for appointments. That is truer in a work environment than a social one, however. Social activities operate according to a different set of "rules" altogether, rules that may be specific to given co-cultures, geographic regions, or even groups of friends. Unlike guide-books for international travel that tell you, say, to expect restaurants in Spain to close for afternoon siestas and to plan on dining at 9:00 or 10:00 in the evening, informal time systems do not come with guidebooks; you have to learn the rules on your own.

The multiple work, social, and familial subgroups to which people belong subject their behavior to a host of these implicit rule systems, often with resultant misunderstandings. Consider, for example, what "in a few minutes" means. If you poll a number of friends and associates on precisely how long a time that is, you may have as many answers as you have respondents. Two friends of one of the authors almost canceled their wedding over this very expression, when one's statement that he would be there to pick her up "in a few minutes" left the other member of the couple standing on a boulevard in the middle of rush hour traffic for more than half an hour.

The various levels of chronemics draw our attention to the various kinds of temporal messages that are commonly recognized in this and other first-world countries. (Less is known about whether they constitute messages in developing countries.) Among the chronemic variables that can be encoded and decoded as messages are these:

- Punctuality (arriving at scheduled events on time)
- Wait time (amount of time before a scheduled event commences)
- Lead time (amount of forewarning for a scheduled event)
- Duration (length of time dedicated to an event)
- Simultaneity (single or multiple activities per time unit)

Norms and Expectations for Chronemics

We now turn to the social and cultural level of the chronemic code. Perhaps the best way to understand the parts of the chronemic code that are most relevant to daily life is to examine time at the cultural level. Elements at this level are those we are most often aware of on a day-to-day basis; they reflect a culture's view of time and include its norms and standards for time. Many of us find it difficult to realize that there is any time orientation other than our own. Yet in many cases, the chronemic code in other cultures has little in common with our own. We begin this section by detailing three important dimensions by which societies and cultures differ—psychological time orientation, orientations toward time and space, and monochronism versus polychronism—and then we look at some specific examples of social and cultural variation in what time means for people and their relationships.

Psychological Time Orientation.   Psychological time orientation relates to the pattern of our ideas and expectations about time, and it varies both from person to person and from culture to culture. Research suggests that there are four basic psychological time orientations (Reinert, 1971). Individuals with a *past orientation* dwell on events in the past, relive old times, and take a sentimental view toward time.

Such people often see events as recurrent and time as circular, an idea captured by Spanish-American writer George Santayana's quote, "Those who cannot remember the past are condemned to repeat it." Individuals with a *time-line orientation* literally see time as a continuum integrating past, present, and future, a linear and systematic progression of events. These people often view time analytically and scientifically. Individuals with a *present orientation* are focused on the here and now. They pay little attention to the past or future and tend to deal with events, activities, and problems spontaneously. Finally, individuals with a *future orientation* are focused on anticipating and planning for future events and relating them to the present.

Cultures appear to vary in their primary psychological time orientations. As Martin and Nakayama (2008) point out, many communities in the United States emphasize a future orientation. This is reflected in behaviors such as investing or saving for retirement, and also in the practice of tearing down historical buildings and areas to make way for newer ones. In contrast, many European and Asian societies (including France, Germany, Japan, and Indonesia) emphasize a past orientation. This encourages behaviors such as preserving oral histories, valuing genealogy and social traditions, and keeping (rather than replacing) historical sites. Still other societies, including Spain, Mexico, and Greece, emphasize a present orientation. This encourages people to "live in the moment" and make decisions with relative indifference to the past or future.

These time orientations can affect communication in many ways. The content of conversation may be affected; those with a past orientation may spend time retelling old stories, whereas those with a future orientation may talk about predictions for the future. The urgency of communication may be affected; those who are present-oriented may be far less concerned about achieving closure on decision or plans, whereas those who are time-line and future-oriented may be insistent upon it. The structure of communication likewise may be affected; people with past or present orientations may see little need for punctuality or adherence to others' time pressures, whereas those with a time-line or future orientation may see schedules, calendars, and deadlines as necessities.

Orientations Toward Time and Space. As we have pointed out, time is an abstract entity, not a concrete one. Research shows that when people reason about something abstract, they have a tendency to imagine something concrete that the abstract entity is similar to, and then reason about that thing instead (Lakoff & Johnson, 1980). For most people, that thing is *space* (Gentner, Imai, & Boroditsky, 2002). Across cultures, people tend to imagine time as though it were a spatial dimension. This is why we say that the future is *in front* of us and the past is *behind* us. We say we are *looking forward* to upcoming events and *looking back* on events already transpired. We say that our lives *pass us by*, in the same way that cars on the freeway would. (To some extent, we also compare time to speed, as when we say time *flies* during fun events or *drags* during boring ones.) Our use of space as a metaphor for time gives us the sense that the present is located at a certain place and that we are moving away from the past and moving toward the future.

BOX 7.4

Time Orientations and Your Career

Has it ever occurred to you that the way you deal with time could affect your choice of career? A *Psychology Today* survey report (Gonzales & Zimbardo, 1985) suggested that time orientation may be related to income, gender, and occupational choice. Although the results, which came from *Psychology Today* readers, may not be representative of the population at large, they do indicate some interesting patterns.

If your time orientation is associated with an occupation that you currently hold or plan to hold in the future, the news is good. Gonzales and Zimbardo showed that people gravitate to jobs with matching time orientations, and job success and satisfaction depend on intensifying that time orientation. Moreover, one's time orientation may depend on one's socioeconomic background and upbringing. Children with skilled and professional parents may acquire the kind of time orientation that allows them to succeed in skilled and professional occupations. Conversely, children raised by unskilled parents may develop a present orientation that predisposes them to unskilled and semiskilled occupations. The researchers recommended remedial time training for those from unskilled backgrounds who aspire to professional-level jobs. Finally, they suggested that we would all be better off if we could be flexible enough to shift time orientations when the situation calls for it. At work, for instance, a future orientation is best for productivity and success—but when it is time to socialize, relax, and enjoy friends, a present orientation is more appropriate. Given the number of workaholics that many of us encounter on a daily basis, this sounds like good advice. More research in this area may support the maxim "Work hard, play hard!"

The tendency to use space as a concrete metaphor for the abstract entity of time appears to be largely cross-cultural. As with many things, however, cultures differ in how they think about the spatial representation of time, and the operative element appears to be a culture's language. To illustrate how, take a minute to draw a timeline on a piece of paper and mark the present with an "X." Now, place a "P" on that line to indicate the past, and an "F" to indicate the future. Where did you put your P and F relative to the X?

If you grew up speaking English, you probably put the past on the left side of your timeline and the future on the right, like this:

If your first language was Arabic, however, then you are accustomed to reading right to left, and your timeline probably looked like this (Tversky, Kugelmass, & Winter, 1991):

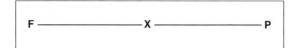

This reflects the idea that the events you have already experienced—like the words you have already read—are to your right, not to your left as they would be to a native English speaker. Likewise, if you grew up speaking Chinese, your time-line probably looked like this (Boroditsky, 2001):

Monochronism vs. Polychronism. Perhaps the most efficient way of under-standing social and cultural differences in norms and expectations for time is by distinguishing between monochronic and polychronic conceptions of time. Soci-eties that have a monochronic concept of time, such as Germans, Swiss, or most Americans, see time as a commodity. We spend time, save time, fill time, invest time, and waste time, as though it were tangible. We treat it as something of value, believe that "time is money," and talk about making time and losing time. Simultaneously, we think of time as invaluable and recognize that it is, in fact, intangible. As American author and businessman Harvey MacKay said, "Time is free, but it's priceless. You can't own it, but you can use it. You can't keep it, but you can spend it. Once you've lost it, you can never get it back."

Examples abound of how monochronic modern American society is. Because we think of time as valuable, we hate to waste it. Therefore, we expect meetings and classes to start on time (within a minute or so), and when they don't, we are only willing to wait for so long before leaving. For many of us, the workday is also strongly governed by the clock. We must arrive at work at an appointed time (certainly within a minute or two), typically take only an hour for lunch, and leave at an appointed time (although working "late" is sometimes acceptable). We value efficiency and prefer things to be fast, from fast food to instant stock quotes to high-speed Internet access.

In sharp contrast, people with a polychronic orientation think of time as more holistic, more fluid, and less structured than do their monochronic counterparts.

Rather than thinking of time as a finite commodity that must be managed properly to avoid being wasted, polychronic societies (which include Latin America, the Arab part of the Middle East, and much of Sub-Saharan Africa) conceive of it more like a never-ending river, flowing infinitely into the future. Because they see time as infinite, therefore, they aren't as obsessed with it as people in monochronic societies are.

One result is that schedules are more fluid and flexible. A business may not open at an appointed time, the way it would be expected to in a monochronic culture, but may simply open whenever the proprietor chooses. Students would not expect their professor to begin class at a predetermined time; instead, the professor and students would arrive to class over a period of time and would begin whenever the professor was ready. Efficiency and punctuality are not prioritized; rather, people give more value to the quality of their lives and their relationships with others.

Polychronic groups can even be found as co-cultures within monochronic societies, including the United States. For example, the Sioux have no words for *late* or *waiting* in their language. Pueblo Indians start many of their ceremonies "when the time is right," not at some scheduled time. For the traditional Navajo, time and space are very much the same; only the here and now is real, and the future is a foreign concept (see Hall, 1959, for a more thorough discussion of these co-cultural differences). Some social groups within monochronic societies also prioritize polychronic principles. As one example, the *Slow Food* movement was founded in Italy in 1986 as an organization promoting long, leisurely dining experiences that encourage conversation and appreciation of the food being eaten, as opposed to quick consumption of mass-produced fast food. The movement now boasts 80,000 members around the world. (Its mascot? The snail.)

Psychological time orientation, orientations toward time and space, and monochronism versus polychronism represent three ways in which societies and cultural groups vary in their norms and expectations for time. Let us look now at some of the implications of these differences for communication between people.

Implications of the Chronemic Code for Communication.

We have discussed three primary ways in which individuals and groups differ with respect to their norms and expectations for time. What implications do these differences have for social interaction? In this section, we will discuss how the use of time reflects three types of relational messages: messages of politeness, messages of value, and messages of power.

Time and Messages of Politeness.   People can use time in both polite and impolite ways. What qualifies as a polite or impolite use of time, however, depends on people's norms and expectations. One of the best examples relates to rules for punctuality. Arriving for an appointment or an event at the appropriate time is often a very important part of having a successful interaction with others, as it signals politeness and acknowledges the value of other people's time. What constitutes being "on time," however, varies across cultures. As we saw previously, people in polychronic societies generally do not expect meetings or other events to begin at a predetermined time, so they would be unlikely to take offense if you showed up at noon for an 11:00 a.m. class, even though the same behavior would be considered irresponsible or disrespectful in a mono-chronic society.

Even within a monochronic society such as the United States, rules for the polite use of time also vary from situation to situation. For instance, being on time for a business appointment most often means literally arriving at the appointed time. Arriving more than five minutes late is a violation of this rule and often requires an apology or an explanation. If you are invited to a friend's party that starts at 8:00 p.m., however, arriving "on time" may mean showing up at 8:30 or 9:00, possibly later. No explanation for lateness is given because you are not per-ceived to be "late." The difference in these rules reflects the task-oriented nature of the business meeting and the social nature of the party; in social settings, polite-ness norms for time are often relaxed.

Some social situations may approximate task-oriented situations in their rules for time, however. For example, if you are invited to dinner at a friend's house at 7:00 p.m., most often the expectation is that you will arrive either at 7:00 or shortly thereafter. The formality of this situation is introduced by the effort your friend goes through to prepare dinner. It is expected that you will respect that effort by arriving promptly so that the food does not spoil. To complicate mat-ters, different regions of the United States often have different versions of these informal rules. In New York City, going to a party that starts at 9:00 p.m. often means arriving at 10:30 and staying until the event is over. Being invited to din-ner in a Mormon community in Utah, however, often means you are expected to arrive early, as members of the Latter-Day Saints community tend to be quite punctual. Since these kinds of rules are rarely communicated explicitly, people who move from one region of the country to another are likely to follow the wrong rules and be perceived negatively.

Time and Messages of Value.   Particularly in monochronic societies, the way people use their time sends signals about what and whom they value. Since time is seen as a finite commodity, giving your time to a person, an activity, or a cause implies that you believe that person, activity, or cause is valuable to you. For instance, who are the five people with whom you voluntarily spend the most time? Chances are, they will be people who matter to you a great deal. The connection between time and value can also be appreciated by considering how you feel when people fail to give you enough of their time. This may occur in a profes-sional setting, as when a physician gives you only three minutes of his or her time, making you feel rushed and unvalued as a patient. It can also occur in personal relationships, such as when one spouse feels that the other doesn't pay him or her adequate attention, or when the time you have set aside to spend with a friend gets occupied by his or her work obligations. In all of these situations, we are likely to feel that, because the other person isn't giving us as much time as we want or expect, that person therefore doesn't value us as much as we thought. This idea directly reflects the notion that time, like money, is a commodity of value that is spent on, and invested in, things we care about.

With respect to parental relationships, specifically, many child development experts have opined that it is not so much the quantity of time parents spend with their children, but rather the quality of that time, that matters. Some suggested, for instance, that giving children 20 minutes a day of undivided attention was just as beneficial for the children's development, and for the parent-child relationship, as 5 hours of divided attention. "Quality time" thus became a part of the national lexicon in the United States (Warner, 2002). Research has provided mixed evidence about whether children feel equally valued by the quantity and quality of their parents' time. In a national representative sample of more than a thousand 3rd through 12th graders in the United States, for instance, Galinsky (1999) found that 60% of children felt they spent enough time with their parents, whereas 40% did not. Older children were more likely than younger children to express a desire for more time, especially with their fathers. As to children's preferences for *how* they spent time with their parents, Galinsky found that both "focused time" (akin to quality time) and "hanging out time" were highly valued.

Societies also send messages of value by the way they allocate and use time. In the United States, for instance, the Family Medical Leave Act allows up to 12 weeks of unpaid, job-protected leave to care for a newborn, newly adopted, or foster child, provided that the employer has at least 50 employees and that the employee requesting the leave is not considered critical to the employer's economic success. In contrast, federal law in Sweden allows for full parental leave at 80% salary until a new child is 18 months old, with an additional 6 months per child if there is a multiple birth. These two approaches represent extremes, with the policies of most countries falling somewhere in between (Kamerman, 2000). They may signal cultural differences in the relative value of family and work productivity, however. Cultures also differ in the value they place on leisure and relaxation. For example, Austrian law guarantees workers at least 30 days of paid vacation, plus 13 paid holidays, every year. In fact, every nation in Europe has collective bargaining agreements guaranteeing between 20 and 36 days of paid vacation annually. This is in sharp contrast to the two weeks of paid vacation granted to workers in the United States and Japan—and then, only to those workers whose jobs afford this benefit. The United States, in fact, is the only industrialized country in the world that does not guarantee paid vacation time, and nearly 25% of American workers receive no paid vacations or holidays at all (Ray & Schmitt, 2007).

Time and Messages of Power.   At least in monochronic cultures, the use of time—and the ability to dictate how others use their time—sends signals about power and status. When people meet or congregate, for instance, their relative status dictates who waits for whom. You have probably had the experience of going to the doctor at a preappointed time, only to wait first in the waiting room and then later in the examination room before he or she appears. Likewise, you have probably had to wait to meet with a professor or a supervisor. Although these experiences can be annoying, we generally do not find them to be violations of our expectations, because we expect that people of higher status have the "right" to make us wait for their time (Schwartz, 1975). By the same token, most of us would not make a higher-status person wait for us.

Making a person wait, therefore, sends a signal about our status and power relative to that person. The story is told about Harry Truman, who, shortly after becoming President of the United States, was visited by a newspaper editor. After waiting 45 minutes in the outer office, the editor asked an aide to tell the president that he was becoming annoyed by the long wait. Truman replied, "When I was a junior senator from Missouri, that same editor kept me cooling my heels for an hour and a half. As far as I'm concerned, the son of a bitch has 45 minutes to go!"

In some situations, the amount of time one is willing to wait for another person varies systematically according to that person's rank. Many American university students, for example, have repeated the unwritten rule that students must wait 30 minutes for a full professor who is late for class, 20 minutes for an associate professor, and only 10 minutes for an assistant professor. The implicit message is that the further removed one is from you in status, the more legitimate it is for him or her to make you wait.

Politeness, value, and power are not the only types of messages that the use of time can send, but they are among the most potent for social interaction. To conclude our discussion of chronemics, let us look more specifically at its communication potential.

Communication Potential of the Chronemic Code

Encoding Potential.   We have seen that the intentional manipulation of time can send signals related to politeness, value, and power. Many chronemic cues are manipulated unintentionally, however, reflecting a person's response to internal cycles or to cultural norms, rather than an intentional message. Such diverse chronemic actions as following a schedule, being early or late for an appointment, and filling time with activity are certainly examples of informative behavior, but they do not qualify as communication if they are unintentional and not used regularly by members of a social community to mean something in particular.

When communicators intend to send messages with the chronemic code, they can find the code's encoding potential limited, because the number of identified elements in the code is relatively low. It is not always clear which forms of time manipulation qualify as messages in a given culture. Moreover, little is known about the possible relevance of chronemic codes to such primary communication functions as emotional expression and message processing. All these factors, then, limit the encoding potential of chronemics.

Decoding Potential.   Given the fact that some chronemic cues are unintentional, there is a great deal of ambiguity in particular behaviors. Also, chronemic cues are often subtle. On the other hand, such cues do have an ability to evoke strong emotional reactions.

Accuracy in the perception of chronemic cues also varies. The formal and technical elements of this code tend to be perceived quite accurately, but the informal time system, which contains the elements most likely to affect behavior, tends to be perceived less accurately. Co-cultural and ethnic background, region of the country, and some individual difference factors complicate our perceptions of the informal elements so that in our culture there is often less than consensual agreement on what a given informal element might be taken to mean. Further, since these elements are often not explicitly taught, there may be additional room for misperception.

All these problems reduce the decoding potential of chronemics. Since there are also limitations in its encoding potential, the chronemic code emerges as lower in overall communication potential than the nonverbal codes discussed in other chapters.

Summary

The environmental code and the chronemic code both play important roles in human communication. Elements from these codes are often used in a communicative fashion and may also provide a great deal of situational and contextual information. Environmental code elements act as communication cues by communicating meaning directly in symbolic form, providing a context for interaction, or guiding behavior by prompting rules for interaction. The elements of the environment and artifacts code can be classified as fixed-feature elements, which are relatively permanent and slow to change, and semifixed-feature elements, which are mobile and easily changed. In general, people in our culture have a much greater degree of control over semifixed than fixed features. Other cultures have a greater degree of control over features in both categories. Finally, some recent analysis indicates that some cultures are more oriented toward the use of elements of this code for communicative purposes (high-context cultures), whereas other cultures are less likely to do so (low-context cultures). Although the U.S. culture qualifies as a low-context culture, this chapter has shown that we still make extensive use of these code elements as part of communication.

We are still discovering the importance of the chronemic code elements, but it is already apparent that they are very relevant to all cultures. Physical and biological cycles appear to provide a fundamental framework for the experience of time. Moreover, individuals and groups vary in their psychological and cognitive constructions of time. Given that the elements of the chronemic code are often learned on an implicit basis and that there is great cultural and co-cultural variation in their use and meaning, many communication difficulties can be explained by an analysis of chronemic elements. Much is yet to be learned about this interesting and subtle code, especially in interpersonal and relational contexts.

SUGGESTED READINGS

Bruneau, T. J. (1990). Chronemics: The study of time in human interaction. In J. A. DeVito & M. Hecht (Eds.), *The nonverbal communication reader* (pp. 301–311). Prospect Heights, IL: Waveland Press.

Freake, D. (1995). The semiotics of wristwatches. *Time & Society* 4(1): 67–90.

Hall, E. T. (1990). *The hidden dimension* (2nd ed.). Garden City, NY: Anchor/Doubleday.

Holahan, C. J. (1982). *Environmental psychology.* New York: Random House.

Mehrabian, A. (1976). *Public places and private spaces: The psychology of work, play, and living environments.* New York: Basic Books.

Rapoport, A. (1990). *The meaning of the built environment: A nonverbal communication approach.* Tucson: University of Arizona Press.

8 Message Production and Processing

While verbal and nonverbal communication may be different, they are not separate. There is a dynamic tension, an inseparable bond between them.
—A. M. Katz & V. T. Katz (1983)

. . . Gestures, like verbal expressions, may be vehicles for the expression of thoughts and so participate in the tasks of language.
—A. Kendon (2007)

. . . Emotional communication proceeds in two simultaneous streams: a spontaneous stream that is biologically based in both its sending and receiving aspect—it constitutes literally a conversation between two limbic systems—and a symbolic stream that is learned and culturally patterned.
—Buck, Losow, Murphy, & Costanzo (1992)

In the popular vernacular, we call nonverbal communication "body language," but is it a "language"? This is one of the questions addressed in this chapter. We consider whether nonverbal signals have enough regularities in form and meaning to create a language of sorts. A related question to be answered is how nonverbal signals work with our verbal language system to create total meaning. We have said that nonverbal signals are closely intertwined with verbal ones. If they are closely aligned, then perhaps nonverbal codes play a critical role in the production, reception, and comprehension of the verbal channel. Thus this chapter starts our examination of nonverbal functions with the most fundamental of them all: the encoding and decoding of messages.

Is Body Language Really a Language?

This question is one that has attracted conjecture and observation for centuries (Kendon, 2007) and is the subject of a lively controversy. You may be wondering why it even matters. Consider the following scenario: Satoko, an international student, enters a highly-regarded graduate program in her chosen field of psychology. In class discussions, following the customs of her high-context Japanese culture, she waits patiently for the professor to recognize that she has the answer and to call upon her. She respectfully averts eye contact whenever he looks directly at her. The professor in turn is perplexed by Satoko's lack of participation because he thought she was coming well prepared for the program, but her silence says otherwise to him. Her avoidance of eye contact in class is further confirmation that she is unwilling to speak up in class, perhaps because she is shy or perhaps because she doesn't know the material. To avoid embarrassing her, he decides not to call on her until she seems more comfortable and engaged in the discussion. He directs his attention to other students instead. Satoko, believing that she is showing respect to the professor and her fellow students, remains silent but wishes that she had the opportunity to show her knowledge. Both student and teacher end up frustrated with this communication—or lack of it.

This too-common scenario points out some knotty issues about whether nonverbal signals qualify as a form of language or not. If the professor had met with Satoko privately and asked her why she was not participating, the misunderstanding probably would have been resolved. But nonverbal behaviors are typically subject to more interpretations than are verbal behaviors, making misunderstanding more likely in many situations. What constitutes a message to one person or culture may merely be taken as information by another, or the same behavior may have different interpretations from one person to the next.

In fact, some experts regard much of nonverbal behavior as not communicative and thus not language-like (e.g., Chawla & Krauss, 1994; Krauss, Morrel-Samuels, & Colasante, 1991; Rimé & Schiaratura, 1991). They offer as evidence nonverbal acts that are merely inadvertent by-products of producing speech. Examples include actions that assist a speaker in retrieving a word from memory or signal when a person is having difficulty putting thoughts into words. Also included among noncommunicative acts are involuntary emotional expressions that are informative to observers but are not intentional messages being transmitted to a receiver (Ekman, 1997). In short, many facial expressions, gestures, and vocalizations accompanying speech are seen as serving primarily an intrapersonal rather than interpersonal function; they are not intended to convey meaning to another but rather are simply "spill-over" from the speech production process or are outward indications of inward feelings.

Experts on the other side of the issue believe nonverbal cues are social signals; that is, they are used deliberately to communicate and are part of the total message. According to this view, advanced throughout the years by many leading nonverbal scholars from communication, psychology, anthropology, and linguistics (e.g., Burgoon, 1994; Clark, 1996; Kendon, 1994; Knapp, 1978; McNeill, 1985; Patterson, 1983), verbal and nonverbal behaviors are like strands in a tapestry, inextricably intertwined; they are not isolated structures but rather form a unified communication system in which nonverbal signals are closely synchronized and integrated with language to form a complex whole (Bavelas, 1994). We can see this in the scenario involving Satoko and her psychology professor. Satoko's interpretation is based both on his nonverbal behavior (e.g., he directs eye contact to other students) but also on his verbal behavior (e.g., he calls on other students). It is this interconnectedness of verbal and nonverbal codes as part of a total communication system that allows us to exchange messages and understand one another.

We have noted already that not all nonverbal codes and cues are alike. The signals that fall under the nonverbal umbrella run the gamut from those that are merely indicative and expressive (noncommunicative) to those that are communicative, so the linguistic nature of nonverbal signals is not an either-or proposition. Nevertheless, the interconnectedness among verbal and nonverbal codes in the formulation, creation, perception, comprehension, and retrieval of messages should become increasingly apparent in this chapter as we consider the elemental place of nonverbal behaviors in communication encoding and decoding.

We begin our in-depth analysis of this issue by starting with key properties of coding systems that are applicable to our verbal and nonverbal signaling systems. This is followed by a brief overview of the human neurophysiology that undergirds the construction, perception, comprehension, and retrieval of messages. We then turn to specifics of message production and processing. Although this material tends to be more technical than that which appears in other chapters, it is becoming an increasingly important foundation for the educated nonverbal student. It is also at the forefront of some of the most intriguing discoveries taking place in fields such as neurosciences, cognitive psychology, and computer vision. We encourage you to "stay with it."

Properties of Coding Systems

Meanings derive from a number of properties of coding systems. Early in the study of nonverbal communication, it was common to treat nonverbal codes as quite distinct from, and lacking many of the characteristics of, our verbal system of communication. With more advanced study and observation, it has become apparent that language is composed of both verbal and nonverbal elements and that many of the "design features" of language pertain to both verbal and nonverbal communication, whereas others are unique to verbal or nonverbal codes.

A detailed analysis of formal design features of verbal human language can be found in Hockett (1960). Other structural and organizing features of language-in-use can be found in Ellis (1982); applications specifically to nonverbal and animal communication can be found in Burgoon (1985), Lyons (1972), and Thorpe (1972), among others. Here we present the most obvious and important properties.

Analogic Versus Digital Coding

A first common distinction is whether a code is analogic or digital. The distinguishing features of an *analogic* code are that it is composed of an infinite, continuous range of naturally occurring values. The color spectrum and the natural number system are good examples of analogic systems. By contrast, a *digital* code consists of a finite set of discrete and arbitrarily defined units. An A-to-E grading system is a good example: It has only five categories, each of which is mutually exclusive and distinguishable from the next, and the number of grade levels is an arbitrary, human decision. There could as easily be 10 grade levels or 100.

Language is a digital coding system. It is composed of recognizable, separable (discrete), and arbitrary units. Spoken language actually has a dual system of sound units (phonemes, phones, allophones, etc.) and symbol units (letters) that combine to form semantically meaningful components called morphemes (words, prefixes, etc.). Units are combined in increasingly complex hierarchies, but at each level, the separate units are distinguishable.

It has been popular to designate nonverbal codes as analogic, but to do so creates a false dichotomy. True, many nonverbal signals have intrinsic, or naturally arising, meaning; they form a continuum; and they may take on an infinite range of values. Among the behaviors that have a natural continuum of values are conversational distance (although we may reduce it to a few simple categories), sociopetal-sociofugal furniture arrangement, length of eye gaze, touch intensity and frequency, colors used in clothing and artifacts, chronemic messages of promptness or tardiness (although a culture may designate a specific range of time when "on time" turns into "late"), emotional expressions, and most vocal features. Because of the infinite range and intensity of values that are possible, analogic codes permit subtle shadings of meanings.

However, many nonverbal signals must be regarded as digital, either because what they represent is designated arbitrarily or because they are discrete actions. All of the nonverbal codes have some discrete elements—gestures such as the A-OK sign in kinesics, vocalized pauses in vocalics, symbolic colors for clothing in physical appearance, formal seating arrangements in proxemics, specific types of touch such as a handshake in haptics, appointment times in chronemics, or status symbols in artifacts. Some of these, such as emblems or status symbols, are created by convention and are therefore arbitrary. Others—such as a laugh or slap—are natural behaviors rather than linguistic inventions but also are regarded as discrete behaviors.

Dittmann (1978) observed that many apparently continuous behaviors become essentially discrete units when used to communicate. Examples of behaviors that we regard as single or stand-alone units include the smile, the nod, eye contact (present or absent), postural shifts, hairstyles, vocal characterizers such as a shriek, emblems, and a wide array of other gestures (e.g., the ear tug, pointing). Moreover, most of the classification schemes for nonverbal codes (e.g., kinemes) reduce behaviors to discrete categories on the assumption that the categories represent what is meaningful. Two different people doing a rhythmic beat gesture may differ in how emphatically they raise and lower their hand and in what spatial plane the movement occurs, but the gesture will still be recognized by onlookers as having the same meaning.

That said, many nonverbal signals when actually enacted lack the clear segmentation that characterizes verbal expression and thus are more analogic in form. With regard to gestures, for example, McNeill (1992) argues that gestures are "multidimensional and present meaning complexes without undergoing segmentation or linearization. Gestures are *global* and *synthetic* and *never hierarchical"* (p. 19). By global he means that the meanings of gestures arise from the whole expression, not from constituent parts that are combined. An example would be

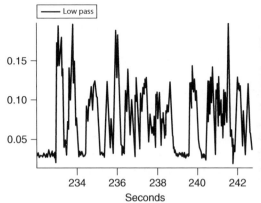 

PHOTO 8.1 *(a) An example of an analogic acoustic signal (low-pass filtered voice) digitized at 8000 kHz. (b) An example of an analogic gesture treated as digital.*

interpreting a negative statement combined with a pleasant face and voice as a joke. By synthetic he means that one gesture may represent multiple meanings at once. A pointing gesture might simultaneously be accusatory but also signal that it is your turn to answer. Interestingly, Goldin-Meadow (2005) found that gestures are more language-like when they stand alone (replacing speech); when they share some of the burden of communication with speech, they lose some of their language-like structure and become more global and synthetic in form.

Hence, nonverbal codes (and it should be emphasized that we are talking in the plural) include a mix of analogic and digital elements. Even though a signal's form may be analogic, our processing of it may be digital. Current computer-based technologies used for capturing nonverbal behavior segment analogic signals into digital ones (as shown in Photo 8.1a), even if the units are as small as picture frames captured at 250 frames per second or sounds captured at a rate of 48,000 kHz. Mentally, we do the same thing. We are accustomed to segmenting a continuous, naturally arising behavior into a more manageable, digital form to make sense of it (as shown in Photo 8.1b). We may be especially inclined to do so the more we regard a given nonverbal behavior or pattern as communicative and symbolic.

Grammar

Grammar refers to the morphological, syntactic, and semantic rules governing the composition of a code. Morphology covers the rules for combining letters into morphemes and morphemes into words. Semantics covers rules for how symbolic forms convey relationships between signs and their referents. Syntax covers rules for the ordering and patterning of elements.

All languages have rules for forming, combining, and sequencing elements, such as rules for what letters can follow each other, rules for noun-verb order in sentences, rules for associating words with their referents, and so on.

Nonverbal coding systems also follow rules. There are morphological rules for forming expressions, syntactic rules for their ordering, and semantic rules for the assignment of meaning. Symbolic expressions are the most obvious examples. The V-for-victory emblem, for instance, must be displayed with the palm facing outward rather than toward the body. A smile and a scowl do not appear together because that would create a bizarre expression. Other facial expressions, hand gestures, and vocal patterns that are not emblems per se have consistently recognized meanings within a given speech community and so are symbolic in that they stand for something else (Bavelas & Chovil, 2006; Burgoon & Newton, 1991).

Nonverbal displays also have rules of combination and ordering, which means that, like language, they have their own syntax. For example, a variety of parakinesic and prosodic cues structure, pattern, and punctuate the stream of communicative behavior and thus have syntactic properties. Beat gestures, for instance, demark phonemic clauses. Head movements, by their direction, signal present, past, or future tense. Illustrator gestures accompany speaking, not listening. Greeting rituals follow the order of eye contact before handshake, not vice versa.

Other nonverbal behaviors follow semantic rules. Laughter may express happiness, anxiety, or contempt; it never means "I want a turn at talk." Sometimes context is needed to restrict the possible meanings. Close proximity may have several meanings, but when combined with smiles, caresses, and constant gaze, becomes restricted to meanings of intimacy or physical attraction. Meanings also derive from larger cue patterns and sequences, as in the departure ritual (see Exline & Fehr, 1978, and Kendon, 1983, for additional examples).

Nonverbal behaviors used in a communicative sense, then, are rule-governed. The best evidence of this is our ability to recognize "ungrammatical" nonverbal expressions—unorthodox combinations of signals and uninterpretable sequences that we immediately spot as strange. However, unlike verbal utterances in which deviations from specific rules for language are viewed as nonstandard, we can enact nonverbal displays in a variety of ways that still qualify as conventionally appropriate. In other words, we tolerate considerable variation in how nonverbal behaviors are performed.

Pragmatic and Dialogic Rules

Just as there are rules for how to construct language and assign meaning to it, so are there rules for actual practice by individual language users (pragmatic rules) and for discourse with others (dialogic rules). These are socially dictated prescriptions for when and how to use language forms. There are also verbal mechanisms for making dialogue coherent. Devices such as prepositions, anaphoric references (repetitive expressions that refer back to an earlier expression), and question-answer sequences allow speakers and listeners to draw connections between a series of utterances in a larger discourse.

Nonverbal signals may follow both kinds of rules (although the rules may be relaxed with spontaneous, improvisational talk; Ellis, 1992). Ekman and Friesen (1969b) introduced the concept of *display rules* to explain how emotional expressions are tempered, modified, masked, or exaggerated in public according to a given culture's norms for emotional displays. These are pragmatic rules. Each culture can easily articulate what behaviors are considered appropriate or inappropriate for use in various contexts. For example, among many Native American tribes, it is impolite to look another person directly in the eye while talking, whereas direct eye contact is expected in Israel.

Dialogic rules are evident in face-to-face conversation, during which gestures are used in a highly collaborative fashion to help people make sense of what is being said. Just as verbal features such as anaphoric references maintain a verbal "thread" across multiple utterances, parakinesic head movements, discursive gestures, and gestures called cohesives bind together thematically related but temporally separated verbal utterances (Bavelas & Chovil, 2006; Kendon, 1994; McNeill, 1992; Streeck, 1994). For example, speakers may look at their own gestures while using words that "point" to the gesture so that listeners attend to them.

Polysemy

Words may have multiple denotations. The word "pot," for instance, may denote a cooking utensil, a container for plants, the act of placing plants in the container, or marijuana, among other meanings. The fact that a nonverbal cue such as gaze has no single meaning is often cited as evidence against nonverbal behavior forming a language. Yet this is no different from the property of polysemy in verbal language. It merely means that for signals with multiple interpretations, one must rely on context and culture to decide which interpretation to select. Both verbal and nonverbal cues may rely on other accompanying signals to reduce ambiguities (Holler & Beattie, 2003).

Universality Versus
Culture- and Context-Bound Meaning

The corollaries of the arbitrariness and polysemy principles are that meanings in verbal communication are not universal. They are tied to a specific culture, language, or speech community and are further constrained by the context in which they occur.

The same is true for many nonverbal behaviors. One may need to know the culture before choosing an interpretation. Downcast eyes may mean sadness in the United States, for example, but respect for elders in an African village. Meanings are also tied to context. A poke in the ribs means one thing during playful teasing. The same poke means something different in the heat of an argument. In this way, verbal and nonverbal communication are similar—they are both culture- and context-bound.

That said, within the nonverbal coding system there are some universally used and understood behaviors. International travelers quickly discover that even when they lack a common language, they can still manage some rudimentary communication across language barriers. This is because there are some nonverbal signals that everyone recognizes. Close approach distances, threat stares, a warm tone of voice, facial expressions of surprise, smiling, crying, fleeting touches to gain attention, provocative clothing—these are just a sampling of the wealth of nonverbal signals that are readily understood the world over.

Displacement

Language can refer to things removed in space and time, to the "not here" and the "not now." For example, verbal languages explicitly index tense through morphemic, phonological, or paralinguistic changes, which allows us to talk about the past or the future rather than just the present. The use of the negative ("no," "not") allows us to talk about things that are absent or nonexistent.

Nonverbally, some parakinesic and paralinguistic behaviors act as verb tense and place markers (e.g., Birdwhistell, 1970). Otherwise, nonverbal codes tend to be tied to the here and now. Although one might display anxiety cues in anticipation of an uncomfortable situation or long after an unpleasant occasion has passed, the time referent of the anxiety, in the absence of further information, would be unclear to an observer. Pantomime narratives occasionally attempt flashes backward or forward in time, but they are usually accompanied by some verbal explanation. Nonverbal communication, then, has limited displacement.

Reflexivity

Language has a special property in that it can be used to talk about itself. In other words, it can reflect on itself, theoretically, an infinite number of times. The sentence "My last statement was nonsensical" is an example of self-reflexivity.

It is difficult to envision an example of nonverbal behavior that can reflect on itself indefinitely. A smile might comment on a preceding smile or a laugh on a previous laugh, but it is hard to imagine this going beyond one iteration. Nonverbal codes are therefore probably best regarded as not self-reflexive.

Prevarication

Language need not be truthful. It can be used to lie and intentionally mislead. As we will see in Chapter 15, one can also dissemble, misrepresent, or misdirect nonverbally. People are continually masking true emotions and constructing self-presentations that are more favorable than reality. It is easy to deceive others through the omission of some nonverbal information or the addition of false information. A defendant in a child molestation case, for instance, shaved his beard, cut his hair, dressed in conservative clothing, and wore a cross so that he would appear to be a moral and upstanding person on the witness stand.

Iconicity

Iconicity is typically regarded as a feature of nonverbal but not verbal coding systems, with the exception of words like "buzz" or "flush," which sound like the thing or action that they represent (Guerrero & Farinelli, 2009). Nonverbal behaviors are iconic to the degree that they resemble directly what they refer to and preserve a one-to-one correspondence in size. A hologram or life-size statue of a person would be the most iconic form of representation; a photograph is less iconic, although it preserves the proportionality of the physical features that are visible; a stick figure would be less iconic; and a verbal description would have no iconicity. The images of the Statue of Liberty shown in Photos 8.2a, 8.2b, and 8.2c also illustrate varying degrees of iconicity.

PHOTO 8.2 *Examples of decreasing iconicity: (a) Three-dimensional sculpture of the Statue of Liberty; (b) two-dimensional drawing of same; and (c) cartoon version of same.*

Many emblems are iconic because they attempt to mimic what they represent. For example, the death emblem of the finger drawn across the throat imitates slashing the throat with a knife. Facial emotion expressions, some illustrators, and some artifacts are iconic. Metaphoric gestures are typically iconic in that they convey an abstraction in an imagistic way. For example, visualize both hands held up to form an imaginary box in which ideas are placed or moved from one time and place to another. The gestures are metaphoric, depicting a container or conduit metaphor since the gesture itself is not intended to be a literal representation of the thoughts or memories being expressed, but rather to conjure up the abstract meaning of location or movement through the gestural imagery. Iconicity confers a vividness to nonverbal expressions that may be lacking from verbal expressions for the same referent.

Simultaneity

Although verbal expression can convey a double entendre, it lacks the degree of simultaneous transmission of multiple messages that characterizes nonverbal communication. Within each nonverbal code, several features can be manipulated at the same time. In kinesics, for instance, gaze and facial expression together may send one message, while posture sends another, and gestures send a third. With touch, one can tickle another person in a playful manner with one hand while holding the victim in a not-so-playful, vise-like grip with the other. If one considers all the nonverbal codes as an interdependent system, the opportunity for a multiplicity of cross-modal messages increases dramatically. Because of this capacity for simultaneous message encoding, nonverbal codes may be used in combination, all sending the same message—thereby greatly increasing message redundancy and the likelihood of accurate reception—or they may modify and complement each other to produce a complex and possibly incongruent message. A variety of thoughts and feelings can be conveyed much faster this way than through the sequential transmission required with verbal expression.

Directness of Sensory Stimulation

Because nonverbal behaviors can impinge directly on the senses, they may produce more rapid, automatic, and emotional responding in receivers than verbal behaviors. In contrast, verbal descriptions require an intermediate cognitive translation step before the individual can respond. The maxim "A picture is worth a thousand words" takes some of its truth from this principle that direct stimulation of the visual scenes has far more impact than the most elaborate verbal description of the same phenomenon. An example of the impact of visual images can be seen in Box 8.1

In sum, it should be clear that verbal communication and nonverbal communication do not have identical linguistic and message properties. Table 8.1 summarizes the similarities and differences between the two types of communication. Nevertheless, the verbal and nonverbal codes do share enough similarities to regard nonverbal acts as integral to the functioning of language. Leach (1972) asserted that nonspeech behavior (nonverbal communication) "does not consist of isolated sets of trigger signals . . . but of gestures and symbols which are related to one another as total system after the fashion of a language" (p. 318). McNeill went a step further to propose that nonverbal behaviors form a single, unified system for expressing human thought (2005; McNeill, Cassell, & McCullough, 1994). A wealth of supporting evidence includes the fact that gestures occur only during speech, coincide with or even precede the verbal utterance, synchronize with parallel linguistic units, develop in tandem with speech in children, and have functions that parallel those of speech (see also Birdwhistell, 1970; Blake & Dolgoy, 1993; Rimé & Schiaratura, 1991). McNeill's growth point theory elaborates on the ways in which imagistic modes of thought, which take the form of gestures, combine with lexicogrammatic modes of thought (verbal forms) to generate meaning and the production of utterances. It promises to spark further investigation into what code properties are significant in achieving human goals and social organization rather than what *linguistic* ones are important.

Neurophysiology of Nonverbal Encoding and Decoding

Another perspective on how nonverbal and verbal codes relate to one another in producing and processing messages comes from the neurophysiology behind message encoding and decoding. Here we offer a quick primer on how the brain handles verbal and nonverbal information in sending and receiving messages. A computer is a useful metaphor here: The neurophysiological aspects are the "hardware" of message processing, whereas the processes themselves are the "software."

BOX 8.1
A Picture Is Worth a Thousand Words

A vivid example of the directness of sensory stimulation comes from the period of the war in Vietnam. Although many people watched news of the war on the television during the dinner hour, one night—much to the horror of viewers—they witnessed a South Vietnamese officer parade a prisoner before the camera, put a pistol to his head without warning, and summarily execute him (Photo 8.3a). Viewers not only saw the man's body crumple to the ground, his blood spattering on the street, but they also heard the gun firing and the shocked vocal responses of the onlookers. Seeing this event produced powerful visceral responses in the viewers that could not be captured by the next day's newspaper account of it. You can partially re-create the experience by viewing the accompanying photos here. Compare the photograph of the moment prior to the shooting to the written account just given. Which is more compelling? Similarly, look at the other photograph (Photo 8.3b). Which is more vivid,

this stark photograph of the innocent victims of war or written newspaper accounts of starving children in Africa?

Other examples of the impact of direct sensory stimulation are becoming daily occurrences. Surveillance cameras and camera phones are now bringing to light a host of shocking events, from health caregiver abuses to bystanders ignoring cries for help to Iranian election protesters being beaten and shot. These images and sounds have far more impact than written reports of the same events. The videotapes and photographs of the torture and humiliation of Abu Ghraib prisoners unleashed an avalanche of outrage throughout the United States and around the world. Imagine if we had all learned of the actions only from written newspaper accounts. Would there have been the international protests, heated political accusations, and extended legal battles if we had all only read about the incidents instead of seeing them?

PHOTO 8.3 *(a) Saigon police chief Ngoc Loan summarily executes a Viet Cong suspect at the height of the Tet offensive, 1968. (b) Starving African refugees.*

TABLE 8.1   Properties of Verbal and Nonverbal Codes

Property	Present in Verbal Code	Present in Nonverbal Codes
Analogic Coding		X
Digital Coding	X	X
Grammar	X	X
Pragmatic and Dialogic Rules	X	X
Polysemy	X	X
Universality		X
Culture- and Context-Bound Meaning	X	X
Displacement	X	
Reflexivity	X	
Prevarication	X	X
Iconicity		X
Simultaneity		X
Directness of Sensory Stimulation		X

One possibility is that differences in the structural features of nonverbal and verbal codes result in them being processed differently by the brain. The crux of this argument lies in the designation of the left hemisphere of the brain as the "verbal" side and the right hemisphere as the "nonverbal" side. There is some basis for this distinction. Many verbally related activities such as word and symbol recognition occur in the left hemisphere, and the left side of the brain is typically dominant for rational, logical, and analytic tasks (which themselves involve verbal abilities). Conversely, the right hemisphere is said to excel at spatial, pictorial, musical, geometric, and emotional tasks, including such nonverbally related activities as voice recognition and depth perception (Hopkins, 2007). Moreover, damage to the left hemisphere often impairs linguistic functioning, whereas damage to the right hemisphere damages recognition of such nonverbal features as vocal intonations, familiar faces, spatial relationships, and emotional expressions. This lateralization of many functions has led some scholars such as Andersen (2008) to conclude that "nonverbal communication is governed by the right brain hemisphere and verbal communication by the left hemisphere" (p. 10).

This view is too simplistic, however (Efron, 1990). Much of the literature applies only to where stimuli are initially *perceived*. It does not address where the stimuli are *interpreted* as communication signals. It is possible, for example, that the right hemisphere initially apprehends that a person is 6 feet away, but the left hemisphere takes over in determining what message is implied by that choice of conversational distance. The lateralization literature also applies largely to the decoding but not the encoding of stimuli. If you choose to stand 6 feet from someone as a message of detachment, where does that communicative decision take place?

BOX **8.2**

Gales of Laughter Greet President's Speech

Oliver Sacks, famed author of *The Man Who Mistook His Wife for a Hat and Other Clinical Tales,* writes of an occasion when he was returning to the aphasia ward at his clinic and was surprised to hear gales of laughter floating up from his patients gathered around the television to hear the President's speech. "There he was, the Old Charmer, the Actor, with his practiced rhetoric, his histrionisms, his emotional appeal—and all the patients were convulsed with laughter" (p. 76). The patients had been eager to hear the speech, so was it a matter of them not understanding the president, or conversely, understanding too well? Aphasia patients do not lack intelligence; what they do lack in the most severe cases of receptive aphasia is the ability to understand individual words. Still, they are fully capable of processing every-

thing else that surrounds the words—the subtle facial mannerisms, the expressive gestures, the tone and intonation of voice, and all the other innuendos and complexities that nonverbal cues supply. The ability to process nonverbal expression and to discern what is authentic versus false remains fully preserved in aphasia.

Says Sacks (1985), "Thus, it was the grimaces, the histrionisms, the false gestures and, above all, the false tones and cadences of the voice, which rang false for these wordless but immensely sensitive patients. It was to these (for them) most glaring, even grotesque, incongruities and improprieties that my aphasic patients responded, undeceived and undeceivable by words.

"This is why they laughed at the President's speech" (p. 79).

Contemporary work on information processing suggests a far more complex, synchronized relationship between the two brain hemispheres in the perception, comprehension, retrieval, and encoding of social information (Borod, 1993; Ross, 2000). (Box 8.2 presents one striking illustration.) For example, both hemispheres are involved in speech production. The left hemisphere governs vocabulary, rhythmic patterns, and free movements that accompany speech. The right hemisphere processes social gestural speech and automatic speech and contributes prosodic and kinesic features that organize discourse. Interpretation responsibilities are also shared. Right hemispheric involvement is necessary to understand jokes, metaphors, stories with a moral, and emotions. People who have right hemispheric damage give inaccurate, disjointed, or overly literal versions of these kinds of communication.

Where interpretation takes place may also shift, depending on how familiar the person is with the code. Most people initially process music in the right hemisphere, responding to it in a gestalt, analogic fashion. However, after musicians become familiar with a particular piece of music, they process it in the left hemisphere, treating it as a digital code. It is a reasonable hypothesis that communicative stimuli that are treated in a holistic fashion are processed initially by the right hemisphere, whereas those that are segmented into finer, discrete categories are processed by the left hemisphere. This conclusion is consistent with the view that the left brain is better for deductive, convergent, discrete, intellectual, objective, literal, and denotative tasks, whereas the right brain is better for imaginative, divergent, continuous, sensuous, subjective, metaphorical, and connotative tasks. As Campbell (1982) noted decades ago:

> The right brain is not a linguistic idiot. It has its own codes, its own rules, and these are worth examining. It does have some comprehension of spoken language, and it is good at detecting pitch, intonation, stress, cadence, loudness, and softness. It knows whether a sentence is asking a question, giving an order, expressing a condition, or making a statement . . . . It can recognize the ridiculous and inappropriate, and be aware that words are embedded in a wide matrix of relationships. (pp. 244–245)

Contemporary neurophysiological research casts further doubt on the simple nonverbal right–verbal left distinction. MacLean (1990; see also Ploog, 2003) proposed a Triune brain, in other words, viewing the brain as tripartite, consisting of the *R-complex*, the most primitive brain, located at the end of the brain stem; the *paleomammalian brain*, composed of the limbic system surrounding the R-complex; and the *neomammalian brain*, which is part of the cerebral cortex.

Each part of the brain controls different aspects of communication and nonverbal behavior (see Photo 8.4). The striatal or R-complex controls instinctive behavioral and aggressive displays such as territorial defense, threat displays, and alarm vocalizations. The paleomammalian brain controls emotional expression and experience, as well as bodily functions. The neomammalian brain controls higher-order thought processes and symbolic activity, including speech production and such nonverbal symbols as emblems.

Although some communicative activities may be primarily controlled by one part of the brain, other activities may require the interplay among multiple regions of the brain. For example, emotional expressions and speech perception may require the careful coordination of the limbic system and neocortex (Newman, 2003). Cortical and subcortical regions of the left hemisphere (the supposed linguistic side of the brain) have been shown to be involved in the production or comprehension of symbolic gestures, pantomimic gestures, and various nonverbal sounds, and the right hemisphere is involved in the processing of language (Beeman & Chiarello, 1997). In short, it is becoming increasingly apparent that the interplay among the three levels of the brain is quite complex (Rinn, 1991). And the idea of a tripartite brain may give way to other ways of viewing brain organization. For instance, a set of neural structures termed the "communication brain" that governs vocal communication in mammals does not fit well into the triune scheme of brain organization (Newman, 2003). Recent advances in functional magnetic resonance imaging (fMRI) and other forms of neurophysiological measurement and observation will undoubtedly resolve some of these issues with the daily discoveries of locations and neural structures in the brain where communication activities are processed. Feyereisen (1991) conjectured that if behavioral categories are large and cover global acts such as gesture production or emotional processing, it is unlikely that corresponding brain functions will be precisely located. Mounting evidence

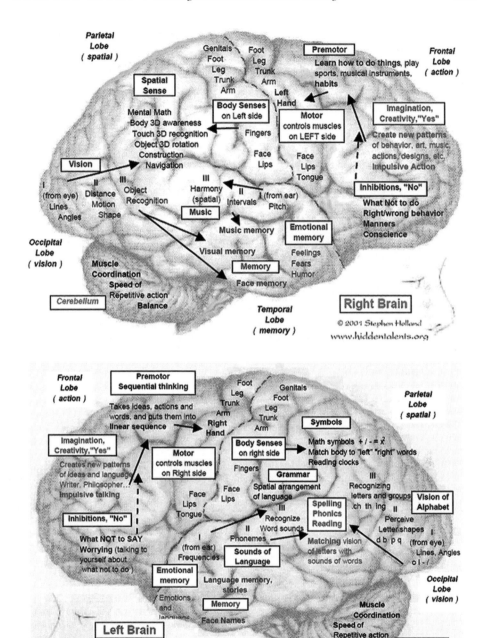

PHOTO 8.4 *Brain structures and regions associated with nonverbal communication.*

Source: Stephen Holland, 2001. Retrieved July 9, 2009, from http://members.shaw.ca/hidden-talents/brain/113-map-print.html

supports this view of diffuse areas of the brain being engaged in what were once thought to be localized tasks. Thus, the interconnection of verbal and nonverbal features of communication may become more solidified.

Nonverbal Behavior and Message Production

Our ability to construct utterances effortlessly is remarkable yet often taken for granted. The speed with which we can produce novel utterances, the amount of information embedded in utterances, and the depth and clarity that utterances can have for other communicators are all qualities that distinguish humans as a species concerned with communication.

Message production consists of three processes (Levelt, 1989). First is *message generation*. Speakers must formulate preverbal ideas and convert plans into intentions to send a message. Nonverbal images may shape the ideas that are to be expressed. Second, ideas must be translated into symbolic expression. This is *semantic encoding*. Nonverbal behaviors may convey the central meaning, may augment or modify the verbally expressed meaning, or may contradict the verbal meaning. Third, when the message is to be conveyed in oral rather than written form, it must also undergo *phonological encoding*—putting the right sounds with the words. Nonverbal cues not only supply the phonological component of speech but also supply "nonverbal punctuation" for communication that is oral rather than written. That is, they supply nonverbal syntax. Additionally, nonverbal cues may be informative about the difficulty speakers are experiencing in constructing their messages. We take up each of these roles in turn.

Message Generation

Have you ever noticed that people talking on the telephone continue to use facial expressions and gestures, even though their listeners cannot see them (Photo 8.5)? It

PHOTO 8.5   *Even when we can't be seen, we use gestures to facilitate our own encoding.*

may look foolish, but researchers are learning that it serves a useful purpose because gestures accompanying speech may assist speakers in "priming the pump," so to speak. They help activate and recall words, thoughts, images, and ideas from memory that become part of the utterance (Chawla & Krauss, 1994; Krauss et al., 1991). They may also shape what is to be said (McNeill, 2005; Parrill, 2008). For example, making circular hand motions may cause a speaker to start using circular metaphors in his or her verbal statements. Or, vocal and facial behaviors may predict what form a subsequent verbal account takes (Manusov & Trees, 2002). Kinesic and vocalic expressiveness are such a natural part of the encoding process that even when they serve no benefit to the listener, they help us translate our meanings into words.

Nonverbal cues may also "prime the pump" in another way, by cementing affective associations with objects. One study found that if people nodded their head affirmatively while being exposed to a neutral object, they came to have greater preference for it, whereas if they shook their head laterally (a negative expression), their preference for the object declined (Tom, Pettersen, Lau, Burton, & Cook, 1991). Apparently, connotations of nonverbal actions can rub off on the objects with which they are associated.

Semantic Encoding

As noted with emblems, some nonverbal cues convey meaning independently of whatever is being said. Young children, for instance, learn to tell a mere look from caregivers that indicates they are just checking a child's activities from "the look"—a longer, fixated gaze—that signals they are "in trouble"(Kidwell, 2005). Other nonverbal cues are an integral part of messages and may contribute to the semantic meaning of a total utterance. Irony and sarcasm, for example, are expressed through changes in pitch, loudness, and/or tempo combined with a "blank face" that marks the words as being sarcastic (Attardo, Eisterhold, & Hay, 2003; Bryant & Fox Tree, 2005; Rockwell, 2000). Gestures also mark the importance of verbal meaning and reinforce the spoken word in a way that produces a different meaning than when each is produced by itself (Bernardis & Gentilucci, 2006; Chieffi & Ricci, 2005). Such a view is consistent with cognitive theories that propose dual coding of mental representation: Information is stored in both a semantic and imagistic form (Paivio, 1971). You can confirm this for yourself by observing that when people give complex directions to others or try to make fine verbal discriminations, they use lots of gestures to fill in meaning. If they are prevented from gesturing, they pause a lot more and replace the missing gestures with more verbiage (Graham & Heywood, 1975). Another illustration comes from a clever experiment by Holler and Beattie (2003) in which speakers distinguished homonyms and words with multiple meanings such as "ring" or "pot," by how they used nonverbal cues to clarify the meaning (see Box 8.3).

The nonverbal displays that accompany speech can be adapted in form and intensity to suit the auditor or situation. For example, people giving directions or presenting a narrative use more illustrator and interactive gestures in a face-to-face situation than when speaking over an intercom, through a

BOX **8.3**

Is It in the Look of Your Face, the Wave of Your Hand, the Tone of Your Voice?

Holler and Beattie (2003) conducted a clever experiment to demonstrate how speakers use gestures to clarify ambiguous meaning of words for listeners. They studied homonyms (words that sound the same but mean different things) and the kinds of gestures used to clarify meaning. A wide range of gestures emerged. But we need not stop at gestures. It is instructive to look at the other kinesic and vocalic expressions speakers use.

Ask 10 volunteers to read each of the following sentences out loud and then explain the ambiguous meaning of the word contained in the sentence to their listener. If

you can, record the answers. Notice how speakers use gestures, facial expressions, and tone of voice to help clarify the meaning. Which nonverbal behaviors were the most helpful?

1. The old man's glasses were filthy.
2. Ann took her housemate's pot without asking.
3. Her pupils were examined to detect possible illness.
4. The solution was right there on the desk.
5. The ring caught his attention.

---

partition, or to a tape recorder or video camera (Bavelas, Chovil, Lawrie, & Wade, 1992; Bavelas, Hagen, Lane, & Lawrie, 1989). This demonstrates that communicators are aware of their listeners' needs and abilities when fashioning their messages.

Syntactic and Phonological Encoding

One characteristic of speech is that utterances occur in "chunks." Conversational speech is not made up of sentences and paragraphs like written language is. Instead, utterances are composed of noticeable segments of speech called *phonemic clauses*. As an example (Boomer, 1978, pp. 246–247), imagine hearing someone say the following:

> The dog that ate my final paper last year just did it again.

How do you hear this phrase being uttered in your mind? Research on phonemic clauses suggests that you hear this in two chunks:

> The dog that ate my final paper last year / just did it again.

The slash indicates where most people are likely to put a break point in the phrase, separating it into two chunks, or phonemic clauses. Three vocal cues identify a phonemic clause: *pitch, rhythm,* and *loudness.* The pitch contour or intonation pattern accompanying our sample phrase should have a characteristic pattern, with the pitch being relatively level over *The dog that ate my final paper,* abruptly rising over *last,* and gliding back down over *year.* A similar though not identical pattern should be found over *just did it again.* A change in the rhythm of the utterance typically coincides with the pitch change just described. *Last year* and *-gain* should be heard as slightly longer and stretched out, the same points at which the pitch changes occur. *Last* and *-gain* also should be slightly louder than the rest of the segment. The simultaneous changes in pitch, rhythm, and loudness produce what is called *primary stress* and mark the whole phrase into two segments. In phonemic clauses, primary stress occurs at or near the end of the clause. Pitch, rhythm, and loudness fall off and assume previous levels, a feature called a *terminal juncture*. A phonemic clause is thus defined by one primary stress and a terminal juncture.

Spoken language, then, is segmented into noticeable units marked by kinesic, vocal, proxemic, and haptic properties. These nonverbal properties form a nonverbal grammar that structures conversation for both speaker and listener. In a series of experiments, Parrill (2008) demonstrated just how tightly coordinated gestures and prosody are with the verbal stream to form an overall "information package." On the speaker side, rhythmic illustrator gestures, parakinesic behaviors such as head nods, self-touching, and other adaptor behaviors may be especially helpful (Hadar, 1989; Harrigan, 1985). Listener backchannel responses such as nods and brief interjections such as *um-hmm* occur primarily at the end of phonemic clauses, immediately after terminal junctures. This suggests that listeners recognize phonemic clause units and coordinate their responses to the units so that they don't "step on" the speaker's lines.

Indicating Difficulty and Complexity of Encoding

Can you tell when someone is thinking or having difficulty putting his or her thoughts into words? Many scholars, believing you can, have gone in search of reliable external indicators of what is variously referred to as *cognitive effort, cognitive load,* or *cognitive taxation*. When communicators are doing cognitively demanding tasks such as speaking (rather than listening), expressing new and unrehearsed ideas, becoming more self-conscious, experiencing social anxiety, or even deceiving, their nonverbal behaviors provide outward indications of those inward processes.

Facial expressions, eye gaze, head movements, gestures, vocal pauses, and other vocal nonfluencies are among the nonverbal cues from which we infer that someone is thinking very hard (or not) (Beattie, 1981a; Chawla & Krauss, 1994; Harrigan, Wilson, & Rosenthal, 2004; Scherer, 1981). Several muscles in the eye and forehead region join to produce the knit eyebrows associated with deep concentration, reflection, or determination. People also typically look away. Gaze aversion, coupled with the eye and brow muscle movements, may restrict visual input while sharpening the acuity of other senses. Gesturally, self-adaptors increase and illustrators decrease or cease temporarily as verbal complexity or difficulty increases.

Vocally, cognitive stress may be revealed through more rapid, louder, and higher-pitched speech. For example, recordings of stressed airline pilots showed these patterns to be common. Nonfluencies are indicative of someone being taxed cognitively. Hesitation (silent) pauses and long response latencies occur more frequently when people are speaking spontaneously and at junctures when it is difficult to anticipate the next word. More difficult tasks requiring greater cognitive planning to encode an utterance also result in longer pauses. Other kinds of vocalic phenomena, including filled pauses and nonfluencies, are also associated with greater cognitive planning.

Although the nonverbal cues do not tell us exactly what is causing the cognitive effort, contextual information often supplies useful clues. For example, if someone is disclosing a very embarrassing episode in his or her life, increased nonverbal markers of cognitive difficulty may be the tip-off that the person is struggling to convey the detail in a socially acceptable, face-saving manner. When speakers are very glib, we take their ease in verbalizing as a sign that the subject matter is a familiar one over which they have mastery. Awkward delivery implies that the speaker lacks expertise with the subject at hand. This is why speech delivery is so critical to speaker credibility.

Message Processing

Message processing is concerned with how humans acquire, store, comprehend, and retrieve messages. It is the decoding side of the message production and processing coin. Nonverbal behaviors are instrumental in each of the processing stages of attention, activation of conceptual knowledge, inference making, short-term and long-term memory storage, and retrieval of messages from memory.

Relative Impact of Nonverbal and Verbal Codes

A substantial amount of research has investigated how much impact nonverbal cues have on message decoding. The question driving the research has been: Do people depend more on nonverbal or verbal channels when deciding what something means? Research has looked at the relative impact of nonverbal and verbal cues when people judge others' credibility or dominance, size up their personality, infer their emotions and attitudes, or determine the "objective meaning" of utterances. Some experiments have manipulated a combination of verbal and nonverbal cues, then measured what interpretation receivers assign to the cue combinations. For example, three versions of a verbal message (positive, neutral, and negative) might be paired with three levels each of facial expression (positive, neutral, and negative) and vocal tone (positive, neutral, and negative), for a total of 27 different verbal-facial-vocal combinations. Receivers are asked to judge the meaning of a given combination on a positive-to-negative continuum. In cases when the cues are not consistent with each other—say, the facial cue is negative and the other two cues are positive—it is possible to determine if the facial cue carries more weight than the verbal and vocal channels by seeing if the meaning is negatively skewed or is judged as positive. Other investigations have looked at naturally occurring conversation or monologues, measured the nonverbal and verbal behaviors that appeared, and then determined statistically which ones most influenced the outcomes. For example, observers might watch videotaped segments from a job interview and rate the applicant on intelligence, personality, and hirability. The nonverbal and verbal behaviors appearing on the tapes could then be coded and correlated with the observer evaluations of the applicants.

The experimental approach can create all possible combinations of a particular subset of cues so that congruent and incongruent combinations can be studied. It also ensures that each cue can be presented with equal frequency and strength. It usually means looking at a very limited number of cues, however. The natural observation approach can study the full range of verbal and nonverbal behaviors that normally occur, but those cues may not arise with equal frequency, extremity, or consistency. Also, cues typically do not appear in all possible combinations, and incongruent patterns are especially rare. The second approach is therefore much more informative about consistent cue patterns than about contradictory ones.

Six Principles of Channel Reliance

On the basis of close to one hundred studies (see summaries in Burgoon, Buller, & Woodall, 1996, and Philpott, 1983), a number of general principles (also called propositions) can be identified.

1. *On average, adults rely more on nonverbal cues than on verbal cues to determine social meaning.* The figure most often cited to support this claim is the estimate that 93% of all meaning in a social situation comes from nonverbal information, whereas only 7% comes from verbal information. This estimate has found its way into almost every popular article on nonverbal communication. As noted in Chapter 1, however, it is an erroneous extrapolation from a study comparing vocal cues to facial cues (Mehrabian & Ferris, 1967) and another comparing vocal tone to single words (Mehrabian & Wiener, 1967), rather than a study comparing all three. In the vocal-verbal study, only single words were used, which provides a very limited test of the impact of verbal information. In the vocal-facial study, the verbal component was held constant, so it never had a chance to make a difference in receivers' interpretations. Hence, the verbal component was not given a fair test. These and other faults have led many scholars to treat the proposed weighting as highly suspect and exaggerated.

Nevertheless, other, more temperate estimates have given priority to nonverbal cues. Birdwhistell (1955), for example, asserted that 60 to 65% of the meaning in a social context is conveyed nonverbally. Philpott's (1983) summary of much of the channel reliance literature provided statistical support for Birdwhistell's claim. It showed that approximately 35% of social meaning derives from verbal behaviors, leaving the remaining 65% accounted for by nonverbal behaviors or their combination with verbal information. Interestingly, a classic series of studies by Argyle and colleagues showed that even when the verbal expressions were made far stronger than the nonverbal displays, people still placed more weight on the nonverbal than the verbal cues when judging a speaker's attitude from videotaped presentations (Argyle, Alkema, & Gilmour, 1971; Argyle, Salter, Nicholson, Williams, & Burgess, 1970).

Among the circumstances under which nonverbal cues prevail over verbal ones are: (1) judging a communicator's leadership ability and credibility, (2) judging

BOX 8.4

Watch What I Do, Not What I Say—Nonverbal Cues in the Clinic

One of the most important contexts in which nonverbal behavior can make a difference is doctor-patient interaction. How doctors communicate with their patients can influence not only how well patients understand their physician's or therapist's information, advice, and instruction but also whether they comply with the practitioner's recommendations.

The research has produced a mix of findings that might be described as equivalent to a Rorschach test (meaning one could read anything into it that you want). Nevertheless, some things are known about the nonverbal part of the equation (Gottman & Levenson, 1992; Harrigan & Rosenthal, 1986; Roter & Hall, 1992).

First, many studies have found that patients give more weight to a therapist's or doctor's nonverbal behavior than to what is said. For example, in the counseling realm, nonverbal cues are far more important than verbal ones in judging a therapist's empathy, genuineness, and respect for the client. When positive verbal statements are accompanied by contradictory negative kinesic and vocal behaviors rather than positive ones, counselors are rated as less effective and as having less regard for their clients. Nonverbal cues may also be more sensitive in distinguishing distressed from nondistressed couples.

Second, a synthesis of eight studies that examined kinesic nonverbal behavior in the doctor-patient interview found that the fol-

lowing behaviors were associated with positive health outcomes: head nodding, forward lean, direct body orientation, uncrossed legs and arms, arm symmetry, and less mutual gaze (Beck, Daughtridge, & Sloane, 2002). Expressions of empathy are also better conveyed through some of the same nonverbal behaviors, such as forward trunk lean but also direct eye contact, a concerned voice, and a concerned facial expression.

Third, the nonverbal stream, especially vocal intonation, becomes increasingly important with more visits (Hall, Roter, & Rand, 1981; Waitzkin, 1984).

Fourth, some socioeconomic factors make a difference. Women physicians spend an average of 2 minutes more with their patients (a chronemic variable) and engage in more positive nonverbal behavior and patient-centered communication (Roter, Hall, & Aoki, 2002). By contrast, when the patient is of lower socioeconomic status, physicians use a more directive, less warm style (Willems, De Maesschalck, Deveugele, Derese, & De Maeseneer, 2005). Patients from lower social classes may be less expressive and more passive than their higher-status counterparts, which may lead doctors to misperceive their desire for information and set up an interaction pattern with the physician that puts such patients at a disadvantage. Thus, the nonverbal behaviors may signal both parties' interest or disinterest in the interaction.

interpersonal styles, (3) completing comprehension and behavioral tasks, (4) answering interpretive questions, and (5) distinguishing true attitudes, feelings, and ideas from inconsistent expressions. Box 8.4 illustrates this vividly in patient-provider relationships.

Although the general research trend points to nonverbal behaviors carrying more weight than verbal ones in forming meaning, a number of circumstances alter the pattern. Thus this generalization needs to be qualified by the specific principles that follow.

2. *Children rely more on verbal cues than adults do.* In fact, most of the research suggests that children believe words more than they do facial expressions or intonations. For example, if you tell your 3-year-old nephew in an affectionate, teasing voice that he is "really strange," he will think you don't like him. A teacher who tempers criticism with a smile will still be regarded as critical, not helpful.

Whether children are truly more literal than adults is hard to say. It may be that they don't discount the verbal content as much as adults do when the verbal and nonverbal channels are in conflict. It is also not clear at what age they make the transition to greater reliance on the nonverbal channel. But it would be safest not to use sarcasm with a young child if you want the true intent of your message to be understood.

3. *Adults rely more on nonverbal cues when verbal and nonverbal channels conflict than when these channels are congruent.* Communicators frequently encounter "mixed" messages in which the combination of nonverbal and verbal cues does not provide a clear, unambiguous message. Sometimes these mixed messages are deliberate. Jokes and sarcasm rely on mixed messages for their effect. Other times, mixed messages are indicative of internal confusion. Uncertainty, indifference, and ambivalence (e.g., simultaneously liking and disliking another person) produce mixed messages. Further, deceptive communicators inadvertently display mixed messages that can clue others in on their duplicity.

Mixed messages are difficult to decode. One must sort out the conflicting cues and make an interpretation based on less certain information than in pure messages. When this happens, receivers are inclined to turn more to the nonverbal cues than the verbal ones to resolve the conflict. When the verbal and nonverbal channels are relatively consistent, the verbal information takes on greater importance. For example, impressions of job interviewees and presidential candidates have been shown to be equally influenced by verbal and nonverbal cues.

4. *Channel reliance depends on the communication function at stake.* Verbal content is more important for factual, cognitive, abstract, and persuasive interpretations. Nonverbal content is more important for judging emotional and attitudinal expressions, relational communication, and impression formation. For example, when people are asked to reconstruct a speaker's overt statements, they rely most on the verbal information; when asked to volunteer impressions of the speaker, they rely more on nonverbal cues. When one is judging objective meanings, verbal content prevails; when one is inferring a speaker's liking, intonation prevails. In a deception context, verbal content is also more useful in detecting factual lying, whereas nonverbal cues are more helpful when detecting emotional deception. In fact, most of the findings cited to support the general superiority of nonverbal cues come from studies involving relational, affective, or impression-leaving outcomes, whereas those showing increasing impact for verbal content come from studies involving interpretations or reconstructions of verbal meanings. Noller (1985) concluded that "the importance of the verbal channel increases with the amount of information contained in the words and is greater for more cognitive (rather than affective) tasks" (p. 44).

5. *When the content in different channels is congruent, the meanings of the cues tend to be averaged together equally; when content is incongruent, there is greater variability in how information is integrated.* It appears that when the information in the various channels is not totally at odds, people tend to add up their individual meanings and arrive at an average meaning based on all the contributing channels. For example, in judging a speaker's nervousness, audiences will tend to add together the separate bits of information presented by the kinesic and vocal cues of anxiety. However, when mixed messages are sent, people may handle such conflicting information differently. In some cases, people use a discounting strategy, in which they ignore one incongruent cue when two others are consistent with each other. In a study of immediacy cues, that is what people did when judging the relational meaning of a set of five cues: If two were consistent, a third inconsistent one failed to reverse or neutralize the interpretation drawn from the other two (Burgoon, Buller, Hale, & deTurck, 1984). Other research has shown that people believe whichever cue is the most extreme or most negative. But this is not always the case. The bulk of the evidence suggests that visual cues are counted more strongly than vocal cues, which in turn are counted more heavily than verbal ones.

6. *Individuals have biases in their channel dependence.* Some people consistently rely on certain nonverbal channels, some usually rely on verbal content, and some are situationally adaptable. One early study showed that people are consistent in relying on either facial cues or language when judging incongruent emotional expressions (Shapiro, 1968). Another showed that people making judgments of a speaker's level of stress can be divided into three groups: those who are verbal-reliant, those who are nonverbal-reliant, and those who shift back and forth in their channel preference, depending on the context or type of judgment being made (Vande Creek & Watkins, 1972).

No doubt people's channel preferences are related to which channel they have the best ability to encode and decode accurately. In as much as people differ in their skill at sending and interpreting linguistic, facial, or auditory information and in decoding pure or mixed messages (Berman, Shulman, & Marwit, 1976), it makes sense that they might come to rely on those channels that they are best able to use and read.

The Primacy of Visual Cues

Throughout this research, an important conclusion that has emerged is that visual cues carry the day for both adults and children. When attempting to resolve the inconsistency in mixed messages, receivers rely heavily on information communicated by visual cues (e.g., kinesic cues) (DePaulo & Rosenthal, 1979a; Philpott, 1983). For example, the classic study by Mehrabian and Ferris (1967) found that people rely most on visual cues, less on vocal cues, and least on verbal cues when decoding inconsistent messages. Bugental, Kaswan, Love, and Fox (1970) found a visual primacy among both adults and children. Research on nonsocial visual cues (e.g., lights) and auditory cues (e.g., tones), in which subjects indicate whether a light flashes or a tone sounds on their right or left, similarly found that perceivers displayed a strong visual bias (Posner, Nissen, & Klein, 1976).

Visual cue primacy is greater under the following conditions: (1) when mixed messages involve the face rather than the body; (2) when decoding emotions related to positivity (agreeableness, conscientiousness, positive or negative attitude); (3) when the discrepancy between the visual and auditory codes is not large; and (4) when the visual cues reside in the face (DePaulo & Rosenthal, 1979a; Posner et al., 1976). The face has long been recognized as a rich source of emotional content, so it is not surprising that receivers place more weight on facial cues when resolving inconsistencies. Body and vocalic cues become more important when receivers are decoding dominance, assertiveness, and anxiety (Scherer, Scherer, Hall, & Rosenthal, 1977; Zuckerman, Amidon, Bishop, & Pomerantz, 1982). Dominance is communicated very well by intense, emphatic body movements and vocal loudness, leading to greater reliance on these two channels when judging mixed messages of dominance, assertiveness, and anxiety. In contrast, the face is particularly important in judging positivity, because receivers associate the smile with positivity, a link that has no analogue in the body and voice.

Men and women differ in their reliance on visual information (DePaulo & Rosenthal, 1979a; Exline & Winters, 1965). Women are more likely to display visual cue primacy, especially when the visual cues involve the face and judgments of positivity. This may be due to greater visual interaction by women. Women use more eye contact than men in interpersonal interactions and are uncomfortable when they cannot see their conversational partner. Further, women increase their visual attention in positively valenced interactions. The attention to visual cues may also be the result of a learned tendency for women to be "polite" communicators by paying less attention to vocalic channels that are likely to "leak" information the source did not intend to send (Rosenthal & DePaulo, 1979b).

Finally, children encountering mixed messages use decoding processes that are somewhat different from those of adults (DePaulo & Rosenthal, 1979a). When positive visual cues are paired with negative vocalic cues, younger children appear to assume the worst, placing more weight on the negative meaning in these mixed messages, whereas adults counterbalance negative voices with positive visual cues. Younger children also have difficulty deciphering mixed messages that communicate dominance (Bugental et al., 1970). However, the ability to decode mixed messages does improve with age.

Explanations of and Speculations About Channel Reliance

As important as who relies most on nonverbal versus verbal channels and when is why the nonverbal stream so often dominates people's determinations of meaning. Several intriguing conjectures have been advanced.

Argyle et al. (1971) offered three possibilities. One is that we are innately programmed to signal affective states nonverbally and are likewise programmed to recognize such signals. As support for this position, they noted that many nonverbal behaviors are universal and unlearned. To the extent that all humans come equipped to send and recognize nonverbal cues, this would give nonverbal behaviors an edge over verbal expressions, which must be learned.

A second possibility is that, because of an efficient division of labor, verbal communication handles more abstract, nonsocial tasks such as problem solving, whereas nonverbal communication handles more social, interpersonal matters. Because verbal and nonverbal signals arise simultaneously, the nonverbal channels can silently monitor the sender, send and receive feedback, express emotions, and define the interpersonal relationship all the while the verbal stream is conveying linguistic content. The nonverbal cues thus become the frame of reference against which verbal interpretations are checked. Scherer (1982) made the same point when he noted:

> Through speech, humans can at the same time communicate symbolic meaning via language, with all the advantages that the design features of language command, and reveal information about their biological and social identity, transitory states, and relationship to the listener via a nonverbal vocal signaling system. (p. 138)

A third, related possibility is that, because of their ambiguity, subtlety, and deniability, the nonverbal channels may be especially well suited to expressing sensitive and risky interpersonal information. As we noted in Chapter 1, nonverbal codes can express what the verbal code cannot or should not. If you offer verbal criticism of a friend's behavior and it is rebuffed, you may find yourself very embarrassed, with little ability to retract your statement. But if you express the same concern through looks, touches, and vocal tones rather than words, this gentle approach may be more effective. If not, you can always disclaim any unkind intentions.

Some other possible reasons for the power of nonverbal cues are mentioned in Chapter 1. The primacy of nonverbal communication as a means of expression for the species and for infants may predispose us to rely more on nonverbal behaviors as dependable and familiar sources of information. The temporary shift in early childhood to greater reliance on words may be due to the novelty and challenge of learning the verbal communication system. We may return to relying on nonverbal cues because we believe they are more spontaneous, uncontrolled expressions of "true" feelings.

One other possible explanation concerns the structure of verbal and nonverbal coding systems and how the brain is able to handle such information. It may be that the more continuous, nonsegmented nature of many nonverbal signals makes them especially well designed for right-hemispheric processing, where more holistic, impressionistic, and affective judgments are made. That is, structural properties of the coding system may determine how and where such information is processed and, consequently, what types of interpretations are made.

As for why receivers are strongly biased toward the visual channel, at least four explanations have been offered (Berman et al., 1976; Keeley-Dyreson, Bailey, & Burgoon, 1988; Posner et al., 1976). First, when it comes to decoding emotional information, visual cues provide more information and possess more meaning than vocal cues. Visual cues are more semantically distinctive and are more efficient transmitters, providing more units of meaning per time unit. Second, humans may attend deliberately to the visual channel because, unlike auditory cues, it is not automatically alerting. This deliberate attention reduces the input from auditory cues, giving visual cues more impact. Third, encoders have greater control over the face, thereby giving decoders more intentional information. Fourth, people may rely more on visual cues because they can quickly scan a face and then concentrate on the most informative facial cues, whereas with the voice, decoders can only process the cues sequentially and fleetingly. Thus the amount of emotional information in the visual channel, its lower alerting capacity, its greater intentionality potential, and the longer duration of facial cues are thought to cause people to rely more on visual cues when decoding mixed messages.

Summary

We have reiterated throughout this chapter that nonverbal and verbal codes are part of an indivisible communication system. Both streams have many linguistic properties in common. Both have semiotic capability, that is, the capacity to convey representational information, but the nonverbal codes also have iconic and imagistic properties that add complementary and sometimes competing meanings.

The differences in linguistic characteristics are paralleled by neurophysiological differences in the production and processing of nonverbal messages. Many parts of the brain are specialized to handle different aspects of communication. The limbic system and R-complex are especially central to emotions and reflexive actions. However, emerging research is confirming a high degree of integration and coordination of verbal and nonverbal processes, especially between the two hemispheres of the neocortex.

The production of oral communication thus depends on nonverbal cues for generating meaning, retrieving lexical items, segmenting discourse into phonemic chunks, and augmenting meaning. Other nonverbal cues signal speaker difficulty in the message construction process. On the receiving end, nonverbal cues also play a major role in the perception, comprehension, and recall of received messages. Although the verbal stream carries important, and sometimes overriding, information for many functions and receivers, nonverbal information prevails over verbal information for much of our interpretation of the meaning of social situations. Despite these differences, verbal and nonverbal codes are well integrated for achieving a variety of communicative functions. To treat them as independent systems is therefore an artificial and counterproductive distinction.

Greater reliance on nonverbal than verbal codes for meaning is the prevailing pattern but also varies with age, gender, communication function at stake, degree of congruence in meaning among channels, and individual biases. Among the nonverbal codes, visual ones often carry more weight than auditory and other ones, but with many exceptions. Reasons offered for these patterns of channel reliance include inborn tendencies, divisions of labor, structural properties that are suited for cerebral processing, units of meaning per time, alerting capacity, controllability, and parallel rather than serial processing.

SUGGESTED READINGS

Andersen, P. A. (2008). *Nonverbal communication: Forms and functions* (2nd ed.). Long Grove, IL: Waveland.

Bavelas, J. B., & Chovil, N. (2006). Hand gestures and facial displays as part of language use in face-to-face dialogue. In V. Manusov & M. L. Patterson (Eds.), *Handbook of nonverbal communication* (pp. 97–115). Thousand Oaks, CA: Sage.

Burgoon, J. K., & Hoobler, G. (2002). Nonverbal signals. In M. L. Knapp & J. Daly (Eds.), *Handbook of interpersonal communication* (pp. 240–299). Thousand Oaks, CA: Sage.

Efron, R. (1990). *The decline and fall of hemispheric specialization*. Hillsdale, NJ: Lawrence Erlbaum Associates.

Guerrero, L. K., & Farinelli, L. (2009). Key characteristics of messages: The interplay of verbal and nonverbal codes. In W. Eadie (Ed.), *21st century communication: A reference handbook* (pp. 239–248). Thousand Oaks, CA: Sage.

Key, M. R. (1980). *The relationship of verbal and nonverbal communication*. The Hague: Mouton.

MacLean, P. D. (1990). *The Triune Brain in evolution: Role of paleocerebral functions*. New York: Plenum.

McNeill, D. (2005). *Gesture and thought*. Chicago: University of Chicago Press.

Poyatos, F. (1993). *Paralanguage: A linguistic and interdisciplinary approach to interactive speech and sound*. Philadelphia: J. Benjamins.

Rimé, B., & Schiaratura, L. (1991). Gesture and speech. In R. S. Feldman & B. Rimé (Eds.), *Fundamentals of nonverbal behavior* (pp. 239–281). Cambridge, England: Cambridge University Press.

9 Social Cognition and Impression Formation

Sometimes one creates a dynamic impression by saying something, and sometimes one creates as significant an impression by remaining silent.

—Dalai Lama

We humans are naturally social beings, and one of our most pervasive activities is forming impressions of each other. Take a look at Photo 9.1. In the second case, you see a clean-cut young man in a suit and tie. What impressions do you have about his personality, his honesty, his intelligence, and his background? How does that compare to the young black woman with braids? What about the elderly woman with the walker, the man in the tuxedo t-shirt, or the barefoot reveler at an outdoor music festival? Chances are that you have distinctly different impressions of each. These first impressions may or may not be accurate, but you form them nonetheless—with relatively little effort—because they guide how you think about this person and how, if at all, you will interact with him or her. Of course, our impressions of others are strongly influenced by what they say, but as the Dalai Lama's quotation reminds us, they are also strongly influenced by nonverbal cues.

In this chapter, we'll take a closer look at social cognition—the processes by which we use social information to form impressions of others—and how it is affected by nonverbal behavior. We will begin by examining three stages that we go through to form perceptions of others and by addressing a host of mental biases and "shortcuts" that often guide our impression-making behaviors. Next, we'll look at how accurately and consistently we form impressions based on nonverbal cues. Finally, we'll discuss how nonverbal characteristics inform three important classes of impressions: physical and demographic impressions, sociocultural impressions, and psychological impressions.

Throughout our discussion, it's important to keep in mind that *impression formation* is somewhat different than *image management*, the topic of the next chapter. In a way, these are two sides of the same coin. Impression formation has to do with *how we form impressions of other people* and the specific verbal and nonverbal cues that inform those impressions. In contrast, image management has to do with *how we enact the images we want others to form of us*. Fortunately for us, we can apply what we learn about each topic to the other. The more we know about how we form impressions of others, for instance, the better we can manage our

PHOTO 9.1   *What impressions do you have of each of these people?*
Source: Bottom center, right: Marilyn Stringer Photography.

appearance and behaviors so that others will form the impressions of us that we want them to form.

The Process of Social Cognition

Folk sayings reveal our culture's interest in social cognition and impression formation. Phrases such as "You can't judge a book by its cover" and "beauty is only skin deep" suggest a cautious and hesitant approach to impression formation. The phrase "what you see is what you get" suggests, however, that impressions are straightforward and reliable. Like many commonsense views of social behavior, these phrases do not quite hit the mark. The principles researchers have found to govern the formation of social impressions provide a more thorough and systematic view. We will begin this section by discussing the three-step process by which we form perceptions of other people. We'll then examine several cognitive heuristics and biases that frequently come to bear on our impressions of others.

Person Perception

The process of person perception involves three separate but related tasks: selection, organization, and interpretation. Usually, we engage in all three of these tasks so quickly and so subconsciously that we think of our perceptions as objective reflections of the world. In reality, however, we create our person perceptions based on the information we select for attention, the way we organize it, and the way we interpret it. We'll take a look at each of these stages of person perception in this section.

Selection.   Person perception begins as a sensory process. Perhaps you see your neighbor wave at you, or you feel your classmate nudge you as he walks past, or you hear your daughter calling out to you from her room. When events such as these stimulate one or more of your senses, they can initiate the process of person perception. It would be impossible to pay attention to everything you are seeing, hearing, smelling, tasting, and feeling at any given moment, however. Consequently, you engage in *selection*, meaning that your mind and body help you select certain stimuli to attend to, and several things make a particular stimulus more noticeable. One is how unusual or unexpected it is. For example, you might not pay attention to people talking loudly in a restaurant or bar, but hearing the same conversation during a church service would probably spark your attention, because it would be more unusual in that environment. Another characteristic that makes a stimulus noticeable is how frequently you're exposed to it. You're more likely to remember faces or voices that you encounter repeatedly than ones you've only encountered once, for instance. Finally, the strength or intensity of a stimulus affects how much we attend to it. We're more likely to notice strong odors than weak ones, for example. Since we can't attend to every stimulus, we must be selective in what we pay attention to.

Organization.   After you've noticed a particular stimulus, the second step in person perception is to classify it in some way. This process, known as *organization*, helps you make sense of the information by understanding how it is similar to, and different from, other pieces of information you have. To classify a stimulus, your mind applies to it a *perceptual schema*, a mental framework for organizing information. According to Duck (1976), people use four specific types of schema to classify information they notice about others. The first, *physical constructs*, emphasizes people's appearance, so we might notice that a particular person is tall, short, fat, skinny, beautiful, ugly, old, young, male, female, Hispanic, or Asian. The second, *role constructs*, focuses on people's social position, so we might notice that a person is a parent, a celebrity, a truck driver, a religious figure, and so on. A third schema, *interaction constructs*, emphasizes people's behavior, so we would notice if a person is shy, outgoing, sarcastic, aggressive, or considerate, for example. The fourth schema, *psychological constructs*, emphasizes people's thoughts and feelings, so we might notice that a person is self-conscious, angry, envious, insecure, or worried. Each of these perceptual schema helps us organize sensory information in some meaningful way so that we can move forward with the process of perception.

Interpretation.   After you have noticed and classified a stimulus, you must assign it an *interpretation* to determine what it means for you. Let's say you wave at a friend from across the street, but all she does is scowl and keep walking. Such a behavior would definitely be noticeable, and you would probably classify it as an interaction construct, since it relates to her behavior. What does the behavior *mean*, however? Is your friend mad at you? Did she just not see you? Is she just being sarcastic? Did she intend to wave back but get distracted in the meantime? Each of these questions has to do with the meaning you assign to her behavior.

Many elements influence how we interpret an event. One is our degree of involvement with the person whose behavior we are interpreting. For instance, we may interpret the same behavior more favorably if enacted by someone we know and care about than if enacted by a stranger (Manusov, 1993). A second influence is our attitudes about the behavior we are witnessing. If you see a mother spanking her toddler, for example, your interpretation of that behavior is likely to be affected by your attitudes about corporal punishment. A third influence is our knowledge about the event. When you witness your co-worker crying at her desk, for instance, your interpretation of her behavior may be shaped by your knowledge that her grandfather has just been stricken with inoperable cancer. Finally, your self-esteem can influence how you interpret nonverbal behaviors, particularly behaviors directed at you. If someone teases you, for example, you'll be more likely to interpret that behavior as friendly instead of hostile if you feel good about yourself than if you do not (see Alberts, Kellar-Guenther, & Corman, 1996).

These three elements of person perception—selection, organization, and interpretation—might seem complicated, but most of us go through these mental processes almost subconsciously. We constantly notice, organize, and interpret information in our physical and social environments, including other people's behaviors, and these perceptions help us form impressions of others around us. Because most of us practice person perception on an ongoing basis, our perceptions can seem to us as though they accurately reflect reality. When we get the impression that someone is upset, for instance, we believe we get that impression because he or she genuinely *is* upset. Subconsciously, we believe we have selected, organized, and interpreted all the relevant information to arrive at our impression, and that's why we are inclined to trust it. In reality, however, our person perception abilities are subject to a number of cognitive biases and "shortcuts," many of which make certain pieces of information more salient than others. This is not necessarily problematic; and in fact, these shortcuts—which are called *heuristics*—often lead us to form relatively accurate impressions of others. They can impair our perceptual accuracy, however, so it is useful for us to understand how. In the next section, we will briefly examine several of the biases and heuristics that most influence the impressions we form of others.

Cognitive Heuristics and Biases

When solving arithmetic problems, many of us use shortcuts to reduce the amount of time and effort required to arrive at the answer. To solve the equation 3×10, for instance, we could take the long route of adding $10 + 10 + 10$, but most of us know that when we multiply any number by 10, all we really need to do is add a zero to that number to arrive at our answer. Either approach will lead us to 30 as the correct answer, but the second approach—the shortcut—requires much less time and cognitive effort. Just as this shortcut allows us to solve a mathematical problem efficiently, cognitive heuristics and biases allow us to form perceptions of others relatively quickly and easily. We'll discuss several of these perceptual shortcuts in this section.

Primacy Bias. Browse the self-help aisle at most any bookstore and you'll discover there is no shortage of advice on how to make a good first impression. Whether you're interviewing for a job or meeting your future in-laws for the first time, it's clear that making a positive first impression is crucial. In contrast, you probably won't find a single book focusing on the importance of making a good *second* impression. What's so special about first impressions, exactly?

According to the *primacy bias*, or *primacy effect*, first impressions are critical because they form a baseline for all future impressions. That is, our initial impression of someone not only seems to stick in our minds more than our second, third, or fourth impressions do, but it can affect the nature of those later impressions. In one of the earliest studies of the primacy effect, Asch (1946) found that a person described as "intelligent, industrious, impulsive, critical, stubborn, and envious" was judged more positively than one described as "envious, stubborn, critical, impulsive, industrious, and intelligent." Most of these adjectives are negative, but when the description begins with a positive one (intelligent), this reduces the effect of the more negative latter items. Subsequent experiments have also shown that the first information we receive about someone has a stronger effect than later information on our judgments about that person, other things being equal (e.g., Parsons, Liden, & Bauer, 2001).

Given how important first impressions are, it might seem as though people would form them slowly and thoughtfully, having carefully considered all the information to which they have access. As you might have gathered from your own experience, just the opposite appears to be true: We usually form first impressions of others quickly, and on the basis of limited information. Psychologist Nalini Ambady and her colleagues use the term *thin slicing* to describe this process, suggesting that people often form their impressions of others on the basis of "thin slices" of information. In one study, for instance, participants watched three 10-second videotapes of college instructors teaching their classes and were asked to predict, on the basis of only 30 seconds of observation, how positively those teachers would be evaluated by their students at the end of the semester (Ambady & Rosenthal, 1993). Participants watched the videotapes without sound, so their judgments were based solely on the teachers' nonverbal behaviors. Not only were the participants able to form impressions of the teachers' effectiveness after watching only 30 seconds of videotape, but their impressions accurately predicted the actual evaluations the teachers received from their students.

The researchers then made the "slices" of information even thinner by reducing the original 10-second videotapes into 5-second and 2-second versions and repeating the study. You might guess that watching 30 seconds of videotape would make someone more accurate at predicting a teacher's evaluations than watching only 15 seconds (three 5-second clips)—and certainly more accurate than watching only 6 seconds (three 2-second clips). As it turned out, however, more information was not better; those watching the shorter video segments were just as accurate at predicting the teacher's evaluations as were those watching the longer ones.

In effect, the researchers demonstrated that observing the nonverbal behaviors of a college instructor for only *6 seconds* gives a person enough information to predict—with significant accuracy—the evaluations that instructor will receive from students who have observed and interacted with him or her all semester long. This finding suggests not only that first impressions can form quickly and on the basis of limited information, but also that those impressions can be remarkably accurate. Subsequent research has demonstrated that thin slices of information—predominantly nonverbal—provide adequate bases for forming accurate impressions of people's personality traits (Kammrath, Ames, & Scholer, 2007), status (Costanzo & Archer, 1989), pathologies (Waxer, 1977), sexual orientation (Ambady, Hallahan, & Conner, 1999), and citizenship (Marsh, Elfenbein, & Ambady, 2007).

Confirmation Bias.   Initial impressions can have lasting impact, but they aren't necessarily permanent. Rather, our impressions can change—sometimes significantly—if we gain new information about others over time. For instance, you can probably name at least one close friend whom you didn't really like at first. As we get to know people, new observations and experiences with them can alter our impressions. Often, however, we process these subsequent forms of information through the lens of our first impressions. Let's say your first impression of your economics professor was that he was absent-minded. That impression establishes an expectation in your mind that he will behave in absent-minded ways, making you more likely to notice behavior that confirms your impression (e.g., he can't find his car keys when class is over) than behavior that doesn't (e.g., he retrieves his keys without having to search for them).

Researchers call this a *confirmation bias*, or the tendency to notice or interpret evidence—such as behaviors you observe—in ways that support what you already believe (Nickerson, 1998). If your first impression of your new boss is that she is sociable and friendly, then you may be more inclined to notice behaviors that conform to that impression (such as smiling and chatting with her employees) than behaviors that do not (such as keeping her office door closed while she's working). Just because you notice confirmatory behavior more than disconfirmatory behavior doesn't mean your impression is inaccurate. You probably notice your boss acting sociable because she *is* sociable. However, the point of the confirmation bias is that we often cling to first impressions even when they're wrong because we pay attention to behavior that supports our impressions while ignoring or minimizing behavior that contradicts them.

What the confirmation bias does, therefore, is to cause our initial impressions of someone to endure even in the face of contradictory evidence. Not all impressions are equally susceptible to the confirmation bias, however. Rather, it appears that some types of impressions are more resistant to contrary information than others. Kammrath et al. (2007) examined the robustness of impressions of five personality traits, known to personality researchers as the Big Five.

These include (1) *agreeableness*, or the extent to which a person seems friendly, sympathetic, and interested in others; (2) *extroversion*, or how outgoing a person is in social situations; (3) *conscientiousness*, or how prepared and detail-oriented a person is; (4) *neuroticism*, or how commonly a person gets upset, irritated, or stressed; and (5) *openness to experience*, or a person's tendency to have new ideas and a vivid imagination. The researchers suspected that some of these impressions would be "high scope" impressions, meaning that they only endure if you frequently observe impression-consistent behaviors. A few inconsistent behaviors could change your mind. They proposed that other impressions would be "low scope" impressions, which are relatively persistent even in the face of impression-inconsistent behavior.

In a series of three studies, Kammrath and colleagues discovered that impressions of agreeableness, conscientiousness, and neuroticism are high scope impressions, vulnerable to even small amounts of contrary evidence. If you meet a new co-worker and find her to be highly agreeable, for instance, you only need to see her behaving in a disagreeable way once or twice before your impression of her is likely to change. Contrarily, the researchers found that impressions of extroversion and openness to experience are more likely to endure even in the face of contradictory evidence. If your new neighbor strikes you as highly extroverted, for example, that impression is likely to stick even if you observe him behaving in quiet, introverted ways on several occasions.

Recency Bias. Many stand-up comedians would say that the two most important jokes in a show are the first joke and the last. We have seen how important it is to make a good first impression, but many entertainers know it is equally important to make a good *final* impression, because that's what the audience is likely to remember. This advice reflects a principle known as the *recency bias* or *recency effect*, which suggests that the most recent impression we have of someone is more influential than our earlier impressions (Berza, Gannon, & Skowronski, 1992).

At first glance, the recency effect and primacy biases may seem to contradict each other. Logically, the first impression and the most recent one cannot both be the most important impression we make of someone, so how can the primacy and recency biases both be operative? The answer is that, whether the initial impression is more influential than the most recent one or vice versa, both are more influential than any impressions that come between them. Think about the last movie you saw, for instance. You probably have a better memory of how the movie started and how it ended than you do of all the events that occurred in between. Our perceptions of people often follow the same pattern: our first impressions and our most recent impressions are often more important than any others we form.

Research suggests that the recency bias is influential not only in face-to-face interaction, but also in computer-mediated communication. In one example, Rintel and Pittam (1997) analyzed text from Internet Relay Chat (IRC) interactions. They found that both the opening and closing phases of IRC conversations are critical for the impressions people form of each other and for the development and maintenance of their online relationships, a finding that reflects the simultaneous importance of both the primacy and recency biases.

Visual Bias.   Most of us use multiple senses—seeing, hearing, feeling, tasting, and smelling—to take in information about the world around us. At the same time, however, most of us give more weight to visual information than to other forms of sensory or social information when forming our impressions of others. Researchers call this a *visual bias* (Noller, 1985) and one of its most pronounced effects is that it leads us to rely heavily on people's physical appearance when forming impressions (particularly first impressions) of them.

You might not find it surprising that our first impressions of people are strongly influenced by their outward appearance, but why do we privilege visual cues this way? One reason may be that, for sighted people, nearly a third of the brain is devoted in some way to visual ability, more than is devoted to any other single ability (Melzer et al., 2001). Because so much of our neurological capacity is devoted to sight, it is understandable that visual cues would play a prominent role in our impressions of others. Another reason for the effect of the visual bias on impression formation is that physical appearance is readily available as a source of information during first encounters. Before you know much else about a new face-to-face acquaintance, you typically know what she looks like. Other nonverbal cues influence your impressions of her over time. Current research indicates that kinesic and vocalic demeanor and proxemic patterns are the next most available sources of information, but physical appearance cues are quite potent initially.

Several studies have illustrated the strong influence of visual cues on person perception. As we discussed in Chapter 4, physical attractiveness—a judgment that is based almost exclusively on visual cues—is directly associated with the extent to which a person is seen as more responsive, sensitive, kind, sexy, modest, poised, sociable, extroverted, intelligent, well adjusted, and interesting than unattractive individuals (e.g., Berscheid & Walster, 1974). Taller and thinner men earn higher salaries than their shorter and heavier counterparts (see Box 9.1). Finally, some jury simulation studies (e.g., Jacobson, 1981) have shown that guilty defendants who are physically attractive receive lighter sentences than unattractive ones unless they were perceived as using their looks to help them commit the crime (Wilson & Nias, 1976), such as a beautiful woman found guilty of blackmailing a wealthy man after having an affair with him.

Stereotyping.   Our impressions of others are a combination of the information we know about an individual and what we know about people in general. To some extent, that is, our impressions are influenced by *stereotypes*, or generalizations about groups of people that are often based on their physical traits, such as ethnicity, hair color, or body type. Stereotyping is a three-part process that begins by identifying a group that you believe a person belongs to (e.g., "you are a blonde"). Next, it involves recalling some generalization that is made about people in that group (e.g., "blondes have more fun"). Finally, it involves applying that

BOX **9.1**

Being Tall Pays

Research regularly shows that the thinner and taller the male executive, the fatter the salary. Professor Irene Frieze and Josephine Olson surveyed 1,200 graduates of the University of Pittsburgh's MBA program. They found that tall men earned more than their shorter colleagues, and that men who were at least 20% overweight made $4,000 less than their thinner coworkers. A typical 6-foot male professional earned $4,200 more than his 5-foot-5 counterpart. When weight and height were combined, the taller and trimmer man earned about $8,200 more than the shorter and heavier man. Olson explained the survey findings by pointing out that "people imagine a male manager as tall, strong and powerful. And the man who meets that image gets rewarded" (*Tucson Citizen*, March 2, 1987, p. 9A).

The results for women were not conclusive because of the small number of female respondents who were significantly tall or overweight. However, Frieze indicated that

"it's more complex for women than men. If a woman is seen as fairly attractive and she is doing these male-dominated jobs . . . there's a suspicion of how she's gotten there, how much she's used her attractiveness to get there." For tall and thin men, social stereotypes about physical appearance attributes and personal characteristics work advantageously. As for the rest of us, the implications are not so positive.

The connection between tallness and trait judgments of dominance and strength gets made early. One study (Montepare, 1995) examined the impact of variations in height in preschool-age children and found that children judged taller male and female targets as stronger and more dominant. When given both male and female targets of different heights to judge, taller female targets were judged to be stronger, more dominant, and smarter when paired with shorter male targets. It would appear that, for both children and adults, tallness pays.

---

generalization to the individual (e.g., "therefore, you must have more fun"). Thus, stereotyping is a way of arriving at a judgment about someone without investing a lot of cognitive effort in the process (Pendry & Macrae, 1994). You can probably think of stereotypes for many different groups of people (Nelson, 2005). What stereotypes come to mind when you think about ethnic minorities, for instance? How about overweight people? Blondes or redheads? Tall or short people? People with physical disabilities? What stereotypes come to mind when you think about yourself?

Research indicates that stereotyping is a pervasive cognitive activity and that many of us implicitly associate certain characteristics with certain types of people, even if we know at a conscious level that such associations have little merit (see Box 9.2). We often find the idea of stereotyping distasteful, particularly when stereotypes have to do with characteristics such as race, sex, disability, or sexual orientation (Hendrix, 2002). Stereotyping often leads us to make inaccurate, even offensive, evaluations of other people. The reason is that stereotypes underestimate the differences between people in a group. Consider, for instance, the stereotype that tall men are more dominant and aggressive than short men. Even if this is

BOX 9.2

The Implicit Association Test

We can all think of offensive stereotypes made about particular groups of people, and many of us like to think that although others might believe such stereotypes, we ourselves do not. Research has shown, however, that even people who reject certain stereotypes at a conscious level nonetheless make associations at the subconscious level that are consistent with those stereotypes. An ingenious procedure known as the *Implicit Association Test* (IAT) demonstrates how. Let's say you're part of a study to examine stereotypes about women and men. Sitting in front of a computer screen, you are shown a series of facial photos, some of women and some of men. Whenever you see a man's face, you hit a key on the left side of the keyboard, and when you see a woman's face, you strike a key on the right side. Second, you are shown a series of evaluative words. You strike a left key whenever you see a positive word (e.g., "intelligent," "wonderful") and a right key whenever you see a negative word (e.g., "boring," "disastrous"). In the third phase, you see pairs of faces and words and are instructed to strike a left key whenever you see either a

man's face or a positive word and a right key for either a woman's face or a negative word. All along, the computer is tracking how long it takes you to hit each key and how accurate you are at hitting the appropriate key.

Now comes the hard part. You are instructed to hit the left key whenever you see a man's face or a negative word and a right key whenever you see a woman's face or a positive word. The computer compares your response times and accuracy rates during the period when men's faces are paired with negative words to the period when women's faces are paired with negative words. If you take more time, and/or make more mistakes, in the first condition than the second, then researchers believe you implicitly associate negative concepts more with women than with men, revealing a subconscious bias against women.

Importantly, the IAT tests mental associations that are implicit or subconscious. Results of research using the IAT demonstrate that many of us carry negative stereotypes subconsciously, even if we believe at a conscious level that we don't. You can take the test for yourself at implicit.harvard.edu.

---

true in general, it doesn't mean that *every* tall man is dominant or that all tall men are dominant to the same extent. People in almost every group vary one from another, but stereotypes focus our attention only on the generalizations.

Even though stereotyping can lead us to form inaccurate impressions of others, it's important to point out that perceptions made on the basis of a stereotype are not *necessarily* inaccurate. In fact, stereotypes often arise and persist because they carry some grains of truth. But stereotypes gloss over individual differences and may take on more the qualities of a caricature than a true depiction of a group of people. Applying a stereotype to the individual case risks making some erroneous assumptions.

Egocentric Bias.   Perhaps you have encountered people who seem genuinely unable to see things from anyone else's perspective but their own. Instead, they assume that whatever they are sensing, thinking, or feeling, others are sensing, thinking, or feeling the same. This inability to take another person's perspective is called *egocentrism.*

You might have noticed that children often behave in egocentric ways. Billy stands right in front of the television, blocking your view; Missy asks you questions while you're talking on the telephone. Developmental psychologists have long believed that egocentrism is a normal stage of development for children ages 2 to 6 (Piaget, 1932). Billy doesn't understand that he is blocking your view of the television because he assumes you can see what he sees. Missy assumes you can hear only what she hears, so she doesn't realize she is interrupting your telephone conversation. As children, Billy and Missy both lack the developmental ability to take someone else's perspective.

Although most of us grow out of the egocentric stage by mid-childhood, even adults can act egocentrically from time to time. When we do, our egocentrism can influence our perceptions of others' nonverbal communication. Perhaps you've had the experience of traveling overseas and finding that people sometimes interpret the same situation differently than you do. Let's say that, during a business trip to China, Dylan stopped at a fast food restaurant for lunch, only to find a big crowd of people trying to get up to the registers to place their orders. Dylan tried to line up in front of one of the registers but was immediately pushed and shoved out of the way by the people around him. As you might imagine, Dylan got angry because he perceived this behavior to be aggressive and mean-spirited. Everyone else in the restaurant perceived this behavior as normal social behavior, however, certainly not as aggressive or mean. Waiting in orderly lines is common in the United States, but it is much less common in China and some other countries.

Being egocentric isn't the same as being selfish. People who are selfish are concerned only about their own needs and desires and are often unwilling to share their resources with others. In contrast, being egocentric simply means assuming that people around us are perceiving and interpreting the world in the same way we are.

Positivity Bias. When we meet and get to know people, our perceptions of them are often influenced more heavily by information that is positive, as opposed to negative or neutral. In such cases, we exhibit what researchers call a *positivity bias* (Mezulis, Abramson, Hyde, & Hankin, 2004). Think back, for instance, to the last time you met someone who is highly attractive. Perhaps you formed a positive overall perception of that person largely because you were emphasizing this positive quality—attractiveness—more than the person's negative or neutral qualities. The "halo effect," which was also discussed in Chapter 4, leads us to notice one positive quality of a person (such as attractiveness) and infer other positive qualities about that person (such as kindness or intelligence). According to the positivity bias, we give a person's positive qualities more weight when forming an impression of the person.

One form of the positivity bias is the tendency of people who are in love to look at each other through "rose-colored glasses" (Murray, Holmes, & Griffin, 1996). This phrase refers to overestimating people's positive characteristics while underestimating their faults or shortcomings (or ignoring them altogether).

Maybe you've been around people who have perceived their romantic partners in this way. Researchers suggest that this is a normal stage of relationship development and that a certain amount of "idealizing" is actually healthy for new relationships (see Fisher, 2004). Most relationships do grow out of this stage, however. People who cling to idealized views of their romantic partners may experience disappointment when they realize their partners are not as perfect as they originally thought.

Negativity Bias.   The opposite of the positivity bias is the *negativity bias*, which is the tendency to weigh negative information about a person more heavily than positive or neutral information. According to the negativity bias, even one piece of negative information can spoil your perception of someone you would otherwise like. Let's say you're meeting a new potential roommate. If other people describe him as "kind," you'd probably form a positive impression of him. If others say he's "dishonest," your impression would probably be negative. What if he's described as both "kind" and "dishonest," however? Most people would still form a negative impression—that is, the negative information would override the positive (Anderson, 1981).

Thus far, we have discussed several cognitive biases and heuristics: primacy, confirmation, recency, visual, stereotyping, egocentric, positivity, and negativity. We've seen how each of these functions as a type of mental shortcut, allowing us to focus on particular pieces of information while minimizing or ignoring others when forming a perception of someone. One point worth reiterating here is that the perceptions we form on the basis of these mental shortcuts are not always accurate, but they often are. We will address the issue of how accurate and consistent our impressions of others are in the next section.

Accuracy and Consistency of Impressions

Most of us are continually engaged in the task of forming impressions of others, and we often operate from the assumption that our impressions are accurate. To some extent, we do this by necessity—if you had to stop and critique the accuracy of every impression you formed, your social interaction would quickly become immobilized. You've probably been in situations, however, when you realized that your first impression of someone wasn't exactly correct. If so, then you've experienced how tricky impression formation can be.

When we talk about an impression being *accurate*, we mean that it reflects a person's "true" characteristics. You perceive that your neighbor is highly intelligent because she *is* highly intelligent. You perceive that your accounting professor is Pakistani because he *is* Pakistani. Thus, to say that an impression is accurate is to imply that the impression is warranted by the facts. Impressions are often also *consistent*, meaning they are shared by several people who know the same individual. Not only do you perceive your neighbor to be intelligent, for instance, but everyone else in the neighborhood does as well. Importantly, therefore, accuracy and consistency are separate issues. Your impression of someone can be accurate even if others don't share it. Likewise, many people can share a consistent, but inaccurate, impression of someone. Research has shown that several factors affect both the accuracy and the consistency of the impressions we form.

First, the level of an impression affects its likelihood of being accurate and consistent. Impressions generally are most accurate and consistent when made at the physical level, somewhat less so at the sociocultural level, and least accurate and consistent at the psychological level. Let's say it's the first day of school and you—along with 100 other students—are forming your first impressions of your nonverbal communication professor. Some of your impressions are about your professor's physical characteristics, such as her age, her sex, and her ethnicity. Most of you will agree on your assessments of these characteristics, and most of your assessments will be accurate. Other impressions will be about her sociocultural background, such as where she grew up, what her political or religious affiliations are, and how much money she makes. These features are not quite as evident, so your impressions will probably be a little less accurate and a little less consistent with those of your classmates. Finally, some of your impressions will relate to her psychological characteristics, such as her personality, her maturity, or her honesty. These are often the hardest to assess accurately, particularly when you are meeting someone for the first time, because they require observation of the person's behavior in various situations. These types of impressions, therefore, are likely to be the least accurate and the most inconsistent (Cook, 1979). For example, if you look at the photographs of the three authors of this text book (see Photos 9.2a, 9.2b, and 9.2c), you will probably be more accurate in guessing age and ethnicity than personality characteristics, such as what music they enjoy.

Second, the amount of information we have access to influences the accuracy and consistency of impressions. As we noted earlier, however, more information does not always increase accuracy or consistency; "thin slices" of information can sometimes support accurate and consistent impressions (Smith,

| a. Judee | b. Laura | c. Kory |

PHOTO 9.2 *How accurately you can identify these characteristics of your three authors? Try to identify the age bracket, (30s, 40s, etc.), sex, height, ethnic heritage, birthplace (region of country), preferred music, and favorite leisure activities of each of them. Answers are at the end of the chapter.*

Archer, & Costanzo, 1991). Judgments of physical characteristics—such as sex, age, or ethnicity—typically are accurate because the characteristic being judged is largely external. Judgments of internal characteristics—such as attitudes, values, beliefs, and some personality traits—tend to be less accurate because these characteristics are more variable and subject to stereotyping. However, *some* personal and interpersonal characteristics can be judged with accuracy. Berry (1991a) found that enduring facial and vocal cues accurately predicted self-ratings of warmth and power. For example, people with "smiley" faces tend to rate themselves as warmer. Kenny et al. (1992) reported high accuracy as well as consensus on judgments of extroversion; Ambady and Rosenthal (1993) showed that observations of nonverbal behavior as brief as 30 seconds predicted supervisors' and students' ratings of teachers' effectiveness.

Berry (1991a) offered three possible explanations for the high degree of accuracy for some internal judgments: (1) There may be direct links between some features of personality and behavior (e.g., "approachable" people may use softer, warmer vocal patterns); (2) Self-fulfilling prophecies occur (e.g., obese people are expected to be jolly, are treated as such, and may then internalize jolliness); and (3) Repetitive expressions of affect become permanent features of appearance (e.g., frequent scowling produces frown wrinkles, or chronic depression produces slumped posture). In addition, many studies that found inaccuracies with respect to impressions examined only single cues or codes rather than the multiple codes that are actually available to people. Impressions founded on combinations of cues, especially dynamic cues available during interpersonal interaction, may be more accurate because the interrelationships among cues provide clearer information (Smith et al., 1991).

In sum, our ability to judge internal characteristics accurately from nonverbal cues is mixed. Some characteristics, such as extroversion, are readily judged from a variety of nonverbal cues; other internal characteristics, such as an attitude toward incumbent politicians, are much more difficult to assess from nonverbal cues.

We should also point out that the term *accuracy* is problematic when it comes to certain types of impressions. To determine the accuracy of any judgment, some reliable information about the judgment must exist. Reliable information usually exists for the physical and sociocultural judgments we make about people. That is, if we think we know Sally as a Caucasian woman from Little Rock, Arkansas, who weighs 115 pounds, stands 5 feet 4 inches tall, has a bachelor's degree in education, and is a member of the Tri-Delta sorority, information is available to verify all these judgments. When we make inferences about Sally's personality and psychological characteristics, however, the reliability and availability of relevant information decreases. If you judge Sally as outgoing, vivacious, flippant, judgmental of others, rigid, and bigoted, what information could verify these judgments? You could cite several examples of Sally's behavior, but you would still be relying on your *perception* of her behavior. Personality tests wouldn't necessarily help much, either. Although some measures of personality traits significantly predict actual behaviors (Mount, Barrick, & Stewart, 1998), others do not (Mischel, 1968), so the results from personality tests would not necessarily be consistent with your impressions.

With psychological impressions, therefore, it may be more useful to focus on whether impressions are consistent than on whether they are accurate. Not surprisingly, many judgments at this level are consistent: People often agree on the personality traits of a given individual. Research on what nonverbal cues produce consensual judgments about personality still says little about what nonverbal cues provide accurate impressions, however.

Two more qualifying comments are in order about the research evidence we will review in the next section. First, since much of this research has investigated only one or two nonverbal cues at a time, what is known is often the effect of a fragmentary set of cues on impression formation. Although researchers have made progress in cementing these nonverbal pieces together into something that corresponds to everyday interaction, much research on large sets of cues is yet to be done. Second, most of the research has not included situational and contextual factors, which can affect impression formation in a variety of ways.

Types of Impressions and Relevant Nonverbal Cues

As you've probably gathered by now, the impressions we develop of people come in a variety of forms. Some relate to a person's physical or demographic characteristics; others reflect a person's social, cultural, and economic background; still others focus on a person's personality and psychological characteristics. We will discuss each form of impression in this section, paying particular attention to the nonverbal cues that help us make each type of assessment.

Physical and Demographic Judgments

Because they rely so heavily on readily available cues, judgments about physical characteristics such as a person's age, sex, ethnicity, body shape, height, and weight should be the easiest to make and the most accurate. They are not infallible, however. These judgments typically are made on the basics of physical appearance and vocal cues, with other codes such as kinesics, proxemics, haptics, and artifacts playing a secondary role.

Age.   Judging the age of someone unknown to you might not seem like a difficult task, but that partly depends on how exact your judgment needs to be. We are most successful at making estimates within broad age categories, such as "infant," "teenager," or "elder." Physical appearance cues are very likely to influence impressions of age; however, they can be misleading. Since our culture values youth so highly, people use a wide variety of cosmetics, drugs, preparations, and cosmetic surgery procedures to take years off their physical appearance (for a review, see Guerrero & Floyd, 2006). Several researchers have pointed out that these factors complicate age judgments and increase errors. Look at the woman in Photos 9.3a and 9.3b. In the first picture, she let her hair dry naturally and wore no makeup. In the second picture, she had her hair and makeup done. How old do you think this woman is in each of these pictures? (See the end of the chapter for

PHOTO 9.3   *Do you think this woman is younger in Photo A or Photo B? The answer is at the end of the chapter.*

Source: Photos supplied by Laura Guerrero.

A   **B**

the answers.) Does she look younger in one of the pictures versus the other? What other personality characteristics might you attribute to her based on which photograph you viewed?

Clothing can also make specific and accurate age judgments difficult. Some clothing styles may identify the wearer as someone older, but this is usually because they emphasize comfort over fashionability. As younger people opt for more comfortable attire or "recycle" previously popular styles, the differences between old and young become less evident.

Researchers have long acknowledged that vocal cues can lead to fairly accurate judgments of age (Schötz, 2003). The accuracy of these judgments is probably due to changes in a variety of vocal parameters that occur with aging (see Chapter 5). As one grows older, for example, the pitch level of the voice drops, although in the elderly, sex may make a difference in this pattern (McGlone & Hollien, 1963). One study (Mysak, 1959) found that speaking rate drops with age: middle-age and older people speak more slowly than college-age people. However, children increase their speaking rate as they get older, because they pause less and become more articulate (Kowal, O'Connel, & Sabin, 1975). These results indicate that vocal cues change with age in ways we can implicitly recognize. Although these changes may allow some broad judgments to be made about age, more research is needed on vocal changes across the entire developmental time span before relationships between age and vocalics can be fully understood.

The relationship of other nonverbal codes to age judgments is speculative. Kinesic cues such as general posture, frequency of gestures, speed of movement, and apparent energy level could be related to age judgments. Similarly, proxemic cues, such as larger or smaller conversational distances, could indirectly indicate differences in age among people in a group.

Of the cues we have covered, vocal cues appear to provide the most reliable information about age. In fact, the combination of vocal and other nonverbal cues may help the observer to make more accurate and specific age judgments than research has suggested so far.

Sex and Sexual Orientation.   Although impressions of a person's biological sex are usually accurate, many people have embarrassing stories to tell about being mistaken in such judgments. Perhaps you have occasionally mistaken a woman for a man, or vice versa, on the basis of what you presumed were reliable cues.

If asked, most of us would probably say we assess a person's sex primarily on the basis of his or her physical appearance, such as the shape of the face, the shape of the body, hairstyle, clothing, jewelry and cosmetics, and other visual cues. In many instances, these cues lead us to reliable assessments—after all, women and men do differ, on average, on all of these traits (see Guerrero & Floyd, 2006). Occasionally, though, these cues lead us to inaccurate judgments. Clothes can often mask sex-related physical characteristics, such as body shape, so to the extent that women and men prefer similar styles of clothing, judging sex from certain angles can be difficult. Body type can also be an unreliable indicator of sex; even though men and women's bodies differ on average, people come in all shapes and sizes. As films such as *Mrs. Doubtfire, Tootsie, She's the Man,* and *Boys Don't Cry* have shown, a "he" can certainly look like a "she" and vice versa. Some styles of physical appearance conform more closely than others to our stereotypical view of masculinity and femininity, and the cues that are part of these styles can lead to impressions about a person's sex that may be consistent but not necessarily accurate.

As with age, vocal cues seem to be reliable indicators of sex (Hollien, Dew, & Philips, 1971). In Chapter 5 we noted many vocal cues that differ between women and men, and this wide variety of physiological and learned differences is probably what allows listeners to distinguish between male and female adult voices with nearly perfect accuracy (see Günzburger, 1984). Most listeners are less able to distinguish between the voices of male and female children (for whom the physiological differences observed in adult male and female voices are not yet developed), but most people can still tell boys' and girls' voices apart at a better-than-chance rate (Bennett & Montero-Diaz, 1982). Other cues from the kinesic, proxemic, and haptic codes confirm our impression that someone is masculine, feminine, or androgynous. For instance, women (at least in North America) are more likely than men to touch other adults in supportive, affectionate ways (Floyd, 2006), and men typically take up more personal space than women when they stand or sit (see Uzzell & Horne, 2006).

Whereas a person's biological sex is relatively easy for others to assess accurately, assessing a person's sexual orientation is often far more difficult. The reason is that the genes that determine biological sex cause women and men to develop different physical characteristics—such as differences in height, bone structure, vocal pitch, facial hair, or body shape—by which they are often accurately distinguished. The same is not necessarily true for sexual orientation; that is, heterosexuals, homosexuals, and bisexuals don't systematically differ from each other in the same physical characteristics. For instance, just as some straight men are tall, strong, and masculine, whereas others are shorter, weaker, and more feminine, the same can be said of gay men, and indeed, of lesbians and bisexual women and men. The lack of readily identifiable physical cues to a person's sexual orientation makes it possible for many homosexual and bisexual people to hide their orientation from others (i.e., "passing" as a straight person). It also makes it likely that some heterosexual people are incorrectly presumed to be homosexual and vice versa.

Even though sexual orientation doesn't have as concrete a set of physical cues as biological sex does, people still use various nonverbal characteristics to form impressions of another's sexual orientation. These include a person's vocal characteristics as well as eye contact behaviors. Multiple studies have examined the association between vocalic characteristics and sexual orientation. Most have demonstrated that people can distinguish heterosexual from homosexual or bisexual adult speakers at greater-than-chance levels on the basis of the voice (e.g., Munson, McDonald, DeBoe, & White, 2006). For instance, when gay men, lesbian women, and heterosexual and bisexual adults of both sexes record a set of predetermined words, listeners successfully distinguished gay, lesbian, and bisexual speakers from heterosexual ones. However, one investigation using only male voices (Smyth et al., 2003) reported that listeners had a harder time correctly identifying the gay voices than the straight voices.

How do people distinguish the voices of heterosexual, homosexual, and bisexual speakers? Several studies have examined whether such voices differ in their acoustic properties. For instance, Pierrehumbert, Bent, Munson, Bradlow, and Bailey (2004) applied acoustic analyses to voice sounds and found that, compared to heterosexual adults, adults who were gay, lesbian, or bisexual articulated vowel sounds more distinctly. After analyzing their vocal samples acoustically, Munson et al. (2006) also found that gay, lesbian, and bisexual adults overarticulated "e," "i," and "u" vowels compared to heterosexual adults. However, other acoustic analyses found that, contrary to the stereotype, gay men's voices were not higher pitched or more varied, nor did they place greater emphasis on "s" sounds than straight men's voices (Smyth et al., 2003). When pitch variation was assessed by listeners' subjective ratings, however, it was significantly higher for gay than straight voices. That is, gay men's voices do not actually have greater pitch variation, but they are perceived to. Moreover, Linville (1998) analyzed the speech sounds of men who were perceived by listeners to "sound gay" (regardless of their actual orientation). She found that, in line with the stereotype, voices that sounded gay used "s" sounds of higher pitch and longer duration than did voices that sounded straight.

Comparatively fewer studies have focused on other nonverbal behaviors by which sexual orientation might be identified. Of these, some have focused on the notion that homosexual people are particularly adept at identifying other homosexual people on the basis of nonverbal signs. The folk term for this ability is *gaydar*, a contraction of "gay radar," and speculation about its behavioral basis has largely focused on the use of prolonged eye contact between homosexual adults. For instance, two gay men—strangers to each other—might notice when they first meet that they hold eye contact longer than is typical for men, and through this longer-than-normal eye contact, they "identify" each other as gay. There is some experimental evidence to support this notion (Nicholas, 2004). Importantly, however,

BOX **9.3**

False Impressions and Not "Telling It Like It Is"

Although we might like to think otherwise, our judgments about a communicator's ethnicity can strongly affect how and what we communicate to that person. One study exemplifies how judgments of ethnicity based on vocal cues alone can color attitudes expressed in an interaction. In an investigation reported in the *Washington Post National Weekly Edition* ("How Perceptions of Race Can Affect Poll Results, Morin, June 26–July 25, 1995), the researchers conducted the National Black Politics Study, a nationwide survey of 1,204 black respondents interviewed by telephone between November 1993 and February 1994. Only black interviewers were used to carry out the phone interview, which queried respondents on their political opinions. Respondents were not told the race of the interviewers, but clearly respondents did infer the race of the interview from vocal and verbal cues during the interview. At the end of the interview, respondents were asked to indicate what they thought the race of the interviewer was. As an aside, answers to this question confirmed what we noted earlier, that judgments of ethnicity from vocal cues are not always correct: 76% of the respondents got it right, but 14% thought their black interviewer was white, and another 10% were not sure. Lynn Sanders, the first author, noted that "respondents make racial assessments even when they cannot see the person interviewing them."

Of interest here is how their assumptions about the interviewer's race affected interviewees' responses to key political attitude questions. These black respondents gave much more conservative answers when they thought they were talking to a white interviewer than when they thought they were talking to a black interviewer. Two examples: (1) 64% of the respondents who thought they were being interviewed by a black interviewer agreed that "black elected officials can best represent the black community," whereas 49% of the respondents agreed with this statement when they thought they were being interviewed by a white interviewer; (2) 14% of the respondents who thought their interviewer was black agreed that "American society is fair to everyone," compared to 31% who agreed when they thought their interviewer was white.

Besides representing a serious challenge to survey researchers, these results tell us a great deal about vocal cues, ethnicity, and attitudes expressed in social interaction. First, we often draw inferences about the ethnicity and racial characteristics of others based on how their voice sounds, and those inferences may not necessarily be accurate (in this case, judgments within one's ethnic group were accurate about three-quarters of the time). Second, the attitudes and views we express are strongly affected by the perceived ethnic characteristics of others. Nonverbal cues play a key role in this sequence of events and show that ethnicity still provides a significant frame of reference for how we act towards others. This became evident most recently during the 2008 U.S. presidential election. Those who regarded Barack Obama, who is multiracial, as a black man heard and interpreted his speeches very differently than those who saw him as a white man or those who thought (erroneously) that he is Muslim rather than Christian.

---

research has shown that no single nonverbal behavior is a reliable indicator of a person's sexual orientation 100% of the time (Carroll & Gilroy, 2002).

Race and Ethnicity. Another fundamental part of an impression has to do with race and ethnicity. It is important to realize that the inferences people make in this

---

BOX **9.4**

Regional and Ethnic Dialects: Speaking Like a "New Yawker"

Whether variants on English such as Ebonics represent regional and ethnic dialects or an entirely distinct language was brought to a head in the 1990s when the Oakland County School Board in California voted to teach Ebonics in the public schools. This decision unleashed a rash of editorials, including this rather satirical commentary from the *New York Times* (Haberman, 1996):

> Here's an idea sure to go nowhere fast: recognize that vast numbers of New Yorkers speak a distinct language that may be called ivonics. It is not named after the former Mrs. Trump. The word combines ivory and phonics, and applies to speech patterns of European origin that virtually define what many Americans think of as a New York accent.
>
> 'e says 'e's troo wit 'er.
> He says he's through with her.
> Note how the H's go off duty like cabs in the rain, and the "th" is pronounced as though it were "t." Classic European patterns. Surely, this idiosyncratic New York speech may be deemed not a patois but a language of its own, meriting respect.
>
> No? Then how about ochonics, for ocher and phonics. It refers to the English spoken by many Asian-American immigrants, whose language structure in their countries of origin has them substituting R's for L's and stumbling over the V sound. Vivaldi is highly popular in Japan, but sons and daughters of that land often cannot pronounce his name right. That's because they speak ochonics.
>
> OK, let's get serious. Obviously, neither language idea is going to catch on soon with New York educators.

More to the point— and many New Yorkers will breathe sighs of relief—neither is ebonics, the combination of ebony and phonics that has stirred angry debate across the country since the school board in Oakland, Calif., declared it to be not black slang but a distinct language. Indeed, not only distinct but "genetically based," rooted in "West and Niger-Congo African language systems." It should be used in the classroom, the Oakland board said, both for teaching black students standard English and for "maintaining the legitimacy" of black English, their "primary language."

• • •

The suggestion from Oakland that many American blacks are somehow handicapped by West African roots particularly galled Michael Meyers, executive director of the New York Civil Rights Coalition and, he admits, an unreconstructed integrationist. How then do you explain the success of a New York resident from West Africa named Kofi Annan? Mr. Annan, a Ghanaian, is the newly elected Secretary General of the United Nations. When last heard, he spoke graceful standard English.

The remainder of the column presents others' assessments of the pros and cons of legitimating Ebonics and the potential stigmatizing effect that encouraging such language use could have. What it underscores for us from the standpoint of social cognition is that preferred and unpreferred dialects—and that includes Southern and Hoosier and Bronx dialects—not only are clearly recognized and associated with one's racial or ethnic identity, but also have profound effects on people's impressions of their users.

---

area are often based on racial stereotypes, not on judgments of racial or ethnic ancestry per se. The extent and impact of this stereotyping from nonverbal cues are illustrated in Box 9.3. Box 9.4 presents a commentary on the use of ethnic dialectics in the classroom and elsewhere.

Physical appearance may allow us to categorize an individual into one of three broad racial groupings, often called *Mongoloid*, *Negroid*, and *Caucasoid*. However, it is often difficult to place people in one of these three broad groupings—much less to make any finer distinctions—on the basis of a person's appearance. Many North Americans, for example, are not very good at distinguishing between Koreans, Japanese, Chinese, Vietnamese, and Thais on the basis of facial structure, skin color, and hair. Note also that even within each broad racial category, there is a great deal of individual variation in appearance, so that any given individual may be difficult to categorize. The celebrity of people such as Tiger Woods—who describes himself as part African American, part Chinese, part Native American, part Thai, and part Caucasian—reminds us that many people represent a mixture of racial and ethnic backgrounds.

Another feature of physical appearance that may be relevant here is clothing. However, variations in dress are also due to other factors, such as geographic region, socioeconomic status, sex, and rural or urban location. In India, for example, distinct differences in the way Sikhs and Hindus dress are immediately recognizable. In North American culture, however, because of the mass production of clothing, dress is not a reliable indicator of race or ethnicity.

Similarly, vocal cues do not provide a good basis for making judgments about race and ethnicity. Ethnic groups do differ systematically in some vocalic characteristics (Grabe & Low, 2002), particularly average pitch (Tom, 2003), and some scholars have suggested that vocal cues allow the determination of an individual's ethnic background, although others contradict this claim. Several factors help to explain this seeming contradiction. First, it may be that some vocal differences are too subtle for the untrained ear to hear and cannot be used by most people to determine another person's race. For example, the finding that African American children pause primarily at pitch changes in utterances, whereas Caucasian children pause at the beginning of clauses or conjunctions (French & von Raffler-Engel, 1973), is probably not noticeable to most people; it would take the trained ear of a sociolinguist and systematic research to pick up on the difference. Second, even though researchers have identified dialects such as Black English/Ebonics that are tied to race and ethnicity, the use of these dialects is a sociological rather than a racial or ethnic phenomenon (see Box 9.4). Not all people of African descent speak Ebonics (also referred to by linguists as African American Vernacular English, or AAVE), which is a mixture of standard English, elements of West African languages, and elements unique to the black experience in America. Some may either code-switch or not speak with a dialect at all. Further, Southern whites in the United States often use AAVE forms (Dillard, 1972). These days, some white celebrities, such as rappers Eminem and Kevin Federline, are known partly for their tendency to speak in stereotypically "black-sounding" ways. When a person hears the vocal cues associated with AAVE, therefore, there is only a moderate probability that the speaker is actually of African heritage.

An additional complicating factor is the trend of different ethnic groups copying each other's styles in music, urban street talk, and slang. For example, although rap mostly originated in the African American community, members of other ethnic groups (such as Anglos and Hispanics) have become successful rap performers, and in doing so, have emulated the vocal style of black rap performers. Much the same has happened in rhythm and blues.

Similar cases of vocal emulation have occurred between different ethnic groups in street talk usage, all in the effort to sound "hip." With so much borrowing of vocal contours between ethnic groups, it has become difficult indeed to use vocal cues to reliably identify an individual's ethnicity. The most reliable information for racial background judgments, therefore, appears to come not from vocal characteristics but from physical appearance. Other codes appear to play supplementary roles at best, and none is highly accurate.

Body Traits.   Although body characteristics are fairly accurately estimated from physical appearance cues, some evidence suggests that they can be derived from other nonverbal cues as well. Studies have shown that extremes in height and weight can be inferred from vocal cues. However, height and weight in the middle ranges are apparently difficult to estimate from vocal cues (Lass & Davis, 1976). Knapp (1978) made two important points about these judgments. First, the precision required for the judgment to be considered accurate can affect whether vocal cues are found to be useful guides for these judgments. In a study by speech and hearing scientists Norman Lass and Margaret Davis (1976), for instance, participants listened to tape-recorded segments of speech and were asked to guess the height and weight of each speaker. The verbal content of each recording was the same, so participants' estimates of each speaker's height and weight were based only on the sound of his or her voice. Participants were not asked to estimate actual height and weight, however. For height, they were asked to indicate whether each speaker was (1) under 5'0", (2) between 5'0" and 5'5", (3) between 5'6" and 6'0", or (4) over 6'0". For weight, they were asked to guess whether each speaker was (1) under 100 lbs., (2) between 100 and 150 lbs., (3) between 151 and 200 lbs., or (4) over 200 lbs. Using these broad categories of height and weight, participants correctly identified speakers' height category 48% of the time and their weight category 57% of the time. Participants were also more accurate at guessing the weight of female than male speakers, but were slightly more accurate at guessing the height of male than female speakers, based only on the sound of the voice. Recall, however, that participants were using broad categories for both height and weight assessments. Had they been asked to specify participants' *actual* heights and weights, the probability is that their accuracy scores would have been lower. It is also still unclear what particular vocal cues are informative for making weight and height judgments. It could be loudness, resonance, intonation, breathiness, or some other vocal cues. This area provides an opportunity for some interesting research.

To summarize, judgments in the physical features category are often accurate, but not as accurate as one might guess. Physical appearance cues are usually good indicators of age, sex, and body shape, but only moderately accurate indicators of race and ethnicity. Vocal cues provide good indicators of age and sex and somewhat accurate indicators of body characteristics, but they do not offer very accurate indicators of race. Other codes appear to play a supporting and contextual role for these judgments.

Sociocultural Judgments

Included in the broad category of *sociocultural* impressions are such judgments as socioeconomic status, region of residence, religion, and political leanings. As with physical judgments, physical appearance and vocal cues are most relevant, although cues from other codes also assist in the perception-making process.

Socioeconomic Status. Judgments about a person's socioeconomic status, occupation, and educational level are highly intercorrelated. As a result, an impression about one of these characteristics can lead us to form inferences about the others. Therefore, we discuss all three together here.

Imagine the following people on a bus or subway: a woman in blue hospital scrubs, a man in a three-piece pinstripe suit with overcoat in hand, a woman dressed in a sweatshirt and jeans, and a woman in a light-gray business suit. Do these clothing cues prompt you to make assumptions about these people's occupations, socioeconomic status (SES), and education? Your answer is probably yes. All other information being equal, you might conclude that the person in jeans is a student, the man in the pinstripe suit is a banker, the woman in the business suit is a middle-level corporate manager, and the woman in hospital scrubs is a surgical nurse. Perhaps you would've come to different conclusions about each person. Your perceptions may or may not be accurate, but the likelihood is that you formed impressions about each person's occupation, SES, and education level fairly effortlessly.

Studies by Behling (1995) and Cox and Dittmar (1995) have shown that observers make consistent status distinctions on the basis of clothing cues. Other research shows that people not only form perceptions of others' education level, SES, and occupation on the basis of clothing cues, but they make their own clothing decisions based on the impressions they want others to form of them (Kwon, 1994). Anecdotal evidence also suggests that many groups and corporations stress clothing as a means of indicating status and prestige through dress codes for employees.

People are acutely aware of the status cues that clothing provides, and they rely on apparel as a means of signaling professional aspirations and personal values. Further, people expect others to recognize their status and socioeconomic aspirations from their clothing. As a result, many individuals believe that if they don't conform to the dress norms for their social level and occupation, advancement up the ladder of success will be slowed, if not blocked. In some sectors of our culture, this is so; many people, rightly or wrongly, take dress seriously. In fact, Sybers and Roach (1962) observed that clothing often communicates not only people's present SES, occupation, and education, but also what they aspire to.

One of the most straightforward clothing indicators of SES, education, and occupation is the uniform. Through specific and widely used clothing styles, societies formalize the status of such occupations as police officer, judge, doctor, and clergy. People not only tend to associate specific uniforms with particular occupations, but they also make judgments about the credibility of people in those professions based on the uniform worn. Several studies, for instance, have shown that how physicians dress—such as in a white coat, hospital scrubs, or in business attire—makes a difference in how competent or credible they are perceived by patients to be (Lill & Wilkinson, 2005). One such study focusing on gynecologists, for example, found that patients rated the credibility of both male and female doctors the highest when the doctors wore a white lab coat over hospital scrubs (Cha, Hecht, Nelson, & Hopkins, 2004). This is further testimony to the need for readily accessible visual information about a communicator's social role.

Vocal cues are informative for some judgments, less so for others. Listeners can accurately identify a speaker's SES from vocal cues (Moe, 1972). Although it is unclear from these studies exactly which vocal cues are responsible, pronunciation and pausing patterns are possibilities (Siegman, 1978). Siegman and Pope (1965), for example, found a correlation between silent pausing and SES in an interview study with female nursing students. In this study, lower-class and lower-middle-class subjects showed more pausing than upper-middle-class and upper-class subjects.

Judgment of occupation from vocal cues, however, is less precise. Some investigations (Allport & Cantril, 1934) have found limited support for accurate judgments of occupational categories. Fay and Middleton (1940) found a great degree of consistency among subjects' occupational judgments but little accuracy. Put in context, these results make a great deal of sense. A person's socioeconomic status is a constant feature of his or her everyday life—people are born into a family at a given social stratum and are socialized by that family. As language researchers have shown, verbal and vocal behaviors are affected by socialization at different levels of SES. Occupational choices, in contrast, typically are only made as an adult and thus do not have the powerful socializing effects that a person's socioeconomic background does. Short of occupations that require very specialized vocal training (such as a radio announcer, professional singer, or auctioneer), it is unlikely that occupation has much recognizable effect on how people use their voices, and thus it is unlikely to affect listeners' judgments.

Both physical appearance and vocal cues can therefore be consistent, if not accurate, indicators of education, occupation, and SES. Being able to judge one of these three characteristics accurately greatly increases the odds of accurately judging the other two.

Region of Residence.   Physical appearance and vocalic cues can also be indicators of the region in which a person resides. Of course, many communicators dress and use vocal cues that are typical of their own region. Cowboy hats and western boots may be at home in Albuquerque and Tucson but might seem out of place in Baltimore or Cincinnati. Similarly, Eastern seaboard "preppie" styles of clothing might look appropriate in Boston but less so in Boise. Although the mass marketing of clothing allows people to adopt almost any style they want, regardless of where they live, certain styles of clothing still exemplify different regions.

Most of us are also aware of the role that regional accent plays as an indicator of geographic residence. Trained and knowledgeable linguists can often accurately determine not only the state a person comes from, but also the county or community, by features of his or her accent. Most of us don't have that precise an ear for accent, and the empirical evidence indicates that the typical listener can accurately determine only the general region from which a person hails (Nerbonne, 1967). These broad regional discriminations may be easiest when a speaker uses a dialect that is not of one's own region. Brooklyn listeners might immediately recognize a speaker's Southern accent, and residents of Mobile, Alabama, will most likely know that a person with a Chicago accent is from the North.

Three factors complicate the judgment of regional residence from vocal cues. First, some parts of the country, such as Florida and California, have experienced great influxes of people from other regions. As a result, it is difficult to determine what the local and regional dialects and accents are, and very mixed patterns of regional accent may result. Second, researchers have discovered that communicators often accommodate to the surrounding linguistic community's accent patterns. A person from Pennsylvania who moves to Oklahoma will most likely begin to sound like an Oklahoman after a while.

Third, evidence suggests that children acquire their accents from their peers—such as their friends and classmates—more so than from their parents. Suppose, for instance, that a couple lives in Boston but moves to Dallas and then has children. You might think the children would grow up with a Boston accent (at least until the parents' own accents have changed, as we discussed previously), because they would hear their parents speaking in the home while they were acquiring their language skills. Instead, the children are more likely to acquire the accent they hear spoken by their peers—a Southern accent in this case (Vandell, 2000). The same process appears to transpire with children of immigrants, who quickly adopt the accent of their peers (rather than retain the accent of their parents) once they enter school and acquire a peer group (see Caldas & Caron-Caldas, 1999). As a result, children's accents tend to correspond more directly to the region in which *they* were raised than to the region from which their parents hailed.

Culture. Cultural judgments can be more difficult than one might think, and to some extent they overlap judgments of race and ethnicity. Although features of physiognomy and skin pigmentation can often help define a person's ethnic and cultural *ancestry*, other physical appearance cues, such as clothing and grooming, are more useful in defining his or her *current* culture. Unfortunately, many observers don't know enough about other cultures to recognize clothing and grooming cues that would indicate a person's culture. For example, many Westerners do not know enough about different traditional Asian folk costumes to distinguish between a *kimono* (traditional Japanese attire) and a *hanbok* (traditional Korean attire). In our own culture, there are many co-cultures whose members would theoretically be identified by clothing cues if traditional forms of clothing were worn. If individuals from Navajo, German, and Italian communities wear traditional cultural costumes, for instance, an observer should be able to identify their ethnic backgrounds. However, since traditional forms of dress are infrequent these days, such cues are often of little use in everyday life.

The ability of a typical observer to make ethnic or cultural judgments on the basis of vocal cues also appears to be limited. Different languages do have different vocal patterns and parameters in terms of rhythm, inflection, rate, and other vocal qualities. One study indicated that listeners may be best at identifying vocal patterns of their own language (Cohen & Starkweather, 1961). American subjects who heard filtered samples of Chinese, English, German, and Italian identified the English voice more accurately than any of the others. However, the extent to which a speaker exhibits these vocal cues and the degree to which a listener is familiar with them may be limited.

Some research also suggests that people can identify the region of a country from which a person hails by listening to the rhythm and intonation of his or her speech. In a series of studies conducted in The Netherlands, for instance, Van Bezooijen and Gooskens (1999) found that listeners could accurately identify which region of The Netherlands or the United Kingdom a speaker was native to by listening to the sounds of his or her language.

Group Membership.   An individual's membership in social, political, religious, civic, and other groups is often communicated nonverbally, primarily through physical appearance cues. Whether the group is the Lions' Club, a local softball team, or a gangster rap band, a variety of physical appearance cues will often identify an individual as a member. Beyond inferences about group membership, observers will also make inferences about an individual's social, political, moral, and religious views, which are linked to these groups. In a study that is now 45 years old (Buckley & Roach, 1974), participants viewed photographs of college students in different clothing styles and were asked to indicate each person's likely stance on various political issues that were hotly contested at the time, including abortion, women's liberation, and the military draft. Study results showed that people wearing unconventional styles of dress were perceived to have politically liberal positions on these controversial issues. Likewise, those wearing more conventional styles were thought to be politically conservative. Although this study is dated, similar results would probably be obtained if it were replicated today. Regardless of what time era we may explore, individuals make judgments about others based, in part, on clothing style and how that clothing style may indicate group membership. On the whole, though, physical appearance cues allow observers a rather straightforward way of making inferences about another person's group membership and related attitudes (see also Davis, 1984).

Psychological Judgments

People make a whole range of judgments about others' psychological states, personalities, traits, and moods. Many psychological judgments are evaluative in that they represent an attitudinal response to another individual. Also, these judgments tend to rely heavily on stereotypes, scripts, implicit personality theories, and other person-relevant information. As a result, these judgments are often more consensual than accurate. Further, unlike physical and sociocultural judgments, these inferences rely on a broader range of nonverbal cues. In a sense, these inferences are among the most interesting to investigate because they show how willing we are to attribute internal characteristics to an individual on the basis of external cues. In this section, we will focus on two important psychological judgments—perceived personality and perceived attractiveness—and review their links to nonverbal behavior and characteristics.

Personality. Perception of a personality trait in another person involves not only relying on one or more nonverbal cues but also linking those cues to a stereotype. Personality traits themselves are stable and enduring internal characteristics that persist across situations. As noted earlier, the accuracy of these judgments is at best difficult to assess. More important is the fact that such inferences and judgments are commonly made by observers about others.

A variety of physical appearance cues can lead to impressions of personality. One of the most basic is body type. Recall that people describe themselves according to a set of stereotypes that are associated with body type or somatotype: endomorphic, mesomorphic, or ectomorphic (see Chapter 4). These stereotypes are used to perceive not only oneself but other people as well. Research by Tucker (1984), for instance, showed that college men rated men with mesomorphic bodies as being more extroverted, less neurotic, more satisfied with themselves, and more satisfied with their bodies than men with endomorphic or ectomorphic bodies. Others have also shown that body types influence perceptions of personality for both women and men (Johnson, 1990). Some research suggests that the connection between body type and perceptions of personality begins early in life. For example, Walker (1963) demonstrated that somatotype stereotypes are used by parents and teachers to evaluate children. Although the accuracy of these stereotypes can be questioned, the more important point is that as part of the impression formation process, people often invoke such stereotypes based on the somatotype of the person being perceived. Further, if such stereotypes are applied early in life, as Walker suggested, children are consistently responded to and interacted with as if they actually possessed the personality traits associated with their particular body type. As a result, a child's self-concept and personality can be shaped by the expectations that others have on the basis of the child's somatotype. This line of reasoning could help to explain why there is some correspondence between somatotype and self-description in terms of these traits.

Another physical feature that may affect personality attributions is facial and cranial hair (see Box 9.5). In an innovative study, Pellegrini (1973) recruited bearded undergraduates to shave off their beards in stages, until they were completely clean shaven. Pellegrini took photos of the men at each stage of the shaving process, and later showed the photos to male and female participants who rated the photographed men on various personality traits. The results consistently showed that the more hair on the face, the higher the ratings on masculinity, maturity, self-confidence, dominance, courage, liberality, nonconformism, industriousness, and good looks. These findings seem a bit curious in light of our discussion of beardedness and careers in Box 9.5. It may be that while some of the traits cited are desirable

BOX **9.5**

When Less Is Better—Hairiness and Job Success

Hair length and beardedness (for males) may affect judgments of occupation and even whether one gets a job in the first place. Surveys of college recruiting officers and managers routinely find that they favor short-haired and clean-shaven males. In the United States, short hair and the absence of facial hair makes a man appear more businesslike and serious and therefore more appropriate for certain types of employment. This preference has prevailed for some time. In a study of physician appearance, for instance, Gjerdingen, Simpson, and Titus (1987) found that patients judged male physicians with long hair as particularly unprofessional. One reason why short hair and a lack

of facial hair are associated with professional success in contemporary society is that people judge men with short hair and no facial hair as more competent and socially mature than men with longer hair, beards, and moustaches (Muscarella & Cunningham, 1996).

Are women's career concerns affected by hairstyles as well? Little systematic evidence is available on this question, but some authors (e.g., Hinsz, Matz, & Patience, 2001; Richmond, McCroskey, & Payne, 1987) have suggested that women with longer hair are perceived as younger and sexier than women with shorter hair, which may contribute to perceptions of incompetence from female coworkers and low intelligence from male coworkers.

---

for males in careers, others, such as nonconformity, liberality, and dominance, are not. So from a personnel manager's point of view, beardedness presents a mixed picture at best. Even the current popularity of the 3-day beard stubble has not altered expectations for the workplace (although, as with any physical appearance feature related to current style trends, what is preferred is subject to change). Take a look at Photo 9.4. Do your perceptions of the man in these photos differ based on whether he is bearded or clean-shaven?

As for hair length, although some organizations and companies still have either written or unwritten codes about hair length and beards, attributions about men who have longer hair (or beards) are not as negative as they once were. Personality stereotypes about hair for females also exist, especially about length and color. However, these stereotypes have so far received little empirical attention. The larger issue

PHOTO 9.4 *How do your perceptions of this man change based on whether he is bearded or clean-shaven? If you were an employer, which look would you prefer?*

Source: Photos supplied by Laura Guerrero.

here may be a matter of what is normative in the workplace. Since men and women have varying hair lengths these days, and shaved heads are currently popular, a variety of hairstyles may be tolerated without evoking negative attributions. However, coming to work with hair dyed in waves of lime green, hot pink, and deep purple is bound to raise many corporate eyebrows. A 60-year-old secretary in one of our workplaces (a business school) routinely came to work with bright purple hair, much to the chagrin of the dean. But the dean was powerless to enforce a "hair code" in an academic environment, and so the secretary daily turned the heads of campus visitors. One wonders if their impression of the entire college was affected in a positive or negative way by the "statement" this secretary made with her hair.

Vocal cues have also been associated with personality. Studies in this area fall into one of three categories: (1) studies that focus on the actual relationship between voice characteristics and personality traits; (2) studies that focus on the accuracy of judges in identifying personality traits; and (3) studies that focus on the perceptions attached to various vocal features. We are concerned with the last category of studies here.

One of the most extensive studies in this area was conducted several decades ago by Addington (1968). Addington understood that certain voice qualities are closely linked to impressions of personality. He devised a study in which male and female speakers simulated breathy, thin, tense, flat, throaty, nasal, and orotund voice qualities. Subjects then rated the perceived personality traits. The results indicate that some rather specific personality stereotypes are associated with voice qualities, as shown in Table 9.1.

Research conducted on the link between the voice and perceived personality over the last several years has focused on two aspects of the voice in particular. One is how attractive the voice sounds. Work by Zuckerman, Miyake, and Hodgins (1991) has established the existence of a *vocal attractiveness stereotype* whereby we attribute positive personality characteristics to people who have nice-sounding voices. In particular, several studies have shown that people with attractive voices are perceived to be more honest, warm, dominant, likeable, and likely to achieve than are people with less attractive voices (e.g., Berry, 1992).

TABLE 9.1   Associations Between Voice Qualities and Perceptions of Women and Men as Reported by Addington (1968)

Voice Quality	Perceptions for Women	Perceptions for Men
Breathiness	Feminine, high-strung, pretty	Young, artistic
Flatness	Masculine, sluggish, cold	Masculine, sluggish, cold
Tenseness	Young, emotional, unintelligent	Old, unyielding
Throatiness	Lazy, unintelligent, unattractive	Old, sophisticated, successful
Richness	Lively, friendly, humorless	Energetic, healthy, artistic, proud
Rate	Animated, extroverted	Animated, extroverted
Pitch variation	Dynamic, extroverted	Dynamic, feminine, artistic

---

BOX **9.6**

Is Beauty Better Than Brains?

It has now been more than four decades since Robert Rosenthal and L. Jacobson published *Pygmalion in the Classroom: Teacher Expectation and Pupils' Intellectual Development* (1968). Rosenthal and Jacobson detailed the effect of teachers' expectations on students' performance and came to the conclusion that the impact was considerable. Subsequent research (see Clifford & Walster, 1973; Elashoff & Snow, 1971) found that students' physical attractiveness was one of the major determinants of teachers' expectations.

This seems unfair to children. A teacher's estimate of a child's abilities should not be so strongly influenced by physical attractiveness; moreover, the child's actual performance will be affected—because of the self-fulfillment prophecy or other such processes. One would hope then that these processes would be taken into account by teachers and schools. Ritts, Patterson, and Tubbs (1992) returned to these issues, reviewing 29 studies on expectations and judgments of physically attractive students, and performing a meta-analysis on 17 of these studies. (A meta-analysis is a statistical review and summary of results of several studies.) They concluded:

> The studies reviewed here clearly show that highly attractive students, compared to their unattractive counterparts, are the beneficiaries of more favorable judgments by teachers. This attractiveness effect is reflected in teachers' more positive expectancies of physically attractive students in terms of their intelligence, academic potential, grades, and other attributes. (p. 422)

The significance of this research is hard to miss. Physical attractiveness has an impact early in our lives. It can determine what others, particularly others that figure largely in our development, think and expect of us. Although it would be overstating the case to indicate that all teachers' expectations are influenced by physical attractiveness, or that other factors don't play much of a role in developing those expectations, physical attractiveness is clearly important, as Rosenthal and Jacobson initially suggested.

The second focus of research has been on vocal maturity, which relates to how babyish or grown-up a voice sounds. Multiple studies have demonstrated that adults who have babyish voices are perceived by others to be more warm and honest than adults with mature voices (Berry, 1991a). In comparison to those with mature voices, however, adults with babyish voices are also perceived to be less powerful and less competent. This is true of children as well as adults (Berry, Hanse, Landry-Pester, & Meier, 1994). So, whereas vocal attractiveness appears to be an advantage across the board when it comes to personality perceptions, vocal babyishness seems to be a mixed blessing (for a review of research on perceived personality and the voice, consult Siegman, 1978).

Attractiveness.   Social scientists have given much attention to the cues that foster perceptions of attractiveness. Being perceived as attractive carries a great deal of clout in our culture (this is true in other cultures as well, although the specific cues that prompt perceptions of attractiveness are sometimes different from those that we encounter in the United States). The power of attractiveness is illustrated by a stereotype that some researchers express as the "what is beautiful is good" hypothesis (see Chapter 4). On the basis of this stereotype, attractive people are credited with more positive attributes, such as intelligence, persuasiveness, poise, sociability, warmth, power, and occupational success, than unattractive people (see Hatfield & Sprecher, 1986, and Box 9.6). Another term for this is the *halo effect*: judgments of attractiveness positively influence judgments in other domains.

Early research in this area demonstrated that a variety of physical appearance cues produce judgments of attractiveness. For instance, Berry (1990b, 1991b) showed that certain characteristics make up a "facially attractive" impression, leading to a variety of other positive judgments. Beyond these facial cues, factors such as nonverbal expressivity, smiling, gaze, nonverbal immediacy and involvement, positivity of facial expressions, and apparent spontaneity contribute to perceived attractiveness (Gallaher, 1992; Reis et al., 1990). Curiously, engaging in self-adaptors has also been perceived positively in terms of honesty, extroversion, and professionalism (Harrigan, Kues, Steffen, & Rosenthal, 1987).

In sum, a variety of physical appearance cues, vocal cues, and facial cues may prompt impressions of attractiveness, extroversion, maturity, or babyishness. Perceptions of attractiveness have an additional effect: prompting positive impressions on other judgmental dimensions. Many of these judgments are attributions of enduring and stable traits, and as such may be the basis for consistent behavior of others toward the person being judged. It is important, then, to keep in mind that nonverbal cues may lead to these impressions, and that such judgments can have effects on other interpersonal outcomes as well.

Summary

The process of person perception involves selecting, organizing, and interpreting available information, which often comes in the form of nonverbal cues. Several cognitive heuristics and biases influence the perceptions that nonverbal cues lead us to form of others, including primacy, confirmation, recency, visual, stereotyping, egocentric, positivity, and negativity. Nonverbal cues from a number of codes have been shown to affect impressions on the physical, sociocultural, and psychological levels. Evidence indicates that impressions are more consensual and less accurate when they are of objective characteristics, but recent research suggests that first impressions of some internal characteristics (such as extroversion) can be accurate. Finally, a wide variety of cues affects impression formation on all three levels of judgment, and cues that affect impression formation are widely distributed in the behavioral flow of interaction. "Don't judge a book by its cover" remains a prudent rule for social behavior, but much social life is nevertheless guided by WYSIWYG: "What you see is what you get."

SUGGESTED READINGS

Ambady, N., Hallahan, M., & Rosenthal, R. (1995). On judging and being judged accurately in zero acquaintance situations. *Journal of Personality and Social Psychology, 69*, 518–529.

Aronson, E. (2007). *The social animal* (10th ed.). New York: Worth.

DePaulo, B. M. (1992). Nonverbal behavior and self-presentation. *Psychological Bulletin, 111*, 203–243.

Gladwell, M. (2005). *Blink: The power of thinking without thinking.* New York: Little Brown & Company.

Kida, T. E. (2006). *Don't believe everything you think: The 6 basic mistakes we make in thinking.* Amherst, NY: Prometheus Books.

London, M. (Ed.) (2001). *How people evaluate others in organizations.* Mahwah, NJ: Lawrence Erlbaum Associates.

Mezulis, A. H., Abramson, L. Y., Hyde, J. S., & Hankin, B. L. (2004). Is there a universal positivity bias in attributions? A meta-analytic review of individual, developmental, and cultural differences in the self-serving attributional bias. *Psychological Bulletin, 130,* 711–747.

Noller, P. (1985). Video primacy—a further look. *Journal of Nonverbal Behavior, 9,* 28–47.

Smith, H. J., Archer, D., & Costanzo, M. (1991). "Just a hunch": Accuracy and awareness in person perception. *Journal of Nonverbal Behavior, 15,* 3–18.

Zebrowitz, L. (1997). *Reading faces: Window to the soul?* Boulder, CO: Westview Press.

A N S W E R S   T O   P H O T O   Q U E S T I O N S

1. Photos 9.3a, 9.3b, and 9.3c:

	Judee	*Laura*	*Kory*
Age Bracket	Over 55	40–49	40–49
Sex	Female	Female	Male
Height	5'9"	5'6"	5'8"
Ethnic Heritage	English, Irish, Scottish	Russian, Hungarian/ Austrian, English, French	Scottish, Welsh, French
Birthplace	Midwest	West Coast	Northwest
Preferred Music	Blues and bluegrass, rock	Classic rock, pop rock	70s
Favorite Leisure Activities	Golfing, traveling, hiking, reading	Reading, writing fiction, traveling, dancing	Reading, singing, traveling

2. Photos 9.4a and 9.4b: The woman is 41 years old in both pictures.

CHAPTER

10 Expressing Real and Desired Identities

Masquerade! Paper faces on parade . . . Masquerade! Hide your face so the world will never find you . . . .
—*The Phantom of the Opera*, Andrew Lloyd Webber and Charles Hart

Just be yourself is advice commonly offered in situations when we want to project a positive image of ourselves, such as during a job interview or a blind date. Regardless of how authentic we try to appear, however, we're constantly engaged in the process of creating and managing an image of ourselves and communicating that image to others. Your image reflects not necessarily how you see yourself, but rather, *how you want others to see you*. As the lyric from *The Phantom of the Opera* suggests, each of us is involved in an ongoing game of social masquerade, showing others only the images of ourselves that we want them to see.

As we pointed out in the last chapter, image management differs from impression formation: Whereas impression formation has to do with how we form impressions of other people, image management relates to how we influence the impressions we want others to form of us. These topics are intimately related, however, since our ability to project a certain image depends on our knowledge of how others will interpret our behaviors. If you want others to see you as credible and trustworthy, for instance, you can project that image effectively if you know which nonverbal behaviors and characteristics will lead others to form an impression of you as credible and trustworthy. Image management and impression formation are therefore two sides of the same coin: Whereas impression formation is a *decoding* process, image management is the process of *encoding* a particular image.

We begin our discussion by identifying several important principles of image management. Next, we peruse three major theories that provide guidance for understanding how communicators create and manage images nonverbally. Finally, we explore how people use nonverbal behaviors to portray three dimensions of image—those related to sex and gender, age, and personality.

Principles of Image Management

This chapter centers on how communicators can manage their images to maximize favorable evaluative outcomes such as liking, attraction, credibility, and power. As we've noted, image management relates to how we want others to see us. The emphasis is on sender behaviors, usually behaviors designed to enhance others' judgments of us, and on the success or failure of those efforts. Before we examine theories that explain the image management process or identify the specific nonverbal behaviors that portray specific images, let's take a look at four important principles of image management.

1. *We manage multiple images.* Depending on the social situation you're in, you might want others to see you as friendly and outgoing, contemplative and reserved, strict and stern, or caring and compassionate. You might also show different sides of your personality to your friends, your professors, your relatives, your co-workers, and to strangers. As a consequence, you project different images depending on whom you're interacting with and in what context. The fact that we manage multiple images doesn't necessarily mean we're being inauthentic or two-faced with others. Rather, it reflects the idea that what we call *The Self* is really a collection of multiple, smaller *selves*, each of which represents a portion of who we are, but none of which represents us completely.

2. *Image management is concerned with cause-and-effect relationships.* That is, successful image management relies on knowledge about which behaviors and characteristics foster which impressions. Which speaking rate do others perceive as denoting the most credibility, for instance? How does physical attractiveness affect perceptions of honesty? The ability to manage images requires us to understand and make use of these and other causal relationships between behaviors, characteristics, and impressions.

3. *Image management techniques are typically directed toward a generalized audience.* We may use specific relational messages, such as those that portray warmth, empathy, or dominance, with particular relational partners. For the most part, however, we portray our image to a general audience. This makes image management pertinent to public and mass media contexts as well as interpersonal ones. For instance, celebrities, politicians, and other public figures spend considerable amounts of attention and money on shaping, projecting, and protecting their public images, which may or may not reflect the images they project in their private lives.

4. *Image management focuses on the single encoder who is enacting image management strategies.* One person might use a dominant communication style to portray an image of power and authority, for instance. Another might use a more immediate, compassionate style to portray an image of empathy and care. This doesn't mean that managing and communicating an image isn't a social experience. Indeed, it is inherently social, since others must recognize and affirm the image you're trying to project in order for your image management to be successful. You can successfully portray an image of being ethical and intelligent, for example, only if others recognize your behaviors as having those meanings. The process of managing and projecting an image, however, is primarily focused on the encoder.

Perhaps more than any other area of nonverbal study, image management has generated a significant amount of theorizing and research. In the next section, we review three major theoretical perspectives on image management and briefly describe the research findings associated with each. These include self-presentation theory, impression management theory, and expectancy violations theory.

Theories of Image Management

Self-Presentation Theory

The first and most comprehensive of the theories related to image management is Goffman's (1959, 1961b, 1963a) dramaturgic analysis of the presentation of self. *Self-presentation* is the process whereby we use nonverbal and verbal communication to put forward positive images of ourselves for public consumption. Perhaps guided by Shakespeare's oft-quoted line, "All the world's a stage and all the men and women, merely players," Goffman's collection of writings offers an implicit theory of self-presentation that builds on analogies between theatre and everyday human interaction. The dramaturgic approach begins with the notion that, much as actors perform theatrical roles, people present themselves in daily life through the roles they adopt and perform. Although most of us play a variety of roles on any given day, the overall goal of promoting positive views of ourselves in others transcends any particular role. In this respect, presentation of self is intrinsically concerned with putting forward a socially acceptable face.

The stage analogy is evident when looking at the terms in Goffman's theory. He variously used the term *performance* or *line* to refer to the totality of people's nonverbal and verbal acts in a given situation. Various situations call for different performances, such as enacting the role of "friend and confidant," "gently chastising parent," or "composed public speaker." Performances occur in the presence of others, who serve as the *audience,* and in particular settings, which are called the *stage.* The *front region* of the stage encompasses the areas the communicator customarily uses to present the performance. Thus, people are seen as actors playing a role when in the front stage area. In the *back region* of the stage, people are less concerned about self-presentation, although to some extent Goffman believed we are always "on stage." Being able to adapt to different situations and audiences is a key component of effective self-presentation. Goffman's ideas laid the foundation for later theories about impression management that consider both the positive and negative images we project to others.

Impression Management Theory

Impression management theory is concerned explicitly with how social actors engender positive views of themselves in others while avoiding negative views. Image management theorists have attempted to identify strategies and tactics that would allow people to achieve these goals. Tedeschi and Norman (1985) synthesized a variety of image management techniques, including those derived from Jones and Pitman's (1982) theory and Jones's (1964) earlier ingratiation theory, into an overall taxonomy of image management behaviors. Although not all tactics they cover are relevant for our purposes, some clearly are, and others have the potential to be applicable.

Tedeschi and Norman's taxonomy rests on two basic distinctions. First, image management techniques can be described as either defensive or assertive.

Defensive image management occurs whenever actors experience or anticipate a predicament in which they believe others will attribute negative qualities to them. They will therefore employ image management techniques to avoid being judged negatively. Conversely, *assertive image management* occurs when actors attempt to establish particular attributes in the eyes of others. An actor who wants to be perceived as a skilled computer hacker, for instance, will engage in behaviors designed to enhance that image.

Second, image management may be either *strategic* or *tactical*. As Tedeschi and Norman use these terms, strategic images have long-term goals and consequences, whereas tactical images have short-term ones. (This usage parallels that in the military. Elsewhere, strategies often refer to overarching plans, whereas tactics refer to specific behaviors deployed to accomplish those objectives.) Crossing assertive-defensive actions with the strategic-tactical distinction results in a 2 × 2 matrix of possible image management behaviors. For example, the assertive-strategic cell includes self-promotive strategies related to attraction, credibility, trustworthiness, status, prestige, and esteem.

Nonverbal image management is most closely associated with the assertive-strategic cell of the table. What follows is a summary of major research findings related to these various strategies. Most of the studies to be reported were not undertaken expressly to test impression management theory. Rather, they represent our analysis of how the empirical studies relate to one another and to the larger communication function of image management. We have grouped our review according to two general image management domains: attraction and likability judgments, and credibility judgments.

Attraction and Likability Judgments.   One of the most basic aims of image management is to get others to be attracted to us and like us. Elsewhere, this fundamental of human interaction goals comes under the heading of conveying or promoting affiliation, affection, warmth, and immediacy (Mehrabian, 1981). Many of the nonverbal cues that promote an attractive image are the same ones we use to communicate to others that we are attracted to them; that is, they serve as relational messages of attraction. Here we focus on ones that can be used to create generalized images of a communicator as attractive, friendly, and likable.

First and perhaps most obvious are those *behaviors that convey physical attractiveness*. As noted in Chapters 4 and 9, a "what is beautiful is good" stereotype operates such that people who are physically attractive (such as the person in Photo 10.1) get the benefit of more positive evaluations on a score of personal attributes. For example, men and women find interactions with the opposite sex more pleasant and like the partner better if the partner is physically attractive (Garcia, Stinson, Ickes, & Bissonnette, 1991). See Box 10.1 for additional information on the benefits of physical attractiveness.

We are also drawn to people who have *attractive voices* and show *positive affect*. For example, some research has shown that impressions of physical beauty are influenced by vocal cues, and impressions of vocal attractiveness are influenced by physical appearance (Raines, Hechtman, & Rosenthal, 1990; Zuckerman,

---

BOX 10.1

Attractiveness and Organizational Survival

We have all heard the old adage that "beauty is only skin deep," and we would like to think we are appreciated more for our inner qualities and talents than our outer appearances. But in a survey of 662 managers in Fortune 500 firms, personal appearance ranked eighth out of 20 main factors determining survival of the fittest in the "organizational jungle" (Nikodym & Simonetti, 1987). Doubtless the results would be similar today.

A review of corporate image seminar material led Nikodym and Simonetti (1987) to propose that those who have the proper "corporate image" are more likely to be promoted in their organizations. Important elements to "looking and playing the part" include the following:

1. *Dress:* conservative in style and color for both women and men; formality of dress matched to the occasion.
2. *Hair:* short and neat style for both sexes; little facial hair for men; clean-shaven legs for women.

3. *Jewelry:* limited and tasteful for both men and women.
4. *Grooming:* pressed clothes, polished shoes; clean and buffed nails for men; manicured nails for women.
5. *Posture and gait:* maintain proper sitting and standing posture (neither overly relaxed or overly tense); confident but not cocky walk.

It should be evident that all of these elements are things everyone can control, regardless of their innate physical endowments. Other good news: even higher on the list of success factors—ranked as third—was *communication skills*, which includes other nonverbal behaviors that promote impressions of credibility and attractiveness. All of this means that anyone who is attentive to these nonverbal elements has the prospect of improving his or her standing in the corporate workplace.

Miyake, & Hodgins, 1991). Positive affect cues, such as smiles, facial pleasantness, vocal resonance, and vocal warmth make an actor look and sound more attractive and likable (Burgoon, Birk, & Pfau, 1990).

Other *immediacy cues* that have been linked to attractiveness and likability judgments include increased use of touch, close proximity, gestural activity, open

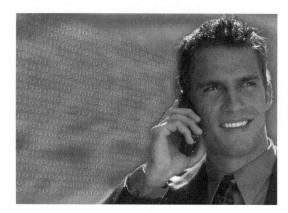

PHOTO 10.1 *The halo effect explains that we attribute more positive qualities to people who are physically attractive than to people who are less attractive.*

body positions, direct body orientation, and forward lean (e.g., Barak, Patkin, & Dell, 1982). Political figures often use immediacy cues to their advantage when trying to connect with voters, as shown in Photo 10.2. One study of effects of judge behavior on juries found that judges who were more nonverbally involved—leaned forward, made more eye contact, and nodded more—were judged as more attractive and credible than those who were less involved (Badzinski & Pettus, 1994). Fortunately for the sake of a fair jurisprudence system, those behaviors did not translate into different jury decisions.

Credibility Judgments.   Concerns about communicator credibility (also called *ethos*) can be traced back to the earliest writings of Greek philosophers and classical rhetoricians, the historical roots of the communication discipline. Contemporary treatments of credibility conceive it to be a set of judgments held by receivers about a sender. Although fostering credibility is often an end in itself, frequently it is designed to enable a communicator to achieve other communication objectives such as message comprehension (see Chapter 8) and social influence (see Chapter 13). The majority of research has focused on the vocal channel, so we will summarize the major findings from this research.

One of the most extensively studied vocal correlates of credibility is *speaking tempo*. Most studies have shown that faster speaking enhances credibility perceptions such as intelligence, objectivity, and knowledge (Buller & Aune, 1988). Marketing research on the effects of time-compressed speech, which essentially speeds up the audio portion of a radio or television broadcast, similarly finds beneficial effects for faster tempo (LaBarbera & MacLachlan, 1979). By contrast, people who speak at a moderate or slow rate generally are perceived as more honest, people-oriented, benevolent, and composed than those who speak fast (Woodall & Burgoon, 1983; but see also Miller, Maruyama, Beaber, & Valone, 1976). It is also possible that people who speak rapidly themselves will prefer rapid tempos, whereas those who speak slowly themselves will prefer slow tempos (Street, Brady, & Putman, 1983).

PHOTO 10.2 *Displaying immediacy behaviors helps many politicians, such as presidents Bill Clinton and George W. Bush, connect with voters and enhance their credibility.*

A second vocal feature affecting credibility is *pausing*. Two types of pauses that have been studied are within-turn pausing, sometimes termed hesitation pauses, and response latencies, which occur between speaking turns. Several studies have shown that credibility is enhanced by shorter pauses within speaking turns and between speaking turns (Newman, 1982). Pauses of one second or less may be best for appearing competent; however, pauses of one to three seconds may be best for appearing trustworthy (Baskett & Freedle, 1974).

Loudness is a third vocal feature that affects credibility. Research indicates that increasing vocal volume or intensity up to a moderately high level improves several credibility judgments, including impressions of dominance, boldness, competence, emotional stability, and extroversion (Burgoon et al., 1990; Ray, 1986).

Research on voice *pitch* has been more inconsistent. Some evidence suggests that higher pitch promotes impressions of competence, dominance, and assertiveness (Scherer, 1978). Other research suggests that higher pitch creates negative impressions and that deeper pitch is more credible (Apple, Streeter, & Krauss, 1979). The conflicting findings may be due partly to different acceptable pitch ranges for male and female voices. Increases in male pitch may result in positive impressions up to the point of beginning to sound like the female register, beyond which impressions may suffer.

Finally, *vocal fluency* contributes positively to a credible image (Burgoon et al., 1990). Dysfluent speech may jeopardize competence and composure impressions; however, it appears not to diminish an image of trustworthiness.

Expectancy Violations Theory

Expectancy violations theory challenges the claim of self-presentation theory that successful performances require conformity to social norms and expectations. It had its genesis in Burgoon and colleagues' initial forays into the realm of proxemic behavior (e.g., Burgoon & Aho, 1982; Burgoon & Jones, 1976; Burgoon, Stacks, & Burch, 1982). Their reviews of proxemic literature turned up an apparent contradiction: People typically respond negatively to personal space invasions but often respond positively to close interaction distances. Trying to make sense of this pattern led to the development of what was first called nonverbal expectancy violations theory and later shortened to expectancy violations theory (EVT). Over the past three decades, the theory has been expanded to apply to numerous nonverbal behaviors and to interaction patterns as well as their outcomes. Here we look at the effect on impressions of credibility and attraction. In Chapter 13, we consider the effects on social influence, and in Chapter 14, we examine the effects on interaction patterns.

Four key elements in EVT are expectancies, expectancy violations, communicator valence, and violation valence. These combine to determine whether it is more advisable to adhere to norms and expectations (as suggested by self-presentation theory) or to violate them (see Figure 10.1).

The theory begins with the assumption that people hold *expectancies*—enduring patterns of anticipated nonverbal (and verbal) behavior—about others' communication (Burgoon & Walther, 1990). Expectations are grounded largely in social norms

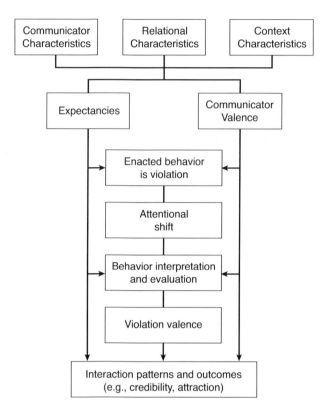

FIGURE 10.1   Expectancy violations theory

but also take into account knowledge of another's unique behavioral patterns. For example, men are expected to interact at farther distances than women, but you may know that a male friend of yours is even more distant than most. A combination of *communicator*, *relationship*, and *context* factors such as one's sex, age, personality, relational familiarity, cultural similarity, status, liking, physical setting, formality of the interaction, and conversational topic all feed into what is expected for a given interchange.

Expectancies have both *predictive* and *prescriptive* components. They are predictive in the sense of reflecting what is typical. We expect (predict) that when we nod hello to someone, he or she will nod hello back. They are prescriptive in the sense of reflecting what is appropriate or not preferred. We expect (prescribe) that people will avoid staring at us in public. Expectancies form a range of customary and preferred behavior. These expectancies may be specific to a particular culture, co-culture, relationship, or situation. For example, Greek citizens often expect interactions with ingroup members to be warm, cooperative, and truthful but expect interactions with outgroup members to be hostile, competitive, and deceitful (Broome, 1990). Expectancies vary in how firmly they are held, but EVT assumes that all communicative situations invoke expectancies.

When another's behaviors fall within the expected range, they are said to *confirm* expectancies. When behaviors fall outside that range, they are called *expectancy violations, deviations,* or *disconfirmations.* Although EVT principles apply to situations in which people do what is expected, the theory's main focus is on what happens when expectancies are violated. Like other novel or vivid acts, violations are thought to draw a receiver's attention away from what is being said and toward the violation act and the person committing it. This shift in focus may be accompanied by heightened physiological arousal.

The heightened attention to the characteristics of the violator and the meaning of the violation act brings into play another important factor: communicator reward valence, or more simply, *communicator valence.* EVT assumes that we implicitly evaluate all communicators on a positive to negative continuum according to their apparent reward value for us. Someone who is physically appealing, has a great sense of humor, holds elevated status, or strokes us with positive feedback, for instance, should be more positively regarded than someone who is physically repulsive, lacks a sense of humor, is of lower status, or gives us negative feedback. EVT posits that we arrive at a net assessment of a communicator's valence at a given point in time. Positively valenced communicators should achieve more favorable impressions just by virtue of these characteristics, but their valence should also affect how we respond to any violations they commit.

According to EVT, when a communicator commits a violation, receivers attempt to make sense of the violation act. They undertake an *interpretation and evaluation appraisal* process. They try to determine what meaning the act has, if any, and whether they like the behavior or not. Suppose, for example, that while talking, an acquaintance unexpectedly moves into close proximity. You might interpret the act as a relational message of interest or intimacy or as one of dominance or aggression. If the violation has multiple or ambiguous meanings (such as the proximity example), EVT contends that you will select the meaning based on how favorably you regard the communicator, with more favorable meanings attributed to the highly regarded than poorly regarded communicators. For example, if the acquaintance is someone you dislike, you might interpret his or her close proximity as a threat; if the acquaintance is someone you like, you might instead interpret moving in as a show of affiliation.

Even when behaviors have unambiguous meanings (e.g., gaze aversion generally has negative connotations), communicator valence can affect how the violation is evaluated. You would probably welcome a move closer from a positively regarded person but find it undesirable from a negatively regarded one. Communicator valence doesn't guarantee what interpretations and evaluations are assigned to nonverbal violations, but it can influence both parts of the appraisal process.

The ultimate evaluation of the violation act determines whether it is a *positive violation* or a *negative violation,* which in turn determines whether a violation helps or harms one's image. EVT predicts that positive violations enhance credibility and attractiveness, and negative violations reduce them, relative to expectancy confirmation. That is, violations can lead to more positive impressions for the violator than if the violator had done what is normative or expected. This is contrary to the claim in many quarters that violations are always negative and harmful to one's self-presentational efforts (see, e.g., Olson et al., 1996).

Numerous studies have tested the effects of proxemic and other nonverbal violations, including ones related to gaze, touch, posture, immediacy, and involvement (e.g., Afifi & Metts, 1998; Burgoon & Le Poire, 1993; Burgoon, Le Poire, & Rosenthal, 1995; Burgoon, Newton, Walther, & Baesler, 1989; Burgoon, Walther, & Baesler, 1992; Floyd & Voloudakis, 1999; Le Poire & Burgoon, 1994b, 1996). So far, the following conclusions seem warranted (with the caveat that they may only apply to Western cultures because that is where the tests have been conducted):

1. *Proxemic violations improve judgments of positively valenced communicators but undermine them for negatively valenced communicators.* The likely reason for this is that close and far conversational distances have numerous meanings associated with them, so the valence of the communicator makes a big difference in how they are interpreted. Also, as with other immediacy cues, proximity has strong arousal potential. People may find the arousal pleasurable when it is associated with someone they like but disconcerting when associated with someone they dislike. However, a far distance coupled with either very tense or very relaxed posture is evaluated negatively, so a positive violation can be transformed into a negative one with the addition of other nonverbal cues.

2. *Unexpectedly high amounts of gaze create favorable judgments and gaze aversion creates negative ones, regardless of communicator valence.* The reason is that maintaining a high amount of gaze connotes interest, attention, friendliness, and composure, whereas gaze avoidance connotes disinterest, nonreceptivity, noncomposure, and possibly disdain. In other words, in the United States and similar cultures, the multiple meanings associated with a high degree of eye contact are largely positive, whereas the multiple meanings associated with limited eye contact are largely negative, and people prefer more gaze regardless of who enacts it. This pattern is unlikely to hold true in countries where averting the eyes is a sign of respect and where gazing too long or too directly is seen as overly forward and personal.

3. *Brief, nonintimate touches are positive violations that promote more favorable images, especially when committed by positively valenced communicators.* The handshake and arm touch carry many favorable relational messages and are evaluated favorably. More intimate and informal touches, such as face touches and an arm around the waist, are best reserved for use by attractive, high-status, or female communicators.

4. *Violations that increase overall conversational involvement have positive effects, regardless of communicator valence, whereas violations that decrease involvement have negative effects.* Involvement, being composed of numerous nonverbal cues, is fairly unambiguous in its meaning and is desired in most conversational settings. Showing high involvement is flattering to the recipient and carries such favorable relational meanings as openness, similarity, liking, composure, and

dominance. Showing detachment has the opposite effect, producing negative interpretations and reductions in credibility and attraction.

5. *Immediacy violations, if extreme, may have negative effects regardless of communicator valence.* Nonimmediacy, including gaze aversion, carries negative connotations, and the presence of multiple behaviors all with the same meaning reduces ambiguity. Extremely high immediacy, such as a personal space invasion, may be overly arousing and disturbing except in highly intimate relationships. What counts as too much or too little immediacy will differ by culture.

Self-presentation theory, impression management theory, and expectancy violations theory each help us understand how people conceive of their images and what behaviors and characteristics enhance or inhibit those images. In the next section, we'll look at three domains of image that each of us manages to signal our personal identity in terms of: sex and gender, age, and personality. These are among the most visible aspects of our personal identities that are displayed to others through nonverbal behavior. Whereas impression management expresses who we want others to think we are, these behaviors "communicate" our unique identities to the world at large.

Three Domains of Identification

Nonverbal Identifiers of Sex and Gender

You may think that differences between women and men are too obvious to require discussion. After all, there are genetic and anatomical differences in the bodies of men and women. Birdwhistell (1970) called genetic differences *primary* sex differences and anatomical differences *secondary* sex differences. However, as he pointed out, there are also many *tertiary*, or behavioral, differences in the nonverbal behavior of women and men that are not necessarily the result of chromosomal, hormonal, or anatomical influences.

One origin of communication differences between men and women is the gender-role differences taught by our society (Dow & Wood, 2006). Some scholars argue that women are trained to be affiliative, to create close relationships characterized by equality, to criticize others in acceptable ways, to be sensitive to others, and to interpret accurately the behavior of others. In contrast, men are socialized to assert their position of dominance, to be proactive, and to attract and maintain an audience (Wood, 2009). Some scholars contend that women and men inhabit different cultures, with different rules for taking part in conversation and interpreting conversational behavior. Men desire independence, whereas women desire involvement (Wood, 2009). Another argument is that some sex differences represent attempts by men to exert power over women, whereas other differences—such as men's lower sensitivity to nonverbal cues—are an outgrowth of their greater social power, which requires less adeptness at communication (Burleson & Kunkel, 2006).

Research on sex differences suggests that although the distinctions based on differences in culture and power may have some merit (Noller, 1993), these explanations may oversimplify sex differences (see Dindia & Canary, 2006). In particular, several studies have challenged the notion that sex differences should be attributed to dominance (see, e.g., Marche & Peterson, 1993; Staley & Cohen, 1988). For example, Mulac (1989) suggested that sex differences in talk are consistent with the *appearance* of power but not necessarily the actual *implementation* of it. More damaging is Halberstadt and Saitta's (1987) failure to find differences in nonverbal behavior consistent with the power-dominance explanation. Power cues appear to be moderated by whether or not a task is linked to participants' sexes. Men display more nonverbal power-related behavior than women when the tasks are masculine in character or lack a gender link. By contrast, women display more nonverbal power-related behavior than men when the task is feminine in character (Dovidio, Brown, Heltman, Ellyson, & Keating, 1988). The difference in power displays appears to be due to familiarity with the experimental task: more familiarity leads to being more assertive. When Brown, Dovidio, and Ellyson (1990) trained their experimental participants and equalized their familiarity with the task, sex differences in power-related behavior were eliminated.

LaFrance, Hecht, and Noyes (1994) introduced *expressivity demand theory* to account for sex differences in nonverbal behavior. Based on reviews and meta-analyses of an enormous amount of research, they concluded that the combination of sex, relationship, and situational features call forth different levels of expressivity. Women are expected to be more expressive and will often meet those expectations. When care-giving social roles are salient, women will also smile more than men. This is especially likely when people are equal in status or power. But when status and power differ, men are more like women: Both smile more when in the lower power position and smile less when in the higher position. And when the situation calls for it, both women and men will be expressive and smile.

One must keep in mind that (1) sex differences are more apparent in children and young adults than in older adults; (2) context frequently overrides sex differences; (3) gender differences vary by culture and co-culture; and, (4) people differ in their acceptance of gender roles (Epstein, 1986; LaFrance & Mayo, 1979). These last two qualifications deserve additional comment. Variance in gender-related communication norms between cultures and co-cultures is very common. In some groups, adherence to very traditional feminine and masculine roles is dictated. Other groups are less strict, allowing women to display masculine traits and men to display feminine ones. Further, gender role expectations are constantly in flux. North American culture, in which much of the research reported in this section was conducted, has experienced significant changes in gender role expectations in the past 50 years. It has become more acceptable for women to assume roles previously reserved for men (especially in the work environment) and for men to assume roles previously reserved for women (especially in the home environment; see Medved & Rawlins, 2007). This adaptation has led to increased androgyny (Bem, 1974; Powell & Butterfield, 1989), the display of both feminine and masculine traits. Thus, one must be careful not to pigeonhole another person solely on the basis of overt biological sex differences. A competent communicator, instead, bases notions of sex and gender role acceptance on the behaviors and opinions expressed by the person.

Kinesics

Emblems.   Limited evidence suggests that social norms may permit women to use emblems more frequently than men. Baglan and Nelson (1982) found that both men and women thought it more appropriate for women than men to use beckoning gestures. This is especially true for physically attractive women, suggesting a norm for usage by this group. Contrary to the social-power explanation, however, use of emblems is greater for dominant than submissive female communicators, especially in opposite-sex interactions.

Illustrators.   Research on sex differences in illustrators has produced mixed results (Ickes & Barnes, 1977; Kennedy & Camden, 1983) but greater general expressivity by women implies women will use more and possibly different types of gestures than men. For example, one study found that women use more palms-up gestures and men use more pointing gestures (Friesen, Ekman, & Wallbott, 1979). Palms-up gestures frequently accompany the shrug emblem, signifying uncertainty or hesitancy. Pointing gestures, conversely, can be interpreted as more dominant. These findings would be consistent with the social-power explanation of sex differences.

Gaze.   Female dyads engage in more eye contact than do male dyads (Mulac, Studley, Wiemann, & Bradac, 1987). The same sex difference has been observed by Wada (1990) in Japan. Female pairs use higher amounts of gaze than do male pairs when speaking, while listening, and even during silence (see Table 10.1). This is consistent with the finding that women are more sensitive communicators (Rosenthal, Hall, DiMatteo, Rogers, & Archer, 1979). Keeley-Dyreson, Burgoon, and Bailey (1991) confirmed women's superior sensitivity to nonverbal cues, although they also found that men's sensitivity improved with practice. Increased visual surveillance is likely to improve sensitivity to nonverbal cues. Mulac et al. (1987) speculated that there may be less mutual awareness in dyads that include a male because of more one-sided gazing in these dyads. Further, there may be a norm or expectation in the North American culture that women engage in more eye contact during conversations than men.

Posture.   Most of the research on posture is dated and so may no longer be valid but seems to be consistent with patterns related to other kinesic cues such as facial expressions. Mehrabian (1981) observed that men assume more potent, more dominant, less affiliative, and less intimate postures than women. In other studies,

TABLE 10.1   Percentages of Time Spent Engaging in Eye Contact

	Mutual Talk	Listening	Speaking	Total Time
Women	7.5	42.4	36.9	37.3
Men	3.0	29.8	25.6	23.2

Source: Exline (1963), p. 11.

men have been observed to use less direct body orientations and more backward leaning than women in interpersonal conversations (Shuter, 1977). It may be more appropriate for men to lean backward and to display more postural relaxation than women. In contrast, in small-group interactions, men were observed to lean forward, whereas women leaned backward. Backward leaning by women may indicate less involvement and lead to more interruptions by men (Kennedy & Camden, 1983). Other studies found that men tilt their heads forward, thrust their chins out, and adopt more direct head orientations than women, whereas women cock their heads to the side (Dovidio et al., 1988; Kendon & Ferber, 1973; Wada, 1990). These patterns are consistent with men adopting more expansive, relaxed and powerful demeanors than women.

Facial Expression.   A prevalent stereotype is that women are more expressive communicators than men. This stereotype is, in general, upheld by research on facial expressions (Kring & Gordon, 1998). Women are more expressive facially than are men (Eakins & Eakins, 1978; LaFrance & Mayo, 1979) and display warmer cues than do men (Weitz, 1976). Compared to men, women appear to be more likely to express positive emotions such as joy (Burgoon & Bacue, 2003; Coats & Feldman, 1996) and affection (Floyd, 2006; Owen, 1987). They are also more likely than men to express sadness and depression (Blier & Blier-Wilson, 1989; Nolen-Hoeksema, 1987). In contrast, some studies have found that men are more likely than women to express anger (Coats & Feldman, 1996), but other studies have failed to find such a difference (Burrowes & Halberstadt, 1987). Women also appear to be better encoders of emotion than are men (Buck, Miller, & Caul, 1974); however, this varies according to the type of emotion being expressed. In a study by Zaidel and Mehrabian (1969), women were more accurate senders of negative emotions and men were more accurate senders of positive emotions. Androgynous men (those who score highly on both masculine and feminine traits) may also be better senders than traditionally masculine men (Weitz, 1976).

One explanation for why encoding ability varies by the type of emotion is that baseline or at-rest facial expressions are different for women and men. That is, women generally have a positive baseline facial expression; therefore, negative emotions are more distinctly displayed by women. Conversely, men generally have a neutral or negative facial expression; thus, their positive facial expressions become more noticeable.

Consistent with this speculation is the general finding that women smile more than men, regardless of the emotion they feel at the moment (Dovidio et al., 1988). In some of these studies, women also encoded more positive head nodding than men. Moreover, communicators expect women to smile more frequently than men, and this expectation is resistant to information to the contrary (Briton & Hall, 1995). This expectation also may be applied to young children. Haviland (1977) showed a group of people pictures of infants and asked them to identify the sex of the infant. Infants with positive facial expressions were more likely to be judged female, whereas those with negative facial expressions were more likely to be judged male. Hecht et al. (1993) also reported that the smiling norm was more apparent in Caucasians and college-age women than among African Americans and high school-age women.

For men, smiling is an emotional expression, whereas for women, it is an interactional phenomenon (LaFrance & Mayo, 1979). Communicators seem to recognize this distinction. Bugental, Love, and Gianetto (1971) found that children attributed greater friendliness to their fathers who smiled than to their mothers who smiled. Another study found that women—who smiled more than men even when alone—increased their rate of smiling when paired with another woman more than did men paired with men. Women were also more likely than men to respond to a smile of greeting with a smile of their own (see also Patterson & Tubbs, 2005). Beekman (1975) found that a woman's smile was associated with her feelings of social anxiety, discomfort, deference, and abasement, whereas a man's smile was correlated with his desire to be affiliative and sociable. It appears, then, that women are socialized to use the smile as an interactional tool. Men, in contrast, are taught to reserve it for times when they feel genuinely happy or friendly.

Proxemics. Compared with men, women are approached more closely, tolerate more spatial intrusions, give way more readily to others, and adopt closer sitting and standing distances in interpersonal and small-group interactions (Patterson & Schaeffer, 1977). Advertisements often depict women as taking up less space than men, and women have even been known to use the armrests in airplanes less often than men (Hai, Khairullah, & Coulmas, 1982). These smaller spaces apparently are not distressing, as women behave more cooperatively and less aggressively than men under conditions of high density (Freedman, 1972).

In opposite-sex interactions, men are also more likely than women to dictate spacing and distancing patterns and are more likely to violate female territorial markers than vice versa (Shaffer & Sadowski, 1975). Typically, female-male interactions are characterized by closer distances than male-male interactions and, sometimes, even female-female interactions (Shuter, 1977).

Haptics. Paralleling proxemic patterns, women give and receive more touch than men (except when initiating courtship, playing sports, or exchanging violence) and appear to seek more physical contact (Jones, 1984). Studies looking at friends, coworkers, and acquaintances have shown that female dyads are characterized by more touching than male dyads or opposite-sex dyads, and women in opposite-sex dyads receive more touch than do men (Stier & Hall, 1984). Partners in romantic relationships touch each other more frequently than do female, male, or opposite-sex friends, with seriously dating couples more likely to display touch in public settings than casually dating or married couples (Guerrero & Andersen, 1991).

Henley (1977) hypothesized that men initiate more touch than women as part of a general pattern of dominant behavior by men and submissive behavior by women, but later research (e.g., Jones, 1984; Stier & Hall, 1984; Hall & Vecchia, 1990) found that women equal or exceed men in the initiation of touch, and that men initiate touch more during courtship, whereas women initiate touch more in marriage (e.g. Guerrero & Andersen, 1994). Women also reciprocate others' touch and have their own touch reciprocated more often than men do (Major & Williams, 1980). The results of one observational study of 799 instances of intentional touch (Major & Williams, 1980), which appear in Table 10.2, are illustrative.

TABLE 10.2   Percentages of Responses to Intentional Touch

	Reciprocate	Fail to Reciprocate	Total
Male to female	21	15	36
Male to male	6	9	15
Female to male	14	13	27
Female to female	11	11	22

Source: Adapted from Major & Williams, 1980.

Jones (1984) proposed that the greater total amount of touch and reciproca-tion of touch for women occurs because touch is a feminine-appropriate role behavior and a masculine-inappropriate one. Indeed, respondents in one study considered touch by women to be more desirable than touch by men (Burgoon & Walther, 1990). Thus, women and girls are encouraged to touch and be touched as part of their feminine, nurturing role. Conversely, men and boys are discour-aged from touching because touch becomes synonymous with feminine rather than masculine behavior. As further evidence, Jones (1984) reported that men who are verbally aggressive are least likely to initiate touch. Major (1981) con-tended that women are expected to be more passive, affiliative, and emotional than men. The patterns of touch between women and men reflect these social expectations (Floyd, 1999).

These sex-specific proxemic and touch differences are believed by some to originate in mother-child interactions (Field, 2001). Mothers have been observed to touch female infants more than male infants (Goldberg & Lewis, 1969), and female children seek and offer more nonaggressive touch than male children (Whiting & Edwards, 1973). It seems that women are taught to have a different attitude toward touch than are men (Stier & Hall, 1984). In a study by Fisher, Rytting, and Heslin (1976), women reacted positively to touch, whereas men reacted ambivalently. Similarly, Whitcher and Fisher (1979) found that touch by nurses in a therapeutic setting resulted in positive evaluations and increased recip-rocal touching by female patients. Male patients, however, gave more negative evaluations of touching nurses and were less likely to reciprocate the nurses' touch. Some research also suggests that patterns of sex difference in touch are influenced by the type of relationship people share. In a study of affectionate behavior, for instance, Floyd and Morman (1997) found that women and men dif-fered in affectionate communication (including touch) in friendships, but that this sex difference was nonsignificant in sibling relationships.

Vocalics.   Perhaps the most obvious sex difference in vocalic behavior is that men's voices have a lower pitch, or fundamental frequency, than do women's. This is partly because men have a larger larynx and longer, thicker vocal folds than women do, as a result of physiological changes at puberty (Marieb, 2003). Men's voices also have lower resonances than women's due to larger supralaryngeal vocal tracts.

Sex differences in pitch are not entirely due to physiological differences, however. Girls and boys are also socialized into different speaking styles at an early age (Siegman, 1978). In line with this idea, Sachs, Lieberman, and Erickson (1973) found that boys and girls who had not yet reached puberty could be distinguished by voice alone. They offered as a further explanation girls' and women's tendency to smile more than boys and men. Smiling changes the vocal cords by shortening them, thereby increasing overall pitch (Meditch, 1975).

Women also seem to encode vocalic patterns containing a more varied range of tone changes than do men (Brend, 1975). One pattern is the "high-low down-glide" frequently used to indicate surprise ("Oh, how awful!"). Another is a "request confirmation pattern" ("You do?"). Still others include the "hesitation pattern" ("Well, I studied . . .") and a "polite cheerful pattern" ("Are you coming?"). Finally, women often answer questions with declarative statements that end in rising pitch, an intonation pattern characteristic of a question. This can make women appear uncertain or hesitant when making statements (Lakoff, 1973).

Women and men's vocalic patterns, then, are not due just to physical differences in their vocal tracts. Social norms prescribe different vocal patterns for men and women, and children learn to encode these patterns at a very early age (LaFrance & Mayo, 1979).

When it comes to overall time spent talking, social stereotypes provide that women are more talkative than men. According to research, however, men dominate the talking time in opposite-sex dyads; they talk more when interacting with women than with other men; and they talk with greater intensity than do women (Mulac, 1989). All three differences conform to the social-power explanation of sex differences, although they also fit the cultural explanation that men are socialized to seek and hold an audience. Although men do talk more than women in certain contexts, recent research shows that men and women do not differ in their overall talk time—that is, in the number of words each sex speaks during an average day (Mehl, Vazire, Ramírez-Esparza, Slatcher, & Pennebaker, 2007).

Several studies with adults show that men also interrupt women more than women interrupt men, another possible indication that men tend to dominate conversations with women (e.g., Aries, 2006). However, interruptions are sometimes invited by women's displays of low involvement, such as backward leaning and lack of eye contact, or displays of facial pleasantness, such as smiling (Kennedy & Camden, 1981, 1983).

The sex differences in interruption behavior are far from consistent, however. Beattie (1981b) failed to observe a sex difference in interruptions, as did Dindia (1987). McCarrick et al. (1981) reported that women interrupted the interrupter. Moreover, Marche and Peterson (1993), in a study of children and adults, did not find that males interrupted females any more than females interrupted males. Further, many of the sex differences reflected the behavior of ninth-grade females, who interrupted their partners. Even though interruption behavior was frequently asymmetrical in the dyad (i.e., one partner interrupted the other more frequently than vice versa), interruption frequency was similar in same- and opposite-sex dyads and sex of the partners did not predict who was likely to interrupt more.

Marche and Peterson concluded that it is unwarranted to believe that this asymmetrical behavior occurs because men consider women to be interruptible, believe that what women have to say is less important than what men have to say, or attempt to exert more power or status by interrupting more.

Finally, there may be a sex difference in pausing during speech. Fitzpatrick, Mulac, and Dindia (1994) reported that male speech contained more pausing—in particular, more vocalized or filled pauses—than did female speech. These authors also showed that women were more likely to converge toward the speech of men than men were to converge toward the speech of women. This implies that women are more likely to code-switch than are men; however, Fitzpatrick et al. also noted that the greatest amount of convergence was witnessed among husbands toward their wives' communication style. So, men are not incapable of code switching and may be motivated to accommodate to the style of intimate female partners.

Box 10.2 gives an overview of some effects of sex differences in nonverbal communication, noting that they can be substantial.

Nonverbal Identifiers of Age

Age produces co-cultures with different nonverbal communication styles. In outlining the origins and acquisitions of each of the nonverbal codes, we noted numerous differences in nonverbal behavior between children and adults. However, there are also differences among adults, especially between young adults and middle-age to elderly people.

Physical Appearance.   Probably the most obvious identifiers are the overt changes in physical appearance that take place as we age. Skin and muscle lose their elasticity, wrinkles and gray hairs appear, the hair grays, and posture becomes more stooped. However, there are other age-related changes in the brain, sensory apparatus, and respiratory and phonatory systems that change the nonverbal communication of older adults (O'Hair, Allman, & Gibson, 1991).

Kinesics.   Loss of neurons in the frontal lobe of the brain can reduce motor control and coordination. This can impair or ultimately eliminate gesturing as a form of nonverbal communication (O'Hair et al., 1991), and can make previously simple tasks such as walking more difficult. Sensory deficits in vision can also impair the encoding and decoding of kinesic behavior, as well as proxemic and physical appearance cues that rely on visual acuity. Sensory abilities can start to decline as early as age 40 but do not seem to impair behavior until around age 60 (Kalymun, 1989). Older adults can still compensate for some of the sensory difficulties, so substantial changes in conversational abilities often do not occur until age 70 or 80 (O'Hair et al., 1991).

On the encoding end, sensory deficits may produce slower conversational styles, including slower body movements (Corso, 1977). On the decoding side, reduction in visual capacity may decrease the accuracy with which kinesic cues, especially facial expressions, are interpreted. Moreover, losses in memory abilities can make it difficult to recognize familiar faces (O'Hair et al., 1991). Research by Stine, Wingfield, and Myers (1990) showed that decoding difficulties associated

BOX 10.2

Nonverbal Battle of the Sexes

Sex differences are interesting and often humorous, but in actual practice, they can cause tension in male-female conversations.

The first place where tension may exist is in the eye behavior of women and men. As noted, women are expected to engage in more eye contact. Moreover, when females fail to make eye contract, they are more likely to be interrupted by males, especially in group situations. Lack of eye contact by women may be interpreted as inattention or disinterest, making them more vulnerable to interruptive attempts. Men, however, do not seem to fall victim to a similar interpretation.

Eye contact and interruption differences may contribute to perceptions of women as submissive and men as dominant. Women may also accede control to men by occupying less space, assuming less relaxed postures, and taking less conversation time. Women are more accommodating than men toward the gaze and speech patterns of opposite-sex partners, consistent with other evidence that women code-switch more than do men (Noller, 1993).

The gender role adopted by parties in an interaction may be more important to communication between males and females than biological sex differences. Ickes, Schermer, and Steeno (1979) showed that interaction patterns changed when the interactants were either gender-typed (i.e., masculine or feminine) or androgynous. That is, an interaction between two masculine men or two feminine women is characterized by less nonverbal involvement than an interaction between two androgynous individuals. Androgynous communicators may have a broader range of conversational skills, being both instrumental (masculine) and expressive (feminine), that they can use to maintain an appropriate level of involvement. Androgynous individuals may compensate for the interaction skills of gender-typed opposite-sex partners but not gender-typed same-sex partners. In turn, people are more satisfied with a conversation when at least one member of the dyad is androgynous.

Other differences in nonverbal behavior can create relational stress between women and men and reduce relational satisfaction. The avoidance of close interactions and touch by men and the desire for more contact by women may produce dissatisfaction (Floyd, 2006). Women may also be uncomfortable with men's common associations of touch and sexual intentions, whereas men may be confused by women's need for touch that does not culminate in sexual intercourse.

Finally, stress between the sexes can arise in group interactions. Women in leadership positions may experience more challenges than men, because they often receive more negative nonverbal emotional responses and fewer positive responses than men when offering the same arguments and suggestions (Butler & Geis, 1990). By comparison, men receive at least as many positive nonverbal emotional reactions as negative ones from other group members. Negative responses to women can devalue their leadership relative to men's leadership.

Sex and gender differences, therefore, are far from trivial. They have the potential to create tension, conflict, and dissatisfaction between women and men. This may be increasingly true as more women move into male-dominated areas in business and politics. In these areas, power and influence are important considerations, and to the extent that women's behaviors inhibit their abilities to exercise control, their success may be limited. On the social front as well, these differences may bode ill for male-female relationships when men's and women's communication styles come into conflict.

with age are particularly acute when older adults just decode two nonverbal channels (e.g., facial expressions and tone of voice) simultaneously. However, decoding impairments may be most evident when older adults interpret the communication of young adults. Parham, Feldman, Oster, and Popoola (1981) observed that older adults were more accurate when judging facial expressions from other older adults than from younger adults. Experience with one's age cohort may make an individual more attuned to subtle nuances in kinesic behavior that helps overcome processing deficits (O'Hair et al., 1991). Another interpretation is that the slowing of muscle movement reduces the number of cues emitted, and the speed with which they are encoded, making it easier for older adults to recognize communicative expressions from other older adults.

Proxemics.   Adults who experience hearing loss often compensate by relying more on sight to interpret communicative behavior. This compensation often leads older adults to adopt closer conversational distances to help them detect visual cues. Thus, hearing loss associated with age may cause older adults to stand closer to conversational partners than they or their partners are used to (Nussbaum, Thompson, & Robinson, 1989).

Vocalics.   Humans experience structural changes in the respiratory and phonatory systems as they age, which alters their vocalic style (Leaf, 1973). Reduced lung capacity may produce speech with inadequate loudness and vocal variation and may make it more difficult to maintain sound production for sufficient periods without pausing. These changes can produce rough, breathy, or hoarse voices, monotone voices, slurred speech, slower speech, or uneven vocal rhythm among older communicators (O'Hair et al., 1991). One study (Smith, Wasowicz, & Preston, 1987) showed that the voices of older adults contained longer sounds (i.e., sentences, syllables, consonants, and vowels). Changes in sensory abilities linked to age can also alter vocal style. Hearing loss can produce louder or poorly articulated speech (O'Hair et al., 1991; Whitbourne, 1985).

Hearing impairment also reduces vocalic decoding skills. Even a slight hearing loss can require a louder and slower conversational style of the partner in order to ensure accurate interpretation (Corso, 1977). Emotional expressions communicated by the voice seem to be particularly problematic to hearing-impaired individuals (Hooyman & Kiyak, 1988). Hearing aids often do not solve the decoding problems because they also amplify background noise, which further interferes with the decoding process (Corso, 1977). These changes in older people's communication style can alter the way younger people communicate with them, and not always for the better.

Nonverbal Identifiers of Personality

At the core of our identities are our individual personalities, those unique traits and characteristics that distinguish us from other members of our same cultural, ethnic, gender, or age cohort. Nonverbal cues are a primary means by which we make public "who we are." Take a look at the women shown in Photo 10.3. What judge-

PHOTO 10.3   *What person-ality traits would you attribute to these women on the basis of their nonverbal communication?*

ments might you make about their personalities on the basis of their nonverbal communication? Two categories of investigation offer insights into the use of nonverbal behavior for image management: (1) research on personality character-istics such as introversion, attachment, and need for affiliation; and (2) studies of psychological disorders such as schizophrenia and paranoia. What follows is a very selective sampling of the ways in which nonverbal cues manifest underlying per-sonality traits and states.

Physical Appearance.   Somatotypes may be related to personality insofar as they indirectly affect one's view of self and others. Stereotypes exist of the jolly, easygoing overweight person and the sensitive, high-strung thin person, and many traits stereotypically associated with each of the somatotypes show up when people rate their own temperament (Cortes & Gatti, 1965, 1970). They also show up in parents' and teachers' evaluations of children (Walker, 1963). The most commonly found associations are listed in Table 10.3.

Why are behaviors and personality traits associated with somatotypes? Temperament has physiological determinants, and the genetic, organic, and metabolic processes that produce a certain somatotype may influence tempera-ment. Alternatively, communicators may respond to children according to their appearance. Plump endomorphs and skinny ectomorphs get negative reactions and teasing, whereas mesomorphs receive more positive reinforcement because they are considered more attractive. Research on somatotypes and body attrac-tiveness as they relate to self-esteem seems to support this view (Berscheid, Wal-ster, & Bohrnstedt, 1973). One should be careful, though, not to overinterpret these associations. There is no direct evidence that possessing a particular soma-totype *causes* one to adopt certain behavioral patterns and personality traits.

**TABLE 10.3   Personality Traits Commonly Associated
with Somatotypes**

Endomorph	Mesomorph	Ectomorph
Affable	Active	Aloof
Affected	Adventurous	Anxious
Affectionate	Argumentative	Awkward
Calm	Assertive	Cautious
Cheerful	Cheerful	Considerate
Complacent	Competitive	Cool
Cooperative	Confident	Detached
Dependent	Determined	Gentle-tempered
Extroverted	Dominant	Introspective
Forgiving	Efficient	Meticulous
Generous	Energetic	Reflective
Kind	Enterprising	Reticent
Leisurely	Hot-tempered	Sensitive
Placid	Impetuous	Serious
Relaxed	Optimistic	Shy
Soft-hearted	Outgoing	Tactful
Soft-tempered	Reckless	Uncooperative
Warm	Social	Withdrawn
	High need for achievement	Low need for achievement
	Nonconforming	Conforming

Source: Compiled from Cortes & Gatti (1970), pp. 32–34, 42–44.

Clothing and other features of adornment are also related to personality. In an early study, Aiken (1963) found that those who showed great interest in clothing were conventional, conscientious, compliant with authority, stereotyped in thinking, persistent, suspicious, insecure, and tense. Although the results may now be outdated, they support the relationship of personality to clothing and adornment. Rosenfeld and Plax (1977) conducted a study that was designed to follow up and extend Aiken's work. Male and female participants were given a clothing questionnaire and an extensive set of personality measures. Again, the dimensions of attitudes identified in the study were related to the personality characteristics of both women and men. Here are some of the results:

- *Clothing consciousness.* "The people I know always notice what I wear." Women strong on this dimension were inhibited, anxious, compliant with authority, kind, sympathetic, and loyal to friends.
- *Exhibitionism.* "I approve of skimpy bathing suits and wouldn't mind wearing one myself." Men strong on this dimension were aggressive, confident, outgoing, unsympathetic, unaffectionate, moody, and impulsive.

- *Practicality.* "When buying clothes, I am more interested in practicality than beauty." Women strong on this dimension were clever, enthusiastic, confident, outgoing, and guarded about personal self-revelations.
- *Designer image.* "I would love to be a clothes designer." Men strong on this dimension were cooperative, sympathetic, warm, helpful, impulsive, irritable, demanding, and conforming.

Kinesics. Eye gaze and direct facing are intuitively recognizable indicators of people's gregariousness and social tendencies (Gifford, 1991; Simpson, Gangestad, & Biek, 1993). Extroverts and people with a high need for affiliation use more eye contact than introverts and those with a low need for affiliation. In fact, introverts often resist visual interaction as if fearing involvement. Men high in sociosexuality also make frequent flirtatious glances and avert gaze less often when interacting with attractive women. The relationship between looking and affiliative tendencies makes sense, as eye contact is a primary means of securing attention and social companionship.

Facing is one of several head and facial cues (e.g., nodding, head tilting, and smiling) that tend to co-occur and together are associated with a host of other personality traits. People who are ambitious, dominant, extroverted, warm, expressive, and generally socially skilled are more likely to display these cues than are people who are aloof, introverted, lazy, submissive, unassuming, or ingenuous (Simpson et al., 1993; Tucker & Friedman, 1993). These cues convey liking, openness, approval, and agreement and so may serve as positive feedback to others. It makes sense, then, that people who want to influence others, to get ahead, or just to be around others will put their expressive skills to use. Extroverts may also have an advantage over introverts because they pay more attention to the nonverbal cues of others due to their greater desire for social stimulation and more extensive experience in social situations.

People with secure attachment styles may also have an advantage over their non-secure counterparts when it comes to displaying nonverbal behavior that communicates liking and demonstrates social skill. An *attachment style* is a style of social interaction that reflects how people feel about themselves and others. People with positive models of themselves are self-confident and have high self-esteem. People with positive models of others are comfortable with intimacy and generally see other people as responsive and trustworthy. Four specific attachment styles have been identified by Bartholomew (1990) based on whether a person's models of self and others are positive or negative. *Secures,* who have positive models of themselves and others, enjoy social interaction and prefer interdependent relationships characterized by both closeness and autonomy. *Preoccupieds,* who have negative models of themselves but positive models of others, desire excessively close relationships and seek social approval from others to validate their self worth. *Fearfuls,* who have negative models of themselves and others, would like to have intimate relationships but avoid getting too close to people because they fear being hurt or rejected. Finally, *dismissives,* who have positive models of themselves but negative models

Table 10.3   Attachment-Style Differences in Nonverbal Communication

	Secure	**Preoccupied**	**Fearful**	**Dismissive**
Nonverbal Intimacy	Relatively high levels of facial and vocal pleasantness, laughter, touch, and smiling	A mix of cues showing intimacy (e.g., smiling, vocal pleasantness) and/or avoidance (e.g., less gaze, facial unpleasantness) depending on the situation	Relatively low levels of facial and vocal pleasantness, expressiveness, and smiling	Relatively low levels of facial and vocal pleasantness, expressiveness, and smiling
Emotional Expression	Readily express positive emotions	More aggressive and passive aggressive displays of negative emotion	Inhibit expression of negative emotion	Experience and express emotions (negative and positive) least
Nonverbal Conflict Behavior	More eye contact, nodding, and gestural animation	Most likely to sound whiny or vocally aggressive	Most likely to exhibit anxiety cues (e.g., more vocal anxiety and adaptors)	Mostly like to use interruptions
Social Skill	High levels of emotional expressiveness and nonverbal responsiveness	Difficulty controlling emotional expressions	Relatively low levels of composure, lack of fluency, and long response latencies	Low levels of emotional expressiveness and nonverbal responsiveness

Source: Information compiled from Guerrero, Andersen & Afifi (2007).

of others, are highly autonomous and tend to put distance between themselves and their relational partners.

Think of people you know who fit each of these attachment styles. Do these people exhibit different types of nonverbal behavior? Research suggests that they do (see Guerrero, Andersen, & Afifi, 2007, for a summary). Some of the key non-verbal differences between people with different attachment styles are shown in Table 10.3. As this Table shows, secure individuals are generally better at showing intimacy and expressing emotion than are individuals with other attachment styles. Skill at controlling these displays is associated with another personality trait: self-monitoring. High self-monitors are better at inhibiting expressions of triumph over an adversary than are low self-monitors (Friedman & Miller-Herringer, 1991). They may conceal their happiness by biting their lips and distorting their mouths in other ways.

Kinesic anxiety cues tend to be associated with negative personality traits and disorders (Gifford, 1991; Gilbert, 1991). For example, lazy, submissive, unassuming, and ingenuous communicators display more object adaptors than dominant and ambitious ones. Adolescents high in neuroticism show more facial anxiety cues than those low in neuroticism when getting a shot but not when giving a speech. Curiously, psychotic adolescents show more positive facial expressions during both presumably anxiety-producing activities.

One stable predisposition that is evidenced through all of these kinesic cues is communication reticence (also referred to as *communication apprehension* or *unwillingness to communicate*). Originally, this was called *stage fright* but has come to mean something much more than freezing in front of an audience. Communication reticence can be prompted by almost any situation calling for interpersonal, group, or public communication. In general, reticent communicators look ill at ease, apathetic or depressed, unanimated, uninvolved, and possibly submissive. Specifically, their kinesic profile includes negative forms of arousal such as increased bodily tension, more self-adaptors, more uncoordinated or random movements, and more protective behaviors such as body blocking, face covering, and leaning or facing away from their communication partner. Their posture is often more rigid and their behavior more restrained, with little facial or gestural expressiveness, nodding, and smiling. They also engage in less eye contact, as well as reduce immediacy through indirect body orientation (Burgoon & Koper, 1984). These kinesic and proxemic patterns are typically accompanied by vocal indicators of anxiety such as nonfluencies (Harper, Wiens, & Matarazzo, 1978). Thus, people who are apprehensive about communicating reveal themselves through an inexpressive, anxious, and detached demeanor, which ironically may lead others to avoid them and perpetuate their anxieties about interacting.

Proxemics and Haptics. People's willingness to approach and be approached, to touch and be touched, is another reflection of their personality. Scott (1988) proposed that people's orientations toward touch, conversational distance, and other communicative behaviors reflect the kind of *personal boundary* they have. Some people have open, permeable personal boundaries that allow exchange between the person and their surroundings (including other people), whereas others have closed boundaries that restrict such interaction. People also may have flexible boundaries that allow them to adapt from one situation or person to the next, or they may have rigid boundaries that lead them to respond the same way across situations and interactions. Scott's conceptualization of boundaries shares much in common with a number of personality traits and attitudes toward contact. As shown in Table 10.4, people who have open, flexible boundaries fit a high-contact profile: They enjoy and seek touch and close interaction, and they exhibit many other nonverbal and verbal behaviors indicative of being sociable, impulsive, and warm. Conversely, those with closed and rigid boundaries exhibit many behaviors indicative of discomfort with, and avoidance of, interaction. Thus, sets of proxemic and haptic behaviors coincide with a collection of personality characteristics.

TABLE 10.4   Characteristics of Communicators with Open/Flexible or Closed/Rigid Personal Space Boundaries and High Touch Comfort or High Touch Avoidance

Individuals with open and flexible personal space boundaries and/or individuals who report being comfortable with touch tend to have the following characteristics:

Behavior	Personality Traits
Talkative	Impulsive, takes risks
Shares self with others	Moves rapidly into relationships
Enjoys being around people	Easily attracted to objects and people
Readily shows emotions	Seeks close relationships
Admits errors easily	Overresponsive
Little control over impulses	Democratic
Spontaneous, with infantile dependence	Easily distracted, short attention span
Assertive	Hypersensitive to the environment
Socially acceptable self-presentation	Satisfied with self and life
Active interpersonal problem-solving style	

Individuals with closed or rigid boundaries and/or who are uncomfortable with touch and avoid opposite-sex touch tend to have the following characteristics:

Behavior	Personality Traits
Adopts large interpersonal distances	Low self-esteem
Infrequent touch in new relationships	Fears closeness in personal relationships
Apprehensive about communicating	Non-risk-taker
Reticent, quiet, shy	Emotionally detached
Nondisclosive	Lacking self-confidence
Protects secrets and territory	Fears not being able to maintain façade
Prefers to be alone	Passive-aggressive conflict
Passive interpersonal style	Negative emotional states (e.g., depression)
Nonopen communication style	Strives for internal and external control
Holds grudges	Autocratic
Highly structured	Long attention span
Negative views of touch	

Sources: Compiled from Andersen, Andersen, & Lustig (1987), Andersen & Leibowitz (1978), Andersen & Sull (1985), Guerrero & Andersen (1991), Landis (1970), and Scott (1988).

Vocalics.   Research on many aspects of the voice has yielded evidence of several significant associations with personality. Early research found that inflection correlated with intelligence and breathiness related to neuroticism, introversion, and submissiveness (Crawford & Michael, 1927; Moore, 1939). In 1934, Allport and Cantrill concluded that (1) the voice conveys correct information about inner as well as outer characteristics of personality; (2) although there is no uniformity in expression of personality from the voice (i.e., certain personality traits are not consistently evidenced by certain vocal features), many features of personality can be determined from the voice; and, (3) more highly organized and deep-seated traits and dispositions are judged more consistently and more accurately than physique and appearance features.

Subsequent research added more information on the relationship between vocalics and personality. Markel, Phillis, Vargas, and Howard (1972) examined loudness and tempo. They found that *loud, fast* voices correlate with being self-sufficient and resourceful, expecting the worst in people, and blaming oneself for problems. The *loud, slow* voice is associated with being aggressive, competitive, confident, self-secure, radical, self-sufficient, and resourceful; tending toward rebelliousness for its own sake; being low on introspection; and responding to stressful situations with hypochondria. The *soft, fast* voice correlates with being enthusiastic, happy-go-lucky, adventuresome, thick-skinned, confident, self-secure, radical, phlegmatic, composed, optimistic, nonconforming, independent, and composed under stress. Finally, the *soft, slow* voice is associated with being competitive, aggressive, enthusiastic, happy-go-lucky, adventurous, thick-skinned, reckless, and carefree, but withdrawn and introspective under stress.

Other investigations that have looked at such vocal features as resonance, loudness, pitch, and tempo have found that vocal profiles correlate with personality profiles (e.g., Markel, 1969). In sum, voices are often good indicators of actual personality traits. You might want to compare your own voice qualities to personality features listed in this section to see if they apply to you.

Summary

The process of image management relates to the ways in which we portray ourselves to others. As we've seen in this chapter, this is an ongoing process that relies on our knowledge of how nonverbal behaviors and characteristics will be interpreted by others. Nonverbal behavior plays a central role in the ways we communicate messages about our sex and gender, age, and personality to those around us. "Just be yourself" may be commonly heard advice, but as you've seen, image management is a complex endeavor that engages multiple elements of nonverbal communication.

SUGGESTED READINGS

Bixler, S., & Dugan, L. S. (2000). *5 steps to professional presence: How to project confidence, competence, and credibility at work.* Avon, MA: Adams Media.

Demarais, A., & White, V. (2005). *First impressions: What you don't know about how others see you.* New York: Bantam.

Etcoff, N. (2000). *Survival of the prettiest: The science of beauty.* New York: Anchor.

Maysonave, S. (1999). *Casual power: How to power up your nonverbal communication & dress down for success.* Austin, TX: Bright Books.

Patzer, G. L. (2006). *The power and paradox of physical attractiveness.* Boca Raton, FL: Brown-Walker Press.

Rhodes, G., & Zebrowitz, L. A. (2002). *Facial attractiveness: Evolutionary, cognitive, and social perspectives.* Westport, CT: Ablex.

Shields, S. H. (2002). *Change your voice, change your image.* San Francisco: Alliance Publishing.

11 Expressing Emotions

*The emotions are all those feelings that so change [humans] as to affect
their judgments, and that are also attended by pain or pleasure.*
—Aristotle, *The Rhetoric*

*Feelings or emotions are the universal language and are to be honored.
They are the authentic expression of who you are at your deepest place.*
—Judith Wright, Australian poet

Think about what life would be like without emotion. Being able to feel and communicate emotion is part of being human; without the experience and expression of emotion, life would be monotonous and human interaction would be uninteresting and unfulfilling. Emotions motivate us to take action. Fear prompts us to move out of the way, happiness leads us to seek contact with people who make us feel good, and guilt motivates us to seek reparation. Emotions are driven by innate, biological forces. They are also shaped by culture and social interaction. Indeed, the experience and expression of emotions are social and relational phenomena. Our social interactions with others often provide the basis for emotion, and we feel and show emotions differently in various types of relationships.

In this chapter we explore the relationship between emotion and nonverbal behavior. First, we discuss the nature of emotional experience, including how emotion is defined. Next, we discuss the nature of emotional expression, followed by a theoretical examination of the link between emotional experience and expression and a summary of nonverbal cues used to express emotion. We conclude the chapter with a discussion of nonverbal skills related to the decoding and encoding of emotion.

The Nature of Emotional Experience

To understand the nature of emotion, researchers have distinguished between *emotional experience*, which is the internal, intrapersonal part of emotion, and *emotional expression*, which is the external, interpersonal part of emotion. Emotional experience is what occurs within our minds and bodies; emotional expression is what we show to others. In this chapter, we discuss both of these facets of emotion, starting with the features that characterize emotional experience.

Emotions as Adaptive Responses to Events

Emotions are the feelings people have in response to precipitating events. For example, parents feel proud when their children get good grades, employees feel angry when their employers treat them unfairly, and patients feel relieved when physicians tell them they will recover from a serious injury. In all these cases, a precipitating event (good grades, unfair treatment, or information about recovery) causes people to feel an emotion. Although the specific events that cause people to experience emotion differ based on each individual's personality and culture, emotion motivates a person to behave in a way that allows him or her to adapt to the situation (Burgoon, Buller, & Woodall, 1996). Emotions also stimulate human cognition and organize information so that people are ready to respond to events in ways that ensure their survival and help them get along with others (Burgoon et al., 1996).

Emotions as Affective Responses

Affect refers to the positive or negative feelings that characterize emotion. Indeed, good or bad feelings are central to the experience of emotion. People generally experience positive affect when something is consistent with their goals and desires (Berscheid, 1983). Winning an award, talking with someone you like, and being complimented by a coworker all probably will produce positive affect, because these events are consistent with goals such as wanting to be respected, liked, and appreciated by others. Negative affect, on the other hand, arises when something blocks or interferes with your goals and desires. An out-of-control car threatens your safety, your roommate's messy habits prevent you from having the tidy home you want, or your friend's harsh criticism makes you question how others see you.

Emotions as Physiological Responses

Physiological change refers to the biological changes in one's body that occur when a person experiences an emotion. Such changes include increased or decreased arousal, warmer or cooler body temperature, and tighter or more relaxed muscles. Some physiological changes are shown nonverbally through behaviors such as sweating or blushing. Other physiological changes, such as changes in blood pressure or heart rate, cannot be seen directly, although they often produce observable bodily changes, such as sweaty palms. Various emotions are associated with different physiological changes. For example, across different cultures, anger is associated with an accelerated heart rate, warm skin temperature, and tense muscles, sadness is associated with tense muscles and a lump in the throat, and fear is associated with an accelerated heart rate, tense muscles, and a cold sweat (Ekman, Levenson, & Friesen, 1983; Scherer & Wallbott, 1994).

Emotions as Cognitive Responses

In the context of emotional experience, *cognitive appraisal* involves interpreting and evaluating an event to make sense of how one is feeling (Frijda, 1993; Lazarus, 1991; Omdahl, 1995). According to the *cognitive appraisal theory of emotion,* people label their feelings as particular emotions by considering all or some of the following: (1) how personally relevant the event is; (2) how pleasant or unpleasant they are feeling; (3) how much they think they can control or cope with the event that caused their feelings; (4) whether they perceive the event to interfere with or help them reach a goal; and (5) who or what is responsible for the situation (Frijda, 1993; Frijda, Kuipers, & ter Schure, 1989; Roseman, 1984; Smith & Ellsworth, 1985). According to Barrett's (2006) *categorization view of emotions,* cognitive processing is essential to the experience of emotion. Barrett argued that categories of emotion do not exist in nature. Instead she believes that people use their learned knowledge to conceptualize and label their feelings as falling under socially constructed categories such as "angry" or "sad."

To illustrate how the various components of emotional experience work together, let's imagine that both Dave and Tamika feel their hearts race when they get up to give a public speech. Dave evaluates his feelings as intensely unpleasant and believes that he cannot cope effectively with the situation, leading him to label the emotion he is feeling as "stage fright." Tamika, on the other hand, evaluates her feelings as more controllable and less unpleasant, leading her to label the emotion she is feeling as "excitement." This categorization process then translates into more nervousness and discomfort for Dave, whereas it generates a sense of enthusiasm for Tamika.

Approaches to Understanding Emotional Experience

Whether the emotion you are experiencing is fear or excitement, happiness or sadness, each emotional experience is unique. To understand how various emotional experiences are similar and different, scholars have described emotions using three approaches: the basic emotions approach, the prototype approach, and the dimensional approach.

The Basic Emotions Approach

According to the basic emotions approach, certain emotions are distinct and universal (Ekman, 1971; Izard, 1977; Tomkins, 1962), and all humans are hardwired to experience and express these emotions similarly, beginning in childhood. Each of the basic emotions is also related to a specific facial expression, which is said to be innate and understood across cultures. The most commonly reported list of basic emotions is from Ekman (1971), who listed happiness, sadness, fear, anger, surprise, and disgust-contempt as the six universal emotions. Other scholars have included interest, shame, distress, pride, love, warmth, and guilt on their lists of basic, universal emotions (e.g., Andersen & Guerrero, 1998; Izard, 1977; Tomkins, 1963). Other emotions are considered "blends" of the basic emotions. For example, hurt may be a mixture of sadness and anger, disappointment may be a combination of sadness and surprise, and jealousy may include anger and fear. According to the basic emotions approach,

PHOTO 11.1   *According to the basic emotions approach, young children and adults encode certain emotions similarly, regardless of culture. Which emotion—anger, disgust, fear, happiness, sadness, or surprise—is each child expressing?*

these blended emotions would not be as easily recognized across cultures as would the basic emotions. Moreover, the facial expressions associated with blended emotions are less distinct and less recognizable.

Take a look at the six photographs of children expressing various emotions in Photo 11.1. Which emotional expressions are easiest to recognize? All of the emotions shown there are basic emotions (anger, disgust, fear, happiness, sadness, and surprise), so they should be relatively easy to interpret. To determine if you were accurate in identifying which emotion each child was expressing, see the answer key at the end of this chapter.

The Emotion Prototypes Approach

Rather than classifying emotions as basic or blended, or dealing with issues related to universality, other scholars have categorized emotions based on the "prototype" or family to which they belong (Rosch, 1977, 1978; Shaver, Schwartz, Kirson, & O'Connor, 1987). Within this approach, a *prototype* can be thought of as the basic emotion that acts as the anchor for an emotion family. These prototypes or anchors are similar in some ways to basic emotions. For example, there is an

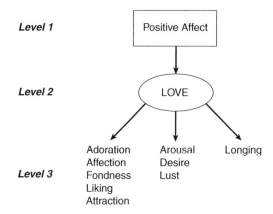

FIGURE 11.1   The Love Emotion Family

"anger" family and a "joy" family. To determine which emotions cluster together within different emotion families, scholars had people write about their emotional experiences, including different emotions they felt and ways they expressed those emotions. Researchers have also had people rate how likely they are to experience different emotions together. The information from these types of studies (e.g., Shaver et al., 1987) has been used to identify families of emotions that tend to be experienced and expressed in similar ways.

Each family of emotions contains three levels (see Figure 11.1). The top level (Level 1) concerns whether the family of emotions is characterized by positive or negative affect. The middle level (Level 2) identifies the prototype or basic emotion that anchors the category. Shaver and his colleagues labeled six emotions as anchors or basic-level emotions: love, joy, anger, sadness, fear, and surprise. Love and joy are both characterized by positive affect. Anger, sadness, and fear are characterized by negative affect. Surprise can be characterized by either positive or negative affect depending on the situation. Finally, the lower level (Level 3) includes groups of emotion that are related to the anchor. For example, the anger family includes emotions such as annoyance (a mild form of anger), rage (an intense form of anger), and frustration and jealousy (blended emotions related to anger). Blended emotions only belong to one emotion family. For example, anger is seen as more central than surprise in defining frustration. Therefore, frustration is classified as part of the anger family rather than the surprise family. Figure 11.1 illustrates how the three levels within the prototype system work together to help define what an emotion family looks like. At Level 3, the most similar emotions are grouped together.

Dimensional Approaches

Other researchers have used dimensions rather than categories or prototypes to describe emotions and distinguish emotions from one another. Russell's (1978, 1980) circumplex model includes two dimensions: activity and valence. The *activity dimension* refers to how aroused or relaxed a person is compared to normal. Thus,

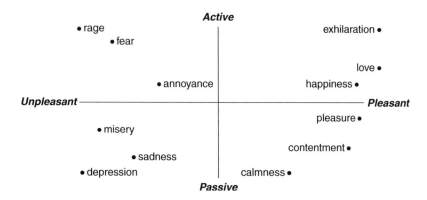

FIGURE 11.2 The Two-Dimensional Model

this dimension gauges the physiological changes that occur in people's bodies when they are experiencing emotion. The *valence dimension* refers to the degree to which people experience pleasant or unpleasant feelings with the emotion. Research on infants has shown that facial muscles respond differently to emotions depending on whether they are positive or negative (Messinger, 2002). Figure 11.2 shows how selected emotions are typically plotted using this dimensional structure. Of course, some emotions are more difficult to plot than others. For example, surprise could be pleasant on the valence dimension (e.g., you are thrilled that your friends planned a surprise party for you) or unpleasant on the valence dimension (e.g., you are dismayed that your friends surprised you with a party that you didn't want).

In addition to the activity and valence dimensions, some researchers use an intensity dimension to help describe emotional experience (e.g., Daly, Lancee, & Polivy, 1983). The *intensity dimension* refers to how strong or weak an emotional experience is. The intensity dimension differs from the activity dimension. For activity, people who are not experiencing an emotion would fall in the middle of this dimension; they would not be more aroused or relaxed than their normal state (aroused—normal—relaxed). For intensity, however, no reaction would constitute the lower end of the continuum (no emotion—weak emotion—strong emotion). Take a look at Figure 11.3 and think about which emotions might fall in various places on the three-dimensional space defined by intensity, activity, and pleasantness. Depression would be categorized as strong, passive, and unpleasant. Anger would be strong, active, and unpleasant. Joy would be strong, active, and pleasant. Where do you think emotions such as contentment, peacefulness, excitement, and relief would fall?

The Nature of Emotional Expression

As noted earlier, *emotional expression* is the external, interpersonal part of emotion that occurs when we communicate our feelings to others, either spontaneously or strategically. The majority of emotional expression is spontaneous and nonverbal.

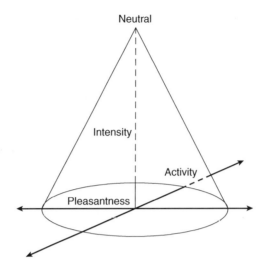

FIGURE 11.3   The Three-Dimensional Model

Source: Daly, Lancee, & Polivy (1983). Reprinted with permission of the American Psychological Association.

In fact, sometimes people have trouble hiding their true emotions from others because they cannot control some of the nonverbal cues, such as giggling or furrowing an eyebrow, that occur automatically in response to an emotion. At other times, emotional expression is strategic. We plan how we will say "I love you" for the first time or try to hold back tears to look tough during a sentimental movie. Both the spontaneous and strategic parts of emotional communication are highlighted next.

Emotional Expression as a Biological Response

Starting with Darwin's (1998/1872) classic work on emotion, research has often focused on the biological or evolutionary roots of emotional expression. Being able to send and interpret nonverbal behavior accurately certainly had adaptive value in our evolutionary history. For example, people who could recognize fear in the faces of other tribesmen and tribeswomen were alerted to possible dangers. In today's world, the ability to recognize expressions of emotion is similarly adaptive. As Andersen (2008) put it:

> Instant nonverbal communication allows us to understand the moods and emotional states of other people and to adjust our behavior accordingly. When people communicate their anger, we can avoid them and thus avert potentially dangerous—and even deadly—conflicts. People who express warm, happy emotions show they are available as friends, partners, or mates. (p. 139)

In addition to being able to recognize and respond adaptively to the emotional displays of others, evolutionary psychologists believe that people developed action tendencies that helped them cope with emotions more effectively. *Action tendencies* are innate, biological impulses that lead people to respond to specific emotions in ways that help them adapt to their environment (Lazarus, 1991). For example, the action tendency for anger is to attack, the action tendency for fear is to escape, and the action tendency for guilt is to make amends. These action tendencies help people react to situations quickly. In fact, in some of the earliest work on emotions, scholars argued that emotion is a motivating force that helps people harness the thoughts and behaviors necessary to respond to changes in their environment in ways that help them survive (Buck, 1984; Darwin, 1998/1872; Izard, 1977; Tomkins, 1963). According to these scholars, the emotion system evolved in humans over time, making children "hardwired" to experience and express emotions in particular ways. Some emotions, such as distress, disgust, and interest, are present at birth (Izard, 1978). Other emotions develop at around the same time in most children. For instance, most infants display their first social smile when they are between 6 and 10 weeks old. By 6 or 7 months old, most babies show anger, surprise, shame, fear, and joy. More complex emotions, such as contempt and guilt, usually emerge later (Izard, 1978).

Emotional Expression as a Social and Relational Response

Emotional expression is more than just a biological reaction. Emotional expression is also influenced by the social situation, including the people within the social environment (Buck, Losow, Murphy, & Costanzo, 1992). Several studies have demonstrated that people are more likely to display certain emotions when with others than when alone (e.g., Chovil, 1991b; Fridlund et al., 1990; Kraut & Johnston, 1979). In the Kraut and Johnston study, bowlers tended not to smile after making a spare or strike until they turned to face their group. In other studies, babies were more likely to smile when facing a caregiver versus a toy (Jones, Collins, & Hong, 1991; Jones & Raag, 1989). Sometimes, however, people suppress the expression of certain emotions when others are present (Buck et al., 1992). For example, you might hide jealousy from your romantic partner or hold back tears in public but then let them out in private.

People also "catch" the emotions being expressed by those around them. For example, you might feel down after talking to a depressed friend or up after being around someone who is excited and happy. The process of catching another person's emotions has been called the *emotional contagion effect* (Hatfield, Cacioppo, & Rapson, 1994). Even babies appear to catch the emotions of others. In one study (Tremine & Izard, 1988), infants displayed more happiness when their mothers expressed joy and more negative affect and interest when their mothers expressed sadness. Additional research on the emotional contagion effect is summarized in Box 11.1.

Social and cultural forces also lead people to *manage* their emotions. When people manage their emotional expression, their communication does not always match what they are feeling inside. The term *cultural display rule* has been used to describe how people manage emotional communication to be socially appropriate within a given situation or culture (Ekman & Friesen, 1975; Planalp, 1999; Saarni, 1993). For example, in the United States, boys are taught to hold

B O X **11.1**

That Look—It's Catching!

Emotions, Like Germs, Are Easily Transmissible. The Trick Is Passing and Receiving the Right Ones.

—by Stacey Colino, *Washington Post*,
May 30, 2006, p. F1.

It takes only a sneeze, a cough or a handshake to spread cold or flu germs from one person to another. But emotions can be transmitted even more easily, faster than the blink of an eye.

Research has found that emotions—both upbeat ones like enthusiasm and joy, and negative ones like sadness, fear and anger—are easily passed from person to person, often without either party's realizing it. Emotional contagion occurs in a matter of milliseconds, says Elaine Hatfield, a professor of psychology at the University of Hawaii and co-author of "Emotional Contagion" (Cambridge University Press, 1994). If you're the receiver, you may not know what exactly happened, just that you feel differently after the encounter than you did before.

It turns out this phenomenon depends on a basic, even primal, instinct: During conversation, humans unconsciously tend to mimic and synchronize with the other person's facial expressions, posture, body language and speech rhythms, explains John T. Cacioppo, professor of psychology and director of the Center for Cognitive and Social Neuroscience at the University of Chicago.

When it comes to this monkey-see, monkey-do dynamic, "the more expressive and sincere someone is, the more likely you are to see that expression and mimic it," Cacioppo says. "The muscle fibers [in your face and body] can be activated unbeknownst to you, at much lower levels than if you were to express those movements yourself initially."

In a study at Uppsala University in Sweden, researchers exposed people to pictures of happy or angry faces for 30 milliseconds, immediately followed by neutral faces. Even though the participants didn't realize they'd just looked at a happy or angry face, they responded with distinct facial muscle reactions of their own that corresponded to the emotion they'd just seen.

Those incremental muscle movements then trigger the actual feeling by causing the same neurons to fire in the brain as if you were experiencing the emotion naturally, according to Hatfield. In other words, the mood feedback loop can travel in both directions: Normally, when you feel happy, your brain might send a signal to your mouth to smile. With the mood-contagion effect, the facial muscles involved in smiling might begin to twitch when you're with a cheerful friend and those tiny muscle movements then send a signal to your brain, telling it to feel happy.

But there may be another mode of transmission: In the course of conversation, people have a tendency to match the emotional tone of their word choices—particularly when it comes to using negatively charged words such as "hate," "worthless," "anger" and "sad"—with the tone being used by whomever they're talking to, according to research presented at the Midwestern Psychological Association's annual meeting.

"Communication requires the matching of specific words and contents so [people] can understand each other," explains study co-author Frank Bernieri, an associate professor of psychology at Oregon State University in Corvallis. "So it's not hard to imagine the language driving some part of this contagion process."

Whether it happens at home, work, school or other settings where you have close interactions with other people, this communicative dance is highly adaptive and functional, experts say, because it allows you to know what other people are feeling or thinking. "It's the very first idea of mind reading," Hatfield says. "For the vast majority of people, you want to know what other people are

(continued)

BOX 11.1 *Continued*

thinking, to be in sync with them, to have sympathy and empathy."

With any luck, people catch the positive emotions—a colleague's enthusiasm for a project at work, a friend's excitement over an athletic event—and miss the negative ones. Some psychologists suspect, however, that negative emotions may be more infectious. "If someone is sharing negative emotions in a self-disclosing, personal realm, you have to be empathic and acknowledge it," Bernieri says, which makes the emotion more likely to spread.

Marta Wiseman, a mother of two in Oakton, has experienced this firsthand. "I try to start my day feeling hopeful and positive," she says, "but some mornings my 15-year-old mopes around, complaining about having to get up so early, and his disposition brings me down."

While the idea of making yourself impervious to other people's emotions may be appealing, putting up an emotional barrier is not the answer.

"There's a cost to it—you lose empathy," Cacioppo says. After all, shutting out other people's dark moods precludes you from catching their good cheer, too.

Source: Permission to reprint this article was granted by the author.

Note: This material is an excerpt from the abovementioned article by Colino (2006).

---

back tears if they get injured on the football field, and women often learn that they will face negative consequences at work if they display negative emotions too aggressively. Researchers have identified five specific types of display rules, as described in Table 11.1. As shown in the table, simulation and inhibition are opposites; one involves acting like you feel an emotion when you actually feel nothing, and the other involves acting like you feel nothing when you actually do feel something. Exaggeration and minimization also involve the opposite process, with a felt emotion intensified in the former case and de-intensified in the latter case. Masking is the only display rule that involves substituting a felt emotion for a very different emotion, and is therefore the most complex. Enacting this display rule is difficult for two reasons—you have to cover up any spontaneous displays of nonverbal behavior related to the emotion you are actually feeling, while also producing nonverbal and/or verbal cues that convince others you are feeling the feigned emotion.

The Link Between Emotional Experience and Emotional Expression

As we have seen, emotions are influenced by both biological and social or cultural forces. The specific link between internal emotional experiences and external emotional expressions, however, is controversial. Scholars have taken various positions. Some researchers argue that there is a direct biological link between emotional experience and emotional expression. Others argue that social and cultural forces curb the influence of biology. Still others believe that internal emotions are best viewed as one of many motivating forces that shape people's nonverbal expressions of emotions. Next, we describe four positions on

TABLE 11.1   Common Cultural Display Rules

Rule	Description	Example
Simulation	Acting like you feel an emotion when you really do not feel anything	Katelyn acts happy when a coworker tells her she is getting married, even though she does not know her coworker very well and does not really care.
Inhibition	Acting like you do not feel any emotion when you actually feel something	Jack walks into a pole while looking at an attractive woman. Although he is embarrassed he keeps walking as if nothing happened.
Exaggeration	Acting like you feel an emotion more intensely than you actually do	One-year-old Isabella falls down on her bottom when trying to walk. It hurts a little, but she cries really hard so her mom will come pick her up.
Minimization	Acting like you feel an emotion less intensely than you actually do	Gustavo is angry that his boss let a coworker take extra family leave after refusing a similar request that he made. Before he talks to his boss, he tries to calm down so he will look annoyed but not overly upset.
Masking	Acting like you feel a different emotion than you actually feel	Jordan is up for best actor at the Academy Awards for the fourth time without ever winning. When a new-comer to the industry wins, Jordan is very upset and envious but smiles and acts happy for the winner.

the link between emotional experience and expression: the universalistic perspective, the neurocultural perspective, the behavioral ecology perspective, and the functionalist perspective.

The Universalist Perspective

The traditional position regarding the link between the experience and expression of emotion is that emotional expressions are innate and inherited (Darwin, 1998/1872; Izard, 1977; Tomkins, 1963). According to this view, both emotions and emotional expressions evolved over time because they were adaptive and helped people survive. Darwin (1998/1872) described the chain of events this way: "Actions, which were at first voluntary, soon became habitual, and at last hereditary, and may then be performed even in opposition to the will" (p. 356). Thus, adaptive expressions of emotion were believed to be hardwired reactions to events in the environment.

Researchers who take a universalistic perspective believe that there is a limited set of basic human emotions that evolved because they were adaptive and helped humans survive. As noted earlier in this chapter, emotions such as happiness,

BOX **11.2**

Universal Expressions of Pride by Olympic and Paralympic Champions

PHOTO 11.2 *At the 2008 Olympics, Nastia Liukin acknowledges the crowd after winning the all-around gold medal in women's gymnastics, and Li Xiaopeng celebrates after hitting a routine that helped secure the team gold for the Chinese men.*

Your favorite athlete has just placed first at the Olympic Games. Can you imagine how he or she will look after securing victory? According to research by Tracy and Matsumoto (2008), you probably can. These researchers suggest that the expression of pride is universal, innate, and easily recognizable. To test this idea, they analyzed photographs of athletes after they won or lost their events at the 2004 Olympic and Paralympic Games. The photos included athletes from 36 countries. Some of the athletes whom they photographed were blind from birth. They found that, regardless of country and whether they were blind or sighted, the athletes expressed pride in very similar ways. Their bodies, in particular, showed universal signs of pride and victory, including raised arms, fisted or outstretched hands, back head tilts, smiles, an expanded chest, and a pushed out

torso. In contrast, those who lost their events tended to show shame by slumping their shoulders and narrowing their chests. Interestingly, the profile of behaviors was more consistent for pride than shame. Tracy and Matsumoto suggested that sighted individuals from individualistic countries—such as the United States and some countries in western Europe—learn to inhibit shame displays more than do congenitally blind people and individuals from collectivist countries—such as Japan or China. The researchers suggest that pride displays may have evolved as a survival mechanism that allows people to telegraph to others that they are strong and powerful, and therefore should not be challenged.

Source: Information summarized from Tracy and Matsumoto (2008).

---

sadness, anger, fear, disgust, and surprise are commonly identified as basic emotions. Some scholars have also classified pride as a universal emotion (see Box 11.2). According to the universalistic perspective, the face is the primary channel used to express these emotions, and facial expressions of basic emotions evolved so that infants, adults, and people from different cultures all display them the same way.

Developmental research provides some evidence supporting the idea that infants display facial expressions of emotion similar to adults. For example, a study by Oster, Hegley, and Nagel (1992) showed that infants displayed facial expressions of positive emotions—such as joy, interest, and surprise—in ways that were highly consistent with adults. Infants, and even newborns, also display facial expressions showing pain using the same specific nonverbal behaviors as adults: a scrunched down brow, tightly shut eyes, wrinkled nose, opened mouth, and tight curved tongue (Grunau & Craig, 1990). Yet infants and adults do not match when it comes to displaying other negative emotions, such as anger, disgust, fear, and sadness (Camras, Sullivan, & Michel, 1993; Oster et al., 1992). It appears, therefore, that some forms of emotional expression may be more innate than others.

More evidence supports the idea that people from different cultures are similar in their facial displays of emotion, although the extent of this consistency has been debated by scholars. People from Argentina, Brazil, Chile, France, Great Britain, Greece, Japan, Spain, Switzerland, and the United States all have been shown to display similar facial expressions of emotion (Ekman, 1971, 1975; Ekman & Oster, 1979; Izard, 1971; Oster & Ekman, 1978). Individuals are also able to identify the emotions that people from other cultures are experiencing by looking at their faces (Boucher & Carlson, 1980; Ekman, 1993; Ekman & Friesen, 1986; Ekman, Friesen, & Ellsworth, 1972; Frank & Stennett, 2001; Russell, 1994; Scherer & Wallbott, 1994; Shimoda, Argyle, & Ricci Bitti, 1978). Typically, studies in this tradition involved showing people from different countries photographs of facial expressions and then having them identify the emotion the person in the photo is feeling, either by having them choose from a list of emotions or having them fill in a blank. In these studies, basic emotions are identified well beyond chance levels.

However, some emotions are identified more easily than others. For example, happiness appears to be particularly easy to identify, perhaps because it stands apart as one of the only positive basic emotions and is marked by the universal and easily recognizable smile. In most cultures, happiness is recognized at a rate of 90% or higher. Surprise is also recognized with a relatively high level of accuracy, from around 82% to 92% of the time, depending on culture. Fear, anger, and sadness vary in their accuracy level with ranges beginning in the 60% range and extending into the 80% range (e.g., Russell, 1994). Blended emotions, although often recognized at a rate better than chance, are less easily identifiable than basic emotions (Ekman et al., 1987).

It is also important to realize that there are cultural differences in the accuracy rates of judging facial expressions of emotion (Matsumoto, 2006). In other words, although people from different cultures are able to identify emotion in faces at a rate better than chance, the accuracy rate varies by culture. In general, people have an *ingroup advantage* when decoding emotions from facial expressions (Dovidio, Hebl, Richeson, & Shelton, 2006; Elfenbein & Ambady, 2002b, 2003). This means that people are better able to decode emotion in the faces of people who are from the same cultural or ethnic group as themselves. For example, Elfenbein and Ambady showed that Chinese individuals are better at decoding emotion in Chinese faces than are people from the United States, who are better at decoding emotion in American faces. They also showed that exposure to a culture makes a difference. U.S. citizens who had a Chinese background were better at decoding the emotional expressions of people from China than were U.S. citizens who did not have an Asian background.

Overall, then, there has been mixed support for the universalistic perspective. This means that although some nonverbal displays of emotion are likely based on brain functioning and innate impulses, cultural and social conditions also play a role, as suggested in the neurocultural perspective presented next.

The Neurocultural Perspective

Ekman's neurocultural theory is an extension of the universalistic perspective (Ekman, 1971, 1975; Ekman, Sorenson, & Friesen, 1969; Oster & Ekman, 1978). Specifically, like Darwin and other universalists, Ekman and his team of researchers believed that there is a connection between people's internal emotional states and their facial expressions of emotion. However, they also argued that cultural displays can alter the way an internal emotion is expressed. The diagram in Figure 11.4 illustrates this process.

As the figure shows, the process begins with *emotional elicitors*. These are events that stimulate emotion in the human brain. According to this theory, some emotional elicitors, such as hunger and fear of heavy falling objects, are universal. Other emotional elicitors are socially and culturally learned. For example, babies often turn away from an angry face, which suggests that such faces could be a universal elicitor of fear or other negative emotions. But babies would not know that bowing is a sign of respect in some cultures or that an unwavering gaze could signal love or a threat. Some emotional elicitors are even related to different emotions in different cultures. As a case in point, in some cultures a funeral is a time to celebrate someone's life, thereby eliciting happy feelings and memories. In other cultures, a funeral is a time to grieve and be sad.

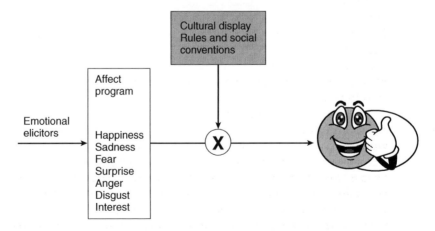

FIGURE 11.4 The Neurocultural Model

The next step in the process involves *the affect program*. Here the emotional elicitors trigger the brain and the physiological changes that accompany emotion. The affect program includes the basic, universal emotions that are theorized to be linked to particular physiological changes and facial expressions. If the process stopped here, the emotional expression would be a pure read-out of what the person was feeling. However, as the circled X in Figure 11.4 represents, the true expression of a person's emotions is often modified or even blocked by cultural display rules.

These display rules are taught within a given culture. Cultural display rules are also based on our observations of others. For instance, mothers tell their children not to get angry much more than they tell them not to look happy, so children learn which expressions are most and least socially appropriate (Casey & Fuller, 1994). Children also learn situational and cultural rules regarding emotional expression, such as not going to bed angry, not looking happy at another person's misfortune, and hiding or at least curbing expressions of love early in a relationship. According to the neurocultural model, knowing these rules and social conventions helps people manage their emotional communication to be more functional and socially appropriate.

The result is that the nonverbal and verbal expression of emotion often (although not always) represents a combination of one's true feelings and the feelings that one wishes to project. Take the following as an example. Mario is at his wife's company picnic. He does not know anyone there, and after an hour or two of listening to "shop talk" about a place where he does not work, he is ready to go home. Then Mario's wife, Michelle, approaches him with her boss, Jim, in tow and says, "Hey honey, great news! Jim and Kelly have invited us to their place to swim after the picnic!" Mario's first reaction is surprise followed by dread. But knowing how important it is to Michelle and how inappropriate it would be to show his negative feelings, Mario puts a polite smile on his face and says, "That sounds fun." Although Michelle can tell that Mario's enthusiasm level is a little low, the smile satisfies Jim, who grins back and says, "Great, see you there."

The Behavioral Ecology Perspective

According to the neurocultural explanation, Mario's emotional expression was a combination of felt emotion and feigned emotion. Researchers taking a *behavioral ecology perspective* (Fridlund & Duchaine, 1996; Fridlund & Russell, 2006), however, look at this example a different way. They argue that Mario's smile and verbal acceptance were not false; rather they were a natural reaction to another competing emotion—the desire to please his wife and to act in a socially appropriate and likeable manner in front of her colleague. According to the behavioral ecology perspective, nonverbal expressions of emotion are influenced by social motives and should therefore be interpreted within the context of interpersonal interaction. Indeed, if Michelle had approached Mario without her boss and no one else was near them, he would likely have had a very different reaction. He might have sighed and told her he was tired and would prefer not to go. Proponents of the neurocultural perspective would say that this reaction would have been a more genuine expression of Mario's emotions. However, proponents of the behavioral ecology perspective would argue that Mario's expression would be a true expression of his feelings in both cases, with the two situations eliciting different combinations of emotions.

Behavioral ecologists also believe that the case for universality has been overstated. According to these researchers, the evidence shows a pattern of *minimal universality* (Fridlund & Russell, 2006), which means that there are both similarities and differences between members of different cultures when it comes to the facial expression of emotion. These researchers also argue that it is overly simplistic to view facial expressions as simple read-outs of the emotions that people are experiencing internally. Instead, facial expressions display more than emotional states; they also reflect people's thoughts, intentions, and physical states. For example, although Kristin might smile because she is happy, she might also smile to appear friendly, to ingratiate herself with someone, or to appease an angry friend. Thus, facial expressions do not always reflect internal emotions. They do, however, provide information about the social interaction at hand. Table 11.2 shows common interpretations of various facial expressions from the behavioral ecology as compared to the universalist perspective.

When you look at this table, think back to the example of Mario at his wife's company picnic. Do you think the universalistic perspective or the behavioral ecology perspective does a better job of explaining Mario's smile? You could argue that Mario's smile was fake; he was tired and wanted to go home. Or you could argue, as the behavioral ecologists would, that his smile was motivated by a readiness to appease, especially if he loves his wife and wants to please her. If that is the case, was the smile really fake, or was it a reflection of the mix of feelings and motivations that Mario experienced—surprise, dread, compassion, empathy, and even love for his wife? Behavioral ecologists argue that social motivations are as central to nonverbal expressions of emotion as are internal feelings.

The Functionalist Perspective

According to Barrett's (1993, 1998) functionalist perspective, emotions represent the relationship between a person and the environment. Emotions are adaptive because they help people cope with their environment and reach their goals. Emotional experience is theorized to be a dynamic process that is highly dependent on the context and consequences. People learn what different events in the environment mean, and they also learn how to react to emotion-eliciting events in ways that help them cope effectively. Thus, according to this perspective, socialization plays a key role in determining how people experience and express emotion. Barrett (1998) put it this way: "the emotion process does not spring forth, fully formed, from a program in the brain, nor is it created completely anew on each occasion" (p. 110). Instead, emotions are functional responses to the environment that people continually refine based on experiences and current events. Experiences provide a blueprint for labeling and expressing emotions; but each situation has its own set of unique consequences.

TABLE 11.2   Common Interpretations of Facial Expressions According to the Universalist and Behavioral Ecology Perspectives

Facial Expression	Probable Meaning Based on the Universalist Perspective	Probable Meaning Based on the Behavioral Ecology Perspective
Felt smile	Expression of happiness	Readiness to play or affiliate ("Let's keep talking.")
False smile	Simulation of happiness when happiness is not felt	Readiness to appease ("Whatever you say.")
Sad face	Expression of internal sadness	Elicitation of support ("Comfort me.")
Angry face	Expression of internal anger	Readiness to attack ("Back off or else.")
Leaked anger	Inhibition of anger	Conflict about attacking ("I want to attack but I'm not sure I should.")
Fear face	Expression of internal fear	Readiness to escape or submit ("I need to get away.")
Contemptuous look	Expression of internal feelings of contempt	Declaration of superiority ("You are inferior to me.")
Poker face	Suppression of emotion	Declaration of neutrality ("I'm not taking a position on this.")

Source: Adapted from Fridlund and Duchaine (1996), p. 279.

Fear is a good example of this. People experience fear when something in their environment threatens their well-being. As such, fear represents a relationship between a person and the environment. According to the functionalist perspective, all emotions, including fear, are associated with a tendency toward engaging in a particular type of behavior. With fear, the tendency is to try to eliminate the threat. This can be accomplished in different ways, and depending on the context, some means for eliminating the threat may be more effective than others. Sometimes hiding or leaving the scene is the best reaction; other times it is necessary to face the threat calmly or to act aggressively toward the threat. Imagine, for example, seeing a large black bear while hiking in the woods. Based on your knowledge and experiences, you might react in a number of different ways. If you had little knowledge, you might run away as fast as you could. Your fear could even help you run faster because of the adrenaline your body would be producing. However, if you responded this way, the bear would be more likely to chase you, so a better response would be to stay hidden (if the bear had not seen you) or to remain calm and tell the bear "Go away" in a firm voice (if you were face-to-face with the bear). Notice that the context and your knowledge of how to best respond would influence your experience and expression of fear.

Whether people are experiencing fear or another emotion, Barrett believes that emotions serve various functions that help people adapt to their environment and achieve their personal and social goals. According to Barrett (1993, 1998), emotions serve three broad types of functions that are significant for a person's adaptive functioning. *Internal-regulatory functions* help people regulate their internal experience of

TABLE 11.3   Functions for Happiness and Sadness

Emotion	Functions
Happiness	*Internal-regulating:* Expend and expand available positive energy; direct positive feelings toward creative thought; maintain motivation toward reaching goals and engaging in activities that promote success. *Behavior-regulatory:* Continue the activity in order to feel positively and further one's goals. *Social-regulatory:* Communicate to other people that ongoing activities are pleasant and enjoyable; encourage others to continue engaging in current activity.
Sadness	*Internal-regulatory:* Conserve energy and resources in the event of loss or an unattainable goal; divert energy to more attainable goals. *Behavior-regulatory:* Stop attempts to acquire an unattainable goal, object, or relationship and focus attention elsewhere. *Social-regulatory:* Communicate sadness, loss or defeat in ways that elicit comfort and support from others.

emotion in ways that help them use resources, such as energy, more effectively within the environment. *Behavior-regulatory functions* help people regulate their own behavior in relation to their goals. Finally, *social-regulatory functions* help people regulate the reactions of others in ways that foster the continuation of positive consequences and inhibit or reverse negative consequences. Table 11.3 provides examples of how these three functions work in relation to happiness and sadness.

The functionalist perspective suggests that the link between emotional experience and emotional expression is dependent on the environment and the consequences of communicating an emotion a certain way. Emotional expressions do not always reflect internal feelings; they also reflect social control, with people regulating their emotional experiences and expressions to adapt to their environment and fulfill goals. Barrett also argues that people express emotions using a variety of nonverbal channels other than the face. These channels are discussed next.

Nonverbal Expressions of Emotion

Although the face is a highly significant channel for communicating emotion, other nonverbal cues are also important (Barrett, 1993). A study by Planalp, DeFrancisco, and Rutherford (1996) showed that people commonly take at least four channels of communication into consideration when trying to determine what emotion someone is experiencing. They also found that people relied more on nonverbal than verbal communication when making judgments about the emotions others were feeling. Nonverbal channels included the face, voice, body, and activity cues (such as slamming a door or taking a walk), as well as physiological cues, such as blushing or crying. Facial and vocal cues were especially common, whereas physiological cues were rare. Next, we summarize the research on emotional expression using each of these types of communication.

Facial Cues of Emotion

The face has been studied more than any other nonverbal channel used to express emotion. Even though people usually get a general impression of the emotions someone is feeling by looking at their face, researchers have broken the face down into different regions and types of expressions to try to understand how specific facial cues communicate emotion.

Early work by Ekman and Friesen (1975) focused on three types of facial cues: static, slow, and rapid. *Static facial cues* are permanent facial features, such as bone structure, skin color, and lip size. Although these features can be changed through means such as cosmetic surgery or tanning, they are stable for long periods of time. Static facial cues do not directly signal emotions, but they provide the canvas on which other facial expressions of emotion occur. For example, the wideness of a happy smile or the contemptuous upward curl of one's lip are affected by the shape of a person's mouth. In addition, people with babyish versus mature facial features are sometimes judged differently when they display negative emotion. Those with babyish faces are more likely to be judged as fearful, whereas people with more mature faces are more likely to be judged as angry (Marsh, Adams, & Kleck, 2005).

Slow facial signals are facial cues that gradually change over time, such as wrinkles, skin texture, and even the shape and size of one's lip and nose (i.e., lips get thinner and the nose gets slightly larger as people age). Again, although slow signals do not transmit emotion themselves, they affect a person's overall facial expression (see Photo 11.3). People with smile lines generally look happier than people with frown lines, and people with a deep indentation between their eyebrows may always look worried or angry. It is no wonder, then, that people spend billions of dollars a year on cosmetic surgery and treatments such as Botox (see Chapter 4).

The most important types of facial cues, however, are *rapid signals,* which involve all of the facial movements that people make while expressing emotion. These rapid signals tend to occur in three regions of the face: (1) eyes, eyelids, and bridge of the nose; (2) eyebrows and forehead; and (3) the cheeks,

PHOTO 11.3 *How do the slow facial signals on this woman's face affect her expressions of emotion?*

nose, mouth, chin, and jaw. Some of the movements that occur in these regions are idiosyncratic, and there are certainly many facial movements that are not associated with emotion (such as looking up while thinking). However, some rapid signals are associated with specific types of emotion, as shown in Table 11.4. For example, a happy facial expression is often marked by the nasolabial folds, which are the creases or wrinkles that form diagonal lines from the sides of the nose to the corners of the mouth, making the shape of a triangle. If these types of rapid movements occur frequently, they may eventually become slow signals.

As the name "rapid signals" suggests, many facial cues of emotion are dynamic and change quickly. Expressions of surprise and fear tend to be especially fleeting (Ervin & Martin, 1986; Gaines et al., 1998). The initial expression of surprise is often rapidly replaced by another expression, such as joy, excitement, anger, relief, or embarrassment. Fear expressions often de-intensify as people think about how to cope with a threatening situation. Hiding one's fear to be inconspicuous or displaying anger to ward off a potential threat are common responses that occur after the initial fear expression has dissipated. Because facial expressions of emotions are rapidly changing, it is relatively uncommon for someone to display the prototypical expressions of emotion shown in Table 11.4 for long periods of time.

Some researchers have also examined *micromomentary facial expressions,* or microexpressions. These rapid facial expressions were first identified by Haggard and Isaacs (1966), who slowed down films of patients communicating with therapists to see what emotions the patients expressed. They found that patients' faces often showed a number of rapidly changing emotions, such as anger, happiness, and disgust, in a short period of time, and that the most fleeting of these emotional expressions (i.e., those lasting 1/5 of a second or less) were not noticeable until the film was slowed down. Researchers have claimed that although such microexpressions are somewhat rare, they can provide tell-tale cues about what people are actually feeling (Ekman, Friesen, & Ellsworth, 1982).

The eyes also provide important cues regarding people's feelings. As shown in Table 11.4, the eyes and eyebrows can express a multitude of emotions. In fact, people are better able to recognize and interpret facial expressions when they take both facial expressions and eye behavior into account. Outwardly positive emotions such as happiness and excitement tend to be interpreted more accurately when they are expressed with direct eye contact, whereas inwardly negative emotions such as sadness and anxiety tend to be interpreted more accurately when gaze is averted (Adams & Kleck, 2005).

Vocal Cues of Emotion

Along with the face, the voice is one of the most important channels for communicating emotion (Guerrero & Floyd, 2006). Vocal emotional cues evolved in humans and other animal species as a way of providing instantaneous information (Juslin & Laukka, 2003). For example, yelling "watch out" conveys the urgency of a dangerous situation much better than calmly speaking the words. Many vocal emotional cues are universal (Juslin & Laukka, 2003; Scherer & Wallbott, 1994). People

TABLE 11.4   Facial Movement Associated with Various Emotions

Happiness
(primarily identified by the eye/eyelid region and the mouth/cheek/nose region) Skin crinkled around eyes; mouth curved upward with the corners of the lips drawn back and up; cheeks raised; wrinkles appear to form a triangle shape from the edges of the nose to the edges of the mouth

Sadness
(primarily identified by the eye/eyelid and eyebrow/forehead regions) Skin between the eyebrows drawn down while the skin around the inner corners of the eyebrows is drawn up; eyes lowered; corners of the lips curved downward; lips sometimes pressed together with the bottom lip looser than the top lip or the bottom lip trembling

Fear
(primarily identified by the eye/eyelid region) Open mouth that is often stretched with tense lips; eyebrows raised and drawn together; eyes wide open and dilated; wrinkles in the center of the forehead; sometimes vertical lines appear between the eyebrows

Anger
(primarily identified by the eyebrow/forehead and mouth/cheek/nose region) Mouth shortened and opened in a square shape or shut with lips pressed together; eyebrows furrowed with vertical lines between the eyebrows; eyes can be bulging or in a fixed stare; nostrils can be flaring

Surprise
(primarily identified by the eye/eyelid and eyebrow/forehead regions) Eyes opened wide so that the whites of the eyes are seen all around the iris; eyebrows raised and arched, with eyelids somewhat raised; horizontal lines across the forehead; jaw dropped so that lips and teeth are parted; sometimes eyes move up and down and pupils dilate

Disgust
(primarily identified by the mouth/cheek/nose region) Nose and eyes scrunched up; mouth can be open with upper lip raised or closed with upper lip pushed down; chin and cheeks are often raised; in extreme cases the tongue is thrust out and downward

Source: Information compiled from Cüceloglu (1972); Boucher & Ekman (1975); Ekman, Friesen, & Tomkins (1971); Forsyth, Kushner, & Forsyth (1981); and Wiggers (1982).

around the globe yell when they are angry; speak with softer, warmer voices to communicate love or affection; and talk more rapidly when they are feeling nervous. Evidence that some vocalic patterns are innate or hardwired in humans also comes from studies on children. Newborns have an amazing repertoire of different crying and cooing behaviors that help them communicate with their caregivers. During the first year of life, babies tend to follow a similar pattern of vocalic behavior, moving from crying to non-crying speech sounds, to making sounds that vary in terms of intonation (Burgoon, Buller & Woodall, 1996). Children from different parts of the world also learn to laugh at around the same time, and both deaf and blind children produce laughter despite having never heard or seen it (Owren & Bachorowski, 2003).

TABLE 11.5 Vocal Characteristics of Emotional Expressions

Emotion	Volume	Tempo	Pitch
Happiness	Moderately loud and varied	Fast	Moderately high pitch Large pitch variation
Sadness	Low	Slow	Low pitch, monotone when speaking High-pitched crying
Fear	Loud (if in attack mode)	Fast	High pitch level (if in attack mode) Quiet (if in escape mode) Small pitch variation
Anger	Loud	Fast	High pitch level (if frustrated) Rising pitch (if frustrated) Low pitch level (if annoyed or threatened) Small pitch variation (if annoyed or threatened)
Surprise	—	Fast	High pitch level
Disgust	—	Slow	Small pitch variation with rising pitch

Sources: Information compiled from Banse & Scherer (1994); Pittam & Scherer (1993); Scherer & Wallbott (1994); and Scherer & Oshinsky (1977).

The voice can communicate emotion in many different ways. Loudness and speaking rate (or tempo) are especially important when people are trying to figure out what emotions another person is experiencing (Planalp et al., 1996). Hostile emotions, such as anger and contempt, are especially likely to be communicated using loud voices, whereas supportive emotions, such as affection and empathy, are more likely to be communicated using soft voices and variations in pitch (Burgoon, Buller, et al., 1996; Floyd & Ray, 2003). The fundamental frequency of the voice, which indexes the number of sound-wave vibrations produced per second, is also an important vocal characteristic related to emotional expression (Floyd & Ray, 2003). The more vibrations a voice produces per second, the higher its pitch. The more varied those vibrations are, the more animated a person sounds. Table 11.5 shows how the volume, tempo, and pitch of voices are related to emotional expressions.

Body and Activity Cues of Emotion

Although the face and the voice are the most important nonverbal cues for expressing emotion, people also show how they are feeling by their body movements and their actions. Common *body cues* of emotion include "clenched fists, walking heavily, stomping feet, throwing arms up, stomping around, and the like" (Planalp, 2008, p. 399). Gait, or the way people move when they walk, may be an especially potent indicator of the emotions a person is experiencing. When people are angry, they tend to walk stronger and heavier, with longer strides. A sad gait is characterized by less arm swing, whereas a happy gait is characterized by bouncier steps and a faster pace (Montepare, Goldstein, & Clausen, 1987).

Body positioning can also communicate emotion. Folding one's arm across one's chest can communicate displeasure and disagreement; crossing one's legs can show positive affect and relaxation; slumped shoulders can indicate sadness; and shuffling feet can betray how nervous a person is (Bull, 1987; Guerrero & Floyd, 2006; Planalp et al., 1996; Segrin, 1998). In an inventive study (Coulson, 2004) in which people viewed computer-generated mannequins posed in different positions, both happiness and anger were associated with a backward head tilt and raised arms. Anger was also associated with an especially erect posture. Sadness was associated with a slumped posture and a lowered head, and fear was associated with a backward head tilt as well as a backward transfer of weight.

Activity cues include more general actions that show emotion, including "solitary activities such as going for a walk, eating, drinking, smoking, throwing things, and changing putters, but also interpersonal activities such as kissing, hugging, tickling, hitting, and touching" (Planalp, 2008, p. 399). People often have a hard time staying on diets or giving up smoking if they are sad, nervous, or worried. Activity cues that involve tactile behavior can be especially powerful ways of communicating emotion. Hertenstein, Keltner, App, Bulleit, and Jaskolka (2006) had people from the U.S. and Spain try to identify the emotions of a person who was touching them on the arm from behind a curtain. From touch alone, people were able to determine the emotions of the person behind the curtain at a rate much better than chance, with sadness identified the most easily. Touch was related to various emotions as follows:

- *Happiness:* swinging, shaking, lifting
- *Sadness:* stroking, squeezing, lifting
- *Fear:* trembling, shaking, squeezing
- *Anger:* squeezing, hitting, trembling
- *Surprise:* squeezing, lifting, shaking
- *Disgust:* pushing, lifting, tapping

Physiological Cues

Earlier in this chapter, we discussed physiological changes as part of the emotional experience. Changes in overall arousal level, blood pressure, heart rate, muscle tenseness, and skin temperature can accompany and help define the type of emotion a person is experiencing. Although these changes are internal, they often manifest themselves in outward behavior. Examples include sweaty palms or face, blushing, pupil dilation, a face that turns white, shaky hands, and a quivering lip. In the study by Planalp et al. (1996), the most commonly mentioned physiological cues were crying and changes in breathing. However, these cues were seldom noticed.

Skill in Encoding and Decoding Nonverbal Expressions of Emotion

Good communicators are able to express their own emotions effectively and appropriately, while also recognizing and accurately interpreting the emotions of others. Thus, competent communication involves being skilled at both encoding and decoding emotions. Considerable research has examined these types of emotional skills, with some work focusing on the broad construct of emotional intelligence and other work focusing on more specific skills related to the decoding and encoding of emotion.

Emotional Intelligence

The concept of *emotional intelligence* refers to the ability to understand, manage, and utilize your emotions to meet goals, and to understand the emotions of others (Goleman, 1995; Mayer, Salovey, & Caruso, 2004; Mayer, Salovey, Caruso, & Sitarenios, 2001; Salovey & Mayer, 1990). People who are emotionally intelligent are more successful in their careers and their personal lives. Research suggests that people have an innate predisposition to be more or less emotionally intelligent, although some skills related to emotional intelligence can be learned. There are four essential components involved in emotional intelligence: recognition, understanding, motivation, and management.

Emotional Recognition. Emotionally intelligent people recognize their own emotions. They are in touch with their emotions in part because they pay attention to what they are thinking and feeling, including nonverbal manifestations of internal emotions. They notice physiological changes such as increased heart rate, sweaty palms, or rapid speech, and they label these emotions based on their feelings and the situation.

Emotionally intelligent people also recognize when other people are experiencing emotions. This ability allows them to comfort a sad friend more easily, reassure a nervous colleague, or reciprocate shared romantic feelings. Importantly, however, emotionally intelligent people avoid the trap of believing that they can always read the emotional expressions of others. Rather than assuming that they know how another person feels, they continue to look for nonverbal and verbal cues that affirm or change their initial impression.

Emotional Understanding. Recognizing emotions is not enough. It is essential also to understand one's own emotions and the emotions of others. Emotionally intelligent people know how to analyze their emotions rationally, and they use their emotions to facilitate thought and problem solving. When interpreting and labeling their emotions, people who are emotionally intelligent also take context into account. They try to understand how the situation affects their emotions and how emotional feelings and expressions might influence the situation. It is more difficult to understand other people's emotions than your own, and it is inadvisable to assume that you can always empathize with other people's feelings. But emotionally intelligent people try to imagine what they would be feeling if they were in someone else's position.

Emotional Motivation. Another part of emotional intelligence involves being able to channel the energy and direction that come with emotions. As noted earlier in this chapter, emotions are accompanied by physiological changes, such as increased or decreased heart rate, blood pressure, and skin temperature. Emotionally intelligent people are able to use these changes to help them accomplish tasks and reach goals. For instance, emotionally intelligent college students might determine that it is best to work on a challenging term paper at the time of day when they feel the most refreshed, alert, and upbeat. Even negative emotions can be channeled in positive directions. For instance, emotionally intelligent people can use nervous energy to their advantage. They can also redirect sadness by immersing themselves in pleasant, distracting activities, and redirect frustration toward finding a solution to problems.

Emotional Management.   Emotionally intelligent people also know how to regulate emotional experiences and expressions. They are able to prevent negative emotions from flooding their thoughts, and they can inhibit the expression of inappropriate or destructive emotions. Indeed, when emotions are intense, it is often better to postpone talking about your feelings until you can think more rationally. Gottman (1994) used the term *emotional flooding* to describe what happens when people become so overwhelmed with emotion during a conflict situation that they become defensive and stop communicating effectively. Emotional flooding can also occur in other situations, such as when you are feeling intense attraction or love for someone. Rather than getting carried away with these emotions, an emotionally intelligent person would be able to determine whether it was the right time to share feelings of love or not.

Emotionally intelligent people are also better able to inhibit, simulate, or mask emotions. For example, during a conflict situation, they know to refrain from engaging in contemptuous behaviors, such as rolling one's eyes or using a sarcastic voice, and instead displaying positive affect. Some research even suggests that people can change the way they are feeling inside by changing their outward expression of emotion (Laird & Apostoleris, 1996). If this is true, then putting a pleasant expression on your face when you are feeling bad will actually make you feel better. This idea, which was first proposed by Charles Darwin, has been called *self-perception theory* (Laird & Bresler, 1992) or the *facial feedback hypothesis* (Cappella, 1993). According to this hypothesis, facial expressions send signals to the brain that produce feelings. Several studies have supported the facial feedback hypothesis, including research in which people were asked to hold a pen in their teeth in one of two different ways—between their teeth or between their lips— and then watch a cartoon. Those who held the pen between their teeth, which approximates a smile, rated the cartoon as more funny than did those who held the pen between their lips, which approximates a frown (Strack, Martin, & Stepper, 1988). Other studies have shown that posing an emotion such as happiness, sadness, or anger also leads people to recall times in their lives when they experienced those emotions (Schnall & Laird, 2003).

In addition to managing their own emotions, people who are emotionally intelligent can influence the emotions of others. For example, they have the ability to cheer up a depressed friend by being sympathetic or deescalate an argument by displaying positive rather than negative affect. Because emotionally intelligent people are usually expressive, they also influence other people through the *emotional contagion effect* discussed earlier in this chapter. In other words, the emotions they experience are especially contagious. They can cheer up a room of sad people or bring energy to a group task when everyone is tired.

Decoding Ability

Consistent with the work on emotional intelligence, research has shown that the ability to recognize and understand the emotions of others is an important communication skill. A study of children showed that girls are perceived as more socially competent if they are good decoders of emotional expressions (Custrini & Feldman, 1989). Another study showed that girls who learn how to decode emotions better reported an improved sense of self and reduced social anxiety (Grinspan, Hemphill, & Nowicki, 2003). Studies of adults have produced similar findings. Socially competent men tend to be especially good at decoding facial expressions of positive emotion, whereas socially competent women tend to be especially good at decoding facial expressions of negative emotion (Zuckerman, Larrance, Hall, DeFrank, & Rosenthal, 1979). People who are able to decode the emotions of their friends and romantic partners accurately also have happier relationships (Burleson & Denton 1997; Gottman & Porterfield, 1981). These positive consequences beg the question—how accurate are most people when decoding the emotions of others?

People appear to be more accurate when decoding certain emotions compared to others. As noted earlier, people from various cultures identify basic emotions with more accuracy than blended emotions, and happiness is, perhaps, the most easily recognizable of all the emotions when people are judging single faces. People often confuse negative emotions, such as anger, fear, and disgust, when decoding negative emotion from facial expressions (Custrini & Feldman, 1989; Horatcsu & Ekinci, 1992; Marsh et al., 2005; Zuckerman, Lipets, Koivumaki, & Rosenthal, 1975). Interestingly, however, it is easier to pick an angry face out of a crowd of happy faces than it is to pick a happy face out of a crowd of angry faces (Hansen & Hansen, 1988), perhaps because humans are hardwired to recognize and decode threatening faces that are looming in their environment.

The intensity of the emotion being expressed also makes a difference. In general, facial expressions of intense emotions are easier to decode than are expressions of milder emotions. This is especially true for negative emotions, such as anger, disgust, and sadness; the more intense these expressions are, the more accurately they are decoded (Hess, Blairy, & Kleck, 1997). Vocal expressions of emotion are also decoded more accurately when the emotion being experienced is intense (Horatcsu & Ekinci, 1992; Zuckerman et al., 1975).

It is also easier to identify posed expressions of emotions than spontaneous expressions. Spontaneous expressions are often more fleeting or subtle than posed facial expressions. For example, during social interaction, surprise is often expressed with a slight raise of the eyebrows rather than the entire face (Reisenzein, Bordgen, Holtbernd, & Matz, 2006), making it harder to decode than when it is posed for a picture. When people are asked to pose emotions, they tend to display more stylized, intense expressions.

Vocal expressions of emotion can also be difficult to decode, with one study showing accuracy rates of about 50% (Pittam & Scherer, 1993). Happiness may be the easiest emotion to recognize in the voice (e.g., Horatcsu & Ekinci, 1992), as well as the face. Mistakes in decoding vocal expressions often occur when people confuse fear with nervousness, love with sadness or sympathy, pride with happiness, surprise with happiness, anger with contempt, or interest with pride or happiness (Apple & Hecht, 1982; Banse & Scherer, 1994).

There are sex and age differences in decoding accuracy. In general, women tend to be better than men at decoding expressions of emotion (Guerrero & Reiter, 1998; Hall, 1979, 1984; McClure, 2000; Zuckerman, Hall, DeFrank, & Rosenthal, 1976; Zuckerman et al., 1975). This sex difference appears early in life and is very consistent, but it is not very large. In other words, across many different studies, women emerge as slightly better decoders of emotional expression than men. Both males and females gain more accuracy in decoding with age, with people becoming increasingly more adept at deciphering emotional cues between age 5 and about age 25 or 30 (e.g., Harrigan, 1984; Markham & Adams, 1992; Nowicki & Duke, 1994). One study showed that children from the United States and Japan were able to decode surprise and sadness accurately before they learned how to decode happiness and anger (Matsumoto & Kishimoto, 1983). Between early and late elementary school, children learn to distinguish between different types of smiles (Gosselin, Perron, Legault, & Campanella, 2002). Another study suggested that children learn to decode vocal expressions of happiness before anger, and that it is particularly difficult for children to interpret neutral voices correctly (Horatcsu & Ekinci, 1992).

Adults may even have trouble decoding neutral voices correctly (Noller, 1980). According to Noller's research, spouses report less marital satisfaction when husbands mistakenly hear their wives' neutral voices as carrying a negative tone. Inaccurate decoding can also be especially problematic in conflict situations. In one study, couples were observed as they discussed a conflict issue. People tended to reciprocate or match the emotional tone that they *perceived* their partner to use (Gaelick, Bodenhausen, & Wyer, 1985). So, for example, if Courtney perceives Marcus to sound angry, she would be more likely to engage in nonverbal behaviors such as rolling her eyes, sighing, or crossing her arms defensively across her chest. If Courtney perceives Marcus to have a pleasant demeanor, she would be more likely to engage in behaviors such as smiling and speaking in a warm voice. The problem, however, is that in the 1985 study by Gaelick et al., people overestimated the amount of negative affect their partners were feeling; at the same time, they underestimated the amount of positive affect. These inaccurate perceptions led to more negative spirals of nonverbal communication. (For more on nonverbal communication in conflict interactions, see Box 11.3.)

Encoding Ability

Perhaps surprisingly, people who are good at decoding emotional expressions are not always skilled in encoding emotional expressions (Burgoon et al., 1996). Encoding involves a different set of skills than decoding. Sometimes being an effective encoder involves expressing emotions spontaneously. Other times being an effective encoder involves inhibiting or masking inappropriate emotions. Still other times, encoding involves strategically sending an emotional message.

BOX 11.3

Nonverbal Communication in Conflict Interaction

Nonverbal communication plays a key role in conflict interactions. John Gottman's research, in particular, has shown that nonverbal behavior related to contempt, defensiveness, and stonewalling are detrimental to effective problem solving and increase the likelihood of spiraling negativity during conflict (Gottman, 1994). Contempt is often communicated via the voice by sounding sarcastic, fed up, disgusted, or patronizing (Gottman, 1994). It is also communicated through kinesic behaviors, such as rolling one's eyes, looking down at someone, or acting astonished (Gottman, 1994; Guerrero & Floyd, 2006). Because these types of behaviors are often interpreted as personal attacks, they lead people to defend themselves—both verbally and nonverbally. Defensive nonverbal behaviors include speaking in a whiney voice, averting gaze, moving farther away, putting hands on one's hips, crossing arms across one's chest, stuffing one's fingers in one's ears while the partner is talking, and shaking one's head while frowning (Guerrero & Floyd, 2006).

According to Gottman, these types of behaviors are especially likely when people experience *emotional flooding* during conflict. Emotional flooding, which occurs when people experience high levels of arousal, confusion, and surprise in response to their partner's negative behavior, is often accompanied by physiological symptoms such as sweating, increased heart rate, and elevated blood pressure. This physiological state makes it difficult to process information and to act in a rational way.

When couples have repeated patterns of negativity in their relationships, one or both partners may start *stonewalling,* which takes defensiveness a step further. With stonewalling, partners protect themselves by withdrawing completely from one another. Like the name implies, it is almost as if they put a stone wall between themselves and their partner. They stop listening and show signs of noninvolvement and disinterest, such as holding long grudges, refusing to look at their partner, engaging in activities such as playing with the remote control when their partner is talking, and acting indifferent when the partner is trying to get them upset. According to Gottman, couples who engage in a pattern of conflict that includes contempt, defensiveness, and especially stonewalling, are more likely to get a divorce. Gottman's research, as well as work on the *demand-withdrawal pattern* (i.e., one partner makes demands, the other partner withdraws), suggests that men are somewhat more likely than women to stonewall, whereas women are more likely to engage in contemptuous communication (Christensen & Heavey, 1990; Sagrestano, Heavey, & Christensen, 2006), in part because women are more likely than men to want to change the status quo in their relationships.

So how can people engage in more productive forms of conflict and avoid expressions of contempt, defensiveness, and stonewalling? You may think that displaying positive emotion is a good place to start. Sometimes this is true, but be careful not to engage in smiles or particularly warm and affectionate behaviors if they could be perceived as insincere or condescending. If your partner wants to have a serious discussion about a conflict issue, he or she wants you to be serious too. Show that you are listening by giving your partner eye contact and trying to be empathetic. Don't be afraid to express your feelings, but try to do so without letting negative nonverbal behaviors throw you and the discussion off track.

Encoding emotions appropriately and effectively is a critical communication skill. People who express too much negative emotion are perceived as less likable (Sommers, 1984). In contrast, people who are good at expressing positive emotions, including affection, are more popular, have better relationships, and are physically and mentally healthier (e.g., Burgoon & Bacue, 2003; Floyd, 2002, 2006; Floyd et al., 2005). Some studies even suggest that people who frequently stifle the expression of emotion may be more likely to have cardiovascular and memory problems, as well as social problems (Berry & Pennebaker, 1993; Buck, 1977; Butler et al., 2003; Richards & Gross, 1999). Sharing emotions, especially when they are strong, can alleviate stress.

Men and women have different skills related to encoding ability. In general, women tend to be more expressive than men (Burgoon & Bacue, 2003; Guerrero & Reiter, 1998; Guerrero, Jones, & Boburka, 2006; Wagner, Buck, & Winterbotham, 1993; Wagner, MacDonald, & Manstead, 1986). Women are particularly good at expressing positive emotions, such as joy and happy surprise. Many studies have shown that women smile more than men do, both to show friendliness and to express happiness (Coates & Feldman, 1996; Ellis, 2006; Hall, 2006; Weisfeld & Stack, 2002). People also expect women to smile more (Hess, Adams, & Kleck, 2005). However, women may not be better than men at encoding all emotions. Men may be slightly better at encoding anger and, perhaps, sadness. Men also have an edge when it comes to inhibiting or controlling emotions (Guerrero et al., 2006). For example, men may be better able to stifle tears or act calm when upset. The ability to spontaneously express emotions may run counter to the ability to control emotions, with women slightly better at spontaneous emotional communication and men slightly better at emotional control (Tucker & Riggio, 1988).

As with decoding ability, encoding ability increases with age. Children's ability to encode specific emotions improves dramatically between early elementary school age and puberty (Cole, 1986; Custrini & Feldman, 1989; Mayo & LaFrance, 1978). There is some evidence that children learn how to encode positive emotions before they master negative emotional expressions (Burgoon et al., 1996). Children also become better at using display rules as they age. Children first learn how to exaggerate emotions. For instance, a 2-year-old is usually adept at crying loudly to get attention even if he or she is only a little hurt. Next, children learn how to inhibit or minimize emotions, so that they look like they are feeling less of a particular emotion than they actually are. Learning how to inhibit or simulate emotions is more difficult, and masking, which involves substituting a different emotional expression for the emotion a child is feeling, is usually learned last (Saarni, 1993).

Summary

Emotions are powerful. They motivate people to take action, bond people together, and sometimes lead people to act in irrational ways. Emotions are adaptive because they help people cope with their changing environment. The internal experience of emotion is characterized by affect, cognition, and physiological changes; whereas the external expression of emotion is shaped by innate action tendencies as well as learned display rules. Researchers have different perspectives regarding the link between emotional experience and emotional expression. They disagree regarding the extent to which facial expressions are universal and provide a direct read-out of a person's internal emotional state. Some researchers see emotional expression as a combination of felt and feigned emotions. Other researchers believe that emotional expressions are shaped by social motives and the emotions that accompany those motives. The most significant nonverbal channels for emotional expression are the voice and the face, although people also communicate emotion nonverbally using body cues, activity cues, and physiological cues. Being able to express and manage emotions is an important communication skill. Emotionally intelligent people are able to recognize, understand, and manage their own emotions as well as the emotions of others.

Women appear to have an advantage over men when it comes to decoding emotional information and expressing positive emotion; men appear to have a small advantage over women when it comes to expressing anger and controlling emotional expressions. For both females and males, encoding and decoding ability increases from childhood through young adulthood. Being skilled at expressing and interpreting emotions is a valuable skill throughout the lifespan.

SUGGESTED READINGS

Barrett, K. C. (1998). A functionalist perspective to the development of emotions. In M. F. Mascolo & S. Griffin (Eds.), *What develops in emotional development?* (pp. 109–133). New York: Plenum Press.

Ekman, P. (1993). Facial expression and emotion. *American Psychologist, 48*, 384–392.

Elfenbein, H. A., & Ambady, N. (2002). On the universality and cultural specificity of emotions. *Science, 164*, 86–88.

Fridlund, A. J., & Duchaine, B. (1996). Facial expressions of emotion and the delusion of the hermetic self. In R. Harrè & W. G. Parrott (Eds.), *The emotions: Social, cultural, and biological dimensions* (pp. 259–284). Thousand Oaks, CA: Sage Publications.

Fridlund, A. J., & Russell, J. A. (2006). The functions of facial expressions: What's in a face? In V. Manusov & M. L. Patterson (Eds.), *The Sage handbook of nonverbal communication* (pp. 299–319). Thousand Oaks, CA: Sage.

Guerrero, L. K., & Floyd, K. (2006). *Nonverbal communication in close relationships.* Mahwah, NJ: Lawrence Erlbaum Associates.

Guerrero, L. K., Jones, S. M., & Boburka, R. R. (2006). Sex differences in emotional communication. In D. J. Canary & K. Dindia (Eds.). *Sex differences and similarities in communication* (2nd ed., pp. 241–261). Mahwah, NJ: Lawrence Erlbaum Associates.

Hatfield, E., Cacioppo, J. T., & Rapson, R. L. (1994). *Emotional contagion.* New York: Cambridge University Press.

Matsumoto, D. (2006). Culture and nonverbal behavior. In V. Manusov & M. L. Patterson (Eds.), *The Sage handbook of nonverbal communication* (pp. 219–235). Thousand Oaks, CA: Sage.

Mayer, J. D., Salovey, J. P., & Caruso, D. R. (2004). Emotional intelligence: Theory, findings, and implications. *Psychological Inquiry, 15*, 197–215.

Planalp, S., DeFrancisco, V. L., & Rutherford, D. (1996). Varieties of cues to emotion in naturally occurring situations. *Cognition and Emotion, 10*, 137–153.

Scherer, K. R., & Wallbott, H. G. (1994). Evidence for universality and cultural variation of differential emotion response patterning. *Journal of Personality and Social Psychology, 66*, 310–328.

ANSWERS TO PHOTO 11.1 QUESTION

(a) surprise, (b) happiness, (c) sadness, (d) fear, (e) anger, and (f) disgust

CHAPTER

12 Relational Messages: Intimacy and Affection

Communication leads to community, that is, to understanding, intimacy, and mutual valuing.

—Rollo May, Psychologist and Author

Caresses, expressions of one sort or another, are necessary to the life of the affections as leaves are to the life of a tree. If they are wholly restrained, love will die at the roots.

—Nathaniel Hawthorne

Perhaps one of the most essential functions that nonverbal communication performs is relational communication. Relational communication refers to how people define the nature of their relationships with one another. It concerns the messages, usually nonverbal, that people exchange telling one another whether they view the relationship as one of love or hate, friendship or enmity, trust or distrust, equality or inequality, and so forth. Although relational communication also occurs in the verbal stream—after all, people do say, "I love you" or "I don't trust you anymore"—most of the process of defining interpersonal relationships takes place in the nonverbal streams.

In their research on fundamental relational themes, Burgoon and Hale (1984, 1987) identified seven key dimensions underlying relational messages: (1) level of intimacy; (2) dominance/submission; (3) degree of similarity; (4) social-task orientation; (5) formality/informality; (6) degree of social composure; and (7) level of emotional arousal. Some scholars have argued that intimacy and dominance/submission are the most important of these dimensions. In this chapter, we focus on nonverbal messages related to intimacy. In Chapter 13, we focus on dominance and the related concepts of power and persuasion.

Nonverbal behaviors play a critical role in communicating intimacy and affection across various types of relationships. Parents tuck their children in and kiss them good night. Potential romantic partners signal interest by flirting with each other and engaging in courtship behavior. New friends show solidarity by adopting one another's mannerisms and listening intently to each other's stories. Smiles, touches, and other intimate nonverbal behaviors can also help keep these various relationships satisfying. In contrast, when people do not wish to develop or maintain a relationship with someone, they often engage in behavior such as refraining from smiling and looking away when the person approaches them. These are subtle yet powerful ways of letting someone know that you are uninterested.

Within this chapter, we describe various types of nonverbal behavior that are associated with intimacy. Specifically, we summarize research on nonverbal cues related to immediacy, affection, courtship, and similarity. We also look at how nonverbal communication reflects formality versus informality and a social versus task orientation. At the end of the chapter, we focus on the environment as a contextual frame in which intimate interactions occur. First, however, we define intimacy and contextualize it as an important relational message.

Intimacy as a Relational Message

According to Burgoon and Hale's (1984) work, intimacy is reflected in messages that show high levels of immediacy, involvement, affection, depth, and trust. Shows of similarity, having a social orientation, and being informal also help make interactions more intimate. But what is intimacy? The term *intimacy* has been defined differently by various scholars, but most researchers agree that intimacy is experienced as an internal state and expressed using nonverbal and verbal behaviors. Prager has argued that people experience intimacy when they share knowledge about one another and feel "liked, accepted, understood, cared for, or loved" (Prager, 2000, p. 231; see also Prager & Roberts, 2004). Interaction is at the heart of intimacy; intimate emotions and behaviors are displayed within the context of intimate interaction, and nonverbal communication is a primary mode for expressing intimate feelings (Andersen, Guerrero, & Jones, 2006).

Nonverbal Immediacy and Positive Involvement

A set of nonverbal behaviors called *immediacy* or *positive involvement* cues helps people communicate intimacy and liking to one another. Immediacy behaviors indicate physical and psychological closeness, approachability, sensory stimulation, interest, and interpersonal warmth (Andersen, 1985; Andersen & Guerrero, 1998). Involvement behaviors, such as leaning toward someone, giving eye contact, and using an expressive voice, show that a person is actively engaged in a conversation (Coker & Burgoon, 1987). When involvement behaviors are coupled with indicators of positive affect, such as smiling and speaking in a warm vocal tone, they send strong messages related to liking and intimacy. Prager (2000; Prager & Roberts, 2004) used the term "positive involvement cues" to refer to the nonverbal behaviors that show both involvement and positive affect. Next, we discuss some of the most frequently studied positive involvement cues. These include haptic, proxemic, and kinesic behaviors, and to a lesser extent, vocal and chronemic cues.

Proxemic and Haptic Cues

As the term "closeness" itself suggests, close proxemic distancing and positive forms of touch communicate intimacy. Indeed, most scholars consider close proxemic distancing and touch to be the most important means for expressing attraction and liking (Andersen & Guerrero, 1998; Burgoon, Buller, Hale, & deTurck, 1984; Burgoon, Walther, & Baesler, 1992; Gilbert, Kirkland, & Rappoport, 1977). People who sit or stand close together are usually rated as more intimate than are those who are farther apart from one another, as are those who touch versus those who do not touch (Patterson, 1983). In one study (Stelzner & Egland, 1995), people rated close proxemic distances as the most important indicator of relational satisfaction in close relationships.

Communicating at eye level is also related to proxemic distancing and intimacy (Andersen, 2008). Researchers suggest that being at eye level minimizes height differentials, sends messages of equality, and reduces power differentials, creating intimacy. Imagine a 7-foot-tall basketball player interacting with a 4-foot-8-inch gymnast in the Olympic Village. Further imagine that they are standing about two feet away from one another while talking. Now imagine that they are still about two feet away from each other, but this time the basketball player is sitting on the floor and the gymnast is on a sofa so that they are talking at eye level. Which interaction would you rate as more intimate? With all other nonverbal cues equal, research suggests that most people would perceive the second interaction to reflect more intimacy than the first (Andersen, 2008).

Of course, if the basketball player and gymnast had been standing closer together—perhaps a foot apart rather than two feet apart—you likely would have rated the interaction as even more intimate. In early work on proxemics, Hall (1990) defined the "intimate zone" as ranging from 0 to 18 inches, suggesting that such close proxemic distancing is typically reserved for intimate relationships such as those between family members, romantic partners, and close friends. This zone includes touch as well as interaction that occurs between two people who are less than an arm's length away from one another. At this distance, people make themselves vulnerable in that their partners can easily touch and smell them.

Positive forms of touch can send strong, instantaneous messages of intimacy by communicating inclusion, support, and affection (Thayer, 1986). Touch that signals *inclusion* draws attention to the act of being together and suggests psychological closeness. Jones and Yarbrough (1985) described several types of inclusion touches, including holding hands, putting arms around one another, sitting together with one person leaning against the other, and sitting across from one another with knees touching. These types of inclusion touches have also been called *body contact tie-signs*, which signal a couple is to be treated as a bonded pair (Morris, 1977). Body contact tie-signs include holding hands, linking arms, and putting arms around someone's waist or shoulder. All of these behaviors tell others that two people are a unit, while also reinforcing intimacy within the couple. See Photo 12.1 for examples of tie-signs.

Mutual grooming is another form of touch that many women, in particular, consider to be a tie-sign (Nelson, 2007). These types of touch include moving a

PHOTO 12.1 *Three variations of body contact tie-signs.*

strand of hair out of someone's eyes, wiping a tear off another person's cheek, fixing someone's tie or collar, or tucking in a tag on the back of someone's shirt. According to Nelson's research, mutual grooming behaviors are a special type of touch that people use to communicate care-giving and attachment rather than flirtation or attraction. Such behaviors are common in parent-child relationships. When people see a couple using mutual grooming behaviors, they tend to assume that they are in an established, intimate relationship rather than a new or causal relationship (Nelson, 2007).

Touch also communicates comfort. In a study in which people described how they would comfort a roommate who was going through a romantic relationship breakup, the vast majority of people reported that they would likely engage in some form of tactile contact. Hugs and pats to the shoulder or arm were commonly reported as ways to comfort the roommate. People also described less common types of comforting touch, such as stroking the roommate's hair or putting the roommate's head on their shoulders. In addition to reporting that touch was an important way to provide comfort, people reported using close proxemic distancing. For example, people wrote that they would decrease distance by sitting down next to and/or leaning closer to the roommate. Jones and Yarbrough's (1985) study on touch produced similar findings. In their study, people kept logs of the touch that they encountered. The most common types of touch used to comfort others involved patting or touching someone's arm, shoulder, or hand. Hugs tended to be used only when comforting people who were extremely distressed.

Kinesic Cues

Many kinesic cues are associated with intimacy, attraction, and likability. These nonverbal behaviors, along with vocalic cues, might be especially important in professional contexts in which touch and close proxemic distances are less acceptable. For example, students rate teachers as more comptetent and likable when

---

BOX 12.1
Nonverbal Immediacy in the Classroom

Do you perceive your favorite teachers to use more nonverbal immediacy than other teachers? According to a long tradition of research, you probably do. Janis Andersen (1979) was the first to apply Mehrabian's (1969) research to the instructional context. Since then, numerous studies have examined the role that nonverbal immediacy plays in the classroom (see Witt, Wheeless, & Allen, 2004, for a review). These studies have found that perceptions of a teacher's nonverbal immediacy are related to positive affective learning, which includes the way students feel about their teacher, their attitudes toward the teacher and the course, and how they expect to behave and perform in the class (Pogue & AhYun, 2006). Hess and his colleagues (2001) believed that nonverbal immediacy behaviors are associated with positive emotions that produce a halo effect. Thus, students perceive teachers who they like to use more smiling, eye contact, warmer voices, and enthusiastic movement, and to be more competent, trustworthy, caring, and credible (e.g., Gorham & Christophel, 1990; Manusov, 1991). In one study, students watched videotapes of college professors giving lectures (Guerrero & Miller, 1998). Some of these professors used high levels of nonverbal immediacy; others used

low levels of nonverbal immediacy. Students rated the teachers who used high levels of immediacy as more competent. They also anticipated that they would like the courses taught by immediate instructors more, and that they would be more likely to take a future course with the immediate instructors than the nonimmediate instructors.

Importantly, a teacher's level of nonverbal immediacy seems to be related to positive attitudes and feelings rather than actual performance on tests or other indices of learning. Research also suggests that there is little correspondence between the immediacy behaviors teachers actually use and the immediacy behaviors that students perceive them to use (e.g., Smythe & Hess, 2005). Nonetheless, students perceive nonverbally immediate teachers more favorably, which could lead to a more positive classroom environment. Nonverbally immediate teachers are also able to demand more from their students and still be rated as likable (Mottet, Parker-Raley, Beebe, & Cunningham, 2007). Think about the various teachers you have had. How much do you think their nonverbal immediacy influenced your feelings toward them and the course, as well as the overall classroom environment?

---

they perceive them to smile, use eye contact, gesture, walk around the classroom, and have an open, relaxed body position (see Box 12.1). These types of behaviors are related to impressions of intimacy and likability across a number of different personal and professional contexts, as discussed next.

Gaze.   Eye behavior is one of the most commonly studied kinesic cues. Increased gaze typically sends messages of liking and friendliness, whereas averted gaze signals disliking and hostility (Burgoon et al., 1984; Burgoon & Le Poire, 1999; Palmer & Simmons, 1995; Simpson, Gangestad, & Biek, 1993). Direct, sustained gaze is also seen as expressing empathy and warmth (McAdams, Jackson, & Kirshnit, 1984) as well as comfort (Dolin & Booth-Butterfield, 1993). Gaze is also a primary cue indicating romantic attraction, although ironically both demure gaze and

---

BOX **12.2**

Nonverbal Immediacy in Doctor-Patient Relationships

Research has shown that the degree to which doctors display nonverbal immediacy is not a trivial matter. As Robinson (2008) summarized, when physicians show more nonverbal immediacy, their patients (1) trust them more, (2) talk to them more about their symptoms and concerns, (3) understand and retain more of the medical information they are given, (4) are more motivated to follow medical advice, and (5) are more generally satisfied with their doctor visits.

Several kinesic and vocal cues are related to these positive outcomes. Doctors are rated as more immediate and effective when they gaze at their patients' faces. Looking at patients' faces helps doctors diagnose patients' psychological problems while also encouraging patients to talk more about their illness (Bensing, 1991; Bensing, Kerrsens, & van der Pasch, 1995; Duggan & Parrott, 2001). Similarly, doctors who face their patients while they are speaking are better at diagnosing psychological problems (Giron et al., 1998). Interestingly, looking toward a patient or at the patients' face appears to be more important for establishing rapport than looking directly in a patient's eyes (Harrigan & Rosenthal, 1983, 1986). In addition to gaze, doctors who smile and use friendly vocal tones may be especially effective in getting

patients to disclose information and trust them (Duggan & Parrott, 2001; Parrott & Le Poire, 1988), even though an angry tone can sometimes communicate concern and motivate a patient to follow a doctor's recommendations (Roter, Hall, & Katz, 1987).

Touch and proxemic distancing also play a role in determining medical outcomes. Patients report being more satisfied when doctors lean toward them (Larsen & Smith, 1981) and sit close to them (Weinberger, Green, & Mamlin, 1981). They also report understanding and retaining more medical information when their doctors spend more time standing or sitting near them (Smith, Polis, & Hadac, 1981). Self-touching may also promote feelings of immediacy during doctor-patient interactions. Specifically, Harrigan's research has shown that doctors who engage in self-touch (such as touching their own face or rubbing hands together) are rated as warmer and more expressive, probably because such actions suggest that the doctor is paying attention to the patient rather than to her or his own communicative performance (Harrigan, 1985; Harrigan, Kues, & Weber, 1986). Although subtle, it appears that these types of nonverbal cues can enhance or detract from a doctor's effectiveness in diagnosing and treating medical conditions.

---

constant gaze are signs of flirtation (Givens, 1983). People engage in more eye contact when they like one another (Maxwell, Cook, & Burr, 1985) or are in love (Rubin, 1970), and romantic partners gaze at each other more than do friends (Guerrero, 1997). People also gaze more at romantic partners, friends, and people they like than at strangers or people they dislike (Coutts & Schneider, 1976). Even in professional contexts, such as patient-therapist interactions, patients report liking and trusting their therapists more if they use high levels of eye contact (Ziegler-Kratz & Marshall, 1990). Gaze also plays a pivotal role in interactions between medical doctors and patients, as discussed in Box 12.2.

High levels of gaze can also be viewed as a dominance move; so depending on the context, moderately high levels of gaze may sometimes be viewed more positively than very high levels of gaze. As a case in point, one study found that moderate eye contact was rated as better at conveying genuineness and empathy than was high eye contact (Reed, 1981). When high levels of gaze are used in conjunction with hostile or neutral facial expressions, gaze is likely to reflect efforts to intimidate rather than to communicate intimacy. Thus, gaze is most likely to communicate intimacy when it is used with other immediacy cues such as smiling.

Smiling.   Like eye behavior, smiling has received considerable attention as an indicator of intimacy and liking. Smiling typically reflects friendliness, social politeness, and/or positive emotional feelings such as liking (Kraut & Johnston, 1979; Palmer & Simmons, 1995). In fact, both the frequency and intensity of smiling help predict how much intimacy people feel toward one another (Guerrero, Andersen, & Afifi, 2007). A smile can also help create an atmosphere of interpersonal warmth and intimacy (Andersen & Guerrero, 1998), perhaps by creating an emotional contagion effect. According to work on emotional contagion, when one person expresses an emotion, the partner is likely to "catch" some of that emotion and experience it as well (Hatfield, Cacioppo, & Rapson, 1994; see also Chapter 11). Thus, a smile might spread from one person to others.

In the context of courtship, small amounts of smiling typically signal friendliness, moderate levels of smiling that range from frequent demure smiles to more constant smiling tend to signal flirtation, and constant smiling often signals seduction (Muehlenhard, Miller, & Burdick, 1983; Walsh & Hewitt, 1985). Smiling is also a key indicator of intimacy within same-sex friendships, especially between women (Guerrero, 1997; LaFrance & Mayo, 1979). Interestingly, smiling and other positive facial expressions may also make a person more facially attractive (Rhodes & Zebrowitz, 2002). An older face with smile lines is more attractive and better able to send messages of warmth and liking than is one with frown lines.

Body Positioning and Positive Reinforcers.   The positioning of the body also sends important messages related to intimacy, even though many of these messages are sent unconsciously (Palmer & Simmons, 1995). In particular, when people adopt open body positions and direct body orientation, they create a sense of closeness. An *open body position* involves leaving the body accessible by removing barriers such as objects or limbs. Imagine a friend crossing her or his arms across her or his chest while telling you "It's not that big of a deal." What would your friend's closed body position tell you? According to Guerrero et al. (2007), "people are most likely to cross their arms, hide their face, or stand behind objects when they lack trust, feel vulnerable, and do not want to interact" (p. 263). As a general rule, most people would interpret your friend's behavior as defensive and unfriendly.

Direct body orientation involves communicating in a face-to-face position. Several researchers have argued that people tend to use more direct body orientation when they are highly involved in the conversation at hand (Coker & Burgoon, 1987; Patterson, 1983). Direct body orientation reduces distraction and allows two people to see one another's facial expressions better. Direct body orientation is also related to proxemics in that the distance between two people's faces is often reduced. Relational partners sometimes let others know they are in a couple by using direct body orientation while simultaneously blocking others out of the conversation. So Kayla and Ryan might sit facing one another at a table in a busy cafeteria, with jackets and paperwork on the seats near them to prevent others from joining them.

Some body positions also help signal that a receiver is listening attentively to a speaker and wants the speaker to continue communicating. These types of behaviors are sometimes referred to as *positive reinforcers* (Coker & Burgoon, 1987). Lean and body orientation can help regulate a conversation and indicate that a receiver is interested (or uninterested) in what a speaker is saying. For example, you might lean forward while someone is telling an exciting story, but face away while someone is telling a boring story. Or you could lean back, smile, and look relaxed while settling in to hear a long story. Head nods can also act as positive reinforcers by signaling agreement and showing liking (Coker & Burgoon, 1987; Palmer & Simmons, 1995).

Facial and Gestural Animation. Both facial animation and gesturing show that a person is involved in the conversation at hand (Coker & Burgoon, 1987). Not surprisingly, facial expressions that convey positive emotion are typically associated with intimacy, interpersonal warmth, and liking (Andersen & Guerrero, 1998; Maxwell et al., 1985). Perhaps more surprisingly, expressions of negative emotion can also foster impressions of intimacy under certain circumstances. For instance, if you are listening to a friend's sad story, having a sad expression on your face shows empathy and promotes perceptions of similarity. Likewise, intimacy and connection can be communicated by having an angry expression on your face when a third party insults your friend or lover.

Expressive gestures, particularly illustrators and emblems, can also convey both conversational involvement and empathy (Burgoon, Buller, & Woodall, 1996). As discussed in Chapter 5, *illustrators* are gestures used to emphasize a point or paint a visual picture of something for a receiver. So showing that someone is "this tall," swinging an imaginary bat, or making a hand gesture to emphasize that something is "really" important are examples of illustrators. Illustrator gestures such as these help keep a conversation lively and maintain the receiver's interest. *Emblems* are gestures that substitute for verbal language, such as waving to say "hello" and "good-bye" and crossing one's fingers to wish someone "good luck." When emblems represent a private language between two people, they are especially intimate. For example, figure skater Michelle Kwan used to touch her ear in a particular way when waiting for her scores after performing. Media commentators noted that this was her unique shorthand way of saying "hi" to some of the special people in her life. (Of course, only Kwan and her loved ones know if this is the correct interpretation of this gesture!)

Vocalic Cues

Vocal cues also affect the intimacy level of a given interaction. When people are highly involved in the conversation at hand, they tend to talk faster and louder, sound more varied in terms of tempo, pitch, and volume, and have fewer silences and non-fluencies. In addition, intimacy is communicated by voices that are warm, expressive, moderately relaxed, resonant, rhythmic, and punctuated with relaxed laughter (Coker & Burgoon, 1987; McAdams et al., 1984; Scott, 1994). Warmth and expressiveness seem to be the key components contributing to a voice that reflects intimacy and liking (Andersen, 2008; Beebe, 1980; Scherer, 1979a). In one study, same-sex high school students who liked one another had more "lively voices" during their interactions than did those who did not like one another (Maxwell et al., 1985).

Soft voices and silences can also communicate intimacy. Lovers often use soft, even slurred, voices during intimate conversations and courtship situations (Givens, 1978; Kimble, Forte, & Yoshikawa, 1981). Soft voices draw people closer together proxemically as people lean near one another to hear. And sometimes the absence of any sound sends a strong message. As Burgoon, Buller, and Woodall (1996) put it, "Silences may be associated with complete harmony . . . When people are comfortable in a relationship, there is no need to talk" (p. 327).

Chronemic Cues

The way people structure and use time also sends subtle messages related to intimacy (Andersen, 2008; Guerrero et al., 2007). Three particularly important messages related to time revolve around rules of punctuality and consideration, time spent together, and the monochronic use of time. Think about the last time a friend or romantic partner showed up late to pick you up, made you wait while he or she got ready to go out, or forgot to call you at a specified time. Chances are that you were not very happy when your friend or romantic partner violated these rules of punctuality and consideration. Such violations signal a lack of intimacy, whereas adherence to these rules communicates respect, equality, and liking. The time that people spend with you is another important immediacy cue. In fact, Egland, Stelzner, Andersen, and Spitzberg (1997) found that spending time with one's partner was a key way of showing relational closeness. Finally, in the United States, having a monochronic focus on your partner is related to closeness and intimacy. Can you remember a time when you were irritated because someone was typing on the computer or watching television while talking on the phone with you? Or perhaps your partner was talking to other people at a party and ignoring you. Having a monochronic focus means that you concentrate on one task or one person at a time, rather than engaging in multiple tasks. When two people concentrate only on one another, rather than on multiple tasks, this monochronic focus communicates interest and attention.

As we have seen, several nonverbal behaviors are used to express immediacy and positive involvement. Another category of nonverbal behavior that plays a big role in relationships is the communication of affection, which we turn our attention to next.

Nonverbal Affection Behaviors

Expressing nonverbal affection helps people form and maintain close relationships with others. You probably have many people in your life for whom you feel affection—it is that sense of fondness and positive regard that draws you to those people and holds your relationships together. Affection is related to intimacy, but it isn't exactly the same thing. Intimacy is a property of relationships—each relationship has a certain amount of intimacy at a given time. By contrast, affection is a property of individuals—each of us feels affection for those friends, family members, and romantic partners who make up our circle of close relationships. In newly forming relationships, in fact, expressions of affection frequently serve as "critical incidents" that denote the development of the relationship (King & Christensen, 1983). Romantic partners, for instance, often remember their first hug, their first kiss, or their first exchange of the words "I love you" (Owen, 1987). Both intimacy and affection are typically developed and maintained in the context of interaction, which includes the exchange of nonverbal messages.

Although there are many ways to express affection verbally, the ways we do it nonverbally are often more provocative, for at least two reasons. First, like other nonverbal behaviors, they may be enacted with less conscious control than verbal behaviors and may therefore reflect the emotional status of the sender more accurately (Burgoon, 1994). Second, they may be less risky for the sender than verbal expressions, since their intended meanings may be easier to deny or downplay if the receiver does not share the sender's affectionate feelings (Floyd, 2006).

Why humans communicate affection in personal relationships is the subject of *affection exchange theory* (AET: Floyd, 2001, 2002, 2006; Floyd et al., 2005; Floyd, Hesse, & Haynes, 2007; Floyd, Mikkelson, Hesse, & Pauley, 2007; Floyd & Morman, 2001; Floyd & Morr, 2003; Floyd & Ray, 2003; Floyd, Sargent, & di Corcia, 2004). AET is a neo-Darwinian theory proposing that the expression of affection promotes human viability and fertility by facilitating the development of significant pair bonds. It offers that, in the course of human evolution, those who engaged in affectionate communication were more successful than those who did not at forming and maintaining relationships, increasing their chances for procreation and their access to the protection those relationships entailed. Because affectionate communication contributes to survival and procreation, according to AET, humans have evolved physiological mechanisms that encourage affection exchange. Specifically, hormonal and neurochemical processes cause sharing affectionate behavior in the context of a close relationship to feel good physically (in the same way that eating when you're hungry, which is also important for survival, feels good). In recent years, researchers have identified particular hormones, such as oxytocin, dopamine, prolactin, and β-endorphins, as among those that may be responsible for causing affectionate behavior to feel good and for promoting its enactment in personal relationships (for review, see Floyd, Mikkelson, & Hesse, 2007).

To understand nonverbal affection behaviors, researchers often separate them into two categories: direct and indirect. A nonverbal behavior is a direct expression if its meaning is overtly affectionate—in many cultures, behaviors such as hugging, kissing, and hand-holding are examples of direct expressions of behavior, because most everyone recognizes them as affectionate behaviors. A nonverbal behavior is an indirect expression if its link to affection is more covert. For instance, doing a favor for someone can be a way of showing your affection for that person, but the behavior itself wouldn't be widely recognized as an affectionate one—it would be widely recognized as a favor. Therefore, the affectionate meaning of the behavior is more indirect. In this section, we'll take a look at several nonverbal behaviors that fall into each category.

Direct Nonverbal Affection Behaviors

Direct nonverbal affection behaviors are those that are generally interpreted by others as being affectionate in nature. Two types of direct behaviors are those associated with touch and those associated with vocalics.

Haptic Cues.   One of the most common direct nonverbal affection behaviors is affectionate touch. People use several forms of touch to express affection to others, such as hugging, kissing, holding hands, touching another's arm or leg, and engaging in sexual intercourse. Several studies have shown that these types of touch behaviors are commonly interpreted as expressions of affection and love, making them direct affection behaviors rather than indirect (see, e.g., Afifi & Johnson, 1999; Burgoon et al., 1992; Floyd, 1999; Rane & Draper, 1995). In one study, for example, Burgoon (1991) showed people photographs of couples depicting one of seven types of touch: shaking hands, holding hands, touching the forearm, putting an arm around the shoulder, putting an arm around the waist, touching the face, or engaging in no touch. She then asked the participants to report their perceptions of how affectionate the people in the photographs were being with each other. Burgoon found that all of the touch conditions were rated as more affectionate than the no-touch group. As you might imagine, some touches were rated as more affectionate than others. Burgoon reported that face touches, hand-holding, and arms around shoulders were generally perceived to be the most affectionate touches, and hand-shaking was rated as the least affectionate—but still more affectionate than not touching at all (see also Floyd, 1997, and Lee & Guerrero, 2001).

Touch is a versatile way to express affection, because many touches can be enacted in several different ways, each of which might mean something slightly different. For instance, think about how many different ways there are to kiss someone. One kiss might be a momentary peck on the cheek, whereas another might be a prolonged mouth-to-mouth encounter. The way you kiss someone probably varies according to the type and intensity of the affection you feel for him or her. Longer kisses might convey romantic affection, for example, whereas shorter ones are used with platonic friends or family members. The location of a kiss also matters. A kiss on the mouth is often more intimate than a kiss on the cheek. Kissing someone on the forehead can show affection or comfort and is a particularly affectionate form of touch.

Hugging is another common affectionate touch, and hugs can also vary on a number of dimensions. One is how long they last; longer hugs are often used to express more intense affection than shorter hugs. Another is how "intense" they are; romantic partners may engage in intense, full-body-contact hugs, whereas casual friends might prefer lighter hugs that are restricted to upper-body contact. Finally, hugs vary in their form, which has to do with relative arm placement. As discussed in Chapter 6, Floyd (1999) compared three forms of hugging: the "criss-cross hug," in which each person has one arm above and one arm below the other's; the "neck-waist hug," in which one person's arms wrap around the other's neck and the other person's arms wrap around the person's waist; and, the "engulfing hug," in which one person's arms are held together on his or her chest and the other's arms are wrapped entirely around this person. The criss-cross hug is especially intimate. However, there are many other varieties of hugs, with many different possible interpretations. For example, in 2005 a story about a middle-school girl who received detention for hugging her boyfriend was in the national spotlight, leading to a debate about what constitutes acceptable forms of touch in middle schools (see Box 12.3).

Some affectionate touches are examples of tie-signs (Morris, 1977), which were discussed earlier in this chapter. In their research, Afifi and Johnson (1999) found that tie-signs are used more frequently in dating relationships than in platonic friendships and that the most common tie-signs in both relationships are patting, shoulder embraces (putting one's arm around another's back shoulder), and hand-holding. Afifi and Johnson also found that people in romantic relationships used tie-signs to express affection more so than people in platonic relationships did.

Vocal Cues. We also express affectionate messages by the way we use our voices when speaking with loved ones. One pattern of vocal behavior that often conveys affection is babytalk. Babytalk involves speaking at a high pitch, using lots of pitch variance, and using exaggerated and highly simplified speech sounds, the way many people do when speaking to babies, the elderly, or pets (Zebrowitz, Brownlow, & Olson, 1992). Research has shown that babytalk is used around the world and is practiced by both men and women, whether or not they are parents (Shute & Wheldall, 1989; Toda, Fogel, & Kawai, 1990). Adults also use babytalk as a means of expressing affection with their romantic partners and, to a lesser extent, their platonic friends. In their research, Bombar and Littig (1996) found that women and men were equally likely to use babytalk with their romantic partners and with their opposite-sex friends, but women were more likely than men to use it with their same-sex friends.

Other research has examined which acoustic characteristics of the voice people modify when they are trying to express liking or affection. Floyd and Ray (2003) paired up same-sex strangers in a get-acquainted exercise and instructed one person in each pair (the confederate) to behave as though he or she really liked or really disliked the other. An observer of the same sex watched the exercise through a closed-circuit television, and then the confederate's voice was analyzed for pitch, pitch variation, and loudness. Participants and observers were then asked to rate how affectionate the confederate in each pair was being during the exercise. The observers thought that confederates were being the most affectionate

B O X   **12.3**   IN THE NEWS

When Do Public Displays of Affection at School Cross the Line?

Reporter Elizabeth Armstrong Moore of the *Christian Science Monitor* described the controversy that occurred when an eighth-grade girl in Oregon was given detention after hugging her boyfriend too long in the school hallway.

Moore reported that many schools across the country have guidelines banning public displays of affection. The problem, however, is that hugs are interpreted in various ways by different people. The Oregon school district where the controversy occurred had this statement in its guidelines:

> Hugging, holding hands, walking arm-in-arm, kissing, and other public displays of affection are not appropriate for middle school. Quick hello and goodbye hugs are OK.

So how do you separate the hello and good-bye hugs from more emotionally–charged hugs? Dr. Rob Horner from the University of Oregon noted that middle school children come from diverse backgrounds, "with very different ideas about 'appropriate' behavior." Hugs also have a variety of meanings, ranging from "hi," to "I'm sorry," "Don't worry, it will be okay," and "I love you."

Because of this ambiguity, school administers argued that they have to hold all children to the same code of conduct regardless of cultural background or intended meaning. Superintendent Douglas Nelson said it wasn't about a hug, but rather about students having to follow the rules whether they agree with them or not.

The girl's mother countered by saying: "When I think about all the terrible things that children could be doing . . . to put hugging in that same category is absolutely absurd to me . . . You've got this collection of things you're not supposed to do—they're wrong, bad—and hugging is one of them? I don't think so."

So what did the offending hug look like? The mother asked her daughter to demonstrate. The girl encircled her mom's waist with both her arms and rested her chin on her mother's shoulder, after which the mother asked, "That's it?" The hug lasted a full five seconds after that.

You be the judge. Should such behavior be considered an appropriate or inappropriate display of public affection for middle school children?

Source: Summarized from E. Moore (2005).

when they used higher-pitched voices, rather than lower ones. For participants, there was a sex difference: women were seen as being the most affectionate when their voices used higher pitches, but men were seen as being the most affectionate when their voices used lower pitches. Both participants and observers also rated the confederates as highest in affection when their voices had lots of pitch variation (instead of being monotone). Loudness wasn't a factor in how affectionate the confederates were judged to be.

Indirect Nonverbal Affection Behaviors

For various reasons, people sometimes choose to express affection indirectly, rather than directly. Indirect nonverbal affection behaviors carry a message of affection for the people engaging in them, but they would not necessarily be interpreted as affectionate behaviors by others. In this section, we will look at two types of indirect nonverbal affection behaviors: support behaviors and idiomatic behaviors.

Support Behaviors.   One of the most common indirect ways of expressing affection for someone is to provide that person with some type of needed support or assistance. Sometimes this involves giving psychological or emotional support; for example, friends might show their affection to a newly widowed mother by providing a sympathetic ear or making her gifts. Other times, it involves providing more instrumental types of support; for instance, the friends of the widowed mother might show their affection by bringing her meals, offering to babysit, or taking care of her yard work.

Support behaviors such as these don't express an affectionate message directly, the way that hugging, kissing, or saying "I love you" do. However, these behaviors can be very valuable ways of showing how much you care for someone. When they are in need of support, people often feel that their true friends are those who don't just *say* they care, but who also *show* their care through their actions. Providing a resource such as money, time and effort, a material resource (like the use of one's house), or even just attention, is often seen by the recipient of the resource as a significant and genuine gesture of affection, even if the affectionate message is indirect.

Idiomatic Behaviors.   Another indirect way of expressing affection nonverbally is to use idioms, or behaviors that have a specific meaning only to people in a particular relationship. Relational partners sometimes come up with idioms so they can express their affection for each other secretly. In the 1997 movie *Bent*, two prisoners in a Nazi camp discover feelings of affection for each other but are too afraid of repercussions from the guards to express their feelings directly. Instead, they decided that whenever one of them scratched his eyebrow, both would recognize it as a sign of affection. What made this behavior an idiom is that only the two prisoners knew what it meant. This type of idiom allows people to express their affection to each other whenever they want to, but in a way that only they recognize. It also allows people to convey affection in situations when more overt affectionate displays are inappropriate (for instance, during a business meeting or a church service).

Bell, Buerkel-Rothfuss, and Gore (1987) studied the use of idioms in heterosexual romantic couples and found that expressing affection was one of the most common reasons why people developed idioms. They found that idioms for affection were more likely to be verbal than nonverbal and were more likely to be used in public than in private. For the couples in their study, it was usually the man who invented the idioms for affection. Moreover, both men and women said they had more idioms for affection if their relationship was more loving, satisfying, and affectionate (see also Hopper, Knapp, & Scott, 1981).

Thus far, we have seen how various nonverbal behaviors can be used to convey immediacy, create intimacy, and express affection in a variety of relationships. Nonverbal communication is also an important part of sexual attraction and the process of courtship, and we will examine these functions in the next section.

Courtship Behavior

As you might suspect, many of the same behaviors described previously as immediacy or affectionate cues are also used to signal romantic interest during courtship. However, research on courtship suggests that flirtatious behavior also has special characteristics related to ambiguity and submissiveness (Givens, 1978, 1983; Scheflen, 1965, 1974). First, flirtatious behaviors are typically indirect and ambiguous at the beginning of interaction, becoming somewhat bolder as interaction progresses. For instance, Emma might smile demurely and look away from Jeff immediately after they make eye contact for the first time. Then, as the interaction unfolds and Emma becomes more confident that her interest is reciprocated, she may become bolder by engaging in more direct smiling and eye contact, and eventually engaging in behaviors such as touching Jeff's arm or kissing him. By contrast, if Emma thinks that Jeff is uninterested, her indirect behaviors allow her to move away from the interaction gracefully without losing face. Second, many flirtatious behaviors appear to resemble submissive forms of intimate interaction that are common in parent-child interaction, such as resting one's head on the partner's shoulder, sharing food with or feeding the partner, moving a stray hair out of the partner's face, and using babytalk. In line with these two principles, research suggests that courtship tends to progress in stages (Givens, 1978, 1983; Scheflen, 1965, 1974).

Stage 1: Attention

Imagine that you are at a party and see someone whom you would like to meet. What would you do to get this person's attention? You might try to catch the person's eye, you might ask someone to formally introduce you, or you might "accidentally" bump into the person, among other options. Givens (1983) claimed that "all the smiling, firm handshakes, excited greetings, nervous laughter, clown-colorful costumes, and scurrying about you see at parties can be viewed in a detached way as attention signals" (p. 11). Women, in particular, tend to engage in behaviors such as giggling and tossing their hair back as ways to get attention (Moore, 1995).

During this initial stage of courtship, people experience mixed emotions. They are excited about the possibility of meeting someone they like, but they are also nervous about being rejected. Thus, in the attention stage, people engage in a lot of seemingly contradictory behavior such as looking at the desired person intently for a couple seconds but then covering one's face with one's hand (see Photo 12.2). Adaptors and self-grooming behaviors, such as nervously twisting a ring, brushing one's hair out of one's eyes, and sucking on a breath mint, are also common in this stage. A study that looked at interactions in bars (Renninger, Wade, & Grammer, 2004) showed that men are most likely to get a woman's attention when they engage in more glancing, more space-maximization movement (such as sitting with arms or legs extended to move closer in the women's personal space zone), and less closed body movements (such as arms crossed against the chest).

PHOTO 12.2 *In the attention and recognition stages, courtship behavior is often shy and ambiguous.*

Stage 2: Recognition

After you have secured someone's attention, the next stage is to determine how receptive he or she is to you. If the person to whom you are attracted looks away and pretends not to see you, chances are that you will stop pursuing her or him. Some research, however, suggests that woman are more sensitive to nonverbal signals of rejection, such as reduced eye contact, yawning, and frowning, than are men (Moore, 2002). In Moore's study, participants viewed interactions with people displaying either friendly or rejecting nonverbal behaviors. Women rated the rejection behaviors as more negative than men did, whereas men rated the friendly behaviors as more positive than the women did.

In the attention and recognition stages, ambiguous cues serve two primary functions—they help you get attention and signal attraction, but they also allow you to walk away from the situation without losing face. If the other person is interested in you, he or she will likely display availability signals. These signals include eyebrow raises and immediacy cues such as gaze, direct body orientation, forward lean, and smiling. However, these immediacy behaviors will be tempered by ambivalence signals such as demurely averting gaze downward and engaging in adaptors such as stretching and tapping one's fingers on a table. Primping behaviors are also as common in this stage as they are in the attention stage.

Although men often initiate courtship by approaching women, research suggests that women often determine whether interaction proceeds beyond the initial stages of courtship. During the recognition stage, women signal availability and interest through subtle behaviors such as darting glances, smiling, primping, nodding, and tossing their head or hair (Moore, 1983; Perper & Weis, 1987). These types of behaviors provide men with signals about whether or not to pursue interaction. Men are likely to pick up on such signals and reciprocate nonverbal displays of intimacy. Men are less likely, however, to pick up on rejection signals, which often makes it necessary for women to use direct, verbal communication to thwart men's advances. Research also shows that nonverbal behaviors play an important role in courtship for lesbian women, who may be especially sensitive to subtle nonverbal cues. In a study by Rose and Zand (2002), lesbians "relied heavily on the nuances of touching, smiling, and maintaining eye contact to convey interest" in each other (pp. 101–102).

Stage 3: Positioning

If courtship proceeds, behaviors become increasingly intimate. During the third stage, people place themselves in close face-to-face positions so that they can have a personal conversation while shutting others out. By leaning forward, crossing legs toward each other, using direct body orientation, and placing chairs and possessions in a way that prevents others from joining them, a couple may become an enclosed unit. During this stage, conversation often becomes highly animated, with both people listening intently when the other is speaking. Behaviors are less ambivalent, with longer gazes and more head nodding and smiling. The couple's behaviors may also become more synchronized, with more similar body positioning, more fluency, and less interruptions. Indeed, Perper (1985) found that courtship behavior often follows a fairly consistent pattern, with approach followed by turning and direct body orientation, first touch, and then increased synchronization of body movement. Despite more expressiveness and synchronization, behaviors are still submissive in that people tend to use soft voices, punctuate gaze with some demure glances downward, shrug their shoulders, and tilt their heads toward the partner.

Voices also change during this stage. One study showed that young men were more successful at attracting women when their voices moved from being high-pitched and animated to more low-pitched and monotone (Anolli & Ciceri, 2002). Men also talked softer and slower as the courtship process progressed. These vocal changes may reflect the more serious tone that courtship takes as people move toward the final two stages. As Anolli and Ciceri explained, men's voices change from being exhibitionist in the initial stages of courtship to more self-disclosive in the later stages of courtship. An exhibitionist voice calls attention to the speaker by conveying excitement, vitality, and confidence, whereas a self-disclosive voice communicates warmth and tenderness.

Stage 4: Sexual Arousal

In this stage, behaviors become more distinctly sexual. Eye contact and flirtatious smiling become more direct and sustained, and people may engage in sexually provocative behaviors such as exposing one's thigh when crossing legs or stroking one's wine glass in a suggestive way. For example, Moore (1985) identified the "skirt hike" as a courtship behavior that is used by women. Intimate forms of touch might also characterize this stage, with vulnerable parts of the body being touched (Abbey & Melby, 1986; Jones & Yarbrough, 1985). Vocally, people often speak in soft, sometimes slurred, tones. Givens (1978) also noted that people sometimes use child-like nicknames such as "babe" and "sweetie" at this point in the courtship process. Other behaviors common in this stage include grooming the partner (such as moving the hair out of your partner's eyes) and carrying and clutching activities (such as playing with someone's fingers or carrying him or her to the bedroom).

Stage 5: Resolution

The courtship process is complete when the couple has sexual intercourse. Importantly, however, there are times when only one person wants to move into this stage. Indeed, many misunderstandings and embarrassing moments have occurred when one person thought it was okay to move into the resolution stage and the other person did not. People flirt for many different reasons, not all of which are related to showing sexual interest. For example, people flirt as a means of gaining attention or compliance, as a way of making a third party jealous, and as an exercise in developing social skills (Afifi, Guerrero, & Egland, 1994; Koeppel, Montagne-Miller, O'Hair, & Cody, 1993). When people flirt without intending to develop a sexual relationship, their flirting behaviors are classified as quasi-courtship rather than courtship behavior. Because courtship and quasi-courtship behaviors look similar, people sometimes misinterpret flirtatious behavior as seductive rather than merely friendly. Men, in particular, may overestimate the extent to which friendly behaviors are intended to show sexual interest (Abbey, 1982, 1987; Abbey & Melby, 1986). Such misinterpretation can lead to serious consequences, including sexual harassment (Lee & Guerrero, 2001) or, worse yet, date rape (Shotland & Craig, 1988). Thus, it is crucial that people remember that friendly or flirtatious behavior is not always meant to convey sexual attraction.

After Resolution: The Principle of Escalation

Researchers have also studied how immediacy behavior and courtship cues change over the course of relationships. This research suggests that there is a drop in immediacy and flirtation after a couple has reached the resolution stage. For example, couples in established relationships display far less self-grooming behavior than do couples in the beginning stages of courtship (Daly et al., 1983). Other studies suggest that couples in serious dating relationships touch more than couples who are casually dating or married. This finding holds for touch occurring in both public and private settings (Emmers & Dindia, 1995; Guerrero & Andersen, 1991). These findings have been interpreted to support a *principle of escalation*, which is based on the idea that nonverbal cues related to immediacy, and particularly those related to courtship, tend to increase as a romantic relationship escalates toward commitment and sexual involvement. When a relationship is committed, immediacy cues decrease somewhat and then level off. Courtship cues decrease even more. As Givens (1978) put it, "courtship seems to be only a *temporary* relationship that occurs between the first meeting and intercourse. After resolution, courting signals become scarce" (p. 353).

Shows of Similarity and Synchrony

Although spouses tend to use fewer courtship cues than they did as daters, research suggests that they compensate for this by engaging in similar, reciprocal behavior. For example, Guerrero and Andersen (1994) found that spouses matched one another's level of touch more than did serious daters or casual daters. If a wife touched her husband five times during a 10-minute interaction, he was also likely to touch her five times. Close friends, family members, and romantic partners also tend to adopt similar mannerisms, body positions, dress, and so forth as a way of signaling cohesion. As you will see, similarity in dress, adornment, and behavior is related to intimacy and liking.

Similarity in clothing and adornment influences social attraction to potential friends as well as romantic partners. University students tend to be attracted to other students who dress similarly to themselves, and to judge students wearing uncommon or counter-fashion clothing styles harshly unless they themselves wear alternative forms of clothing (Pinaire-Reed, 1979; Reid, Lancuba, & Morrow, 1997). Similarity in clothing and adornment can also indicate group or team membership, as is the case with team uniforms, sorority/fraternity pins, and some kinds of tattoos. For example, one study focused on the experiences of 12 tattooed cadets at a military college (Coe et al., 1993). All of these cadets reported getting their tattoos with a group of men as a way of promoting friendship while proving to one another that they could withstand pain. Another study focused on the reasons why college-age women get body piercings (Beauregard, 2001). Similar to the cadets with tattoos, women reported getting body piercings as a means both of developing relationships and expressing their identities. Interestingly, research also suggests that group alliances are strengthened when outsiders discriminate against those with body piercings or tattoos (Jetten, Branscombe, Schmitt, & Spears, 2001). So friends who get tattoos may feel particularly close to one another if they consider themselves to be a minority group that is different from the mainstream.

Similarity in nonverbal behaviors such as accent, speech rate, gestures, posture, and facial expression also promote intimacy in most circumstances. According to communication accommodation theory, people are likely to *converge* toward the nonverbal style of a liked other by becoming more similar vocally and behaviorally (Giles, Mulac, Bradac, & Johnson, 1987; Giles & Wadleigh, 2008). So as you develop a new friendship with someone, you will probably adopt some of her or his nonverbal characteristics. For example, as Jose and Miguel develop their friendship, Jose might start to talk a little faster (which is Miguel's speaking style) and Miguel might become more vocally and kinesically expressive (which is Jose's style) as a result of interacting with one another. Their speech patterns and behaviors may also become more coordinated. In initial encounters, Jose might have accidentally interrupted Miguel a few times because he had mistakenly thought that Miguel was ending his speaking turn. Both men might have also started talking at the same time following a pause in the conversation. Now, however, they know one another's speech rhythms and are able to coordinate speaking turns smoothly.

Body synchrony also communicates intimacy. Such synchrony occurs when two or more people adopt the same or similar posture, such as crossing their legs the same way, walking together in rhythm, or jumping up at the same time. When people like one another and have similar attitudes, they also tend to echo each other's body positions or adopt mirror-image postures (Morris, 1977; Scheflen, 1964). In turn, when people are asked to adopt similar positions, they perceive themselves to be more similar in attitudes (Navarre, 1982). In one study, same-sex pairs of high school students were videotaped as they conversed for the first time. Students who reported liking one another were more likely to display synchrony in body movements, including positioning and gestures (Maxwell et al., 1985).

Reciprocity

In addition to synchrony, researchers have shown that reciprocity is a key determinant of attraction and relational closeness. *Reciprocity* occurs when a person responds to another person's behavior by engaging in similar behavior. For example, if someone smiles at you, you might smile back. Or if someone looks lovingly into your eyes, you might put your head on her or his shoulder. Notice that the behaviors do not have to be exactly the same for reciprocity to occur; instead, the behaviors must communicate similar messages. Patterns of reciprocity can occur for either positive or negative behaviors. The examples given here are all of positive reciprocity. In contrast, if you frown at a friend and your friend frowns back, or if you yell at your sibling and your sibling storms out of the room, negative reciprocity has occurred.

Patterns of positive reciprocity are essential for developing and maintaining intimate relationships. According to the *principle of reciprocity*, immediacy often begets more immediacy, and people are likely to feel more attraction and intimacy as a result of engaging in these behaviors (Burgoon, Stern, & Dillman, 1995). In other words, if one person engages in warm, friendly behaviors, the other person is more likely to follow suit, and both people are likely to feel more positively toward each other. The principle of reciprocity also works for negative behaviors—if one person engages in cold or rude behavior, the other person often feels a natural inclination toward engaging in similarly negative behavior, leading both people to feel less positive toward the other. Satisfying relationships tend to be defined by strong patterns of positive reciprocity and infrequent patterns of negative reciprocity (Guerrero & Floyd, 2006).

The concept of positive reciprocity illustrates another important point—when it comes to creating an intimate interaction, it is not enough for one person to increase immediacy. If Jessica smiles and tries to start a conversation with Brent, and Brent looks at his watch, says he has to go, and backs away, Jessica's attempt to increase intimacy has failed. Reciprocity is the key to creating truly intimate interaction and developing close relationships.

As this example shows, people do not always respond to increases in immediacy positively. Most people can readily think of situations in which they have felt uncomfortable or even insulted when someone engaged in too much immediacy. For example, if your romantic partner tries to hug you when you are mad at her or him, you might pull back; if your boss touches you inappropriately, you might be offended and angry; and if your enemy glances at you and smiles, you might be suspicious. In each of these cases, you would have compensated for the other person's immediacy behavior. In contrast to reciprocity, *compensation* occurs when a person responds to another person's change in behavior with the opposite behavior.

Both expectancy violations theory (Burgoon & Hale, 1988) and cognitive valence theory (Andersen, 1985, 2008), describe the conditions under which reciprocity is most likely. According to expectancy violation theory, the valence of the behavior and the reward value of the partner work together to predict whether people will reciprocate or compensate when another person increases nonverbal immediacy. *Valence* refers to whether the behavior is perceived to be positive or negative compared to what was expected. *Reward value* refers to how favorably or unfavorably the person who increased intimacy is regarded. Increases in nonverbal immediacy are most likely to lead to reciprocity when both the behavior and the person who engaged in the behavior are evaluated positively. So imagine that Chris unexpectedly walks up and gives you a hug. If you like Chris, you are more likely to see the hug as a positive behavior and to reciprocate. But if you dislike Chris, you are likely to see the hug as a negative behavior (and perhaps as a violation of your personal space) and to compensate by backing away.

Cognitive valence theory (Andersen, 1985, 2008) suggests that there at least six conditions that influence how people respond to most increases in immediacy. According to this theory, most increases in immediacy are moderately arousing, leading people to evaluate the behavior and the situation before deciding how to respond. As in expectancy violations theory, the *interpersonal valence* of the partner is important. Interpersonal valence refers to how attractive, credible, and likable a person is. Thus, interpersonal valence is very similar to reward value in expectancy violations theory. The more positively you regard someone, the more likely you are to reciprocate his or her intimacy behaviors.

The other five conditions that help determine how people respond to increases in nonverbal immediacy are personality, the situation, the relationship, culture, and temporary states (Andersen, 1985, 2008). *Personality* refers to the characteristics of the person who is the recipient of the increased immediacy behavior. For example, a shy person is likely to react differently than an extroverted person. The *situation* can also make a difference. Imagine being winked at during a fun social gathering versus a formal business meeting. Chances are that you would respond quite differently. The *relationship* is critical in determining how people respond to immediacy behavior. The closer the relationship, the more accepted and welcome immediacy behavior usually is. Think about being unexpectedly kissed on the cheek by a family member versus a friend, casual acquaintance, or ex-lover. How would you react in each situation? *Culture* may also influence your reaction. If you grew up in an affectionate, contact-oriented culture, such as those found in the Mediterranean area (see Chapter 6), you might be more receptive to public displays of affection than if you grew up in a less contact-oriented culture. Finally, your mood and temporary physical or cognitive state could affect how you respond to another person's immediacy behavior.

If you have a headache, feel depressed, or are preoccupied with a problem, you may be less likely to respond positively to other people's attempts to increase nonverbal intimacy.

Formality-Informality and Social Versus Task Orientation

So far, this chapter has focused primarily on how people use nonverbal communication to send messages of intimacy and affection. Communication scholars, such as Burgoon and Hale (1984, 1988), regard intimacy/affection to be a fundamental theme underlying nonverbal behavior. In addition, Burgoon and Hale identified informality/formality and social versus task orientation as important themes that characterize most nonverbal communication. In general, intimate interactions tend to be characterized by more informality as well as a social orientation. Each of these dimensions is discussed in the following sections.

Informality/Formality

Informal interaction is characterized by closer proxemic distancing, looser rules regarding what constitutes acceptable communication, and a casual versus serious atmosphere. Verbal behaviors, such as form of address, reflect the formality level of a given interaction. For example, which form of address would you be most likely to use with a professor you are meeting with for the first time outside of class (let's say her name is Michelle Stevens)? Would you be more likely to call her Dr. Stevens, Professor Stevens, Ms. Stevens, Dr. S., or Michelle? Using her title would denote respect and formality. Many nonverbal behaviors also reflect the level of formality within an interaction. In one study, people were more likely to judge an interaction as formal if people displayed anxiety cues, such as saying "um," fidgeting, and speaking too fast, coupled with low levels of eye contact and a lack of nonverbal expressiveness (Burgoon & Newton, 1991). This combination of cues suggests that people expect others to be more nervous and on their guard in formal settings. In informal settings, people are freer to relax and express themselves verbally and nonverbally.

Social-Task Orientation

Burgoon and Newton (1991) also examined nonverbal behaviors related to the social-task orientation of an interaction. They found that interactions were rated as higher in task orientation when people seemed sincere and were focused on the task rather than the conversation at hand. Of course, sharing tasks in a fair and equitable manner can help couples maintain close relationships (Stafford & Canary, 1991); however, if people engage in only task-oriented interaction rather than relating to one another on a social level, the relationship is unlikely to be very intimate. Some research even suggests that computer-mediated communication is perceived as more socially oriented when nonverbal surrogates are used along with text. For example, in a study examining the social versus task orientation of communication posted on a discussion board, the use of emoticons (e.g., smiley faces, winks) and signifiers (e.g., use of ellipses . . . and exaggerated punctuation !!!!!!, ?!?!) were positively related to perceptions that the interaction was more socially oriented (Schiefelbein, 2006).

Creating an Intimate Environment

Environmental cues also play a key role in determining the formality, task versus social orientation, and intimacy level of an interaction. Intuitively, most people can identify some environmental features that promote intimate interaction. Low lighting, especially when augmented with candlelight or a fire in a fireplace, can create a romantic or cozy mood, as can certain kinds of music (Andersen, 2008; May & Hamilton, 1980). Imagine going to an expensive elegant restaurant compared to a fast food restaurant. The elegant restaurant likely features comfortable chairs and dim lighting, with soft music playing and flowers on the tables. This kind of environment encourages people to sit and talk for a while. In contrast, in a fast food restaurant the chairs or booths are usually fairly hard and uncomfortable and the lighting is usually bright. Such an atmosphere contributes to the fast food industry's goal of servicing many people in a short time. Room temperature is also important; environments that are too cool or too warm tend to discourage interaction (Griffit, 1970). Similarly, environments that are too densely crowded may lessen interpersonal attraction (Tripathi, 1996).

Seating arrangements also influence social interaction. Early work on nonverbal communication described two kinds of seating arrangements that mirror Burgoon and Hale's (1984, 1987) distinction between task and social orientation. *Sociofugal* seating arrangements prevent or discourage the formation and maintenance of interpersonal relationships and allow people to maintain privacy boundaries and engage in individual tasks or activities; *sociopetal* seating arrangements encourage social interaction and the development of close relationships (Sommer, 1969). Take a classroom as an example. If you are seated in a long rectangular room with all the desks arranged in rows, you are much less likely to interact with others than if you are in a square room with desks arranged in a semi-circle. Similarly, living room furniture can be arranged so that there is a common focal point and everyone in a group can easily see one another (a sociopetal arrangement), or it can be arranged so that people sit farther apart and have to exert effort to carry on a conversation with others (a sociofugal arrangement). Even subtle differences in furniture and furniture arrangement can affect perceptions of intimacy. A smaller table literally brings people closer together, and having people sit around a circle creates perceptions of intimacy and equality, as was the purpose behind King Arthur's famous round table. Photo 12.3 shows environments that differ in how sociopetal versus sociofugal they are.

Intimacy is also affected by the type of activity and emotion occurring within an environment. In one famous study, men were greeted by a female research assistant after crossing either a stable or an unstable bridge (Dutton & Aron, 1974). So that perceptions of security and safety would differ, the stable bridge was not very high, but the unstable bridge was over a deep ravine. Men who

PHOTO 12.3 *How do the various environments shown in these photos encourage or discourage intimate interaction?*

crossed the "scary bridge" were more sexually attracted to the research assistant than were men who crossed the "safe bridge." The researchers argued that the high levels of arousal the men experienced when crossing the unstable bridge played a role in heightening their attraction to the research assistant. Similarly, work on *excitation transfer* has shown that people experience stronger emotions toward others after engaging in activities such as exercising vigorously (Zillman, 1990). Other researchers have discussed an emotional contagion effect, whereby people can "catch" emotions from one another much like people catch colds from others (Hatfield et al., 1994; see also Chapter 11). If a particular environment is conducive to positive emotions, the people within that environment may catch those emotions and spread them to others. Using this logic, people are more likely to be attracted to one another at a festive party than at a somber business meeting.

Summary

Relational communication is one of the principal functions that nonverbal communication accomplishes. Through nonverbal messages, people define and maintain their interpersonal relationships. Of the multifaceted themes of relational communication, intimacy and dominance are the two superordinate ones.

Among the nonverbal cues that signal whether people have an intimate or nonintimate relationship are immediacy cues. Key immediacy cues include positive forms of touch, close proxemic distancing, direct body orientation, gaze, kinesic and vocalic expressiveness, and spending time together. Many of these immediacy cues are also used when people flirt with one another, although they tend to be more ambiguous and submissive during courtship. People also communicate intimacy by showing affection toward one another, both directly and indirectly, by engaging in similar behaviors, and by reciprocating immediacy. Finally, the environment sets the stage for intimate communication. Factors such as lighting, temperature, and furniture arrangement can affect social interaction, as can the emotions people are experiencing within a given environment. Clearly, nonverbal communication is rich in its ability to create intimate interactions and foster close relationships. By the same token, nonverbal relational messages can express hostility, dislike, exclusion, or distrust. Thus, the nonverbal expressions of relational messages are potent means by which people gauge their own relationship and that of others.

SUGGESTED READINGS

Abbey, A. (1987). Misperceptions of friendly behavior as sexual interest: A survey of naturally occurring incidents. *Psychology of Women Quarterly, 11*, 173–194.

Andersen, P. A. (1998). The cognitive valence theory of intimate communication. In M. Palmer & G. A. Barnett (Eds.), *Progress in communication sciences, Vol. 14: Mutual influence in interpersonal communication theory and research in cognition, affect, and behavior* (pp. 39–72). Norwood, NJ: Ablex.

Andersen, P. A., Guerrero, L. K., & Jones, S. M. (2006). Nonverbal behavior in intimate interaction and intimate relationships. In V. Manusov & M. L. Patterson (Eds.), *The Sage handbook of nonverbal communication* (pp. 259–277). Thousand Oaks, CA: Sage.

Burgoon, J. K., & Hale, J. L. (1984). The fundamental topoi of relational communication. *Communication Monographs, 51*, 193–214.

Burgoon J. K., & Hale, J. L. (1988). Nonverbal expectancy violations: Model elaboration and application to immediacy behaviors. *Communications Monographs, 55*, 58–79.

Floyd, K. (2006). *Communicating affection: Interpersonal behavior and social context.* Cambridge, England: Cambridge University Press.

Givens, D. B. (1978). The nonverbal basis of attraction: Flirtation, courtship, and seduction. *Psychiatry, 41*, 346–359.

Moore, M. M. (1995). Courtship signaling and adolescents: "Girls just wanna have fun?" *Journal of Sex Research, 32*, 319–328.

Moore, M. M. (2002). Courtship communication and perception. *Perceptual and Motor Skills, 94*, 97–105.

Palmer, M. T., & Simmons, K. B. (1995). Communicating intentions through nonverbal behaviors: Conscious and nonconscious encoding of liking. *Human Communication Research, 22*, 128–160.

Robinson, J. D. (2008). Nonverbal communication in doctor-patient relationships. In L. K. Guerrero & M. L. Hecht (Eds.), *The nonverbal communication reader: Classic and contemporary readings* (3rd ed., pp. 384–394). Long Grove, IL: Waveland Press.

Witt, P. L., Wheeless, L. R., & Allen, M. (2004). A meta-analytical review of the relationship between teacher immediacy and student learning. *Communication Monographs, 71*, 184–207.

13 Relational Messages: Power, Dominance, and Influence

The successful leader does not talk down to people. He lifts them up.

—Richard Nixon

He who has great power should use it lightly.

—Seneca

Power and persuasion are all around us. In a given day, most people are bombarded with requests to do something for someone, purchase a product or service, or support a particular candidate, proposition, or position. At work you might try to persuade your supervisor that you are the best person for a promotion. You might also try to use persuasion and dominant communication to initiate a new relationship or gain more power in an established relationship. Most people are also exposed to dozens of advertisements each day, on television and the radio, in magazines and newspapers, on the Internet, and even on billboards. As these examples suggest, dominance-submission (or powerfulness versus powerlessness) is one of the most fundamental dimensions underlying all types of relationships and interactions (e.g., Burgoon & Hale, 1984, 1987; McDonald, 1980).

Nonverbal behavior can promote perceptions of power and reflect one's level of status. Nonverbal communication also plays an instrumental role in the persuasion process. However, there is no easy formula for determining what constitutes an appropriate and effective dominance display or influence attempt. For example, high levels of gaze can show power and dominance (especially when someone gazes at others while speaking), but gaze can also communicate meekness and submission if someone is listening intently to a powerful person. Similarly, smiling can signal appeasement, or it can contribute to perceptions of likability and dynamism that make a person more persuasive. There is also a fine line between nonverbal behavior that is perceived as dominant and credible, and nonverbal behavior that is perceived as coercive and intimidating. The latter form of behavior is usually less influential in the long run. Thus, as you read through this chapter, it is important to remember that nonverbal cues reflecting power, dominance, status, and credibility do not occur in a vacuum. The context, as well as the total package of nonverbal behavior that a person uses, work together to create perceptions related to power and dominance.

In this chapter, we first define several related terms—power, dominance, credibility, status, and influence. The remainder of the chapter then concentrates on explicating how nonverbal communication is related to each of these terms. We examine six principles of power, followed by a discussion of five facets of credibility. The chapter ends with a discussion of the role that nonverbal communication plays in the process of persuasion and social influence.

Defining Power and Related Terms

Scholars have given various definitions for power, status, dominance, credibility, and social influence, and they sometimes use these terms interchangeably. However, there are important distinctions between these concepts. Power is generally regarded as the broadest term (Burgoon, Johnson, & Koch, 1998), with status, credibility, and dominant communication contributing to perceptions of power. Social influence, which is related to persuasion, is sometimes an outcome or consequence of being powerful, having credibility, and/or using dominant communication. Each of these terms is described in more detail in the following sections.

Power

Power has been defined in terms of three specific abilities: the ability to do what one wants without inference from others, the ability to influence other people, and the ability to resist the influence attempts of others (Burgoon, Johnson, & Koch, 1998; Huston, 1983). According to Burgoon and Bacue (2003), these abilities arise from "actual or implied authority, expertise, capacity to bestow rewards, capacity to withhold or apply punishments, persuasive abilities, or possession of interpersonal qualities with which others may identify" (p. 200). People who are perceived as powerful also tend to control valuable resources (Ellyson & Dovidio, 1985), such as time, money, and affection. Although some people possess *objective power* because they own or control certain resources, it is important to recognize that power is ultimately a perception (Guerrero, Andersen, & Afifi, 2007). For *actual power* to be exercised, other people must value the resources someone controls and be influenced by the person who controls those resources. Researchers have also discussed *relative power,* which refers to the amount of power that one person possesses in relation to another person. Box 13.1 provides a summary of how relative power is theorized to function in romantic relationships.

Classic work by French and Raven (1959) identified five types of power: coercive, reward, legitimate, expert, and referent. *Coercive power* can be exercised when a person has the ability to punish others or take away something they value. A boss can demote an employee, a parent can ground a child, and a teacher can deduct points when a student's work is late. *Reward power,* on the other hand, is the ability to provide someone with valued resources or outcomes. Instead of demoting an employee, a supervisor can give raises and promotions. Teachers can give good grades, and parents can give love, affection, and material goods to their children. People in high-status positions, such as superiors, parents, and teachers, often have *legitimate power,* which is based on the perception that they have the "right" or "authority" to be in charge. *Expert power,* in comparison, is rooted in a

---

BOX 13.1

Relative Power in Relationships

Norah Dunbar and Judee Burgoon (Dunbar, 2004; Dunbar & Burgoon, 2005) developed *dyadic power theory* to explain patterns of dominant and submissive behavior in romantic relationships. This theory is an extension of earlier work by Rollins and Bahr (1976). According to dyadic power theory, people make judgments about how much power they have in relation to their partner. Judgments of relative power are based partially on how resources are distributed in the relationship, with "perceptions of legitimate authority and access to resources" influencing how much power partners believe they have in comparison to each other (Burgoon & Dunbar, 2005).

Perceptions of relative power are theorized to influence how dominant or submissive relational partners act during situations such as decision-making and conflict. The partner who is low in relative power is theorized to act passive and submissive. This prediction is in line with research on the *chilling effect*, which has shown that the less-powerful person in a relationship often hesitates to communicate grievances to her or his partner (Cloven & Roloff, 1993; Roloff & Cloven, 1990; Solomon, Knobloch, & Fitzpatrick, 2004). Dyadic power theory also predicts that a partner who is high in relative power may not have to use dominant behavior, because

she or he already has control. The highest levels of dominant behavior may be used by partners who have similar levels of power and, therefore, compete for resources. Partners who have similar levels of power are also likely to use dominant communication to try to influence one another during the decision-making process.

Dunbar and Burgoon (2005) found some support for their predictions. In their study, people who perceived themselves as having slightly more or less power than their partners displayed more nonverbal dominance cues than did those who perceived themselves as quite high or low in relative power. Moreover, partners who perceived themselves as high in relative power appeared pleasant and relaxed rather than overtly dominant. Contrary to Dunbar and Burgoon's predictions, however, people who perceived themselves as low in power tended to interrupt more and use more illustrator gestures, perhaps in an effort to be more powerful. This finding may be related to the *demand-withdrawal sequence*, which specifies that the person in the less-powerful position is more demanding during conflict and decision-making because he or she wants the relationship to change (Christensen & Heavey, 1990; Heavey, Christensen, & Malamuth, 1995).

---

person's level of specialized knowledge. Sometimes, the person with the highest level of authority is not the person with the most specialized knowledge. For instance, a father may have more overall authority than his teenage son, but if the son is a computer whiz, the father might ask the son for help with a word-processing problem. In this situation, the son would have expert power, but the father would still have legitimate power, which might make it more likely that the son will comply with the father's request for help. Finally, some people have *referent power*, which relates to how dynamic and likable they are. People gravitate toward and pay attention to individuals with referent power because they like, respect, and admire them, or because they are exciting to be around.

As you might expect, different types of nonverbal behavior are associated with various forms of power. People with coercive power are more likely to use intimidating nonverbal behaviors including a lowered brow and a lack of smiling. Aguinis, Simonsen, and Pierce (1998) found that people were perceived as having more referent, reward, legitimate, and expert power when they were portrayed as having a relaxed expression on their face. The opposite was found for coercive power, with less relaxed facial expressions associated with this type of power. People who possess high levels of referent power are also more likely to use affiliative or friendly nonverbal behaviors, such as smiling, vocal warmth, and positive forms of touch, to influence others (Burgoon, 1994). Some research also suggests that people who have legitimate or expert power do not have to display their power nonverbally; they are influential simply because of their position and/or knowledge (Guerrero & Floyd, 2006).

Dominance

Dominance refers to a communication style that is effective in influencing others. As Burgoon and Hoobler (2002) put it, "*dominance* refers to actual interactional behaviors by which power and influence can be accomplished" (p. 268). Dominance is a social and relational phenomenon. If a person tries to exert influence on others but no one complies, then the person's attempts to dominate are unsuccessful; communication can only be classified as dominant if it is effective. Dominance is often communicated by verbal behaviors, such as requests, directives, and other assertive statements (Dillard, Anderson, & Knobloch, 2002), but nonverbal cues are also a critical part of dominant communication.

Some researchers associate dominance with threatening or intimidating nonverbal communication, such as hostile facial expressions and stares (e.g., Aguinis et al., 1998). Other researchers have studied how dominance can be communicated via a set of nonverbal behaviors that show social skill and competence (Burgoon & Dunbar, 2000; Burgoon et al., 1998; Guerrero & Floyd, 2006). These socially skilled behaviors can be grouped into three broad categories: (1) poise and self-assurance; (2) panache or dynamism; and (3) conversational control. The nonverbal behaviors related to each of these categories appear in Table 13.1.

When dominance is communicated using social skill rather than intimidation, a person's influence is likely to be more enduring (Burgoon, 1994). For example, children may do their homework on a given day because a parent yells and threatens punishment. However, when the child is not being threatened, homework may not get done. A parent who engages in dominant yet socially skilled communication to convince a child to do homework (e.g., pointing out the advantages of studying in a confident, expressive voice) is more likely to instill good, long-term studying habits. Research on conflict in dating relationships and marriages also suggests that people are more likely to resort to threats and violent forms of communication to control their partners when they do not have the skill required to communicate their needs in an assertive manner (Christopher & Lloyd, 2001).

TABLE 13.1   Nonverbal Cues Perceived as Reflecting Dominance and Social Skill

Poise and Self-Assurance	Panache or Dynamism	Conversational Control
Asymmetrical leg and arm positions	Close distancing	Attention-getting techniques (e.g., demure
Sideways leaning	Gaze and direct body orientation	eye contact, bumping
Open arms and body position	Forward lean	into someone)
Kinesic expressiveness	Vocal and kinesic	Fluent speech with
Low amount of swiveling,	expressiveness	unsmooth turn-switching
adaptors, and random	Faster, louder speech	and interruptions
movement		Backchannelling and nodding
Fluent speech		Increased talk time
Facial pleasantness/smiling		Eye contact (especially
Eye contact		when speaking)
Moderately fast and loud voice		Rejection and leave-taking
Increased talk time		behaviors (e.g., ignoring
		someone, increasing distance)

Source: Adapted from Guerrero and Floyd (2006), p. 141.

Credibility

In many cases, credibility is a prerequisite to being powerful and influential. Without credibility, people are not taken seriously. *Credibility* is a set of perceptions about a person's levels of competence and character. The most credible individuals are perceived to have both of these characteristics—they have high levels of expertise, authority, and status, and they are also perceived as being trustworthy and having integrity (Hovland, Janis, & Kelley, 1953).

Although competence and character are the primary determinants of credibility, perceptions of composure, likability, and dynamism are also important. A study by Burgoon and her colleagues (Burgoon, Birk, & Pfau, 1990) examined how different facets of credibility are associated with persuasion. First, they determined which nonverbal cues are associated with five different components of credibility: (1) character and trustworthiness; (2) competence and expertise; (3) composure; (4) sociability and likability; and (5) dynamism. They found that all five aspects of credibility were related to persuasion, with perceptions of competence associated particularly strongly. Dynamism was associated the least strongly with persuasion, possibly because both too much and too little dynamism or extroversion are undesirable in terms of fostering credibility.

Status

Status refers to one's position in a hierarchy. Groups, organizations, and societies are all built on hierarchical structures (Hofstede, 1991; Pettit, Bakshi, Dodge, & Coie, 1990). In organizational hierarchies, some people are subordinates, and others are superiors. In social hierarchies, people vary in terms of leadership and popularity. Even in families, there are hierarchies based on age and authority. People with high status in organizations possess "privileged access to restricted resources" (Mast & Hall, 2004, p. 146). For example, the CEO of a company controls more resources than does a mid-level manager, who controls more resources than does an entry-level employee. High social status has been defined as "the prestige an individual has within the group; it is related to popularity" (Coats & Feldman, 1996, p. 1014). People with high status tend to have more referent power and perhaps more reward or coercive power, but they do not necessarily have more authority or expertise.

Although it is possible for a high-status person to have little power and to engage in few dominant behaviors, high status typically fosters power and dominance (Patterson, 1985). This may be particularly true in organizations in which high-status individuals often control resources such as money and time spent on various tasks. Importantly, however, high status does not equate to power in all domains. In fact, some people with high status are figureheads who lack real power. Imagine working for a company president who owns a business that has been handed down from generation to generation in his family. You have little contact with him since he is rarely at work, and based on the few times you have worked with him, you determine that he doesn't know very much about the inner workings of the company. Although the company president would still have high status and control resources tied to wages and other perks, he would be unlikely to influence you much on a daily basis.

Social Influence

Social influence involves preserving or changing someone's thoughts, emotions, or behaviors, including persuading someone to comply with a request or agree to a decision (Burgoon, Buller, & Woodall, 1996). Dillard and colleagues (2002) specified that behavior is usually the primary focus of influence attempts, but that maintaining or modifying a person's thoughts, emotions, or identities is often a critical component in preserving or changing behavior. Social influence is sometimes an outcome of dominant communication; in other words, people use dominant communication (along with other means) to try to influence others. People who have power and high status are more likely to be persuasive and to wield influence, but status and power cannot compensate for poor communication. Successful influence often requires skilled communication, with nonverbal behavior playing a critical role (Segrin, 1993). In fact, after summarizing the compliance-gaining literature, Segrin concluded that "nonverbal behaviors are as powerful, and in some cases, more powerful" than verbal communication . . . "[F]or example, . . . whether a source gazes at and touches a target while attempting to gain compliance will be as influential in determining the outcome as whether the source gives supportive information" or uses other specific types of verbal messages (pp. 183–184).

As our definition suggests, social influence is motivated behavior. Three general motives are highly relevant to the process of social influence: self-presentational goals, relational goals, and instrumental goals (Canary & Cody, 1994; O'Keefe & Delia, 1982). Self-presentational goals revolve around our identities and the images we present to others. Projecting a credible image and making a good impression are often critical for persuasion to take place. Relational goals focus on the establishment, maintenance, and sometimes termination of particular relationships. Canary and Cody (1994) offer several examples of behavior that fulfills relational goals, such as influencing someone to spend time and do activities with you, wanting to initiate, escalate, maintain, or end a relationship, and giving advice and social support to friends and family. Finally, instrumental goals involve trying to accomplish specific tasks, such as getting a good grade, negotiating a good deal on a car, finding a ride to the airport, seeking advice or social support (rather than giving it), and getting your partner or roommate to do more around the house. These three motivations are present in most attempts at social influence, although each fluctuates in importance. At times the goals compete with each other (e.g., maintaining a positive image while ending a relationship with someone); at other times they complement one another (e.g., getting advice from someone helps the two of you build a better friendship); and at still other times the motivations are irrelevant to one another (e.g., getting someone to purchase a product from you, regardless of what they think of you).

Principles of Power and Dominance

One pathway to social influence is through power and/or dominant communication. Many different nonverbal cues are related to power and dominance. Because these terms are interrelated, it is sometimes difficult to disentangle which nonverbal cues are related more to dominance than power, and more to power than dominance. Therefore, some of the behaviors that we discuss next can be used to communicate power and dominance simultaneously. To provide a framework for discussing nonverbal behaviors related to power and dominance, we present six principles of power. A discussion of sex differences in nonverbal behavior reflecting power is also included in Box 13.2.

The Principle of Space and Access

Powerful people are given access to more space and larger, more luxurious territories (Remland, 1981). This principle is evident within various organizations, including universities. For example, if you visited the office of a university president, a professor, and then a graduate teaching assistant, you would likely notice that office space decreased along with status. The president's office would likely be largest, followed by the professor's office. The graduate student's office might not only be smallest, but this space might be shared with other graduate students. People who have larger, more private territories also typically have more room to display status symbols such as luxurious furnishings, artwork, framed diplomas and awards, and so forth. In the military, for instance, rank determines size of office, size of desk, number of filing cabinets, and even the type of wastebasket (metal or wood). One study (Leffler, Gillespie, & Conaty, 1982) even suggests that people in high-status positions point toward their possessions more often than

BOX **13.2**

Sex Differences in Power and Dominance: Subordination or Social Skill?

Since the 1970s, scholars have used a power or dominance framework to explain sex differences in nonverbal communication. In her famous book, *Body Politics,* Nancy Henley (1977) proposed that women's nonverbal behavior is characterized by submissiveness, whereas men's nonverbal behavior is characterized by dominance (see also Henley, 1995, 2001). Thus, sex differences in nonverbal communication are thought to reflect a power dimension, with behavior between men and women paralleling that between superiors and subordinates. According to this perspective, women are also more likely to be nonverbally sensitive, because having less social power necessitates developing survival skills related to listening and becoming affiliated with others. Other scholars have attributed sex differences in communication, including nonverbal behavior, to power. For example, in a commentary based on debate between Julia Wood and Kathryn Dindia (1998), Wood remarked that "Many, if not most, differences between the sexes reflect women's and men's unequal social power and the disparate behavior and attitudinal tendencies their respective degrees of power promote" (p. 21).

Henley's theoretical position, which has been labeled the *subordination hypothesis,* is supported by empirical studies showing that men talk more often and in louder voices (e.g., Kimble & Musgrove, 1988), display more visual dominance, interrupt more, and initiate touch more often than women (Henley, 1995). Studies have also shown that women smile more, are more facially and vocally expressive, let people move closer to them, and take up less physical space than men (Burgoon, 1994; Hall, 1984, 1998; Henley, 1977, 1995).

Of course, the behaviors listed above are not always interpreted as dominant or submissive. Burgoon (1994) argued that some behaviors labeled "submissive," such as smiling and vocal expressiveness, may reflect friendliness or even dynamism more than submission (see also Hall, 1998). Burgoon and her colleagues have also shown that expressive, friendly behaviors are influential, and thus may represent a form of social skilled dominant behavior

(e.g., Burgoon & Bacue, 2003). Because women are sometimes perceived to have more referent power than men (Carli, 1999), using friendly, expressive nonverbal behavior may actually be an effective strategy when women seek to gain power and influence others. In contrast, because men are often perceived as having more expert and legitimate power than women (Carli, 1999), dominant behaviors such as interruptions and increased talk time might be more effective for males.

In an effort to do a systematic analysis of the existing research on the *vertical dimension* of relationships, Judith Hall, Erik Coats, and Lavonia Smith LeBeau decided to conduct a meta-analysis of the literature. To their surprise, they found about 150 independent studies involving around 14,000 perceivers on perceived relations between status or power and nonverbal behavior, and about 125 studies involving around 10,000 participants on actual relations. Although quite a few behaviors correlated with perceptions of verticality, they found very few nonverbal behaviors that were actually associated with it. They concluded that there was no evidence that actual verticality was correlated across the board with smiling, gazing, raised brows, nodding, self-touching, touching others, gestures, postural relaxation, overlapped speech, pausing, backchanneling, vocal nonfluencies, or speaking tempo. The only four behaviors to show overall effects were closer proximity, open body postures, interrupting more, and speaking loudly. This analysis is more supportive of a social skills interpretation than the subordination hypothesis because women tend to establish closer distances and more open postures, behaviors associated with being more, not less, powerful. Hall et al. caution that interpretations of behaviors need to be grounded in an understanding of the social context and people's motivations before nonverbal behavior patterns are interpreted as indicative of power or something else. This cautionary note is equally applicable to most interpretations of nonverbal cues.

Sources: Guerrero & Floyd (2006), pp. 145–146; Hall, Coats, & Smith LeBeau (2005).

those in lower status positions. In this study, people were assigned to play the role of a "teacher" or a "student." Those assigned to the teacher role pointed to their possessions more often.

The spaces of powerful people are also more likely to be protected by territorial markers and gatekeepers. In many organizations, entry-level employees share a large workspace. Sometimes they are separated into "cubbyholes" that are created by putting up movable barriers; other times they are not separated at all. Thus, there is little privacy. Upper-level managers, in contrast, are likely to have private offices that are marked with name plaques. Doors and secretaries block their territory, helping them to regulate who has access to them and who does not. In some organizations, to see the most senior people you have to get through several different rooms and gatekeepers.

Although it is usually difficult for a subordinate to gain access to a superior, a powerful person has easy access to a wide variety of people and places. Corporate presidents do not need to make an appointment to speak with one of their managers and in some cases may not need to knock on doors before entering. A high-status person also has access to perks such as country club memberships, company cars, limousines, and jets. If you can command a company jet, you are obviously in a position of power. If you get to ride occasionally in the jet, you are still part of an inner circle. If you fly commercial airlines but go first class, you have some rank even though you haven't made "the big time" yet. And if you fly coach or don't fly at all, you are down somewhere in the lower echelons.

In addition to having more private office space, powerful individuals can communicate dominance by taking up more physical space. Dominant individuals often sit in more open body positions (as opposed to defensive positions), and use more expansive gestures (Andersen, 2008; Hall, Coats, & Smith LeBeau, 2005). High-status individuals can put their feet up on a desk while talking to a subordinate, but a subordinate would be wise not to engage in the same behavior. Other people also give high-status others more space. For example, if organizational members are sitting at a round table, the individuals with the highest status are often positioned so they have the most space around them.

The Principle of Centrality

Dominance and status are also signaled by centrality of position. Leaders sit or stand in more central positions in a group, such as at the head of a table or wherever visual access to the most people is maximized (Andersen, 2008). People also look at high-status individuals more than low-status individuals, especially when the high-status person is speaking. This relates to Exline, Ellyson, and Long's (1975) idea of a *visual dominance ratio*. According to this idea, powerful people look more at others when speaking than when listening. On the other side of the coin, submissive or low-status individuals look at superiors more when they are listening (as a sign of attention and respect) than when they are speaking. Through central positioning at a table or in a room, high-status individuals can maximize the amount of control they have. They can look around to ensure that everyone is listening when they are speaking, and they can regulate conversation more easily. People can also look at them more easily. Take a look at Photo 13.1. Who appears to be in the most central position?

PHOTO 13.1   *The person in the most central position is often at the head of the tables, where everyone can easily look at him or her.*

The idea of centrality also relates to the placement of a person's office or workspace. Offices that are located closer to the "center of power" are typically inhabited by high-status organizational members, with the center of power defined by the office inhabited by the highest ranking member of all. A promotion might not just entail a more prestigious title and larger office space, but an office closer to the seat of power. Indeed, an excerpt from Gay Talese's *The Kingdom and the Power* (1969) relates how the principle of centrality functioned at the *New York Times*:

> Where one sits in *The Times'* newsroom is never a causal matter. It is a formal affair on the highest and lowest level. Young reporters of no special status are generally assigned to sit near the back of the room, close to the Sports department; and as the years go by and people die and the young reporter becomes more seasoned and not so young, he is moved up closer to the front. (p. 131)

In this case, the front of the newsroom is the center of power.

The Principle of Elevation

Just as size and position can convey power, so too can height or vertical space. High-ranking organizational members often have offices on the upper floor or in the "penthouse." Residing in the top floors of a building denotes status while also providing separation and privacy from the mass of lower-level employees who often occupy the bottom floors. This principle extends to other professional settings, such as courtrooms, where the judge's bench is often higher than the rest of the courtroom, or undergraduate classrooms, where everyone is typically seated except the professor. Monuments also reflect the principle of elevation. If you have ever been to Washington, D.C., and have seen the Washington, Jefferson, and Lincoln Memorials, you were probably impressed by the height and size of these monuments, which symbolize the greatness of these presidents.

Behaviors that increase height differentials can also convey power. For example, standing over another person or "looking down at someone" often function as dominant behaviors. It follows then that tall people would be seen as more powerful than short people (Frieze, Olson, & Russell, 1991; Henley, 1977). Indeed, as reported in *The Economist,* most presidents of the United States have been taller than the average American man, and the taller candidate typically wins the election. This power bias toward height "is deeply embedded in the visual grammar of western civilization. For a speaker, it has functional advantages. The elevation . . . gives him or her a much larger field of vision. Elevation gathers and keeps attention" (King as cited in Jaworski, 1993, p. 14). Taller people, especially tall men, generally earn higher salaries than people of average and short stature (Pierce, 1996). Some research even suggests that taller people act differently than shorter people. A study by Yee and Bailenson (2007) compared the behaviors of avatars, which are digital representations of oneself, in a virtual environment. People who were assigned taller avatars acted more confident than people who were assigned shorter avatars.

The principle of elevation is also applicable in other cultures, although the mechanisms for producing height differentials vary. For example, in many Asian cultures people bow to show respect for someone. The degree to which a person bows reflects the status of the interactional partner. The higher your partner's status in comparison to your own, the lower you are expected to bow. Across many different cultures and generations, rulers (such as kings, queens, and emperors) have sat in elevated thrones. In the classic musical *The King and I,* there is a comical scene in which the King of Siam warns Anna, his children's schoolteacher, that her head should never be higher than his. Anna has great difficulty keeping her head lower than the king's when he purposely maneuvers his face near the ground.

The Principle of Prerogative

When a person is climbing the metaphorical organizational ladder, it is usually best to stay within the norms and avoid violating expectancies. This advice ranges from the way an employee should dress (in terms of the expected company attire) to how an employee should use time (such as showing up on time or a little early to meetings) and territories (always knocking before entering a superior's office). Interestingly, however, the need to follow company norms often fades when a person has achieved high status and power within an organization. A powerful person has the prerogative to dress casually or show up late without being questioned or scrutinized. The more powerful the person, the more she or he can violate the norms that are in place for "ordinary" employees and still be seen in a positive light. In fact, when powerful people engage in actions such as failing to call a subordinate back or leaving a meeting early, subordinates often assume that the superior had something especially important to do, thereby increasing the powerful person's stature even more. One of our students offered this example of how the prerogative principle works. Everyone in her company always knew when the boss had an important meeting with an equal- or higher-status manager from another department or organization, because on those days he would dress much more professionally than normal. On the days he stayed in his office surrounded only by his subordinates, he dressed more casually than the average worker.

The principle of prerogative extends to various aspects of time. In addition to being able to show up later or leave earlier than subordinates, high-status individuals often have more flexibility to set their own hours. Moreover, high-status individuals often keep others waiting even though others do not keep them waiting. For example, people commonly arrive on time and then wait for appointments with high-status individuals such as doctors, dentists, and attorneys. Having to wait often signifies that the professional is in high demand and that her or his time is valuable. In contrast, if a low-status individual keeps people waiting, he or she is more likely to be seen as rude, inconsiderate, and irresponsible. University folk wisdom applies a similar line of reasoning to waiting time in classrooms. That is, in many colleges and universities there are unwritten rules about how long to wait for a late professor before leaving class. Students might wait 15 or 20 minutes for a full professor, but only 5 or 10 minutes for a graduate student teacher.

This principle also extends to proxemic and haptic behavior. In terms of proxemics, both close and far interaction distances have been associated with being perceived as high status and dominant (Burgoon, 1991; Burgoon, Buller, Hale, & deTurck, 1984; Burgoon & Hale, 1988; Hall et al., 2005). This is because dominant individuals are freer to deviate from normative distances than are submissive individuals. High-status individuals may initiate a more formal or more intimate interaction pattern, whereas low-status individuals must maintain deferential intermediate distances in conversation, letting the high-status person dictate any changes from that intermediate norm. Haptic behavior follows a similar pattern. Dominant individuals are usually given the prerogative to initiate touch as well as to determine the frequency, intensity, and intimacy of touch. Think about the following scenario: Anne, a senior-level manager, calls Lindsay into her office to tell her that she has just been promoted from an entry-level position to a supervisory position. Which would be more likely—Lindsay touches Anne when she hears the good news, or Anne touches Lindsay to congratulate her? Most people would agree that the latter scenario is more likely than the former. Notice also that in this example the employee went to the manager's office rather than the other way around. This illustrates the next principle—the principle of interactional control.

The Principle of Interactional Control

Related to the idea of having the prerogative to break norms and initiate spatial violations, powerful people are able to control the interaction around them. Powerful people can summon others to their office, call for and adjourn meetings, and change the direction of a conversation or discussion more easily than less powerful people can. As noted previously, powerful people's central positions at tables, in office buildings, and so forth, enable them to practice interactional control.

Another way to reinforce power through interaction control is to insist that important negotiations occur within one's own territory. People entering someone else's domain automatically become more deferent and submissive (Edney, 1976), whereas those on their "home court" gain confidence from the familiarity of their surroundings. Moreover, the artifacts and furnishings in one's office (such as awards, diplomas, and expensive furniture) can add to one's powerful image. In contrast, to allow oneself to be summoned voluntarily to someone else's home turf can be taken as a sign of weakness. Inexperienced diplomats and politicians often learn this only after having made too many concessions to adversaries or having lost the respect of allies. The recognized territorial advantage is the reason for insisting on a neutral locale for summit meetings and other serious talks, as was the case when U.S. President Bush, British Prime Minister Blair, and Spanish Prime Minister José Maria Aznar met in the Azores (off the coast of Portugal) before the second Gulf War was launched in 2003. Holding the Azores Summit in a location other than the United States or Great Britain was necessary to show a powerful, unified front against a backdrop of world dissent. Of course, not issuing an invitation at all is another type of power move. After the split in the United Nations regarding the 2003 Gulf War, much was made in the U.S. press about who was and was not invited to President Bush's Texas ranch for a visit.

The principle of interactional control can be seen in operation at meetings, wherein dominant individuals often control the conversational floor by initiating and switching topics (Wiemann, 1985). Dominant people also talk more and interrupt others more, both in groups and in relationships (Dunbar & Burgoon, 2005; Hall et al, 2005; Leffler et al., 1982; Schmid Mast, 2002). In turn, people who use these behaviors are often perceived as the leader of a group (Kleinke, Lenga, Tulley, Meeker, & Staneski, 1976; Lustig, 1977). This principle also applies to courtrooms and classrooms. In courtrooms, people rise and stand in response to a judge's actions, and those who interrupt proceedings can be held in contempt of court. In classrooms, students often raise their hands and wait for the instructor to call on them.

The Principle of Intimidation and Threat

Height is also related to the principle of intimidation or threat, in that people who are higher or taller can "look down" at others. Size can be intimidating, as can gaze, angry facial expressions, loud vocal tones or silence, and spatial invasion.

The face and eyes can also signal intimidation and threat. The threatening stare is a primary dominance display that cuts across various species and is universally understood by humans (Dovidio & Ellyson, 1985). People in positions of power or status are more likely to engage in unwavering, direct looks or stares (Exline et al., 1975). Steady, extended gaze is generally perceived as dominant and threatening, especially when used by a high-status or powerful person (Burgoon et al., 1984; Le Poire & Burgoon, 1994). Consider how the power of the stare is captured in Secretary of State Dean Rusk's metaphor for the Soviets' response to President John Kennedy's blockade during the Cuban missile crisis: "Eyeball to eyeball, they blinked first." In addition to the eyes, other parts of the face can convey intimidation. A study by Montepare and Dobish (2003) showed that angry faces are rated as more dominant than sad or fearful faces. Other research has shown that non-smiling faces are perceived as more dominant than smiling faces (Keating, 1985), or that smiling is associated with less dominance (Hall et al., 2005). Indeed, some research suggests that smiling can signal appeasement, deference, and submission, which is the opposite of intimidation (Henley, 1977; Keating, 1985).

Interestingly, two seemingly opposite types of vocalic behavior can be intimidating—loudness and silence. Loud voices are often heard as dominant and intimidating (Hall et al., 2005), particularly when they convey anger. Thus, some researchers have cautioned that although loud voices send messages of power and dominance, they can also show disrespect and inconsideration (Remland, 1982). On the other side of the vocalic spectrum, silence can sometimes be intimidating and threatening. The ultimate forms of silence—such as failing to acknowledge another person's presence with a greeting, failing to recognize someone's contribution, or ignoring someone's suggestions during a meeting—can be very potent reminders of a superior's power. Because the "silent treatment" causes frustration, it can provoke behavior that reinforces power. As Bruneau (1973) put it, silence can force

> subordinates into awkward positions whereby they exhibit behaviors detrimental to their own cause—because their frustration is aggravated by silent response to their efforts. Silence as absence of response to or lack of recognition of subordinates may very well be the main source of protection of power in socio-political orders where physical restraint has lost repute. (p. 39)

Simply put, silence can be used as a weapon that intimidates subordinates and traps them in their low-status positions.

Powerful people can also intimidate others by engaging in spatial violations. When people approach others' territory in a rapid and deliberate fashion, they display dominance. In contrast, people display submission when they hesitantly approach others (Mehrabian, 1981). To intrude on someone else's territory is the boldest of power ploys. One popular book on nonverbal communication advises power seekers to spread their briefcase and possessions on another person's desk to gain the upper hand or at least tip the balance of power in their favor. A woman executive reported that a salesperson carried this idea to the extreme by sweeping into her office and taking over her desk. She was so unsettled by this violation of her territory that she lost control of the business deal. Clearly this intimidating maneuver shifted the power balance toward the salesperson rather than the executive.

Although intimidating behaviors are sometimes successful in securing compliance, these types of behaviors should be used judiciously. For example, there are instances in which managers may need to intimidate employees to enhance productivity or to get a lazy or incompetent worker to improve performance. Many times, however, intimidation strategies backfire because they alienate employees, increase status differentials, and reduce job satisfaction (e.g., Remland, 1981). Studies have even showed that staring can decrease people's willingness to help others. In a classic study by Horn (1974), people were less likely to help a researcher on a computer problem if the researcher had stared at them.

Credibility

Intimidation is one of several different routes to persuasion. Rather than (or in addition to) intimidating others, people often present a credible image as a way to gain power and influence others. As noted previously, there are at least five facets of credibility: (1) competence, which is related to authority and status; (2) character and trustworthiness; (3) composure and poise; (4) likability; and (5) dynamism or charisma. Research has shown that various nonverbal behaviors are related to each of these components of credibility.

Competence, Status, and Authority

Judgments of competence are related to a person's level of status and authority, as well as how much expert knowledge a person has. Importantly, a person's level of competence is a perception; sometimes people appear to know more than they really do. Moreover, authority and status are sometimes unrelated to the other major component of credibility—good character. This has led researchers to ask: How much are people influenced by individuals who have authority and status? Although the answer to this question varies based on the situation and the people involved, both research and anecdotal evidence suggests that authority figures can have a frightening amount of influence on people.

A famous series of experiments by Milgram (1963, 1974) illustrates this point. Milgram had people come into a research laboratory at Yale University where they were asked to play the role of a "teacher." Another person played the part of a "learner." The experimenter, who wore a gray technician's lab coat and white shirt and tie, told the teacher to administer electric shock to the learner whenever the learner gave a wrong answer. The learner did not really receive any shocks, but pretended to feel pain. As learners got more answers wrong, teachers were told to increase the level of electric shock. Even when teachers were told that the level of shock was reaching a dangerous level, 65% of them continued to administer the shock when the experimenter told them to. The experimenter even told people that the learner had a heart condition and the learner sometimes groaned and fell silent, yet some teachers continued giving shocks.

Although Milgram was not directly testing the influence of attire, it is likely that the setting (Yale University) and the appearance of the experimenter as a high-status individual wearing a lab coat contributed to the continued shocking of the so-called learners. As disturbing as the results of this study are, real-life examples are even more disturbing. In fact, one reason that Milgram conducted his experiment was to try to understand what mentality might lead people to commit the kinds of inhuman, heinous acts that occurred during World II under Hitler. In war and in other situations, Milgram argued that people sometimes give blind obedience to authority figures. Clothing and uniforms are often the most compelling symbols of that authority.

Several other studies have examined how clothing and other adornment cues influence perceptions of status, with particular attention given to uniforms. Pilots, businesspeople, firefighters, doctors, and construction workers, among other occupations, are often easily identifiable by dress (see Photo 13.2). When

PHOTO 13.2   *What stereotypes do you have of these people based on the uniforms they are wearing?*

people are dressed in these types of uniforms, they are often stereotyped based on perceptions about their occupation. Paradoxically, uniforms can reflect high or low status. In the classic movie *Fast Times at Ridgemont High,* there is a scene in which one of the characters is sitting in his car at a stop sign. He notices an attractive girl in the car next to him smiling at him. He smiles back and then she starts laughing. He catches a glimpse of himself in his rearview mirror and realizes that he is wearing the pirate uniform, complete with a parrot on the shoulder, that he is required to wear at the fast food fish restaurant where he works. Embarrassed and frustrated, he pulls the hat off and throws it out the window. As this example illustrates, uniforms sometimes reflect low-status positions. In fact, in some organizations, including some retail and grocery stores, the lower-level employees such as cashiers, baggers, and cart-attendants wear smocks or vests, whereas the supervisors wear professional clothing, such as a shirt and tie or a dress.

Of course, uniforms can also connote high status and authority. Doctors, nurses, police officers, firefighters, military personnel, and even professional athletes create an image of authority when they wear uniforms that help people associate them with their occupations. A classic set of field studies by Bickman (1971a, 1971b, 1974) examined how people reacted to men wearing one of three outfits: civilian clothes consisting of a sport coat and tie, a milkman's uniform, or a nondescript security guard's uniform that looked similar to a police officer's uniform. The men approached people on the street in Brooklyn and made various requests, including asking them to pick up a small paper bag lying on the ground, give change to someone whose parking meter had expired, and stand on the wrong side of a "Bus Stop—No Standing" sign. In all these situations, people were most likely to comply with the request when the man was wearing the guard uniform. Bushman (1988) replicated these findings for women who were dressed in a generic blue uniform, business attire, or casual attire. In this study, people were more likely to give change to a third party whose parking meter had expired if the woman making the request was wearing a uniform.

Professional forms of dress, other than uniforms, are also related to status and authority. People are more likely to donate money (Bull & Gibson-Robinson, 1981), sign a petition (Suedfeld, Bochner, & Matas, 1971), and complete questionnaires (Harris et al., 1983) when the requestor is formally dressed and well groomed. However, in some situations, formal dress may actually *decrease* perceptions of competence and authority. Leigh and Summers (2002) found salespersons were rated as less capable and professional if they were dressed in highly formal attire. In certain contexts, dressing too formally may be perceived as overcompensating for a lack of competence. Some research also suggests that salespeople are rated as more competent when their style of dress is similar to the buyer's (Campbell, Graham, Jolibert, & Meissner, 1988).

Researchers such as Mast and Hall (2004) have argued that people are fairly good at determining who has more and less status in an interaction based on clothing and other nonverbal cues. To test this idea, Mast and Hall recruited coworkers at a university to participate in a discussion about work-life issues. They then took photographs of pairs of coworkers during the discussion and had the coworkers report on their status relative to each other. As they hypothesized, observers were fairly accurate in determining who had higher status. Moreover, nonverbal cues played an important part in these judgments. For women, tilting one's head upward and raising one's eyebrow were related to perceptions of low status; for men, age, forward lean, and formal dress were related to perceptions of high status.

Another study examined perceptions of competence during re-enacted verbal examinations of medical students. The students who used more direct eye contact and a moderate rate of speaking were judged as more competent than the students who used less eye contact and spoke slowly, even though the answers they gave were exactly the same (Rowland-Morin, Burchard, Garb, & Coe, 1991).

Character and Trustworthiness

Although eye contact is not a reliable indicator of deception (see Chapter 15), people are judged as more trustworthy and sincere when they maintain eye contact with listeners. In the courtroom, witnesses are judged as less trustworthy if they look downward slightly instead of looking directly at the attorney while they are being questioned (Hemsley & Doob, 1978). Eye contact appears to have the strongest effects on judgments of trustworthiness when it is used with other nonverbal cues that show affiliation and expressiveness. In a study by Burgoon et al. (1990), people were rated as more trustworthy when they used high levels of eye contact, vocal variety, more smiling and facial pleasantness, and more overall facial expressiveness. In another study (Leigh & Summers, 2002), salespeople were judged as more trustworthy when they used more eye contact. Bettinghaus and Cody (1994) summarized research on nonverbal indicators of trustworthiness and concluded that:

> To build the perception of *trustworthiness,* the speaker should maintain high eye-contact, nod frequently, smile, display open arms and hands, and employ other behaviors associated with affiliation. The speaker should also avoid exhibiting anxiety-related behaviors, and use a conversational style of delivery.

Facial features are also related to perceptions of honesty and sincerity. In particular, research suggests that both attractive and average-looking people are more likely to be judged as honest, sincere, and warm when they have babyish facial features compared to mature facial features (Berry, 1991b; Brownlow, 1992; Brownlow & Zebrowitz, 1990). In a simulated courtroom trial, people with babyish facial features were convicted less often of intentional crimes that involved manipulation, whereas people with mature faces were convicted less often for unintentional crimes than involved negligence (Berry & McArthur, 1986). Thus, people with babyish adult faces may be perceived as sincere and trustworthy, but also somewhat unintelligent or unsophisticated. In a study of women in politics, Rosenberg, Kahn, and Tran (1991) found that women tended to be rated as more trustworthy when they had triangular, almond-shaped, or upper-curved-shaped eyes.

Composure, Poise, and Relaxation

Relaxation and composure are communicated nonverbally through a set of behaviors that includes asymmetrical leg and arm positions, sideways leaning, arm openness, expressive gestures, less swiveling, and less random leg and foot movement (Mehrabian, 1969; Mehrabian & Ksionzkey, 1972). Facial pleasant-ness, smiling, eye contact, verbal fluency, and close proximity also send messages of calmness, relaxation, and composure (Burgoon et al., 1990). Thus, nonverbal behaviors that combine to show openness, expressiveness, lack of nervousness, and positive affect communicate relaxation and poise.

Powerful individuals typically appear more relaxed than their less-powerful counterparts, and people who appear poised and relaxed are perceived as more dominant, powerful, and persuasive (Andersen & Bowman, 1999; Burgoon et al., 1998; Henley, 1977; Weisfeld & Linkey, 1985). In a mixed-status group, people with higher rank exhibit more relaxation and feel freer to stretch out, slump in their chairs, or put their feet up on a sofa. Those of lower rank tend to mirror the postures and level of relaxation of high-status members, but they don't match it fully. Instead they maintain some degree of postural restraint and possibly some level of nervousness, and the latter is sometimes displayed through adaptor gestures and random movement. A study by Dunbar and Burgoon (2005) also demonstrated that relaxation is a key component of dominance. In their study of romantic couples, men were rated as more dominant if their bodies looked relaxed, their facial expressions were pleasant, and their voice was fluent. Women were rated as more dominant if their bodies looked relaxed and they used fewer adaptors. Hall et al. (2005) also found that having a relaxed voice and an open body position were related to both perceived and actual power. Take a look at Photo 13.3. What do the facial expressions and body positions of these two world leaders tell us about how relaxed and composed they were during their meeting?

The importance of nonverbal behaviors that reflect composure and poise is documented in an interesting analysis of the 1976 presidential debates between Gerald Ford and Jimmy Carter. Exline (1985) objectively coded such tension-release adaptors as lip licking, postural sway, shifting gaze, eye blinks, and speech

PHOTO 13.3 *In 1985, U.S. President Ronald Reagan and Soviet leader Mikhail Gorbachev try to warm up relations between their two countries during the Cold War by engaging in a series of fireside chats in a relaxing environment.*

nonfluencies and then had observers rate various segments of the speeches. Observers rated more favorably the segments that showed less tension, and Ford—the winner of the first debate—showed fewer of these tension-related adaptors at the outset of his speech. The implication is that power and credibility correlate with greater relaxation and poise. To look composed and poised, a person must minimize adaptor behaviors, such as twisting a ring or wringing one's hands together. Gestures that are purposeful and expansive communicate power; random, nervous gestures do not.

Finally, although relaxation is clearly an important part of projecting a composed and confident image, it is important to recognize that too much relaxation can communicate apathy rather than dominance. As Burgoon and Bacue (2003) explained, "extremes in postural relaxation function as negative expectancy violations and therefore would presumably constitute unskillful performances" (p. 201). So moderately relaxed bodies, faces, and voices likely signal confidence without also signaling boredom or disengagement. Thus, moderate relaxation probably conveys more dominance than extremely relaxed or unrelaxed behavior.

Likability

Likability, which includes perceptions of sociability and friendliness, also contributes to judgments about credibility. When people like or admire someone, they are more likely to rate that person as trustworthy. People are also more likely to pay attention to those whom they like. Indeed, one of the questions that political pundits often ask the general public is "Which candidate would you most like to have a beer with (or go on a picnic with)?" Such a question may seem superfluous when trying to determine who your next mayor, senator, or president will be, but the question gets at the issue of likability, which is an important component of credibility and social influence.

Likability, friendliness, and interpersonal warmth are communicated through a set of nonverbal immediacy cues, including gaze, smiling, close distancing, and direct body orientation (see also Chapter 12). Numerous studies have demonstrated links between persuasion, credibility, and nonverbal immediacy cues (Burgoon, Segrin & Dunbar, 2002). Immediacy cues lead to changes in arousal and sometimes increased attention and liking. Andersen (2008) proposed a *direct effects model* for nonverbal immediacy, such that "both single-channeled immediacy increases, such as increased eye contact, and multi-channeled immediacy increases are associated with increased persuasion" (p. 248). For example, smiling, nodding, expressive gesturing, facial pleasantness, and direct body orientation are associated with greater dominance and persuasiveness, and well as greater likability (Burgoon et al., 1990; Liss, Walker, Hazelton, & Cupach, 1993; Mehrabian, 1981). Take a look at Photo 13.4 of Barack Obama interacting with the audience at a rally during the 2008 U.S. presidential campaign. What nonverbal behaviors is he using to project images of dominance and likability?

Some research suggests that gaze and smiling are key components in projecting a friendly image and increasing liking. Palmer and Simmons (1995) examined which nonverbal cues people use to communicate liking, and which of those cues induced the most liking in receivers. People reported liking their partners most when they used eye contact, smiling, and illustrator gestures. A similar study by Ray and Floyd (2000; see also Floyd & Ray, 2003) found that people's level of liking for their partners was influenced by how much they used eye contact, smiled, nodded their heads, and looked facially animated, with all of these nonverbal cues contributing to increased liking. Other studies have shown that smiling people are rated as more likable and more persuasive than non-smiling people (Liss et al., 1993; Burgoon & Bacue, 2003).

At this point, you may have noticed that the findings for smiling are contradictory. Earlier in this chapter, we mentioned that non-smiling, angry faces are often rated as dominant, whereas smiling faces are sometimes rated as submissive.

PHOTO 13.4 *Smiling and shaking hands helps President Barack Obama create a sense of immediacy and rapport, while at the same time, his high elevation and the presence of Secret Service and police officers communicate power.*

One way to understand this contradiction is to focus on the type of power or credibility being communicated. Angry, non-smiling faces are most likely when power or authority is communicated via intimidation. In contrast, smiling and facial pleasantness are most likely when dominance is wielded through likability. In a study by Montepare and Dobish (2003), both angry and happy faces were rated as more dominant than sad or fearful faces. Another important issue may be how much and when a person smiles. A person who smiles too much, especially in response to others, may be viewed as submissive. A person who smiles occasionally and at appropriate times may be perceived as more personable and likable.

Appropriate and friendly forms of touch are also related to both likability and persuasion. In a classic study by Fisher, Rytting, and Heslin (1976), librarians were instructed to touch some college students lightly and inconspicuously when they checked out their books but not to touch others. The students who had been touched reported more positive feelings about the library and its staff. Other studies have shown that waitresses receive larger tips when they touch their customers (Crusco & Wetzel, 1984). The effect of touching on tips appears to be stronger in casual bar-oriented restaurants than in more formal restaurants (Hubbard, Tsuiji, Williams, & Seatriz, 2003). People also tend to tip the most when touched by a server of the opposite sex. In bar-style restaurants, Hubbard and her colleagues found that men tipped an average of 31% when touched by a female server versus 24% when touched by a male server. When they were not touched, they tipped at an average rate of about 11%, regardless of whether the server was a man or a woman. For women customers, the trend was reversed, with women giving male servers who touched them an average tip of 36% versus 24% for a female server who touched them. Women tipped servers (both male and female) who did not touch them around 15%. Other studies have produced similar results highlighting the importance of touch and close interpersonal distancing in the service industry. For example, people believe that they will be more satisfied with products and services when a salesperson stands close to a client (Hashimoto & Borders, 2005), and shoppers buy more when touched by salesclerks (Smith, Gier, & Willis, 1982), presumably because they like and trust the salespeople more. Box 13.3 describes other ways that touch is used in marketing and sales.

Dynamism and Charisma

Dynamism, or charisma, is an elusive form of credibility that is difficult, but not impossible, to learn (Taylor, 2002). Friedman, Riggio, and Casella (1988) defined *personal charisma* as "a dramatic flair involving the desire and ability to communicate emotions and thereby inspire others" (p. 204). Charismatic people are dynamic communicators who have qualities that draw other people to them and their message. These qualities include energy, enthusiasm, expressiveness, and self-confidence. As Burgoon, Johnson, et al. (1998) found, "panache" or dynamism is often a critical feature of dominant communication. People who communicate in a dynamic fashion have a "dramatic, memorable, and attention-grabbing communication style that is immediate, expressive, and energetic" (Guerrero & Floyd, 2006, p. 156; see also Burgoon et al., 1998).

BOX 13.3
Touch in Marketing and Sales

Since the mid-1970s, researchers have known that, in certain circumstances, salespeople can use appropriate and friendly touch to help them sell products and services. More recently, Joann Peck and her colleagues (Peck & Childers, 2003, 2006; Peck & Wiggins, 2006) have discovered that customers are more likely to have positive attitudes toward certain products if they can touch them. Being able to touch a product may also lead customers to buy a product that they had not originally considered purchasing. These connections between touch and product marketability help explain why product placement is important for products, as well as why some products are difficult to sell via the Internet.

A series of three studies by Peck and Wiggins (2006) looked more deeply into this issue. These researchers argued that touch serves two marketing functions: an instrumental function that allows customers to evaluate a product or service; and an autotelic function that allows customers to enjoy the sensory stimulation provided by touch. People can have one or both of these orientations toward touch. As they explained, a person who is oriented toward fulfilling instrumental needs might touch "a sweater to learn if the material is thick enough to provide warmth," whereas a person who is oriented toward fulfilling autotelic needs might finger "the sleeve of a cashmere sweater that he or she has no intention of purchasing, simply because the

cashmere feels pleasant to touch" (p. 57). Peck and Wiggins's studies showed that touch has a more positive effect on people who are autotelically oriented. For example, in one study people were presented with a pamphlet that asked them to "Feel the warmth of a warm winter blanket" and to volunteer to deliver blankets to families in need. Touching the blanket led to positive emotional responses, but only for people who had high autotelic needs for touch. People who had high instrumental needs for touch were only likely to respond favorably to touch if the element they felt was consistent with the message, such as feeling something soft representing a warm blanket. If the touch element was inconsistent with the message (e.g., it felt rough) then touch actually reduced the persuasiveness of the message.

Peck and Wiggins suggest that their findings have several implications for marketing. Including touch elements that are consistent with a message or with one's expectations about a product appear to produce positive effects for almost everyone. They also suggest that product packaging and print advertising could benefit by including touch elements, and that in-store product displays that encourage touch may lead customers to interact with products that they otherwise would have ignored, which in turn may increase impulse and unplanned purchases.

Energy and enthusiasm are conveyed through a variety of kinesic cues, including expansive gestures, facial expressiveness, head shaking and nodding, wide smiles, erect posture, quick and vigorous movement, and fluid movement (Bettinghaus & Cody, 1994; Gallaher, 1992). Taylor (2002) compared the nonverbal communication of 10 charismatic leaders to that of 10 non-charismatic leaders. The leaders who were considered charismatic used more gesturing, smiling, eyebrow raises, and body shifts than the leaders who were considered non-charismatic. The charismatic leaders also used fewer eye blinks and stiff head turns. When people were trained to exhibit this pattern of nonverbal behaviors, they were rated as more charismatic than they were before they were trained.

Speaking in a moderately loud, rapid, expressive, and fluent voice is also associated with dynamism, confidence, competence, and dominance (Apple, Streeter, & Krauss, 1979; Buller & Aune, 1988, 1992). An early study contrasted a conversational speaking style with a dynamic speaking style by having an actor record two versions of a speech (Pearce & Brommel, 1972). For the dynamic version, the actor used a fast speaking rate, with more inflections and higher pitch levels than he used for the conversational version. Students then listened to one of the speeches. Half the time, students were told that the speaker had high credibility; the other half of the time, they were told the student had low credibility. As expected, students rated the speaker as more friendly, trustworthy, and pleasant when he used a conversational style, and more exciting when he used the more expressive speaking style. Interestingly, students were more persuaded by the conversational style when the speaker had been presented as low in credibility, but when the speaker had been presented as high in credibility, the dynamic speaking style was more persuasive. In fact, the speaker was most effective when he was introduced as highly credible and used a dynamic speaking style, and least effective when he was introduced as low in credibility and used a dynamic speaking style. When people who are nonexperts are dynamic, they may come across as "all flash and no substance."

Physical attractiveness also contributes to perceptions of dynamism and charisma, although being good looking is not a prerequisite for dynamism. In other words, attractiveness is only one of many nonverbal cues related to dynamism, and people can be dynamic without being good looking. In one study, physical attractiveness was related to perceptions of both charisma and likability, but nonverbal cues related to expressiveness were better predictors of both of those types of credibility than were appearance (Friedman et al., 1988). Bettinghaus and Cody (1994) suggest that physical attractiveness is a factor in dynamism for at least three reasons. First, people in the United States and other Western cultures have a beauty bias that leads people to stereotype good-looking people as more popular, exciting, and friendlier than average or plain-looking people (see also Chapter 4). Second, because of this beauty bias, people admire and respect people who are physically attractive, which leads people to pay more attention to them. Third, some evidence suggests that because good-looking people receive more positive feedback from others, they develop more self-confidence and optimism, which can translate into a more dynamic style of presentation.

Social Influence

Several nonverbal behaviors are consistently associated with social influence. In fact, many of the same nonverbal cues we discussed in relation to power, dominance, and credibility are also associated with persuasion. For example, nonverbal behaviors such as smiling may prompt perceptions of likability, which enhances persuasive ability. In other cases, a non-smiling face might communicate threat, which leads to

BOX 13.4

Do Voices Persuade?

Do voices persuade? Based on a long tradition of research, the answer is a resounding "yes." Mehrabian and Williams (1969) identified four vocal cues that are both encoded and decoded as persuasive: (1) louder amplitude; (2) more intonation; (3) greater fluency; and (4) faster tempo. Studies of legal presentations and job interviews have confirmed the beneficial effects of loudness and fluency. They revealed that louder, more fluent voices communicate confidence, are more persuasive, and earn more favorable decisions (Hollandsworth, Kazelski, Stevens, & Dressel, 1979; Kimble & Seidle, 1991). Research specifically on nonfluencies (sentence corrections, slips of the tongue, repetitions, vocalized pauses, and stutters) indicated that nonfluent speech results in lower ratings of a speaker's competence (Burgoon, Buller, et al., 1996) and that this reduction in credibility often but not always translated into being less

persuasive. In studies of public speaking, nonfluent speakers produced less attitude change and were rated as less persuasive than fluent speakers (Burgoon, Birk, & Pfau, 1990).

Finally, faster tempos generally produce higher assessments of the speaker's expertise and competence and can be more persuasive (Buller & Aune, 1988, 1992: Buller & Burgoon, 1986; Buller, Le Poire, Aune, & Eloy, 1992). However, there is an upper limit to tempo (around 375 syllables per minute) beyond which judgments of competence plateau or even decrease (Buller & Aune, 1992). In some cases, especially when influence is based on a speaker's character or social attractiveness, matching one's partner's tempo might be the best bet for persuasion. Similarity in tempo appears to enhance perceptions of the persuader's sociability, likability, and general social attractiveness (Buller & Aune, 1988, 1992; Street & Brady, 1982).

---

compliance. Thus, scholars have described credibility, threat, and other dominant behaviors as means for attempting to influence others (e.g., Burgoon et al., 1990).

Segrin (1993) summarized the research on nonverbal communication and compliance-gaining—a specific form of social influence that involves getting someone to comply with a request. Segrin found that people were more likely to comply when the person making the request used direct gaze, engaged in positive and appropriate forms of touch, had a professional, well-groomed appearance, and stood close, but not too close, to them. Other studies show that kinesic and vocal expressiveness (Burgoon et al., 1990), smiling (Liss et al., 1993), and vocal similarity between the person who makes the request and the person who receives the request (Buller & Aune, 1988, 1992; Buller, Le Poire, Aune, & Eloy, 1992) all lead to more compliance. (See Box 13.4 for more on how the voice is related to persuasion.)

Although Segrin's summary is straightforward, the relationship between some of these nonverbal behaviors and persuasion is actually quite complex. Several factors are important in determining how nonverbal cues such as gaze, close proxemic distancing, and smiling affect persuasion. Next, we discuss three of these factors: the legitimacy of the request, the role of expectations and reward level, and how nonverbal information is processed.

The Legitimacy of Requests

Legitimate requests involve clear problems and remedies, such as helping a falling person (Shotland & Johnson, 1978) and asking someone to help with a research project by completing a questionnaire (Hornik & Ellis, 1988). Illegitimate requests include situations such as asking someone to pick up a shopping bag you dropped even though it is clear that you could do it yourself. Several studies have shown that the legitimacy of a request influences how effective nonverbal behaviors are in securing compliance.

For example, gaze has a positive effect on compliance-gaining in many situations that involve an important task or legitimate request. Studies have shown that people are more likely to donate to charity (Linkey & Firestone, 1990), help a disabled person who dropped change (Valentine, 1980), and accept leaflets being distributed on a street corner (Kleinke & Singer, 1979) when the person who needs their help or compliance looks at them. Similarly, people are more likely to influence fellow group members if they use consistently high levels of gaze, especially when they are speaking (Bull & Gibson-Robinson, 1981). Another study involved a simulated trial, with people pretending to be jurors engaging in discussion. The "jurors" who gave the group more eye contact were most likely to be persuasive regarding the verdict (Timney & London, 1973).

However, prolonged gaze or staring can be counterproductive for people who are not perceived to have authority or high status, and in situations in which requests are not seen as legitimate (e.g., Horn, 1974). Kleinke (1980) had requestors use high versus low intimacy (gaze and touch versus no gaze or touch) when making legitimate versus illegitimate requests. Men complied more in the high-intimacy condition when the request was legitimate, but more in the low-intimacy condition when the request was illegitimate. Krapfel (1988) also found that, in general, requests were evaluated as less legitimate if pressed too assertively. For example, if someone stares at you and tells you, "Pick that up. I need help," you are likely to react defensively, because you do not want someone telling you what to do. Gaze can also backfire when a persuader's position is counter to an audience's attitude (Giesen, 1973). Thus, staring and prolonged gaze are most likely to be effective when used by a high-status or powerful person, when a request is considered legitimate, and when receivers agree with the persuader's position. In most cases, gaze is probably most effective when combined with affiliative cues, such as smiling, forward leans, and expressiveness (Burgoon & Bacue, 2003).

Similar findings have emerged for touch and close proxemic distancing. People are more likely to sign a petition or fill out a questionnaire if the requestor touches them (Willis & Hamm, 1980). Specifically, in Willis and Hamm's first study, 81% of the people who were touched signed a petition, compared to only 50% of the people who were not touched. In their second study, 60% of the people who were touched completed a questionnaire, compared to only 40% of those who were not touched. Buller (1987) had individuals stay within a normative distance, move closer, or move farther away from someone who they asked to sign a petition. People were most likely to comply when the requesters moved closer. Similarly, Baron and Bel (1976) found that helping behavior was more likely when the person requesting help violated spatial norms by standing closer than is customary.

Despite these findings, touch and close proxemic distancing can also be perceived as pushy and intimidating, causing discomfort and resulting in less persuasion. A study by Baron (1978) showed that the legitimacy of the request makes a difference. In this study, people who violated spatial norms by getting close to someone were more likely to receive help, but only when their apparent need for assistance was high. When their apparent need for assistance was low, getting close to someone actually decreased the likelihood of receiving help. Research in the area of sales also suggests that some requests are considered illegitimate because they are made prematurely. In other words, a relationship has not yet been forged between the potential client and salesperson. In cases in which a salesperson invades a potential client's space prematurely, clients often feel dominated, uncomfortable, and awkward, which makes it unlikely that a relationship will develop or a sale will be made (Futrell, 1984; Hashimoto & Borders, 2005).

Expectations and Reward Value

Research on *expectancy violations theory* (Burgoon & Hale, 1988) suggests that a person's level of rewardingness may affect how close he or she should stand to others in persuasive situations. According to expectancy violations theory, people hold expectations about how others will and should behave in a given situation. When a sender violates these expectations, receivers try to make sense of the violation by evaluating both the behavior and the person who committed the violation. For example, if someone unexpectedly moves closer to you, your reaction to the change in distance would be influenced by your perceptions of that person. If he or she is rewarding (e.g., attractive, likable, and high-status) you would be more likely to evaluate the move favorably than if he or she is non-rewarding. According to expectancy violations theory, the reward level of the sender influences how people interpret unexpected behavior, especially when behaviors are ambiguous and could be judged as positive or negative.

Research suggests that expectancy violation theory can help explain why various levels of proxemic distancing are effective for different people in various situations. In one of these studies, Burgoon, Stacks, and Burch (1982) had three-person groups discuss a murder trial. Two of the group members were confederates who were helping the researcher. The confederates were either presented as highly rewarding (attractive, well-groomed, and interested in the case, with a prestigious major and previous jury experience) or relatively unrewarding (physically unattractive, not interested in the case, with an undisclosed major and no previous jury experience). During each group interaction, one of the confederates violated distance norms by moving either closer to or farther away from the participant. The other confederate stayed within a normative distance. The highly rewarding confederates were most persuasive when they violated proxemic norms, especially at far distances. The non-rewarding confederates were most persuasive when they stayed within proxemic norms.

A second series of studies by Burgoon and Aho (1982) considered whether distance affects a salesperson's communication and willingness to comply with a request to use the telephone. Student experimenters approached salespeople and asked for help with a purchase or interviewed them about consumer behavior. Some experimenters presented themselves as rewarding by saying they were interested in buying a big-ticket item, dressing more formally and attractively, or verbally indicating their expertise. Other experimenters presented themselves as relatively unrewarding by saying they were interested in buying an inexpensive item, dressing as if lower in status, or indicating that they lacked expertise. The experimenters also manipulated proxemic distancing. Not surprisingly, salespeople smiled more at, spent more time with, and showed greater interest in the students who projected a more rewarding image. Distance also played a role, with salespeople communicating especially high levels of interest and talking louder with rewarding students who violated distance norms by moving farther away. Salespeople also spoke louder when non-rewarding students increased proxemic distances, but rather than showing increased interest, they showed increased tension.

A more recent study examined how proxemic distancing influences perceptions of salespersons (Hashimoto & Borders, 2005). In this study, students were shown black-and-white service advertisements of salespeople interacting with clients at hotels. For each of three scenes, the salesperson and client were shown interacting at one of three distances: intimate (closer than normal), personal (normative), and social (farther than normal). The results from this study suggest that people do indeed evaluate salespeople differently based on conversational distance, at least as depicted in pictures. Students rated the salespeople as most competent, professional, and confident when they were shown interacting at the social (farthest) distance, followed by the intimate (close) distance. Perceptions of competence were lowest at the personal distance. For perceptions of honesty, likability, friendliness, and enthusiasm, salespeople were rated highest at the intimate distance. However, at the intimate distance, people were also more likely to rate salespeople as pushy and anxious.

Hashimoto and Borders (2005) concluded that "intimate distances will enhance whatever personality traits the buyer already portrays" (p. 59). If a friendly looking salesperson moves in close, she or he will be seen as even friendlier. An anxious salesperson, however, will look even more anxious at an intimate distance. These findings are consistent with the principles guiding expectancy violations theory, in that rewarding (or friendly looking) salespeople can enhance their image by violating expectations, whereas non-rewarding (or in this case, anxious-looking) salespeople are better off staying with the norms. This study also suggests that when it comes to projecting a competent image, salespeople who violate norms by standing either closer or farther from the client than normal are evaluated more favorably. Box 13.5 lists other tips for using nonverbal communication effectively as a salesperson or customer service representative.

Information Processing: Attention, Distraction, and Elaboration

One reason expectancy violations can promote persuasion is that they capture the receiver's attention and provide her or him with new information to process and evaluate. Since the 1950s, researchers have acknowledged that gaining a receiver's

BOX 13.5

Tips for Effective Nonverbal Communication During Employee-Customer Interactions

In their article on "The Role of Nonverbal Communication in Service Encounters," Professors D. S. Sundaram and Cynthia Webster (2000) offer the following propositions that contain advice for using nonverbal communication effectively when providing service to customers:

- Smiling, light laughter, and frequent eye contact enhance perceptions of friendliness and courtesy.
- Head nodding enhances perceptions of empathy, courtesy, and trust.
- Frequent eye contact enhances perceptions of general credibility.
- Speaking relatively slow, in a low pitch, with moderate pauses and less inflection, enhances customers' perceptions of friendliness.

- Speaking relatively quickly, in a high pitch, with vocal intensity and higher inflection, enhances perceptions of competence, but reduces perceptions of friendliness.
- Using appropriate forms of touch can enhance perceptions of friendliness and empathy.
- Physical attractiveness enhances perceptions of friendliness, competence, and overall credibility.
- Wearing cool colors such as green and blue reinforces customers' perceptions of friendliness, whereas wearing warm colors such as red or yellow, and dark colors, such as black and navy, reinforces perceptions of dominance.

---

attention is the first step toward persuasion (Hovland et al., 1953). In one of the first systematic investigations of persuasive processes, Hovland and his colleagues identified attention, comprehension, yielding, retention, and action as the four sequential processes that prompt enduring changes in beliefs, attitudes, and behaviors.

Many nonverbal behaviors can be used to get attention. For example, immediacy behaviors, such as smiling, standing close to someone, and looking someone straight in the eye are often arousing, leading to increased attention (Andersen, 1985). People also pay more attention to attractive individuals than unattractive or average-looking people (see Chapter 4). Vocal expressiveness and varied tempo can also help secure and maintain attention, leading to more comprehension of a message (Glasgow, 1952; MacLachlan & Siegel, 1980). In the MacLachlan and Siegel study, students who watched a sped-up version of the television news show *60 Minutes* were better able to recall the content of the program two days later than if they had watched the normal version.

Importantly, however, some of these same nonverbal cues can be distracting, which can, in some cases, lead to less persuasion. If someone smiles at you and touches you, your increased arousal could distract you from the message. In some cases, high levels of nonverbal immediacy can produce too much arousal, leading to flight-or-fight responses, such as withdrawal or defensiveness (Andersen, 1992). Similarly, if speaking tempo is too fast, it becomes distracting and any persuasive advantage associated with faster speech is lost (Woodall & Burgoon, 1983). A study by Buller (1986) provided a summary of the relationship between distraction and persuasion. Buller's analysis showed that certain kinds of distractions, such as noise and nonfluencies, hurt a receiver's ability to pay attention and comprehend a message. Distractions that are relevant to one's judgment of a sender, such as his or her level of attractiveness or credibility, can either enhance or impede persuasion. Senders who were judged as attractive or credible benefited from the receiver being distracted by their personal characteristics; however, senders who were judged as low in attractiveness or credibility had a difficult time persuading others, regardless of the validity of their arguments.

Petty and Cacioppo's (1986) *elaboration likelihood model of persuasion* provides a related explanation for how nonverbal cues are processed. This model was advanced to explain better the perceptual and cognitive processes related to social influence. *Elaboration* refers to how much thinking goes into making persuasion decisions. *Likelihood* refers to the probability that persuasion will take place. A central tenet of this model is that people can process persuasive information through a central or peripheral route. The *central route* involves "careful and thoughtful consideration of the true merits of the information presented" (Petty & Cacioppo, 1986, p. 3). People are most likely to process information through the central route when they perceive the message to be relevant and are both capable and motivated to put effort into understanding and evaluating the message. However, people are not always motivated or capable of attending to and processing information. Sometimes persuasive messages are not personally relevant; other times people have a limited amount of time to make a decision. In these cases, people are more likely to process information through the *peripheral route,* which involves focusing on "some simple cue in the persuasion context" such as the attractiveness of a sender (Petty & Cacioppo, 1986, p. 3).

Nonverbal cues can be processed centrally, such as when a receiver carefully scrutinizes a sender's nonverbal communication to look for clues of deception, or when the voices and gestures of two political candidates or two job applicants are carefully compared and contrasted (Trent, Short-Thompson, Mongeau, Nusz, & Trent, 2001). In many cases, however, nonverbal cues are processed peripherally (Kopacz, 2006). Advertisers often uses nonverbal cues such as an attractive appearance, a loud voice, laughing, or other emotional displays to try to get attention and secure positive attitudes toward products quickly. When people are viewing a 30- or 60-second commercial, there is not much time to process information in the central route, so people usually make sense of the information quickly. Kopacz (2006) also suggests that the elaboration likelihood model can help explain why physical appearance, a charismatic speaking style, and other nonverbal cues play critical roles in political elections. Most people do not spend a lot of time listening to debates or reading about candidates' positions on issues; instead they rely on peripheral cues. Petty and Wegener (1998) also noted that nonverbal cues may activate heuristic reasoning. For example, if a candidate is wearing professional dress, the heuristic rule associates this type of clothing with competence. "By functioning as peripheral cues, nonverbal behaviors may inform judgments through affective responses, for instance, a candidate's speaking tone may convey a sense of warmth or an air of superiority, arousing distinct emotions in the listeners" (Kopacz, 2006, p. 6).

Summary

Powerfulness-powerlessness and dominance-submission are fundamental components underlying communication. Principles of space and access, centrality, elevation, prerogative, interactional control, and intimidation/threat help explain why certain nonverbal cues are perceived as powerful or dominant. Credibility can also foster impressions of power and pave the way for persuasion. Scholars have identified five facets of credibility: (1) competence and authority; (2) character and trustworthiness; (3) composure and poise; (4) likability; and (5) dynamism or charisma. Physical appearance cues, such as uniforms and formal dress, are associated with authority. People are rated as more trustworthy and likable when they use eye contact, are vocally and facially pleasant, and speak in a conversational style. Composure and poise are conveyed through behaviors showing pleasantness, fluency, and a lack of anxiety.

Finally, dynamic or charismatic individuals communicate energy, enthusiasm, expressiveness, and self-confidence. Many of the same nonverbal behaviors that are related to power and credibility are also related to social influence. These include a well groomed appearance, kinesic and vocal expressiveness, smiling, appropriate forms of touch, and vocal similarity. Several factors affect whether various nonverbal behaviors are successful in persuading others. These factors include how legitimate a request is, how expected a behavior was, and how the information was processed. After reading this chapter, it should be apparent that there is a fine line between power that is gained through intimidation, and power that is gained through social skill. People who gain power through the use of skilled nonverbal communication are usually more influential over time than those who use intimidation or threat.

SUGGESTED READINGS

Aguinis, H., Simonsen, M. M., & Pierce, C. A. (1998). Effects of nonverbal behavior on perceptions of power bases. *Journal of Social Psychology, 138,* 455–469.

Andersen, P. A. (2008). Positions of power: Nonverbal influence in organizational communication. In L. K. Guerrero & M. L. Hecht (Eds.), *The nonverbal communication reader: Classic and contemporary readings* (3rd ed., pp. 450–467). Long Grove, IL: Waveland Press.

Burgoon, J. K., Segrin, C., & Dunbar, N. E. (2002). Nonverbal communication and social influence. In J. P. Dillard & M. Pfau (Eds.), *The persuasion handbook: Developments in theory and practice* (pp. 445–473). Thousand Oaks, CA: Sage.

Dunbar, N. E., & Burgoon, J. K. (2005). Perceptions of power and dominance in interpersonal encounters. *Journal of Social and Personal Relationships, 22,* 207–233.

Ellyson, S. L., & Dovidio, J. F. (1985). Power, dominance, and nonverbal behavior: Basic concepts and issues. In S. L. Ellyson & J. F. Dovidio (Eds.), *Power, dominance, and nonverbal behavior* (pp. 1–27). New York: Springer-Verlag.

Hall, J. A., Coats, E., & Smith LeBeau, L. (2005). Nonverbal behavior and the vertical dimen-sion of social relations: A meta-analysis. *Psychological Bulletin, 131,* 898–924.

Henley, N. M. (1995). Body politics revisited: What do we know today? In P. J. Kalbfleisch & M. J. Cody (Eds.), *Gender, power, and communication in human relationships* (pp. 27–61). Hillsdale, NJ: Lawrence Erlbaum Associates.

Hubbard, A. S. E., Tsuiji, A. A., Williams, C., & Seatriz, V. (2003). Effects of touch on gratuities received in same-gender and cross-gender dyads. *Journal of Applied Social Psychology, 33,* 2427–2438.

Mast, M. S., & Hall, J. A. (2004). Who is the boss and who is not? Accuracy of judging status. *Journal of Nonverbal Behavior, 28,* 145–165.

Peck, J., & Wiggins, J. (2006). It just feels good: Customers' affective response to touch and its influence on persuasion. *Journal of Marketing, 70,* 56–69.

Schmid Mast, M. (2002). Dominance as expressed and inferred through speaking time: A meta-analysis. *Human Communication Research, 28,* 420–450.

Segrin, C. (1993). The effects of nonverbal behavior on outcomes of compliance-gaining attempts. *Communication Studies, 44,* 169–187.

14 Managing Conversations

When people interact, their behaviors intertwine as do the sounds from different instruments in a band.

—Bernieri & Rosenthal (1991, p. 404)

Imagine listening to an orchestra warming up before a performance. You're likely to hear cellos, clarinets, drums, trombones, cymbals, and other instruments, each producing sounds in their own rhythm and time. When the conductor takes the stage and waves the first downbeat of her baton, however, all the sounds converge around a unified purpose. No longer do you hear individual trumpets or piccolos; instead, you hear the coordinated sound of the orchestra. As Bernieri and Rosenthal's quotation suggests, people's interactions are also more than the sum of their parts. Like the music of the orchestra depicted in Photo 14.1, they represent a convergence of purpose in which there is not simply you and me, but *us*. As you might guess, managing these interactions requires a broad array of skills. And, as we'll see in this chapter, many of these skills are nonverbal in nature.

Setting the Stage for Interaction

Before a word is ever uttered, nonverbal cues are setting the stage for interaction. They are framing what is expected and how conversations will proceed. For many people, it is a significant self-revelation that people behave differently in various

PHOTO 14.1 *Just as individual sounds converge in an orchestra, people's conversational behaviors converge to create coordinated interaction.*

situations. Depending on the situation in which we find ourselves, we may adjust how, with whom, and about what we communicate. In many situations, we merely respond to contingencies that are presented to us. We enter a doctor's examining room and passively accept the solitary wait, the uncomfortable seating on an examining table, and the impersonal probing of our body by the physician. In other situations, we take control of various aspects of the social situation to achieve our own goals. When we invite guests for dinner, we may make decisions about such nonverbal features as what time they should arrive, where they should congregate before the meal, whether the meal is to be formal or informal, what seating arrangement at the dinner table will enhance conversation, and what attire guests should be told is appropriate. These decisions are not trivial, because they can affect how enjoyable the evening turns out to be. Failure to provide sufficient structure may result in immense discomfort for the friend who arrives promptly, dressed in suit and tie for a formal dinner party, only to find the other guests arriving an hour later, dressed in jeans for a casual outdoor barbecue.

The nonverbal features that frame and regulate interactions elicit behavior largely outside of people's conscious awareness. That is, people respond to them in relatively passive, subconscious ways. Although most of these nonverbal features can also be used deliberately to structure a situation to accomplish some instrumental goal, for the moment our interest lies primarily in those elusive background elements of which we are at once consciously unaware and yet unconsciously, profoundly aware. Such features, like a puppet's strings, appear to invisibly control our actions but are readily detectable if we choose to look closely.

Aspects of the Framing Process

Nonverbal code elements function to frame interactions in at least three ways. First, *some nonverbal elements control the occurrence of interaction*. They affect with whom we interact, when, and how often. They can control whether interaction even takes place.

Second, *nonverbal cues set expectations for unfamiliar situations*. They often "telegraph" upcoming interactions by suggesting what a given situation will be like. Environmental designs, for example, evolve out of a culture's customs and expectations and therefore evoke anticipations of what behaviors will be exhibited in a previously unencountered setting. Our ability to prepare for new interactions and situations is strongly based on nonverbal codes.

Third, *nonverbal elements set the stage for current interactions*. As an episode unfolds, nonverbal elements embedded in the situation provide elaboration of its definition. They may prompt certain kinds of behavior, identify or clarify role relationships among interactants, and imply rules for behavior (Goffman, 1967, 1974). In so doing, the totality of situational features, including the nonverbal cues that are present, creates a *frame of reference* or lens through which to see and understand a situation, providing structure for the interaction that occurs. Moreover, when people arrive at an understanding of what the situation is, they typically conform in a habitual and relatively mindless fashion to the behavioral routines associated with it. This further reinforces the prevailing definition of the situation.

Erickson and Shultz (1982) refer to this process of cuing the appropriate behavioral programs as *telling the context*:

> People of varying ages and cultural backgrounds all seem to be actively engaged as they interact, telling one another what is happening as it is happening. The particular ways this telling is done—what signals are used and how the signals are employed and interpreted by the interactional partners—may vary developmentally across the life cycle and may also vary from one culture to another. But some ways of telling the context seem to be present in all instances of face-to-face interaction among humans. People seem to use these ways to keep one another on track, to maintain in the conduct of interaction what musicians call "ensemble" in the playing of music. (p. 71)

Making Connections

One of the chief ways that nonverbal behaviors structure interaction is by determining whether interaction will occur at all. Three nonverbal signals are posited to be especially influential in determining if and how much people will interact: propinquity, gaze, and physical attractiveness.

Propinquity. One of the more intriguing discoveries of social scientists is just how much pressure *propinquity*, or geographic proximity, exerts on people to interact (Mehrabian & Diamond, 1971). Propinquity controls the opportunities for interaction. Environments can facilitate communication by placing people in relatively close proximity when engaged in similar activities. Moreover, proximity encourages interaction. You may have noticed your own urge to exchange pleasantries with someone who shares a bus seat or sauna with you. Workers in businesses and medical offices who are seated within 12 feet of each other purportedly seek interaction (Goffman, 1963a). The happenstance of propinquity often leads to communication.

Several studies conducted in the 1940s, 1950s, and 1960s (e.g., Byrne, 1961; Festinger, Schachter, & Back, 1950; Kennedy, 1943) found that people in residences, classrooms, or naval bunk quarters were much more likely to interact, develop friendships, and even marry those who were physically closest to them. In an apartment building, those who lived adjacent to one another, resided on the same hall, or shared the same elevator or stairwell were far more likely to become acquainted than those who lived on different floors. The likelihood of interacting was directly proportional to the physical and psychological distance between dwellings. A study of Maryland police trainees (cited in Wegner & Vallacher, 1977) similarly found that propinquity fosters interaction and friendship. The trainees were assigned classroom seats and living quarters alphabetically, so that those whose names were closest together in the alphabet sat and lived together. After six weeks of training, "the Andersons and Bakers preferred each other to the Youngs and Zimmermans" (p. 201).

Mann (1959) attempted to determine if increased contact between people could decrease racial prejudice. Black and white students were placed in leaderless groups (which gave everyone equal status) and interacted with one another for a three-week period. Afterward, students were asked to rank-order those whom they would like to have as continuing friends. Their choices indicated that interracial exposure reduced their tendency to use race as a criterion for choosing friends. In other words, the sheer force of physical proximity and the interaction it fostered broke down some racial prejudices. Such findings led scientists (e.g., Festinger, 1951) to encourage architects and planners to take greater account of propinquity when planning and anticipating the social consequences of various housing developments and residential designs.

One reason that proximity promotes interaction is that it connotes belonging: "Our expectancies about proximity—called *spatial schemata*—are closely related to our belong schemas" (Wegner & Vallacher, 1977). We use spatial relationships to infer with whom we are affiliated and to signal to others our belonging expectancies. The result is that we tend to feel we "belong" with those close to us and use communication to express that bond.

Of course, the probability of interacting with others need not be a chance occurrence. By intentionally increasing or decreasing physical distance, people can control their own or others' interaction availability. The use of such privacy-gaining mechanisms as fences, walls, and hedges can override the power of propinquity. Conversely, the absence of territorial markers or an "open door" policy in an office may promote the kinds of accidental contacts that open communication channels. Men and women who are successful at picking someone up in a singles bar rely in part on others feeling the obligation to speak to them when at close range. In these ways, it is possible to structure the communication situation actively rather than passively react to it.

Gaze.   In most unfocused social situations, where there is no intention to carry on a conversation, the rule is to engage in *civil inattention*. It is impolite to stare at strangers in a restaurant or department store. Although it is often unavoidable to look briefly at passersby on the street, this usually occurs while at a distance and is followed by "casting the eyes down as the other passes—a kind of dimming of lights" (Goffman, 1963a, p. 84). The mere act of making eye contact, then, creates a temporary union between people and serves as an invitation to interact.

Physical Attractiveness.   We have noted elsewhere that beauty may be only skin deep, but physical attractiveness often influences whom we choose to approach or avoid. The fact that attractive people are often viewed as more curious, complex, outspoken, assertive, flexible, candid, amiable, happy, active, confident, and perceptive than unattractive people (Miller, 1970) suggests we may be more willing to interact with attractive strangers because we attribute appealing characteristics to them.

More direct evidence comes from the first-ever computer dating studies conducted in the 1970s (Berscheid & Walster, 1974) in which experimenters paired subjects with members of the opposite sex and asked them to spend 30 minutes getting acquainted over a soda at the student union. Afterward, students evaluated their dates. Results showed that students were much more attracted to their date if the date was physically attractive (both as rated by the partner and the experimenters). A follow-up study at the end of the semester also revealed that students were more inclined to see their partner again if the partner was hand-some or pretty. Thus, physical attractiveness may affect not only with whom we interact but also the likelihood and amount of subsequent contact.

In Chapters 3 and 12, we noted the biological bases for many courtship prac-tices. The importance of physical attractiveness in approach-avoidance decisions is strongly linked to sexual attraction and the mating process. It is natural for men and women to size up potential partners on physical appeal. It may be, however, that the sizing-up process works overtime, extending to social interactions that do not have sexual undercurrents. It would be interesting to study whether physical attractiveness governs same-sex interactions to the same extent that it does oppo-site-sex relations.

Situation and Context

The term *situation* probably has intuitive meaning for you, but what is really meant by it? Although it has been treated as synonymous with other terms that range from the microscopic (e.g., small sequences of events known as episodes) to the macroscopic (e.g., physical settings or types of occasions), most scholars see situations as some intermediate combination of physical, temporal, and psycho-logical frames of reference tied to particular occasions. According to Furnham and Argyle (1981), a situation includes:

- *The elements of behavior used.* These are the specific verbal utterances and non-verbal behaviors accompanying the situation.
- *The goals or motivations of the participants.* For example, is this a learning, a sell-ing, or a socializing situation?
- *The rules of behavior.* The rules for carrying on a dinner party differ from those for a classroom lecture, for instance.
- *The roles different people must play.* A committee chair plays a different role and follows different rules than the secretary of that committee.
- *The physical setting and equipment.* A classroom with a chalkboard, overhead projector, and straight row seating creates a different situation than a living room with overstuffed chairs and a coffee table.
- *Cognitive concepts associated with the situation.* Dominance may be relevant to meetings and to people fulfilling a leadership role; supportiveness may be relevant to a confidential conversation with a troubled friend.
- *Relevant social skills.* Providing leadership invokes a different set of skills, for example, than does comforting someone over a personal loss.

Situation, then, refers to an overall gestalt that is the sum of all the above factors. This is also often what is meant by "context." To talk of nonverbal behav-ior in context is to talk about how such factors as setting, role expectations, and rules governing the situation affect what nonverbal behaviors are enacted. In turn, the nonverbal behaviors establish what the context is by signaling to those present what the definition of the situation is. Because the nonverbal cues work in concert and so much redundancy is built in across codes, we are able to

Fright

Sensed confinement. An apparent trap. No points of orientation. No means by which to judge position or scale. Hidden areas and spaces. Possibilities for surprise. Sloping, twisted, or broken planes. Illogical, unstable forms. Slippery, hazardous base plane. Danger. Unprotected voids. Sharp, protruding elements. Contorted spaces. The unfamiliar. The shocking. The startling.

Gaiety

Free spaces. Smooth, flowing forms and patterns. Looping, tumbling, swirling motion accommodated. Movement and rhythm expressed in structure. Lack of restrictions. Forms, colors, and symbols that appeal to emotion rather than intellect. Temporal. Casual. Lack of restraint. Pretense is acceptable. The fanciful is applauded. Warm, bright colors. Exuberant or lilting sound.

Spiritual awe

Overwhelming scale that transcends normal human experience and submerges one in a vast well of space. Soaring forms in contrast with low horizontal forms. A volume so contrived as to hold man transfixed on a broad base plane and lift his eye and mind high along the vertical. Orientation upward to or beyond some symbol of the infinite.

Tension

Unstable forms. Split composition. Illogical complexities. Wide range of values. Clash of colors. Intense colors without relief. Visual imbalance about a line or point. No point at which the eye can rest. Hard, rough, or jagged surfaces. Unfamiliar elements. Harsh, binding, or quavering light. Uncomfortable temperatures in any range. Piercing, jangling sound.

FIGURE 14.1   Sampling of environmental features that can create various moods

instantly and effortlessly determine what kind of situation is presenting itself and what our own behavioral obligations are. Take, for example, Simonds's (1961) sample environmental designs, shown in Figure 14.1. Through a combination of volume of space, linear perspective, materials, artifacts, lighting, color, and sound, radically different moods and types of interaction are created.

The Case of Privacy

The definitions of privacy are quite varied, but most stress that privacy includes the ability to exert control over self, objects, spaces, information, and behavior, to regulate interactions with others, and to deny unwanted access to or influence by others (Bok, 1982). Thus, privacy may pertain to an individual, dyad, or group. Four major types or *dimensions of privacy* are physical, social, psychological, and informational (Burgoon, 1982). *Physical privacy* refers to the degree to which an

Relaxation

Simplicity. Volume may vary in size from the intimate to the infinite. Fitness. Familiar objects and materials. Flowing lines. Curvilinear forms and spaces. Evident structural stability. Horizontality. Agreeable textures. Pleasant and comfortable shapes. Soft light. Soothing sound. Volume infused with quiet colors—whites, grays, blues, greens.

Sensuous love

Complete privacy. Inward orientation of room. Subject the focal point. Intimate scale. Low ceiling. Horizontal planes. Fluid lines. Soft, rounded forms. Juxtaposition of angles and curves. Delicate fabrics. Voluptuous and yielding surfaces. Exotic elements and scents. Soft rosy pink to golden light. Pulsating, titillating music.

Contemplation

Scale is not important since the subject will withdraw into his own sensed well of consciousness. The total space may be mild and unpretentious or immense and richly ornate—so long as the structural forms are not insistent. No insinuating elements. No distractions of sharp contrast. Symbols, if used, must relate to subject of contemplation. Soft, diffused light.

FIGURE 14.1 *(Continued)*

individual, dyad, or group is physically accessible or inaccessible to others (Kira, 1966). Physical privacy brings freedom from surveillance, overcrowding, overstimulation, and intrusion on one's "body buffer zone." The more nonverbal sensory channels (e.g., sight, sound, touch, smell) through which one is accessible to others, the less privacy he or she presumably has.

Social privacy refers to the ability of individuals, dyads, and groups to control the who, when, and where of communication. Individuals need to keep the number of social encounters to a reasonable number so that they can maximize gratifications and minimize conflicts and annoyances. When the number of social contacts becomes excessive, the amount of stimulation "overloads" the system, creating stress and a desire to withdraw. At the dyadic or small group level, social privacy becomes a means for facilitating intimacy within the relationship while inhibiting social overtures from others. A dating couple, for example, displays courtship behaviors that foster togetherness while simultaneously alerting others that their company is unwelcome.

Psychological privacy refers to the ability to control affective and cognitive inputs and outputs so as to prevent intrusions on one's intellectual and emotional "private property." On the input side, psychological privacy means a person is free to think, formulate attitudes, hold beliefs and values, develop an individual identity, engage in emotional catharsis, assimilate new experiences, and make plans without interference, undue influence, or distraction from others. On the output side, it means determining with whom and under what circumstances one will share thoughts and feelings, disclose intimate or secret information about the self, offer emotional support, and seek advice.

Finally, *informational privacy* refers to the right to determine how, when, and to what extent personal data are released to others. It is grounded in legalistic concerns such as protections over the gathering, computerization, and dissemination of information about private citizens. Informational privacy differs from psychological privacy in that it is less under personal control (and also not as likely to be managed through nonverbal communication).

Although verbal behavior also plays a significant role in establishing or restoring privacy, our interest here is in how privacy can be achieved through managing nonverbal behaviors. Here we consider some specific features, by code.

Environment and Artifacts.   We already know that environments can vary along a general *sociofugal-sociopetal* continuum (Osmond, 1957). Sociofugal environments thrust people apart, while sociopetal ones bring them together and encourage interaction. Architectural design can further foster physical privacy by creating barriers (walls, fences, partitions, gated parking lots) and insulation that protect the individual from visual, auditory, olfactory, and bodily intrusions (Derlega & Chaikin, 1977). Architectural design may make a space seem forbidding or welcoming. Through the imposition of distance and gatekeepers, buildings can make access to a locale's occupants difficult. Corporate executives often have offices in largely impenetrable spaces. They may be buffered by several stories, winding corridors, private elevators, multiple secretarial offices or desks, and personal receptionists that separate them from the public and from subordinates.

The design of fixed-feature space also signals implicitly whether spaces are private or semi-public by the number of enclosures and the degree of functional differentiation associated with them. The design of most American homes, for example, creates separate spaces for sleeping, bathing, elimination and personal hygiene, cooking, and so forth. The more spatial divisions in a setting and the smaller the volume of space in each, the greater the sense of physical and psychological privacy and social intimacy. Large, open spaces create a feeling of vulnerability and tend to define a situation as more public. Greater differentiation of the functions of each space also results in some spaces such as bedrooms and bathrooms being defined as highly private, intimate locales (Edney, 1976; Goffman, 1963a).

Floor plans and arrangements of other semifixed features such as furniture may also create sociofugal or sociopetal environments (Osmond, 1957). Institutional arrangements of benches along a wall, church pews, and rows of rigid, connected seats in airports inhibit interaction, whereas small conversational groupings of chairs facing each other in a home or hotel lobby encourage interaction. The arrangement therefore signals whether social encounters are permissible and expected. Doors are particularly significant barriers in our everyday experience. Schwartz (1968) referred to doors as "a human event of significance equal to the discovery of fire" because they can be used deliberately and selectively to regulate physical and social intrusion. Those who trespass when a door is closed are in some ways violating our selfhood because their entry implies we have lost control of our territory.

Furnishings provide additional barriers and insulation in such forms as drapes, blinds, lamps, room dividers, bookshelves, and white noise from air conditioners or radios. These can carve settings into smaller spaces, block visual and auditory access, and cushion noise. Personal artifacts are a common means of demarcating a particular place as someone's territory. Having clearly defined territory affords its occupants not only physical protection but also the ability to regulate social interaction, reduce anonymity, create a sense of personal identity, and promote group identity and bonding (Altman & Chemers, 1980). Any parent of teenagers knows the great lengths to which they will go to establish privacy, often using signs, padlocks, and other barriers to prevent intrusion by curious siblings and parents. Patterson (1978) found that when elderly people used such territorial markers as "no trespassing" signs, welcome mats, and electronic surveillance devices, they had less fear of assault and property loss. Conversely, students who use fewer decorations such as posters, pictures, and mementos to personalize a dorm room are less likely to remain in school (Vinsel, Brown, Altman, & Foss, 1980). This suggests that territorial markers are indicative of one's sense of belonging and security in an environment.

Proxemics and Haptics. How people space themselves within an environment and the amount of touching that is present or absent can likewise define a situation as private or public. Recall that Hall's (1973) distance categories range from intimate (0–18") to public (12' and beyond). Intimate distances tend to correspond to situations that are regarded as private. As conversational distance increases, so does the perception of the situation as more public. By the same token, frequent touch and touches to more "intimate" body regions are more likely to occur in private contexts and therefore to define those situations as private (Rosenfeld, Kartus, & Ray, 1976). We are often surprised and offended by a couple's prolonged fondling and kissing in public precisely because such behavior is "out of place" in a nonprivate setting.

A number of other proxemic behaviors may color a situation as one of physical, social, or psychological privacy. In libraries and other public settings, people who want privacy select seating positions at tables that are farther from others, permit greater surveillance of the entrances, and reduce their own vulnerability to surveillance (Sommer, 1970). When we enter a library or museum, we recognize the relatively private quality of what is otherwise a "public" setting and respond with appropriately quiet, unobtrusive behavior. We use nonimmediacy behaviors such as indirect body orientation, gaze avoidance, and extreme sideways or backward lean to signal our desire for individual privacy. When people feel threatened physically or psychologically, or when the amount of social involvement is excessive, they may attempt to compensate by increasing nonimmediacy (which increases psychological distance), plus they may erect body and artifact barriers (Argyle & Dean, 1965; Sundstrom & Sundstrom, 1977). If these fail, they may resort to flight, or rarely, to fight (Smith & Knowles, 1979). In couples, however, people may face each other directly or sit side by side to signal they want social and physical privacy from others (Bond & Shiraishi, 1974).

BOX 14.1
Prison Codes

Within the prison setting, where verbal communication is tightly controlled, an awareness and sensitivity to all types of nonverbal messages is vital to successful functioning. One may communicate invasion of privacy and rudeness by looking into another's cell without invitation. This is especially true if it occurs on a range other than one's own. When in the yard or other open space, someone crossing the 8- to 10-foot barrier is perceived as trespassing. In closed quarters, depending on the need for privacy, the distance is reduced to 2 or 3 feet. The outer limits become important when approached from the rear or when an approach is combined with direct constant eye contact. Conversational distance between two inmates is approximately 2 feet; between an inmate and a guard it increases to 3 feet. Invasion of boundaries communicates disrespect and violation of one's person.

Although one's cell is the only claim to privacy available, some inmates or groups of inmates stake out rights to seats in the auditorium and cafeteria. New inmates learn very quickly that violation of such space is strongly dealt with. When the auditorium is filled, there is usually a seat between every two men. An inmate would rather stand in the back than sit down right beside a stranger.

Even though most of the time spent in the cell is behind locked doors, the individual cell is perceived as an extension of one's self. It is the only place where an inmate may even begin to relax. Locked doors keep one inside, but they also keep others out. Any uninvited intrusion into the cell is considered a direct assault. Only guards have continual access, and as long as their visits fall into expected patterns, the feeling of relaxation is not disturbed.

Source: Ramsey, 1976, pp. 39, 43–44.

Finally, people may use a proxemic shift (Erickson, 1975) to signal their desire to end an episode within an encounter. If, for example, people find a discussion becoming embarrassing or too invasive of their psychological privacy and informational privacy, they may shift their posture away from another person as a cue that they are ready to change the subject. The use of these proxemic as well as artifactual elements to make privacy statements is nowhere more evident than in prison, as Box 14.1 illustrates.

Chronemics.   There are at least three ways time can be manipulated to regulate privacy. One is to *segregate use of a particular setting by time*. In the animal kingdom, different species may have territories that overlap but use the commonly held space at different times (Leyhausen, 1971). With humans, this may take the form of maximizing privacy in an otherwise heavily trafficked area by using it at times when one expects other people to be absent. A prime example is coordinating the use of a solitary bathroom in a large household when guests come to visit. Those who want maximum privacy may choose to use the bathroom either before others awaken or after they retire to bed.

A second way is by *using interactional or public territories during non-peak hours.* A person who truly wants solitude may seek out a church sanctuary during the week, when it is not in use. A dating couple may seek out a secluded corner of a public park late at night when there is little traffic. Early risers or late-night workers may consciously alter their work schedule to avoid rush–hour traffic.

Finally, a setting may be *assigned different functions by time*. In many parts of the world and in lower socioeconomic households, what is the living room during the day may become a bedroom at night. In dormitories, fraternities, and sororities, a common room may be designated as a study room during certain hours and a place for entertaining guests during other hours. Thus, the kinds of social interactions that are permissible vary by time. When the time-space pattern for a setting affords inadequate privacy, people may cope by changing schedules or making more explicit rules about what functions are acceptable at what time. We know of a graduate student who became so annoyed by his office mate's public displays of affection with a girlfriend that he began coming to his office late in the day and working until the middle of the night. Both students saw the office as a private place, but the use of it for intimate behavior by one office mate intruded on the felt privacy of the other. The radical change in schedule should have been a tip-off to the office mate that something was awry.

Kinesics and Vocalics. A wide variety of facial, body, and vocal behaviors can be used not only as relational messages but also as signals of how private or public the situation is viewed by the participants. Especially important are turf defense and exclusion cues. These include (1) threat displays such as staring or tongue showing, (2) dominance displays such as expansive postures and loud voices, (3) body blocks and face covering, (4) emblems such as "go away" that express unapproachability, (5) dyadic postures and orientations that create a closed unit, (6) silences, (7) gaze aversion or reduced facial regard, and (8) other forms of reduced immediacy (Burgoon, 1982; Burgoon et al., 1989).

Another sign that a situation is being viewed as private is people "letting down their mask" and violating normal social rules for appropriate conduct. Goffman (1959), in his self-presentational approach to human interaction, distinguished between frontstage and backstage behavior. When you are "frontstage," your conduct conforms to the various roles you are performing for your audience. When you are "backstage," you are free to drop your role, blow off steam, slouch in furniture, and commit socially taboo behaviors such as tugging at underwear or picking your nose, among other things (see also Chapter 10). When people engage in backstage behavior, it often signifies that they view the situation as a private one.

Physical Appearance and Attire. Finally, physical appearance may signal individual or group privacy. At the individual level, clothing offers physical insulation that carries psychological connotations: In psychiatric settings it has been recognized that more layers of clothing symbolize a closing-off of self from others and a greater desire for psychological privacy. Clothing may also establish anonymity, which minimizes self-identity but contributes to individual psychological privacy. Goffman (1961) has observed that institutions strip people of individual identities by issuing regulation attire, giving standard haircuts and forbidding facial hair, and enforcing restrictions on other aspects of personal grooming. The military and prisons rely on the same kinds of uniformity in appearance to create mass rather than individual identities. Organizations such as the Ku Klux Klan and militia groups also achieve individual anonymity and hence privacy through the use of identical garb.

Conversely, clothing may establish one's identity and status, which affect how much social and physical privacy the individual is accorded (Altman, 1975). Occupational uniforms and other role-related dress denote levels of social status. As status increases, approachability decreases. Military uniforms, police uniforms, business suits, or surgical scrubs are far less likely to invite approach than are jeans or a factory apron. Veils worn by women in the Middle East cue strangers that they are not to be spoken to, whereas the near-nudity of beach attire in the West invites conversation and possibly physical contact.

This detailed analysis of privacy is meant to be illustrative of how nonverbal patterns define and structure interaction. Other dimensions of situations, such as their dominance, informality, or competitiveness, can be examined in a similar fashion. The important point is that nonverbal codes and cues—especially those that are relatively stable during and across encounters—are critical to defining situations in ways that constrain or encourage various communication patterns.

Managing Conversations

The term *conversational management* may seem incongruous. After all, "management" seems to imply a deliberate attempt to control or affect something, and having a conversation with another person may not seem to take on that quality very often. But throughout this chapter you will find that participants use a wide variety of nonverbal behaviors to regulate many aspects of interpersonal interactions. Indeed, Cappella (1987) claimed that coordination of interpersonal behavior is the defining feature of interpersonal communication. If the ability to use these cues to regulate conversations were somehow taken away, it would be difficult, perhaps impossible, to have conversations at all.

What kinds of conversational phenomena do we regulate nonverbally? Among other things, we manage how we enter and leave conversations, who speaks when, how we change topics, and how we coordinate our actions with others throughout the conversation. As we shall see, nonverbal regulative cues have a profound effect on the whole communication process.

Principles of Conversation Management

One reason it may seem odd to think of conversations as managed is that *we take much of the regulative process for granted* as we converse. This makes conversations seem almost automatic and effortless, and in fact, much interaction activity is habitual and routine. We think about it only when something goes wrong, such as when someone monopolizes the floor and we make strategic choices to regain our speaking turn.

Another basic characteristic is that *conversational management is typically rule-bound*. That is, we follow a set of social rules, acquired through modeling and explicit instruction, that tell us how to organize and conduct conversations (Pearce, 2005). Among some of the basic, often unstated rules in many industrialized cultures are:

- Conversations are preceded by a greeting.
- The conversational "channel" is opened with eye contact.
- Only one speaker may speak at a time in a conversation; interruptions are unwelcome.
- Possession of the floor must change during conversations.
- Silences are a cue for someone to speak.
- Listeners must signal that they are paying attention to the speaker.

Different cultures and co-cultures may follow different rules. For example, during storytelling in some African cultures, listeners echo and overlap the speaker's utterances in a musical cadence. Among some Native American tribes, eye contact may be unnecessary to engage in talk, and lengthy silences are expected rather than avoided.

Of course, rules are merely guidelines for conversational behavior. As the old adage suggests, "rules are made to be broken," and we do break these rules during conversations with others. We do so, however, at the risk of negative sanctions from other people, although we're typically reluctant to confront others directly about their rule violations. Telling someone to pay attention to what you are saying signifies a conversational process already in trouble and such statements are typically a last resort—an indication that we prefer to regulate conversations nonverbally.

A third basic characteristic is that *conversational management is linked to other interpersonal functions* such as relational communication. That is, how we manage interpersonal interactions with others allows us to coordinate conversations and accomplish other interpersonal objectives as well. Wiemann (1985) summarized evidence showing that, among other things, turn-taking is very important in defining power and control in personal relationships, and behaviors that gain the conversational floor may facilitate changing another's attitudes.

Fourth, *interaction management is capable of provoking strong emotional reactions.* When others break conversational rules, it can be infuriating. Students complain about instructors they find difficult to follow because they cannot tell when the teacher changes from one topic to another. Workers complain about a boss who interrupts their work, starts a conversation, and then leaves just as abruptly. Patients complain of inadequate medical care when doctors don't listen to them and cut off the consultation too soon. One of the frustrations of teleconferencing is that the brief delays in signal transmission cause people to "step on" each other's talk. A major consulting business is being launched at the time of this writing to help companies mitigate the problems such talkovers cause. These examples illustrate that poor interaction management can provoke strong reactions and lead to relational difficulties.

This brings up a final point: *Interaction management behaviors are a fundamental part of one's competence as a communicator.* Exchanging the conversational floor smoothly, shifting topics without losing everyone, and initiating and terminating conversations skillfully are interaction management skills that, like the other

BOX **14.2**

Hanging Out Your Tongue as a "Do Not Disturb" Sign

Although a variety of cues indicate approachability and a willingness to interact, some indicate just the opposite—in effect, saying "Don't bother me now!" Research at the University of Western Australia identified the protruded tongue as a particularly effective cue for this message. Researchers had participants take a test, the last page of which was indecipherable. Participants had to get another copy of the test from a proctor in order to finish. The proctors had headphones on, kept their eyes closed, and tried to appear absorbed, either with tongues showing or not. Participants took significantly longer to disturb proctors whose tongues were showing than those whose tongues were not showing.

To make sure this wasn't just nervous test-taking behavior, the researchers set up a similar experiment, this time using a campus stall selling cacti manned by two salesclerks. The salesclerks read books and pretended to concentrate on their reading, one with the tongue showing and one without. As before, customers approaching the stall were more likely to disturb the salesclerk whose tongue was not showing. Although hanging your tongue out may not be the most pleasant or hygienic way to avoid being disturbed, it does appear to be effective.

Source: Adapted from McCarthy, 1988, p. 16.

---

nonverbal and verbal social skills identified earlier, go a long way toward defining a person as a competent communicator. We tend to be most aware of these skills in their absence—in the person who ignores all efforts to terminate a telephone conversation or ends conversations without warning, for example. These individuals may simply lack skill as communicators, but such behavior may lead to a number of other attributions about them. Thus effective conversational management has implications for achieving other desired communication outcomes.

Beginning and Ending Interactions

The first task confronting communicators is to know how to start and stop interactions. Nonverbal behaviors such as smiling and gaze can encourage interaction. Other times nonverbal behaviors can discourage or delay interaction (see Box 14.2 for an example). Some conversations begin and end smoothly and effortlessly; others are difficult, uncomfortable, and problematic. Ending a conversation in a skillful way makes subsequent interactions more likely. Nonverbal cues play a central role in getting conversations off on the right foot. The right initiation cues set the stage for effective communication. The popularity of etiquette books, self-help manuals, and advice columns on how to start conversations "properly" is an indication of the premium this and other cultures place on appropriate greeting and leave-taking behavior.

Initiating Interaction

Although we're often unaware of it, nonverbal cues are busy at work long before the first "hello" is said. These cues signal awareness of the presence of others

PHOTO 14.2 *The handshake is a common component of social greetings in many Western cultures. Social greetings in other cultures often involve hugging, kissing on the cheeks, and kissing on the lips.*

and willingness to become involved in conversation. Greeting cues are highly ritualized and habitual, producing what Goffman (1971) called an "access ritual." Morris (1977) captures the importance of this ritual:

> Whenever two friends meet after a long separation . . . they amplify their friendly signals to super-friendly signals. They smile and touch, often embrace and kiss, and generally behave more intimately and expansively than usual. They do this because they have to make up for lost time—lost friendship time. While they have been apart it has been impossible for them to send the hundreds of small, minute-by-minute friendly signals to each other that their relationship requires, and they have, so to speak, built up a backlog of these signals. This backlog amounts to a gestural debt that must be repaid without delay. (p. 77)

Some researchers, primarily ethologists, have found similarities in human and primate greetings that suggest an evolutionary and biological base for such behavior. For example, eye behavior during greetings is similar for adults, infants, children, blind persons, and nonhuman primates (Pitcairn & Eibl-Eibesfeldt, 1976). The eyebrow flash, a quick raising of the eyebrows held for about one-sixth of a second before lowering, is part of greetings among a wide range of cultures, including Europeans, Balinese, Papuans, Samoans, South American Indians, and Bushmen (Eibl-Eibesfeldt, 1979), and may be universal (Morris, 1977). Other greeting rituals are specific to given cultures, such as a handshake (as depicted in Photo 14.2), cheek kissing, or a full embrace.

Greetings are designed to signal greater availability for interaction and determine or reestablish the intimacy level of the relationship. They are highly ritualized and typically progress through some common stages (Kendon, 1990). You can confirm this for yourself. The next time you are traveling, watch for this sequence among passengers being greeted in a public place:

1. *Sighting, orientation, and initiation of approach.* After spotting the person to be greeted, one or both parties engage in a distant salutation such

as smiling, waving or nodding that ratifies that the greeting ritual
has begun.

2. *The head dip.* A head movement common at this stage is to lower the head,
followed by a slow rise, or to "toss" it in a somewhat rapid back-and-forth
movement. This behavior indicates a shift in activities and/or psychological
orientation. With it comes an averting of gaze so that greeters can escape the
awkwardness of maintaining eye contact while traversing the distance
between them.

3. *Approach.* Increased gazing and grooming behaviors such as straightening
clothing or patting hair take place as greeters move toward each other.

4. *Final approach and close salutation.* When people are within 10 feet of each
other, mutual gazing and smiling can resume, along with a verbal salutation.
Forms of contact that are culture-specific such as a handshake or embrace
can then occur.

Terminating Interaction

It would be very efficient to end conversations by just walking away. But social
norms call for balancing efficiency with appropriateness (see Kellermann,
Reynolds, & Chen, 1991). Abruptly getting up and saying good-bye is seen as rude
and/or incompetent. If future interaction with the other is likely and maintaining
a decent relationship with the person is important, greater effort must be mus-
tered to conclude interactions in an acceptable fashion.

Leave-taking rituals in some ways look like greeting rituals in reverse
(Floyd, Melcher, & Zhong, 2000). First, like initiation rituals, they are designed to
signal supportiveness. Typically, people prefer to leave conversations on a positive
note, indicating points of agreement, satisfaction with the encounter, and positive anticipation of the next interaction. This conforms to a "politeness maxim"
of avoiding offensive, vulgar, or rude language and projecting mutual support
(McLaughlin, 1984). Second, leave-taking may *entail summarization*—summing
up what has been said during the conversation—perhaps as a way to achieve
psychological closure. Third, rather than signaling heightened accessibility,
leave-taking cues are designed to *signal impending inaccessibility.* Usually one can
tell that people are preparing to bring a conversation to a close before anything is
said because their nonverbal cues convey that they are closing down their availability for conversation.

In a now-classic experiment, Knapp et al. (1973) explored how verbal and
nonverbal leave-taking behaviors accomplish these functions. Participants were
paid to conduct information-gathering interviews in the shortest time possible
and were told that the shorter their interviews, the more money they would
make. Unbeknownst to them, the interviewee was actually a confederate
instructed to prolong the encounter. Thus the situation was designed to motivate
the display of numerous leave-taking cues by interviewers.

Knapp et al. (1973) found that the coded verbal and nonverbal cues fit these
functional categories well. The specific nonverbal and verbal termination cues,
ranked from most to least frequent, appear in Table 14.1. All in one way or another

TABLE 14.1   **Verbal and Nonverbal Leave-Taking Behaviors**

Rank	Nonverbal Variables	Verbal Variables
1	Breaking Eye Contact	Reinforcement
2	Left Positioning	Professional Inquiry
3	Forward Lean	Buffing
4	Nodding Behavior	Appreciation
5	Major Leg Movements	Internal Legitimizer
6	Smiling Behavior	Tentativeness
7	Sweeping Hand Movements	External Legitimizer
8	Explosive Foot Movements	Filling
9	Leveraging	Superlatives
10	Major Trunk Movements	Reference to Other
11	Handshake	Personal Inquiry
12	Explosive Hand Contact	Welfare Concern
13	—	Continuance
14	—	Terminating

signal supportiveness, summarization, or inaccessibility. Other leave-taking cues include unequal weight stances, breaking eye contact, hand gesturing, and, near the end of conversations, a general increase in nonverbal activity, with increases in mutual smiling, leaning forward, and leveraging by departing interactants (O'Leary & Gallois, 1985). Other cues the authors would add to the list from classroom observations include a general shuffling of feet, shifting of bodies, symmetrical stacking of books in the absolute center of the desk, and longing looks toward the door. Of course, experienced teachers know when to acknowledge these cues and when not to. Skilled communicators also know how to use leave-taking cues such as these most effectively. (See Box 14.3 for more advice on how to end conversations).

Turn-Taking in Conversations

Sandwiched between the hellos and good-byes is the conversation itself, which also must be managed. The task confronting communicators is how to weave the fabric of conversation without becoming entangled in it. Here again, nonverbal cues help to organize and sequence interactions. Organization occurs on several different levels, ranging from the microscopic to the macroscopic. One of the most socially meaningful units is the *turn*.

It has been said that a wise person knows when to speak and when to keep silent. So, too, does the skilled communicator. A key to gaining the conversational floor when you want it and recognizing when others want a chance to speak is the skillful use of nonverbal cues, which are the traffic cops of conversation.

Conversations and Turns

A *conversation* is a series of opportunities to speak and listen. It is composed of *turns*, or times during which one speaker has sole possession of the floor. Conversations

---

BOX **14.3**

Ending Conversations

Having trouble ending conversations? Part of the problem may be that polite verbal expressions such as "I'll let you go" sound insincere and condescending, but more direct ones such as "Are we finished here?" lack a supportive ring. It is tricky to signal unavailability for talk yet also maintain positivity.

Instead, try relying on nonverbal cues to wind the conversation down to a close:

Break eye contact. Begin attending to other activities—shuffling papers, clearing dishes from a dinner table, or taking phone calls. These polychronic activities may seem rude but are effective.

With the most recalcitrant visitors, use the great movers—proxemics and haptics. Stand, invade their personal space, shake

their hand, and if necessary, with a hand on their shoulder, propel them to the door. A final handshake can be a most effective dismissive but supportive gesture.

Eventually, these cut-off tactics should become automatic. Just remember that they won't work to end phone conversations. For those, flat pitch and long silences may signal waning interest but may also prompt the other person to reenergize the conversation and fill the void with yet more talk. Effective verbal closings may be essential—such as, "It's been wonderful talking with you. I hope we can do it again soon." Said with the proper vocal warmth, such closings summarize and support while closing off accessibility.

---

have variable turn order, size, and content peculiar to the occasion and participants involved (West & Zimmerman, 1982), but average turn length is a mere 6 seconds (Jaffe & Feldstein, 1970). Typically, who speaks first, about what, and for how long are not determined in advance but are negotiated by the participants.

Although the concept of turns is straightforward, just where turns begin and end is not always so clear. Researchers disagree on how to tell when someone has a turn or not (Feldstein & Welkowitz, 1978), with definitions varying in the extent to which they rely on vocalic, semantic, and/or gestural information to mark where a turn begins and ends (Rosenfeld, 1978). Some definitions are based on the physical change of vocalization from one person to another: "A speaking turn begins when one interlocutor starts solo talking and ends when a different interlocutor starts solo talking" (Markel, 1975, p. 190). Others rely on some consensual notion of when a person has finished a verbal contribution or conveyed substantial information to demarcate turns (Matarazzo & Wiens, 1972). Sacks, Schegloff, and Jefferson (1974) define the turn as a period of time during which one has the right or obligation to speak. According to this view, turns are constructed out of unit types, which can include words, phrases, clauses, or sentences. A speaker, upon gaining the floor, can produce at least one of these unit types before losing the floor. Finally, others rely on a reading of the speaker's and listener's intentions based on the occurrence of gestural and vocalic information to determine where a turn occurs: "A speaker is a participant who claims the speaking turn. An auditor is a participant who does not claim the speaking turn at a given moment" (Duncan & Fiske, 1977, p. 177). Knowing when an interactant claims the speaking turn is based on the occurrence of "turn-requesting cues." Let's take a look at how people typically exchange speaking turns.

The Turn-Taking Process

That people routinely exchange turns rapidly and seamlessly is remarkable. This turn exchange process is enabled by the display of multiple nonverbal cues, some of which speakers employ and some of which listeners employ.

Speaker Cues. Speaker cues fall into two categories: turn-suppressing cues and turn-yielding cues. *Turn-suppressing cues* are ones that a speaker uses to maintain possession of the floor. Early research (Duncan, 1972) identified five turn suppressing cues: (1) audible inhalation of breath by the speaker; (2) continuation of a gesture; (3) facing away, or diverting gaze from the listener; (4) sustained intonation, which lets the listener know that more vocalization is yet to come; and, (5) fillers (also known as vocalized pauses) such as "hmmm" and "uhhh" that fill pauses in the speaking turn so that listeners will not use the silence as an opportunity to gain the floor. Other possible turn-suppressing cues include increased loudness, light touch (Knapp, 1978), or use of the "stop" hand gesture emblem.

Turn-yielding cues are ones that speakers use to give up the floor. Many turn-yielding cues are simply the opposite of turn-suppressing cues. Termination of gesturing, facing the listener, making eye contact, falling intonation (such as at the end of a declarative statement) or rising intonation (such as at the end of a question), and silences are prime turn-yielding cues. Decreased loudness and slowed tempo also may be used to relinquish the turn. In conversations among three or more people, eye contact, gesturing, and head nodding in the direction of a given listener all serve to increase the probability of that person being the next speaker.

Listener Cues. Listeners employ cues from three categories: turn-requesting cues, backchannel cues, and turn-denying cues. *Turn-requesting cues* are behaviors the listener uses to gain possession of the conversational floor. It is clear that listeners do not sit idly by, waiting for a chance to speak. Rather, they indicate their intention to speak by the display of this type of cue. In a classroom setting, one of the most common turn-requesting cues is the raised hand, as shown in Photo 14.3. In interpersonal interactions, Wiemann (1973; Wiemann & Knapp, 1975) found that listeners use gaze directed at the speaker, head nods, forward leans, the raised index finger, and an inhalation of breath coupled with a straightened back to gain the floor. Duncan (1974) found that turn-requesting cues occurred primarily at the end of phonemic clause units.

Backchannel cues are behaviors the listener uses to communicate a variety of messages to the speaker without gaining access to the conversational floor (Rosenfeld, 1978). These cues can communicate agreement and confirmation or disagreement and disconfirmation, involvement and interest or boredom and

PHOTO 14.3 *Raising our hands when we want to speak is one of the first turn-requesting behaviors many of us learn.*

disinterest. Some backchannel cues can also be used to pace the speaker, as when a listener continuously nods at a fast pace to hurry the speaker up. Specific backchannel cues include smiling, frowning, head nodding and shaking, raised eyebrows, short vocalizations ("uh-huh," "mm-hmm"), and verbal statements ("yep," "right," "I see," "oh good"). These short verbal statements do not constitute turns according to most researchers, especially if they are simultaneous with speaker vocalization. Instead, they allow a listener to communicate a variety of meanings without having to gain access to the conversational floor. Duncan (1974) found that backchannel cues are distributed fairly evenly throughout the listening turn. Sometimes backchannel and turn-requesting cues are confused with one another. See Box 14.4 for tips on how to differentiate these cues.

Backchannel or listener responses underscore the dynamic and simultaneous nature of face-to-face interaction. Further, speakers *expect* listeners to display some level of these cues, particularly cues that fall into the involvement category. Speakers find it disconcerting when listeners fail to signal attentiveness by smiling, leaning toward the speaker, or gazing. In fact, listeners may suppress backchannel cues as a means of signaling that they don't follow what a speaker is saying (Chen, cited in Krauss, Fussell, & Chen, 1996). Ethnic differences in the kinds of listener responses Caucasians and African Americans give also can lead to misinterpretations and awkward interchanges. Clearly, backchannel cues play a potent role in conversation.

Finally, *turn-denying cues* provide a way for a listener to refuse a turn nonverbally. Although they have not been widely studied, Knapp (1978, p. 217) suggested that relaxed posture, silence, and staring away from the speaker are cues that qualify as turn-denying cues.

Research has shown that floor exchanges are smoothest when speakers display many turn-yielding cues. Listeners are more likely to take the floor the more turn-yielding cues the speaker displays (Duncan, 1972). Also, when speakers change their minds, turn-suppressing cues—even just one—are highly effective in eliminating listener turn-taking attempts, regardless of how many turn-yielding cues appear simultaneously.

B O X 14.4

Getting the Floor When You Want It

Some people feel like they are always sitting on the conversational sidelines, not knowing how or when to jump into the conversational stream. Knowing how to negotiate nonverbal "traffic signals" can help. Confusion sometimes arises because cues such as head nods may be either a backchannel cue or a turn request. This can result in awkward or failed turn-switching if speakers "read" the cue differently than listeners intend. Speakers who monopolize conversations may conveniently fail to recognize turn-request cues, treating them instead as backchannel support. This often happens to women, as they employ nods more frequently than men as a socially facilitative style.

How can speakers and listeners alike distinguish turn-request cues from backchannel or turn-denial cues? Two points might be helpful. First, other cues that occur with these multipurpose cues may clarify their role. A nod, when accompanied by other turn-requesting cues, will be seen as desire to gain the floor. Second, the point at which these cues occur may clarify their function. Backchannel cues can appear in a number of places during a turn, though typically not at the beginning. Turn-requesting and turn-denying cues are more likely to occur at turn junctures when the conversational floor could potentially be exchanged.

The advice for those having difficulty "getting a word in edgewise" is to use multiple cues when requesting a turn and to minimize use of those that serve the dual function of signaling supportiveness.

Topic Management and Exchange

On a broader level, conversations consist of one or more topics. Although much of our maneuvering through topics is the result of following routine verbal patterns (see Kellermann & Lim, 1990), nonverbal cues may also help to segment and organize topics. They do so by marking the boundaries between episodes and positions. *Episodes* are periods within conversations when discussion focuses on a particular topic, whereas *positions* are segments of interaction within an episode during which a person maintains a consistent disposition toward the topic and other communicators (Scheflen, 1974). As interest in a given topic wanes, or as attitudes shift, one's position changes.

Four classes of nonverbal cues serve as *boundary markers*. First, *proxemic shifts*—changes in leaning forward or backward and toward or away from other communicators—have been found to be reliable indicators of episode and position changes (Erickson, 1975). Second, *extrainteractional activities* include behaviors that are not directly part of the stream of communication, such as lighting a cigarette, reaching for a drink, rearranging personal articles (a jacket, purse, etc.), adjusting a chair cushion, and so on (Pittenger, Hockett, & Danehy, 1960). These cues are more likely to occur at episode and position boundaries, perhaps because if they appeared elsewhere, they might be perceived as inappropriate and indicative of low involvement. Third, *silences* mark episode and position boundaries, often closing topics that participants are no longer interested in pursuing (Schegloff &

Sacks, 1973) and allowing participants to relax physically and mentally before pursuing the next segment of interaction. These are the awkward silences that often develop as participants let one topic die and cast about for another one to pick up. Finally, other *paralinguistic cues*, such as sighs, gasps, and clearing the throat, mark episode and position boundaries (Pittenger et al., 1960). Such cues may facilitate changes in speaking style by releasing air from the lungs and relaxing the vocal cords, thereby allowing loudness, pitch, and tempo also to change. Interactants can then "start fresh" vocally with the next topic.

Some research (e.g., Planalp & Tracy, 1980) has suggested that people only need verbal information to decide where topic switches are appropriate. Although that may be true when reading transcripts, it is likely that in actual conversation, nonverbal boundary markers reinforce verbal topic change signals as well as bolster perceptions of communicator competence in managing conversation. They may also alert participants that the relevant background information required to comprehend the upcoming topic is about to change.

Interaction Adaptation Patterns

It should be clear from the preceding sections that conversation is clearly a joint venture that requires intricate coordination by the involved parties. Nowhere is this more evident than in the larger behavioral patterns that capture how people adapt their behavior to one another.

Have you ever stopped to notice two people talking: How their bodies move in similar rhythms, their eyes make and break contact at regular intervals, their postures and gestures often fall into identical patterns? This conversational "dance" has intrigued scholars for decades, but knowledge advanced slowly because researchers focused on the individual as the unit of analysis, thus failing to observe properties of interpersonal systems and relationships. More recent theorizing and research has made important advances by explicitly examining what communicators do together as a unit and by considering sequential patterns. Additionally, much of the newer research focuses on multiple nonverbal and verbal cues, giving a more comprehensive view of the behavioral stream and thereby avoiding the historical problem of focusing on a single behavior or code.

The Patterns Defined

Several different interaction adaptation patterns have been observed. When two people display a similar behavior (or set of behaviors) such as pause lengths, gesturing rates, or linguistic elaboration, they are said to *match* one another. When the matching takes the form of identical visual behavior, such as adopting the same posture, it is called *mirroring* (or sometimes postural congruence). Mirroring usually refers to static or slow signals, whereas dynamic ones are usually described as matching. If one person's behavior becomes increasingly like the other's, the pattern is described as *convergence.* If the behavioral change appears to be contingent on, directed toward, and/or in exchange for the other's behavior, it is called *reciprocity.* For example, if Person A leans forward and smiles at Person B, and B responds by leaning forward and nodding, then a reciprocal pattern has occurred. One special form of contingent behavior is *motor mimicry*, in which a person displays an empathic behavior in response to another's actual or imagined circumstance. When a friend recounts accidentally running into a low-hanging tree branch and we wince, that's motor mimicry.

If behavioral similarity is based on communicators coordinating dynamic behaviors temporally and rhythmically, *interactional synchrony* exists. (Another type of synchrony, *self-synchrony*, involves individuals coordinating their own kinesic behavior to their own verbal-vocal stream.) Interactional synchrony may occur *simultaneously*, as when the listener's behavior synchronizes with the speaker's behavior, or it may occur *concatenously*, as when the coordination is sequential from speaker to speaker (as in the first person's use of baton gestures being echoed by the next speaker's use of the same gestures).

The opposites of these patterns are *complementarity* (wherein behaviors are dissimilar or opposite to one another (such as one person gazing and the other avoiding gaze), *divergence* (wherein behaviors become increasingly dissimilar), *compensation* (wherein one person responds to another's behavior with a behavioral change in the opposite direction), and *dissynchrony* (wherein behaviors fail to mesh and are out of sync). Of course, people may also fail to adapt to one another, in which case the pattern is described as *nonaccommodation* or nonadaptation. (See Burgoon, Dillman, & Stern, 1993; Burgoon, Stern, & Dillman, 1995; Giles, Coupland, & Coupland, 1991; and Street & Giles, 1982, for more detailed discussion of these patterns.)

Research Evidence of Interpersonal Adaptation

The research on these patterns has produced impressive evidence that communicators mutually influence and adjust to each other's interaction style. This adaptation occurs at both microscopic and macroscopic levels and appears to include biologically based, automatic forms of coordination as well as more deliberate, socially learned ones (Burgoon, Stern et al., 1995).

From the microscopic level comes evidence that humans can converge toward or diverge from another's speech within milliseconds (Street, 1990) and may begin at birth (or perhaps even in utero) to synchronize their movements and communication to one another. Classic work by Condon and his associates (Condon, 1976; Condon & Sander, 1974) filmed interactions with high-speed film, then coded the onset, offset, and changes in body movements frame by frame. The behavioral changes were matched with simultaneous verbal changes recorded in a phonetic transcript. Because the film speed ranged from 30 to 48 frames per second, behavior was analyzed down to 1/48th of a second. This work revealed not only that adults entrain their communication with one another but also that neonates synchronize their movements to their mothers' voices.

People not only adapt their behavior to each other quickly, they also appear to identify coordinated behavior fairly quickly in others. In three experiments, Cappella (1997) showed 1-minute clips of dyadic interaction to naïve judges who were asked to rate the clips for the degree of interaction synchrony. Half the clips were taken from conversations between communicators whose vocal and kinesic behaviors were highly coordinated with each other; the other half portrayed conversations in which communicators' behaviors were highly uncoordinated with each other. After watching only one minute of each interaction, the naïve judges were able to distinguish reliably between coordinated and uncoordinated conversations, but only when they were watching male-male pairs. The judges were not reliable in discriminating between coordinated and uncoordinated conversations when the communicators were both female. As explanation, Cappella (1997) suggested that the judges were evaluating the coordination of female-female pairs largely on the basis of whether the females smiled in synchrony. He also pointed out that, among female-female pairs, even coordinated conversations do not necessarily involve synchronous smiling. At least for male-male pairs, however, judges were able to identify whether the conversation was coordinated or not after only a brief view.

Although some writers have engaged in a lively debate about whether synchrony actually exists (Gatewood & Rosenwein, 1981), the accumulating research findings suggest extensive meshing and synchronization of activity (Cappella & Planalp, 1981; Hatfield, Cacioppo, & Rapson, 1994). In fact, the rhythmicity between two people often exceeds that between a speaker's own vocal rate and heart rate, which suggests a strong predisposition for people to adapt to each other's communication rhythms (Warner, Malloy, Schneider, Knoth, & Wilder, 1987).

At the same time, abundant research also demonstrates that compensation and complementarity often occur. It is common for increased proximity to provoke a compensatory decrease in gaze or in directness of body orientation. Apart from the natural complementarity on behaviors related to speaker and listener roles, interactants tend to compensate for the combined floor-holding behaviors of gaze, vocalization, and illustrator gestures. Compensation may also occur in negatively toned situations or ones of dissimilarity and inequality. For example, when you are interacting in a positive situation with friends, you will likely match their eye contact patterns. However, when having a disagreement with your employer at work, you will likely look less if your boss is looking more. Additionally, people may simultaneously reciprocate some behaviors and compensate others. Hale and Burgoon (1984) found that interactants responded to a partner's reduction in nonverbal immediacy with reciprocal decreases in some nonverbal immediacy behaviors but a compensatory increase in verbal immediacy. Burgoon, Le Poire, and Rosenthal (1995) found that when a confederate greatly reduced involvement and pleasantness, it had a reciprocal, depressive effect on the partner's involvement and pleasantness, but partners compensated for the confederate's overly relaxed, blasé demeanor by being more erect and tense. And Iizuka, Mishima, and Matsumoto (1989) found that participants interacting with a negative (disagreeing) partner compensated increased gaze but reciprocated increased smiling.

Theories of Interaction Adaptation

The mix of behavioral patterns has led scholars to develop a variety of theories to explain and predict them. Knowing when each pattern is likely to occur has important implications. Consider that if you are attracted to someone, it is important to know when your intimate overtures are likely to be reciprocated and when they are likely to be rebuffed (Floyd, 2006). Doctors and therapists need to know if adopting too verbal or dominant an interview style will lead patients to become more submissive and reticent, which are compensatory patterns that may prevent patients from disclosing relevant information. Employment interviewers need to know if the behavior they are observing in prospective employees is an indication of the person's own style or just a reflection of the interviewer's own style (i.e., the natural result of reciprocation).

Much of the earliest theorizing focused on biological factors. Work on synchrony and motor mimicry supported the conclusion that human behavior is innately rhythmic and cyclical and that humans are inherently predisposed to synchronize their rhythms and behaviors to one another (Chapple, 1970). As the progenitor of many contemporary theories, Argyle and Dean (1965) proposed *affiliative conflict theory* (also called equilibrium theory), which states that humans seek to bring competing drives to approach others and to avoid others into balance. The point at which two communicators are comfortable with the level of immediacy defines an equilibrium point. Deviations from that point were posited to cause arousal, discomfort, and a compensatory effort to bring the interaction back to its previous level. Thus, if Person A moves close to whisper something to Person B, B should compensate by breaking eye contact and adopting an indirect body orientation. (Compensation can also occur within the individual, as when someone moves farther away while talking and simultaneously increases eye contact to offset the physical distance.) Although this theory generated a tremendous amount of research and earned some support, a chief shortcoming was its inability to account for patterns of reciprocity. After all, we know that every time someone increases intimacy with us, we don't back away. If that were the case, no relationships or conversations would ever progress beyond the first polite and distant stage! Sociological evidence indicates that people follow a *norm of reciprocity* by treating others as they treat us and returning good for good (Gouldner, 1960). A substantial body of evidence that verbal self-disclosures beget self-disclosures from the partner (Derlega, Metts, Petronio, & Margulis, 1993) also raised doubts about interactions principally following a compensatory or complementary pattern.

As an alternative, Patterson (1976) proposed the *arousal-labeling model*. Deviations from a comfortable interaction level are still posited to create discomfort and arousal. The arousal is nonspecific and needs to be identified as pleasant or unpleasant. Interactants are said to examine the situation for cues to label the arousal positively or negatively. Positive arousal is predicted to produce reciprocity and negative arousal to produce compensation. On the surface, this model is simple and intuitively appealing. If people label the situation as a pleasant one, they should reciprocate the partner's behavior, but if they label it as negative, they should compensate. But a moment's reflection raises some wrinkles in this theory. If an unattractive person moves to a far distance, what then? Will that actually be arousing? If so, such detachment normally would be labeled negatively. But that would lead to a prediction of a compensatory increase in proximity. Intuitively, most of us probably would not expect to respond that way. Other problems with the model led Patterson himself to repudiate it and offer a *sequential functional model* that tries to identify numerous factors that precipitate arousal changes during interaction, assessments of those changes, and reactions to them (Patterson, 1983). However, that model lacks specificity as to when compensatory versus reciprocal responses will occur.

Five other theories that have attempted to further refine predictions are *discrepancy-arousal theory* (Cappella & Greene, 1982, 1984), *expectancy violations theory* (Burgoon, 1993; Hale & Burgoon, 1984), *cognitive-valence theory* (Andersen, 1985, 1989), *communication accommodation theory* (Giles et al., 1991), and *interaction adaptation theory* (Burgoon, Stern, & Dillman, 1995). The first two share as a starting point that communicators have expectations about the communicative styles of others and that behaviors that are discrepant from, or violative of, those expectations activate behavioral change. Discrepancy-arousal theory posits that discrepancies produce arousal change, that moderate arousal change produces positive affect, and that large arousal changes produce negative affect. Positive affect is variously described as producing reciprocity or approach and negative affect as producing compensation or avoidance. This theory thus hinges on the size of arousal change and its concomitant affective reaction to predict the interaction patterns. It is unclear whether extreme nonimmediacy would generate avoidance (a reciprocal response) or approach (a compensatory response).

Expectancy violations theory posits that the valence of the communicator must be factored in as well. For example, increased intimacy by an attractive person is hypothesized to be a positive violation that elicits reciprocated intimacy, whereas the same approach from a repulsive person is hypothesized to be a negative violation that produces a compensatory reduction in intimacy. Some predictions are straightforward, but others are less clear, especially when the valence of the communicator is at odds with the valence of the behavior. Take, for instance, the case of someone you like a great deal unexpectedly becoming increasingly detached during a conversation. Will you do the same or try to "pull the person back" to a high level of involvement by becoming more involved yourself (a compensatory move)?

Cognitive valence theory is less ambitious in scope, being limited only to cases in which one person increases intimacy behaviors. The theory begins like arousal-labeling theory in arguing that changes in one person's intimacy behaviors prompt arousal changes in the other which must be valenced. The theory identifies six classes of factors that are said to determine the valence of behavioral changes: (1) culture; (2) individual predispositions (3) interpersonal evaluations; (4) relational expectations; (5) situational features; and (6) transitory states. If any one of them is negative, the valence is predicted to be negative. Only when arousal change is moderate are these valencers predicted to affect outcomes, with positive valence producing reciprocity and negative valence producing compensation. Like discrepancy-arousal theory, this theory predicts that large arousal changes are always aversive and produce compensation.

Communication accommodation theory is also more limited in scope in that it centers on vocalic and linguistic features such as dialect, response latencies, and language style. Adaptation, or accommodation, to another is considered to be a deliberate act that is influenced by social factors such as one's status as an ingroup or outgroup member. Convergence is designed to promote similarity and rapport, usually among ingroup members, whereas divergence is designed to create distance. This theory has also generated a tremendous amount of research and support, but in addition to not encompassing a wide range of nonverbal cues, it may not account adequately for highly automatic forms of adaptation.

Based on a review of the theories and research evidence, Burgoon, Stern et al. (1995) arrived at the following conclusions:

1. *At a biological level, there appears to be an innate pressure to adapt and synchronize interaction patterns but also to make compensatory adjustments when physical safety and comfort are at stake.* People are innately programmed to adapt and synchronize with others. That adaptation may include compensation to ensure one's safety.

2. *At the social level, the pressure is also toward reciprocity and matching.* Exceptions include role or status relationships (such as soldier and commander) and competence differences (such as parent and infant) that dictate complementary patterns. Biological and social forces thus jointly predispose people to coordinate interactions through use of similar behaviors.

3. *At the communication level, both reciprocity and compensation may occur.* Salespeople, for example, may attempt to win over a buyer with a friendly, reciprocal style or an obsequious, ingratiating one that places them in a submissive role relative to the buyer's dominant one. These voluntary forms of adaptation are aimed at achieving communicators' goals such as putting forward a desirable image, facilitating information processing, creating a personal relationship, or persuading someone to comply with a request.

4. *Several factors may limit interaction adaptation: (1) internal causes of adjustments; (2) individual style; (3) poor self-monitoring; (4) poor skills; and (5) cultural differences.* People may fail to adapt because they are hungry or tired, because they are adhering to their own or their culture's typical behavioral pattern, or because they lack the necessary skills to adjust to their partners. Thus, the degree of adaptation observed may be subtle.

5. *Biological, psychological, social, and communicative forces set up boundaries within which most interaction patterns will operate, producing mostly matching, synchrony, and reciprocity.* Behavioral changes outside these boundaries will often be met with nonaccommodation as a means of retarding movement away from the normative range, or with compensation to return interaction to its previous style.

6. *Patterns of adaptation are more readily predicted for constellations of interrelated behaviors rather than individual ones.* It is easier to anticipate how interactants will respond to changes in overall levels of involvement, intimacy, dominance, or formality than to specific proxemic, haptic, or vocalic cues.

These principles formed the foundation for *interaction adaptation theory* (Burgoon, Stern et al., 1995), which attempts to take into account the complexities of interpersonal interaction by considering people's needs, expectations, and desires or goals as precursors to their degree and form of adaptation. For instance, people with strong affiliation needs seek social contact, may expect others to maintain a polite level of involvement and pleasantness during conversation, and may prefer a high degree of nonverbal immediacy when interacting with friends. Their combined required, expected, and desired levels of interaction yield what is called an *interaction position* (IP) (Burgoon, Allspach, & Miczo, 1997). The IP refers to the behavior they are likely to adopt. The IP, which can be positively or negatively valued, is compared to the partner's *actual behavior* (A). If the partner's A is different than the IP, it is going to be either more or less positive. Suppose, for example, that the partner chooses to interact at a very close distance. For extroverts and those with high affiliation needs, this is a positive; for introverts, it is a negative.

Based on the relative valence of the A and IP, the theory makes two simple predictions: (1) If A differs from the IP and is more positively valenced, people should converge toward the partner's desirable behavior (which might even be seen as a positive violation). The result is reciprocity. (2) If, instead, A is more negatively valenced than the IP, people should diverge from the partner's behavior or maintain their existing behavior. If they diverge, the result is compensation. If they maintain their existing behavior, their nonadaptation still functions like compensation to retard changes in the dyad's level of a given behavior. Examples of these predictions are presented in Figure 14.2.

This cursory introduction to IAT shows how many different elements can be brought together to predict one person's response to another's actual or anticipated communicative behavior. The theory can also account for what happens when two people's patterns are at odds with one another. For example, if one person is predicted to approach the partner, but the other is predicted to avoid the partner, we should expect a compensatory pattern between the two of them. This theory represents an attempt to integrate other theories while providing a simpler model of interpersonal adaptation processes. Although IAT is still a relatively new theory, several studies have already found support for its principles (Burgoon, Le Poire et al., 1995; Floyd & Burgoon, 1999; Guerrero & Burgoon, 1996; White & Burgoon, 2001).

Effects of Interaction Adaptation

Identifying how and when interactants adapt to one another is important in itself. But equally as important is how adaptation or nonadaptation affects other interaction outcomes such as attraction, satisfaction, commitment, and persuasion. Interaction coordination heightens perceptions of rapport (Bernieri & Rosenthal, 1991). Research on romantic and married couples' interactions has shown that reciprocity of nonverbal expressions of negative emotions can lead to severe discord and negative relational consequences. Distressed couples tend to reciprocate more negative affect than nondistressed ones, whereas happy couples are quicker to reciprocate positive expressions (Manusov, 1994). Whether

Sample Predictions from Interaction Adaptation Theory

Bob has spent the weekend by himself, taking a solitary hiking trip in the mountains. Come Monday morning, what interaction style might we predict between Bob and a coworker?
Bob's *Interaction Position* (IP) will be based on the following:

Required behavior: Bob is feeling lonely and in need of sensory stimulation after his weekend of isolation. Bob should seek out others (be highly involved) to meet his biological needs for affiliation and sensory stimulation.

Expected behavior: Moderate affiliation with coworkers is generally expected as typical and appropriate in a work environment. Smaller distances are expected from liked than disliked coworkers.

Desired behavior: Bob believes in separation of work and play. He usually prefers a formal, nonaffiliative interaction style during work hours but likes to engage in small talk with friends over lunch. He is also a shy and private person, which leads him to be reticent with liked coworkers and to avoid disliked coworkers.

Combining these elements, Bob's *IP* should be for moderately high involvement with a liked coworker, especially at lunch, and moderately low involvement with a disliked coworker (because the required and expected elements take precedence over the desired elements). This leads to the following patterns, depicted below:

Example 1: A liked coworker's actual behavior, A, reflects high involvement. This makes A more positively valenced than IP. The model predicts Bob will converge toward and reciprocate that involvement.

converge/match/reciprocate (approach)

Example 2: A liked coworker's behavior instead is somewhat low involvement. This makes the IP more positively valenced than A. The theory predicts Bob will diverge from the coworker's behavior or maintain his own level of involvement in hopes of it eliciting a similar response from the coworker.

compensate or maintain

Example 3: A disliked coworker's A is detached and uninvolved, making A more positively valenced than IP. Bob should again reciprocate but to a lesser degree because of his need for affiliation and sensory stimulation.

match/reciprocate (avoid)

Example 4: A disliked coworker's A is highly involved, making A more negatively valenced than Bob's IP. Bob should compensate for that with a relatively uninvolved interaction style.

compensate or maintain (avoid)

Higher Inv ————————————————— Lower Inv
(-)   A   IP   (+)

Adapted from Burgoon, Stern, and Dillman (1995), *Interaction Adaptation: Dyadic Interaction Patterns.* Cambridge, England: Cambridge University Press.

FIGURE 14.2   Sample predictions from interaction adaptation theory (IAT).

couples' discord is the chicken or the egg (i.e., the cause or the result of limited positive reciprocity) is unclear, but it may be part of a cycle of each influencing the other (Huston & Vangelisti, 1991). For the moment, at least we know a little about what cues are part of expressing positive feelings. In addition to those implicated in Chapters 10 and 11 on emotional expression and relational communication, some research specifically on conflict and reciprocity has discovered that gaze, involvement behaviors generally, submissiveness, and relaxation cues tend to accompany positive expressions of affect (Newton & Burgoon, 1990). Conversely, the lack of such behaviors can signal discord, as depicted in Photo 14.4.

Of course, divergence dictated by social norms (such as showing deference to someone of high status) is judged positively unless outgroup members do it. Then it may be evaluated as impolite or hostile (Deprez & Persoons, 1984), something that both communication accommodation theory and expectancy violations theory would predict, because actions of nonrewarding communicators are judged more harshly than those of rewarding communicators. One other exception to the general desirability of reciprocating is that newly formed pairs may be more attracted to one another when they compensate on floor-holding behaviors (Cappella, 1994), which allows one person to take the lead and another to follow.

Finally, adaptation may influence other interaction behaviors. Kikuchi (1994) wanted to see what would happen if convergence toward another's backchannel behavior would facilitate smoother interaction in an intercultural interaction. He found that convergence did indeed increase the tempo of the interaction, whereas divergence led to a slowing of the tempo and more efforts by the other to check for indications of understanding.

These are just a few examples of how adaptation to the communication patterns of others can have positive or negative consequences.

PHOTO 14.4 *It's not uncommon for people with opposing viewpoints to fail to adapt their nonverbal behaviors to each other, as seen in this photograph from a debate between Senators Hillary Clinton and Barack Obama during the 2008 U.S. presidential campaign.*

Summary

Nonverbal behaviors play a major part in managing conversations during all phases and at all levels. They are instrumental in initiating and terminating conversations. Coupled with verbal behaviors, they signal approachability (during greetings) or pending inaccessibility (during terminations), convey supportiveness, and reaffirm the definition of the interpersonal relationship. During leave-taking, they also bolster verbal behaviors that summarize and bring closure to the interaction.

Within the conversation itself, nonverbal cues regulate turn-taking. Speakers employ them to signal their intentions to keep or relinquish the floor. Listeners use them to request or deny a turn and to provide backchannel support to the speaker. The manner in which communicators utilize these cues determines whether turn exchanges are smooth, overlapped, or interruptive. There are several models of how the turn exchange process works, one of the most promising of which appears to be the resource model.

Nonverbal cues also assist topic switches. Proxemic shifts, extra-interactional activities, silences, and paralinguistic cues are used to signal changes in conversational topics. This is important not only in preparing listeners for the new information to be introduced but also as an indicator of speaker competence.

Finally, conversations are coordinated through dyadic interactional sequences and patterns. Substantial evidence documents that people adapt to one another, producing synchrony, convergence, matching, mirroring, and reciprocity or dissynchrony, divergence, complementarity, and compensation. Many of the patterns appear to be biologically based or acquired early in life as infants and children first interact with caretakers. Several theories have been forwarded to explain and predict these interaction patterns; among them are affiliative conflict theory, arousal labeling theory, the sequential functional model, expectancy violations theory, discrepancy arousal theory, communication accommodation theory, and interaction adaptation theory. Research has recently begun to verify the effects of adaptation on such interaction outcomes as relational satisfaction and evaluations of communicators. It is clear that adaptation patterns have long-term implications for successful human relationships.

SUGGESTED READINGS

Burgoon, J. K., Stern, L. A., & Dillman, L. (1995). *Interpersonal adaptation: Dyadic interaction patterns.* Cambridge, England: Cambridge University Press.

Fine, D. (2005). *The fine art of small talk: How to start a conversation, keep it going, build networking skills, and leave a positive impression.* New York: Hyperion.

Garner, A. (1997). *Conversationally speaking: Tested new ways to increase your personal and social effectiveness.* New York: McGraw-Hill.

Patterson, K., Grenny, J., McMillan, R., & Switzler, A. (2002). *Crucial conversations: Tools for talking when stakes are high.* New York: McGraw-Hill.

Shepherd, M. (2005). *The art of civilized conversation: A guide to expressing yourself with style and grace.* New York: Broadway.

15 Deceiving Others

And after all, what is a lie? 'Tis but a truth in masquerade.
—Byron, *Don Juan* (1818)

If language was given to men to conceal their thoughts, then gesture's purpose was to disclose them.
—John R. Napier, *Hands* (1933)

What I hide by language my body utters.
—John Barthes

We trust the eye even when the tongue and hand speak a different language.
—Thomas Hyde and William Hyde (1886)

Trust everybody, but always cut the cards.
—Finley Peter Dunne's Credo

Renter on the phone to calling landlord: "The rent check is coming in the mail."
Gallery visitor at an artist's first showing: "Your paintings are quite unusual."
Elderly mother in nursing home to her visiting children: "I'm okay, really I am."

Sound familiar? You have no doubt heard, or even said, such things to skirt the truth about an overdue rent check, to sidestep a hurtful appraisal of a friend's artistic talent, or to avoid telling family you're feeling blue. These oh-so-common forms of white lies, equivocations, and evasions are part and parcel of the larger communication function of deception that is the topic of this chapter.

The Pervasiveness of Deception

You may be wondering why this topic merits an entire chapter in a nonverbal communication textbook. Its pervasiveness is one reason. Much as we would like to disavow it, deceit is a natural part of the human condition. As D. L. Smith put it, "deceit is the Cinderella of human nature; essential to our humanity but disowned by its perpetrators at every turn" (2004, p. 2). Newspapers and television broadcasts daily report some form of deception, whether it be corporate executives covering up fraudulent business dealings, courtroom witnesses trying to discredit contenders for an heiress's fortunes, spies creating false identities, or athletes lying about doping to improve their performance. And deceit is not just the stuff of sensational headlines. It is everywhere in our daily lives and our daily encounters. It might surprise you to learn that people may lie as often as once or twice a day, and one-fourth to one-third of all conversations involve some form of deception (Turner, Edgley, & Olmstead, 1975). Some of the estimates of the frequency of deceit come from diary studies of college students' interactions with their acquaintances, friends, and family (e.g., DePaulo & Kashy, 1998; George & Robb, 2006; Hancock, Thom-Santelli, & Ritchie, 2004; Marett & George, 2004). Students have reported rates of lying in up to 77 out of every 100 interactions with strangers and a high likelihood of lying to their mother. If one counts not just big lies but also all the little white lies, exaggerations, misrepresentations, flattery, and so forth that populate our day-to-day communication, then one realizes that deceit is an intrinsic part of the fabric of everyday life.

Another reason to devote a chapter to deception is that deception is often enacted, detected, and perceived from nonverbal cues. Although we think of deceit as a verbal activity, and what people say is obviously a central component of most deceptions, deceptions are also carried out through nonverbal channels and depend on nonverbal cues to pull them off. Sometimes the nonverbal cues are intended to bolster a sender's believability or benign intent, as when delivering an equivocal art appraisal with a winning smile so that the recipient believes it is a sincere compliment. Sometimes the nonverbal cues create mixed messages by contradicting the words, as when an aging relative's verbal declaration that she is okay is accompanied by sad eyes and a monotone voice. Other times the deception is entirely nonverbal, as when Angel, the flamboyant female dancer in *Rent*, turns out to be a "he," not a "she." And sometimes it is verbal and nonverbal cues combined that create a believable impression. Take, for instance, Professor Quirrell in the *Harry Potter* series. His character is a study in effective nonverbal deception. Nonverbal cues are thus instrumental to successful deceit. The animal kingdom is chock full of evidence of nonverbal forms of deception that have contributed to survival of various nonhuman species (see Box 15.1). The human species is no different.

On the receiving end, people also rely heavily on nonverbal channels to size up another's credibility and honesty. Sometimes this serves them well (Forrest & Feldman, 2000). But more often, people overlook the most valid and reliable nonverbal cues and rely on faulty ones when judging another's veracity (Burgoon, Blair, & Strom, 2008; Vrij, 2000, 2006). Take, for instance, the Detroit judge who insisted that a Muslim woman remove her veil in his courtroom—not as a show of respect for him but because he believed he could not judge her truthfulness if her face was partially hidden. As we shall see, the face and eyes are a very poor place to look for clues to deception. How deceit gets enacted and judged, then, is of direct importance to us in understanding nonverbal communication, and yet it is a topic that is seldom included when other communication functions—such as relationship development, conversation management, impression management, or social influence—are addressed. Deception is actually relevant to all of these functions, which makes it an appropriate topic on which to conclude a textbook.

B O X **15.1**

Deception in Nature

". . . the tendency to deceive has an ancient pedigree. We find it in many forms, at all levels in the natural kingdom. Even viruses, organisms so simple that it is a struggle to think of them as living things, have subtle strategies for deceiving the immune systems of their hosts: nature is awash with deceit," says David Livingstone Smith in his book *Why We Lie* (2004, p. 1).

Mark Knapp, author of *Lying and Deception in Human Interaction* (2007), explains that nature tends to favor those who practice deception effectively as well as those who become effective deception detectors. Either through fortuitous mutations in perceptual abilities or through learning, organisms that are better able to process information from the environment in order to acquire resources and avoid danger will improve their chances of adapting to and surviving ever-changing circumstances. The traits that enable those adaptations will thus tend to be preserved in future generations. Organisms that detect the fakery, misdirection, false mimicry, and so forth will also improve the chances of their own and their progeny's survival. Deception is thus an intrinsic part of the life–and–death struggle to survive.

It comes as no surprise, then, that the natural world is rife with examples of deception. Here is a sampling from Knapp's compilation of nonhuman deception:

- The virus that causes sleeping sickness circulates in the blood stream. Every time the body's immune system sends out antibodies to combat it, the virus changes its identity by changing its surface glycoprotein, and thus it evades detection. These viruses supposedly are capable of producing a thousand such variations.
- Angler fish, some turtles, and catfish put out an appendage just outside their mouth that looks like a worm. The "worm" lures other fish. Once in range, the predator fish become prey.

- The American avocet is a bird that uses a clever feint to divert predators from its nest. It fakes an injured wing, limping away from its eggs or young so that predators like the fox follow it instead. When the fox goes in for the kill, the bird flies away. Captive gorillas have been known to use a similar trick—in this case, an arm stuck through the bars of their cage—to gain the attention of their human caregivers.
- Chimps are known to use clever diversions to protect hidden food sources and draw more dominant chimps to fake locations.

The strategies that are used in the nonhuman world are quite varied but also quite familiar. Some, like *camouflage* and *mimicry*, are based on appearance, or morphology. Organisms can either take on the appearance of other organisms or blend into the background. Others, like *illusion, evasion*, and *perversion*, are behavioral and may be acquired through trial-and-error, instrumental, or observational learning. Some organisms are even able to plan and reprogram their actions to adapt to changing circumstances. Deception, then, is—in a very real sense—a natural part of life.

The Nature of Nonverbal Deception

Numerous definitions have been offered for deception. Most experts agree that it is an intentional act in which *senders knowingly transmit messages (verbal or nonverbal) to mislead another by fostering false impressions, beliefs, or understandings or by actively concealing the truth* (Buller & Burgoon, 1994; Ekman, 1985; Knapp & Comadena, 1979; Zuckerman, DePaulo, & Rosenthal, 1981). This definition rules out self-deception, intentionally transparent lies (e.g., sarcasm, joking, polite comments, tall tales, role-playing), and mistaken information (i.e., telling something that is false but that the sender believes is true).

It does rule in those forms of deception that benefit others, not just ones that benefit the self. Scholars have long noted that deception occurs for a variety of reasons, not all of which would be considered morally reprehensible. Some lies are altruistic (as in soldiers concealing sensitive information to protect national security), some benefit both the deceiver and the target by preserving the relationship (as in keeping hurtful attitudes about the partner private), and some are strictly for the benefit of self (as in concealing embarrassing secrets or fraudulently obtaining someone's identity information) (Anderson, Ansfield, & DePaulo, 1999; Camden, Motley, & Wilson, 1984; DePaulo, Wetzel, Sternglanz, & Wilson, 2003; Metts & Chronis, 1986). Table 15.1 lists some of the motives for which people report lying.

Our definition also rules in a wide variety of deception forms. Stop for a moment and think of all the terms we have for ways of misleading others. Did all of these come to mind—white lies, fabrication, falsification, evasion, equivocation, concealment,

TABLE 15.1 Motives for Deception

I. Self-focused motives
   A. Protect, retain, or gain resources
   B. Ensure continuation of rewards or services from target
   C. Protect or enhance self-image and self-esteem
   D. Avoid abuse, conflict, punishment, or negative repercussions from target
   E. Maintain privacy/avoid disclosure of secrets and risky information
   F. Control conversational direction, length, or termination
II. Partner-focused motives
   A. Protect target's self-image or self-esteem
   B. Protect target's mental and emotional state (e.g., avoiding worry, hurt, fear, embarrassment)
   C. Protect target's physical state
   D. Protect target's relationship with third party
III. Relationship-focused motives
   A. Avoid conflict
   B. Avoid relational trauma
   C. Avoid unpleasant, repetitive episodes
   D. Avoid violation of role expectations
   E. Avoid relational breakup
   F. Obligatory acceptance

dissembling, omission, bluffing, charade, con, scam, impostership, phishing, fakery, masquerade, trickery, strategic ambiguity, exaggeration, obfuscation, grifting, camouflage? Clearly we have a vast repertoire of possibilities for misrepresenting and putting forward a false front. Most of these boil down to what sociolinguists, psychologists, and communication scholars have identified as five dimensions along which people can alter messages so that they depart from "the truth, the whole truth, and nothing but the truth" (Bavelas, Black, Chovil, & Mullett, 1990; Burgoon, Buller, Guerrero, Afifi, & Feldman, 1996; Grice, 1989; McCornack, 1992). Messages can be altered in terms of their (1) "quantity" or *completeness* of information presented, (2) "quality" or *veridicality* (degree of truth), (3) "manner" or *clarity*, (4) *relevance*, and (5) *personalism* or ownership and connection to the statement. These dimensions for managing information in messages do not rely exclusively on verbal elements. Nonverbal features are also instrumental in successfully perpetrating deceit. Before delving into these specific features and the accuracy with which deception is recognized, we first review some major theories that relate to nonverbal deception.

Theories of Deception

Physiognomic Perspective

A century ago, a book was published called *Vaught's Practical Character Reader* (1902). In it, the author promised to identify who could be trusted as honest and forthright and who could not on the basis of the shapes of their heads, ears, eyes, and so on (see Figure 15.1). According to this view, deceptiveness or truthfulness would be an inborn trait that would be revealed through one's outward appearance. We might find this notion completely laughable were it not for the fact that many people today are still promoting the notion that your physiognomy—the structural aspects of your head and face—can reveal your inner character. One of

FIGURE 15.1   Samples of physiognomic indicators of (a) deceptiveness, (b) genuineness, and (c) honesty, from *Vaught's Practical Character Reader* (1902)

the authors had occasion to debate an individual who claimed he could help attorneys select the best juries during *voie dire* by identifying from appearance which prospective jurors would be leaders, which would be devious and untrustworthy, and so on. Though he claimed to have thousands of studies to back up his "research," he balked when asked to produce any and yet was still "hawking his wares" as a consultant to the legal community. As we saw in Chapter 9, many of our implicit assumptions about others' personality and character are formed from these appearance cues, so it is not entirely far-fetched to believe that such outward features could be handy guides to inward tendencies. No scientific data, however, are available to support this perspective.

Evolutionary Perspective

Another nature-oriented approach with far more believability is the evolutionary perspective. Its impetus springs from Darwin's ground-breaking and meticulous observations about expressions of emotions in humans and animals, which paved the way for so many scientific lines of nonverbal inquiry (Scherer & Ekman, 2005). As we saw in Chapter 3, this perspective proposes that many nonverbal signals have innate origins and were "selected for" (retained) in our communication repertoire because they contributed to survival. In the case of deception, an evolutionary perspective holds that deception evolved as an effective means of aiding the ablest tricksters and manipulators to gain goods, resources, and mates through illicit means and thus perpetuated the bloodlines of those individuals and groups who were skilled at deception (Smith, 1987). Bond and Robinson (1988) wrote:

> Deception has evolved under natural selection, as has the capacity to detect deceit. In conflicts between predator and prey, in competitions for reproduction, deception confers a selective advantage: liars leave behind more offspring, and the progeny inherit their parents' advantage. (p. 295)

Under this view, deception need not be intentional—natural proclivities may be "released" or called forth by circumstances (such as the chameleon that changes colors to match its background)—and they need not be learned. Thus, even small children can generate some remarkable lies without having been taught to do so. We have frequently witnessed this ourselves. Two examples are a two-year-old claiming that his tears at a basketball game were due not to his own fears but to "Grandpa being afraid of Wilbur," the basketball team mascot; and a three-year-old hiding a prized toy from a sibling and then claiming not to know where it is.

Among the common forms of deception are ones that occur elsewhere in nature, where many species use camouflage and mimicry to evade detection, adopt false guises to lure an unsuspecting prey, or use bluffing to settle dominance disputes. Human deception often relies on the same tactics. Many of the most successful spies in history were masters of disguise, changing every feature of their physical appearance—from eyebrows, eye and hair color, and hairstyle to clothing, accessories, and gait—to prevent their true identity from being uncovered. (See Box 15.2.) Con artists operate on the same principle, donning

BOX 15.2

The World of Spies

In the heart of downtown Washington, D.C., sits the International Spy Museum, the world's greatest collection of history and trade craft from the art and intrigue of international espionage (http://www.spymuseum.org/about/exhibits.php). Spies live a life of lies, so what better window into the world of deception than through the strategies, cover stories, disguises, and subterfuge that have populated the history of spying by the United States, its allies, and its adversaries? Here you will see an astonishing cavalcade of successful spies throughout history, such as Lia de Beaumont, a lovely young girl who visited the 18th century Russian court, and with whom Empress Elizabeth was quite taken. But her demure visitor was actually Charles-Genevieve-Louis-Auguste-Andre-Timothee d'Eon de Beaumont, a male spy.

Or consider Josephine Baker, one of many film and stage stars who used their dazzling charm and celebrity to mask their watchful eyes, gain access to sensitive information, and feed disinformation to the enemy.

In *The Master of Disguise* (1999), retired CIA operative and former "chief of disguises"

Antonio Mendez recounts how, over the course of his 25-year history with the CIA, he and his subordinates changed the identities and appearance of thousands of clandestine operatives—and how his own use of disguise and illusion enabled him to succeed against the overwhelming forces of the KGB during the Cold War era.

Now Hollywood has gotten into the act, helping agents with more elaborate prostheses, wigs, makeup, mannerisms, and other ploys to transform young into old, male into female, able-bodied into frail. New technologies even allow these master manipulators to view digitally enhanced photographs to see how certain individuals might look with different disguises. During the search for Saddam Hussein, U.S. armed forces were equipped with several different versions of what the normally black-haired, mustached Hussein might look like if disguised with full beard and Arab headdress or as an older man with and without facial hair. Videos of Hussein were also studied for specific speech patterns so that if one of Hussein's doubles, and not the real Iraqi leader, were found, the imposter could be unmasked.

the attire and demeanor of trusted professions such as the clergy to extract money from the unsuspecting elderly, for example. Frank Abagnale, the mastermind thief who was the subject of the true-story movie *Catch Me If You Can*, reports having an elaborate wardrobe of disguises that would allow him to pass himself off as an old man, a physician, a bank employee, or even a woman. Humans attempting to ward off a bear attack likewise may attempt to make themselves look larger and more forbidding so that the bear takes flight. Impersonators, imposters, and fakers who rely on these age-old techniques for deceit stand as tacit evidence that the evolutionary advantage conferred by deception is anything but lost.

Although some forms of falsehoods are unsuccessful and may even backfire, an evolutionary perspective holds that these would not be selected for, so that over time, only the most successful practices and their perpetrators would survive. At the same time, the evolutionary perspective holds that natural selection would also have favored those who are particularly successful at detecting cheating and deceit (Shackleford, 1997), thus producing rough parity between deceivers and detectors.

Other important principles from an evolutionary perspective include the expectation that deception has a fairly infrequent rate of occurrence, or else it would not succeed, and its occurrence is subject both to environmental constraints and to the relative rewards and costs for deceivers and their targets. Additionally, an evolutionary view does not imply that everyone is alike. Ontogeny plays a role such that individuals should improve their ability to deceive and to detect deceit as they mature, and deception and its detection are expected to show intra-individual and inter-individual variability (Smith, 1987).

So far, our discussion of the evolution of deception has focused more on voluntary and intentional acts of deceit. However, evolution has also equipped us with involuntary physiological signals. Darwin's observations about emotional displays underpin the next hypothesis as regards telltale signs of deception (Ekman, 2003).

The Leakage Hypothesis

As early as the 1920s, research was being conducted on nonverbal behaviors associated with deception, but it began in earnest with a program of research by Ekman and Friesen (1969a) guided by the leakage hypothesis. Ekman and Friesen speculated that the act of deception is associated with a host of internal physiological, emotional, and cognitive responses that give rise to external displays. Like Pinocchio's nose (see Figure 15.2), these telltale signs "leak out" of the body unbidden and are a "giveaway" that the communicator is hiding something. Deceivers attempt to control these telltale external displays to avoid giving receivers any behavioral clues that deception is occurring (*deception cues*) or that reveal the true nature of their feelings (*leakage cues*). The success of such attempts is determined by senders' internal reactions to the deception and by

FIGURE 15.2   Pinocchio's nose

the controllability, sending capacities, and external feedback provided by the nonverbal channels.

Ekman and Friesen (1969a) speculated that deception is an arousing action, one that usually is accompanied by negative emotional states such as guilt, fear, or disgust (although deceivers may occasionally experience overeagerness and "duping delight" at fooling someone). These emotional states, as well as general arousal, may be manifested involuntarily and unintentionally, hence they are described as "leaking out" of the body. These leaked emotions are under the control of the lower parts of the brain (the limbic system) rather than the motor cortex and should include such difficult-to-inhibit expressions as eyebrow raises that show fear, lip presses that show anger, or cheek raises and crinkling eye muscles that show enjoyment (Ekman, 2003).

Some channels may be "leakier" than others. Among the factors that may determine which channels or body regions give off the most telltale signs are controllability, ability to monitor, perceived importance, sending capacity, and feedback capacity (Ekman & Friesen, 1969a; Hocking & Leathers, 1980). *Controllability* relates to which channels are amenable to suppression of unwanted behaviors and which permit a sender to call up or repeat specific sequences of cues that are "honest-looking." *Monitoring ability* concerns how easily a sender or receiver can observe the specific behaviors being emitted. People, for instance, may be less aware or able to observe foot bobbing than hair twisting. *Perceived importance* relates to which channels and cues a sender believes are most salient and likely to be noticed by receivers. *Sending capacity* refers to the communication channel itself, specifically how visible it is, how many different messages can be sent, and how quickly messages can be transmitted. *Feedback capacity* refers to the extent to which a receiver attends to, comments on, reacts to, and holds a sender responsible for the messages in a given channel.

In general, deceivers should be less likely to display telltale nonverbal cues in channels that are highly controllable, easily monitored by self or others, include cues that stereotypically are associated with deceit, have large sending capacity, or receive extensive feedback. These factors produce a *leakage hierarchy* among the various nonverbal channels, but just what that hierarchy is has been a point of dispute. Within the kinesic channel, Ekman (2003; Ekman & Friesen, 1969) proposed that facial cues present a complex picture but on balance are the least likely to leak information about deception. He reasoned that facial expressions (1) are highly visible and (2) can send a variety of signals rapidly. This means that (3) receivers are likely to attend to them and react to them, (4) senders will be quite conscious of them, and (5) senders will attempt to suppress micro-expressions while managing macro-expressions to best effect. Gross bodily movements, though more easily controlled, are also more likely to leak information because they have a lower sending capacity (i.e., they can send fewer messages and at a slower rate), receive less external feedback, and thus are less likely to be censored. Empirical evidence bears this out: Facial cues typically are the least diagnostic in identifying deception (Hocking, Bauchner, Kaminski, & Miller, 1979; Zuckerman, Larrance, Spiegel, & Klorman, 1981), yet people pay closer attention to face than body or voice cues (Bauchner, Kaplan, & Miller, 1980; Buller, Strzyzewski, & Hunsaker, 1991; Ekman & Friesen, 1974).

Many characteristics of the voice suggest it should be the least "leaky" channel, because senders manage their vocal cues along with their verbalizations, senders can control many aspects of their vocalizations, the voice has excellent sending capacity, and senders receive excellent internal auditory feedback to let them know how their voice is sounding. However, empirical evidence indicates that the voice is at least as "leaky" as the body and in fact may be the most diagnostic (informative) channel as to a sender's veracity (Burgoon et al., 2008; Hocking & Leathers, 1980; Burgoon, Stoner, Moffitt, Humpherys, & Jensen, 2007). Innate alerting qualities of the voice and its strong connection to emotional states may account for some of its telltale qualities.

Finally, the verbal channel is considered least likely to reveal deception; however, many scholars have speculated to the contrary, and recent research on linguistic and meta-content features of language (e.g., Burgoon & Qin, 2006; Vrij, 2000) may rewrite that conclusion.

Four-Factor Theory

Zuckerman, DePaulo, and Rosenthal (1981) extended the original leakage hypothesis by analyzing more deeply what kinds of internal events can cause outward deception displays. They grouped the possible factors into four classes: (1) *arousal*; (2) *negative affect*; (3) *cognitive processing*; and (4) *attempted control*. Deception is thought to be physiologically arousing. The autonomic arousal that deceivers experience is thought to produce behavioral indicators such as dilated pupils and rapid blinking. Deception is also thought to be associated with negative emotions such as guilt or anxiety. These emotions should produce nonverbal affect displays such as higher vocal pitch, less facial pleasantness, or more adaptors. Further, deception is thought to be more cognitively challenging than telling the truth. The greater cognitive effort involved with concocting plausible lies and other deceptive responses should show up as longer delays in responding (response latencies), more pauses, more speech disturbances, and fewer gestures. Finally, deceivers are thought to be aware of these possible telltale signs and to attempt to control them, but in their zealousness, to overcontrol their behavior. The resultant behavior patterns may be stiff, rigid, awkward, inexpressive, and lacking in spontaneity.

One challenge that has been posed to this perspective is that telling the truth may sometimes also elicit arousal, anxiety, fear, and cognitive effort (McCornack, 1997). Ekman (1985), for example, proposed that innocent individuals who are wrongly accused may also be distressed and flustered at trying to prove their innocence and thus show many of the same behaviors that are attributed to deceivers. He called the resultant erroneous judgment by receivers the *Othello error*, after Shakespeare's character who murdered innocent Desdemona because his accusations of her infidelity made her so overwrought that she appeared guilty.

The other significant challenge is that many everyday lies simply do not induce leakage. They are so commonplace, and are run off with such ease, that they do not cause any internal angst by their senders nor require any extra cognitive effort to produce (DePaulo, Kashy, Kirkendol, Wier, & Epstein, 1996). Thus, deception need not instigate a lot of arousal, emotion, cognitive effort, and need to control one's behavior. By the same token, situations that trigger these internal psychological experiences for deceivers—such as being accused of being a thief—may trigger the same responses for truthful people. This means that if you see someone with a calm exterior, it doesn't necessarily mean he or she is innocent. And if you see someone being very nervous, it doesn't mean he or she is a liar.

Interpersonal Deception Theory

Interpersonal deception theory (IDT; Buller & Burgoon, 1996) was developed to offer an alternative to the more psychologically oriented models. IDT defines fundamental principles of interpersonal communication and applies them to deception. It deemphasizes intrapsychic and physiological factors, instead placing greater emphasis on the social, interactive, and process-oriented nature of interpersonal deception. Deception, for example, is viewed as dynamic and iterative, not static: Displays and judgments change as senders put out their initial messages, receivers form judgments and react verbally or nonverbally, senders read receivers' signals as feedback and adjust what they say and do next, and so on through additional iterations as communication proceeds. The fact that sender thoughts and behaviors depend on what receivers do and vice versa also makes deception an interdependent process of moves and countermoves that enables senders to make ongoing adaptations to receiver feedback so as to evade detection. Put differently, what you see as a deception display may depend as much on how the receiver is communicating as on what the sender is feeling.

IDT also assumes that one cannot predict or explain the production and reception of deceptive messages without taking into account such factors as the kind of communication episode taking place (e.g., an interview, a high-level business discussion, diplomatic negotiations), the modality through which communication is taking place (e.g., text, telephone, videoconference), the culture of the interactants, and the relationship between sender and receiver (e.g., strangers, friends, enemies).

Another important distinction is between *strategic* (deliberate) and *nonstrategic* (unintended) activity. Deception is by definition an intentional act. Therefore, at least part of a deceptive message should be deliberate or "strategic," even though strategic activity may not be highly conscious. For deceivers, the goal is to appear credible and evade detection. For detectors, the goal is to peer behind the mask and determine sender veracity. Deceivers and receivers alike think about what they say and do and monitor the other person's reactions for signs of acceptance, skepticism, or disbelief. For example, the strategy of appearing subservient and without culpability may involve such nonverbal tactics as smiling, attentive eye gaze, symmetrical and stooped posture, constrained gesturing, and a high-pitched voice.

This is not to say that deception doesn't also include nonstrategic activity. IDT agrees that deceivers also display inadvertent telltale signs of arousal, cognitive effort, and emotion identified in the leakage hypothesis and four-factor theory. They also may have a generally poorer communication performance.

In addition to spelling out *assumptions* about deception and interpersonal communication, IDT presents 18 *propositions*, or general statements of empirical relationships, about interpersonal deception. Table 15.2 summarizes the propositions. Based on these propositions, numerous hypotheses have been generated and tested. For example, the first two overarching propositions call attention to the importance of context and relationship in influencing the entire deceptive interchange. Context includes a variety of factors such as culture, setting, and type of communication episode (e.g., formal or informal, business or social), which means that hypotheses could test whether cultures differ in their deception displays and their judgments of deception.

Several criticisms have been directed at IDT. One is that IDT is not really a specific theory because it does not invoke a single causal mechanism. Another is that some of the propositions are quite general and do not make specific predictions, which makes it difficult to say what counts as contrary evidence. Other criticisms concern the experiments themselves.

Self-Presentation Theory

Verbal and nonverbal behaviors can be used to bolster one's general credibility and create an honest appearing demeanor (Bond, Kahler, & Paolicelli, 1985; Zuckerman, DeFrank, Hall, Larrance, & Rosenthal, 1979). By making oneself appear unruffled, cooperative, and sincere, one can boost credibility in terms of competence, trustworthiness, and openness. Self-presentation theory (SPT) (DePaulo, 1992; DePaulo & Friedman, 1998; DePaulo et al., 2003; Levin & Zickar, 2002; Vrij, 2006) draws on individuals' goals of presenting themselves in a favorable light and their inclination to behave strategically to achieve their goals. As we have seen in Chapter 10, the self-presentational aspect of nonverbal communication has many adherents and has attracted a significant amount of research and theorizing. Work specifically on deception also confirms that deceivers consciously employ many

TABLE 15.2   Propositions of Interpersonal Deception Theory

1. *Degree of interactivity influences cognitions, affective states, and behaviors in deceptive interchanges.* How senders and receivers think, feel, and behave depends on whether the communication context is interactive or not.
2. *Relationship status influences cognitions, affective states, and behaviors in deceptive interchanges.* How senders and receivers think, feel, and behave varies systematically with relationship (a) familiarity (relational, informational, and behavioral) and (b) valence (positivity or negativity).
3. *Veracity affects strategic and nonstrategic activity.* Compared with truth-tellers, deceivers (a) engage in greater strategic activity designed to manage information, behavior, and image, and (b) display more nonstrategic arousal cues, negative and dampened affect, noninvolvement, and performance decrements.
4. *Context interactivity affects strategic and nonstrategic activity.* The more interactive the communication context, the more deceivers display (a) more strategic activity (information, behavior, and image management) and (b) less nonstrategic activity (arousal, negative or dampened affect, and performance decrements) over time.
5. *Initial expectations for honesty are positively related to degree of context interactivity and positivity of relationship between sender and receiver.*
6. *The higher the initial expectations for truthfulness, the less deceivers will fear detection and the less they will engage in strategic activity; the higher the level of initial suspicion, the more deceivers will fear detection and engage in strategic activity.*
7. *Goals and motivations moderate strategic and nonstrategic behavior.* Senders deceiving for self-gain will exhibit more strategic activity and nonstrategic leakage than senders deceiving for other-benefit. Receivers' priorities among instrumental, relational, and identity objectives and their initial intent to uncover deceit will also affect their behavior.
8. *Receiver familiarity increases deceiver detection apprehension, strategic activity, and nonstrategic behavior.* As receivers' informational, behavioral, and relational familiarity increases, deceivers not only (a) experience more detection apprehension and (b) exhibit more strategic information, behavior, and image management, but also (c) display more nonstrategic leakage.
9. *Social skill aids deception success through increased strategic activity and reduced nonstrategic activity.* Skilled senders are better at conveying a truthful demeanor through management of their behavior.
10. *Judgments of sender credibility are related to context interactivity, receiver truth biases, sender encoding skills, and sender deviations from expected patterns.* The more interactive the context, the higher the truth biases of receivers; the more skilled the sender and the less deviant the sender's communication patterns, the more the sender will be judged as credible.
11. *Detection accuracy is related to context interactivity, receiver truth biases, receiver familiarity, receiver decoding skills, sender encoding skills, and sender deviations from expected patterns.* Receivers will be less accurate if (a) the context is interactive, (b) they hold strong truth biases, (c) they are more acquainted with the sender, (d) they are less familiar with the sender's background, with the sender's typical communication, and with diagnostic deception cues, (e) the sender has strong encoding skills, and (f) the sender adheres to expected communication patterns.
12. *Receivers reveal their suspicions through a combination of strategic and nonstrategic behavior.* Like senders, receivers also behave strategically in their choice of demeanor and what they say, but they too can inadvertently signal their true feelings through their nonverbal behavior.
13. *Senders perceive suspicion when it is present.* Senders recognize suspicion when receivers' communication deviates from their usual or generally expected patterns and when it expresses disbelief, uncertainty, or the desire for additional information.
14. *Suspicion (perceived or actual) increases senders' strategic and nonstrategic behavior.* If senders think the receiver is suspicious, they will do more to manage their verbal and nonverbal behavior. This may result in some performance impairment and further efforts to repair their performance, especially if it is met with skepticism rather than acceptance.

15. *Deception and suspicion displays change over time.* Displays are not static. They are continuously changing as conversations progress.
16. *The predominant interaction adaptation pattern between deceivers and receivers is reciprocity.* If, for example, receivers appear engaged and involved, deceivers are likely to do the same; if receivers are unpleasant, deceivers may also show some initial unpleasantness. However, deceivers will attempt to overcome non-normative and dispreferred communication styles.
17. *Judgments of sender credibility and detection accuracy at the end of an interaction are a function of final receiver cognitions and sender performance.* What matters is not what receivers thought or how senders acted at the outset, but where the thoughts and behavior processes end up. That is, there is a recency effect.
18. *Senders' judgments of their own success are a function of their final perceived suspicion and final receiver performance.* Senders will believe that they have been successful if they no longer perceive any suspicion and receivers' final behavioral displays bolster that conclusion.

Source: Adapted from Buller & Burgoon (1996).

detection-evading tactics (see, e.g., Burgoon, Buller, Floyd, & Grandpre, 1996; Forrest & Feldman, 2000).

One important implication of SPT is that both truth-tellers and deceivers are concerned with their self-image and will work to put forward a credible front. When jeopardy or other aversive consequences are involved, both truth-tellers and deceivers may be fearful of being disbelieved and so may exhibit many of the same behavioral signs of stress and anxiety. Conversely, when the stakes for deceiving are low, neither truth-tellers nor deceivers may be overly concerned with their self-presentations, because they can each rely on overlearned repertoires of verbal and nonverbal behaviors to produce mundane lies. Where differences may be most evident between deceivers and truth-tellers is in the conviction and sincerity with which truth-tellers embrace their messages compared to deceivers. Like Buller and Burgoon's (1994) categories of strategic communication, deceivers are predicted to be more reticent, hesitant, and uncertain, perhaps because deceivers' statements are illegitimate, because they may have some moral compunction about lying, because they may lack emotional commitment to what they are saying, or because they lack the rich details with which to back up their claims. In DePaulo's version of SPT, deceivers' verbal and nonverbal messages are also predicted to be more pallid, inexpressive, or rehearsed, leading to some verbal and speech performance decrements that are not experienced by truth-tellers. IDT predicts similar performance decrements initially but predicts these will dissipate over the course of an interaction as deceivers strategically attempt to become more expressive, immediate, involved, dominant, and assertive.

Motivation Impairment Effect

The *motivation impairment effect* (MIE) is not really a theory; it is just a hypothesis, but one that has garnered a fair amount of press in the deception arena. Advanced by DePaulo and Kirkendol (1989), the MIE is actually a dual hypothesis of nonverbal impairment and verbal facilitation due to motivation. It states that the lies of motivated deceivers will be more detectable when told in channels that include nonverbal cues than when told in verbal-only channels. In other words, the harder people try, the more they will fail nonverbally. Conversely, lies of less motivated deceivers will be more detectable when told in verbal-only channels than when told in channels that accord access to nonverbal information. The idea is that when people are motivated to deceive, they will attempt to manage their demeanor and will succeed at the verbal level but overcontrol nonverbal performances, resulting in greater nonverbal leakage that makes their lies detectable. Comparatively, unmotivated deceivers will not be anxious and will not have extra cognitive workload. They will not give off leakage but will also have less-believable, less-polished verbal messages.

DePaulo and Kirkendol (1989) summarize several experiments that they believe support the MIE, and other scholars subsequently have often interpreted their own research as consistent with this provocative hypothesis. For example, experiment participants who are given incentives to deceive decrease blinking, have more neutral facial expressions, make fewer head movements, use fewer adaptors, make fewer postural shifts, give shorter responses to questions, and talk more slowly (Bauchner, Brandt, & Miller, 1977; Zuckerman & Driver, 1985).

Burgoon (2005) has raised several questions regarding the validity of the MIE. Based on a review of the original MIE studies and several other investigations, she concluded that some aspects of a motivated performance may look more like poise than suspicious conduct. Only under extreme motivation or jeopardy does impairment occur, a pattern that better fits with a choking-under-pressure explanation, because both verbal and nonverbal behavior suffer. Otherwise, motivation seems to facilitate rather than impair nonverbal performance. Recent studies (e.g., Burgoon, Blair, & Hamel, 2007; Burgoon, Blair, & Moyer, 2003; Burgoon & Floyd, 2000) have shown that motivated deceivers do report being more nervous, experiencing more cognitive effort, and working harder to control their behavior than unmotivated deceivers, but those efforts paid off in that their deception went undetected. Deceivers who self-report high motivation have been judged by observers to be more credible than those reporting moderate to low motivation (Burgoon, Buller, & Guerrero, 1995). Thus, moderate motivation appears to be more beneficial than harmful. The jury is still out on how extreme forms of motivation might affect behavior in real-world circumstances, but we anticipate that, consistent with the choking-under-pressure idea, extreme stress or extreme consequences associated with high motivation will take a toll.

Actual and Perceived Indicators of Deceit

It has been suggested in some quarters (e.g., Park, Levine, McCornack, Morrison, & Ferrara, 2002) that people discover another's dissembling not from the deceiver's verbal and nonverbal behavior but from third-party reports. No doubt much deceit does get uncovered in this way. But as Vrij (2006) points out, there are many situations in which people do not have other information or sources to check out. Moreover, we may just be less aware of the information we are picking up from nonverbal clues because our focus is more on what people say when we are trying to ferret out truth. Yet we can be continuously gleaning nonverbal information, even when another person is silent. When the time comes to consciously size up another's veracity, we may notice both verbal and nonverbal clues but may not pay attention to the right ones. That does not mean that nonverbal cues are not influencing our judgments. But it may mean that we are responding to stereotypical rather than useful cues. And, the ones that we think are the tip-offs may not be the same ones that actually influence our judgments.

So what cues are actually reliable indicators of deception? Most people, when asked, will tell you it is the eyes that give away deceivers. One of your authors oversaw a class project in which students and faculty were intercepted on campus and videorecorded as the "reporter" asked, "How can you tell when people are lying?" The number one answer was "the eyes: people look away." Other answers were "nervous," "shaky voice," "body movements," and "facial expressions."

But are these truly diagnostic? Will they actually allow you to reliably determine who is truthful and who isn't? In reality, the eyes are not a reliable indicator, and there are no single cues that by themselves are highly reliable and produce consistent results across all circumstances and people. So, researchers over the last several decades have been empirically sorting out which behaviors are actual versus stereotypical influences on deception detection. Several meta-analyses (quantitative summaries of estimates from the collected research studies) have identified which behaviors are (1) stereotypical cues to deceit—that is, what receivers report using to form their judgments, (2) actual indicators to deceit—that is, the behaviors that accurately distinguish truthful from deceptive communication, and (3) cues that influence judgments—that is, what cues contribute to receivers' judgments of truthfulness or deceptiveness, regardless of their accuracy (see DePaulo et al., 2003; Vrij, 2000; Zuckerman & Driver, 1985).

Far more experiments have examined actual cues to deceit. The DePaulo et al. meta-analysis, for example, reports the results of 1,338 estimates of 158 cues from 120 different reports comparing truthful to deceptive verbal and nonverbal behavior. Because the data in that analysis include only three studies published since 1996 and because very few truly interactive experiments were included, we have combined those results with more recent summaries and experiments. We have also combined the results on deception stereotypes from previous meta-analyses with the global deception team's results and other recent summaries. The relationships are summarized in Table 15.3, where they are listed within each of the body regions in the order of the strength of their relationship to veracity or the percentage of people relying on them. Although less often measured, it may be that the inconsistency among indicators rather than the specific indicators themselves determine perceptions of deception. A communicator's style may be perceived as insincere or "fishy" when it violates communication norms or when the various cues are at odds with one another (Bond et al., 1992; Buller & Burgoon, 1996; Henningsen, Cruz, & Morr, 2000; Zuckerman & Driver, 1985).

TABLE 15.3   Actual and Stereotypical Nonverbal Indicators of Deceit

Nonverbal Behavior	Associated with Actual Deception	Stereotypically Associated with Deception
Eyes		
Pupil dilation	+	
Blinking	+	+
Gaze aversion	0	+
Face and Head		
Fake smile	0	+
Head movement	−	+
Lip presses/adaptors	+	
Facial expressiveness	−	
Micromomentary emotional expressions	0	+
Body and Limbs		
Illustrator gestures	−	+
Adaptor gestures	+	+
Hand shrugs	0	
Postural shifts	0	+
Postural rigidity/tension	+	−
Voice		
Elevated pitch	+	+
Response latency	+	+
Response length/talk time	−	+
Rapid speech tempo	0	+
Speech errors/dysfluencies	+	+
Filled pauses	+	+
Vocal tension	+	+
Vocal uncertainty	+	
Loud voice	0	
Global Patterns		
General nervousness/tension	+	+
General unpleasantness	0	+
Immediacy/involvement	−	

Note: + indicates a positive relationship with actual or perceived deception, − indicates a negative relationship (e.g., less involvement is associated with deception), 0 indicates that the relationship was tested but not supported or produced mixed results, and an empty cell means the relationship has not been investigated.

Factors Influencing Deception Displays

So far, we have noted that there are very few reliable indicators of deception that are applicable in all circumstances. That is to say, there are no sure-fire individual nonverbal signs that someone is lying. One reason there are so few is that deception displays are responsive to a variety of factors scientists refer to as *moderators* (because they interact with deception to modify or "moderate" the general behavioral pattern). Several of the deception theories explicitly note that deception displays are affected by several moderator variables.

Some moderators should exert a stable influence across interactions. Some social-level variables like one's culture or native language and some individual-level variables like age, personality, and general social skills or demeanor bias should have a fairly consistent impact on behavior. Other factors, like motivations, incentives/consequences, and opportunities for planning or rehearsal, are more situation–specific and so should produce highly variable behavioral patterns across contexts.

Following is a brief synopsis of some of the major moderators of deception displays that have been proposed and supported through research. We begin with sociocultural and psychological variables that people "bring" to the interaction (i.e., they are pre-interaction factors), then move to ones related specifically to the interaction itself.

Culture. Although many studies have examined beliefs about and moral evaluations of deceit by children and adults of varied cultural backgrounds (e.g., Bussey, 1999; Lee, Xu, Fu, Cameron, & Chen, 2001; Robinson, 1996), very little is known about how culture affects actual deceptive displays. It stands to reason that cultures that are more low-context or far more expressive and "immediate" might respond differently than cultures that are normally reticent or high-context. At least one investigation has found that the more independent one's cultural orientation (as would be very true of the United States and far less true of Japan), the more the person is likely to show high involvement, pleasantness, and relaxation during truth-telling but to display reduced involvement, vocal and kinesic pleasantness, and vocal relaxation and more nervousness when lying (Kam, 2003). How culture affects deceptive communication is an area ripe for further investigation.

Sex/Gender. Men and women differ in the kinds of lies they tell (DePaulo et al., 1996), which may affect the nonverbal accompaniments of those lies. For instance, women tell more polite lies; men tell more self-serving ones. Lies of women are more easily detected than lies of men (Forrest & Feldman, 2000; Forrest, Feldman, & Tyler, 2004); in other words, men are better liars than women. One reason might be that males cover their distress with smiles more than females do (Ansfield, 2007) and thus mask deception-related fear or anxiety. Perhaps inauthenticity is also more evident in the smiles of women telling polite lies.

Age. Children are not as skilled at lying as are adults. First graders, for example, are more easily detected when telling lies than seventh graders or college students (Feldman, Jenkins, & Popoola, 1979), so deceit is partly an acquired skill that increases with age (DePaulo, Stone, & Lassiter, 1985a; Feldman & White, 1980), especially around fourth or fifth grade. Children do better lying to peers or strangers than to parents (Allen & Atkinson, 1978; DePaulo, Stone, & Lassiter, 1985b; Morency & Krauss, 1982).

Communication Skills/Demeanor Bias.   Have you noticed how some people always seem to look innocent no matter how guilty they are, and others always have that guilty look about them even when they've done nothing wrong? Perhaps you are someone who gets away with telling a lot of untruths, or maybe you are someone who is easily found out. This is what researchers have described as *honest demeanor bias*—some people consistently are viewed as truthful or sincere or trustworthy, and others as lacking credibility (Kraut, 1978; Zuckerman et al., 1981). Demeanor bias is a reflection of a person's communication skills, and skilled senders are better at pulling off successful deception than their less skilled counterparts. Just what contributes to this bias was the subject of a series of studies (Burgoon et al., 1995; Riggio, Tucker, & Throckmorton, 1987; Riggio, Tucker, & Widaman, 1987). Researchers discovered that people with more emotional control (i.e., skills involving regulation of nonverbal affective displays) are more believable when telling the truth but not when deceiving. Those with more social control (i.e., verbal and role-playing skills) are more believable during both truth-telling and deceit. But, the best combination for garnering credibility is higher nonverbal expressivity, higher verbal control, and *less* verbal expressivity, that is, being more of a chameleon and restrained verbally but more demonstrative nonverbally. Skilled deceivers are more fluent, less hesitant, and better able to appear "normal."

Personality.   Several personality traits have been linked to deception ability. Machiavellianism and self-monitoring have received the most attention. Machiavellians (named after a famous Italian political philosopher) are highly manipulative and see lying as a justifiable means to an end. Thus, they should not experience the same negative feelings of guilt, fear, or remorse that less Machiavellian individuals experience. They are also better at controlling their spontaneous expressions and hence should be more successful liars (Christie & Geis, 1970). However, the actual research evidence for these claims has been mixed. Sometimes no differences have been found. Where there have been differences, Machiavellian liars have used more eye contact and looked their interlocutors in the eye, "hammed it up" more, and were believed more (DePaulo & Rosenthal, 1979b; Exline, Thibaut, Hickey, & Gumpert, 1970; Geis & Moon, 1981; O'Hair, Cody, & McLaughlin, 1981).

Self-monitoring is related to the social skill of expressive control in that it concerns how well a person can regulate expressive behavior. Self-monitoring in principle should make people better deceivers, but empirical results have been mixed. Sometimes high self-monitors have been less detectable than low self-monitors, but sometimes the reverse has been true (Zuckerman et al., 1981). For example, people high in self-control make fewer hand movements during deception than during truth-telling (Vrij, Akehurst, & Morris, 1997), which may disguise nervousness but might also impair illustrative gesturing. Deceivers who are self-conscious in public are overly concerned with being socially appropriate and become less fluent verbally, make less eye contact, display fewer head and hand movements, and show more emotional reactions when deceiving than less self-conscious communicators (Riggio & Friedman, 1982; Riggio, Tucker, & Widaman, 1987; Vrij, Akehurst, & Morris, 1997).

Other personality traits thought to relate to skill at deception include dominance, extroversion, and exhibitionism. Dominant, extroverted, and exhibitionist individuals are better at overcoming and suppressing signs of nervousness and at increasing facial animation.

Motivation. The motivation to succeed, as noted previously, can have both beneficial and deleterious effects on performance and often works in complex ways. For example, highly motivated women are perceived as less sincere than low-motivated ones, although the reverse is true for men (Forrest & Feldman, 2000). As for the influence of specific motives on deception displays, deception can often share the same motives as truthful communication, but motivation may affect *how* deception is enacted (Buller & Burgoon, 1996; Metts & Chronis, 1986). For example, falsification is most common when deception is motivated by a desire to avoid hurting a partner, avoid relational trauma, or protect the deceiver's image. If deception is motivated by a desire to protect another, it should also have less leakage associated with it, because there should be little apprehension about being detected.

Incentives/Consequences. Traditionally we have expected that higher stakes, potential jeopardy such as going to prison, adverse consequences such as failure to win a job, or large incentives such as money should produce differences in deceptive behavior compared to low-stakes situations (Ekman, 1992; Frank & Feeley, 2003). After all, we often have no qualms about lying to a friend that we like his paintings or perhaps fibbing about how much effort we invested in picking out a gift for a family member. Presumably, low-stakes lies are told with ease and therefore should have little nonverbal leakage of arousal, negative emotion, or cognitive effort associated with them (DePaulo & Kashy, 1998). However, some intriguing new research might reverse thinking on this matter. It finds that higher demands produce less, not more, arousal (Leal, 2005). Higher stakes might suppress some forms of arousal.

Planning/Rehearsal. Ability to plan or mentally rehearse deception increases success by allowing more control over nonverbal behavior, although its effect may not be as great as those of motivation. Compared with lies that receive little or no forethought, planned lies are characterized by increased pupil dilation, fewer unfilled pauses, shorter response latencies, and faster speech (Buller, Burgoon, White, Buslig, & Ebesu, 1995; diBattista, 1995; O'Hair et al., 1981). Thus speech appears credible and unimpaired.

Interactivity. One proposition that is central to IDT states that the degree of interactivity alters how deceptive episodes unfold. Communication is more interactive if senders and receivers engage in mutual message exchange rather than one-way transmissions; communication occurs in real time rather than being delayed; each person's message is responsive to the other person's, as in a threaded conversation; and participants have full access to nonverbal cues from each other. As communication contexts depart from this benchmark by, say, reducing the number of channels available for message exchange, they begin to lose the essence of full interpersonal interactivity. Many deception experiments fall at or near the noninteractive end of an interactivity continuum, because senders wrote out their lies, or they gave their deception as a monologue to a silent audience or video camera, or observers viewed a delayed videotape presentation. The issue of interactivity is a centerpiece of IDT, because if much of what has been written about deception derives from experiments that involved little or no interactivity, it may not be informative about what happens during typical interactive deception. Experiments have established that noninteractive deception differs from interactive deception (e.g., Burgoon, Buller, & Floyd, 2001; Dunbar, Ramirez, & Burgoon, 2003). What is written about deception, then, needs to specify whether it applies to interactive or noninteractive contexts.

Deception Strategy. Displays vary according to which deception strategy deceivers are employing (Buller, Burgoon, White, & Ebesu, 1994).

Suspicion. Deceivers recognize suspicion when it is present, presumably because receivers inadvertently "telegraph" their skepticism through their own nonverbal and verbal behavior (Burgoon, Buller, Dillman, & Walther, 1995; Burgoon, Buller, Ebesu, Rockwell, & White, 1996).

Time. Deception displays are dynamic (Burgoon & Buller, 1994). Deceivers adapt their nonverbal performance over time to more closely approximate that of truth-tellers (Burgoon, Buller, White, Afifi, & Buslig, 1999; White & Burgoon, 2001). As a result, the net advantage typically goes to deceivers rather than receivers (Burgoon, Buller, & Floyd, 2001).

Audience Size. Few studies have examined the size of the target audience for its impact on deceit, but we do know from Goffman's (1959) self-presentation theory that failing to keep one's audiences segregated can lead to real challenges when they are then brought together. Now comes some evidence that this makes deception particularly challenging. In a series of experiments, Bond, Thomas, and Paulson (2004) asked students to describe a particular teacher truthfully to one peer, then describe the same teacher deceptively to another peer. When the two receivers were brought together and the sender had to repeat the task, the multiple-audience predicament caused even truth-tellers to look deceptive. Most responsible for piquing suspicion were vocal rather than visual cues, especially dysfluencies. Other studies conducted in an online environment found that deceivers issued fewer lies to group members when face to face than when online, and especially were less likely to tell lies when receivers were suspicious, suggesting that having multiple skeptical receivers alters a deceiver's communication (George & Marett, 2004).

Detecting Deception

We have seen that how and why senders construct their deceptive displays depends on a variety of factors. We turn now to the flip side of the coin, to receivers' ability to accurately detect deception from nonverbal cues. Plenty of research has shown that receivers tune in to nonverbal cues when making their judgments of deception (Burgoon & Buller, 1994; Henningsen, Valde, & Davies, 2005). The question is how well they pay attention to reliable as opposed to bogus indicators.

Accuracy in Detecting Deceit

On the one hand, it seems as if the availability of reliable indicators to detect deceit should give receivers an edge. Consistent with that speculation, Vrij and colleagues (e.g., Mann, Vrij, & Bull, 2004; Vrij, Evans, Akehurst, & Mann, 2004) have found that people who tune in to the right cues, rather than the stereotypical ones, can achieve good rates of success at distinguishing truths from lies. However, the general accuracy picture is not a pretty one—overall, accuracy in detecting deception is poor. On average, people are accurate in judging truth or falseness at an overall rate of about 54%, which is only slightly better than chance (which would be 50%, equivalent to flipping a coin) (Bond & DePaulo, 2006). And that number masks a deeper, more disturbing truth: Detection of deception, as compared to detection of truth, is far worse, averaging 47%.

This poor performance generally holds true for both experts and nonexperts (Burgoon, Buller, Ebesu, & Rockwell, 1994; Hartwig, Granhag, Stromwall, & Vrij, 2004). Some research has suggested that subgroups of professionals such as Secret Service agents, police officers, and clinical psychologists, not to mention criminals (!) achieve higher accuracy rates on some tests (Ekman & O'Sullivan, 1991; Ekman, O'Sullivan, & Frank, 1999; Mann et al., 2004). However, a recent meta-analysis (statistical summary) of 108 studies covering 16,537 participants concluded that "professional lie catchers" such as police officers, detectives, judges, and psychologists were no more accurate at detecting deception than were students and other citizens (Aamodt & Custer, 2006). The experts averaged 55% accuracy and the lay subjects averaged 54% overall. Ironically, then, people who are the least involved in making such judgments are the most accurate in making them. Pooling the judgments of multiple individuals can improve accuracy (Vrij et al., 2004), but that is seldom an option.

One somewhat more encouraging finding is that if you ask the question differently, asking receivers to judge another's veracity on indirect measures such as sincerity or believability, they show a fair degree of sensitivity to sender veracity (Bond & DePaulo, 2006; Vrij, Edward, & Bull, 2001). For example, in an experiment in which senders alternated giving blocks of truthful or deceptive responses, receivers' judgments of veracity closely followed the changes from truthful to deceptive responding and back again (Burgoon et al., 2007). Receivers, then, are clearly not clueless; they recognize when something is amiss, which may lead to greater scrutiny of subsequent communication. They are just unwilling to declare someone else an outright liar.

Stereotypes, Biases, and Heuristics

One reason for the inaccuracy is that people hold deeply entrenched views of how children and adults will lie (Taylor & Hill-Davies, 2004). For example, virtually everyone the world over (not just the Detroit judge we referred to in an earlier example) holds the stereotype that when people are lying, they avert their eyes. When lifelong residents of 63 countries, speaking 45 different languages, were asked, "How can you tell when someone is lying to you?" 72% of them said that people look away (Global Deception Research Team, 2006). Other common beliefs about nonverbal tip-offs to deception—shifting posture, nervous touching of self (adaptors), more stuttering, longer or shorter responses, longer pauses, more gesturing, more nervousness, and nonverbal or verbal inconsistencies—were consistent with previous investigations in the United States, Great Britain, Germany, the Netherlands, Spain, and Sweden (e.g., Akehurst, Köhnken, Vrij, & Bull, 1996; Garrido & Masip, 2000; Köhnken, 1990; Strömwall & Granhag, 2003; Vrij & Semin, 1996; Zuckerman, Koestner, & Driver, 1981). These stereotypes get in the way of paying attention to more reliable information.

Of course the lack of success in detecting deceit is partially a function of the inferential process by which receivers perceive deception. In everyday interaction, detecting deception requires first perceiving and attending to relevant cues and then interpreting them. Even if reliable cues are noticed, they still must be interpreted, and deception is only one of several possible interpretations. Nonverbal cues do not indicate deception directly; thus, receivers must make an inferential leap from the constellation of behaviors they perceive to a judgment of deception. Receivers may be reluctant to call another person a liar, given that deception is socially undesirable, and may opt instead for "safer" interpretations such as ambivalence, discrepancy, tension, or indifference (DePaulo, Rosenthal, Green, & Rosenkrantz, 1982).

When making their judgments, receivers also rely on a number of heuristics—mental shortcuts or rules of thumb—that are sometimes helpful but can also interfere with accurate detection of truth and deceit by systematically biasing judgments in one direction or another. Here we summarize five of the most persistent and robust heuristics and biases.

Truth Bias.   The truth bias refers to the tendency to overestimate the truthfulness of others. Specifically, people typically enter interactions with a strong tendency to expect the truth, and they tend to judge more messages as truths than as lies, independent of their actual veracity (Burgoon & Levine, 2009; McCornack & Parks, 1986; Zuckerman et al., 1981). The opposite, the lie bias, reflects an underestimate of the truthfulness of others' communication. It is sometimes referred to as the *Othello error*, after Shakespeare's Othello fatally mistaking Desdemona's denials of unfaithfulness as lies rather than truths. Presence of a truthfulness expectation or heuristic and/or truth bias has been demonstrated in a variety of contexts (e.g., Anolli, Balconi, & Ciceri, 2003; Buller, Burgoon, White, & Ebesu, 1994; Buller, Strzyzewski, & Hunsaker, 1991; McCornack & Parks, 1986; Stiff, Kim, Ramesh, 1992; Vrij & Mann, 2001) and regardless of whether the actual number of deceptive messages being judged is few or many (Levine, Kim, Park, & Hughes, 2006; Levine, Park, & McCornack, 1999). The lie bias is far less common, but it is more likely to be found among professionals whose job it is to ferret out "bad guys"—imposters, smugglers, criminals, terrorists, and so forth.

Visual Bias.   This is another very potent bias. It refers to a tendency to assign primacy to visual information over other forms of nonverbal and verbal information (Buller et al., 1991; DePaulo & Rosenthal, 1979b; Noller, 1985; Stiff et al., 1989).

Extensive research has shown that when receivers are exposed to only the words, an audio-only recording, a video-only recording, or a full audiovisual version of a sender's communication, they pay more attention to, and are more influenced by, visual rather than other forms of information (Burgoon et al., 2008; Rosenthal, DePaulo et al., 1982). They are especially likely to tune in to the face instead of the body, voice, or words, despite the fact that facial cues typically are the least diagnostic in identifying deception (e.g., Ekman & Friesen, 1974; Feldman, 1976; Hocking et al., 1979; Zuckerman et al., 1981). In a recent experiment, participants watched, heard, or read part of an interview during which interviewees responded deceptively or truthfully to a series of questions. Even though those who received the full audiovisual version were hearing the same voices as those in the audio-only condition and the same words as those in the transcript condition, they were far more inclined to judge the interviewee as truthful than were their counterparts. Fully 82% of the interviewees were judged as truthful when observers had access to visual information, compared to 71% for those who had only the words and voice, and 47% for those who received the text presentation (Burgoon, Blair, & Strom, 2008). Inasmuch as about half of the interviews they watched were deceptive, those in the visual condition ended up being the most inaccurate. The explanation offered for deceivers' ability to evade detection was that they utilized all their nonverbal resources to strategically manage their messages and demeanor to appear credible, and it paid off. Deceivers were judged as the most trustworthy, sociable, competent, and composed, and their messages were judged as the most truthful, complete, clear, and persuasive in the AV presentation—that is, when judges had access to the visual cues. These results are also consistent with a distraction explanation offered by Stiff et al. (1989), that nonverbal visual cues distract from processing diagnostic (reliable) verbal information.

Demeanor Bias. This bias reflects a tendency to judge some senders' communication styles as credible irrespective of their actual truthfulness (Zuckerman et al., 1981). Individuals who are judged as truthful and sincere in one situation earn the same ratings in another situation; in other words, demeanor bias generalizes across situations (Frank & Ekman, 2004). This bias actually stems not from some processing errors on the part of receivers but rather from the skillful management of one's demeanor by senders, that is, from their ability to create the appearance of sincerity, trustworthiness, honesty, and so forth as more nonverbal cues are added to the mix. As Burgoon et al. (2008) note, "Access to visual nonverbal cues should magnify demeanor bias by exposing observers to those controllable cues such as smiles, facial expressions, eye contact, gestures, spacing, and dress that are deceivers' stock in trade when attempting to 'put their best face forward.'"

Facial Maturity Bias. In Chapter 4, we introduced the concept of facial neoteny. This is the basis for yet another visually based bias, in this case, reliance on the degree to which a face is "baby-faced" or mature to make judgments of credibility. Baby-faced adults (but not children) are judged to be more truthful and credible than more mature-faced individuals (Masip, Garrido, & Herrero, 2003). Speculatively, a babyish face may connote lack of guile, whereas a mature face may connote expertise.

Expectancy Violations Bias/Nonverbal Conspicuousness.   This bias focuses on suspicion-provoking behavior. It is the tendency to infer deception from abnormal, "fishy-looking," or atypical behavior (Bond et al., 1992). Fiedler (1989; Fiedler & Walka, 1993) labeled this a nonverbal conspicuousness bias. Expectancy violations theory, interpersonal deception theory, and many other theories of deception assert that deceptive behavior is often unexpected, anomalous, deviant, and attention-arousing (Afifi & Weiner, 2004; Burgoon, 1983; Johnson, Grazioli, Jamal, & Berryman, 2001; Swets, 1996). Thus, nonverbal behaviors that are atypical and conspicuous unduly influence judgments, usually in the direction of judging the person as deceptive.

Accuracy in Detecting Suspicion

Suspicion is the belief, held with moderate uncertainty, that another person may be deceptive. The more certain, the more the judgment shifts from mere suspicion to firm belief in another's untruthfulness. In principle, receivers might never make their suspicions known, but in reality, they often "telegraph" their suspicions through their nonverbal feedback or their verbal expressions. Can deceivers tell when a receiver is skeptical? Yes. Research indicates that senders often detect suspicion when it is present (Burgoon et al., 1995; Burgoon et al., 1996).

Factors Influencing Detection
Accuracy and Credibility Attributions

Adding to the complexity of detecting deception is the fact that the ability to judge another's veracity depends on a number of factors. Some people seem to be better at it than others (although Bond & DePaulo, 2006, find there is far less variability across individuals than originally thought). Some of the key factors that may affect accuracy follow.

Sex/Gender.   Although men are more confident in their judgment of truths and lies than are women, women actually enjoy a modest advantage over men in detecting deception (Burgoon, Buller, Blair, & Tilley, 2006; DePaulo, Charlton, Cooper, Lindsay, & Muhlenbruck, 1997). Accuracy is higher if the lies being detected are those of women or of opposite-sex senders, though this advantage may not hold for less clear-cut forms of deception like equivocation (Bell & Edwards, 2005). The female superiority apparently is tied more to actual sex than to gender (i.e., femininity-masculinity) inasmuch as femininity in itself is not highly correlated with decoding accuracy (Isenhart, 1980), possibly because feminine women are taught to ignore others' unintended communication. It may also be related to what cues people attend to: Women report paying more attention to nonverbal cues; men, to verbal ones (Anderson, DePaulo, Ansfield, & Tickle,

1999). As for actual interpretations and reactions to lies, men and women appear to be quite similar (Gordon & Miller, 2000).

Age. If deception is partly an acquired skill that improves with age, so should detection be. There is some evidence that is the case. Children's detection ability improves with age, and they are not as gullible as one might believe. Even 5- and 6-year-olds disbelieve implausible statements and will infer that the teller is lying (Bussey, 1999; DePaulo, Jordan, Irvin, & Laser, 1982; Lee, Cameron, Doucette, & Talwar, 2002).

Personality. Very little research has examined whether personality matters. One study found that people who score higher on self-awareness are more accurate at detecting deception (Malcolm & Keenan, 2003). Other research examining individual social skills has found minimal differences in decoding ability and limited effects of self-reported decoding sensitivity on detection accuracy (Burgoon, Buller, & Guerrero, 1995).

Behavioral and Relational Familiarity. Earlier in the chapter, we described three types of familiarity—informational, behavioral, and relational. Behavioral and relational familiarity can both have pronounced effects on accuracy in detecting deceit, albeit in opposite directions.

Behavioral familiarity can take the form of exposure to the individual's baseline or normal behavior, general knowledge of behavioral norms for truthfulness, or formal training. Experts such as judges, law enforcement officers, customs agents, and fraud investigators want some exposure to an individual's typical communication pattern on the presumption that such exposure is essential to recognizing deviations. Indeed, polygraph exams and other technologies for detecting deceit rely on having a truthful baseline against which to compare potentially deceptive answers. The research evidence indicates that baseline exposure does improve accuracy (Bond & DePaulo, 2006).

Familiarity with general norms is a poor second choice, because it is error-prone. It does not take into account the unique features of each person's physiology and communication style. Formal training is intended to "codify" which nonverbal and verbal indicators are most reliable. The effects of expertise and training are discussed in the section titled "Expertise/Training" later in the chapter.

Relational familiarity refers to how well acquainted deceiver and deceived are. One would think that the more you know someone, the more you should be able to catch him or her in lies. However, the research has been quite mixed on whether we are better at detecting the lies of strangers, friends, or intimates. The results of a major meta-analysis (Bond & DePaulo, 2006) point to us putting on blinders with those we are close to. Thus, unlike behavioral familiarity, relational familiarity can be detrimental to accurate detection.

Planning/Rehearsal. We have said that when people have time to plan or rehearse their lies, their behavior looks normal. It follows that prepared lies should be less detectable than impromptu, unprepared ones. Several studies manipulated the amount of time liars had to prepare. As expected, detection of lies and truths was better when the lies were unprepared, and planned messages appeared more truthful (Bond & DePaulo, 2006).

Suspicion.   The notion that suspicious receivers should be better detectors is intuitively appealing. However, what little research has been conducted has been inconclusive, with some studies finding positive effects, others finding negative effects, and yet others discovering no effect (see e.g., Burgoon, Buller, et al., 1995; McCornack & Levine, 1990; Toris & DePaulo, 1985). Some of the conflicting findings may be due to the role of other factors such as whether the suspicious receiver is an expert or novice, how much suspicion the person is feeling, and whether it is chronic or situational. Overall, suspicion is not always advantageous. Detection accuracy is undermined rather than aided by receivers being highly suspicious (Burgoon et al., 1996). Moderate state suspicion coupled with a strong dose of trait-like suspicion may improve overall detection accuracy among committed partners (McCornack & Levine, 1990). But if the goal is to accurately detect both truth and deceit, suspicion is unhelpful, because it may simply lead to missing the truth.

Expertise/Training.   Although we have said that even professionals often do little better than the naïve judges in accurately detecting deceit, there is some evidence that police officers with more experience are more accurate than their inexperienced counterparts (Mann et al., 2004). As for formal training, several studies have investigated the effects of training on improving detection accuracy. A major summary of much of that literature produced a dismal record of success (Frank & Feeley, 2003). Making for an even muddier picture, bogus training has been found to improve detection (Levine, Feeley, McCornack, Hughes, & Harms, 2005), which raises doubts about whether training is truly making a difference or is just a placebo effect that makes people pay closer attention.

Other research offers some glimmers of hope. People who hold more accurate beliefs about deception displays and have those activated are more successful at detection (Forrest et al., 2004). It stands to reason that people who rely on stereotypical rather than actual indicators of deceit may be error-prone. A study of police officers found that those who relied on stereotypical cues of fidgeting and looking away were least accurate (Mann et al., 2004). This suggests that if training assists in activating the right schemas, it may aid detection. Newer research is addressing specific features of training that may improve success (George et al., in press; Vrij et al., 2004).

Confidence.   Time and again, research has documented that confidence is totally unrelated to accuracy (Aamodt & Custer, 2006; Bond & DePaulo, 2006; DePaulo et al., 1997; Jensen, 2007). That is to say, people who are supremely confident in their detection ability are no better on average than those who lack all confidence. In fact, overconfidence can lead to more error.

Modality.   The modality through which communication is delivered to receivers has already been shown to affect people's truth biases. The Bond and DePaulo (2006) meta-analysis found that most modalities did not differ from one another in differentiating truth from deception, the exception being that accuracy was poorest when only the visual information was available. However, other research has found that receivers are more accurate in discriminating lies for truths and in recognizing cross-modality inconsistencies from audio rather than other modalities (Burgoon et al., 2008; Davis, Markus, & Walters, 2006; Heinrich & Borkenau, 1998). For example, people judging portions of criminal confessions are the most accurate when hearing rather than seeing or reading the lies. It seems that the presence of visual information leads to reliance on stereotypic rather than "true" indicators of deception, whereas verbal-only media lead to greater distrust. The audio modality may also have the advantage of revealing true emotional states and cognitive difficulty.

In sum, detecting deception is a very challenging enterprise for humans. Vrij (2007) offers a number of guidelines shown in Table 15.4 that may reduce the challenge somewhat.

TABLE 15.4   Guidelines for Catching a Liar

1. Don't expect to find a single obvious sign to deceit like Pinocchio's growing nose. There are no such sure-fire indicators.
2. Liars are only likely to reveal cues to deceit if they experience strong emotions, are being taxed cognitively, or are attempting to control themselves. Absent these conditions, deception cues are less likely to be present.
3. Some cues are more likely than others. You must be familiar with which indicators are reliable and diagnostic and which are not.
4. The more diagnostic indicators that are present, the more likely the person is lying. If only a few are present, caution is indicated.
5. Avoid the *Othello error*. Be sensitive to the possibility that adopting an accusatory stance may make even truthful people look deceptive and lead you to misjudge them.
6. Pay attention to mismatches between speech content and nonverbal behavior and try to explain them. If you can't conjure up a good explanation, deception may be involved.
7. Watch for people's deviations from their usual speech and nonverbal behavior and try to explain them. No good explanation? Deception may be present.
8. Encourage suspected liars to talk. This may increase their cognitive load if they have to come up with plausible and noncontradictory statements.
9. Have the person repeat what he or she has said. Mismatches and deviations may become more evident this way.
10. Have the person tell his or her story in a non-chronological order. This should be more taxing for deceivers than truth-tellers.
11. Be suspicious and on guard against the truth bias, but do not reveal your suspicions.
12. Pay attention to vocal cues and speech content when detecting deceit. Downgrade attention to visual cues.
13. Use implicit or indirect methods for detecting deceit.
14. Detecting deception may be easier earlier rather than later. It may work better during a first rather than later interview, for example, or in the earlier phase of an interview—before the deceiver has adapted to your feedback.
15. Check the information you obtain. Lie detection from behavioral observation cannot substitute for checking out corroborating evidence.

Source: Adapted from Vrij (2007).

New Methods of Detecting Deception

The difficulties humans face as lie detectors has fanned the desire to develop alternative tools for detecting deception. The polygraph is the most familiar. It measures respiratory, cardiac, and electrodermal responses. Other devices like fMRI (functional magnetic resonance imaging), ERP (event-related potentials), thermal imaging, laser Doppler vibrometry, NIRS (near-infrared spectroscopy), and LVSA (layered vocal stress analysis) also measure physiological responses and are predicated on deception causing stress and/or emotional responses. Photo 15.1 shows several of them. However, an alternative approach that is emerging is to measure outward nonverbal behavior using computer vision techniques that automatically identify and track various body movements, gestures, and facial expressions (see Photo 15.1d). Development of all of these technologies is being guided by research and theory on nonverbal communication. At issue will be whether they can improve significantly on human detection accuracy, how they can be implemented, and whether they should replace or augment human judgment. (See Box 15.3 for more on the latest approaches to detecting deception.)

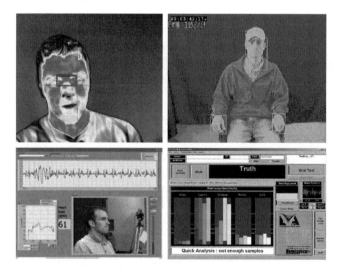

PHOTO 15.1   *Potential lie detection technologies: counterclockwise from top left, (a) thermal imaging, (b) Nemesysco Layered Voice Analysis, (c) laser Doppler vibrometry, and (d) computer vision behavioral tracking*

BOX 15.3

Will Mind-Reading Replace Human Deception Detection?

Minority Report, a science-fiction movie starring Tom Cruise, put forward the provocative notion that a combination of dazzling technology and "pre-cogs" (humans with super clairvoyant abilities) could read people's minds and their criminal intentions before they actually took action. The long arm of the law would swoop in and arrest them *before* they committed their intended crime—no need to interview anyone or detect deception.

Now the Department of Homeland Security (DHS) is hoping to implement something similar to this by using a wide variety of high-tech sensors to replace human detectors. They see it as a replacement for the current SPOT (Screening Passengers through Observation Techniques) program, which is being utilized at selected airports by the Transportation Security Agency (TSA). SPOT relies on trained human observers, who attempt to note micro-expressions and other suspicious nonverbal behaviors among the millions of passengers who pass through major airports daily. Newly trained Behavior Detection Officers scan the crowds looking for signs of fear or disgust in people's micro-expressions or for other suspicious conduct. If someone's nonverbal or verbal behavior seems amiss, the TSA agents will detain the person for further questioning and may turn him or her over to law enforcement (http://www.mcclatchydc.com/homepage/story/18923.html). In a nine-month period at Dulles International Airport, of the roughly seven million people who flew out of that airport, "several hundred" were referred for intense screening, and "about 50" were turned over to law enforcement for follow-up questioning (Lipton, 2006).

Enter Project Hostile Intent (PHI). Instead of depending on human observers, PHI will use an array of lasers, sensors, cameras, microphones, and other remote sensing devices. It aims to identify facial expressions, gait, blood pressure, pulse, and perspiration rates that are characteristic of hostility or the desire to deceive. With this technology, the DHS is hoping to automate the SPOT program, so that computers, not humans, search for micro-expressions, and at the same time beef up the range of bodily signs that can be investigated. Machines will not just look for micro-expressions, they will also attempt to sense whether someone is hiding something. For this they might use a remote-controlled, noncontact version of the polygraph, bouncing lasers or microwaves off a person's skin (Marks, 2007).

Many researchers (not to mention journalists; see Patti Davis's commentary at Global Research: http://www.globalresearch.ca/index.php?context=va&aid=6576) are already skeptical of detecting danger from facial expressions. Emotional expressions of terrorists, for instance, are likely to be highly complex, ranging from excitement about their impending violent act, fear of being caught before they can act, sadness about being killed, contempt for authorities who might detain them, or—in the case of Islamic jihadists—joy about heading to paradise. And innocent passengers are bound to show a full gamut of expressions—stress over delayed flights and long lines, irritation with crying children, boredom—that could be mistaken for hostile emotions. Even a smile can be misleading. People who are emotionally distressed often smile, especially if they are male and the stress is intense (Ansfield, 2007). Thus, whether this program will actually be ready for deployment by its target date of 2012 or will face public resistance as an Orwellian assault on privacy remains to be seen.

Summary

Deception is a frequent, essential, and adaptive strategy in human communication. It takes many guises—from bald-faced lies to fibs to evasions and equivocations to concealment of relevant information. It is motivated by needs for resources, affiliative desires, relational considerations, and self-protection, and it is these motives that determine its morality and acceptability.

A mountain of research on deception displays has yet to find a consistent profile of nonverbal behaviors that signal deception. Deceivers engage in a combination of strategic and nonstrategic activities, the former to manage informational contents, behaviors, and overall image; the latter as inadvertent indications of emotional stress, cognitive effort, memory challenges, speech interference, or attempted suppression of leakage. However, the exact combination depends on the relational and cultural context, the preinteraction expectations, knowledge, goals, motivations, and communication skills of the actors, and characteristics of the interaction itself. Nonetheless, there are some indicators that can probabilistically suggest deception.

Accuracy in detecting deception is poor among experts and novices alike. It is hampered partly by stereotypes, biases, and heuristics that receivers apply when making judgments, but it is also hindered by the absence of a consistent set of indicators and by deceivers' savvy adaptation to receiver-signaled suspicions. Receivers' accuracy will be affected by the communication modality, their familiarity with the actor's baseline behavior, relational familiarity with the actor, suspicion level, personality, and sociodemographic factors of sex and age, among others. It will not be aided by an increase in confidence but it may be improved through training.

SUGGESTED READINGS

Bond, C. F., Jr., & DePaulo, B. M. (2006). Accuracy of deception judgments. *Review of Personality and Social Psychology, 10,* 214–234.

Burgoon, J. K., & Buller, D. B. (2004). Interpersonal deception theory. In J. S. Seiter & R. H. Gass (Eds.), *Readings in persuasion, social influence and compliance-gaining* (pp. 239–264). Boston: Allyn & Bacon.

DePaulo, B. M., Lindsay, J. J., Malone, B. E., Muhlenbruck, L., Charlton, K., & Cooper, H. (2003). Cues to deception. *Psychological Bulletin, 129,* 74–118.

Ekman, P. (1992). *Telling lies: Clues to deceit in the marketplace, politics, and marriage.* New York: Norton.

Knapp, M. L. (2007). *Lying and deception in human interaction.* Boston: Allyn & Bacon.

Vrij, A. (2006). Nonverbal communication and deception. In V. Manusov & M. L. Patterson (Eds.), *The Sage handbook of nonverbal communication* (pp. 341–359). Thousand Oaks, CA: Sage.

REFERENCES

Aamodt, M. G., & Custer, H. (2006). Who can best catch a liar?: A meta-analysis of individual differences in detecting deception. *The Forensic Examiner, 15*(1), 6–11.

Abbey, A. (1982). Sex differences in attributions for friendly behavior: Do males misperceive females' friendliness? *Journal of Personality and Social Psychology, 42*, 830–838.

Abbey, A. (1987). Misperceptions of friendly behavior as sexual interest: A survey of naturally occurring incidents. *Psychology of Women Quarterly, 11*, 173–194.

Abbey, A., & Melby, C. (1986). The effects of nonverbal cues on gender differences in perceptions of sexual intent. *Sex Roles, 15*, 283–298.

Ackerman, D. (1990). *A natural history of the senses.* New York: Van Nostrand.

Acking, C. A., & Kuller, R. (1972). The perception of an interior as a function of its colour. *Ergonomics, 15*, 645–654.

Adams, R. B., & Kleck, R. E. (2005). Effects of direct and averted gaze on the perception of facially communicated emotion. *Emotion, 5*, 3–11.

Addington, D. W. (1968). The relationship of selected vocal characteristics to personality perception. *Speech Monographs, 35*, 492–503.

Afifi, W. A., Guerrero, L. K., & Egland, K. L. (1994, June). *Maintenance behaviors in same- and opposite-sex friendships: Connections to gender, relational closeness, and equity issues.* Paper presented at the annual meeting of the International Network on Personal Relationships, Iowa City, IA.

Afifi, W. A., & Johnson, M. L. (1999). The use and interpretation of tie signs in a public setting: Relationship and sex differences. *Journal of Social and Personal Relationships, 16*, 9–38.

Afifi, W. A., & Metts, S. (1998). Characteristics and consequences of expectation violations in close relationships. *Journal of Social and Personal Relationships, 15*, 365–392.

Afifi, W. A., & Weiner, J. L. (2004). Toward a theory of motivated information management. *Communication Theory, 14*, 167–190.

Aguinis, H., Simonsen, M. M., & Pierce, C. A. (1998). Effects of nonverbal behavior on perceptions of power bases. *Journal of Social Psychology, 138*, 455–469.

Aiello, J. R., Baum, A., & Gormley, F. P. (1981). Social determinants of residential crowding stress. *Personality and Social Psychology Bulletin, 7*, 643–649.

Aiello, J. R., Epstein, Y. M., & Karlin, R. A. (1975). Effects of crowding on electrodermal activity. *Sociological Symposium, 14*, 43–57.

Aiken, L. R. (1963). The relationship of dress to selected measures of personality in undergraduate women. *Journal of Social Psychology, 59*, 119–128.

Ainsworth, M. D. S., Blehar, M. C., Waters, E., & Wall, S. (1978). *Patterns of attachment: A psychological study of the strange situation.* Hillsdale, NJ: Lawrence Erlbaum Associates.

Akehurst, L., Köhnken, G., Vrij, A., & Bull, R. (1996). Lay persons' and police officers' beliefs regarding deceptive behavior. *Applied Cognitive Psychology, 10*, 461–471.

Albana, K. F., Knapp, M. L., & Thenue, K. E. (2002). Interaction appearance theory: Changing perceptions of physical attractiveness through social interaction. *Communication Theory, 12*, 8–40.

Alberts, J. K., Kellar-Guenther, Y., & Corman, S. R. (1996). That's not funny: Understanding recipients' responses to teasing. *Western Journal of Communication, 60*, 337–357.

Allen, V. L., & Atkinson, M. L. (1978). Encoding of nonverbal behavior by high-achieving and low-achieving children. *Journal of Educational Psychology, 70*, 298–305.

Allport, G. W., & Cantril, H. (1934). Judging personality from voice. *Journal of Social Psychology, 5*, 37–54.

Almaney, A. J., & Alwan, A. J. (1982). *Communicating with the Arabs: A handbook for the business executive.* Prospect Heights, IL: Waveland Press.

Altemus, M., Deuster, E. G., Carter, C. S., & Gold, P. (1995). Suppression of hypothalamic-pituitary-adrenal axis responses to stress in lactating women. *Journal of Clinical Endocrinology and Metabolism, 80*, 2954–2959.

Altman, I. (1975). *The environment and social behavior.* Monterey, CA: Brooks/Cole.

Altman, I., & Chemers, M. M. (1980). *Culture and environment.* Monterey, CA: Brooks/Cole.

Altman, I., & Haythorn, W. W. (1967). The ecology of isolated groups. *Behavioral Science, 12*, 169–182.

Ambady, N., Hallahan, M., & Conner, B. (1999). Accuracy of judgments of sexual orientation from thin slices of behavior. *Journal of Personality and Social Psychology, 77*, 538–547.

Ambady, N., & Rosenthal, R. (1993). Half a minute: Predicting teacher evaluations from thin slices of nonverbal behavior and physical attractiveness. *Journal of Personality and Social Psychology, 64*, 431–441.

American Society of Plastic Surgeons. (2002). Plastic Surgery Information Service. Retrieved from http://www.plasticsurgery.org.

Andersen, J. F., Andersen, P. A., & Lustig, M. W. (1987). Opposite sex touch avoidance: A national replication and extension. *Journal of Nonverbal Behavior, 11*, 89–109.

Andersen, J. F., Andersen, P. A., Murphy, M. A., & Wendt-Wasco, N. (1985). The development of nonverbal communication in the classroom: A development study in grades K–12. *Communication Education, 34*, 292–307.

Andersen, P. A. (1985). Nonverbal immediacy in interpersonal communication. In A. W. Siegman & S. Feldstein (Eds.), *Multichannel integrations of nonverbal behavior* (pp. 1–36). Hillsdale, NJ: Lawrence Erlbaum Associates.

Andersen, P. A. (1988). Nonverbal communication in the small group. In R. S. Cathcart & L. A. Samovar (Eds.), *Small group communication: A reader* (5th ed., pp. 333–350). Dubuque, IA: Wm. C. Brown.

Andersen, P. A. (1989, May). *A cognitive valence theory of intimate communication.* Paper presented at the annual conference of the International Network on Personal Relationships, Iowa City, IA.

Andersen, P. A. (1991). When one cannot not communicate: A challenge to Motley's traditional communication postulates. *Communication Studies, 42*, 309–325.

Andersen, P. A. (1992, July). *Excessive intimacy: An account analysis of behaviors, cognitive schemata, affect, and relational outcomes.* Paper presented at the International Conference on Personal Relationships, Orono, ME.

Andersen, P. A. (1998a). *Nonverbal communication: Forms and functions.* New York: McGraw-Hill.

Andersen, P. A. (1998b). The cognitive valence theory of intimate communication. In M. Palmer & G. A. Barnett (Eds.), *Progress in communication sciences, Vol. 14: Mutual influence in interpersonal communication theory and research in cognition, affect, and behavior* (pp. 39–72). Norwood, NJ: Ablex.

Andersen, P. A. (2008). *Nonverbal communication: Forms and functions* (2nd ed). Long Grove, IL: Waveland Press.

Andersen, P. A., & Bowman, L. L. (1999). Positions of power: Nonverbal influence in organizational communication. In L. K. Guerrero, J. A. DeVito, & M. L. Hecht (Eds.), *The nonverbal communication reader: Classic and contemporary readings* (2nd ed., pp. 317–334). Prospect Heights, IL: Waveland Press.

Andersen, P. A., & Guerrero, L. K. (1998). The bright side of relational communication: Interpersonal warmth as a social emotion. In P. A. Andersen & L. K. Guerrero (Eds.), *Handbook of communication and emotion: Research, theory, applications, and contexts* (pp. 303–329). San Diego, CA: Academic Press.

Andersen, P. A., Guerrero, L. K., & Jones, S. M. (2006). Nonverbal behavior in intimate interaction and intimate relationships. In V. Manusov & M. L. Patterson (Eds.), *The Sage handbook of nonverbal communication* (pp. 259–277). Thousand Oaks, CA: Sage.

Andersen, P. A., Guerrero, L. K., Buller, D. B., & Jorgensen, P. F. (1998). An empirical comparison of three theories of nonverbal immediacy exchange. *Human Communication Research, 24*, 501–535.

Andersen, P. A., Hecht, M. L., Hoobler, G. D., & Smallwood, M. (2002). Nonverbal communication across culture. In W. B. Gudykunst & B. Mody (Eds.), *Handbook of international and intercultural communication* (pp. 89–106). Thousand Oaks, CA: Sage.

Andersen, P. A., & Liebowitz, K. (1978). The development and nature of the construct touch avoidance. *Environmental Psychology and Nonverbal Behavior, 3*, 89–106.

Andersen, P. A., Lustig, M. W., & Andersen, J. F. (1990). Changes in latitude, changes in attitude: The relationship between climate and interpersonal communication predispositions. *Communication Quarterly, 38*, 291–311.

Andersen, P. A., & Sull, K. K. (1985). Out of touch, out of reach: Tactile predispositions as predictors of interpersonal distance. *Western Journal of Speech Communication, 49*, 57–72.

Andersen, P. A., & Wang, H. (2006). Unraveling cultural cues: Dimensions of nonverbal communication across cultures. In L. A. Samovar, R. E. Porter, & E. R. McDaniel (Eds.), *Intercultural communication: A reader* (pp. 250–266). Belmont, CA: Wadsworth.

Anderson, C. A. (1989). Temperature and aggression: Ubiquitous effects of heat on occurrence of human violence. *Psychological Bulletin, 106*, 1161–1173.

Anderson, D. E., Ansfield, M. E., & DePaulo, B. M. (1999). Love's best habit: Deception in the context of relationships. In P. Philippot & R. S. Feldman (Eds.), *Social context of nonverbal behavior* (pp. 372–409). New York: Cambridge University Press.

Anderson, D. E., DePaulo, B. M., Ansfield, M. E., & Tickle, J. J. (1999). Beliefs about cues to deception: Mindless stereotypes or untapped wisdom? *Journal of Nonverbal Behavior, 23*, 67–100.

Anderson, N. (1981). *Foundations of information integration theory.* New York: Academic Press.

Anolli, L., & Ciceri, R. (2002). Analysis of the vocal profiles of male seduction: From exhibition to self-disclosure. *The Journal of General Psychology, 129*, 149–169.

Anolli, L., Balconi, M., & Ciceri R. (2003). Linguistic styles in deceptive communication: dubitative ambiguity and elliptic eluding in packaged lies. *Social Behavior and Personality, 31*, 687–710.

Ansfield, M. E. (2007). Smiling when distressed: When a smile is a frown turned upside down. *Personality and Social Psychology Bulletin, 33*, 763–775.

Apple, W., & Hecht, K. (1982). Speaking emotionally: The relation between verbal and vocal communication of affect. *Journal of Personality and Social Psychology, 42,* 864–875.

Apple, W., Streeter, L. A., & Krauss, R. M. (1979). Effects of pitch and speech rate on personal attributions. *Journal of Personality and Social Psychology, 37,* 715–727.

Aragonés, J. I., Francescato, G., & Gärling, T. (Eds.). (2001). *Residential environments: Choice, satisfaction and behavior.* Westport, CT: Greenwood.

Argyle, M. (1967). *The psychology of interpersonal behaviour.* London: Penguin Books.

Argyle, M. (1972). *Non-verbal communication in human social interaction.* Indianapolis: Bobbs-Merrill.

Argyle, M. (1975). *Bodily communication.* London: Methuen.

Argyle, M., Alkema, F., & Gilmour, R. (1971). The communication of friendly and hostile attitudes by verbal and nonverbal signals. *European Journal of Social Psychology, 1,* 385–402.

Argyle, M., & Cook, M. (1976). *Gaze and mutual gaze.* Cambridge, England: Cambridge University Press.

Argyle, M., & Dean, J. (1965). Eye contact, distance, and affiliation. *Sociometry, 28,* 289–304.

Argyle, M., Salter, V., Nicholson, H., Williams, M., & Burgess, P. (1970). The communication of inferior and superior attitudes by verbal and non-verbal signals. *British Journal of Social and Clinical Psychology, 9,* 221–231.

Aries, E. (2006). Sex differences in interaction: A reexamination. In K. Dindia & D. J. Canary (Eds.), *Sex differences and similarities in communication* (2nd ed., pp. 21–36). Mahwah, NJ: Lawrence Erlbaum Associates.

Armstrong, M. L., & Pace-Murphy, K. (1997). Tattooing: Another risk behavior in adolescents warranting national health teaching. *Applied Nursing Research, 10,* 181–189.

Armstrong, M. L., Pace-Murphy, K., Salle, A. S., & Watson, M. G. (2000). Tattooed army soldiers: Examining the incidence, behaviors, and risks. *Military Medicine, 165,* 37–40.

Asch, S. (1946). Forming impressions of personality. *Journal of Abnormal and Social Psychology, 41,* 258–290.

Asthana, S. (2000). Female judgement of male attractiveness and desirability for relationships: Role of waist-to-hip ratio. *Psycho-Lingua, 30,* 60–64.

Attardo, S., Eisterhold, J., & Hay, J. (2003). Multimodal markers of irony and sarcasm. *Humor: International Journal of Humor Research, 16,* 243–260.

Aune, R. K., & Aune, K. S. (2008). The effects of perfume use on perceptions of attractiveness and competence. In L. K. Guerrero & M. L. Hecht (Eds.), *The nonverbal communication reader: Classic and contemporary readings* (3rd ed., pp. 94–102). Long Grove, IL: Waveland Press.

Averett, S., & Korenman, S. (1996). The economic reality of the beauty myth. *Journal of Human Resources, 31,* 304–330.

Axtell, R. E. (1998). *Gestures: Do's and taboos of body language around the world.* New York: John Wiley & Sons.

Badzinski, D. M., & Pettus, D. M. (1994). Nonverbal involvement and sex: Effects on jury decision making. *Journal of Applied Communication Research, 22,* 309–321.

Baglan, T., & Nelson, D. J. (1982). A comparison of the effects of sex and status on the perceived appropriateness of nonverbal behaviors. *Women's Studies in Communication, 5,* 29–38.

Bailenson, J. N., & Yee, N. (2007). Virtual interpersonal touch and digital chameleons. *Journal of Nonverbal Behavior, 31,* 225–242.

Bailenson, J. N., Yee, N., Brave, S., Merget, D., & Koslow, D. (2007). Virtual interpersonal touch: Expressing and recognizing emotions through haptic devices. *Human-Computer Interaction, 22,* 325–353.

Baker, M. A., & Holding, D. H. (1993). The effects of noise and speech on cognitive task performance. *Journal of General Psychology, 120,* 339–355.

Banse, R., & Scherer, K. R. (1994). *Acoustic profiles in vocal emotion expression.* Unpublished manuscript, Humboldt University, Berlin, Germany.

Barak, A., Patkin, J., & Dell, D. M. (1982). Effects of certain counselor behaviors on perceived expertness and attractiveness. *Journal of Counseling Psychology, 29,* 261–267.

Bardack, N. R., & McAndrew, F. T. (1985). The influence of physical attractiveness and manner of dress on success in stimulated personnel decisions. *Journal of Social Psychology, 125,* 777–778.

Bargh, J. A. (1989). Conditional automaticity: Varieties of automatic influence in social perception and cognition. In J. S. Uleman & J. A. Bargh (Eds.), *Unintended thought* (pp. 3–51). New York: Guilford.

Barnett, D. L., & Nichols, A. C. (1982). The effects of open-space versus traditional, self-contained classrooms on the auditory selective attending skills of elementary school children. *Language, Speech, and Hearing Services in Schools, 13,* 138–143.

Barnlund, D. C. (1975). Communicative styles in two cultures: Japan and the United States. In A. Kendon, R. M. Harris, & M. R. Key (Eds.), *Organization of behavior in face-to-face interaction* (pp. 427–456). The Hague: Mouton.

Barnlund, D. C. (1978). Communication styles in two cultures: Japan and the United States. In A. Kendon, R. M. Harris, & M. R. Key (Eds.), *Organizational behavior in face to face interaction* (pp. 427–456). The Hague Mouton.

Barnlund, D. C. (1989). *Communicative styles of Japanese and Americans: Images and realities.* Belmont, CA: Wadsworth/Thomson Learning.

Baron, R. A. (1978). Invasions of personal space and helping: Mediating effects of the invader's apparent need. *Journal of Experimental Social Psychology, 14,* 304–312.

Baron, R. A. (1981). Olfaction and human social behavior: Effects of a pleasant scent on attraction and social perception. *Personality and Social Psychology Bulletin, 7,* 611–616.

Baron, R. A., & Bel, P. A. (1976). Physical distance and helping: Some unexpected benefits of crowding in on others. *Journal of Applied Social Psychology, 6,* 95–104.

Barrett, K. C. (1993). The development of nonverbal communication of emotion: A functionalist perspective. *Journal of Nonverbal Behavior, 17,* 145–169.

Barrett, K. C. (1998). A functionalist perspective to the development of emotions. In M. F. Mascolo & S. Griffin (Eds.), *What develops in emotional development?* (pp. 109–133). New York: Plenum Press.

Barrett, L. F. (2006). Solving the emotion paradox: Categorization on the experience of emotion. *Personality and Social Psychology Review, 10,* 20–46.

Basabe, N., Paez, D., Valencia, J., Rimé, B., Pennebaker, J., Diener, E., & Gonzalez, J. L. (2000). Sociocultural factors predicting subjective experience of emotion: A collective level analysis. *Psicotherma, 12,* 55–69.

Basdogan, C., Ho, C. H., Slater, M., & Srinavasan, M. A. (1998). The role of haptic communication in shared virtual environments. In J. K. Salisbury & M. A. Srinavasan (Eds.), *Proceedings of the Third PHANToM users group workshop* (pp. 443–460). Cambridge, MA: MIT Press.

Baskett, G. D., & Freedle, R. O. (1974). Aspects of language pragmatics and the social perception of lying. *Journal of Psycholinguistic Research, 3,* 117–131.

Bauchner, J. E., Brandt, D. R., & Miller, G. R. (1977). The truth-deception attribution: Effects of varying levels of information availability. In B. R. Ruben (Ed.), *Communication yearbook 1* (pp. 229–243). New Brunswick, NJ: Transaction Books.

Bauchner, J. E., Kaplan, E. A., & Miller, G. R. (1980). Detecting deception: The relationship of available information to judgmental accuracy in initial encounters. *Human Communication Research, 6,* 253–264.

Baum, A., Aiello, J. R., & Calesnick, L. E. (1978). Crowding and personal control: social density and the development of learned helplessness. *Journal of Personality and Social Psychology, 36,* 1000–1011.

Bavelas, J. B. (1990). Behaving and communicating: A reply to Motley. *Western Journal of Speech Communication, 54,* 593–602.

Bavelas, J. B. (1994). Gestures as part of speech: Methodological implications. *Research on Language and Social Interaction, 27,* 201–221.

Bavelas, J. B., Black, A., Chovil, N., & Mullett, J. (1990). *Equivocal communication.* Newbury Park, CA: Sage.

Bavelas, J. B., & Chovil, N. (2000). Visible acts of meaning: An integrated message model of language in face-to-face dialogue. *Journal of Language and Social Psychology, 19,* 163–194.

Bavelas, J. B., & Chovil, N. (2006). Hand gestures and facial displays as part of language use in face-to-face dialogue. In V. Manusov & M. L. Patterson (Eds.), *The Sage handbook of nonverbal comunication* (pp. 97–115). Thousand Oaks, CA: Sage.

Bavelas, J. B., Chovil, N., Lawrie, D. A., & Wade, A. (1992). Interactive gestures. *Discourse Processes, 15,* 469–489.

Bavelas, J. B., Hagen, D., Lane, L., & Lawrie, D. A. (1989, May). *Interactive gestures and a systems theory of conversation.* Paper presented at the annual meeting of the International Communication Association, San Francisco, CA.

Baxter, R. R., & Bellis, M. A. (1993). Human sperm competition: Ejaculate manipulation by females and a function for the female orgasm. *Animal Behavior, 46,* 887–909.

Beattie, G. W. (1981a). A further investigation of the cognitive interference hypothesis of gaze paterns during conversation. *British Journal of Social Psychology, 20,* 243–248.

Beattie, G. W. (1981b). Interruption in conversational interaction and its relation to the sex and status of the interactants. *Linguistics, 21,* 742–748.

Beaupre, M., & Hess, U. (2005). Cross-cultural emotion recognition among Canadian ethnic groups. *Journal of Cross-Cultural Psychology, 36,* 355–370.

Beauregard, J. A. (2001). Embodied identities: College women's perspectives on body piercing using developmental models of psychology. *Dissertation Abstracts International, 62(2-B):* 1138.

Beck, R. S., Dautridge, R., & Sloane, P. D. (2002). Physician-patient communication in the primary care office: a systematic review. *The Journal of the American Board of Family Practice, 15,* 25–38.

Beebe, S. A. (1980). Effects of eye contact, posture and vocal inflection upon credibility and comprehension. *Australian SCAN: Journal of Human Communication, 7–8,* 57–70.

Beekman, S. (1975, August). *Sex differences in nonverbal behavior.* Paper presented at the annual meeting of the American Psychological Association, Chicago, IL.

Beeman, M., & Chiarello, C. (Eds.). (1997). *Right hemisphere language comprehension: Perspectives from cognitive neuroscience.* Hillsdale, NJ: Lawrence Erlbaum Associates.

Behling, D. (1995). Influence of dress on perception of intelligence and scholastic achievement in urban schools with minority populations. *Clothing and Textiles Research Journal, 13,* 11–16.

Belkin, D. (2006, October 17). Don't it make my blue eyes brown: Americans are seeing a dramatic color change. *The Boston Globe,* 3rd ed., p. E1.

Bell, R. A., Buerkel-Rothfuss, N. L., & Gore, K. E. (1987). "Did you bring the yarmulke for the cabbage patch kid?" The idiomatic communication of young lovers. *Human Communication Research, 14,* 47–67.

Bell, R., & Edwards, R. (2005). Interpretations of messages: The influence of various forms of equivocation, face concerns, and sex differences. *Journal of Language and Social Psychology, 24,* 160–181.

Bell, S. (1999). Tattooed: A participant observer's exploration of meaning. *Journal of American Culture, 22,* 53–58.

Bem, S. L. (1974). The measurement of psychological androgyny. *Journal of Consulting and Clinical Psychology, 42,* 155–162.

Ben Ze'ev, A. (2000). *The subtlety of emotions.* Cambridge, MA: MIT Press.

Bennett, S., & Montero-Diaz, L. (1982). Children's perceptions of speaker sex. *Journal of Phonetics, 10,* 113–121.

Bensing, J. (1991). Doctor-patient communication and the quality of care. *Social Science & Medicine, 32,* 1301–1310.

Bensing, J., Kerssens, J. J., & van der Pasch, M. (1995). Patient-directed gaze as a tool for discovering and handling psychosocial problems in general practice. *Journal of Nonverbal Behavior, 19,* 223–242.

Berger, C. R. (1977). The covering law perspective as a theoretical basis for the study of human communication. *Communication Quarterly, 25,* 7–18.

Berman, H. J., Shulman, A. D., & Marwit, S. J. (1976). Comparing multidimensional decoding of affect from audio, video, and audio-video recordings. *Sociometry, 39,* 83–89.

Bernardis, P., & Gentilucci, M. (2006). Speech and gesture share the same communication system. *Neuropsychologia, 44,* 178–190.

Bernieri, F. J., & Rosenthal, R. (1991). Interpersonal coordination: Behavior matching and interactional synchrony. In R. S. Feldman & B. Rimé (Eds.), *Fundamentals of nonverbal behavior* (pp. 401–432). Cambridge, England: Cambridge University Press.

Bernstein, I. L., Zimmerman, J. C., Czeisler, C. A., & Weitzman, E. D. (1981). Meal patterns in "free-running" humans. *Physiology and Behavior, 27,* 621–623.

Berry, D. S. (1990a). Vocal attractiveness and vocal babyishness: Effects on stranger, self, and friend impressions. *Journal of Nonverbal Behavior, 14,* 141–153.

Berry, D. S. (1990b). What can a moving face tell us? *Journal of Personality and Social Psychology, 58,* 1004–1014.

Berry, D. S. (1991a). Accuracy in social perception: Contributions of facial and vocal information. *Journal of Personality and Social Psychology, 61,* 298–307.

Berry, D. S. (1991b). Attractive faces are not all created equal: Joint effects of facial babyishness and attractiveness on social perception. *Personality and Social Psychology Bulletin, 17,* 523–531.

Berry, D. S. (1992). Vocal types and stereotypes: Joint effects of vocal attractiveness and vocal maturity on person perception. *Journal of Nonverbal Behavior, 16,* 41–54.

Berry, D. S., Hansen, J. S., Landry-Pester, J. C., & Meier, J. A. (1994). Vocal determinants of first impressions of young children. *Journal of Nonverbal Behavior, 18,* 187–197.

Berry, D. S., & McArthur, L. Z. (1986). Perceiving character in faces: The impact of age-related craniofacial changes on social perception. *Psychological Bulletin, 100,* 3–18.

Berry, D. S., & Pennebaker, J. W. (1993). Nonverbal and verbal emotional expression and health. *Psychotherapy and Psychosomatics, 59,* 11–19.

Berscheid, E. (1983). Emotion. In H. H. Kelley, E. Berscheid, A. Christensen, J. H. Harvey, T. L. Huston, G. Levinger, E. McClintock, L. A. Peplau, & D. R. Peterson (Eds.), *Close relationships* (pp. 110–168). San Francisco: Freeman.

Berscheid, E., Dion, K. K., Walster, E., & Walster, G. W. (1971). Physical attractiveness and dating choice: A test of the matching hypothesis. *Journal of Experimental Social Psychology, 7,* 173–189.

Berscheid, E., & Walster, E. H. (1974). Physical attractiveness. In L. Berkowitz (Ed.), *Advances in experimental social psychology* (Vol. 7, pp. 158–215). New York: Academic.

Berscheid, E., Walster, E. H., & Bohrnstedt, G. (1973, November). Body image: The happy American body. *Psychology Today, 7,* 119–131.

Berza, A. L., Gannon, K. M., & Skowronski, J. J. (1992). The moment of tenure and the moment of truth: When it pays to be aware of recency effects in social judgments. *Social Cognition, 10,* 397–413.

Bettinghaus, E. P., & Cody, M. J. (1994). *Persuasive communication* (5th ed.). Fort Worth, TX: Harcourt Brace.

Bickman, L. (1971a). Effect of different uniforms on obedience in field situations. *Proceedings of the 79th Annual American Psychological Association Convention,* 359–360.

Bickman, L. (1971b). The effect of social status on the honesty of others. *Journal of Social Psychology, 4,* 47–61.

Bickman, L. (1974). The social power of a uniform. *Journal of Applied Social Psychology, 4,* 47–61.

Birdwhistell, R. (1955). Background to kinesics. *ETC., 13,* 10–18.

Birdwhistell, R. (1970). *Kinesics and context: Essays on body motion communication.* Philadelphia: University of Pennsylvania Press.

Birren, F. (1950). *Color psychology and color therapy.* New York: McGraw-Hill.

Bjorklund, D. F. (1987). A note on neonatal imitation. *Developmental Review, 7,* 86–92.

Blake, J., & Dolgoy, S. J. (1993). Gestural development and its relation to cognition during the transition to language. *Journal of Nonverbal Behavior, 17,* 87–102.

Blier, M. J., & Blier-Wilson, L. A. (1989). Gender differences in sex-rated emotional expressiveness. *Sex Roles, 21,* 287–295.

Bohannon, J. (2005, May 9). A nose for sexual preference. *Science Now,* pp. 4–5.

Bok, S. (1982). *Secrets: On the ethics of concealment and revelation.* New York: Pantheon.

Bombar, M. L., & Littig, L. W. (1996). Babytalk as a communication of intimate attachment: An initial study in adult romances and friendships. *Personal Relationships, 3,* 137–158.

Bond, C. F., & DePaulo, B. M. (2006). Accuracy of deception judgments. *Review of Personality and Social Psychology, 10,* 214–234.

Bond, C. F., Kahler, K. N., & Paolicelli, L. M. (1985). The miscommunication of deception: An adaptive perspective. *Journal of Experimental Social Psychology, 21,* 331–345.

Bond, C. F., Omar, A., Pitre, U., Lashley, B. R., Skaggs, L. M., & Kirk, C. T. (1992). Fishy-looking liars: Deception judgment from expectancy violation. *Journal of Personality and Social Psychology, 63,* 969–977.

Bond, C. F., & Robinson, M. (1988). The evolution of deception. *Journal of Nonverbal Behavior, 12,* 295–307.

Bond, C. F., Thomas, B. J., & Paulson, R. M. (2004). Maintaining lies: The multiple-audience problem. *Journal of Experimental Social Psychology, 40,* 29–40.

Bond, M. H., & Shiraishi, D. (1974). The effect of interviewer's body lean and status on the nonverbal behavior of interviewees. *Japanese Journal of Experimental Social Psychology, 13,* 11–21.

Boomer, D. S. (1978). The phonemic clause: Speech unit in human communication. In A. W. Siegman & S. Feldstein (Eds.), *Nonverbal behavior and communication* (pp. 245–262). Hillsdale, NJ: Lawrence Erlbaum Associates.

Borod, J. C. (1993). Emotion and the brain—anatomy and theory: An introduction to the special section. *Neuropsychology, 7,* 427–432.

Boroditsky, L. (2001). Does language shape thought? Mandarin and English speakers' conceptions of time. *Cognitive Psychology, 43,* 1–22.

Boucher, J. D., & Carlson, G. E. (1980). Recognition of facial expression in three cultures. *Journal of Cross-Cultural Psychology, 11,* 263–280.

Boucher, J. D., & Ekman, P. (1975). Facial areas and emotional information. *Journal of Communication, 25,* 21–29.

Boyatzis, C. J., & Watson, M. W. (1993). Preschool children's symbolic representation of objects through gestures. *Child Development, 64,* 729–735.

Boyer, L. M., Thompson, C. A., Klopf, D. W., & Ishii, S. (1990). An intercultural comparison of immediacy among Japanese and Americans. *Perceptual and Motor Skills, 71,* 65–66.

Brend, R. M. (1975). Male-female intonation patterns in American English. In B. Thorne & N. M. Henley (Eds.), *Language and sex: Difference and dominance* (pp. 84–87). Cambridge, MA: Newbury House.

Briton, N. J., & Hall, J. A. (1995). Gender-based expectancies and observer judgments of smiling. *Journal of Nonverbal Behavior, 19,* 49–65.

Broadstock, M., Borland, R., & Gason, R. (1992). Effects of suntan on judgments of healthiness and attractiveness by adolescents. *Journal of Applied Psychology, 22,* 157–172.

Broome, B. J. (1990). "Palevome": Foundations of struggle and conflict in Greek interpersonal communication. *The Southern Communication Journal, 55,* 260–275.

Brown, C. E., Dovidio, J. F., & Ellyson, S. L. (1990). Reducing sex differences in visual displays of dominance: Knowledge is power. *Personality and Social Psychology Bulletin, 16,* 358–368.

Brown, F. (in press). Morningness/eveningness concordance with the rhythms of life. In D. Lloyd & E. L. Rossi (Eds.), *Ultradian rhythms in life processes: An inquiry into fundamental principles of chronobiology and psychobiology* (2nd ed.). New York: Springer-Verlag.

Brownlow, S. (1992). Seeing is believing: Facial appearance, credibility, and attitude change. *Journal of Nonverbal Behavior, 16,* 101–115.

Brownlow, S., & Zebrowitz, L. A. (1990). Facial appearance, gender, and credibility in television commercials. *Journal of Nonverbal Behavior, 14,* 51–60.

Bruneau, T. J. (1973). Communicative silence: Forms and functions. *Journal of Communication, 23,* 17–46.

Bruneau, T. J. (2007). Communicative silences: Forms and functions. In C. D. Mortensen (Ed.), *Communication theory* (2nd ed., pp. 306–334). New Brunswick, NJ: Transaction Publishers.

Bruneau, T. J. (in press). Time, change, and sociocultural communication: A chronemic perspective. *Sign Systems Studies.*

Bryant, G. A., & Fox Tree, J. E. (2005). Is there an ironic tone of voice? *Language and Speech, 48,* 257–277.

Buck, R. (1977). Nonverbal communication of affect in preschool children: Relationships with personality and skin conductance. *Journal of Personality and Social Psychology, 35,* 225–236.

Buck, R. (1983). Nonverbal receiving ability. In J. M. Wiemann & R. P. Harrison (Eds.), *Nonverbal interaction* (pp. 209–242). Thousand Oaks, CA: Sage.

Buck, R. (1984). *The communication of emotion.* New York: Guilford.

Buck, R. (1991). Social factors in facial display and communication: A reply to Chovil and others. *Journal of Nonverbal Behavior, 15,* 155–161.

Buck, R. (1994). *The communication of emotion.* New York: Guilford.

Buck, R. (2003). Interview during the annual meeting of the National Communication Association, Miami Beach, November 2003.

Buck, R., Losow, J. I., Murphy, M. M., & Costanzo, P. (1992). Social facilitation and inhibition of emotional expression and communication. *Journal of Personality and Social Psychology, 63*, 962–968.

Buck, R., Miller, R. E., & Caul, W. F. (1974). Sex, personality and physiological variables in the communication of emotion via facial expression. *Journal of Personality and Social Psychology, 30*, 587–596.

Buck, R., & VanLear, C. A. (2002). Verbal and nonverbal communication: Distinguishing symbolic, spontaneous, and pseudo-spontaneous communication. *Journal of Communication, 52*, 522–541.

Buckley, H. M., & Roach, M. E. (1974). Clothing as a nonverbal communicator of social and political attitudes. *Family and Consumer Sciences Research Journal, 3*, 94–102.

Bugental, D. E., Kaswan, J. W., Love, L. R., & Fox, M. N. (1970). Child versus adult perception of evaluative messages in verbal, vocal, and visual channels. *Developmental Psychology, 2*, 367–375.

Bugental, D. E., Love, L. R., & Gianetto, R. M. (1971). Perfidious feminine faces. *Journal of Personality and Social Psychology, 17*, 314–318.

Bull, P. E. (1987). *Posture and gesture.* Oxford, England: Pergamon.

Bull, R., & Gibson-Robinson, E. (1981). The influence of eye-gaze, style of dress, and locality on the amounts of money donated to charity. *Human Relations, 34*, 895–905.

Buller, D. B. (1986). Distraction during persuasive communication: A meta-analytic review. *Communication Monographs, 53*, 91–114.

Buller, D. B. (1987). Communication apprehension and reactions to proxemic violations. *Journal of Nonverbal Behavior, 11*, 13–25.

Buller, D. B., & Aune, R. K. (1988). The effects of vocalics and nonverbal sensitivity on compliance: A speech accommodation theory explanation. *Human Communication Research, 14*, 301–332.

Buller, D. B., & Aune, R. K. (1992). The effects of speech rate similarity on compliance: Application of communication accommodation theory. *Western Journal of Communication, 56*, 37–53.

Buller, D. B., & Burgoon, J. K. (1986). The effects of vocalics and nonverbal sensitivity on compliance: A replication and extension. *Human Communication Research, 13*, 126–144.

Buller, D. B., & Burgoon, J. K. (1994). Deception: Strategic and nonstrategic behavior. In J. Daly & J. Wiemann (Eds.), *Strategic interpersonal communication* (pp. 191–223). Hillsdale, NJ: Lawrence Erlbaum Associates.

Buller, D. B., & Burgoon, J. K. (1996). Interpersonal deception theory. *Communication Theory, 6*, 203–242.

Buller, D. B., Burgoon, J. K., White, C., Buslig, A., & Ebesu, A. S. (1995, November). *Interpersonal deception: XIV. Effects of planning on verbal and nonverbal behavior during deception.* Paper presented at the annual meeting of the Speech Communication Association, San Antonio, TX.

Buller, D. B., Burgoon, J. K., White, C., & Ebesu, A. S. (1994). Interpersonal deception: VII. Behavioral profiles of falsification, concealment, and equivocation. *Journal of Language and Social Psychology, 13*, 366–395.

Buller, D. B., Le Poire, B. A., Aune, K. R., & Eloy, S. V. (1992). Social perceptions as mediators of the effect of speech rate similarity on compliance. *Human Communication Research, 19*, 286–311.

Buller, D. B., Strzyzewski, K. D., & Hunsaker, F. G. (1991). Interpersonal deception: II. The inferiority of conversational participants as deception detectors. *Communication Monographs, 58*, 25–40.

Bureau International des Poids et Mesures. (2006). *The International System of Units (SI) (8th ed.).* Downloaded May 18, 2007, from: http://www.bipm.fr/utils/common/pdf/si_brochure_8_en.pdf

Burgoon, J. K. (1982). Privacy and communication. In M. Burgoon (Ed.), *Communication yearbook 6* (pp. 206–249). Beverly Hills, CA: Sage.

Burgoon, J. K. (1983). Nonverbal violations of expectations. In J. M. Wiemann & R. P. Harrison (Eds.), *Nonverbal interaction* (pp. 77–111). Beverly Hills, CA: Sage.

Burgoon, J. K. (1985). The relationship of verbal and nonverbal codes. In B. Dervin & M. J. Voight (Eds.), *Progress in communication sciences* (Vol. 6, pp. 263–298). Norwood, NJ: Ablex.

Burgoon, J. K. (1991). Relational message interpretations of touch, conversational distance, and posture. *Journal of Nonverbal Behavior, 15*, 233–259.

Burgoon, J. K. (1993). Interpersonal expectations, expectancy violations, and emotional communication. *Journal of Language and Social Psychology, 12*, 30–48.

Burgoon, J. K. (1994). Nonverbal signals. In M. L. Knapp & G. R. Miller (Eds.), *Handbook of interpersonal communication* (2nd ed., pp. 229–285). Newbury Park, CA: Sage.

Burgoon, J. K. (2005). The future of motivated deception detection. In P. Kalbfleisch (Ed.), *Communication yearbook 29* (pp. 49–95). Mahwah, NJ: Lawrence Erlbaum Associates.

Burgoon, J. K., & Aho, L. (1982). Three field experiments on the effects of violations of conversational distance. *Communication Monographs, 49*, 71–88.

Burgoon, J. K., Allspach, L. E., & Miczo, N. (1997, February). *Needs, expectancies, goals and initial interaction: A view from interaction adaptation theory.* Paper presented at the annual meeting of the Western States Communication Association, Monterey, CA.

Burgoon, J. K., & Bacue, A. (2003). Nonverbal communication skills. In B. R. Burleson & J. O. Greene (Eds.), *Handbook of communication and social interaction skills* (pp. 179–219). Mahwah, NJ: Lawrence Erlbaum Associates.

Burgoon, J. K., Birk, T., & Pfau, M. (1990). Nonverbal behaviors, persuasion, and credibility. *Human Communication Research, 17,* 140–169.

Burgoon, J. K., Blair, J. P., & Hamel, L. (2007). *Factors influencing deception detection: Impairment or facilitation?* Manuscript submitted for publication.

Burgoon, J. K., Blair, J. P., & Moyer, E. (2003, November). *Effects of communication modality on arousal, cognitive complexity, behavioral control and deception detection during deceptive episodes.* Paper presented at the annual meeting of the National Communication Association, Miami, FL.

Burgoon, J. K., Blair, J. P., & Strom, R. (2008). Cognitive biases, modalities and deception detection. *Human Communication Research, 34,* 572–599.

Burgoon, J. K., & Buller, D. B. (1994). Interpersonal deception: IV. Effects of deceit on perceived communication and nonverbal behavior dynamics. *Journal of Nonverbal Behavior, 18,* 155–184.

Burgoon, J. K., Buller, D. B., Blair, J. P., & Tilley, P. (2006). Sex differences in presenting and detecting deceptive messages. In D. Canary & K. Dindia (Eds.), *Sex differences and similarities in communication* (2nd ed., pp. 263–280). Mahwah, NJ: Lawrence Erlbaum Associates.

Burgoon, J. K., Buller, D. B., Dillman, L., & Walther, J. (1995). Interpersonal deception: IV. Effects of suspicion on perceived communication and nonverbal behavior dynamics. *Human Communication Research, 22,* 163–196.

Burgoon, J. K., Buller, D. B., Ebesu, A., & Rockwell, P. (1994). Interpersonal deception: V. Accuracy in deception detection. *Communication Monographs, 61,* 303–325.

Burgoon, J. K., Buller, D. B., Ebesu, A., Rockwell, P., & White, C. (1996). Testing interpersonal deception theory: Effects of suspicion on nonverbal behavior and relational messages. *Communication Theory, 6,* 243–267.

Burgoon, J. K., Buller, D. B., & Floyd, K. (2001). Does participation affect deception success? A test of the inter-activity effect. *Human Communication Research, 27,* 503–534.

Burgoon, J. K., Buller, D. B., Floyd, K., & Grandpre, J. (1996). Deceptive realities: Sender, receiver, and observer perspectives in deceptive communication. *Communication Research, 23,* 724–748.

Burgoon, J. K., Buller, D. B., & Guerrero, L. K. (1995). Interpersonal deception: IX. Effects of social skill and nonverbal communication on deception success and detection accuracy. *Journal of Language and Social Psychology, 14,* 289–311.

Burgoon, J. K., Buller, D. B., Guerrero, L. K., Afifi, W. A., & Feldman, C. M. (1996). Interpersonal deception XII: Information management dimensions underlying deceptive and truthful messages. *Communication Monographs, 63,* 51–69.

Burgoon, J. K., Buller, D. B., Hale, J. L., & deTurck, M. A. (1984). Relational messages associated with nonverbal behaviors. *Human Communication Research, 10,* 351–378.

Burgoon, J. K., Buller, D. B., White, C. H., Afifi, W. A., & Buslig, A. L. S. (1999). The role of conversational involvement in deceptive interpersonal communication. *Personality and Social Psychology Bulletin, 25,* 669–685.

Burgoon, J. K., Buller, D. B., & Woodall, W. G. (1996). *Nonverbal communication: The unspoken dialogue* (2nd ed). New York: McGraw-Hill.

Burgoon, J. K., Dillman, L., & Stern, L. A. (1993). Adaptation in dyadic interaction: Defining and conceptualizing patterns of reciprocity and compensation. *Communication Theory, 3,* 295–316.

Burgoon, J. K., & Dunbar, N. E. (2000). Interpersonal dominance as a situationally, interactionally, and relationally contingent social skill. *Communication Monographs, 67,* 96–121.

Burgoon, J. K., & Floyd, K. (2000). Testing for the motivation impairment effect during deception and truthful interaction. *Western Journal of Communication, 64,* 243–267.

Burgoon, J. K., & Hale, J. L. (1984). The fundamental topoi of relational communication. *Communication Monographs, 51,* 193–214.

Burgoon, J. K., & Hale, J. L. (1987). Validation and measurement of the fundamental themes of relational communication. *Communication Monographs, 54,* 19–41.

Burgoon, J. K., & Hale, J. L. (1988). Nonverbal expectancy violations theory: Model elaboration and application to immediacy behaviors. *Communication Monographs, 55,* 58–79.

Burgoon, J. K., & Hoobler, G. (2002). Nonverbal signals. In M. L. Knapp & J. Daly (Eds.), *Handbook of interpersonal communication* (pp. 240–299). Thousand Oaks, CA: Sage.

Burgoon, J. K., Johnson, M. L., & Koch, P. T. (1998). The nature and measurement of interpersonal dominance. *Communication Monographs, 65,* 308–335.

Burgoon, J. K., & Jones, S. B. (1976). Toward a theory of personal space expectations and their violations. *Human Communication Research, 2,* 131–146.

Burgoon, J. K., & Koper, R. J. (1984). Nonverbal and relational communication associated with reticence. *Human Communication Research, 10,* 601–626.

Burgoon, J. K., & Le Poire, B. A. (1993). Effects of communication expectancies, actual communication, and expectancy disconfirmation on evaluations of communicators and their communication behavior. *Human Communication Research, 20,* 67–96.

Burgoon, J. K., & Le Poire, B. A. (1999). Nonverbal cues and interpersonal judgments: Participant and observer perceptions of intimacy, dominance, composure, and formality. *Communication Monographs, 66*, 105–124.

Burgoon, J. K., Le Poire, B. A., & Rosenthal, R. (1995). Effects of preinteraction expectancies and target communication on perceiver reciprocity and compensation during dyadic interaction. *Journal of Experimental Social Psychology, 31*, 287–321.

Burgoon, J. K., & Levine, T. R. (2009). Advances in deception detection. In S. Smith & S. R. Wilson (Eds.), *New directions in interpersonal communication* (pp. 201–220). Thousand Oaks, CA: Sage.

Burgoon, J. K., & Newton, D. A. (1991). Applying a social meaning model to relational messages of conversational involvement: Comparing participant and observer perspectives. *Southern Communication Journal, 56*, 96–113.

Burgoon, J. K., Newton, D. A., Walther, J. B., & Baesler, E. J. (1989). Nonverbal expectancy violations and conversational involvement. *Journal of Nonverbal Behavior, 13*, 97–119.

Burgoon, J. K., & Qin, T. (2006). The dynamic nature of deceptive verbal communication. *Journal of Language and Social Psychology, 25*, 76–96.

Burgoon, J. K., & Saine, T. J. (1978). *The unspoken dialogue: An introduction to nonverbal communication.* Boston: Houghton-Mifflin.

Burgoon, J. K., Segrin, C., & Dunbar, N. E. (2002). Nonverbal communication and social influence. In J. P. Dillard & M. Pfau (Eds.), *The persuasion handbook: Developments in theory and practice* (pp. 445–473). Thousand Oaks, CA: Sage.

Burgoon, J. K., Stacks, D. W., & Burch, S. A. (1982). The role of interpersonal rewards and violations of distancing expectations in achieving influence in small groups. *Communication: Journal of the Communication Association of the Pacific, 11*, 114–128.

Burgoon, J. K., Stern, L. A., & Dillman, L. (1995). *Interpersonal adaptation: Dyadic interaction patterns.* Cambridge, England: Cambridge University Press.

Burgoon, J. K., & Walther, J. B. (1990). Nonverbal expectancies and the evaluative consequences of violations. *Human Communication Research, 17*, 232–265.

Burgoon, J. K., Walther, J. B., & Baesler, E. J. (1992). Interpretations, evaluations, and consequences of interpersonal touch. *Human Communication Research, 19*, 237–263.

Burleson, B. (2003). Interview during the annual meeting of the National Communication Association, Miami Beach, November 2003.

Burleson, B. R., & Denton, W. H. (1997). The relationship between communication skill and marital satisfaction: Some moderating effects. *Journal of Marriage and the Family, 59*, 884–902.

Burleson, B. R., & Kunkel, A. W. (2006). Revisiting the different cultures thesis: An assessment of sex differences and similarities in supportive communication. In K. Dindia & D. J. Canary (Eds.), *Sex differences and similarities in communication* (2nd ed., pp. 137–160). Mahwah, NJ: Lawrence Erlbaum Associates.

Burns, J. (1972). Development and implementation of an environmental evaluation and redesign process for a high school science department. In W. J. Mitchell (Ed.), *Environmental design: Research and practice* (Vol. 1, pp. 12.3.1–12.3.9). Los Angeles: University of California Press.

Burrowes, B. D., & Halberstadt, A. G. (1987). Self- and family-expressiveness styles in the experience and expression of anger. *Journal of Nonverbal Behavior, 11*, 254–268.

Bushman, B. J. (1988). The effects of apparel on compliance: A field experiment with a female authority figure. *Personality and Social Psychology Bulletin, 14*, 459–467.

Buslig, A. L. S. (1991). *Architects' and laypeople's perceptions of interaction environments.* Unpublished master's thesis, University of Arizona.

Buss, D. M. (1989). Sex differences in human mate preferences: Evolutionary hypotheses tested in 37 cultures. *Behavioral and Brain Sciences, 12*, 1–49.

Buss, D. M. (1994). *The evolution of desire: Strategies of mate selection.* New York: Basic Books.

Buss, D. M. (1999). *Evolutionary psychology: The new science of the mind.* Boston: Allyn & Bacon.

Bussey, K. (1999). Children's categorization and evaluation of different types of lies and truths. *Child Development, 70*, 1338–1347.

Butler, D., & Geis, F. L. (1990). Nonverbal affect responses to male and female leaders: Implications for leadership evaluations. *Journal of Personality and Social Psychology, 58*, 48–59.

Butler, E. A., Egloff, B., Wilhelm, F. H., Smith, N. C., Erickson, E. A., & Gross, J. J. (2003). The social consequences of expressive suppression. *Emotion, 3*, 48–67.

Byers, P., & Byers, H. (1972). Nonverbal communication and the education of children. In C. B. Cazden, V. P. John, & D. Hymes (Eds.), *Functions of language in the classroom* (pp. 3–31). New York: Teachers College Press.

Byrne, D. (1961). The influence of propinquity and opportunities for interaction on classroom relationships. *Human Relations, 14*, 63–70.

Cüceloglu, D. M. (1972). Facial code in affective communication. In D. C. Speer (Ed.), *Nonverbal communication* (pp. 395–407). Beverly Hills, CA: Sage.

Cahnman, W. J. (1968). The stigma of obesity. *Sociological Quarterly, 9*, 283–299.

Caldas, S. J., & Caron-Caldas, S. (1999). Language immersion and cultural identity: Conflicting influences and values. *Language, Culture, and Curriculum, 12*, 42–58.

Calhoun, J. B. (1962). Population density and social pathology. *Scientific American, 206,* 139–150.

Calhoun, J. B. (1966). The role of space in animal sociology. *Journal of Social Issues, 22,* 46–59.

Camden, C., Motley, M. T., & Wilson, A. (1984). White lies in interpersonal communication: A taxonomy and preliminary investigation of social motivations. *Western Journal of Speech Communication, 48,* 309–325.

Campbell, J. (1982). *Grammatical man.* New York: Simon & Schuster.

Campbell, N. C. G., Graham, J. L., Jolibert, A., & Meissner, H. G. (1988). Marketing negotiations in France, Germany, the United Kingdom, and the United States. *Journal of Marketing, 52,* 49–62.

Camras, L. A. (1988, May). *Darwin revisited: An infant's first emotional facial expressions.* Paper presented at the International Conference on Infant Studies, Washington, DC.

Camras, L. A., Sullivan, J., & Michel, G. (1993). Do infants express discrete emotions? Adult judgments of facial, vocal, and body actions. *Journal of Nonverbal Behavior, 17,* 171–186.

Canary, D. J. (2003). Interview during the annual meeting of the National Communication Association, Miami Beach, November 2003.

Canary, D. J., & Cody, M. J. (1994). *Interpersonal communication: A goals-based approach.* New York: St. Martin's Press.

Cappella, J. N. (1981). Mutual influence in expressive behavior: Adult-adult and infant-adult dyadic interaction. *Psychological Bulletin, 89,* 101–132.

Cappella, J. N. (1987). Interpersonal communication: Definitions and questions. In C. R. Berger & S. Chaffee (Eds.), *Handbook of communication science* (pp. 184–238). Beverly Hills, CA: Sage.

Cappella, J. N. (1993). The facial feedback hypothesis in human interaction: Review and speculation. *Journal of Language and Social Psychology, 12,* 13–29.

Cappella, J. N. (1994). The management of conversations. In M. L. Knapp & G. R. Miller (Eds.), *Handbook of interpersonal communication* (2nd ed., pp. 380–419). Newbury Park, CA: Sage.

Cappella, J. N. (1997). Behavioral and judged coordination in adult informal social interactions: Vocal and kinesic indicators. *Journal of Personality and Social Psychology, 72,* 119–131.

Cappella, J. N., & Greene, J. O. (1982). A discrepancy-arousal explanation of mutual influence in expressive behavior for adult-adult and infant-adult dyadic interaction. *Communication Monographs, 49,* 89–114.

Cappella, J. N., & Greene, J. O. (1984). The effects of distance and individual differences in arousability on nonverbal involvement: A test of discrepancy-arousal theory. *Journal of Nonverbal Behavior, 8,* 259–286.

Cappella, J. N., & Planalp, S. (1981). Talk and silence sequences in informal conversations: III. Interspeaker influence. *Human Communication Research, 7,* 117–132.

Carli, L. L. (1999). Gender, interpersonal power, and social influence. *Journal of Social Issues, 55,* 81–99.

Carmichael, M. S., Humbert, R., Dixen, J., Palmiana, G., Greenleaf, W., & Davidson, J. M. (1987). Plasma oxytocin increase in the human sexual response. *Journal of Clinical Endocrinology and Metabolism, 64,* 27–31.

Carroll, L., & Anderson, R. (2002). Body piercing, tattooing, self-esteem, and body investment in adolescent girls. *Adolescence, 37,* 627–637.

Carroll, L., & Gilroy, P. J. (2002). Role of appearance and nonverbal behavior in the perception of sexual orientation among lesbians and gay men. *Psychological Reports, 91,* 115–122.

Carter, N., Henderson, R., Lal, S., Hart, M., Booth, S., & Hunyor, S. (2002). Cardiovascular and autonomic response to environmental noise during sleep in night shift workers. *Sleep, 25,* 457–464.

Casey, R. J., & Fuller, L. L. (1994). Maternal regulation of children's emotions. *Journal of Nonverbal Behavior, 18,* 57–89.

Cash, T. F. (1988). The psychology of cosmetics: A research bibliography. *Perceptual and Motor Skills, 66,* 455–460.

Cash, T. F., Dawson, K., Davis, P., Bowen, M., & Galumbeck, C. (1989). Effects of cosmetics use on the physical attractiveness and body image of American college women. *Journal of Social Psychology, 129,* 349–355.

Cash, T. F., & Derlega, V. (1978). The matching hypothesis: Physical attractiveness among same-sexed friends. *Personality and Social Psychology Bulletin, 4,* 240–243.

Cash, T. F., & Henry, P. E. (1995). Women's body images: The results of a national survey in the U.S.A. *Sex Roles, 33,* 19–28.

Cash, T. F., & Janda, L. H. (1984, December). The eye of the beholder. *Psychology Today,* pp. 46–52.

Cash, T. F., & Kilcullen, R. N. (1985). The eye of the beholder: Susceptibility to sexism and beautyism in the evaluation of managerial applicants. *Journal of Applied Social Psychology, 15,* 591–605.

Cash, T. F., & Szymanski, M. L. (1995). The development and validation of the Body-Image Ideas Questionnaire. *Journal of Personality Assessment, 64,* 466–477.

Caudill, W., & Weinstein, H. (1972). Maternal care and infant behavior in Japan and America. *Psychiatry: Journal for the Study of Interpersonal Processes, 32,* 12–43.

Caulfield, R. (2000). Beneficial effects of tactile stimulation on early development. *Early Childhood Education Journal, 27,* 255–257.

Cha, A., Hecht, B. R., Nelson, K., & Hopkins, M. P. (2004). Resident physician attire: Does it make a difference to our patients? *American Journal of Obstetrics and Gynecology, 190,* 1484–1488.

Chaplin, W. F., Phillips, J. B., Brown, J. D., Clanton, N. R., & Stein, J. L. (2000). Handshaking, gender, personality, and first impressions. *Journal of Personality and Social Psychology, 70,* 110–117.

Chapple, E. D. (1970). *Cultural and biological man: Exploration in behavioral anthropology.* New York: Holt, Rinehart & Winston.

Charlesworth, W. R., & Kreutzer, M. A. (1973). Facial expressions of infants and children. In P. Ekman (Ed.), *Darwin and facial expression* (pp. 91–168). New York: Academic Press.

Charpied, G. L. (2007). *Anatomy and physiology of voice and speech production: Elements of human communication.* San Diego: Plural Publishing.

Chawla, P., & Krauss, R. M. (1994). Gesture and speech in spontaneous and rehearsed narratives. *Journal of Experimental Social Psychology, 30,* 580–601.

Cherry, C. (1957, 1964). *On human communication.* Cambridge, MA: MIT Press.

Chieffi, S., & Ricci, M. (2005). Gesture production and text structure. *Perceptual and Motor Skills, 101,* 435–439.

Chovil, N. (1991a). Discourse-oriented facial displays in conversation. *Journal of Language and Social Interaction, 25,* 163–194.

Chovil, N. (1991b). Social determinants of facial displays. *Journal of Nonverbal Behavior, 15,* 141–153.

Chovil, N. (2004). Measuring conversational facial displays. In V. Manusov (Ed.), *The sourcebook of nonverbal measures: Going beyond words* (pp. 173–188). Hillsdale, NJ: Lawrence Erlbaum Associates.

Christensen, A., & Heavey, C. L. (1990). Gender and social structure in the demand/withdrawal pattern of marital conflict. *Journal of Personality and Social Psychology, 59,* 73–81.

Christian, J. J., Flyer, V., & Davis, D. E. (1961). Phenomena associated with population density. *Proceedings of the National Academy of Sciences, 47,* 428–449.

Christie, R., & Geis, F. L. (1970). *Studies in Machiavellianism.* New York: Academic.

Christopher, F. S., & Lloyd, S. A. (2001). Physical and sexual aggression in relationships. In C. Hendrick & S. S. Hendrick (Eds.), *Close relationships* (pp. 331–343). Thousand Oaks, CA: Sage.

Ciolek, T. M. (1983). The proxemics lexicon: A first approximation. *Journal of Nonverbal Behavior, 8,* 55–79.

Clark, H. H. (1996). *Using language.* Cambridge, England: Cambridge University Press.

Clevenger, T., Jr. (1991). Can one not communicate? A conflict of models. *Communication Studies, 42,* 340–353.

Clifford, M. M., & Walster, E. H. (1973). The effect of physical attractiveness on teacher expectation. *Sociology of Education, 46,* 248–258.

Cloven, D. H., & Roloff, M. E. (1993). The chilling effect of aggressive potential on the expression of complaints in intimate relationships. *Communication Monographs, 60,* 199–219.

Coan, J. A., Schaefer, H. S., & Davidson, R. J. (2006). Lending a hand: Social regulation of the neural response to threat. *Psychological Science, 17,* 1032–1039.

Coats, E. J., & Feldman, R. S. (1996). Gender differences in nonverbal correlates of social status. *Personality and Social Psychology Bulletin, 22,* 1014–1022.

Coe, K., Harmon, M. R., Verner, B., & Tonn, A. (1993). Tattoos and male alliances. *Human Nature, 4,* 199–204.

Cohen, A., & Starkweather, J. (1961). Vocal cues to the identification of language. *American Journal of Psychology, 74,* 90–93.

Cohen, S., & Weinstein, N. (1981). Nonauditory effects of noise on behavior and health. *Journal of Social Issues, 37,* 36–70.

Cohn, D. (2006, June 5). Scent of a terrorist. *Seed Magazine.* Retrieved from http://www.seedmagazine.com

Cohn, J. F., & Ekman, P. (2006). Measuring facial action. In J. A. Harrigan, R. Rosenthal, & K. R. Scherer (Eds.), *The new handbook of methods in nonverbal behavior research* (pp. 9–64). New York: Oxford University Press.

Cohn, J., & Schmidt, K. L. (2004). The timing of facial motion in posed and spontaneous smiles. *International Journal of Wavelets, Multiresolution, and Information Processing, 2,* 1–12.

Coker, D. A., & Burgoon, J. K. (1987). The nature of conversational involvement and nonverbal encoding patterns. *Human Communication Research, 13,* 463–494.

Cole, P. M. (1986). Children's spontaneous control of facial expression. *Child Development, 57,* 1309–1321.

Colino, S. (2006, May 30). That look—it's catching! Emotions, like germs, are easily transmissible. The trick is passing and receiving the right ones. *The Washington Post,* p. F1.

Collins, G. M., & McNicholas, J. (1998). A theoretical basis for health benefits of pet ownership: Attachment versus psychological support. In C. C. Wilson & D. C. Turner (Eds.), *Companion animals in human health* (pp. 105–122). Thousand Oaks, CA: Sage.

Condon, W. S. (1976). An analysis of behavior organization. *Sign Language Studies, 13,* 285–318.

Condon, W. S., & Sander, L. W. (1974). Synchrony demonstrated between movement of the neonate and adult speech. *Child Development, 45,* 456–462.

Conroy, J. (2001). *Unspeakable acts, ordinary people: The dynamics of torture.* Berkeley: University of California Press.

Cook, M. (1979). *Perceiving others: The psychology of interpersonal perception.* London: Methuen.

Corn, J. J., & Horrigan, B. (1996). *Yesterday's tomorrows: Past visions of the American future.* Baltimore, MD: Johns Hopkins University Press.

Corso, J. F. (1977). Auditory perception and communication. In J. E. Birren & K. W. Schaie (Eds.), *Handbook of the psychology of aging* (pp. 535–553). New York: Van Nostrand Reinhold.

Cortes, J. B., & Gatti, F. M. (1965). Physique and self-description of temperament. *Journal of Consulting Psychology, 29,* 432–439.

Cortes, J. B., & Gatti, F. M. (1970, October). Physique and propensity. *Psychology Today, 4,* 32–34 & 42–44.

Costanzo, M., & Archer, D. (1989). Interpreting the expressive behavior of others: The interpersonal perception task. *Journal of Nonverbal Behavior, 13,* 225–245.

Costigan, K. (1984). How color goes to your head. *Science Digest, 47,* 24.

Coulson, M. (2004). Attributing emotion to static body postures: Recognition accuracy, confusions and viewpoint dependency. *Journal of Nonverbal Behavior, 24,* 117–139.

Coutts, L. M., & Schneider, F. W. (1976). Affiliative conflict theory: An investigation of the intimacy equilibrium and compensation hypothesis. *Journal of Personality and Social Psychology, 34,* 1135–1142.

Cowley, J. J., Johnson, A. L., & Brooksbank, B. W. L. (1977). The effect of two odorous compounds on performance in an assessment-of-people test. *Psychoneuroendrocrinology, 2,* 159–172.

Cox, C. L., & Glick, W. H. (1986). Resume evaluations and cosmetics use: When more is not better. *Sex Roles, 14,* 51–58.

Cox, J., & Dittmar, H. (1995). The functions of clothes and clothing (dis)satisfaction: A gender analysis among British students. *Journal of Consumer Policy, 18,* 237–265.

Crawford, C. C., & Michael, W. (1927). An experiment in judging intelligence by the voice. *Journal of Educational Psychology, 18,* 107–114.

Crozier, W. R. (1999). The meanings of colour: Preferences among hues. *Pigment and Resin Technology, 28,* 6–14.

Crusco, A. H., & Wetzel, C. G. (1984). The midas touch: The effects of interpersonal touch on restaurant tipping. *Personality and Social Psychology Bulletin, 10,* 512–517.

Culos-Reed, S. N., Brawley, L. R., Martin, K. A., & Leary, M. R. (2002). Self-presentation concerns and health behaviors among cosmetic surgery patients. *Journal of Applied Social Psychology, 32,* 560–569.

Cunningham, M. R., Barbee, A. R., & Pike, C. L. (1990). What do women want? Facialmetric assessment of multiple motives in the perception of male facial physical attractiveness. *Journal of Personality and Social Psychology, 59,* 61–72.

Custrini, R. J., & Feldman, R. S. (1989). Children's social competence and nonverbal encoding and decoding of emotion. *Journal of Clinical Child Psychology, 18,* 336–342.

Cutler, A. (2002). Phonological processing. In C. Gussenhoven & N. L. Warner (Eds.), *Papers in laboratory phonology VII* (pp. 275–296). Berlin: Mouton De Gruyter.

Cutler, A., Dahan, D., & van Donselaar, W. (1997). Prosody in the comprehension of spoken language: A literature review. *Language and Speech, 40,* 141–201.

Daly, E. M., Lancee, W. J., & Polivy, J. (1983). A conical model for the taxonomy of emotional experience. *Journal of Personality and Social Psychology, 45,* 443–457.

Darwin, C. (1859). *On the origin of species by means of natural selection, or the preservation of favoured races in the struggle for life.* London: John Murray.

Darwin, C. (1872/1998). *The expression of emotion in man and animals.* New York: Oxford University Press.

Davidoff, J. (1991). *Cognition through color.* Cambridge, MA: MIT Press.

Davis, J. L. (2007). What's so great about kissing? Retrieved January 7, 2007 from the World Wide Web: http://www.webmd.com/content/article/11/1687_51154.htm

Davis, L. L. (1984). Clothing and human behavior: A review. *Home Economics Research Journal, 12,* 325–339.

Davis, M. (Ed.). (1982). *Interaction rhythms: Periodicity in communicative behavior.* New York: Human Sciences Press.

Davis, M., Markus, K. A., & Walters, S. B. (2006). Judging the credibility of criminal suspect statements: Does mode of presentation matter? *Journal of Nonverbal Behavior, 30,* 181–198.

Davis, R. L., Wiggins, M. N., Mercado, C. C., & Sullivan, P. S. (2007). Defining the core competency of professionalism based on the patient's perception. *Clinical & Experimental Ophthalmology, 35,* 51–54.

de Botton, A. (2006). *The architecture of happiness.* New York: Pantheon.

Dellinger, K., & Williams, C. L. (1997). Makeup at work: Negotiating appearance rules in the workplace. *Gender and Society, 11,* 151–177.

Delsarte, F. (1882). *The art of oratory.* New York: E. S. Werner.

Denham, S. A., & Grout, L. (1993). Socialization of emotion: Pathway to preschoolers' emotional and social competence. *Journal of Nonverbal Behavior, 17,* 205–227.

DePaulo, B. M. (1992). Nonverbal behavior and self-presentation. *Psychological Bulletin, 111,* 203–243.

DePaulo, B. M., Charlton, K., Cooper, H., Lindsay, J. J., & Muhlenbruck, L. (1997). The accuracy-confidence correlation in deception detection. *Personality and Social Psychology Review, 1*, 346–358.

DePaulo, B. M., & Friedman, H. S. (1998). Nonverbal communication. In D. T. Gilbert, S. T. Fiske, & L. Gardner (Eds.), *The handbook of social psychology* (Vols. 1–2, 4th ed., pp. 3–40). New York: McGraw-Hill.

DePaulo, B. M., Jordan, A., Irvine, A., & Laser, P. S. (1982). Age changes in the detection of deception. *Child Development, 53*, 701–709.

DePaulo, B. M., & Kashy, D. A. (1998). Everyday lies in close and casual relationships. *Journal of Personality and Social Psychology, 74*, 63–79.

DePaulo, B. M., Kashy, D. A., Kirkendol, S. E., Wyer, M. M., & Epstein, J. A. (1996). Lying in everyday life. *Journal of Personality and Social Psychology, 70*, 979–995.

DePaulo, B. M., & Kirkendol, S. E. (1989). The motivational impairment effect in the communication of deception. In J. Yuille (Ed.), *Credibility assessment* (pp. 51–70). Deurne, Belgium: Kluwer.

DePaulo, B. M., Lindsay, J. J., Malone, B. E., Muhlenbruck, L., Charlton, K., & Cooper, H. (2003). Cues to deception. *Psychological Bulletin, 129*, 74–118.

DePaulo, B. M., & Rosenthal, R. (1979a). Ambivalence, discrepancy, and deception in nonverbal communication. In R. Rosenthal (Ed.), *Skill in nonverbal communication: Individual differences* (pp. 204–248). Cambridge, MA: Oelgeschlager, Gunn & Hain.

DePaulo, B. M., & Rosenthal, R. (1979b). Telling lies. *Journal of Personality and Social Psychology, 37*, 1713–1722.

DePaulo, B. M., Rosenthal, R., Green, C., & Rosenkrantz, J. (1982). Diagnosing deceptive and mixed messages from verbal and nonverbal cues. *Journal of Experimental Social Psychology, 18*, 433–446.

DePaulo, B. M., Stone, J. I., & Lassiter, G. D. (1985a). Deceiving and detecting deceit. In B. R. Schlenker (Ed.), *The self and social life* (pp. 323–370). New York: McGraw-Hill.

DePaulo, B. M., Stone, J. I., & Lassiter, G. D. (1985b). Telling ingratiating lies: Effects of target sex and target attractiveness on verbal and nonverbal deceptive success. *Journal of Personality and Social Psychology, 48*, 1191–1203.

DePaulo, B. M., Wetzel, C., Sternglanz, R. W., & Wilson, M. J. W. (2003). Verbal and nonverbal dynamics of privacy, secrecy, and deceit. *Journal of Social Issues, 59*, 391–410.

Deprez, K., & Persoons, K. (1984). On the identity of Flemish high school students in Brussels. *Journal of Language and Social Psychology, 3*, 273–296.

Derlega, V. J., & Chaikin, A. L. (1977). Privacy and self-disclosure in social relationships. *Journal of Social Issues, 33*, 102–122.

Derlega, V. J., Lewis, R. J., Harrison, S., & Costanza, R. (1989). Gender differences in the initiation and attribution of tactile intimacy. *Journal of Nonverbal Behavior, 13*, 83–96.

Derlega, V. J., Metts, S., Petronio, S., & Margulis, S. T. (1993). *Self-disclosure*. Newbury Park, CA: Sage.

Dermer, M., & Thiel, D. L. (1975). When beauty may fail. *Journal of Personality and Social Psychology, 31*, 1168–1176.

deTurck, M. A., Harszlak, J. J., Bodhorn, D. J., & Texter, L. A. (1990). The effects of training social perceivers to detect deception from behavioral cues. *Communication Quarterly, 38*, 189–199.

Dew, D., & Jensen, P. J. (1977). *Phonetic processing: The dynamics of speech*. Columbus, OH: Merrill.

di Battista, P. (1995, May). *Preparation, familiarity, control, and deceivers' responses to challenges of their truthfulness*. Paper presented at the annual meeting of the International Communication Association, Albuquerque, NM.

Dillard, J. L. (1972). *Black English*. New York: Random House.

Dillard, J. P., Anderson, J. W., & Knobloch, L. K. (2002). Interpersonal influence. In M. L. Knapp & J. A. Daly (Eds.), *Handbook of interpersonal communication* (3rd ed., pp. 423–474). Thousand Oaks, CA: Sage.

Dindia, K. (1987). The effects of sex of subject and sex of partner on interruptions. *Human Communication Research, 13*, 345–371.

Dindia, K., & Canary, D. J. (Eds.). (2006). *Sex differences and similarities in communication* (2nd ed.). Mahwah, NJ: Lawrence Erlbaum Associates.

Dion, K. K. (1972). Physical attractiveness and evaluations of children's transgressions. *Journal of Personality and Social Psychology, 24*, 207–213.

Dion, K. K. (1986). Stereotyping based on physical attractiveness: Issues and conceptual perspectives. In C. P. Herman, M. P. Zanna, & E. T. Higgins (Eds.), *Physical appearance, stigma, and social behavior: The Ontario Symposium* (Vol. 3, pp. 7–21). Hillsdale, NJ: Lawrence Erlbaum Associates.

Dion, K. K., Berscheid, E., & Walster, E. (1972). What is beautiful is good. *Journal of Personality and Social Psychology, 24*, 285–290.

Dittmann, A. T. (1978). The role of body movement in communication. In A.W. Siegman & S. Feldstein (Eds.), *Nonverbal behavior and communication* (pp. 69–95). Hillsdale, NJ: Lawrence Erlbaum Associates.

Dolin D., & Booth-Butterfield, M. (1993). Reach out and touch someone: Analysis of nonverbal comforting responses. *Communication Quarterly, 41*, 383–393.

Dortch, S. (1997). Women at the cosmetics counter. *American Demographics, 19*, 4.

Dosey M. A., & Meisels, M. (1969). Personal space and self-protection. *Journal of Personality and Social Psychology, 11*, 93–97.

Dovidio, J. F., Brown, C. E., Heltman, K., Ellyson, S. L., & Keating, C. F. (1988). Power displays between women and men in discussions of gender-linked tasks: A multichannel study. *Journal of Personality and Social Psychology, 55*, 580–587.

Dovidio, J. F., & Ellyson, S. L. (1985). Patterns of visual dominance behavior in humans. In S. L. Ellyson & J. F. Dovidio (Eds.), *Power, dominance, and nonverbal behavior* (pp. 129–149). New York: Springer-Verlag.

Dovidio, J. F., Hebl, M., Richeson, J. A., & Shelton, J. N. (2006). Nonverbal communication, race, and intergroup interaction. In V. Manusov & M. L. Patterson (Eds.), *The Sage handbook of nonverbal communication* (pp. 481–500). Thousand Oaks, CA: Sage.

Dow, B. J., & Wood, J. T. (Eds.). (2006). *The Sage handbook of gender and communication.* Thousand Oaks, CA: Sage.

Drescher, V. M., Gantt, W. H., & Whitehead, W. E. (1980). Heart rate response to touch. *Psychosomatic Medicine, 42*, 559–565.

Drews, D. R., Alison, C. K., & Probst, J. R. (2000). Behavioral and self-concept differences in tattooed and nontattooed college students. *Psychological Reports, 86*, 475–481.

Droogsma, R. A. (2007). Redefining hijab: American Muslim women's standpoints on veiling. *Journal of Applied Communication Research, 35*, 294–319.

Duchenne, B. (1991/1862). *The mechanism of human facial expression or an electro-physiological analysis of the expression of the emotions* (A. Cuthbertson, Trans.). New York: Cambridge University Press.

Duck, S. (1976). Interpersonal communication in developing acquaintances. In G. R. Miller (Ed.), *Explorations in interpersonal communication* (pp. 127–147). Beverly Hills, CA: Sage.

Duggan, A. P., & Parrott, R. L. (2001). Physicians' nonverbal rapport building and patients' talk about the subjective component of illness. *Human Communication Research, 27*, 299–311.

Dunbar, N. E. (2004). Dyadic power theory: Constructing a communication-based theory of relational power. *Journal of Family Communication, 4*, 235–248.

Dunbar, N. E., & Burgoon, J. K. (2005). Perceptions of power and dominance in interpersonal encounters. *Journal of Social and Personal Relationships, 22*, 207–233.

Dunbar, N. E., Ramirez, A., Jr., & Burgoon, J. K. (2003). Interactive deception: Effects of participation on participant-receiver and observer judgments. *Communication Reports, 16*, 23–33.

Duncan, S. D. (1972). Some signals and rules for taking speaking turns in conversations. *Journal of Personality and Social Psychology, 23*, 283–292.

Duncan, S. D. (1974). On the structure of speaker-auditor interaction during speaker turns. *Language in Society, 2*, 161–180.

Duncan, S. D., & Fiske, D. W. (1977). *Face-to-face interaction: Research, methods, and theory.* Hillsdale, NJ: Lawrence Erlbaum Associates.

Dunlap, J. C., Loros, J. J., & DeCoursey, P. J. (Eds.). (2004). *Chronobiology: Biological timekeeping.* Sunderland, MA: Sinauer.

Dutton, D. G., & Aron, A. P. (1974). Some evidence for heightened sexual attraction under conditions of high anxiety. *Journal of Personality and Social Psychology, 30*, 510–517.

Eagly, A. H., Ashmore, R. D., Makhijani, M. G., & Longo, L. C. (1991). What is beautiful is good, but…: A meta-analytic review of research on the physical attractiveness stereotype. *Psychological Bulletin, 110*, 109–128.

Eakins, B. W., & Eakins, R. G. (1978). *Sex differences in human communication.* Boston: Houghton Mifflin.

Edney, J. J. (1976). Human territories: Comment on functional properties. *Environment and Behavior, 8*, 31–47.

Edwards, D. J. A. (1981). The role of touch in interpersonal relations: Implications for psychotherapy. *South African Journal of Psychology, 11*, 29–37.

Efron, D. (1941). *Gesture and environment.* New York: King's Crown Press.

Efron, D. (1972). *Gesture, race and culture.* The Hague: Mouton.

Efron, R. (1990). *The decline and fall of hemispheric specialization.* Hillsdale, NJ: Lawrence Erlbaum Associates.

Egland, K. L., Stelzner, M. A., Andersen, P. A., & Spitzberg, B. H. (1997). Perceived understanding, nonverbal communication, and relational satisfaction. In J. Aitken & L. Shedletsky (Eds.), *Intrapersonal communication processes* (pp. 386–395). Annandale, VA: Speech Communication Association.

Eibl-Eibesfeldt, I. (1972). Similarities and differences between cultures in expressive movements. In R. A. Hinde (Ed.), *Nonverbal communication* (pp. 297–314). Cambridge, England: Cambridge University Press.

Eibl-Eibesfeldt, I. (1973). Expressive behaviour of the deaf and blind born. In M. von Cranach & I. Vine (Eds.), *Social communication and movement* (pp. 163–194). New York: Academic Press.

Eibl-Eibesfeldt, I. (1974). *Love and hate: The natural history of behavior patterns.* New York: Holt, Rinehart & Winston.

Eibl-Eibesfeldt, I. (1979). Similarities and differences between cultures in expressive movements. In S. Weitz (Ed.), *Nonverbal communication* (2nd ed., pp. 37–48). New York: Oxford University Press.

Eisenberg, A. M., & Smith, R. R., Jr. (1971). *Nonverbal communication.* Indianapolis: Bobbs-Merrill.

Ekman, P. (1971). Universal and cultural differences in facial expressions of emotion. In J. K. Cole (Ed.),

Nebraska symposium on motivation (pp. 207–283). Lincoln: University of Nebraska Press.

Ekman, P. (1975, September). The universal smile: Face muscles talk every language. *Psychology Today, 9*, pp. 35–39.

Ekman, P. (1976). Movements with precise meanings. *Journal of Communication, 26*, 14–26.

Ekman, P. (1985). *Telling lies.* New York: Norton.

Ekman, P. (1992). *Telling lies: Clues to deceit in the marketplace, politics, and marriage.* New York: Norton.

Ekman, P. (1993). Facial expression and emotion. *American Psychologist, 48*, 384–392.

Ekman, P. (1997). Should we call it expression or communication? *European Journal of Social Sciences, 10*, 339–359.

Ekman, P. (2003). Darwin, deception, and facial expression. *Annals of the New York Academic of Sciences, 1000*, 205–221.

Ekman, P., & Friesen, W. V. (1969a). Nonverbal leakage and clues to deception. *Psychiatry, 32*, 88–106.

Ekman, P., & Friesen, W. V. (1969b). The repertoire of nonverbal behavior: Categories, origins, usage, and coding. *Semiotica, 1*, 49–98.

Ekman, P., & Friesen, W. V. (1972). Hand movements. *Journal of Communication, 22*, 353–374.

Ekman, P., & Friesen, W. V. (1974). Detecting deception from the body or face. *Journal of Personality and Social Psychology, 29*, 288–298.

Ekman, P., & Friesen, W. V. (1975). *Unmasking the face: A guide to recognizing emotions from facial clues.* Englewood Cliffs: NJ: Prentice-Hall.

Ekman P., & Friesen W. V. (1982). Felt, false, and miserable smiles. *Journal of Nonverbal Behavior, 6*, 238–252.

Ekman, P., & Friesen, W. V. (1986). A new pan-cultural facial expression of emotion. *Motivation and Emotion, 10*, 159–168.

Ekman, P., Friesen, W. V., & Ellsworth, P. (1972). *Emotion in the human face.* New York: Pergamon.

Ekman, P., Friesen, W. V., & Ellsworth, P. (1982). Methodological decisions. In P. Ekman (Ed.), *Emotion in the human face* (2nd ed., pp. 22–38). Cambridge, England: Cambridge University Press.

Ekman, P., Friesen, W. V., O'Sullivan, M., Chan, A., Diacoyanni-Tarlatzis, I., Heider, K., Krause, R., LeCompete, W. A., Pitcairn, T., Ricci-Bitti, P. E., Scherer, K., Tomita, M., & Tzavaras, A. (1987). Universals and cultural differences in the judgments of facial expressions of emotion. *Journal of Personality and Social Psychology, 53*, 712–717.

Ekman, P., Friesen, W. V., & Tomkins, S. S. (1971). Facial affect scoring technique: A first validity study. *Journal of Communication, 3*, 37–58.

Ekman, P., Levenson, R. W., & Friesen, W. V. (1983). Autonomic nervous system activity distinguishes among emotions. *Science, 221*, 1208–1210.

Ekman, P., & O'Sullivan, M. (1991). Who can catch a liar? *American Psychologist, 46*, 913–920.

Ekman, P., O'Sullivan, M., & Frank, M. G. (1999). A few can catch a liar. *Psychological Science, 10*, 263–266.

Ekman, P., & Oster, H. (1979). Facial expression of emotion. *Annual Review of Psychology, 30*, 527–554.

Ekman, P., Sorenson, E. R., & Friesen, W. V. (1969). Pan-cultural elements in facial displays of emotion. *Science, 164*, 86–88.

Elashoff, J. D., & Snow, R. E. (1971). *Pygmalian reconsidered: A case study in statistical inference: Reconsideration of the Rosenthal & Jacobsen data on teacher expectancy.* Worthington, OH: Charles A. Jones.

Elfenbein, H. A., & Ambady, N. (2002a). On the universality and cultural specificity of emotional recognition: A meta-analysis. *Psychological Bulletin, 128*, 205–235.

Elfenbein, H. A., & Ambady, N. (2002b). On the universality and cultural specificity of emotions. *Science, 164*, 86–88.

Elfenbein, H. A., & Ambady, N. (2003). When familiarity breeds accuracy: Cultural exposure and facial emotion recognition. *Journal of Personality and Social Psychology, 85*, 276–290.

Ellis, D. G. (1982). Language and speech communication. In M. Burgoon (Ed.), *Communication yearbook 6* (pp. 34–62). Beverly Hills, CA: Sage.

Ellis, L. (2006). Gender differences in smiling: An evolutionary neuroandrogenic theory. *Physiology and Behavior, 88*, 303–308.

Ellisworth, P. C., & Ludwig, L. M. (1972). Visual behavior in social interactions. *Journal of Communication, 22*, 375–403.

Ellyson, S. L., & Dovidio, J. F. (1985). Power, dominance, and nonverbal behavior: Basic concepts and issues. In S. L. Ellyson & J. F. Dovidio (Eds.), *Power, dominance, and nonverbal behavior* (pp. 1–27). New York: Springer-Verlag.

Emmers, T. M., & Dindia, K. (1995). The effect of relational stage and intimacy on touch: An extension of Guerrero and Andersen. *Personal Relationships, 2*, 225–236.

Enid, J. (1993). The impact of body type on perceptions of attractiveness by older individuals. *Communication Reports, 6*, 101–108.

Epstein, C. F. (1986). Symbolic segregation: Similarities and differences in the language and non-verbal communication of women and men. *Sociological Forum, 1*, 27–49.

Erickson, F. (1975). One function of proxemic shifts in face-to-face interaction. In A. Kendon, R. Harris, & M. R. Key (Eds.), *The organization of behavior in face-to-face interaction* (pp. 175–187). The Hague: Mouton.

Erickson, F. (1979). Talking down: Some cultural sources of miscommunication in interracial interviews. In A. Wolfgang (Ed.), *Nonverbal behavior: Applications and cultural implications* (pp. 99–126). New York: Academic.

Erolgu, S. A., & Machleit, K. A. (1990). An empirical study of retail crowding: Antecedents and consequences. *Journal of Retailing, 66,* 201–221.

Ervin, F. R., & Martin, J. (1986). Neuropsychological bases of the primary emotions. In R. Plutchik & H. Kellerman (Eds.), *Emotion: Theory, research, and experience* (Vol. 3, pp. 145–170). Orlando, FL: Academic Press.

Etcoff, N. (1999). *Survival of the prettiest: The science of beauty.* New York: Doubleday.

Evans, C. (1996). *The casebook of forensic detection.* New York: John Wiley & Sons.

Evans, G. W., & Lovell, B. (1979). Design modification in an open-plan school. *Journal of Educational Psychology, 71,* 41–49.

Exline, R. V. (1963). Explorations in the process of person perception: Visual interaction in relation to competition, sex, and the need for affiliation. *Journal of Personality, 31,* 1–20.

Exline, R. V. (1985). Multichannel transmission of nonverbal behavior and the perception of powerful men: The presidential debates of 1976. In S. L. Ellyson & J. F. Dovidio (Eds.), *Power, dominance, and nonverbal behavior* (pp. 183–206). New York: Springer Verlag.

Exline, R. V., Ellyson, S. L., & Long, B. (1975). Visual behavior as an aspect of power role relationships. In P. Pliner, L. Krames, & T. Alloway (Eds.), *Nonverbal communication of aggression* (pp. 2–52). New York: Plenum.

Exline, R. V., & Fehr, B. J. (1978). Applications of semiosis to the study of visual interaction. In A.W. Siegman & S. Feldstein (Eds.), *Nonverbal behavior and communication* (pp. 117–158). Hillsdale, NJ: Lawrence Erlbaum Associates.

Exline, R. V., Thibaut, J., Hickey, C., & Gumpert, P. (1970). Visual interaction in relation to Machiavellianism and an unethical act. In P. Christie & F. Geis (Eds.), *Studies in Machiavellianism* (pp. 53–75). New York: Academic.

Exline, R. V., & Winters, L. C. (1965). Affective relations and mutual glances in dyads. In S. S. Tomkins & C. E. Izard (Eds.), *Affect, cognition, and personality* (pp. 319–305). New York: Springer-Verlag.

Extinction of blondes vastly overreported. (2002, October 2). *The Washington Post,* p. C01.

Eysenck, H. J. (1981). Aesthetic preferences and individual differences. In D. O'Hare (Ed.), *Psychology and the arts* (pp. 76–101). Atlantic Highlands, NJ: Humanities Press.

Fauss, R. (1988). Zur begeutung des gesichts für die partnerwahl. [The significance of facial features in the choice of a partner.] *Homo, 37,* 188–201.

Fay, P. J., & Middleton, W. G. (1940). Judgment of intelligence from the voice as transmitted over a public address system. *Sociometry, 3,* 186–191.

Feghali, E. K. (1997). Arab cultural communication patterns. *International Journal of Intercultural Relations, 21,* 345–378.

Feingold, A. (1988). Matching for attractiveness in romantic partners and same-sex friends: A meta-analysis and theoretical critique. *Psychological Bulletin, 104,* 226–235.

Feingold, A. (1992). Good-looking people are not what we think. *Psychological Bulletin, 111,* 304–341.

Feinman, S., & Gil, G. W. (1978). Sex differences in physical attractiveness preferences. *Journal of Social Psychology, 105,* 43–32.

Feldman, R. S. (1976). Nonverbal disclosure of teacher deception and interpersonal affect. *Journal of Educational Psychology, 68,* 807–816.

Feldman, R. S. (1991). A functional approach to nonverbal exchange. In R. S. Feldman & B. Rimé (Eds.), *Fundamentals of nonverbal behavior* (pp. 458–495). New York: Cambridge University Press.

Feldman, R. S., Jenkins, L., & Popoola, O. (1979). Detection of deception in adults and children via facial expressions. *Child Development, 50,* 350–355.

Feldman, R. S., Philipott, P., & Custrini, R. J. (1991). Social competence and nonverbal behaviour. In R. S. Feldman & B. Rimé (Eds.), *Fundamentals of nonverbal behaviour* (pp. 329–350). New York: Cambridge University Press.

Feldman, R. S., & White, J. B. (1980). Detecting deception in children. *Journal of Communication, 30,* 121–139.

Feldstein, S., & Welkowitz, J. (1978). A chronography of conversation: In defense of an objective approach. In A. W. Siegman & S. Feldstein (Eds.), *Nonverbal behavior and communication* (pp. 329–378). Hillsdale, NJ: Lawrence Erlbaum Associates.

Fernández-Dols, J. M., & Ruiz-Belda, M. A. (1995). Are smiles a sign of happiness? Gold medal winners at the Olympic Games. *Journal of Personality and Social Psychology, 69,* 1113–1119.

Festinger, L. (1951). Architecture and group membership. *Journal of Social Issues, 7,* 152–163.

Festinger, L. (1954). A theory of social comparison processes. *Human Relations, 7,* 117–140.

Festinger, L., Schachter, S., & Back, K. (1950). *Social pressures in informal groups: A study of human factors in housing.* New York: Harper & Row.

Feyereisen, P. (1991). Brain pathology, lateralization, and nonverbal behavior. In R. S. Feldman & B. Rimé (Eds.), *Fundamentals of nonverbal communication* (pp. 31–70). New York: Cambridge University Press.

Fiedler, K. (1989). Suggestion and credibility: Lie detection based on content-related cues. In V. Gheorghiu, P. Netter, H. J. Eysenck, & R. Rosenthal (Eds.), *Suggestibility, theory, and research* (pp. 323–335). New York: Springer.

Fiedler, K., & Walka, I. (1993). Training lie detectors to use nonverbal cues instead of global heuristics. *Human Communication Research, 20,* 199–223.

Field, T. (1999). American adolescents touch each other less and are more aggressive toward their peers as compared with French adolescents. *Adolescence, 34,* 753–758.

Field, T. (2001). *Touch*. Cambridge, MA: MIT Press.

Field, T., Henteleff, T., Hernandez-Reif, M., Martinez, E., Mavunda, K., Kuhn, C., & Schanberg, S. (1998). Children with asthma have improved pulmonary functions after massage therapy. *Journal of Pediatrics, 132*, 854–858.

Field, T., & Hernandez-Reif, M. (2001). Sleep problems in infants decrease following massage therapy. *Early Child Development and Care, 168*, 95–104.

Filsinger, E. E., & Fabes, R. A. (1985). Odor communication, pheromones, and human families. *Journal of Marriage and the Family, 47*, 349–359.

Fink, B., Grammer, K., & Thornhill, R. (2001). Human (Homo Sapiens) facial attractiveness in relation to skin texture and color. *Journal of Comparative Psychology, 115*, 92–99.

Fisher, B. A. (1978). *Perspectives on human communication*. New York: Macmillan

Fisher, H. (2004). *Why we love: The nature and chemistry of romantic love*. New York: Henry Holt.

Fisher, J. D., Rytting, M., & Heslin, R. (1976). Hands touching hands: Affective and evaluative effects of an interpersonal touch. *Sociometry, 39*, 416–421.

Fitzpatrick, M. A., Mulac, A., & Dindia, K. (1994, July). *Convergence and reciprocity in male and female communication patterns in spouse and stranger interaction*. Paper presented at the Fifth International Conference on Language and Social Psychology, Brisbane, Australia.

Floyd, K. (1997). Communicating affection in dyadic relationships: An assessment of behavior and expectancies. *Communication Quarterly, 45*, 68–80.

Floyd, K. (1999). All touches are not created equal: Effects of form and duration on observers' perceptions of an embrace. *Journal of Nonverbal Behavior, 23*, 283–299.

Floyd, K. (2000). Affectionate same sex touch: The influence of homophobia on observers' perceptions. *Journal of Social Psychology, 140*, 774–788.

Floyd, K. (2001). Human affection exchange: I. Reproductive probability as a predictor of men's affection with their sons. *Journal of Men's Studies, 10*, 39–50.

Floyd, K. (2002). Human affection exchange: V. Attributes of the highly affectionate. *Communication Quarterly, 50*, 135–154.

Floyd, K. (2004). An introduction to the uses and potential uses of physiological measurement in the study of family communication. *Journal of Family Communication, 4*, 295–318.

Floyd, K. (2006). *Communicating affection: Interpersonal behavior and social context*. Cambridge, England: Cambridge University Press.

Floyd, K., & Burgoon, J. K. (1999). Reacting to nonverbal expressions of liking: A test of interaction adaptation theory. *Communication Monographs, 66*, 219–239.

Floyd, K., & Haynes, M. T. (2005). Applications of the theory of natural selection to the study of family communication. *Journal of Family Communication, 5*, 79–101.

Floyd, K., Hess, J. A., Miczo, L. A., Halone, K. K., Mikkelson, A. C., & Tusing, K. J. (2005). Human affection exchange: VIII. Further evidence of the benefits of expressed affection. *Communication Quarterly, 53*, 285–303.

Floyd, K., Hesse, C., & Haynes, M. T. (2007). Human affection exchange: XV. Metabolic and cardiovascular correlates of trait expressed affection. *Communication Quarterly, 53*, 285–303.

Floyd, K., Melcher, C., & Zhong, M. (2000). Exceptional ways to end conversations. In C. G. Waugh, W. I. Gorden, & K. M. Golden (Eds.), *Let's talk: A cognitive-skills approach to interpersonal communication* (pp. 327–329). Newark, DE: Kendall/Hunt.

Floyd, K., Mikkelson, A. C., & Hesse, C. (2007). *The biology of human communication* (2nd ed.). Florence, KY: Thomson Learning.

Floyd, K., Mikkelson, A. C., Hesse, C., & Pauley, P. M. (2007). Affectionate writing reduces total cholesterol: Two randomized, controlled trials. *Human Communication Research, 33*, 119–142.

Floyd, K., Mikkelson, A. C., Tafoya, M. A., Farinelli, L., La Valley, A. G., Judd, J., Davis, K. L., Haynes, M. T., & Wilson, J. (2007). Human affection exchange: XIV. Relational affection predicts resting heart rate and free cortisol secretion during acute stress. *Behavioral Medicine, 32*, 151–156.

Floyd, K., & Morman, M. T. (1997). Affectionate communication in nonromantic relationships: Influences of communicator, relational, and contextual factors. *Western Journal of Communication, 61*, 279–298.

Floyd, K., & Morman, M. T. (1998). The measurement of affectionate communication. *Communication Quarterly, 46*, 144–162.

Floyd, K., & Morman, M. T. (2001). Human affection exchange: III. Discriminative parental solicitude in men's affectionate communication with their biological and nonbiological sons. *Communication Quarterly, 49*, 310–327.

Floyd, K., & Morr, M. C. (2003). Human affection exchange: VII. Affectionate communication in the sibling/spouse/sibling-in-law triad. *Communication Quarterly, 51*, 247–261.

Floyd, K., & Ray, G. B. (2003). Human affection exchange: IV. Vocalic predictors of perceived affection in initial interactions. *Western Journal of Communication, 67*, 56–73.

Floyd, K., Sargent, J. E., & Di Corcia, M. (2004). Human affection exchange: VI. Further tests of reproductive probability as a predictor of men's affection with their fathers and their sons. *Journal of Social Psychology, 144*, 191–206.

Floyd, K., & Voloudakis, M. (1999). Affectionate behavior in adult platonic friendships: Interpreting and evaluating expectancy violations. *Human Communication Research, 25*, 341–369.

Forbes, G. B. (2001). College students with tattoos and piercings: Motives, family experiences, personality factors, and perception by others. *Psychological Reports, 89,* 774–786.

Forrest, J. A., & Feldman, R. S. (2000). Detecting deception and judge's involvement: Lower task involvement leads to better lie detection. *Personality and Social Psychology Bulletin, 26,* 118–125.

Forrest, J. A., Feldman, R. S., & Tyler, J. M. (2004). When accurate beliefs lead to better lie detection. *Journal of Applied Social Psychology, 34,* 764–780.

Forsyth, G. A., Kushner, R. I., & Forsyth, P. D. (1981). Human facial expression judgment in a conversational context. *Journal of Nonverbal Behavior, 6,* 115–130.

Frank, L. K. (1971). Tactile communication. *Genetic Psychology Monographs, 56,* 204–255.

Frank, L. K. (1972). Cultural patterning of tactile experiences. In L. A. Samovar & R. E. Porter (Eds.), *Intercultural communication: A reader* (pp. 200–204). Belmont, CA: Wadsworth.

Frank, M. G., & Ekman, P. (2004). Appearing truthful generalizes across different deception situations. *Journal of Personality and Social Psychology, 86,* 486–495.

Frank, M. G., & Feeley, T. H. (2003). To catch a liar: Challenges for research in lie detection training. *Journal of Applied Communication Research, 31,* 58–75.

Frank, M. G., & Stennett, J. (2001). The forced-choice paradigm and the perception of facial expressions of emotion. *Journal of Personality and Social Psychology, 80,* 75–85.

Franklin, T. W., Franklin, C. A., & Pratt, T. C. (2006). Examining the empirical relationship between prison crowding and inmate misconduct: A meta-analysis of conflict research results. *Journal of Criminal Justice, 34,* 401–412.

Frederick, C. M., & Bradley, K. A. (2000). A different kind of normal? Psychological and motivational characteristics of young adult tattooers and body piercers. *North American Journal of Psychology, 2,* 380–394.

Freedman, D. G. (1965). Hereditary control of early social behavior. In B. Foss (Ed.), *Determinants of infant behavior* (pp. 149–156). London: Murray.

Freedman, N. (1972). The analysis of movement behavior during the clinical interview. In A. Siegman & B. Pope (Eds.), *Studies in dyadic communication* (pp. 153–175). New York: Pergamon.

French, J. R. P., Jr., & Raven, B. (1959). The bases of social power. In D. Cartwright (Ed.), *Studies in social power* (pp. 150–167). Ann Arbor, MI: Institute for Social Research.

French, P., & von Raffler-Engel, W. (1973). *The kinesics of bilingualism.* Unpublished manuscript, Vanderbilt University. Cited in M. LaFrance & C. Mayo (1978), *Moving bodies.* Monterey, CA: Brooks/Cole.

Fridlund, A. J. (1991). Evolution and facial action in reflex, social motive, and paralanguage. *Biological Psychology, 32,* 3–100.

Fridlund, A. J. (1994). *Human facial expression: An evolutionary view.* San Diego: Academic Press.

Fridlund, A. J., & Duchaine, B. (1996). Facial expressions of emotion and the delusion of the hermetic self. In R. Harré & W. G. Parrott (Eds.), *The emotions: Social, cultural, and biological dimensions* (pp. 259–284). Thousand Oaks, CA: Sage.

Fridlund, A. J., & Russell, J. A. (2006). The functions of facial expressions: What's in a face? In V. Manusov & M. L. Patterson (Eds.), *The Sage handbook of nonverbal comunication* (pp. 299–319). Thousand Oaks, CA: Sage.

Fridlund, A. J., Sabini, J. P., Hedlund, L. E., Schaut, J. A., Shenker, J. I., & Knauer, M. J. (1990). Social determinants of facial expressions during affective imagery: Displaying to the people in your head. *Journal of Nonverbal Behavior, 14,* 113–137.

Friedman, H. S., & Miller-Herringer, T. (1991). Nonverbal display of emotion in public and in private: Self-monitoring, personality, and expressive cues. *Journal of Personality and Social Psychology, 61,* 766–775.

Friedman, H. S., Riggio, R. E., & Casella, D. F. (1988) Nonverbal skill, personal charisma, and initial attraction. *Personality and Social Psychology Bulletin, 14,* 203–211.

Friesen, W. V. (1972). *Cultural differences in facial expressions in a social situation: An experimental test of the concept of display rules.* Unpublished doctoral dissertation, University of California, San Francisco.

Friesen, W. V., Ekman, P., & Wallbott, H. (1979). Measuring hand movements. *Journal of Nonverbal Behavior, 4,* 97–112.

Frieze, I., Olson, J., & Russell, J. (1991). Attractiveness and income for men and women in management. *Journal of Applied Social Psychology, 21,* 1039–1057.

Frijda, N. H. (1993). Moods, emotion episodes, and emotions. In M. Lewis & J. M. Haviland (Eds.), *Handbook of emotions* (pp. 381–403). New York: Guilford.

Frijda, N. H., Kuipers, P., & ter Schure, E. (1989). Relations between emotion, appraisal, and emotional action readiness. *Journal of Personality and Social Psychology, 57,* 212–228.

Fulwood, R., Abraham, S., & Johnson, C. (1986). *Height and weight of adults ages 18–74 by socioeconomic and geographic variables.* DHHS Publication No. 81–1674. Washington, DC: U.S. Government Printing Office.

Furlow, B. F., Armijo-Prewitt, T., Gangestad, S. W., & Thornhill, R. (1997). Fluctuating asymmetry and psychometric intelligence. *Proceedings of the Royal Society of London, Series B, 264,* 823–829.

Furnham, A., & Argyle, M. (1981). *The psychology of social situations: Selected readings.* New York: Pergamon.

Futrell, C. (1984). *Fundamentals of selling*. Homewood, IL: Richard Irwin Publications.

Gaelick, L., Brodenshauser, G. V., & Wyer, R. S., Jr. (1985). Emotional communication in close relationships. *Journal of Personality and Social Psychology, 49*, 1246–1265.

Gaines, S. O., Jr., Bledsoe, K. L., Farris, K. R., Henderson, M. C., Kuland, G. J., Lara, J. K., Marelich, W. D., Page, M. S., Palucki, L. J., Steers, W. N., & West, A. M. (1998). Communication of emotions in friendships. In P. A. Andersen & L. K. Guerrero (Eds.), *Handbook of communication and emotion* (pp. 507–531). San Diego: Academic Press.

Galati, D., Scherer, K. R., & Ricci-Bitti, P. (1997). Voluntary facial expression of emotion: Comparing congenitally blind to normal sighted encoders. *Journal of Personality and Social Psychology, 73*, 1363–1379.

Galgan, R. J., Mable, H. M., Ouellette, T., & Balance, W. D. G. (1989). Body image distortion and weight preoccupation in college women. *College Student Journal, 23*, 13–15.

Galinsky, E. (1999). *Ask the children: What America's children really think about working parents*. New York: William Morrow.

Gallaher, P. E. (1992). Individual differences in nonverbal behavior: Dimensions of style. *Journal of Personality and Social Psychology, 63*, 133–145.

Garcia, S., Stinson, L., Ickes, W., & Bissonnette, V. (1991). Shyness and physical attractiveness in mixed-sex dyads. *Journal of Personality and Social Psychology, 61*, 35–49.

Garrido, E., & Masip, J. (2000, April). *Criminologists' beliefs about indicators of deception and truthfulness*. Paper presented at the 10th European Conference of Psychology and Law, Limassol, Cyprus.

Gatewood, J. B., & Rosenwein, R. (1981). Interactional synchrony: Genuine or spurious? A critique of recent research. *Journal of Nonverbal Behavior, 6*, 12–29.

Geertz, C. (1973). *The interpretations of cultures*. New York: Basic Books.

Geis, F. L., & Moon, T. H. (1981). Machiavellianism and deception. *Journal of Personality and Social Psychology, 41*, 766–775.

Gentner, D., Imai, M., & Boroditsky, L. (2002). As time goes by: Evidence for two systems in processing space time metaphors. *Language and Cognitive Processes, 17*, 537–565.

George, J. F., Biros, D. P., Burgoon, J. K., Crews, J. M, Cao, J., Marett, K., Akins, M., Kruse, J., & Lin, M. (in press). Defeating deception through e-training. *Management Information Systems Quarterly Executive*.

George, J. F., & Marett, K. (2004, January). *Inhibiting deception and its detection*. Paper presented at the 39th Hawaii International Conference on System Sciences, Kauai, HI.

George, J. F., & Robb, A. (2006, January). *Deception and communication technology: A diaries study replication*. Paper presented at the 39th Hawaii International Conference on System Sciences, Kauai, HI.

Gerhart, S. (2004). *Why love matters: How affection shapes a baby's brain*. New York: Brunner-Routledge.

Giesen, J. M. (1973). *Effects of eye contact, attitude agreement, and presentation mode on impressions and persuasion*. Upublished doctoral dissertation, Kent State University.

Gifford, R. (1991). Mapping nonverbal behavior on the interpersonal circle. *Journal of Personality and Social Psychology, 61*, 279–288.

Gilbert, B. O. (1991). Physiological and nonverbal correlates of extraversion, neuroticism, and psychoticism during active and passive coping. *Personality and Individual Differences, 12*, 1325–1331.

Gilbert, G. S., Kirkland, K. D., & Rappoport, L. (1977). Nonverbal assessment of interpersonal affect. *Journal of Personality Assessment, 41*, 43–48.

Giles, H. (1973). Accent mobility: A model and some data. *Anthropological Linguistics, 12*, 193–212.

Giles, H., Bourhis, R. Y., & Taylor, D. M. (1977). Towards a theory of language in ethnic group relations. In H. Giles (Ed.), *Language, ethnicity, and intergroup relations* (pp. 307–348). London: Academic.

Giles, H., Coupland, N., & Coupland, J. (1991). Accommodation theory: Communication, context, and consequence. In H. Giles, J. Coupland, & N. Coupland (Eds.), *Contexts of accommodation: Developments in applied sociolinguistics* (pp. 1–68). Cambridge, England: Cambridge University Press.

Giles, H., Mulac, A., Bradac, J. J., & Johnson, P. (1987). Speech communication theory: The next decade and beyond. In M. McLaughlin (Ed.), *Communication yearbook 10* (pp. 13–48). Newbury Park, CA: Sage.

Giles, H., & Wadleigh, P. M. (1999). Accommodating nonverbally. In L. K. Guerrero, J. A. DeVito, & M. L. Hecht (Eds.), *The nonverbal communication reader: Classic and contemporary readings* (pp. 425–436). Prospect Heights, IL: Waveland Press.

Giles, H., & Wadleigh, P. M. (2008). Accommodating nonverbally. In L. K. Guerrero & M. L. Hecht (Eds.), *The nonverbal communication reader: Classic and contemporary readings* (3rd ed., pp. 491–502). Long Grove, IL: Waveland Press.

Giron, M., Manjon-Arce, P., Puerto-Barver, J., Sanchez-Garcia, E., & Gomez-Beneyto, M. (1998). Clinical interview skills and identification of emotional disorders in primary care. *American Journal of Psychiatry, 155*, 530–535.

Givens, D. B. (1978). The nonverbal basis of attraction: Flirtation, courtship, and seduction. *Psychiatry, 41*, 346–359.

Givens, D. B. (1983). *Love signals*. New York: Crown.

Gjerdingen, D. K., Simpson, D. E., & Titus, S. L. (1987). Patients' and physicians' attitudes regarding the physician's professional appearance. *Archives of Internal Medicine, 147,* 1209–1212.

Glasgow, G. M. (1952). A semantic index of vocal pitch. *Speech Monographs, 19,* 64–68.

Goffman, E. (1959). *The presentation of self in everyday life.* Garden City, NY: Anchor/Doubleday.

Goffman, E. (1961). *Encounters: Two studies in the sociology of interaction.* Indianapolis: Bobbs-Merrill.

Goffman, E. (1963a). *Behavior in public places.* New York: Free Press.

Goffman, E. (1963b). *Stigma: Notes on the management of spoiled identity.* Upper Saddle River, NJ: Prentice-Hall.

Goffman, E. (1967). *Interaction ritual: Essays on face-to-face behavior.* Garden City, NY: Anchor/Doubleday.

Goffman, E. (1971). *Relations in public: Microstudies of the public order.* New York: Basic Books.

Goffman, E. (1974). *Frame analysis.* New York: Harper & Row.

Goldberg, S., & Lewis, M. (1969). Play behavior in the year-old infant: Early sex differences. *Child Development, 40,* 21–31.

Goldin-Meadow, S. (2005). The two faces of gesture: Language and thought. *Gesture, 5*(1–2), 241–257.

Goleman, D. (1991, May 7). Kids who got hugs found to be happy adults. *Arizona Daily Star,* pp. 1C, 3C.

Goleman, D. (1995). *Emotional intelligence: Why it can matter more than IQ.* New York: Bantam Books.

Gonzales, A., & Zimbardo, P. G. (1985, March). Time in perspective. *Psychology Today,* 21–26.

Gordon, A. K., & Miller, A. G. (2000). Perspective differences in the construal of lies: Is deception in the eye of the beholder? *Personality and Social Psychology Bulletin, 26,* 46–55.

Gorham, J., & Christophel, D. (1990). The relationship of teachers' use of humor in the classroom to immediacy and student learning. *Communication Education, 39,* 46–62.

Gosselin, P., Perron, M., Legault, M., & Campanella, P. (2002). Children's and adults' knowledge of the distinction between enjoyment and nonenjoyment smiles. *Journal of Nonverbal Behavior, 26,* 83–108.

Gottman, J. M. (1994). *What predicts divorce? The relationship between marital processes and marital outcomes.* Hillsdale, NJ: Lawrence Erlbaum Associates.

Gottman, J. M., & Levenson, R. W. (1992). Marital processes predictive of later dissolution: Behavior, physiology, and health. *Journal of Personality and Social Psychology, 63,* 221–233.

Gottman, J. M., Markman, H., & Notarius, C. (1977). The topography of marital conflict: A sequential analysis of verbal and nonverbal behavior. *Journal of Marriage and the Family, 39,* 461–477.

Gottman, J. M., & Porterfield, A. L. (1981). Communicative competence in the nonverbal behavior of married couples. *Journal of Marriage and the Family, 43,* 817–824.

Gottman, J. M., Woodin, E., & Coan, J. A. (1998). *The specific affect coding system, 20-code version (4.0).* Unpublished manuscript, University of Washington.

Gouldner, A. W. (1960). The norm of reciprocity: A preliminary statement. *American Sociological Review, 25,* 161–178.

Grabe, E., & Low, E. L. (2002). Durational variability in speech and the rhythm class hypothesis. In C. Gussenhoven & N. Warner (Eds.), *Laboratory phonology* (Vol. 7, pp. 515–546). Berlin: Mouton de Gruyter.

Graham, J. A., & Heywood, S. (1975). The effects of elimination of hand gestures and of verbal codability on speech performance. *European Journal of Social Psychology, 5,* 189–195.

Grammer, K., Fink, B., & Neave, N. (2005). Human pheromones and sexual attraction. *European Journal of Obstetrics, Gynecology and Reproductive Biology, 118,* 135–142.

Grammer, K., & Thornhill, R. (1994). Human (*Homo sapiens*) facial attractiveness and sexual selection: The role of symmetry and averageness. *Journal of Comparative Psychology, 108,* 233–242.

Grassian, S. (1983). Psychopathological effects of solitary confinement. *American Journal of Psychiatry, 140,* 1450–1454.

Greene, J. O. (2003). Interview during the annual meeting of the National Communication Association, Miami Beach, November 2003.

Gregory, S. W., & Webster, S. (1996). A nonverbal signal in voices of interview partners effectively predicts communication accommodation and social status perceptions. *Journal of Personality and Social Psychology, 70,* 1231–1240.

Grewen, K. M., Girdler, S. S., Amico, J., & Light, K. C. (2005). Effects of partner support on resting oxytocin, cortisol, norepinephrine, and blood pressure before and after warm partner contact. *Psychosomatic Medicine, 67,* 531–538.

Grice, P. (1989). *Studies in the way of words.* Cambridge, MA: Harvard University Press.

Grieser, D. L., & Kuhl, P. K. (1988). Maternal speech to infants in a tonal language: Support for universal prosodic features in motherese. *Developmental Psychology, 24,* 14–20.

Griffit, W. (1970). Environmental effects on interpersonal affective behavior: Ambient effective temperature and attraction. *Journal of Personality and Social Psychology, 15,* 240–244.

Griffit, W., & Veitch, R. (1971). Hot and crowded: Influence of population density and temperature on interpersonal affective behavior. *Journal of Personality and Social Psychology, 17,* 92–98.

Grinspan, D., Hemphill, A., & Nowicki, S. (2003). Improving the ability of elementary school-age children to identify emotion in facial expression. *Journal of Genetic Psychology, 164,* 88–100.

Groër, M., Mozingo, J., Droppleman, P., Davis, M., Jolly, M. L., Boynton, M., Davis, K., & Kay, S. (1994). Measures of salivary secretory immunoglobulin A and state anxiety after a nursing back rub. *Applied Nursing Research, 7,* 2–6.

Grunau, R. V. E., & Craig, K. D. (1990). Facial activity as a measure of neonatal pain perception. In D. C. Tyler & E. J. Krane (Eds.), *Advances in pain research and therapy: Proceedings of the 1st International Symposium on Pediatric Pain* (pp. 147–156). New York: Raven.

Gudykunst, W. B., & Kim, Y. Y. (1992). *Communicating with strangers: An approach to intercultural communication* (2nd ed.). New York: McGraw-Hill.

Guerrero, L. K. (1994, November). *Nonverbal immediacy and involvement in friendships and romantic relationships: Untangling the effects of communicator sex, target sex, and relationship type.* Paper presented at the annual meeting of the Speech Communication Association, New Orleans, LA.

Guerrero, L. K. (1997). Nonverbal involvement across interactions with same-sex friends, opposite-sex friends, and romantic partners: Consistency or change? *Journal of Social and Personal Relationships, 14,* 31–58.

Guerrero, L. K. (2000). Intimacy. In D. Levinson, J. Ponzetti, & P. Jorgensen (Eds.), *Encyclopedia of human emotions* (pp. 403–409). New York: Macmillan Reference.

Guerrero, L. K., & Andersen, P. A. (1991). The waxing and waning of relational intimacy: Touch as a function of relational stage, gender and touch avoidance. *Journal of Social and Personal Relationships, 8,* 147–166.

Guerrero, L. K., & Andersen, P. A. (1994). Patterns of matching and initiation: Touch behavior and touch avoidance across relational stages. *Journal of Nonverbal Behavior, 18,* 137–154.

Guerrero, L. K., Andersen, P. A., & Afifi, W. A. (2007). *Close encounters: Communication in relationships* (2nd ed.). Thousand Oaks, CA: Sage.

Guerrero, L. K., & Burgoon, J. K. (1996). Attachment styles and reactions to nonverbal involvement change in romantic dyads: Patterns of reciprocity and compensation. *Human Communication Research, 22,* 335–370.

Guerrero, L. K., & Ebesu, A. S. (1993, May). *While at play: An observational analysis of children's touch during interpersonal interaction.* Paper presented at the annual meeting of the International Communication Association, Washington, D.C.

Guerrero, L. K., & Farinelli, L. (2009). Key characteristics of messages: The interplay of verbal and nonverbal codes. In W. Eadie (Ed.), *21st Century communication: A reference handbook* (pp. 239–248). Thousand Oaks, CA: Sage.

Guerrero, L. K., & Floyd, K. (2006). *Nonverbal communication in close relationships.* Mahwah, NJ: Lawrence Erlbaum Associates.

Guerrero, L. K., Jones, S. M., & Boburka, R. R. (2006). Sex differences in emotional communication. In D. J. Canary & K. Dindia (Eds.). *Sex differences and similarities in communication* (2nd ed., pp. 241–261). Mahwah, NJ: Lawrence Erlbaum Associates.

Guerrero, L. K., & Miller, T. A. (1998). Associations between nonverbal behaviors and initial impressions of instructor competence and course content in videotaped distance education courses. *Communication Education, 47,* 30–42.

Guerrero, L. K., & Reiter, R. L. (1998). Expressing emotion: Sex differences in social skills and communicative responses to anger, sadness, and jealousy. In D. J. Canary & K. Dindia (Eds.), *Sex differences and similarities in communication* (pp. 321–350). Mahwah, NJ: Lawrence Erlbaum Associates.

Günzburger, D. (1984). Perception of some male-female voice characteristics. *Progress Report Institute of Phonetics Utrecht, 9,* 15–26.

Guyton, A. C. (1977). *Basic human physiology: Normal function and mechanisms of disease.* Philadelphia: Saunders.

Haberman, C. (1996, December 21). Straight talk in the debate over ebonics. *New York Times.*

Hadar, U. (1989). Two types of gesture and their role in speech production. *Journal of Language and Social Psychology, 8,* 221–228.

Hager, J. C., & Ekman, P. (1997). The asymmetry of facial actions is inconsistent with models of hemispheric specialization. In P. Ekman & E. Rosenberg (Eds.), *What the face reveals* (pp. 40–62). New York: Oxford University Press.

Haggard, E. A., & Isaacs, F. S. (1966). Micromomentary facial expressions as indicators of ego mechanisms in psychotherapy. In L. A. Gottschalk & A. H. Auerback (Eds.), *Methods of reseach in psychotherapy.* New York: Appleton-Century-Crofts.

Hai, D. M., Khairullah, Z. Y., & Coulmas, N. (1982). Sex and the single armrest: Use of personal space during air travel. *Psychological Reports, 51,* 743–749.

Halberstadt, A. G., & Saitta, B. M. (1987). Gender, nonverbal behavior, and perceived dominance: A test of the theory. *Journal of Personality and Social Psychology, 53,* 257–272.

Hale, J. L. (2003). Interview during the annual meeting of the National Communication Association, Miami Beach, November 2003.

Hale, J. L., & Burgoon, J. K. (1984). Models of reactions to changes in nonverbal immediacy. *Journal of Nonverbal Behavior, 8,* 287–314.

Hall, E. T. (1959, 1973). *The silent language.* Garden City, NY: Anchor/Doubleday.

Hall, E. T. (1981, 1976). *Beyond culture.* Garden City, NY: Anchor/Doubleday.

Hall, E. T. (1990, 1966). *The hidden dimension* (2nd ed.). New York: Anchor Press.

Hall, E. T., & Hall, M. R. (1990). *Understanding cultural differences: Germans, French, and Americans.* Yarmouth, ME: Intercultural Press.

Hall, E. T., & Whyte, W. F. (1966). Intercultural communication: A guide to men of action. In A. G. Smith (Ed.), *Communication and culture* (pp. 567–575). New York: Holt, Rinehart & Winston.

Hall, J. A. (1979). Gender, gender roles, and nonverbal communication skills. In R. Rosenthal (Ed.), *Nonverbal communiation* (pp. 32–67). Cambridge, MA: Oelgeschlager, Genn, & Hain.

Hall, J. A. (1984). *Nonverbal sex differences: Communication accuracy and expressive style.* Baltimore, MD: John Hopkins University Press.

Hall, J. A. (1998). How big are nonverbal sex differences? The case of smiling and sensitivity to nonverbal cues. In D. J. Canary & K. Dindia (Eds.), *Sex differences and similarities in communication* (pp. 155–177). Mahwah, NJ: Lawrence Erlbaum Associates.

Hall, J. A. (2006). How big are nonverbal sex differences? The case of smiling and nonverbal sensitivity. In K. Dindia & D. J. Canary (Eds.), *Sex differences and similarities in communication* (pp. 59–82). Mahwah, NJ: Lawrence Erlbaum Associates.

Hall, J. A., Coats, E., & Smith LeBeau, L. (2005). Nonverbal behavior and the vertical dimension of social relations: A meta-analysis. *Psychological Bulletin, 131,* 898–924.

Hall, J. A., Roter, D. L., & Rand, C. S. (1981). Communication of affect between patient and physician. *Journal of Health and Social Behavior, 22,* 18–30.

Hall, J. A., & Veccia, E. M. (1990). More "touching" observations: New insights on men, women, and interpersonal touch. *Journal of Personality and Social Psychology, 59,* 1155–1162.

Hamermesh, D. S., & Biddle, J. E. (1994). Beauty and the labor market. *American Economic Review, 84,* 1174–1194.

Hamermesh, D. S., Meng, X., & Zhang, J. (2002). Dress for success—does primping pay? *Labour Economics, 9,* 361–273.

Hamermesh, D. S., & Parker, A. (2005). Beauty in the classroom: Instructors' pulchritude and putative pedagogical productivity. *Economics of Education Review, 24,* 369–376.

Hamilton, W. D. (1964). The genetical evolution of social behavior. I & II. *Journal of Theoretical Biology, 7,* 1–52.

Hancock, J., Thom-Santelli, J., & Ritchie, T. (2004). Deception and design: The impact of communication technology on lying behavior. *CHI 2004, 6*(1), 29–134.

Hannan, T. E. (1992). An examination of spontaneous pointing in 20- to 50-month-old children. *Perceptual and Motor Skills, 74,* 651–658.

Hansen, C. H., & Hansen, R. D. (1988). Finding the face in the crowd: An anger superiority effect. *Journal of Personality and Social Psychology, 54,* 917–924.

Hansen, J. (2007). The truth about teaching and touching. *Childhood Education, 83,* 158–162.

Hanzal, A., Segrin, C., & Dorros, S. (2008). The role of marital status and age on men's and women's reactions to touch from a relational partner. *Journal of Nonverbal Behavior, 32,* 21–32.

Harlow, H. F. (1958). The nature of love. *American Psychologist, 13,* 673–685.

Harlow, H. F., Harlow, M. K., & Hansen, E. W. (1963). The maternal affectional system of rhesus monkeys. In H. L. Rheingold (Ed.), *Maternal behaviors in mammals* (pp. 254–281). New York: John Wiley & Sons.

Harlow, H. F., & Zimmerman, R. R. (1958). The development of affectional responses in infant monkeys. *Proceedings of the American Philosophical Society, 102,* 501–509.

Harper, B. (2000). Beauty, stature and the labor market: A British cohort study. *Oxford Bulletin of Economics and Statistics, 62,* 771–800.

Harper, R. G., Wiens, A. N., & Matarazzo, J. D. (1978). *Nonverbal communication: The state of the art.* New York: John Wiley & Sons.

Harrigan, J. A. (1984). The effects of task order on children's identification of facial expressions. *Motivation and Emotion, 8,* 157–169.

Harrigan, J. A. (1985). Self-touching as an indicator of underlying affect and language processes. *Social Science & Medicine, 29,* 1161–1168.

Harrigan, J. A., Kues, J. R., Steffen, J. J., & Rosenthal, R. (1987). Self-touching and impressions of others. *Personality and Social Psychology Bulletin, 13,* 497–512.

Harrigan, J. A., Kues, J. R., & Weber, J. G. (1986). Impressions of hand movements: Self-touching and gestures. *Perceptual and Motor Skills, 63,* 503–516.

Harrigan, J. A., & Rosenthal, R. (1986). Nonverbal aspects of empathy and rapport in physician-patient interaction. In P. D. Blanck, R. Buck, & R. Rosenthal (Eds.), *Nonverbal communication in the clinical context* (pp. 36–73). University Park: Pennsylvania State University Press.

Harrigan, J. A., Wilson, K., & Rosenthal, R. (2004). Detecting state and trait anxiety from audiotry and visual cues: A meta-analysis. *Personality and Social Psychology Bulletin, 30,* 56–66.

Harris, M. B., James, J., Chavez, J., Fuller, M. L., Kent, S., Massanari, C., Moore, C., & Walsh, F. (1983). Clothing: Communication, compliance, and choice. *Journal of Applied Social Psychology, 13,* 88–97.

Harris, M. J. (1989). Personality moderators of interpersonal expectancy effects. Replication of Harris and Rosenthal (1986). *Journal of Research in Personality, 23,* 381–397.

Harris, M. J., & Rosenthal, R. (1985). Mediation of interpersonal expectancy effects: 31 meta-analyses. *Psychological Bulletin, 97,* 363–386.

Harris, M. J., & Rosenthal, R. (1986). Counselor and client personality as determinants of counselor expectancy effects. *Journal of Personality and Social Psychology, 50,* 362–369.

Harris, R. M., & Rubinstein, D. (1975). Paralanguage, communication, and cognition. In A. Kendon, R. M. Harris, & M. R. Key (Eds.), *Organization of behavior in face-to-face interaction* (pp. 251–276). The Hague: Mouton.

Harrison, R. P. (1974). *Beyond words: An introduction to nonverbal communication.* Englewood Cliffs, NJ: Prentice Hall.

Hart, S., Field, T., Hernandez-Reif, M., Nearing, G., Shaw, S., Schanberg, S., & Kuhn, C. (2001). Anorexia symptoms are reduced by massage therapy. *Eating Disorders, 9,* 289–299.

Hartwig, M., Granhag, P. A., Strömwall, L. A., & Vrij, A. (2004). Police officers' lie detection accuracy: Interrogating freely versus observing video. *Police Quarterly, 7,* 429–456.

Hashimoto, K., & Borders, A. L. (2005). Proxemics and its effect on travelers during the sales contact in hotels. *Journal of Travel and Tourism Marketing, 18,* 49–61.

Hatfield, E. (1984). The dangers of intimacy. In V. J. Derlega (Ed.), *Communication, intimacy, and close relationships* (pp. 207–220). New York: Academic Press.

Hatfield, E., Cacioppo, J. T., & Rapson, R. L. (1994). *Emotional contagion.* New York: Cambridge University Press.

Hatfield, E., & Sprecher, S. (1986). *Mirror, mirror . . . the importance of looks in everyday life.* Albany: State University of New York Press.

Haviland, J. M. (1977). Sex-related pragmatics in infants' nonverbal communication. *Journal of Communication, 27,* 80–84.

Hayduk, L. A. (1978). Personal space: An evaluative and orienting overview. *Psychological Bulletin, 85,* 117–134.

Hecht, M. A., LaFrance, M., & Haertl, J. C. (1993, August). *Gender differences in smiling: A meta-analysis of archival data.* Paper presented at the annual conference of the American Psychological Association, Toronto, Canada.

Hecht, M. L., Andersen, P. A., & Ribeau, S. A. (1989). The cultural dimensions of nonverbal communication. In M. K. Asatne & W. B. Gundykunst (Eds.), *Handbook of international and intercultural communication* (pp. 163–185). Newbury Park, CA: Sage.

Hediger, H. P. (1961). The evolution of territorial behavior. In S. L. Washburn (Ed.), *Social life of early man* (pp. 34–57). Chicago: Aldine.

Heilman, M. E., & Saruwatari, L. R. (1979). When beauty is beastly: The effects of appearance and sex on evaluations of job applicants for managerial and non-managerial jobs. *Organizational Behavior and Human Performance, 23,* 360–372.

Heinrich, C. U., & Borkenau, P. (1998). Deception and deception detection: The role of cross-modal inconsistency. *Journal of Personality, 66,* 687–712.

Hemsley, G. D., & Doob, A. N. (1978). The effect of looking behavior on perceptions of a communicator's credibility. *Journal of Applied Psychology, 8,* 136–144.

Hendrix, K. G. (2002). "Did being Black introduce bias into your study?" Attempting to mute the race-related research of black scholars. *Howard Journal of Communication, 13,* 153–171.

Henley, N. M. (1973). Status and sex: Some touching observations. *Bulletin of the Psychonomic Society, 2,* 91–93.

Henley, N. M. (1977). *Body politics: Power, sex, and nonverbal communication.* Englewood Cliffs, NJ: Prentice Hall.

Henley, N. M. (1995). Body politics revisited: What do we know today? In P. J. Kalbfleisch & M. J. Cody (Eds.), *Gender, power, and communication in human relationships* (pp. 27–61). Hillsdale, NJ: Lawrence Erlbaum Associates.

Henley, N. M. (2001). Body politics. In A. Branaman (Ed.), *Self and society: Blackwell readers in sociology* (pp. 288–297). Malden, MA: Blackwell Publishers.

Henningsen, D. D., Cruz, M. G., & Morr, M. C. (2000). Pattern violations and perceptions of deception. *Communication Reports, 13,* 1–9.

Henningsen, D. D., Valde, K. S., & Davies, E. (2005). Exploring the effect of verbal and nonverbal cues on perceptions of deception. *Communication Quarterly, 53,* 359–375.

Hertenstein, M. J. (2002). Touch: Its communicative functions in intimacy. *Human Development, 45,* 70–94.

Hertenstein, M. J., Keltner, D., App, B., Bulleit, B. A., & Jaskolka, A. R. (2006). Touch communicates distinct emotions. *Emotion, 6,* 528–533.

Hertenstein, M. J., Verkamp, A. M., Kerestes, A. M., & Holmes, R. M. (2006). The communicative functions of touch in humans, nonhuman primates, and rats: A review and synthesis of the empirical research. *Genetic, Social, and General Psychology Monographs, 132,* 5–94.

Heslin, R., & Alper, R. (1983). Touch: A bonding gesture. In J. M. Wiemann & R. P. Harrison (Eds.), *Nonverbal interaction* (pp. 47–75). Beverly Hills, CA: Sage.

Hess, E. H. (1972). Pupillometrics: A method of studying mental, emotional, and sensory processes. In N. Greenfield & R. Sternback (Eds.), *Handbook of psychophysiology* (pp. 491–531). New York: Holt, Rinehart & Winston.

Hess, E. H. (1975). The role of pupil size in communication. *Scientific American, 233*, 110–119.

Hess, U., Adams, R. B., & Kleck, R. E. (2005). Who may frown and who should smile? Dominance, affiliation, and the display of anger and happiness. *Cognition and Emotion, 19*, 515–536.

Hess, U., Blairy, S., & Kleck, R. E. (1997). The intensity of emotional facial expressions and decoding accuracy. *Journal of Nonverbal Behavior, 21*, 241–257.

Hess, U., Kappas, A., McHugo, G. J., Kleck, R. E., & Lanzetta, J. T. (1989). An analysis of the encoding and decoding of spontaneous and posed smiles: The use of facial electromyography. *Journal of Nonverbal Behavior, 13*, 121–137.

Hewes, G. W. (1957). The anthropology of posture. *Scientific American, 196*, 123–132.

Higgenbotham, D. J., & Yoder, D. E. (1982). Communications with natural conversational interaction: Implications for severe communicatively impaired persons. *Topics in Language Disorders, 2*, 1–19.

Hill, E. M., Nocks, E. S., & Gardner, L. (1987). Physical attractiveness: Manipulation by physique and status displays. *Ethology and Sociobiology, 8*, 143–154.

Hinz, V. B., Matz, D. C., & Patience, R. A. (2001). Does women's hair signal reproductive potential? *Journal of Experimental Social Psychology, 37*, 166–172.

Hirsch, A. R. (1998). Scent and sexual arousal: Could fragrance help relieve sexual dysfunction? *Medical Aspects of Human Sexuality, 1*, 9–12.

Hockett, C. F. (1960). The origin of speech. *Scientific American, 203*, 86–96.

Hocking, J. E. (1982). Sports and spectators: Intra-audience effects. *Journal of Communication, 32*, 100–108.

Hocking, J. E., Bauchner, J., Kaminski, E. P., & Miller, G. R. (1979). Detecting deceptive communication from verbal, visual, and paralinguistic cues. *Human Communication Research, 6*, 33–46.

Hocking, J. E., & Leathers, D. G. (1980). Nonverbal indicators of deception: A new theoretical perspective. *Communication Monographs, 47*, 119–131.

Hofstede, G. (1980). *Culture's consequences: International differences in work-related values.* Beverly Hills, CA: Sage.

Hofstede, G. (1984). *Culture's consequences: International differences in work-related values* (2nd ed.). Beverly Hills, CA: Sage.

Hofstede, G. (1991). *Cultures and organizations: Software of the mind.* New York: McGraw-Hill.

Hofstede, G. (2001). *Culture's consequences: Comparing values, behaviors, institutions, and organizations across nations.* Thousand Oaks, CA: Sage.

Holahan, C. J. (1982). *Environmental psychology.* New York: Random House.

Hollandsworth, J. G. Jr., Kazelski, R., Stevens, J., & Dressel, M. E. (1979). Relative contributions of verbal, articulative and nonverbal communication to employment decisions in the job interview setting. *Personnel Psychology, 32*, 359–367.

Holler, J., & Beattie, G. (2003). Pragmatic aspects of representational gestures. *Gesture, 3*, 127–154.

Hollien, H., Dew, D., & Philips, P. (1971). Phonational frequency ranges of adults. *Journal of Speech and Hearing Research, 14*, 755–760.

Hollinger, L. M., & Buschmann, M. B. (1993). Factors influencing the perception of touch by elderly nursing home residents and their health caregivers. *International Journal of Nursing Studies, 30*, 445–461.

Holmes, B. (2005). Wonders within WIN Wyoming. *Journal of Nutrition Education & Behavior, 37*, S145.

Honig, A. S. (2005). Take time to touch. *Scholastic Parent & Child, 12*(5), 32–34.

Hoots, M. A., McAndrew, F. T., & Francois, G. R. (1989). Decoding of gestures by kindergarten, first-, and third-grade children. *Journal of Genetic Psychology, 150*, 117–118.

Hooyman, N. R., & Kiyak, H. A. (1988). *Social gerontology.* Boston: Allyn & Bacon.

Hopkins, W. D. (Ed.). (2007). *The evolution of hemispheric specialization in primates.* New York: Academic Press.

Hopper, R., Knapp, M. L., & Scott, L. (1981). Couples' personal idioms: Exploring intimate talk. *Journal of Communication, 31*, 23–33.

Horatçsu, N., & Ekinci, B. (1992). Children's reliance on situational and vocal expression of emotions: Consistent and conflicting cues. *Journal of Nonverbal Behavior, 16*, 231–247.

Horn, P. (1974, April). Newsline. *Psychology Today, 7*, p. 27.

Hornik, J., & Ellis, S. (1988). Strategies to secure compliance for a mall intercept interview. *Public Opinion Quarterly, 52*, 539–551.

Horowitz, M. J., Duff, D. F., & Stratton, L. O. (1964). Body-buffer zones. *Archives of General Psychiatry, 11*, 651–656.

Hovland, C. I., Janis, I. L., & Kelley, H. H. (1953). *Communication and persuasion.* New Haven, CT: Yale University Press.

Hubbard, A. S. E., Tsuji, A. A., Williams, C., & Seatriz, V. (2003). Effects of touch on gratuities received in same-gender and cross-gender dyads. *Journal of Applied Social Psychology, 33*, 2427–2438.

Hugdahl, K. (1995). *Psychophysiology: A mind-body perspective.* Cambridge, MA: Harvard University Press.

Hume, D. K., & Montgomerie, R. (2001). Facial attractiveness signals different aspects of "quality" in women and men. *Evolution and Human Behavior, 22*, 93–112.

Huon, G. F., Morris, S. E., & Brown, L. B. (1990). Differences between male and female preferences for female body size. *Australian Psychologist, 25*, 314–317.

Huston, T. L. (1983). Power. In H. H. Kelley, E. Berscheid, A. Christensen, J. H. Harvey, T. L. Huston, G. Levinger, E. McClintock, L. A. Peplau, & D. R. Peterson (Eds.), *Close relationships* (pp. 169–219). New York: W. H. Freeman.

Huston, T. L., & Vangelisti, A. L. (1991). Socioemotional behavior and satisfaction in marital relationships: A longitudinal study. *Journal of Personality and Social Psychology, 61,* 721–733.

Huxley, A. (1954). *The doors of perception.* New York: Harper & Row.

Hyde, T. A., & Hyde, W. (1886). *A natural system of elocution and oratory founded on an analysis of the human constitution considered in its three-fold nature-mental, physiological and expressional.* New York: Fowler & Wells.

Ickes, W. (1984). Compositions in black and white: Determinants of interaction in interracial dyads. *Journal of Personality and Social Psychology, 47,* 330–341.

Ickes, W., & Barnes, R. (1977). The role of sex and self-monitoring in unstructured dyadic interactions. *Journal of Personality and Social Psychology, 35,* 315–330.

Ickes, W., Schermer, B., & Steeno, J. (1979). Sex and sex-role influences in same-sex dyads. *Social Psychology Quarterly, 42,* 373–385.

Iizuke, Y., Mishima, K., & Matsumoto, T. (1989). A study of the arousal model of interpersonal intimacy. *Japanese Psychological Research, 31,* 127–136.

Iliffe, A. H. (1960). A study of preferences in feminine beauty. *British Journal of Psychology, 51,* 267–273.

Irving, L. M. (1990). Mirror images: Effects of the standard of beauty on self- and body-esteem of women exhibiting varying levels of bulimic symptoms. *Journal of Social and Clinical Psychology, 9,* 230–242.

Isenhart, M. A. (1980). An investigation of the relationship of sex and sex role to the ability to decode nonverbal cues. *Human Communication Research, 6,* 309–318.

Izard, C. E. (1971). *The face of emotion.* Englewood Cliffs, NJ: Prentice-Hall.

Izard, C. E. (1977). *Human emotions.* New York: Plenum.

Izard, C. E. (1978). Emotions as motivations: An evolutionary-developmental perspective. In R. A. Dienstbier (Ed.), *Nebraska symposium on motivation* (Vol. 25, pp. 163–200). Lincoln: University of Nebraska Press.

Jackson, L. A., & Ervin, K. S. (1992). Height stereotypes of women and men: The liabilities of shortness for both sexes. *Journal of Social Psychology, 132,* 433–445.

Jacobi, L., & Cash, T. F. (1994). In pursuit of the perfect appearance: Discrepancies among self-perceived and idealized perceptions of multiple physical attributes. *Journal of Applied Social Psychology, 24,* 379–396.

Jacobson, M. B. (1981). Effects of victim's and defendant's physical attractiveness on subjects' judgments in a rape case. *Sex Roles, 7,* 247–255.

Jaffe, J., & Feldstein, S. (1970). *Rhythms of dialogue.* New York: Academic.

Jandt, F. E. (1995). *Intercultural communication: An introduction.* Thousand Oaks, CA: Sage.

Jasper, C. R., & Klassen, M. L. (1990). Stereotypical beliefs about appearance: Implications for retailing and consumer issues. *Perceptual and Motor Skills, 71,* 519–528.

Jaworski, A. (1993). *The power of silence: Social and pragmatic perspectives.* Newbury Park, CA: Sage.

Jensen, M. L. (2007). The effects of an expert system on novice and professional decision making with application in deception detection. *Dissertation Abstracts International Section A: Humanities and Social Sciences* (Vol 68(5-A)).

Jetten, J., Branscombe, N. R., Schmitt, M. T., & Spears, R. (2001). Rebels with a cause: Group identification as a response to perceived discrimination from the mainstream. *Personality and Social Psychology Bulletin, 27,* 1204–1213.

Johnson, F. J. (2007). Tattooing: Mind, body and spirit. The inner essence of the art. *Sociological Viewpoints, 23,* 45–61.

Johnson, K. K. P. (1990). Impressions of personality based on body forms: An application of Hillestad's model of appearance. *Clothing and Textiles Research Journal, 8,* 34–39.

Johnson, P. E., Grazioli, S., Jamal, K., & Berryman, R. G. (2001). Detecting deception: Adversarial problem solving in a low base-rate. *Cognitive Science: A Multidisciplinary Journal, 25,* 355–392.

Johnston, D. (1981, June). The pink jail. *Corrections Magazine,* pp. 28–32.

Johnston, V. S., & Franklin, M. (1993). Is beauty in the eye of the beholder? *Ethology and Sociobiology, 14,* 183–199.

Jones, D. (1995). Sexual selection, physical attractiveness, and facial neoteny. *Current Anthropology, 36,* 723–748.

Jones, D., & Hill, K. (1993). Criteria of facial attractiveness in five populations. *Human Nature, 4,* 271–296.

Jones, E. E. (1964). *Ingratiation.* New York: Appleton-Century-Crofts.

Jones, E. E., & Pittman, T. S. (1982). Toward a general theory of strategic self-presentation. In J. Suls (Ed.), *Psychological perspectives on the self* (Vol. 1, pp. 231–262). Hillsdale, NJ: Lawrence Erlbaum Associates.

Jones, S., Carrère, S., & Gottman, J. M. (2004). Specific Affect Coding System. In V. Manusov (Ed.), *The sourcebook of nonverbal measures: Going beyond words* (pp. 163–172). Hillsdale, NJ: Lawrence Erlbaum Associates.

Jones, S. E. (1984, November). *An exploratory study of sex differences in tactile communication.* Paper presented at the annual meeting of the Speech Communication Association, Chicago, IL.

Jones, S. E., & Brown, B. C. (1996). Touch attitudes and behaviors, recollections of early childhood touch, and social self-confidence. *Journal of Nonverbal Behavior, 20,* 147–163.

Jones, S. E., & Yarbrough, A. E. (1985). A naturalistic study of meanings of touch. *Communication Monographs, 52,* 19–56.

Jones, S. S., Collins, K., & Hong, H. (1991). An audience effect on smile production in 10-month-old infants. *Psychological Science, 2,* 45–49.

Jones, S. S., & Raag, T. (1989). Smile production in older infants: The importance of a social recipient for the facial signal. *Child Development, 69,* 811–818.

Jourard, S. M. (1966). An exploratory study of body accessibility. *British Journal of Social and Clinical Psychology, 5,* 221–231.

Juslin, P. N., & Laukka, P. (2003). Communication of emotions in vocal expression and musical performance: Different channels, same code? *Psychological Bulletin, 12,* 770–814.

Kaiser, S. B. (1997). *The social psychology of clothing: Symbolic appearances in context* (3rd ed.). New York: Fairfield Publications.

Kalymun, M. (1989). Relationships between sensory decline among the elderly and the physical environment: Implications for health care. *Rhode Island Medical Journal, 79,* 161–167.

Kamerman, S. B. (2000). Parental leave policies: An essential ingredient in early childhood education and care policies. *Social Policy Report, 14,* 3–15.

Kammrath, L. K., Ames, D. R., & Scholar, A. A. (2007). Keeping up impressions: Inferential rules for impression change across the Big Five. *Journal of Experimental Social Psychology, 43,* 450–457.

Kanazawa, S., & Kovar, J. L. (2004). Why beautiful people are more intelligent. *Intelligence, 32,* 227–243.

Karlson, P., & Luscher, M. (1959). "Pheromones": A new term for a class of biologically active substances. *Nature, 183,* 55–56.

Katz, D. (1937). *Animals and men.* White Plains, NY: Longman.

Kaufman, M. (1980). Prime-time nutrition. *Journal of Communication, 30,* 37–46.

Kaye, S. A., Folsom, A. R., Prineas, R. J., Potter, J. D., & Gapstur, S. M. (1990). The association of body fat distribution with lifestyle and reproductive factors in a population study of postmenopausal women. *International Journal of Obesity, 14,* 583–591.

Keasar, T., Bilu, Y., Motro, U., & Shmida, A. (1997). Foraging choices of bumblebees on equally rewarding artificial flowers of different colors. *Israel Journal of Plant Sciences, 45,* 223–233.

Keating, C. F. (1985). Gender and the physiognomy of dominance and attractiveness. *Social Psychology Quarterly, 48,* 61–70.

Keeley, M. (2003). Interview during the annual meeting of the National Communication Association, Miami Beach, November 2003.

Keeley-Dyreson, M. P., Bailey, W., & Burgoon, J. K. (1988, May). *The effect of stress on decoding of kinesic and vocalic channels.* Paper presented at the annual meeting of the International Communication Association, New Orleans, LA.

Keeley-Dyreson, M., Burgoon, J. K., & Bailey, W. (1991). The effects of stress and gender on nonverbal decoding accuracy in kinesic and vocalic channels. *Human Communication Research, 17,* 584–605.

Kelber, A. (1997). Innate preferences for flower features in the hawkmoth *Macroglossum stellatarum. Journal of Experimental Biology, 200,* 827–836.

Kellermann, K. (1992). Communication: Inherently strategic and primarily automatic. *Communication Monographs, 59,* 288–300.

Kellerman, K., & Lim, T. (1990). The conversation MOP: Part 3. Timing of scenes in discourse. *Journal of Personality and Social Psychology, 59,* 1163–1179.

Kellerman, K., Reynolds, R., & Chen, J. B. (1991). Strategies of conversational retreat: When parting is not sweet sorrow. *Communication Monographs, 58,* 362–383.

Kendon, A. (1978). Looking in conversation and the regulation of turns at talk: A comment on the papers of G. Beattie and D. R. Rutter et al. *British Journal of Social and Clinical Psychology, 17,* 23–24.

Kendon, A. (1981). Geography of gesture. *Semiotica, 37,* 129–163.

Kendon, A. (1983). Gesture and speech: How they interact. In J. M. Wiemann & R. P. Harrison (Eds.), *Nonverbal interaction* (pp. 13–45). Beverly Hills, CA: Sage.

Kendon, A. (1990). *Conducting interaction: Patterns of behavior in focused encounters.* Cambridge, England: Cambridge University Press.

Kendon, A. (1994). Do gestures communicate? *Research on Language and Social Interaction, 27,* 175–200.

Kendon, A. (2007). On the origins of modern gesture studies. In S. D. Duncan, J. Cassell, & E. T. Levy (Eds.), *Gesture and the dynamic dimension of language* (pp. 13–28). Philadelphia: John Benjamins.

Kendon, A., & Ferber, A. (1973). A description of some human greetings. In R. P. M. Michael & J. H. Crook (Eds.), *Comparative ecology and behavior of primates* (pp. 591–668). New York: Academic.

Kennedy, C. W., & Camden, C. (1981). Gender differences in interruption behavior: A dominance perspective. *Journal of Women's Studies, 4,* 18–25.

Kennedy, C. W., & Camden, C. (1983). Interruptions and nonverbal gender differences. *Journal of Nonverbal Behavior, 8,* 91–108.

Kennedy, R. (1943). Premarital residential propinquity. *American Journal of Sociology, 48,* 580–584.

Kenny, D. A., Horner, C., Kashy, D. A., & Chu, L. (1992). Consensus at zero acquaintance: Replication, behavioral cues, and stability. *Journal of Personality and Social Psychology, 62,* 88–97.

Kent, S. (1991). Partitioning space: Cross-cultural factors influencing domestic spatial segmentation. *Environment and Behavior, 23,* 438–473.

Kidwell, M. (2005). Gaze as social control: How very young children differentiate 'the look' from a 'mere look' by their adult caregivers. *Research on Language and Social Interaction, 38,* 417–449.

Kikuchi, T. (1994, July). *Effects of backchannel convergence on a speaker's speech rate and track-checking behavior.* Paper presented at the annual meeting of the International Communication Association, Sydney, Australia.

Kimata, H. (2006). Kissing selectively decreases allergen-specific IgE production in atopic patients. *Journal of Psychosomatic Research, 60,* 545–547.

Kimble, C. E., Forte, R. A., & Yoshikawa, J. C. (1981). Nonverbal concomitants of enacted emotional intensity and positivity: Visual and vocal behavior. *Journal of Personality, 49,* 271–283.

Kimble, C. E., & Musgrove, J. I. (1988). Dominance in arguing mixed-sex dyads: Visual dominance patterns, talking time, and speech loudness. *Journal of Research in Personality, 22,* 1–16.

Kimble, C. E., & Seidel, S. D. (1991). Vocal signs of confidence. *Journal of Nonverbal Behavior, 15,* 99–106.

King, C. E., & Christensen, A. (1983). The relationship events scale: A Guttman scaling of progress in courtship. *Journal of Marriage and the Family, 45,* 671–678.

Kira, A. (1966). *The bathroom: Criteria for design.* New York: Center for Housing and Environmental Studies, Cornell University.

Kirk-Smith, M., Booth, M. A., Carroll, D., & Davies, P. (1978). Human social attitudes affected by androstenol. *Research Communications in Psychology, Psychiatry, and Behavior, 3,* 379–384.

Kirschner, M. A., & Samojilik, E. (1991). Sex hormone metabolism in upper and lower body obesity. *International Journal of Obesity, 15,* 101–108.

Kjellgren, A., Sundequist, U., Norlander, T., & Archer, T. (2001). Effects of flotation-REST on muscle tension pain. *Pain Research Management, 6,* 181–189.

Klein, J. (1986). *Natural history of the major histocompatibility complex.* New York: John Wiley & Sons.

Kleinke, C. L. (1980). Interaction between gaze and legitimacy of request on compliance in a field setting. *Journal of Nonverbal Behavior, 5,* 3–12.

Kleinke, C. L., Lenga, M. R., Tulley, T. B., Meeker, F. B., & Staneski, R. A. (1976, April). *Effect of talking rate on first impressions of opposite-sex and same-sex interactions.* Paper presented at the annual meeting of the Western Psychological Association, Los Angeles, CA.

Kleinke, C. L., & Singer, D. A. (1979). Influence of gaze on compliance with demanding and conciliatory requests in a field setting. *Personality and Social Psychology Bulletin, 5,* 386–390.

Knapp, M. L. (1978). *Nonverbal communication in human interaction* (2nd ed.). New York: Holt, Rinehart & Winston.

Knapp, M. L. (1983). Dyadic relationship development. In J. M. Wiemann & R. P. Harrison (Eds.), *Non-verbal interaction* (pp. 179–207). Beverly Hills, CA: Sage.

Knapp, M. L. (1984b). The study of nonverbal behavior vis-à-vis human communication theory. In A. Wolfgang (Ed.), *Nonverbal behavior: Perspectives, applications, and intercultural insights* (pp. 15–40). Toronto, Canada: Hogrefe.

Knapp, M. L. (2007). *Lying and deception in human interaction.* Boston: Allyn & Bacon.

Knapp, M. L., & Comadena, M. E. (1979). Telling it like it isn't: A review of theory and research on deceptive communication. *Human Communication Research, 5,* 270–285.

Knapp, M. L., Hart, R. P., Freidrich, G. W., & Shulman, G. M. (1973). The rhetoric of goodbye: Verbal and nonverbal correlates of human leave-taking. *Speech Monographs, 40,* 182–198.

Knapp, M. L., Wiemann, J. M., & Daly, J. A. (1978). Nonverbal communication: Issues and appraisal. *Human Communication Research, 4,* 271–280.

Kobayashi, H., & Sato, M. (1992). Physiological responses to illuminance and color temperature of lighting. *Annals of Physiological Anthropology, 11,* 45–49.

Koch, J. R., Roberts, A. E., Armstrong, M. L., & Owen, D. C. (2005). College students, tattoos, and sexual activity. *Psychological Reports, 97,* 887–890.

Koeppel, L. B., Montagne-Miller, Y., O'Hair, D., & Cody, M. J. (1993). Friendly? Flirting? Wrong? In P. Kalbfleisch (Ed.), *Interpersonal communication: Communication in evolving relationships* (pp. 13–32). Hillsdale, NJ: Lawrence Erlbaum Associates.

Koeslag, J. H., & Koeslag, P. D. (1994). Koinophilia. *Journal of Theoretical Biology, 167,* 55–65.

Kohfeld, D. L., & Goedecke, D. W. (1974, November). *Why does background noise debilitate simple task performance?* Paper presented at the annual meeting of the Psychonomic Society, Boston, MA.

Köhnken, G. (1990). *Glaubwürdigkeit: Untersuchungen zu einem psychologischen Konstrukt.* [Credibility: Investigations of a psychological construct.] Munich, Germany: Psychologie Verlag Union.

Kopacz, M. A. (2006). Nonverbal communication as a persuasion tool: Current status and future directions. *Rocky Mountain Communication Review, 3,* 1–19.

Kowal, S., O'Connel, D. C., & Sabin, E. J. (1975). Development of temporal patterning and vocal hesitations in spontaneous narratives. *Journal of Psycholinguistic Research, 4,* 195–207.

Krapfel, R. E. (1988). Customer compliant and salesperson response: The effect of the communication source. *Journal of Retailing, 64,* 181–198.

Krauss, R., Morrel-Samuels, P., & Colasante, C. (1991). Do conversational hand gestures communicate? *Journal of Personality and Social Psychology, 61,* 743–754.

Krauss, R. M., Fussell, S., R., & Chen, Y. (1996). Coordination of perspective dialogue: Intrapersonal and interpersonal processes. In I. Markovà, C. F. Graumann, & K. Foppa (Eds.), *Mutualities in dialogue* (pp. 124–145). Cambridge, England: Cambridge University Press.

Kraut, R. E. (1978). Verbal and nonverbal cues in the perception of lying. *Journal of Personality and Social Psychology, 36,* 380–391.

Kraut, R. E., & Johnston, R. E. (1979). Social and emotional messages of smiling: An ethological approach. *Journal of Personality and Social Psychology, 37,* 1539–1553.

Kring, A. M., & Gordon, A. H. (1998). Sex differences in emotion: Expression, experience, and physiology. *Journal of Personality and Social Psychology, 74,* 686–703.

Krotkiewski, M., & Björntorp, P. (1978). The effects of estrogen treatment of carcinoma of the prostate on regional adipocyte size. *Journal of Endocrinological Investigation, 1,* 365–366.

Krout, M. H. (1954a). An experimental attempt to determine the significance of unconscious manual symbolic movements. *Journal of General Psychology, 51,* 93–120.

Krout, M. H. (1954b). An experimental attempt to produce unconscious manual symbolic movements. *Journal of General Psychology, 51,* 121–152.

Kuller, R., Ballal, S., Laike, T., Mikellides, B., & Tonello, G. (2006). The impact of light and colour on psychological mood: A cross-cultural study of indoor work environments. *Ergonomics, 49,* 1496–1507.

Kurzban, R., & Weeden, J. (2005). HurryDate: Mate preferences in action. *Evolution and Human Behavior, 26,* 227–244.

Kusmer, K. L. (2003). *Down and out, on the road: The homeless in American history.* New York: Oxford University Press.

Kwon, Y. H. (1994). The influence of appropriateness of dress and gender on the self-perception of occupational attributes. *Clothing and Textiles Research Journal, 12,* 33–39.

Kyle, D. G., & Mahler, H. I. M. (1996). The effects of hair color and cosmetic use on perceptions of a female's ability. *Psychology of Women Quarterly, 20,* 447–455.

Laban, R. (1974/1956). *Laban's principles of dance and movement notation* (2nd ed.). Boston: Plays, Inc.

LaBarbera, P., & MacLachlan, J. (1979). Time compressed speech in radio advertising. *Journal of Marketing, 43,* 30–36.

Laeng, B., Mathisen, R., & Johnsen, J. (2007). Why do blue-eyed men prefer women with the same eye color? *Behavioral Ecology and Sociobiology, 61,* 371–384.

LaFrance, M., Hecht, M. A., & Noyes, A. (1994, October). *Who's smiling now? A meta-analysis of sex differences in smiling.* Paper presented at the annual meeting of the Society of Experimental Social Psychology, Lake Tahoe, NV.

LaFrance, M., & Mayo, C. (1978a). Cultural aspects of nonverbal communication. *International Journal of Intercultural Relations, 2,* 71–89.

LaFrance, M., & Mayo, C. (1978b). *Moving bodies.* Monterey, CA: Brooks/Cole.

LaFrance, M., & Mayo, C. (1979). A review of nonverbal behaviors of women and men. *Western Journal of Speech Communication, 43,* 96–107.

Laird, J. D., & Apostoleris, N. H. (1996). Emotional self-control and self-perception: Feelings are the solution, not the problem. In R. Harré & W. G. Parrott (Eds.), *The emotions: Social, cultural, and biological dimensions* (pp. 285–301). Thousand Oaks, CA: Sage.

Laird, J. D., & Bresler, C. (1992). The process of emotional experience: A self-perception theory. In M. S. Clark (Ed.), *Emotion: Review of personality and social psychology* (Vol. 13, pp. 213–234). Newbury Park: Sage.

Lakoff, G., & Johnson, M. (1980). *Metaphors we live by.* Chicago: University of Chicago Press.

Lakoff, R. (1973). Language and women's place. *Language in Society, 2,* 45–79.

Landis, B. (1970). Ego boundaries. *Psychological issues* (Monograph No. 24). New York: International Universities Press.

Langlois, J. H., & Roggman, L. A. (1990). Attractive faces are only average. *Psychological Science, 1,* 115–121.

Langlois, J. H., Roggman, L. A., & Musselman, L. (1994). What is average and what is not average about attractive faces? *Psychological Science, 5,* 214–220.

Lannutti, P. J., Laliker, M., & Hale, J. L. (2001). Violations of expectations and social-sexual communication in student/professor interaction. *Communication Education, 50,* 69–82.

Larose, H., & Standing, L. (1998). Does the halo effect occur in the elderly? *Social Behavior and Personality, 26,* 147–150.

Larsen, K. M., & Smith, C. K. (1981). Assessment of nonverbal communication in the patient-physician interview. *The Journal of Family Practice, 12,* 481–488.

Lass, N. J., & Davis, M. (1976). An investigation of speaker height and weight identification. *Journal of the Acoustical Society of America, 60,* 700–707.

Lavrakas, P. J. (1975). Female preferences for male physiques. *Journal of Research in Personality, 9,* 324–333.

Lazarus, R. S. (1991). *Emotion and adaptation.* New York: Oxford University Press.

Le Poire, B. A., & Burgoon, J. K. (1994a). *Participant and observer perceptions of relational messages associated with nonverbal involvement and pleasantness.* Manuscript submitted for publication.

Le Poire, B. A., & Burgoon, J. K. (1994b). Two contrasting explanations of involvement violations: Expectancy violations theory versus discrepancy arousal theory. *Human Communication Research, 20,* 560–591.

Le Poire, B. A., & Burgoon, J. K. (1996). Usefulness of differentiating arousal responses within communication theories: Orienting response of defensive arousal within theories of expectancy violation. *Communication Monographs, 63,* 208–230.

Leach, E. (1972). The influence of cultural context on non-verbal communication in man. In R. A. Hinde (Ed.), *Non-verbal communication* (pp. 315–347). Cambridge: Cambridge University Press.

Leaf, A. (1973, September). Getting old. *Scientific American, 229,* pp. 45–52.

Leal, S. (2005). *Central and peripheral physiology of attention and cognitive demand: Understanding how brain and body work together.* Unpublished doctoral thesis, University of Portsmouth, Department of Psychology.

Lee, J. W., & Guerrero, L. K. (2001). Types of touch in cross-sex relationships between coworkers: Perceptions of relational and emotional messages, inappropriateness, and sexual harassment. *Journal of Applied Communication Research, 29,* 197–220.

Lee, K., Cameron, C. A., Doucette J., & Talwar, V. (2002). Phantoms and fabrications: Young children's detection of implausible lies. *Child Development, 73,* 1688–1702.

Lee, K., Xu, F., Fu, G., Cameron, C. A., & Chen, S. (2001). Taiwan and Mainland Chinese and Canadian children's categorization and evaluation of lie- and truth-telling: A modesty effect. *British Journal of Developmental Psychology, 19,* 525–542.

Leffler, A., Gillespie, D. L., & Conaty, J. C. (1982). The effects of status differentiation on nonverbal behavior. *Social Psychology Quarterly, 45,* 153–161.

Leigh, T. W., & Summers, J. O. (2002). An initial evaluation of industrial buyers' impressions of salespersons' nonverbal cues. *Journal of Personal Selling and Sales Management, 22,* 41–53.

Levelt, W. J. M. (1989). *Speaking: From intention to articulation.* Cambridge, MA: MIT Press.

Levenson, R. W. (1992). Autonomic nervous system differences among emotions. *Psychological Science, 3,* 23–27.

Levin, R. A., & Zickar, M. J. (2002). Investigating self-presentation, lies, and bullshit: Understanding faking and its effects on selection decisions using decision theory, field research, and simulation. In J. M. Brett & F. Drawgow (Eds.), *The psychology of work: Theoretically based empirical research* (pp. 253–276). Mahwah, NJ: Lawrence Erlbaum Associates.

Levine, R., & Wolff, E. (1985, March). Social time: The heartbeat of culture. *Psychology Today,* pp. 28–35.

Levine, T. R., Feeley, T. H., McCornack, S. A., Hughes, M., & Harms, C. M. (2005). Testing the effects of nonverbal behavior training on accuracy in deception detection with the inclusion of a bogus training control group. *Western Journal of Communication, 69,* 203–217.

Levine, T. R., Kim R. K., Park, H. S., & Hughes, M. (2006). Deception detection accuracy is a predictable linear function of message veracity baserate: A formal test of Park and Levine's probability model. *Communication Monographs, 73,* 243–260.

Levine, T. R., Park, H. S., & McCornack, S. A. (1999). Accuracy in detecting truths and lies: Documenting the "veracity effect." *Communication Monographs, 66,* 125–144.

Lewis, M., Sullivan, M., & Brooks-Gunn, J. (1985). Emotional behavior during the learning of a contingency in early infancy. *British Journal of Developmental Psychology, 3,* 307–316.

Leyhausen, P. (1971). Dominance and territoriality as complemented in mammalian social structure. In A. H. Esser (Ed.), *Behavior and environment* (pp. 22–33). New York: Plenum.

Lill, M. M., & Wilkinson, T. J. (2005). Judging a book by its cover: Descriptive survey of patients' preferences for doctors' appearance and mode of address. *British Medical Journal, 331,* 1524–1527.

Linkey, H. E., & Firestone, I. J. (1990). Dyad dominance composition effects, nonverbal behaviors, and influence. *Journal of Research in Personality, 24,* 206–215.

Linville, S. E. (1998). Acoustic correlates of perceived versus actual sexual orientation in men's speech. *Folia Phoniatrica et Logopaedica, 50,* 35–48.

Lipton, E. (2006, August 17). Faces, too, are searched as U.S. airports try to spot terrorists. *New York Times,* A1.

Liska, J. (1990). Dominance-seeking strategies in primates: An evolutionary perspective. *Human Evolution, 5,* 75–90.

Liss, B., Walker, M., Hazelton, V., & Cupach, W. D. (1993, February). *Mutual gaze and smiling as correlates of compliance-gaining success.* Paper presented at the annual meeting of the Western States Communication Association, Albuquerque, NM.

Livio, M. (2002). *The golden ratio: The story of phi, the world's most astonishing number.* New York: Broadway.

Luscher, M., & Scott, I. (1969). *The Luscher Color Test.* New York: Random House.

Lustig, M. W. (1977). *The relationship between verbal reticence and verbal interaction in triads.* Unpublished doctoral dissertation, University of Wisconsin.

Lustig, M. W., & Koester, J. (2003). *Intercultural competence: Interpersonal communication across cultures.* New York: Harper Collins.

Lyman S. M., & Scott, M. B. (1967). Territoriality: A neglected sociological dimension. *Social Problems, 15,* 236–249.

Lynn, M., & Shurgot, B. A. (1894). Responses to lonely hearts advertisements: Effects of reported physical attractiveness, physique, and coloration. *Personality and Social Psychology Bulletin, 10,* 349–357.

Lyons, J. (1972). Human language. In R. A. Hinde (Ed.), *Non-verbal communication* (pp. 49–85). Cambridge, England: Cambridge University Press.

Lysaght, R. J., Warm, J. S., Dember, W. N., & Loeb, M. (1983). The effects of noise on a cognitive valence task. *Journal of the Acoustical Society of America, 73,* S105.

MacFarlane, A. (1975). Olfaction in the development of social preferences in the human neonate. In A. MacFarlane (Ed.), *Ciba Foundation Symposium 33: The human neonate in parent-infant interaction* (pp. 103–117). Amsterdam: Associated Scientific Publishers.

Machleit, K. A., Eroglu, S. A., & Mantel, S. P. (2000). Perceived retail crowding and shopping satisfaction: What modifies this relationship? *Journal of Consumer Psychology, 9,* 29–42.

MacLachlan, J., & Siegel, M. H. (1980). Reducing the cost of TV commercials by use of time compressions. *Journal of Marketing Research, 17,* 52–57.

MacLean, P. D. (1990). *The triune brain in evolution: Role of paleocerebral functions.* New York: Plenum.

Major, B. (1981). Gender patterns in touching behavior. In C. Mayo & N. M. Henley (Eds.), *Gender and nonverbal behavior* (pp. 15–37). New York: Springer-Verlag.

Major, B., Schmidlin, A. M., & Williams, L. (1990). Gender patterns in social touch: The impact of setting and age. *Journal of Personality and Social Psychology, 58,* 634–643.

Major, B., & Williams, L. (1980). *Frequency of touch by sex and race: A replication of some touching observations.* Unpublished manuscript, State University of New York, Buffalo.

Makoul, G., Zick, A., & Green, M. (2007). An evidence-based perspective on greetings in medical encounters. *Archives of Internal Medicine, 167,* 172–176.

Malcolm, S., & Keenan, J. P. (2003). My right I: Deception detection and hemispheric differences in self-awareness. *Social Behavior and Personality, 31,* 767–772.

Mann, J. M. (1959). The effect of interracial contact on sociometric choices and perceptions. *Journal of Social Psychology, 50,* 143–152.

Mann, S., Vrij, A., & Bull, R. (2004). Detecting true lies: Police officers' ability to detect suspects' lies. *Journal of Applied Psychology, 89,* 137–149.

Manuel, L., & Sheehan, E. P. (2007). Getting inked: Tattoos and college students. *College Student Journal, 41,* 1089–1097.

Manusov, V. (1991). Perceiving nonverbal messages: Effects of immediacy and encoded intent on receiver judgments. *Western Journal of Speech Communication, 55,* 235–253.

Manusov, V. (1993). It depends on your perspective: Effects of stance and beliefs about intent on person perception. *Western Journal of Communication, 57,* 27–41.

Manusov, V. (1994, February). *Reacting to changes in nonverbal behaviors: Relational satisfaction and adaptation patterns in romantic dyads.* Paper presented at the annual meeting of the Western States Communication Association, San Jose, CA.

Manusov, V., & Patterson, M. L. (Eds.). (2006). *The Sage handbook of nonverbal communication.* Thousand Oaks, CA: Sage.

Manusov, V., & Trees, A. R. (2002). 'Are you kidding me?' The role of nonverbal cues in the verbal accounting process. *Journal of Communication, 52,* 640–656.

Marangoni, C., Garcia, S., Ickes, W., & Teng, G. (1995). Empathic accuracy in a clinically relevant setting. *Journal of Personality and Social Psychology, 68,* 854–869.

Marche, T. A., & Peterson, C. (1993). The development and sex-related use of interruption behavior. *Human Communication Research, 19,* 388–408.

Marieb, E. N. (2003). *Essentials of human anatomy and physiology* (7th ed.). San Francisco: Benjamin Cummings.

Marin, R. (1995, February 6). Lifestyle: Turning in the badges of rebellion. *Newsweek,* p. 46.

Markel, N. N. (1969). Relationship between voice-quality and MMPI profiles in psychiatric patients. *Journal of Abnormal Psychology, 74,* 61–66.

Markel, N. N. (1975). Coverbal behavior associated with conversational turns. In A. Kendon, R. Harris, & M. R. Key (Eds.), *The organization of behavior in face-to-face interaction* (pp. 189–197). The Hague: Mouton.

Markel, N. N., Phillis, J. A., Vargas, R., & Howard, K. (1972). Personality traits associated with voice types. *Journal of Psycholinguistic Research, 1,* 249–255.

Markham, R., & Adams, K. (1992). The effect of type of task on children's identification of facial expressions. *Journal of Nonverbal Behavior, 16,* 21–39.

Marks, P. (2007, August 11). Can you catch a killer before they commit a crime? *New Scientist, 2616.* (http://www.newscientisttech.com/channel/tech/forensic-science/mg19526166.400)

Marsh, A. A., Adams, R. B., & Kleck, R. E. (2005). Why do fear and anger look the way they do? Form and social function in facial expressions. *Personality and Social Psychology Bulletin, 31,* 73–86.

Marsh, A. A., Elfenbein, H. A., & Ambady, N. (2003). Nonverbal "accents": Cultural difference in facial expressions of emotion. *Psychological Science, 14,* 373–376.

Marsh, A. A., Elfenbein, H. A., & Ambady, N. (2007). Separated by a common language: Nonverbal accents and cultural stereotypes about Americans and Australians. *Journal of Cross-Cultural Psychology, 38,* 284–301.

Marshall, L. L. (1994). Physical and psychological abuse. In W. R. Cupach & B. H. Spitzberg (Eds.), *The dark side of interpersonal communication* (pp. 281–311). Hillsdale, NJ: Lawrence Erlbaum Associates.

Marston, P. J., Hecht, M. L., & Robers, T. (1987). True love ways: The subjective experience and communication of romantic love. *Journal of Social and Personal Relationships, 4,* 387–407.

Martin, J. N., & Nakayama, T. K. (1997). *Intercultural communication in contexts.* Mountain View, CA: Mayfield Publishing.

Martin, J. N., & Nakayama, T. K. (2008). *Experiencing intercultural communication* (3rd ed.). New York: McGraw-Hill.

Martin, M. C., & Kennedy, P. F. (1993). Advertising and social comparison: Consequences for female preadolescents and adolescents. *Psychology and Marketing, 10,* 513–530.

Masip, J., Garrido, E., & Herrero, C. (2003). Facial appearance and judgments of credibility: the effects of facial babyishness and age on statement of credibility. *Genetic Social and General Psychology Monographs, 129,* 269–311.

Mast, M. S., & Hall, J. A. (2004). Who is the boss and who is not? Accuracy of judging status. *Journal of Nonverbal Behavior, 28,* 145–165.

Matarazzo, J. D., & Wiens, A. N. (1972). *The interview: Research on its anatomy and structure.* Chicago: Aldine.

Matsumoto, D. (1991). Cultural influences on facial expressions of emotion. *Southern Communication Journal, 56,* 128–137.

Matsumoto, D. (2006). Culture and nonverbal behavior. In V. Manusov & M. L. Patterson (Eds.), *The Sage handbook of nonverbal communication* (pp. 219–235). Thousand Oaks, CA: Sage.

Matsumoto, D., & Kishimoto, H. (1983). Developmental characteristics in judgments of emotion from nonverbal vocal cues. *International Journal of International Relations, 7,* 415–424.

Matsumoto, D., & Kupperbusch, C. (2001). Idiocentric and allocentric differences in emotional expression and experience. *Asian Journal of Social Psychology, 4,* 113–131.

Matsumoto, D., Takeuchi, S., Andayani, S., Kouznetsova, N., & Krupp, D. (1998). The contribution of individualism-collectivism to cross-national differences in display rules. *Asian Journal of Social Psychology, 1,* 147–165.

Matsumoto, D., Yoo, S. H., Hirayama, S., & Petrova, G. (2005). Validation of an individual-level measure of display rules: The display rule assessment inventory (DRAI). *Emotion, 5,* 23–40.

Maxwell, G. M., Cook, M. W., & Burr, R. (1985). The encoding and decoding of liking from behavioral cues in both auditory and visual channels. *Journal of Nonverbal Behavior, 9,* 239–263.

May, J. L., & Hamilton, P. A. (1980). Effects of musically evoked affect on women's interpersonal attraction toward and perceptual judgments of physical attractiveness of men. *Motivation and Emotion, 4,* 217–228.

Mayer, J. D., Salovey, P., & Caruso, D. R. (1999). Models of emotional intelligence. In R. J. Sternberg (Ed.), *Handbook of human intelligence* (2nd ed., pp. 396–420). New York: Cambridge University Press.

Mayer, J. D., Salovey, P., & Caruso, D. R. (2004). Emotional intelligence: Theory, findings, and implications. *Psychological Inquiry, 15,* 197–215.

Mayer, J. D., Salovey, P., Caruso, D. R., & Sitarenios, G. (2001). Emotional intelligence as a standard intelligence. *Emotion, 1,* 232–242.

Mayo, C., & LaFrance, M. (1978). On the acquisition of nonverbal communication: A review. *Merrill Palmer Quarterly, 24,* 213–228.

McAdams, D. P., Jackson, R. J., & Kirshnit, C. (1984). Looking, laughing, and smiling in dyads as a function of intimacy motivation and reciprocity. *Journal of Personality, 52,* 261–273.

McBrayer, D. J., Johnson, W. R., & Purvis, D. (1992). Gestural behavior: Causes and questions. *Perceptual and Motor Skills, 74,* 239–242.

McBride, G. (1975). Interactions and the control of behavior. In A. Kendon, R. M. Harris, & M. R. Key (Eds.), *Organization of behavior in face-to-face interaction* (pp. 415–425). The Hague: Mouton.

McCarrick, A. K., Manderscheid, R. W., & Silbergeld, S. (1981). Gender differences in competition and dominance during married-couples group therapy. *Social Psychology Quarterly, 44,* 164–177.

McCarthy, M. M., & Becker, J. B. (2002). Neuroendocrinology of sexual behavior in the female. In J. B. Becker, S. M. Breedlove, D. Crews, & M. M. McCarthy (Eds.), *Behavioral endocrinology* (2nd ed., pp. 117–151). Cambridge, MA: MIT Press.

McCarthy, P. (1988, January). Mind openers. *Psychology Today,* p. 16.

McClintock, M. K. (1971). Menstrual synchrony and suppression. *Nature, 229,* 244–245.

McClure, E. B. (2000). A meta-analytic review of sex differences in facial expression processing and their development in infants, children, and adolescents. *Psychological Bulletin, 126,* 424–453.

McCormick, E. J. (1976). *Human factors in engineering and design.* New York: McGraw-Hill.

McCornack, S. A. (1992). Information manipulation theory. *Communication Monographs, 59,* 1–16.

McCornack, S. A. (1997). The generation of deceptive messages: Laying the groundwork for a viable theory of interpersonal deception. In J. O. Greene (Ed.), *Message production: Advances in communication theory* (pp. 91–126). Mahwah, NJ: Lawrence Erlbaum Associates.

McCornack, S. A., & Levine, T. R. (1990). When lovers become leery: The relationship between suspicion and accuracy in detecting deception. *Communication Monographs, 57,* 219–230.

McCornack, S. A., & Parks, M. R. (1986). Deception detection and relationship development: The other side of trust. In M. L. McLaughlin (Ed.), *Communication yearbook 9* (pp. 377–389). Beverly Hills, CA: Sage.

McDaniel, E. R., & Andersen, P. A. (1998). Intercultural variations in tactile communication: A field study. *Journal of Nonverbal Behavior, 22,* 59–75.

McDonald, G. W. (1980). Family power: The assessment of a decade of theory and research, 1970–1979. *Journal of Marriage and the Family, 42,* 841–854.

McGlone, R. E., & Hollien, H. (1963). Vocal pitch characteristics of aged women. *Journal of Speech and Hearing Research, 6,* 164–170.

McLaughlin, M. L. (1984). *Conversation: How talk is organized.* Beverly Hills, CA: Sage.

McLeod, P. L., & Rosenthal, R. (1983). Micromomentary movement and the decoding of face and body cues. *Journal of Nonverbal Behavior, 8,* 83–90.

McNeill, D. (1970). *The acquisition of language: The study of developmental psycholinguistics.* New York: Harper & Row.

McNeill, D. (1985). So you think gestures are nonverbal? *Psychological Review, 92,* 350–371.

McNeill, D. (1992). *Hand and mind: What gestures reveal about thought.* Chicago: University Chicago Press.

McNeill, D. (2005). *Gesture and thought.* Chicago: University of Chicago Press.

McNeill, D., Cassell, J., & McCullough, K. (1994). Communicative effects of speech-mismatched gestures. *Research on Language and Social Interaction, 27,* 223–237.

Meditch, A. (1975). The development of sex-specific speech patterns in young children. *Anthropological Linguistics, 17,* 421–433.

Medved, C. E., & Rawlins, W. K. (2007, November). *Constructing gender, identity, and power in at-home father/breadwinning mother couples.* Paper presented at the annual meeting of the National Communication Association, Chicago, IL.

Mehl, M. R., Vazire, S., Ramírez-Esparza, N., Slatcher, R. B., & Pennebaker, J. W. (2007). Are women really more talkative than men? *Science, 317,* 82.

Mehrabian, A. (1969). Significance of posture and position in the communication of attitude and status relationships. *Psychological Bulletin, 71,* 359–372.

Mehrabian, A. (1976). *Public places and private spaces: The psychology of work, play, and living environments.* New York: Basic Books.

Mehrabian, A. (1981). *Silent messages: Implicit communication of emotions and attitudes* (2nd ed.). Belmont, CA: Wadsworth.

Mehrabian, A., & Diamond, S. G. (1971). Seating arrangement and conversation. *Sociometry, 34,* 281–289.

Mehrabian, A., & Ferris, S. R. (1967). Inference of attitudes from nonverbal communication in two channels. *Journal of Consulting Psychology, 31,* 248–252.

Mehrabian, A., & Ksionzky, S. (1972). Categories of social behavior. *Comparative Group Studies, 3,* 425–436.

Mehrabian, A., & Russell, J. A. (1974). *An approach to environmental psychology.* Cambridge, MA: MIT Press.

Mehrabian, A., & Wiener, M. (1967). Decoding of inconsistent communication. *Journal of Personality and Social Psychology, 6,* 109–114.

Mehrabian, A., & Williams, M. (1969). Nonverbal concomitants of perceived and intended persuasiveness. *Journal of Personality and Social Psychology, 13,* 37–58.

Meltzoff, A. N., & Moore, M. K. (1989). Imitation in newborn infants: Exploring the range of gestures imitated and the underlying mechanisms. *Developmental Psychology, 25,* 954–962.

Melzer, P., Morgan, V. L., Pickens, D. R., Price, R. R., Wall, R. S., & Ebner, F. F. (2001). Cortical activation during Braille reading is influenced by early visual experience in subjects with severe visual disability: A correlation fMRI study. *Human Brain Mapping, 14,* 186–195.

Mendez, A. J. (1999). *The master of disguise: My secret life in the CIA.* New York: William Morrow and Company.

Menyuk, P. (1972). *The development of speech.* Indianapolis, IN: The Bobbs Merrill Studies in Communication Disorders.

Merkin, R. S. (2006). Power distance and facework strategies. *Journal of Intercultural Communication Research, 35,* 139–160.

Messinger, D. S. (2002). Positive and negative: Infant facial expressions and emotions. *Current Directions in Psychological Science, 11,* 1–6.

Metts, S., & Chronis, H. (1986, May). *An exploratory investigation of relational deception.* Paper presented at the annual meeting of the International Communication Association, Chicago, IL.

Meyer, J., & Driskill, G. (1997). Children and relationship development: Communication strategies in a day care center. *Communication Reports, 10,* 78–87.

Mezulis, A. H., Abramson, L. Y., Hyde, J. S., & Hankin, B. L. (2004). Is there a universal positivity bias in attributions? A meta-analytic review of individual, developmental, and cultural differences in the self-serving attributional bias. *Psychological Bulletin, 130,* 711–747.

Milgram, S. (1963). Behavioral study of obedience. *Journal of Abnormal and Social Psychology, 67,* 371–378.

Milgram, S. (1974). *Obedience to authority: An experimental view.* New York: Harper & Row.

Miller, A. (1970). Role of physical attractiveness in impression formation. *Psychonomic Science, 19,* 241–243.

Miller, A. G., Ashton, W. A., McHoskey, J. W., & Gimbel, I. (1984). What price attractiveness? Stereotype and risk factors in suntanning behavior. *Journal of Applied Social Psychology, 20,* 1272–1300.

Miller, L. C., & Cox, C. L. (1982). For appearances' sake: Public self-consciousness and makeup use. *Personality and Social Psychology Bulletin, 8,* 748–751.

Miller, N., Maruyama, G., Beaber, R. J., & Valone, K. (1976). Speed of speech and persuasion. *Journal of Personality and Social Psychology, 34,* 615–624.

Mischel, W. (1968). *Personality and assessment.* New York: John Wiley & Sons.

Mobias, M. M., & Rosenblat, T. (2006). Why beauty matters. *American Economic Review, 96,* 222–235.

Moe, J. D. (1972). Listener judgments of status cues in speech: A replication and extension. *Speech Monographs, 39,* 144–147.

Molinsky, A. L., Krabbenhoft, M. A., & Ambady, N. (2005). Cracking the nonverbal code: Intercultural competence and gesture recognition across cultures. *Journal of Cross-Cultural Psychology, 36,* 380–395.

Molloy, J. T. (1977). *The woman's dress for success book.* Chicago: Follett.

Montagu, A. (1978). *Touching: The human significance of the skin* (2nd ed.). New York: Harper & Row.

Montepare, J. M. (1995). The impact of variations in height on young children's impressions of men and women. *Journal of Nonverbal Behavior, 19,* 31–47.

Montepare, J. M., & Dobish, H. (2003). The contribution of emotion perceptions and their overgeneralizations to trait impressions. *Journal of Nonverbal Behavior, 27,* 237–254.

Montepare, J. M., Goldstein, S. B., & Clausen, A. (1987). The identification of emotions from gait information. *Journal of Nonverbal Behavior, 11,* 33–42.

Moon, J., & Cho, K. (2001). The effects on handholding on anxiety in cataract surgery patients under local anesthesia. *Journal of Advanced Nursing, 35,* 407–415.

Moore, E. A. (2005, May 23). Policing displays of affection at school. *Christian Science Monitor, 97,* p. 3.

Moore, M. M. (1983). Nonverbal courtship patterns in women: Context and consequences. *Ethology and Sociobiology, 6,* 237–247.

Moore, M. M. (1985). Nonverbal courtship patterns in women: Context and consequences. *Ethology and Sociobiology, 6,* 237–247.

Moore, M. M. (1995). Courtship signaling and adolescents: "Girls just wanna have fun?" *Journal of Sex Research, 32,* 319–328.

Moore, M. M. (2002). Courtship communication and perception. *Perceptual and Motor Skills, 94,* 97–105.

Moore, W. E. (1939). Personality traits and voice quality deficiencies. *Journal of Speech and Hearing Disorders, 4,* 33–36.

Morency, N. L., & Krauss, R. M. (1982). Children's nonverbal encoding and decoding of affect. In R. S. Feldman (Ed.), *Development of nonverbal behavior in children* (pp. 181–199). New York: Springer-Verlag.

Morris, D. (1967). *The naked ape.* New York: McGraw-Hill.

Morris, D. (1971). *Intimate behavior.* New York: Random House.

Morris, D. (1977). *Manwatching: A field guide to human behavior.* New York: Abrams.

Morris, D. (1994). *Bodytalk: The meaning of human gestures.* New York: Crown Trade Publications.

Morris, D., Collett, P., Marsh, P., & O'Shaughnessy, M. (1979). *Gestures.* New York: Stein & Day.

Morrison, T. G., Kalin, R., & Morrison, M. A. (2004). Body-image evaluation and body-image investment among adolescents: A test of sociocultural and social comparison theories. *Adolescence, 39,* 571–592.

Morsbach, H. (1973). Aspects of nonverbal communication in Japan. *Journal of Nervous and Mental Disease, 157,* 262–277.

Moszkowski, R. J., & Stack, D. M. (2007). Infant touching behaviour during mother-infant face-to-face interactions. *Infant & Child Development, 16,* 307–319.

Motley, M. T. (1990). On whether one can(not) communicate: An examination via traditional communication postulates. *Western Journal of Speech Communication, 54,* 1–20.

Motley, M. T. (1991). How one may not communicate: A reply to Andersen. *Communication Studies, 42,* 326–339.

Mottet, T. P., Parker-Raley, J., Beebe, S. A., & Cunningham, C. (2007). Instructors who resist "college lite": The neutralizing effect of instructor immediacy on students' course-workload violations and perceptions of instructor credibility and affective learning. *Communication Education, 56,* 145–167.

Mount, M. K., Barrick, M. R., & Stewart, G. L. (1998). Five-factor model of personality and performance in jobs involving interpersonal interactions. *Human Performance, 11,* 145–165.

Møller, A. P. (1997). Developmental stability and fitness: A review. *American Naturalist, 149,* 916–942.

Muehlenhard, C. L., Miller, C. L., & Burdick, C. A. (1983). Are high-frequency daters better cue readers? Men's interpretations of women's cues as a function of dating frequency and SHI scores. *Behavior Therapy, 14,* 626–636.

Mulac, A. (1989). Men's and women's talk in same-gender and mixed-gender dyads: Power or polemic? *Journal of Language and Social Psychology, 8,* 249–270.

Mulac, A., Studley, L. B., Wiemann, J. W., & Bradac, J. J. (1987). Male/female gaze in same-sex and mixed-sex dyads: Gender-linked differences and mutual influence. *Human Communication Research, 13*, 323–344.

Mundell, H. (1993, November). How the color mafia chooses your clothes. *American Demographics,* 21–23.

Munson, B., McDonald, E. C., DeBoe, N. L., & White, A. R. (2006). The acoustic and perceptual bases of judgments of women and men's sexual orientation from read speech. *Journal of Phonetics, 34,* 202–240.

Murray, K. G., Winnett-Murray, K., Cromie, E. A., Minor, M., & Meyers, E. (1993). The influence of seed packaging and fruit color on feeding preferences of American robins. *Vegetation, 108,* 217–226.

Murray, S. L., Holmes, J. G., & Griffin, D. W. (1996). The benefits of positive illusions: Idealization and the construction of satisfaction in close relationships. *Journal of Personality and Social Psychology, 70,* 79–98.

Murstein, B. I. (1972). Physical attractiveness and marital choice. *Journal of Personality and Social Psychology, 22,* 8–12.

Muscarella, F., & Cunningham, M. R. (1996). The evolutionary significance and social perception of male pattern baldness and facial hair. *Ethology and Sociobiology, 17,* 99–117.

Muth, J. L., & Cash, T. F. (1997). Body-image attitudes: What difference does gender make? *Journal of Applied Social Psychology, 27,* 1438–1452.

Myers, J. (1992). Nonmainstream body modification. *Journal of Contemporary Ethnography, 21,* 267–306.

Myers, P. N., & Biocca, F. A. (1992). The elastic body image: The effect of television advertising and programming on body image distortions in young women. *Journal of Communication, 42,* 108–118.

Mysak, E. D. (1959). Pitch and duration characteristics of older males. *Journal of Speech and Hearing Research, 2,* 46–54.

Navarre, D. (1982). Posture sharing in dyadic interaction. *American Journal of Dance Therapy, 5,* 28–42.

Nelson, H. (2007). Encoding and decoding mutual grooming: Communication with a specialized form of touch. *Dissertation Abstracts International, Section B: The Sciences and Engineering,* Vol. 68 (4-B), p. 2664.

Nelson, T. D. (2005). Ageism: Prejudice against our featured future self. *Journal of Social Issues, 61,* 207–221.

Nerbonne, G. P. (1967). *The identification of speaker characteristics on the basis of aural cues.* Unpublished doctoral dissertation, Michigan State University.

Newman, H. M. (1982). The sounds of silence in communicative encounters. *Communication Quarterly, 30,* 142–149.

Newman, J. D. (2003). Vocal communication and the triune brain. *Physiology and Behavior, 79,* 495–502.

Newman, O. (1972). *Defensible space: Crime prevention through urban design.* New York: Collier.

Newton, D. A., & Burgoon, J. K. (1990). Nonverbal conflict behaviors: Functions, strategies, and tactics. In D. A. Cahn (Ed.), *Intimates in conflict: A communication perspective* (pp. 77–104). Hillsdale, NJ: Lawrence Erlbaum Associates.

Nicholas, C. L. (2004). Gaydar: Eye-gaze as identity recognition among gay men and lesbians. *Sexuality and Culture, 8,* 60–86.

Nickerson, R. S. (1998). Confirmation bias: A ubiquitous phenomenon in many guises. *Review of General Psychology, 2,* 175–220.

Niolaides, N. (1974). Skin lipids: Their biochemical uniqueness. *Science, 186,* 19–26.

Nolen-Hoekscma, S. (1987). Sex differences in unipolar depression: Evidence and theory. *Psychological Bulletin, 101,* 259–282.

Noller, P. (1980). Misunderstanding in marital communication: A study of couples' nonverbal communication. *Journal of Personality and Social Psychology, 41,* 272–278.

Noller, P. (1985). Video primacy: A further look. *Journal of Nonverbal Behavior, 9,* 28–47.

Noller, P. (1993). Gender and emotional communication in marriage: Different cultures or different social power? *Journal of Language and Social Psychology, 12,* 92–112.

Noller, P. (2004). Behavioral coding of visual affect behavior. In V. Manusov (Ed.), *The sourcebook of nonverbal measures: Going beyond words* (pp. 141–150). Hillsdale, NJ: Lawrence Erlbaum Associates.

Noller, P., & Gallois, C. (1986). Sending emotional messages in marriage: Nonverbal behavior, sex and communication clarity. *British Journal of Social Psychology, 25,* 287–297.

Nowicki, S., & Duke, M. P. (1994). Individual differences in the nonverbal communication of affect: The diagnostic analysis of nonverbal accuracy scale. *Journal of Nonverbal Behavior, 18,* 9–35.

Nussbaum, J. F., Thompson, T., & Robinson, J. D. (1989). *Communication and aging.* New York: Harper & Row.

Nykodym, N., & Simonetti, J. L. (1987). Personal appearance: Is attractiveness a factor in organizational survival and success? *Journal of Employment Counseling, 24,* 69–78.

O'Hair, D., Allman, J., & Gibson, L. A. (1991). Nonverbal communication and aging. *Southern Communication Journal, 56,* 147–160.

O'Hair, H. D., Cody, M. J., & McLaughlin, M. L. (1981). Prepared lies, spontaneous lies, Machiavellianism, and nonverbal communication. *Human Communication Research, 7,* 325–339.

O'Keefe, B. J., & Delia, J. G. (1982). Impression formation and message production. In M. E. Roloff & C. R. Berger (Eds.), *Social cognition and communication* (pp. 33–72). Beverly Hills, CA: Sage.

O'Leary, M. J., & Gallois, C. (1985). The last ten turns: Behavior and sequencing in friends' and strangers' conversational findings. *Journal of Nonverbal Behavior, 9,* 8–27.

Oller, K., & Eilers, R. E. (1988). The role of audition in infant babbling. *Child Development, 59,* 441–449.

Olson, J. M., Roese, N. J., & Zanna, M. P. (1996). Expectancies. In E. T. Higgins & A. W. Kruglanski (Eds.), *Social psychology: Handbook of basic principles* (pp. 211–238). New York: Guilford.

Omdahl, B. L. (1995). *Cognitive appraisal, emotion, and empathy.* Mahwah, NJ: Lawrence Erlbaum Associates.

Osborn, D. R. (1996). Beauty is as beauty does? Makeup and posture effects on physical attractiveness judgments. *Journal of Applied Social Psychology, 26,* 31–51.

Osmond, H. (1957). Function as the basis of psychiatric ward design. *Mental Hospitals, 8*(4), 23–32.

Oster, H., & Ekman, P. (1978). Facial behavior in child development. In W. A. Collins (Ed.), *Minnesota symposia on child psychology* (pp. 231–276). Hillsdale, NJ: Lawrence Erlbaum Associates.

Oster, H., Hegley, D., & Nagel, L. (1992). Adult judgments and fine-grained analysis of infant facial expressions: Testing the validity of a priori coding formulas. *Developmental Psychology, 28,* 1115–1131.

Owen, W. F. (1987). The verbal expression of love by women and men as a critical communication event in personal relationships. *Women's Studies in Communication, 10,* 15–24.

Owren, M. J., & Bachorowski, J. (2003). Reconsidering the evolution of nonlinguistic communication: The case of laughter. *Journal of Nonverbal Behavior, 27,* 183–200.

Paivio, A. (1971). *Imagery and verbal processes.* New York: Holt, Rinehart & Winston.

Palmer, M., T., & Simmons, K. B. (1995). Communicating intentions through nonverbal behaviors: Conscious and nonconscious encoding of liking. *Human Communication Research, 22,* 128–160.

Parham, I. A., Feldman, R. S., Oster, G. D., & Popoola, O. (1981). Intergenerational differences in nonverbal disclosure of deception. *Journal of Social Psychology, 113,* 261–269.

Park, H. S., Levine, T. R., McCornack, S. A., Morrison, K., & Ferrara, M. (2002). How people really detect lies. *Communication Monographs, 69,* 144–157.

Parkinson, B. (2005). Do facial movements express emotions or communicate motives? *Personality and Social Psychology Review, 9,* 278–311.

Parrill, F. (2008). The hands are part of the package: Gesture, common ground, and information packaging. In J. Newman & S. Rice (Eds.), *Empirical and experimental methods in cognitive/functional research* (pp. 1–17). Chicago: University of Chicago Press.

Parrott, R., & Le Poire, B. A. (1988, February). *The pediatrician's voice: Impact on the pediatrician-parent relationship.* Paper presented at the annual meeting of the Western States Communication Association, San Diego, CA.

Parsons, C. K., Liden, R. C., & Bauer, T. N. (2001). Personal perception in employment interviews. In M. London (Ed.), *How people evaluate others in organizations* (pp. 67–90). Mahwah, NJ: Lawrence Erlbaum Associates.

Paterson, M. (2006). Feel the presence: Technologies of touch and distance. *Environment & Planning D: Society and Space, 24,* 690–708.

Patterson, A. H. (1978). Territorial behavior and fear of crime in the elderly. *Environmental Psychology and Nonverbal Behavior, 2,* 131–144.

Patterson, M. L. (1976). An arousal model of interpersonal intimacy. *Psychological Review, 83,* 235–245.

Patterson, M. L. (1983). *Nonverbal behavior: A functional perspective.* New York: Springer-Verlag.

Patterson, M. L. (1985). Social influences and nonverbal exchange. In S. L. Ellyson & J. F. Dovidio (Eds.), *Power, dominance, and nonverbal behavior* (pp. 207–217). New York: Springer-Verlag.

Patterson, M. L. (1990). Functions of non-verbal behavior in social interaction. In H. Giles & W. P. Robinson (Eds.), *Handbook of language and social psychology* (pp. 101–120). Chichester, England: John Wiley & Sons.

Patterson, M. L. (1991). A functional approach to nonverbal exchange. In R. S. Feldman & B. Rimé (Eds.), *Fundamentals of nonverbal behavior* (pp. 458–495). Cambridge, England: Cambridge University Press.

Patterson, M. L., & Schaeffer, R. E. (1977). Effects of size and sex composition on interaction distance, participation, and satisfaction in small groups. *Small Group Behavior, 8,* 433–442.

Patterson, M. L., & Tubbs, M. E. (2005). Through a glass darkly: Effects of smiling and visibility on recognition and avoidance in passing encounters. *Western Journal of Communication, 69,* 219–231.

Patterson, M. L., Yuichi, I., Tubbs, M. E., Ansel, J., Masao, T., & Anson, J. (2007). Passing encounters East and West: Comparing Japanese and American pedestrian interactions. *Journal of Nonverbal Behavior, 31,* 155–166.

Patzer, G. L. (1985). *The physical attractiveness phenomena.* New York: Plenum.

Pawlowski, B., Dunbar, R. I. M., & Lipowicz, A. (2000). Tall men have more reproductive success. *Nature, 403,* 156.

Pearce, W. B. (2005). The coordinated management of meaning (CMM). In W. B. Gudykunst (Ed.), *Theorizing about intercultural communication* (pp. 35–54). Thousand Oaks, CA: Sage.

Pearce, W. B., & Brommel, B. J. (1972). Vocalic communication in persuasion. *Quarterly Journal of Speech, 58,* 298–306.

Peck, J., & Childers, T. L. (2003). To have and to hold: The influence of haptic information on product judgments. *Journal of Marketing, 67,* 35–48.

Peck, J., & Childers, T. L. (2006). If I touch it I have to have it: Effects of need for touch on impulse purchasing. *Journal of Business Research, 59,* 765–769.

Peck, J., & Wiggins, J. (2006). It just feels good: Customers' affective response to touch and its influence on persuasion. *Journal of Marketing, 70,* 56–69.

Pei, M. (1965). *The story of language* (2nd ed). Philadelphia: Lippincott.

Pellegrini, R. J. (1973). The virtue of hairiness. *Psychology Today, 6,* 14.

Pellegrini, R. J., Schauss, A. G., & Miller, M. E. (1978). Room color and aggression in a criminal detention holding cell: A test of the "tranquilizing pink" hypothesis. *Journal of Orthomolecular Psychiatry, 10,* 174–181.

Pendry, L. F., & Macrae, C. N. (1994). Stereotypes and mental life: The case of the motivated but thwarted tactician. *Journal of Experimental Social Psychology, 30,* 303–325.

Pennebaker, J. W., Rimé, B., & Blankenship, V. E. (1996). Stereotype of emotional expressiveness of northerners and southerners: A cross-cultural test of Montesquieu's hypothesis. *Journal of Personality and Social Psychology, 70,* 372–380.

Perper, T. (1985). *Sex signals: The biology of love.* Philadelphia: ISI Press.

Perper, T., & Weis, D. L. (1987). Proceptive and rejective strategies of U.S. and Canadian college women. *Journal of Sex Research, 23,* 455–480.

Perrett, D. I., Burt, D. M., Penton-Voak, I. S., Lee, K. J., Rowland, D. A., & Edwards, R. (1999). Symmetry and human facial attractiveness. *Evolution and Human Behavior, 20,* 295–307.

Perrett, D. I., May, K. A., & Yoshikawa, S. (1994). Facial shape and judgments of female attractiveness. *Nature, 368,* 239–242.

Perry, B. D. (2002). Childhood experience and the expression of genetic potential: What childhood neglect tells us about nature and nurture. *Brain and Mind, 3,* 79–100.

Peterson, A. M., Cline, R. J. W., Foster, T. S., Penner, L. A., Parrott, R. L., Keller, C. M., Naughton, M. C., Taub, J. W., Ruckdeschel, J. C., & Albrecht, T. L. (2007). Parents' interpersonal distance and touch behavior and child pain and distress during painful pediatric oncology procedures. *Journal of Nonverbal Behavior, 31,* 79–97.

Petronio, S. (1991). Communication boundary management: A theoretical model of managing disclosure of private information between marital couples. *Communication Theory, 1,* 311–335.

Pettit, C. S., Bakshi, A., Dodge, K. A., & Coie, J. D. (1990). The emergence of social dominance in young boys' play groups: Developmental differences and behavioral correlates. *Developmental Psychology, 26,* 1017–1025.

Petty, R. E., & Wegener, D. T. (1998). Attitude change. In D. T. Gilbert, S. T. Fiske, & G. Lindzey (Eds.), *Handbook of social psychology* (4th ed., Vol. 1, pp. 323–390). New York: Oxford University Press.

Petty, R. E., Wells, G. L., Heesacker, M., Brock, T. C., & Cacioppo, J. T. (1983). The effects of recipient posture on persuasion: A cognitive response analysis. *Personality and Social Psychology Bulletin, 9,* 209–222.

Philipsen, G. (1992). *Speaking culturally: Explorations in social communication.* Albany: State University of New York Press.

Philpott, J. S. (1983). *The relative contribution to meaning of verbal and nonverbal channels of communication: A meta-analysis.* Unpublished master's thesis, University of Nebraska.

Piaget, J. (1932). *The moral judgment of the child.* New York: Harcourt, Brace & World.

Piaget, J. (1981). Time perception in children. In J. T. Fraser (Ed.), *The voices of time* (2nd ed., pp. 202–216). Amherst: University of Massachusetts Press.

Pierce, C. A. (1996). Body height and romantic attraction: A meta-analytic test of the male-taller norm. *Social Behavior and Personality, 24,* 143–149.

Pierrehumbert, J., Bent, T., Munson, B., Bradlow, A. R., & Bailey, M. (2004). The influence of sexual orientation on vowel production. *Journal of the Acoustical Society of America, 116,* 1905–1908.

Pika, S., Nicoladis, E., & Marentette, P. F. (2006). A cross-cultural study on the use of gestures: Evidence for cross-linguistic transfer? *Bilingualism: Language and Cognition, 9,* 319–327.

Pinaire-Reed, J. A. (1979). Interpersonal attraction: Fashionability and perceived similarity. *Perceptual and Motor Skills, 48,* 571–576.

Pisano, M. D., Wall, S. M., & Foster, A. (1986). Perceptions of nonreciprocal touch in romantic relationships. *Journal of Nonverbal Behavior, 10,* 29–40.

Pitcairn, T. K., & Eibl-Eibesfeldt, I. (1976). Concerning the evolution of nonverbal communication in man. In M. E. Hahn & E. C. Simmel (Eds.), *Communicative behavior and evolution* (pp. 81–113). New York: Academic Press.

Pittam, J., & Scherer, K. R. (1993). Vocal expression and communication of emotion. In M. Lewis & J. M. Haviland (Eds.), *Handbook of emotions* (pp. 185–197). New York: Guildford Press.

Pittenger, R. E., Hockett, C. F., & Danehy, J. J. (1960). *The first five minutes.* Ithaca, NY: Martineau.

Planalp, S. (1999). *Communicating emotion: Social, moral, and cultural processes.* New York: Cambridge University Press.

Planalp, S. (2008). Varieties of emotional cues in everyday life. In L. K. Guerrero & M. L. Hecht (Eds.), *The nonverbal communication reader: Classic and contemporary readings* (pp. 397–401). Long Grove, IL: Waveland Press.

Planalp, S., DeFrancisco, V. L., & Rutherford, D. (1996). Varieties of cues to emotion in naturally occurring situations. *Cognition and Emotion, 10,* 137–153.

Planalp, S., & Tracy, K. (1980). Not to change the topic but . . .: A cognitive approach to the management of conversation. In D. Nimmo (Ed.), *Communication yearbook 4* (pp. 237–258). New Brunswick, NJ: Transaction.

Ploog, D. W. (1995). Mutualities in dialogue in nonhuman primate communication. In I. Markovà, C. F. Graumann, & K. Foppa (Eds.), *Mutualities in dialogue* (pp. 27–57). Cambridge, England: Cambridge University Press.

Ploog, D. W. (2003). The place of the triune brain in psychiatry. *Physiology and Behavior, 79,* 487–493.

Poggi, I. (2001–2). Towards the alphabet and the lexicon of gesture, gaze and touch. In P. Bouissac (Ed.), *Multimodality of human communication: Theories, problems and applications.* Virtual Symposium. http://www.semioticon.com/virtuals/index.html.

Poggi, I. (2002a). From a typology of gestures to a procedure for gesture production. In I.Wachsmuth & T. Sowa (Eds.), *Gesture and sign language in human-computer interaction* (pp. 158–168). Berlin: Springer.

Poggi, I. (2002b). Mind markers. In M. Rector, I. Poggi, & N. Trigo (Eds.), *Gestures, meaning and use.* Porto: Universidad Fernando Pessoa.

Poggi, I. (2002c). Symbolic gestures: The case of the gestionary. *Gesture, 2,* 71–98.

Poggi, I., & Chirico, R. (1998). The meanings of smile. In S. Santi, B. Guaitella, C. Cavé, & G. Konopczynski (Eds.), *Oralité et gestualité, communication multimodale, interaction* (pp. 159–164). Paris: L'Harmattan.

Poggi, I., & Magno Caldognetto, E. (1997). *Mani che parlano.* Padova: Unipress.

Pogue, L. L., & AhYun, K. (2006). The effect of teacher nonverbal immediacy and credibility on student motivation and affective learning. *Communication Education, 55,* 331–344.

Pointer, M. R., & Attridge, G. G. (1998). The number of discernible colours. *Color Research and Application, 23,* 52–54.

Porter, C. P. (1991). Social reasons for skin tone preferences of black school-age children. *American Journal of Orthopsychiatry, 61,* 149–154.

Porter, R. H., Cernock, J. M., & McLaughlin, F. J. (1983). Maternal recognition of neonates through olfactory cues. *Physiology and Behavior, 30,* 151–154.

Porter, R. H., & Moore, J. D. (1981). Human kin recognition by olfactory cues. *Physiology and Behavior, 27,* 493–495.

Porter, T., & Mikellides, B. (1976). *Color for architecture.* New York: Van Nostrand Reinhold.

Posner, M. I., Nissen, M. J., & Klein, R. M. (1976). Visual dominance: An information-processing account of its origins and significance. *Psychological Review, 83,* 157–171.

Powell, G. N., & Butterfield, D. A. (1989). The "good manager": Did androgyny fare better in the 1980s? *Group & Organization Management, 14,* 216–233.

Poyatos, F. (1991). Paralinguistic qualifiers: Our many voices. *Language and Communication, 11,* 181–195.

Poyatos, F. (1993). *Paralanguage: A linguistic and interdisciplinary approach to interactive speech and sounds.* Amsterdam: John Benjamins.

Prager, K. J. (1995). *The psychology of intimacy.* New York: Guilford.

Prager, K. J. (2000). Intimacy in personal relationships. In C. Hendrick & S. S. Hendrick (Eds.), *Close relationships: A sourcebook* (pp. 229–242). Thousand Oaks, CA: Sage.

Prager, K. J., & Roberts, L. J. (2004). Deep intimate connection: Self and intimacy in couple relationships. In D. J. Mashek & A. P. Aron (Eds.), *Handbook of closeness and intimacy* (pp. 43–60). Mahwah, NJ: Lawrence Erlbaum Associates.

Prescott, J. W. (1971). Early somatosensory deprivation as an ontogenetic process in abnormal development of the brain and behavior. In I. E. Goldsmith & J. Morr-Jankowski (Eds.), *Medical primatology* (pp. 356–375). New York: S. Karger.

Purcell, A. T. (1986). Environmental perception and affect: A schema discrepancy model. *Environment and Behavior, 18,* 3–30.

Raines, R. S., Hechtman, S. B., & Rosenthal, R. (1990a). Nonverbal behavior and gender as determinants of physical attractiveness. *Journal of Nonverbal Behavior, 14,* 253–267.

Raines, R. S., Hechtman, S. B., & Rosenthal, R. (1990b). Physical attractiveness of face and voice: Effects of positivity, dominance, and sex. *Journal of Applied Social Psychology, 20,* 1558–1578.

Ramsey, S. J. (1976). Prison codes. *Journal of Communication, 26,* 39–45.

Ramsey, S. J. (1981). The kinesics of femininity in Japanese women. *Language Sciences, 3,* 104–123.

Rane, T. R., & Draper, T. W. (1995). Negative evaluations of men's nurturant touching of young children. *Psychological Reports, 76,* 811–818.

Rapoport, A. (1982). *The meaning of the built environment: A nonverbal communication approach.* Beverly Hills, CA: Sage.

Rapoport, A. (1990). *The meaning of the built environment: A nonverbal communication approach* (2nd ed.). Tucson: University of Arizona Press.

Ray, G. B. (1986). Vocally cued personality prototypes: An implicit personality theory. *Communication Monographs, 53,* 266–276.

Ray, G. B., & Floyd, K. (2000, May). *Nonverbal expressions of liking and disliking in initial interaction: Encoding and decoding perspectives.* Paper presented at the annual meeting of the Eastern States Communication Association, Pittsburgh, PA.

Ray, R., & Schmitt, J. (2007). *No-vacation nation.* Washington, DC: Center for Economic and Policy Research.

Reddy, D. M., Baum, A., Fleming, R., & Aiello, J. R. (1981). Mediation of social density by coalition formation. *Journal of Applied Social Psychology, 11,* 529–537.

Reed, C. (1981). *The impact of consistent-inconsistent combinations of visual and verbal cues on communication of empathy and genuineness in the therapeutic situation.* Unpublished doctoral dissertation. Texas Tech University.

Regan, P. C., Jerry, D., Narvaez, M., & Johnson, D. (1999). Public displays of affection among Asian and Latino heterosexual couples. *Psychological Reports, 84,* 2101–1202.

Reid, A., Lancuba, V., & Morrow, B. (1997). Clothing style and formation of first impressions. *Perceptual and Motor Skills, 84,* 237–238.

Reifman, A. S., Larrick, R. P., & Fein, S. (1991). Temper and temperature on the diamond: The heat-aggression relationship in major league baseball. *Personality and Social Psychology Bulletin, 17,* 580–585.

Reinert, J. (1971). What your sense of time tells you. *Science Digest, 69,* 8–12.

Reis, H. T., Wilson, I. M., Monestere, C., Bernstein, C., Clark, K., Seidl, E., Franco, M., Gioioso, E., Freeman, L., & Radoane, K. (1990). What is smiling is beautiful and good. *European Journal of Social Psychology, 20,* 259–267.

Reisenzein, R., Bordgen, S., Holtbernd, T., & Matz, D. (2006). Evidence for strong dissociation between emotion and facial displays: The case of surprise. *Journal of Personality and Social Psychology, 91,* 295–315.

Reite, M. (1990). Touch, attachment, and health: Is there a relationship? In K. E. Barnard & T. B. Brazelton (Eds.), *Touch: The foundation of experience: Full revised and expanded proceedings of Johnson & Johnson Pediatric Round Table X. Clinical infant reports* (pp. 195–225). Madison, CT: International Universities Press.

Remland, M. S. (1981). Developing leadership skills in nonverbal communication: A situational perspective. *Journal of Business Communication, 18,* 17–29.

Remland, M. S. (1982, November). *Leadership impressions and nonverbal communication in a superior subordinate situation.* Paper presented at the annual meeting of the Speech Communication Association, Louisville, KY.

Remland, M. S., Jones, T. S., & Brinkman, H. (1995). Interpersonal distance, body orientation, and touch: Effects of culture, gender, and age. *Journal of Social Psychology, 135,* 281–297.

Renninger, L., Wade, T. J., & Grammer, K. (2004). Getting that female glance: Patterns and consequences

of male non-verbal behavior in courtship contexts. *Evolution and Human Behavior, 25,* 416–431.

Rhodes, G., Harwood, K., Yoshikawa, S., Nishitani, M., & McLean, I. (2002). The attactiveness of average faces: Cross-cultural evidence and possible biological basis. In G. Rhodes & L. A. Zebrowitz (Eds.), *Facial attractiveness: Evolutionary, cognitive, and social perspectives* (pp. 239–259). Westport, CT: Ablex.

Rhodes, G., Proffitt, F., Grady, J. M., & Sumich, A. (1998). Facial symmetry and the perception of beauty. *Psychonomic Bulletin and Review, 5,* 659–669.

Rhodes, G., & Zebrowitz, L. A. (Eds.). (2002). *Facial attractiveness: Evolutionary, cognitive and social perspectives.* Westport, CT: Ablex.

Richards, J. M., & Gross, J. J. (1999). Composure at any cost? The cognitive consequences of emotional suppression. *Personality and Social Psychology Bulletin, 25,* 1033–1044.

Richmond, V. P., McCroskey, J. C., & Payne, S. K. (1987). *Nonverbal behavior in interpersonal relations.* Englewood Cliffs, NJ: Prentice-Hall.

Riedl, B. I. M. (1990). Morphologisch-metrische merkmale des männlichen und weiblichen partnerleitbildes in ihrer bedeutung für die wahl des ehegatten. [Morphological-metric attributes of male or female partner imagery and their significance for choosing a spouse.] *Homo, 41,* 72–85.

Riggio, R. E. (1986). Assessment of basic social skills. *Journal of Personality and Social Psychology, 51,* 649–660.

Riggio, R. E. (1992). Social interaction skills and nonverbal behavior. In R. S. Feldman (Ed.), *Applications of nonverbal behavioral theories and research* (pp. 3–30). Hillsdale, NJ: Lawrence Erlbaum Associates.

Riggio, R. E., & Friedman, H. S. (1982). The interrelationships of self-monitoring factors, personality traits, and nonverbal skills. *Journal of Nonverbal Behavior, 7,* 33–45.

Riggio, R. E., Tucker, J., & Throckmorton, D. (1987). Social skills and deception ability. *Personality and Social Psychology Bulletin, 13,* 568–577.

Riggio, R. E., Tucker, J., Widaman, K. F. (1987). Verbal and nonverbal cues as mediators of deception ability. *Journal of Nonverbal Behavior, 11,* 126–145.

Riggio, R. E., Watring, K., & Throckmorton, B. (1993). Social skills, social support, and psychosocial adjustment. *Personality and Individual Differences, 15,* 275–280.

Rimé, B., & Schiaratura, L. (1991). Gesture and speech. In R. S. Feldman & B. Rimé (Eds.), *Fundamentals of nonverbal behavior* (pp. 239–281). Cambridge, England: Cambridge University Press.

Rinn, W. E. (1991). Neuropsychology of facial expression. In R. S. Feldman & B. Rimé (Eds.), *Fundamentals of nonverbal communication* (pp. 3–30). Cambridge, England: Cambridge University Press.

Rintel, E. S., & Pittam, J. (1997). Strangers in a strange land: Interaction management on Internet relay chat. *Human Communication Research, 23,* 507–534.

Ritts, V., Patterson, M. L., & Tubbs, M. E. (1992). Expectations, impressions, and judgments of physically attractive students: A review. *Review of Educational Research, 62,* 413–426.

Robinson, J. D. (2008). Nonverbal communication in doctor-patient relationships. In L. K. Guerrero & M. L. Hecht (Eds.), *The nonverbal communication reader: Classic and contemporary readings* (3rd ed., pp. 384–394). Long Grove, IL: Waveland Press.

Robinson, W. P. (1996). *Deceit, delusion, and detection.* Thousand Oaks: Sage.

Robson, K. S. (1967). The role of eye-to-eye contact in maternal-infant attachment. *Journal of Psychology and Psychiatry, 8,* 13–25.

Rockwell, P. (2000). Lower, slower, louder: Vocal cues of sarcasm. *Journal of Psycholinguistic Research, 29,* 83–495.

Rohles, F. H. (1971). Thermal sensations of sedentary man in moderate temperatures. *Human Factors, 13,* 553–560.

Roland, R. C. (1993). What colors are your school supplies? *Direct Marketing,* 60–62.

Rollins, B. C., & Bahr, S. J. (1976). A theory of power relationships in marriage. *Journal of Marriage and the Family, 38,* 619–627.

Roloff, M. E., & Cloven, D. H. (1990). The chilling effect in interpersonal relationships: The reluctance to speak one's mind. In D. D. Cahn (Ed.), *Intimates in conflict: A communication perspective* (pp. 49–76). Hillsdale, NJ: Lawrence Erlbaum Associates.

Rosch, R. (1977). Human categorization. In N. Warren (Ed.), *Studies in cross-cultural psychology* (pp. 1–49). San Diego: Academic Press.

Rosch, R. (1978). Principles of categorization. In E. Rosch & B. B. Lloyd (Eds.), *Cognition and categorization* (pp. 27–48). Hillsdale, NJ: Lawrence Erlbaum Associates.

Rose, S. M., & Zand, D. (2002). Lesbian dating and courtship from young adulthood to midlife. *Lesbian Studies, 6,* 85–109.

Roseman, I. J. (1984). Cognitive determinants of emotion: A structural theory. In P. Shaver (Ed.), *Emotions, relationships, and health* (pp. 11–36). Beverly Hills, CA: Sage.

Rosenberg, S. W., Kahn, S., & Tran, T. (1991). Creating a political image: Shaping appearance and manipulating the vote. *Political Behavior, 13,* 345–367.

Rosenblatt, P. C. (1974). Cross-cultural perspective on attraction. In T. L. Huston (Ed.), *Foundations of interpersonal attraction* (pp. 79–95). New York: Academic Press.

Rosenbloom, S. (2006, November 16). In certain circles, two is a crowd. *The New York Times, Late Edition,* vol. 156, pp. G1, G10.

Rosenfeld, H. M. (1978). Conversational control functions of nonverbal behavior. In A. W. Siegman & S. Feldstein (Eds.), *Nonverbal behavior and communication* (pp. 291–328). Hillsdale, NJ: Lawrence Erlbaum Associates.

Rosenfeld, L. B., Kartus, S., & Ray, C. (1976). Body accessibility revisited. *Journal of Communication, 26,* 27–30.

Rosenfeld, L. B., & Plax, T. G. (1977). Clothing as communication. *Journal of Communication, 27,* 24–31.

Rosenstein, D., & Oster, J. (1988). Differential facial response to four basic tastes in newborns. *Child Development, 59,* 1555–1568.

Rosenthal, R. (Ed.). (1979). *Skill in nonverbal communication: Individual differences.* Cambridge, MA: Oelgeschlager, Gunn & Hain.

Rosenthal, R., Hall, J. A., DiMatteo, M. R., Rogers, P. L., & Archer, D. (1979). *Sensitivity to nonverbal communication: The PONS test.* Baltimore: Johns Hopkins University Press.

Rosenthal, R., & Jacobson, L. (1968). *Pygmalion in the classroom: Teacher expectations and pupils' intellectual development.* New York: Holt, Rinehart & Winston.

Ross, E. D. (2000). Affective prosody and the aprosodias. In M. Mesulam (Ed.), *Principles of behavioral and cognitive neurology* (2nd ed., pp. 316–331). New York: Oxford University Press.

Roter, D. L., & Hall, J. A. (1992). *Doctors talking with patients/Patients talking with doctors: Improving communication in medical visits.* Westport, CT: Auburn House.

Roter, D. L., Hall, J. A., & Aoki, Y. (2002). Physician gender effects in medical communication: A meta-analytic review. *Journal of the American Medical Association, 288,* 756–764.

Roter, D. L., Hall, J. A., & Katz, N. R. (1987). Relations between physicians' behaviors and analogues patients' satisfaction, recall, and impressions. *Medical Care, 25,* 437–451.

Routasolo, P. (1999). Physical touch in nursing studies: A literature review. *Journal of Advanced Nursing, 30,* 843–850.

Rowatt, W. C., Cunningham, M. R., & Druen, P. B. (1999). Lying to get a date: The effect of facial physical attractiveness on the willingness to deceive prospective dating partners. *Journal of Social and Personal Relationships, 16,* 209–223.

Rowland-Morin, P. A., Burchard, K. W., Garb, J. L., & Coe, N. P. (1991). Influence of effective communication by surgery students on their oral examination scores. *Academic Medicine, 66,* 169–171.

Rubenstein, A. J., Langlois, J. H., & Roggman, L. A. (2002). What makes a face attractive and why: The role of averageness in defining facial beauty. In G. Rhodes & L. A. Zebrowitz (Eds.), *Facial attractiveness: Evolutionary, cognitive, and social perspectives* (pp. 1–33). Westport, CT: Ablex.

Rubin, Z. (1970). Measurement of romantic love. *Journal of Personality and Social Psychology, 16,* 265–273.

Rucker, M., Anderson, E., & Kangas, A. (1999). Clothing, power, and the workplace. In K. P. Johnson & S. J. Lennon (Eds.), *Appearance and power: Dress, body and culture* (pp. 59–77). New York: Berg.

Rucker, M., Taber, D., & Harrison, A. (1981). The effect of clothing variation on first impressions of female job applicants: What to wear when. *Social Behavior and Personality, 9,* 53–64.

Ruesch, J., & Kees, W. (1956). *Nonverbal communication: Notes on the visual perception of human relations.* Berkeley: University of California Press.

Russell, J. A. (1978). Evidence of convergent validity on the dimensions of affect. *Journal of Personality and Social Psychology, 36,* 1152–1168.

Russell, J. A. (1980). A circumplex model of affect. *Journal of Personality and Social Psychology, 39,* 1161–1178.

Russell, J. A. (1994). Is there universal recognition of emotion from facial expressions? A review of the cross-cultural studies. *Psychological Bulletin, 115,* 102–141.

Russell, M. J. (1976). Human olfactory communication. *Nature, 260,* 520–522.

Russell, M. J., Switz, G. M., & Thompson, K. (1980). Olfactory influences on the human menstrual cycle. *Pharmacology Biochemistry and Behavior, 13,* 737–738.

Rutter, D. R., Pennington, D. C., Dewey, M. E., & Swain, J. (1984). Eye contact as a chance product of individual looking: Implications for the intimacy model of Argyle and Dean. *Journal of Nonverbal Behavior, 8,* 250–258.

Rutter, D. R., & Stephenson, G. M. (1979). The functions of looking: Effects of friendship on gaze. *British Journal of Social and Clinical Psychology, 18,* 203–205.

Rymer, R (1994). *Genie: A scientific tragedy.* New York: HarperCollins.

Ryu, K., & Jang, S. C. S. (2007). The effect of environmental perceptions on behavioral intentions through emotions: The case of upscale restaurants. *Journal of Hospitality and Tourism Research, 31,* 56–72.

Saarni, C. (1993). Socialization of emotion. In M. Lewis & J. M. Haviland (Eds.), *Handbook of emotion* (pp. 435–446). New York: Guilford Press.

Sachs, F. (1988). The intimate sense. *Sciences, 28*(1), 28–34.

Sachs, J., Lieberman, P., & Erickson, D. (1973). Anatomical and cultural determinants of male and female speech. In R. W. Shuy & R. W. Fasold (Eds.), *Language attitudes: Current trends and prospects* (pp. 74–84). Washington, DC: Georgetown University Press.

Sacks, H., Schegloff, E., & Jefferson, G. (1974). A simplest systematics for the organization of turn-taking for conversation. *Language, 50,* 696–735.

Sacks, O. W. (1985). *The man who mistook his wife for a hat and other clinical tales.* New York: Summit.

Sadalla, E. K. (1978). Population size, structural differentiation, and human behavior. *Environment and Behavior, 10,* 271–291.

Sadalla, E. K., Kenrick, D. T., & Vershure, B. (1987). Dominance and heterosexual attraction. *Journal of Personality and Social Psychology, 52,* 730–738.

Sadalla, E. K., & Sheets, V. L. (1993). Symbolism in building materials: Self-presentational and cognitive components. *Environment and Behavior, 25,* 155–180.

Sadalla, E. K., Vershure, B., & Burroughs, J. (1987). Identity symbolism in housing. *Environment and Behavior, 19,* 569–587.

Sagrestano, L. M., Heavey, C. L., & Christensen, A. C. (2006). Individual differences versus social structural approaches to explaining demand-withdraw and social influence behaviors. In K. Dindia & D. J. Canary (Eds.), *Sex differences and similarities in communication* (2nd ed., pp. 379–395). Mahwah, NJ: Lawrence Erlbaum Associates.

Sallnas, E., Rassmus-Grohn, K., & Sjostrom, C. (2000). Supporting presence in collaborative environments. *ACM Transactions on Computer-Human Interaction.* New York: AMC.

Salovey, P., & Mayer, J. D. (1990). Emotional intelligence. *Imagination, Cognition, and Personality, 9,* 185–211.

Sapir, E. (1949). *Selected writings of Edward Sapir in language, culture and personality.* Berkeley: University of California Press.

Scanlon, B. (1985). Race differences in selection of cheese color. *Perceptual and Motor Skills, 61,* 314.

Schötz, S. (2003). Towards synthesis of speaker age: A perceptual study with natural, synthesized and resynthesized stimuli. *PHONUM, 9,* I–X.

Schachner, L., Field, T., Hernandez-Reif, M., Duarte, A., & Krasnegor, J. (1998). Atopic dermatitis symptoms decrease in children following massage therapy. *Pediatric Dermatology, 15,* 390–395.

Scheflen, A., & Scheflen, A. E. (1972). *Body language and the social order: Communication as behavior control.* Englewood Cliffs, NJ: Prentice-Hall.

Scheflen, A. E. (1964). The significance of posture in communication systems. *Psychiatry, 27,* 320–323.

Scheflen, A. E. (1965). Quasi-courtship behavior in psychotherapy. *Psychiatry, 28,* 245–257.

Scheflen, A. E. (1974). *How behavior means.* Garden City, NY: Anchor/Doubleday.

Schegloff, E., & Sacks, H. (1973). Opening up closings. *Semiotica, 8,* 289–327.

Scherer, K. R. (1978). Personality inference from voice quality: The loud voice of extroversion. *European Journal of Social Psychology, 8,* 467–487.

Scherer, K. R. (1979a). Nonlinguistic vocal indicators of emotion and psychopathology. In C. E. Izard (Ed.), *Emotions in personality and psychopathology* (493–529). New York: Plenum.

Scherer, K. R. (1979b). Voice and speech correlates of perceived social influence in simulated juries. In H. Giles & R. N. St. Clair (Eds.), *Language and social psychology* (pp. 88–120). Oxford, England: Blackwell.

Scherer, K. R. (1981). Vocal indicators of stress. In J. K. Darby (Ed.), *Speech evaluation in psychiatry* (pp. 171–187). New York: Grune & Stratton.

Scherer, K. R. (1982). Methods of research on vocal communication: Paradigms and parameters. In K. R. Scherer & P. Ekman (Eds.), *Handbook of methods in nonverbal behavior research* (pp. 136–198). Cambridge, England: Cambridge University Press.

Scherer, K. R. (1984). Emotion as a multicomponent process: A model and some cross-cultural data. *Review of Personality and Social Psychology, 5,* 37–63.

Scherer, K. R. (1986). Vocal affect expression: A review and a model for future research. *Psychological Bulletin, 99,* 143–165.

Scherer, K. R. (2003). Vocal communication of emotion: A review of research paradigms. *Speech Communication, 40,* 227–256.

Scherer, K. R., & Ekman, P. (2005). Methodological issues in studying nonverbal behavior. In J. A. Harrigan, R. Rosenthal, & K. R. Scherer (Eds.), *The new handbook of nonverbal behavior research* (pp. 471–512). New York: Oxford University Press.

Scherer, K. R., & Oshinsky, J. S. (1977). Cue utilization in emotion attribution from auditory stimuli. *Motivation and Emotion, 1,* 331–346.

Scherer, K. R., Scherer, U., Hall, J. A., & Rosenthal, R. (1977). Differential attribution of personality based on multi-channel presentation of verbal and nonverbal cues. *Psychological Research, 39,* 221–247.

Scherer, K. R., & Wallbott, H. G. (1994). Evidence for universality and cultural variation of differential emotion response patterning. *Journal of Personality and Social Psychology, 66,* 310–328.

Schiefelbein, J. S. (2006). *Conversational involvement in CMC: Signifiers and emoticons in discussion boards.* Unpublished master's thesis, Arizona State University.

Schmid Mast, M. (2002). Dominance as expressed and inferred through speaking time: A meta-analysis. *Human Communication Research, 28,* 420–450.

Schmidt, K. L., Ambadar, Z., Cohn, J. F., & Reed, L. I. (2006). Movement differences between deliberate and spontaneous facial expressions: Zygomaticus major action in smiling. *Journal of Nonverbal Behavior, 30,* 37–52.

Schnall, S., & Laird, J. D. (2003). Keep smiling: Enduring effects of facial expressions and postures on emotional experience and memory. *Cognition and Emotion, 17,* 787–797.

Schwartz, B. (1968). The social psychology of privacy. *American Journal of Sociology, 73,* 741–752.

Schwartz, B. (1975). *Queuing and waiting: Studies in the social organization of access and delay.* Chicago: University of Chicago Press.

Schwartz, D. M., Thompson, M. G., & Johnson, C. L. (1982). Anorexia nervosa and bulimia: The sociocultural context. *International Journal of Eating Disorders, 1,* 20–36.

Schwartz, G., Izard, C. E., & Ansul, S. (1982, May). *Heart rate and facial response to novelty in 7- and 13-month-old infants.* Paper presented at the International Conference on Infant Studies, Austin, TX.

Scott, A. L. (1988). Human interaction and personal boundaries. *Journal of Psychosocial Nursing, 26,* 23–27.

Scott, A. L. (1994). *What exactly did you mean to say?* Unpublished manuscript, University of Arizona, Tucson.

Sebeok, T. A. (1964). Indiana University conference on paralinguistics and kinesics. In T. A. Sebeok, A. S. Hayes, & M. C. Bateson (Eds.), *Approaches to semiotics: Transactions of the Indiana University conference on paralinguistics and kinesics.* The Hague: Mouton.

Segrin, C. (1993). The effects of nonverbal behavior on outcomes of compliance-gaining attempts. *Communication Studies, 44,* 169–187.

Segrin, C. (1998). Interpersonal communication problems associated with depression and loneliness. In P. A. Andersen & L. K. Guerrero (Eds.), *Handbook of communication and emotion: Research, theory, applications, and contexts* (pp. 215–242). San Diego: Academic Press.

Shackelford, T. K. (1997). Perceptions of betrayal and the design of the mind. In J. A. Simpson & D. T. Kenrick (Eds.), *Evolutionary social psychology* (pp. 73–108). Hillsdale, NJ: Lawrence Erlbaum Associates.

Shackelford, T. K., & Larsen, R. J. (1997). Facial asymmetry as indicator of psychological, emotional, and physiological distress. *Journal of Personality and Social Psychology, 72,* 456–466.

Shaffer, D. R., & Sadowski, C. (1975). This table is mine: Respect for marked barroom tables as a function of gender of spatial marker and desirability of locale. *Sociometry, 38,* 408–419.

Shahani, C., & Plumitallo, D. (1993, August). *The influence of physical attractiveness and gender on disciplinary decisions.* Paper presented at the annual convention of the American Psychological Society, Chicago, IL.

Shahani-Denning, C. (2003). Physical attractiveness bias in hiring: What is beautiful is good. *Hofstra Horizons* (Spring Issue, pp. 14–17).

Shapiro, J. G. (1968). Responsivity to facial and linguistic cues. *Journal of Communication, 18,* 11–17.

Shaver, P. R., Schwartz, J., Kirson, D., & O'Connor, C. (1987). Emotion knowledge: Further explorations of a prototype approach. *Journal of Personality and Social Psychology, 52,* 1061–1086.

Sheldon, W. H. (1940). *The varieties of human physique: An introduction to constitutional psychology.* New York: Harper & Row.

Sheldon, W. H., Stevens, S. S., & Tucker, S. (1942). *The varieties of temperament: A psychology of constitutional differences.* New York: Harper & Row.

Shepard, C. A., Giles, H., & Le Poire, B. A. (2001). Communication accommodation theory. In W. P. Robinson & H. Giles (Eds.,) *The new handbook of language and social psychology* (pp. 33–56). Chichester, England: John Wiley & Sons.

Sheppard, J. A., & Strathman, A. J. (1989). Attractiveness and height: The role of stature in dating preference, frequency of dating, and perceptions of attractiveness. *Personality and Social Psychology Bulletin, 15,* 617–627.

Shimoda, K., Argyle, M., & Ricci Bitti, P. (1978). The intercultural recognition of emotional expressions by three national racial groups: English, Italian, and Japanese. *European Journal of Social Psychology, 8,* 169–179.

Shotland, R. L., & Craig, J. M. (1988). Can men and women differentiate between friendly and sexually interested behavior? *Social Psychology Quarterly, 51,* 66–73.

Shotland, R. L., & Johnson, M. P. (1978). Bystander behavior and kinesics: The interaction between the helper and victim. *Environmental Psychology and Nonverbal Behavior, 2,* 181–190.

Shriberg, E. E. (2005). *Spontaneous speech: How people really talk, and why engineers should care.* Proc. Eurospeech, pp. 1781–1784, Lisbon. [Overview paper to accompany keynote address].

Shriberg, E., Bates, R., Stolcke, A., Taylor, P., Jurafsy, D., Ries, K., Cocaro, N., Martin, R., Meteer, M., & Van Ess-Dykema, C. (1998). Can prosody aid in automatic classification of dialog acts in conversational speech? *Language and Speech, 41,* 439–487.

Shute, B., & Wheldall, K. (1989). Pitch alterations in British motherese: Some preliminary acoustic data. *Journal of Child Language, 16,* 503–512.

Shuter, R. (1976). Proxemics and tactility in Latin America. *Journal of Communication, 26,* 46–52.

Shuter, R. (1977). A field study of nonverbal communication in Germany, Italy, and the United States. *Communication Monographs, 44,* 298–305.

Shuter, R. (1979). A study of nonverbal communication among Jews and Protestants. *Journal of Social Psychology, 109,* 31–41.

Siegman, A. W. (1978). The telltale voice: Nonverbal messages of verbal communication. In A. W. Siegman & S. Feldstein (Eds.), *Nonverbal behavior and communication* (pp. 183–243). Hillsdale, NJ: Lawrence Erlbaum Associates.

Siegman, A. W., & Pope, B. (1965). Effects of question specificity and anxiety producing messages on verbal fluency in the initial interview. *Journal of Personality and Social Psychology, 4,* 188–192.

Simonds, J. O. (1961). *Landscape architecture.* New York: McGraw-Hill.

Simpson, J. A., & Gangestad, S. W. (2001). Evolution and relationships: A call for integration. *Personal Relationships, 8,* 341–355.

Simpson, J. A., Gangestad, S. W., & Biek, M. (1993). Personality and nonverbal social behavior: An ethological perspective of relationship initiation. *Journal of Experimental Social Psychology, 29,* 434–461.

Simpson, J. A., Lerma, M., & Gangestad, S. W. (1990). Perception of physical attractiveness: Mechanisms involved in the maintenance of romantic relationships. *Journal of Personality and Social Psychology, 59,* 1192–1201.

Singh, D. (1993). Adaptive significance of waist-to-hip ratio and female physical attractiveness. *Journal of Personality and Social Psychology, 65,* 293–307.

Singh, D., & Luis, S. (1995). Ethnic and gender consensus for the effect of waist-to-hip ratio on judgments of women's attractiveness. *Human Nature, 6,* 51–65.

Singh, D., & Young, R. K. (1995). Body weight, waist-to-hip ratio, breasts, and hips: Role in judgments of female attractiveness and desirability for relationships. *Ethology and Sociobiology, 16,* 483–507.

Smith, B. L., Wasowicz, J., & Preston, J. (1987). Temporal characteristics of the speech of normal elderly adults. *Journal of Speech and Hearing Research, 30,* 522–529.

Smith, C. A., & Ellsworth, P. C. (1985). Patterns of cognitive appraisal in emotion. *Journal of Personality and Social Psychology, 48,* 813–838.

Smith, C. K., Polis, E., & Hadac, R. R. (1981). Characteristics of the initial medical interview associated with patient satisfaction and understanding. *The Journal of Family Practice, 12,* 283–288.

Smith, D. E., Gier, J. A., & Willis, F. N. (1982). Interpersonal touch and compliance with a marketing request. *Basic and Applied Social Psychology, 3,* 35–38.

Smith, D. L. (2004). *Why we lie: The evolutionary roots of deception and the unconscious mind.* New York: St. Martin's Griffin.

Smith, E. O. (1987). Deception and evolutionary biology. *Cultural Anthropology, 2,* 50–64.

Smith, H. J., Archer, D., & Costanzo, M. (1991). "Just a hunch": Accuracy and awareness in person perception. *Journal of Nonverbal Behavior, 15,* 3–18.

Smith, R. J., & Knowles, E. S. (1979). Affective and cognitive mediators of reactions to spatial invasions. *Journal of Experimental Social Psychology, 15,* 437–452.

Smith, W. J., Chase, J., & Lieblich, A. K. (1974). Tongue-showing: A facial display of humans and other primate species. *Semiotica, 11,* 201–246.

Smyth, R., Jacobs, G., & Rogers, H. (2003). Male voices and perceived sexual orientation: An experimental and theoretical approach. *Language in Society, 32,* 329–350.

Smythe, M., & Hess, J. A. (2005). Are student self-reports a valid method for measuring teacher nonverbal immediacy? *Communication Education, 54,* 170–179.

Soldat, A. S., Sinclair, R. C., & Mark, M. M. (1997). Color as an environmental processing cue: External affective cues can directly affect processing strategy without affecting mood. *Social Cognition, 15,* 55–71.

Solnick, S., & Schweitzer, M. E. (1999). The influence of physical attractiveness and gender on ultimatum game decisions. *Organizational Behavior and Human Decision Processes, 79,* 199–215.

Solomon, D. H., Knobloch, L. K., & Fitzpatrick, M. A. (2004). Relational power, marital schema, and decisions to withhold complaints: An investigation of the chilling effect of confrontation in marriage. *Communication Studies, 55,* 146–167.

Sommer, R. (1959). Studies in personal space. *Sociometry, 22,* 247–260.

Sommer, R. (1966). Man's proximate environment. *Journal of Social Issues, 22,* 59–70.

Sommer, R. (1969). *Personal space: The behavioral basis of design.* Englewood Cliffs, NJ: Prentice-Hall.

Sommer, R. (1970). The ecology of privacy. In H. M. Proshansky, W. H. Ittelson, & L. G. Rivlin (Eds.), *Environmental psychology: Man and his physical setting* (pp. 256–266). New York: Holt, Rinehart & Winston.

Sommer, R. (1974). *Tight spaces: Hard architecture and how to humanize it.* Englewood Cliffs, NJ: Prentice-Hall.

Sommers, S. (1984). Reported emotions and conventions of emotionality among college students. *Journal of Personality and Social Psychology, 46,* 207–215.

Spitz, R. A. (1945). Hospitalism: An inquiry into the genesis of psychiatric conditions in early childhood. *Psychoanalytic Study of the Child, 1,* 53–74.

Spitz, R. A. (1946). Hospitalism: A follow-up report on investigation described in Volume 1, 1945. *Psychoanalytic Study of the Child, 1,* 113–117.

Sprecher, S. (1989). The importance to males and females of physical attractiveness, earning potential, and expressiveness in initial attraction. *Sex Roles, 12,* 449–462.

Sprecher, S., & Regan, P. C. (2002). Liking some things (in some people) more than others: Partner preferences in romantic relationships and friendships. *Journal of Social and Personal Relationships, 19,* 463–481.

Sroufe, L. A. (1984). The organization of emotional development. In K. R. Scherer & P. Ekman (Eds.), *Approaches to emotion* (pp. 109–128). Hillsdale, NJ: Lawrence Erlbaum Associates.

Stafford, L., & Canary, D. J. (1991). Maintenance strategies and romantic relationship type, gender and relational characteristics. *Journal of Social and Personal Relationships, 8,* 217–242.

Staley, C. C., & Cohen, J. L. (1988). Communicator style and social style: Similarities and differences between the sexes. *Communication Quarterly, 36,* 192–202.

Stamp, G. H., & Knapp, M. L. (1990). The construct of intent in interpersonal communication. *Quarterly Journal of Speech, 76,* 282–299.

Stansfeld, S. A., Haines, M. M., & Brown, B. (2000). Noise and health in the urban environment. *Reviews on Environmental Health, 15,* 43–82.

Stea, D. (1965). Territoriality, the interior aspect: Space, territory, and human movements. *Landscape, 15,* 13–17.

Stelzner, M. A., & Egland, K. L. (1995, February). *Perceived understanding, nonverbal communication, relational satisfaction, and relational stage.* Paper presented at the annual meeting of the Western States Communication Association, Portland, OR.

Stenberg, C., Campos, J., & Emde, R. (1983). The facial expression of anger in seven month old infants. *Child Development, 54,* 178–184.

Stern, D. N. (1980). *The first relationship: Mother and infant.* Cambridge, MA: Harvard University Press.

Stier, D. S., & Hall, J. A. (1984). Gender differences in touch: An empirical and theoretical review. *Journal of Personality and Social Psychology, 47,* 440–459.

Stiff, J. B., Kim, H., & Ramesh, C. (1992). Truth biases and aroused suspicion in relational deception. *Communication Research, 19,* 326–345.

Stiff, J. B., Miller, G. R., Sleight, C., Mongeau, P. A., Garlick, R., & Rogan, R. (1989). Explanations for visual cue primacy in judgments of honesty and deceit. *Journal of Personality and Social Psychology, 56,* 555–564.

Stine, E. A., Wingfield, A., & Myers, S. D. (1990). Age differences in processing information from television news: The effects of bisensory augmentation. *Journal of Gerontology, 45,* 1–8.

Stinson, L., & Ickes, W. (1992). Empathic accuracy in the interactions of male friends versus male strangers. *Journal of Personality and Social Psychology, 62,* 787–797.

Stokols, D., Ohlig, W., & Resnick, S. M. (1978). Perception of residential crowding, classroom experiences, and student health. *Human Ecology, 6,* 233–252.

Strömwall, L. A., & Granhag, P. A. (2003). How to detect deception? Arresting the beliefs of police officers, prosecutors, and judges. *Psychology, Crime & Law, 9,* 19–36.

Strack, F., Martin, L. L., & Stepper, S. (1988). Inhibiting and facilitating conditions of facial expressions: A nonobtrusive test of the facial feedback hypothesis. *Journal of Personality and Social Psychology, 54,* 768–776.

Streeck, J. (1994). Gestures as communication II: The audience as co-author. *Research on Language and Social Interaction, 27,* 239–267.

Street, R. L. (1990). The communicative functions of paralanguage and prosody. In H. Giles & W. P. Robinson (Eds.), *Handbook of language and social psychology* (pp. 121–140). Chichester, England: John Wiley & Sons.

Street, R. L., & Brady, R. M. (1982). Speech rate acceptance ranges as a factor of evaluative domain, listener speech rate, and communication context. *Communication Monographs, 49,* 290–308.

Street, R. L., Brady, R. M., & Putman, W. B. (1983). The influence of speech rate stereotypes and rate similarity on listeners' evaluations of speakers. *Journal of Language and Social Psychology, 2,* 37–56.

Street, R. L., & Giles, H. (1982). Speech accommodation theory: A social cognitive approach to language and speech behavior. In M. Roloff & C. Berger (Eds.), *Social cognition and communication* (pp. 193–226). Beverly Hills, CA: Sage.

Suedfeld, P., Bochner, S., & Matas, C. (1971). Petitioners' attire and petition signing by peace demonstrators: A field experiment. *Journal of Applied Social Psychology, 1,* 278–283.

Sullins, E. S. (1989). Perceptual salience as a function of nonverbal expressiveness. *Personality and Social Psychology Bulletin, 15,* 584–595.

Sullivan, M., & Lewis, M. (1989). Emotion and cognition in infancy: Facial expressions during contingency learning. *International Journal of Behavioral Development, 12,* 221–237.

Sundaram, D. S., & Webster, C. (2000). The role of nonverbal communication in service encounters. *Journal of Services Marketing, 14,* 378–391.

Sundstrom, E., & Sundstrom, M. G. (1977). Personal space invasions: What happens when the invader asks permission? *Environmental Psychology and Nonverbal Behavior, 2,* 76–82.

Swets, J. A. (1996). *Signal detection theory and ROC analysis in psychology and diagnostics.* Mahwah, NJ: Lawrence Erlbaum Associates.

Sybers, R., & Roach, M. E. (1962). Clothing and human behavior. *Journal of Home Economics, 54,* 184–187.

Tak, J., Kaid, L. L., & Khang, H. (2007). The reflection of cultural parameter on videostyles of televised political spots in the U.S. and Korea. *Asian Journal of Communication, 17,* 58–77.

Talese, G. (1969). *The kingdom and the power.* New York: World Publishing.

Tate, J. C., & Shelton, B. L. (2008). Personality correlates of tattooing and body piercing in a college sample: Kids are alright. *Personality and Individual Differences, 45,* 281–285.

Taylor, R., & Hill-Davies, C. (2004). Parents' and non-parents' beliefs about the cues to deception in children. *Psychology, Crime & Law, 10,* 455–464.

Taylor, S. E., Klein, L. C., Lewis, B. P., Gruenewald, T. L., Guring, R. A. R., & Updegraff, J. A. (2000). Biobehavioral responses to stress in females: Tend-and-befriend, not fight-or-flight. *Psychological Review, 107,* 411–429.

Taylor, S. J. (2002). Effects of a nonverbal skills training program on perceptions of personal charisma. *Dissertation Abstracts International: Section B: The Sciences and Engineering* (vol. 62, 2-B), p. 1091.

Tedeschi, J. T., & Norman, N. (1985). Social power, self-presentation, and the self. In B. R. Schlenker (Ed.), *The self and social life* (pp. 293–322). New York: McGraw-Hill.

Teven, J. J., & Comadena, M. E. (1996). The effects of office aesthetic quality on students' perceptions of teacher credibility and communicator style. *Communication Research Reports, 13,* 101–108.

Thakerar, J. N., & Giles, H. (1981). They are so they spoke: Noncontent speech stereotypes. *Language and Communication, 1,* 255–261.

Thayer, S. (1986). Touch: Frontier of intimacy. *Journal of Nonverbal Behavior, 10,* 7–11.

The Global Deception Research Team. (2006). A world of lies. *Journal of Cross-Cultural Psychology, 37,* 60–74.

Thomson, J. A., Knorr, N. J., & Edgerton, M. T. (1978). Cosmetic surgery: The psychiatric perspective. *Psychosomatics: Journal of Consultation Liaison Psychiatry, 19,* 7–15.

Thornhill, R., & Gangestad, S. W. (1994). Human fluctuating asymmetry and sexual behavior. *Psychological Science, 5,* 297–302.

Thornhill, R., & Gangestad, S. W. (1999). The scent of symmetry: A human sex pheromone that signals fitness? *Evolution and Human Behavior, 20,* 175–201.

Thornhill, R., Gangestad, S. W., & Comer, R. (1995). Human female orgasm and mate fluctuating asymmetry. *Animal Behavior, 50,* 1601–1615.

Thornhill, R., & Møller, A. P. (1997). Developmental stability, disease, and medicine. *Biological Reviews, 72,* 497–548.

Thornton, B., & Moore, S. (1993). Physical attractiveness contrast effect: Implications for self-esteem and evaluations of the social self. *Personality and Social Psychology Bulletin, 19,* 474–480.

Thorpe, W. H. (1972). The comparison of vocal communication in animals and man. In R. A. Hinde (Ed.), *Non-verbal communication* (pp. 27–47). Cambridge, England: Cambridge University Press.

Tiersma, P. M. (1993). Nonverbal communication and the freedom of "speech." *Wisconsin Law Review, 6,* 1525–1589.

Timney, B., & London, H. (1973). Body language concomitants of persuasiveness and persuasibility in dyadic interaction. *International Journal of Group Tensions, 3,* 48–67.

Toda, S., Fogel, A., & Kawai, M. (1990). Maternal speech to three-month-old infants in the United States and Japan. *Journal of Child Language, 17,* 279–294.

Tom, G., Pettersen, P., Lau, T., Burton, T., & Cook, J. (1991). The role of overt head movement in the formation of affect. *Basic and Applied Social Psychology, 12,* 281–289.

Tom, K. (2003, November). *Vocal fundamental frequency characteristics of ethnic Chinese speakers.* Paper presented at the annual meeting of the American Speech-Language-Hearing Association, Chicago, IL.

Tomkins, S. S. (1962). *Affect, imagery, consciousness: Vol. 1. The positive affects.* New York: Springer-Verlag.

Tooke, W., & Camire, L. (1991). Patterns of deception in intersexual and intrasexual mating strategies. *Ethology and Sociobiology, 12,* 345–364.

Toris, C., & DePaulo, B. M. (1985). Effects of actual deception and suspiciousness of deception interpersonal perceptions. *Journal of Personality and Social Psychology, 47,* 1063–1073.

Tracy, J. C., & Robins, R. W. (2008). The nonverbal expression of pride: Evidence for cross-cultural recognition. *Journal of Personality and Social Psychology, 94,* 516–530.

Tracy, J., C., & Matsumoto, D. (2008). The spontaneous expression of pride and shame: Evidence for biologically innate nonverbal displays. *Proceedings of the National Academy of Sciences, 105,* 11665–11660.

Trager, G. L. (1958). Paralanguage: A first approximation. *Studies in Linguistics, 12,* 1–12.

Trager, G. L. (1961). The typology of paralanguage. *Anthropological Linguistics, 3,* 12–21.

Trees, A. R., & Manusov, V. (1998). Managing face concerns in criticism: Integrating nonverbal behaviors as a dimension of politeness in female friendship dyads. *Human Communication Research, 24,* 564–583.

Tremine, N. T., & Izard, C. E. (1988). Infants' responses to their mothers' expressions of joy and sadness. *Developmental Psychology, 24,* 223–229.

Trent, J. S., Short-Thompson, C., Mongeau, P. A., Nusz, A. K., & Trent, J. D. (2001). Image, media bias, and voter characteristics: The ideal candidate from 1998–2000. *American Behavioral Scientist, 44,* 2101–2124.

Trent, L. (1993). Color can affect success of products. *Marketing News, 27,* 4.

Tripathi, H. G. R. (1996). Effect of quality of surrounding on crowding stress. *Journal of Personality and Clinical Studies, 12,* 49–54.

Tripathi, H. G. R., & Tripathi, S. R. (2005). Spatial and non-spatial influences on crowding stress. *Psychological Studies, 50,* 317–321.

Triplett, T. (1995). Carmakers driven by quest to find tomorrow's color. *Marketing News, 29,* 38–39.

Tucker, J. S., & Friedman, H. S. (1993). Sex differences in nonverbal expressiveness: Emotional expression, personality and impressions. *Journal of Nonverbal Behavior, 17,* 103–117.

Tucker, J. S., & Riggio, R. E. (1988). The role of social skills in encoding posed and spontaneous facial expressions. *Journal of Nonverbal Behavior, 12,* 87–97.

Tucker, L. A. (1984). Physical attractiveness, somatotype, and the male personality: A dynamic interactional perspective. *Journal of Clinical Psychology, 40,* 1226–1234.

Turner, R. E., Edgley, C., & Olmstead, G. (1975). Information control in conversations: Honesty is not always the best policy. *Kansas Journal of Speech, 11,* 69–89.

Tusing, K. J., & Dillard, J. P. (2000). The sounds of dominance: Vocal precursors of perceived dominance during interpersonal influence. *Human Communication Research, 26,* 148–171.

Tversky, B., Kugelmass, S., & Winter, A. (1991). Cross-cultural and developmental trends in graphic productions. *Cognitive Psychology, 23,* 515–557.

Uvnäs-Moberg, K. (1998). Oxytocin may mediate the benefits of positive social interaction and emotions. *Psychoneuroendocrinology, 23,* 819–835.

Uzzell, D., & Horne, N. (2006). The influence of biological sex, sexuality and gender role on interpersonal distance. *British Journal of Social Psychology, 45,* 579–597.

Valentine, M. E. (1980). The attenuating influence of gaze upon the bystander intervention effect. *Journal of Social Psychology, 3,* 197–203.

Van Bezooijen, R., & Gooskens, C. (1999). Identification of language varieties: The contribution of different linguistic levels. *Journal of Language and Social Psychology, 18,* 31–48.

van Dierendonck, D., & Te Nijenhuis, J. (2001). Flotation restricted environmental stimulation therapy (REST) as a stress-management tool: A meta-analysis. *Psychology and Health, 20,* 405–412.

van Hooff, J. A. R. A. M. (1972). A comparative approach to the phylogeny of laughter and smiling. In Hinde (Ed.), *Non-verbal communication* (pp. 207–242). Cambridge, England: Cambridge University Press.

Vande Creek, L., & Watkins, J. T. (1972). Responses to incongruent verbal and nonverbal emotional cues. *Journal of Communication, 22,* 311–316.

Vandell, D. L. (2000). Parents, peer groups, and other socializing influences. *Developmental Psychology, 36,* 699–710.

Vaught, L. A. (1902). *Vaught's practical character reader.* Whitefish, MT: Kessinger Publishing.

Vine, I. (1975). Territoriality and the spatial regulation of interaction. In A. Kendon, R. M. Harris, & M. R. Key (Eds.), *Organization of behavior in face-to-face interaction* (pp. 357–387). The Hague: Mouton.

Vinsel, A., Brown, B. B., Altman, I., & Foss, C. (1980). Privacy regulation, territorial displays, and effectiveness of individual functioning. *Journal of Personality and Social Psychology, 39,* 1104–1115.

Von Cranach, M., & Ellgring, J. H. (1973). Problems in the recognition of gaze direction. In M. Von Cranach & I. Vine (Eds.), *Social communication and movement* (pp. 419–443). New York: Academic.

Vrij, A. (2000). *Detecting lies and deceit: The psychology of lying and the implications for professional practices.* West Sussex, England: John Wiley & Sons.

Vrij, A. (2006). Nonverbal communication and deception. In V. Manusov & M. L. Patterson (Eds.), *The Sage handbook of nonverbal communication* (pp. 341–359). Thousand Oaks, CA: Sage.

Vrij, A. (2007). *Guidelines to catch a liar.* Unpublished paper.

Vrij, A., Akehurst, L., & Morris, P. (1997). Individual differences in hand movements during deception. *Journal of Nonverbal Behavior, 21,* 87–103.

Vrij, A., Edward, K., & Bull, R. (2001). Police officers' ability to detect deceit: The benefit of indirect deception detection measures. *Legal and Criminological Psychology, 6,* 185–196.

Vrij, A., Evans, H., Akehurst, L., & Mann, S. (2004). Rapid judgments in assessing verbal and nonverbal cues: Their potential for deception researchers and lie detection. *Applied Cognitive Psychology, 18,* 283–296.

Vrij, A., & Mann, S. (2001). Who killed my relative? Police officers' ability to detect real-life high stake lies. *Psychology, Crime & Law, 7,* 119–132.

Vrij, A., & Semin, G. R. (1996). Lie experts' beliefs about nonverbal indicators of deception. *Journal of Nonverbal Behavior, 20,* 65–80.

Vrij, A., & Winkel, F. W. (1991). Cultural differences in Dutch and Surinam nonverbal behavior: An analysis of simulated police/citizen encounters. *Journal of Nonverbal Behavior, 15,* 169–184.

Wada, M. (1990). The effects of interpersonal distance change on nonverbal behaviors: Mediating effects of sex and intimacy levels in a dyad. *Japanese Psychological Research, 32,* 86–96.

Wagner, H. L., Buck, R., & Winterbotham, M. (1993). Communication of specific emotions: Gender differences in sending accuracy and communication measures. *Journal of Nonverbal Behavior, 17,* 29–53.

Wagner, H. L., MacDonald, C. J., & Manstead, A. S. R. (1986). Communication of individual emotions by spontaneous facial expressions. *Journal of Personality and Social Psychology, 50,* 737–743.

Waitzkin, H. (1984). Doctor-patient communication: Clinical implications of social scientific research. *Journal of the American Medical Association, 252,* 2441–2446.

Walker, R. N. (1963). Body build and behavior in young children: II. Body build and parents' ratings. *Child Development, 34,* 1–23.

Walsh, D. G., & Hewitt, J. (1985). Giving men the come-on: Effect of eye contact and smiling in a bar environment. *Perceptual and Motor Skills, 61,* 873–874.

Warner, P. (2002). *Quality time anytime: How to make the most of every moment with your child.* Minnetonka, MN: Meadowbrook Press.

Warner, R. M., Malloy, D., Schneider, K., Knoth, R., & Wilder, B. (1987). Rhythmic organization of social interaction and observer ratings of positive affect and involvement. *Journal of Nonverbal Behavior, 11,* 57–74.

Watson, O. M. (1970). *Proxemic behavior: A cross-cultural study.* The Hague: Mouton.

Watzlawick, P., Beavin, J. H., & Jackson, D. D. (1967). *Pragmatics of human communication: A study of interactional patterns, pathologies and paradoxes.* New York: Norton.

Waxer, P. (1977). Nonverbal cues for anxiety: An examination of emotional leakage. *Journal of Abnormal Psychology, 86,* 306–314.

Wedekind, C., & Furi, S. (1997). Body odor preferences in men and women: Do they aim for specific MHC combinations or simply heterozygosity? *Proceedings of the Royal Society of London, Series B, 264,* 1471–1479.

Wedekind, C., Seebeck, T., Bettens, F., & Paepke, A. J. (1995). MHC-dependent mate preferences in humans. *Proceedings of the Royal Society of London, Series B, 260,* 245–249.

Wegner, D. M., & Vallacher, R. R. (1977). *Implicit psychology: An introduction to social cognition.* New York: Oxford University Press.

Weinberger, M., Greene, J. Y., & Mamlin, J. H. (1981). The impact of clinical encounter events on patient and physician satisfaction. *Social Science & Medicine, 15E,* 239–244.

Weir, S. R., & Fine-Davis, M. (1989). "Dumb blonde" and "temperamental redhead": The effect of hair colour on some attributed personality characteristics of women. *Irish Journal of Psychology, 10,* 11–19.

Weisfeld G. E., & Linkey, H. E. (1985). Dominance displays as indicators of a social success motive. In S. L. Ellyson & J. F. Dovidio (Eds.), *Power, dominance, and nonverbal behavior* (pp. 109–128). New York: Springer-Verlag.

Weisfeld, C. C., & Stack, M. A. (2002). When I look into your eyes: An ethnological analysis of gender differences in married couples' nonverbal behaviors. *Psychology, Evolution and Gender, 4,* 125–147.

Weiss, S. J. (1979). The language of touch. *Nursing Research, 28,* 76–80.

Weiss, S. J. (1990). Effects of differential touch on nervous system arousal of patients recovering from cardiac disease. *Heart and Lung, 19,* 474–480.

Weiss, S. J., Wilson, P., & Morrison, D. (2004). Maternal tactile stimulation and the neurodevelopment of low birth weight infants. *Infancy, 5,* 85–107.

Weiss, S. J., Wilson, P., St. Jonn-Seed, M., & Paul, S. (2001). Early tactile experience of low birth weight children: Links to later mental health and social adaptation. *Infant and Child Development, 10*, 93–115.

Weitz, S. (1976). Sex differences in nonverbal communication. *Sex Roles, 2*, 175–184.

Wells, W., & Siegel, B. (1961). Stereotyped somatotypes. *Psychological Reports, 8*, 77–78.

Werner, C. M., Peterson-Lewis, S., & Brown, B. B. (1989). Inferences about homeowner's sociability: Impact of Christmas decorations and other cues. *Journal of Environmental Psychology, 9*, 279–296.

West, C., & Zimmerman, D. H. (1982). Conversational analysis. In K. R. Scherer & P. Ekman (Eds.), *Handbook of methods in nonverbal behavior research* (pp. 506–541). Cambridge, England: Cambridge University Press.

Wheeler, L., & Miyake, K. (1992). Social comparison in everyday life. *Journal of Personality and Social Psychology, 62*, 760–773.

Wheeler, L., Reis, H. T., & Bond, M. H. (1989). Collectivism-individualism in everyday social life: The middle kingdom and the melting pot. *Journal of Personality and Social Psychology, 57*, 79–86.

Whitbourne, S. K. (1985). *The aging body: Physiological changes and psychological consequences.* New York: Springer-Verlag.

Whitcher, S. J., & Fisher, J. D. (1979). Multidimensional reaction to therapeutic touch in a hospital setting. *Journal of Personality and Social Psychology, 37*, 87–96.

White, C. (2003). Interview during the annual meeting of the National Communication Association, Miami Beach, November 2003.

White, C., & Burgoon, J. K. (2001). Adaptation and communicative design: Patterns of interaction in truthful and deceptive conversations. *Human Communication Research, 27*, 9–37.

Whiting, B., & Edwards, C. (1973). A cross-cultural analysis of sex differences in the behavior of children aged three through 11. *Journal of Social Psychology, 91*, 171–188.

Wiemann, J. M. (1973). *An exploratory study of turn-taking in conversations: Verbal and nonverbal behavior.* Unpublished master's thesis, Purdue University.

Wiemann, J. M. (1985). Power, status and dominance: Interpersonal control and regulation in conversation. In R. L. Street & J. N. Cappella (Eds.), *Sequence and pattern in communicative behavior* (pp. 85–102). London: Arnold.

Wiemann, J. M., & Knapp, M. L. (1975). Turn-taking in conversations. *Journal of Communication, 25*, 75–92.

Wiener, M., Devoe, S., Rubinow, S., & Geller, J. (1972). Nonverbal behavior and nonverbal communication. *Psychological Review, 79*, 185–214.

Wiggers, M. (1982). Judgments of facial expressions of emotion predicted from facial behavior. *Journal of Nonverbal Behavior, 7*, 101–116.

Willems, S., De Maesschalck, S., Deveugele, M., Derese, A., & De Maesener, J. (2005). Socio-economic status of the patient and doctor-patient communication: Does it make a difference? *Patient Education and Counseling, 56*, 139–146.

Willis, F. N., & Briggs, L. E. (1992). Relationship and touch in public settings. *Journal of Nonverbal Behavior, 16*, 55–62.

Willis, F. N., & Dodds, R. A. (1998). Age, relationship, and touch initiation. *Journal of Social Psychology, 138*, 115–123.

Willis, F. N., & Hamm, H. K. (1980). The use of interpersonal touch in securing compliance. *Journal of Nonverbal Behavior, 5*, 49–55.

Willis, F. N., & Rawdon, V. A. (1994). Gender and national differences in attitudes toward same-gender touch. *Perceptual and Motor Skills, 78*, 1027–1034.

Wilson, G., & Nias, D. (1976). *The mystery of love: The hows and whys of sexual attraction.* New York: Quadrangle Books.

Winkel, F. W., & Vrij, A. (1990). Nonverbal behavior in a cross-cultural dyad: The frequency and effects of gaze aversion in police-black encounters. *Social Behaviour: An International Journal of Applied Psychology, 5*, 335–350.

Witt, P. L., Wheeless, L. R., & Allen, M. (2004). A meta-analytical review of the relationship between teacher immediacy and student learning. *Communication Monographs, 71*, 184–207.

Wohlrab, S., Stahl, J., Rammsayer, T., & Kappeler, P. M. (2007). Differences in personality characteristics between body-modified and non-modified individuals: Associations with individual personality traits and possible evolutionary implications. *European Journal of Personality, 21*, 931–951.

Woll, S. (1986). So many to choose from: Decision strategies in videodating. *Journal of Social and Personal Relationships, 3*, 43–52.

Wood, B. S. (1981). *Children and communication: Verbal and nonverbal language development* (2nd ed.). Englewood Cliffs, NJ: Prentice-Hall.

Wood, J. T. (2009). *Gendered lives: Communication, culture, and gender* (8th ed.). Belmont, CA: Cengage/Wadsworth.

Wood, J. T., & Dindia, K. (1998). What's the difference? A dialogue about differences and similarities between women and men. In D. J. Canary & K. Dindia (Eds.), *Sex differences and similarities in communication* (pp. 19–39). Mahwah, NJ: Lawrence Erlbaum Associates.

Woodall, W. G., & Burgoon, J. K. (1983). Talking fast and changing attitudes: A critique and clarification. *Journal of Nonverbal Behavior, 8*, 126–142.

Wright, G. (1981). *Building the dream: A social history of housing in America*. Cambridge, MA: MIT Press.

Yee, N., & Bailenson, J. (2007). The Proteus effect: The effect of transformed self-representation on behavior. *Human Communication Research, 33*, 271–290.

Yerkes, R. M., & Dodson, J. D. (1908). The relation of strength of stimulus to rapidity of habit-formation. *Journal of Comparative and Neurological Psychology, 18*, 459–482.

Yuki, M., Maddux, W. W., & Masuda, T. (2007). Are the windows to the soul the same in East and West? Cultural differences in using the eyes and mouth as cues to recognize emotions in Japan and the United States. *Journal of Experimental Social Psychology, 43*, 303–311.

Zaadstra, B. M., Seidell, J. C., van Noord, P. A. H., te Velde, E. G., Habbema, J. D. F., Vrieswijk, B., & Karbaat, J. (1993). Fat and female fecundity: Prospective study of effect of body fat distribution on conception rates. *British Medical Journal, 306*, 484–487.

Zaidel, D. W., Chen, A. C., & German, C. (1995). She is not a beauty even when she smiles: Possible evolutionary basis for a relationship between facial attractiveness and hemispheric specialization. *Neuropsychologica, 33*, 649–655.

Zaidel, D. W., & Choi, D. (2007). Attractiveness of natural faces compared to computer-generated perfectly symmetrical faces. *International Journal of Neuroscience, 117*, 423–431.

Zaidel, D. W., & Cohen, J. A. (2005). The face, beauty, and symmetry: Perceiving asymmetry in beautiful faces. *International Journal of Neuroscience, 115*, 1165–1173.

Zaidel, S. F., & Mehrabian, A. (1969). The ability to communicate and infer positive and negative attitudes facially and vocally. *Journal of Experimental Research in Personality, 3*, 233–241.

Zajonc, R. B., Adelman, P. K., Murphy, S. T., & Niedenthal, P. M. (1987). Convergence in the physical appearance of spouses. *Motivation and Emotion, 11*, 335–346.

Zebrowitz, L. A., Brownlow, S., & Olson, K. (1992). Baby talk to the babyfaced. *Journal of Nonverbal Behavior, 16*, 143–158.

Ziegler-Kratz, N., & Marshall, L. L. (1990). Impressions of therapists: The effects of gaze, smiling, and gender. *Journal of Psychology and the Behavioral Sciences, 5*, 115–129.

Zillman, D. (1990). The interplay of cognition and excitation in aggravated conflict. In D. D. Cahn (Ed.), *Intimates in conflict: A communication perspective* (pp. 187–208). Hillsdale, NJ: Lawrence Erlbaum Associates.

Zuckerman, M., Amidon, M. D., Bishop, S. E., & Pomerantz, S. D. (1982). Face and tone of voice in the communication of deception. *Journal of Personality and Social Psychology, 43*, 347–357.

Zuckerman, M., DeFrank, R. S., Hall, J. A., Larrance, D. T., & Rosenthal, R. (1979). Facial and vocal cues of deception and honesty. *Journal of Experimental Social Psychology, 15*, 378–396.

Zuckerman, M., DePaulo, B. M., & Rosenthal, R. (1981). Verbal and non-verbal communication of deception. In L. Berowitz (Ed.), *Advances in experimental social psychology* (Vol. 14, pp. 1–59). New York: Academic.

Zuckerman, M., & Driver, R. E. (1985). Telling lies: Verbal and nonverbal correlates of deception. In A. W. Siegman & S. Feldstein (Eds.), *Multichannel integrations of nonverbal behavior* (pp. 129–147). Hillsdale, NJ: Lawrence Erlbaum Associates.

Zuckerman, M., & Hodgins, H. S. (1993). Developmental changes in the effects of the physical and vocal attractiveness stereotypes. *Journal of Research in Personality, 27*, 349–369.

Zuckerman, M., Koestner, R., & Driver, R. (1981). Beliefs about cues associated with deception. *Journal of Nonverbal Behavior, 6*, 105–114.

Zuckerman, M., Larrance, D. T., Hall, J. A., DeFrank, R. S., & Rosenthal, R. (1979). Posed and spontaneous communication of emotion via facial and vocal cues. *Journal of Personality, 47*, 712–733.

Zuckerman, M., Larrance, D. T., Spiegel, N. H., & Klorman, R. (1981). Controlling nonverbal displays: Facial expressions and tone of voice. *Journal of Experimental Social Psychology, 17*, 506–524.

Zuckerman, M., Lipets, M. S., Koivumaki, J. H., & Rosenthal, R. (1975). Encoding and decoding nonverbal cues of emotion. *Journal of Personality and Social Psychology, 32*, 1068–1076.

Zuckerman, M., & Miyake, K. (1993). The attractive voice: What makes it so? *Journal of Nonverbal Behavior, 17*, 119–135.

Zuckerman, M., Miyake, K., & Hodgins, H. S. (1991). Cross-channel effects of vocal and physical attractiveness and their implications for interpersonal perception. *Journal of Personality and Social Psychology, 60*, 545–554.

SUBJECT INDEX

NAME INDEX

PHOTO CREDITS